MW01640048

A THOUSAND WORDS
PHOTOS FROM THE FIELD

TWENTY–FIVE YEARS OF **INTERNATIONAL MEDICAL CORPS**

A THREE HAWKS PRESS BOOK

ISBN 978-0-615-25937-6

WRITTEN & EDITED BY STACY TWILLEY

ART DIRECTION BY ANN SONG

PREPRESS AND PRODUCTION BY MODERN LUXURY MEDIA

PRINTED IN ITALY

PUBLISHED BY THREE HAWKS PRESS

LOS ANGELES, CALIFORNIA

www.threehawkspress.com

Three Hawks Press publishes art books and electronic photo journals to raise awareness about humanitarian concerns, endangered environments and social conflicts around the world and in our own communities. Our philosophy is simple: Photography has the power to expand our worldview, take us to places we are unable to go, deepen our understanding of issues and ideas, and provoke us to become involved. The mission of Three Hawks Press is to present the work of photographers, artists, humanitarians and volunteers who dedicate their lives to making a difference in our increasingly connected world and who do so with creativity, courage and compassion.

INTERNATIONAL MEDICAL CORPS (IMC) IS A GLOBAL, HUMANITARIAN, NONPROFIT ORGANIZATION DEDICATED TO SAVING LIVES AND RELIEVING SUFFERING THROUGH HEALTH CARE TRAINING AND RELIEF AND DEVELOPMENT PROGRAMS. ESTABLISHED IN 1984 BY VOLUNTEER DOCTORS AND NURSES, INTERNATIONAL MEDICAL CORPS IS A PRIVATE, VOLUNTARY, NONPOLITICAL, NONSECTARIAN ORGANIZATION. ITS MISSION IS TO IMPROVE THE QUALITY OF LIFE THROUGH HEALTH INTERVENTIONS AND RELATED ACTIVITIES THAT BUILD LOCAL CAPACITY IN UNDERSERVED COMMUNITIES WORLDWIDE. BY OFFERING TRAINING AND HEALTH CARE TO LOCAL POPULATIONS AND MEDICAL ASSISTANCE TO PEOPLE AT HIGHEST RISK, AND WITH THE FLEXIBILITY TO RESPOND RAPIDLY TO EMERGENCY SITUATIONS, IMC REHABILITATES DEVASTATED HEALTH CARE SYSTEMS AND HELPS BRING THEM BACK TO SELF-RELIANCE.

THE PROCEEDS FROM THIS BOOK WILL BE DONATED TO INTERNATIONAL MEDICAL CORPS.

A THOUSAND WORDS
PHOTOS FROM THE FIELD

TWENTY–FIVE YEARS OF **INTERNATIONAL MEDICAL CORPS**

WRITTEN AND EDITED BY **STACY TWILLEY**

FOREWORD BY **CHRISTIANE AMANPOUR**
CNN CHIEF INTERNATIONAL CORRESPONDENT

PHOTOGRAPHS SELECTED FROM THE ARCHIVES OF INTERNATIONAL MEDICAL CORPS

INTERNATIONAL MEDICAL CORPS

NANCY A. AOSSEY, PRESIDENT & CEO

I had the privilege of joining International Medical Corps to head up its efforts in 1986, shortly after its founding by Dr. Bob Simon in 1984. Many remarkable people joined our cause; I only wish that I could list them all. Among them were doctors including Henry Hood, Bill Moore and Bill Robinson—doctors who still serve in the field and on our board today. With a house donated by Dick Riordan as our office and a small group of staff and volunteers, we helped millions of Afghan people devastated by the Soviet Union.

Since that time, International Medical Corps has grown to more than 3,500 staff and volunteers, including doctors, nurses, public health professionals, administrators, logisticians, mental health specialists and community health workers. I am proud to say that over the years we have provided life-saving medical care and training in more than 50 countries and regions.

Through it all, I have witnessed some of the worst human tragedies—and the remarkable resilience of the human spirit. I am still inspired every day by the extraordinary compassion of our staff and volunteers who labor in the world's most difficult environments. Each photograph is a profound reminder of the incredible journey of International Medical Corps, the people who work with us and the people we serve.

In Angola, during the devastating civil war, we faced rebel leaders in an underground bunker and convinced them to let us deliver vital supplies and medical care, saving countless lives. During the height of the fighting and famine in Somalia, we were the first U.S. medical team to assist the stricken civilian population, braving mortar fire to train hundreds of Somali doctors and nurses; our work there continues to this day. At the onset of the Rwandan genocide, our team entered the country and had to bury the bodies of doctors and nurses so that we could reopen the hospital and treat the flood of injured. In Bosnia and Kosovo, our local staff, many of whom had lost loved ones in the ethnic cleansing, put their own grief aside to rehabilitate hospitals and operate ambulances and mobile clinics. Responding to the needs of the millions of people

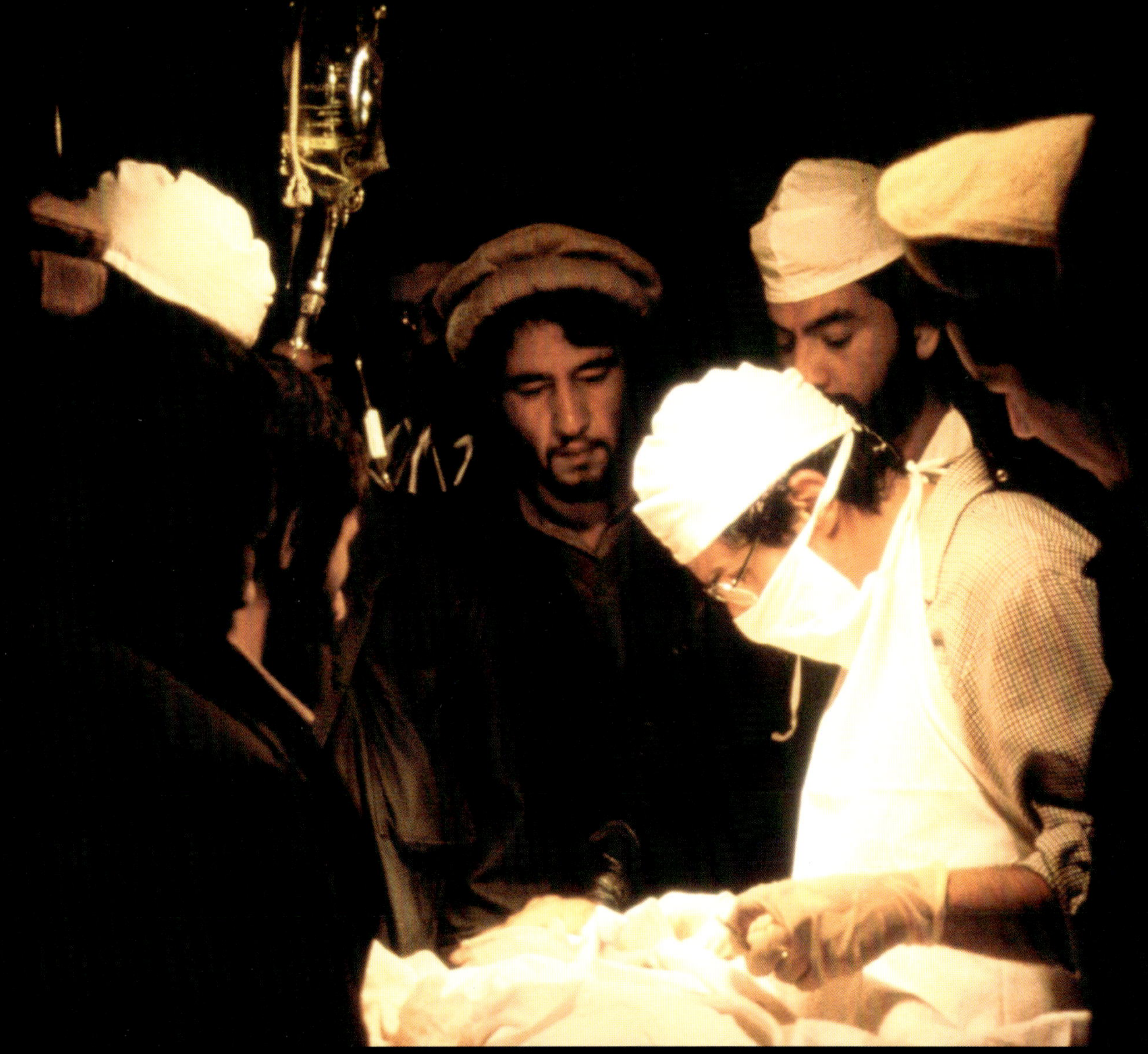

Dr. Robert Simon, *International Medical Corps Founder,* teaching surgery techniques in Afghanistan, 1986

impacted by the violence in Darfur and neighboring Chad, we set up a network of health clinics that are still operating today.

These photographs demonstrate the enduring principle upon which International Medical Corps was founded—that emergency medical relief paired with training offers the best chance to achieve self-reliance and rebuild healthy futures.

This book is a tribute to the exceptional efforts of my colleagues, who have cared for hundreds of millions of people in these fragile, often dangerous environments. It also honors those who have supported our work—the many individuals, corporations, foundations, governmental agencies and others who make it possible. Together, we remain committed to reaching those who bear the brunt of the world's conflicts and disasters and helping them reclaim their lives with dignity and hope.

FOREWORD

CHRISTIANE AMANPOUR

CNN CHIEF INTERNATIONAL CORRESPONDENT

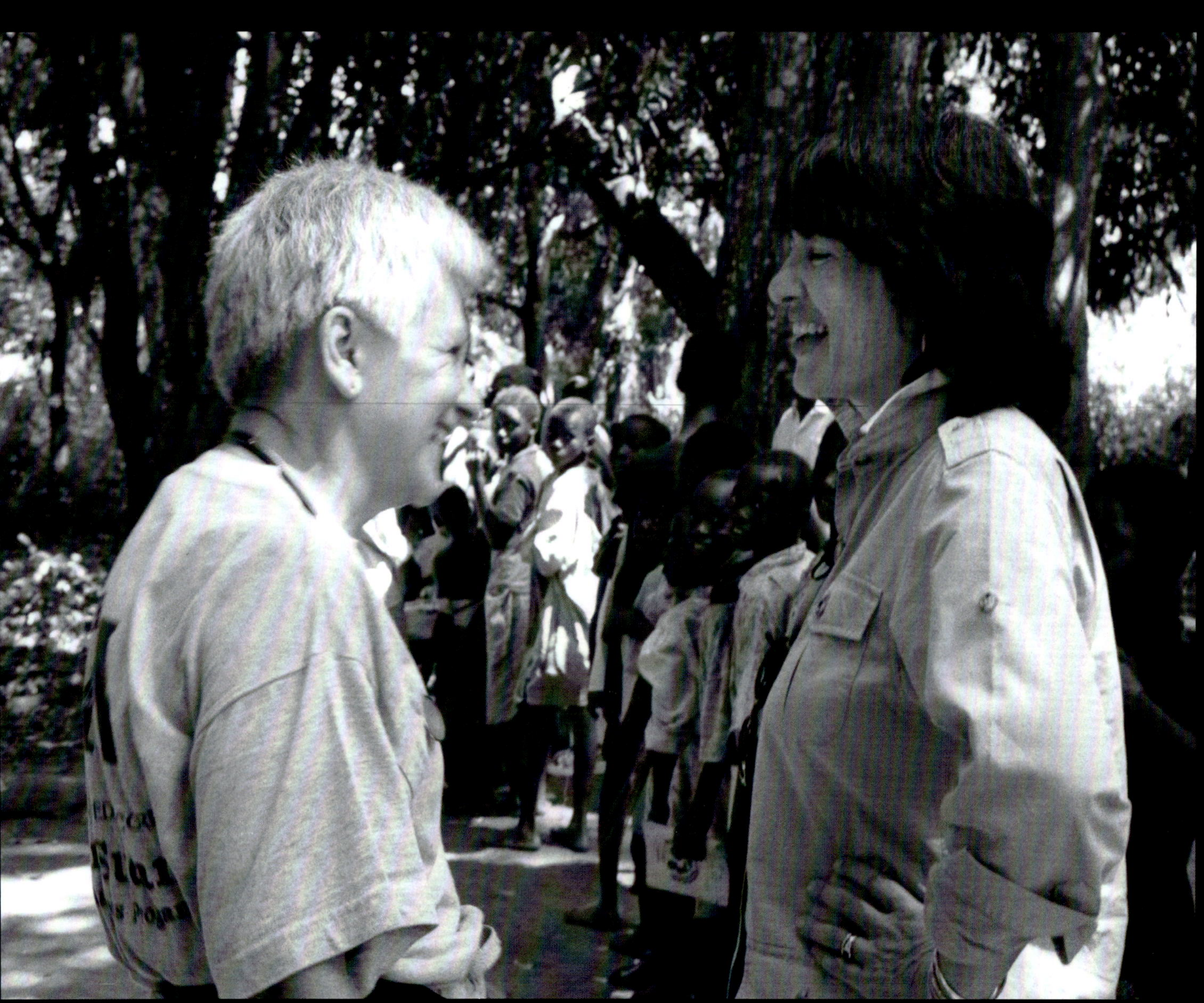

Christiane Amanpour, *CNN Chief International Correspondent*, with International Medical Corps' Dr. Mickey Richer in South Sudan

IN TWO DECADES AS A FOREIGN CORRESPONDENT, MY PATH HAS repeatedly intersected with International Medical Corps. The emergencies to which they responded were often the emergencies I covered.

I reported from the frontlines of the conflicts in Rwanda, Sierra Leone, Somalia, the Balkans, Afghanistan and Iraq. In all of these places, International Medical Corps doctors and nurses were tending to the wounded and the displaced, who were caught in the crossfire.

I reported from Tsunami-hit Sri Lanka and covered the destruction wrought by Hurricane Katrina in Louisiana. There, while I was reporting on all that had been lost, International Medical Corps teams were already at work, helping those devastated communities recover and rebuild.

And I have covered the crisis in Sudan. In Darfur, one of the most dangerous regions of Sudan, International Medical Corps has been delivering health care services and operating mobile clinics for those fleeing the fighting. They are still there—whether I am there or not—risking their lives everyday.

International Medical Corps' stories have been my stories. In fact, there were times when International Medical Corps itself was my story, like when I profiled their heroic work in Sierra Leone during its decade-long civil war. Soldiers—many of them children—were forced into warfare and their chests branded with the initials "RUF", or "Revolutionary United Front". International Medical Corps doctors performed surgeries to remove those scars of war and help both victims and perpetrators reconcile and recover.

More often, though, International Medical Corps was an untold part of my stories, working quietly behind the scenes to ease the pain of human suffering during a crisis we journalists were trying to bring to light.

The photos in this book are familiar to me because I have been to these places, met these people and heard their accounts. I have witnessed the results of International Medical Corps' hard work.

I am honored to be a part of this commemorative photography book, and I encourage you to view these photos with the same compassionate spirit in which I believe that many of them were taken—and with the same hope that International Medical Corps brings to the lives they touch every day.

INTRODUCTION

STACY TWILLEY

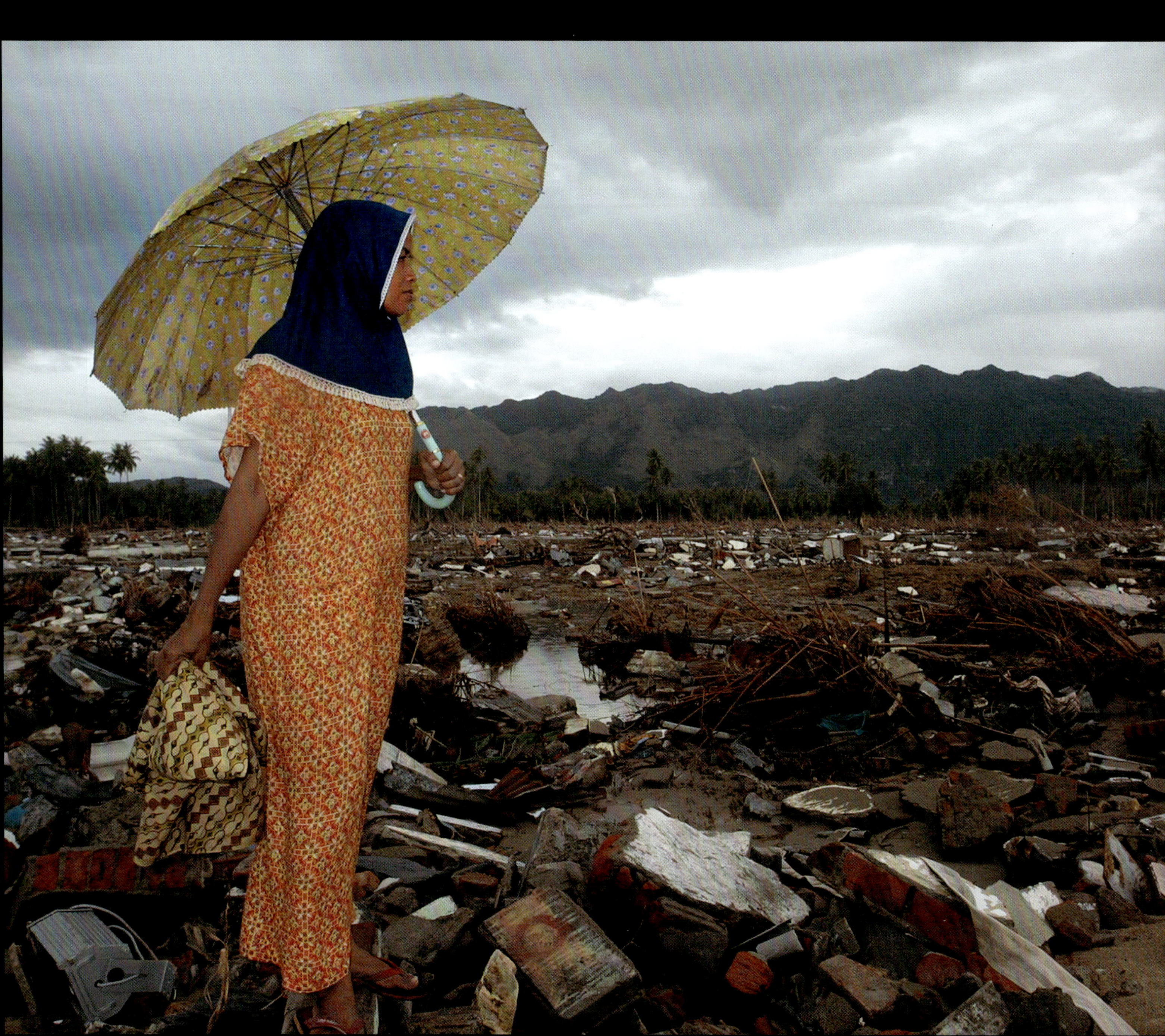

ON CHRISTMAS DAY, 1979, THE SOVIET Union invaded Afghanistan, and for one young American doctor on the other side of the world, it was a call to action. UCLA emergency room doctor Bob Simon assembled a small group of doctors and nurses who, together, risked their lives to enter Afghanistan and set up an emergency medical unit for civilians caught in the crossfire. With no intention of forming a permanent organization, Dr. Simon found the needs were greater than he expected. The group returned to Afghanistan several times, and in 1984, they officially became International Medical Corps.

THE DAY AFTER CHRISTMAS, 2004, A tsunami hit Southeast Asia while the rest of the world watched in horror. That's when I first learned about International Medical Corps. Under the 23-year leadership of its President and CEO, Nancy Aossey, it had become one of the world's largest humanitarian relief organizations. International Medical Corps was headquartered right in my own backyard, Los Angeles, already had teams of doctors working in Indonesia and was one of the first to respond to the tsunami devastation. Like so many others who wanted to help, I donated money to their relief efforts. And that small donation grew into an impassioned, long-term involvement with an impressive group of people. I became a volunteer and began working on small projects at International Medical Corps headquarters.

AND THAT'S WHEN I FOUND THE PHOTOGRAPHS.

MORE THAN 10,000 PHOTOS, STORED in eight large file cabinets along the back wall of the International Medical Corps office. Photo prints in manila folders and wrapped in envelopes, some with handwritten notes on the back, others with typed captions. I found negatives folded in between old field notes, slides with cryptic markings along the borders, and dog-eared prints still in the envelopes with postmarks from villages and towns I had never heard of. I found beautiful professional black and white prints in archival boxes and color prints professionally mounted. I discovered a digital archive with emailed images sent in from the farthest corners of the globe… and on a tucked-away bookshelf in the corner, I found Dr. Simon's original 1980s drugstore-style photo albums filled with snapshots. It was exciting, compelling… and overwhelming.

MANY OF THE IMAGES I FOUND WERE taken by amateur photographers: International Medical Corps doctors and nurses who happened to be at a critical place at a critical time and felt compelled to capture the moment. Other photographs were clearly the work of professionals—well-known photojournalists who could only work in these dangerous places under the protection afforded to the International Medical Corps teams. Some of the photos International Medical Corps directors hadn't ever seen; others had become iconic to them and copies could be found framed in many staff members' offices. The more than 10,000 photographs documented 25 years of International Medical Corps' work in the field all over the world. The images, and the stories they told, were fascinating.

archive became my history course in humanitarian aid: I learned about the Soviet invasion and how it devastated the Afghan health care system, particularly for women and children. I saw how Rwandans came back from the horrible genocide to rebuild their hospitals. I learned that host nations like Albania and Chad were strained by the influx of refugees from neighboring wars, but they continued to receive them anyway. I saw that International Medical Corps remained committed to helping survivors in parts of the world like Darfur and Iraq—places many other humanitarian agencies had long left behind. I saw that the aftermath of Hurricane Katrina had startling similarities to that of many developing nations confronted wtih disaster. I learned that the stigma of HIV/AIDS prevented many Kenyans from seeking the medical help they needed. I saw that the need for clean water—everywhere—is a growing crisis and a constant concern. I learned that there is a little silver package containing something called Plumpy' Nut that can fight famine like nothing else. And I found that there were still more International Medical Corps programs that weren't in the archives because some places where they worked were just too dangerous to take pictures.

I believed that the International Medical Corps photographs could become a book, so over the next year, I began to edit the archive. An avid photographer and art collector myself, I was able to narrow the archive down to 800 images, but then I needed help. I called on some experts well known in the world of photography to help select the final photos for the book. Curators from three of Los Angeles' world-class art museums—The Museum of Contemporary Art Los Angeles, Los Angeles County Museum of Art, and The J. Paul Getty Museum—joined noted Los Angeles collectors and artists including Richard Gere, Anjelica Huston, Mario Testino, Ruth Bloom and Eugenio Lopez to help choose the best of these photographs.

IN SELECTING THE FINAL PHOTOS, WE were keenly aware of the voyeuristic and exploitative nature of this kind of photography, where so many images were of victims of war, poverty and violence. In every selection and with every photograph we were concerned with preserving the dignity and respecting the feelings of International Medical Corps beneficiaries depicted in these images. We tried to avoid the sentimental, the cliché and the stereotype. We eliminated the photographs that we felt might endanger, embarrass or diminish the honor of anyone who appeared in them. And while some of those photographs we omitted may have been considered more beautiful or more powerful works of art, I believe that their absence here makes this photography book all the more poignant because it respects our common humanity. That is perhaps the true power of the 255 International Medical Corps photographs on these pages.

This book commemorates International Medical Corps' 25-year commitment to easing human suffering

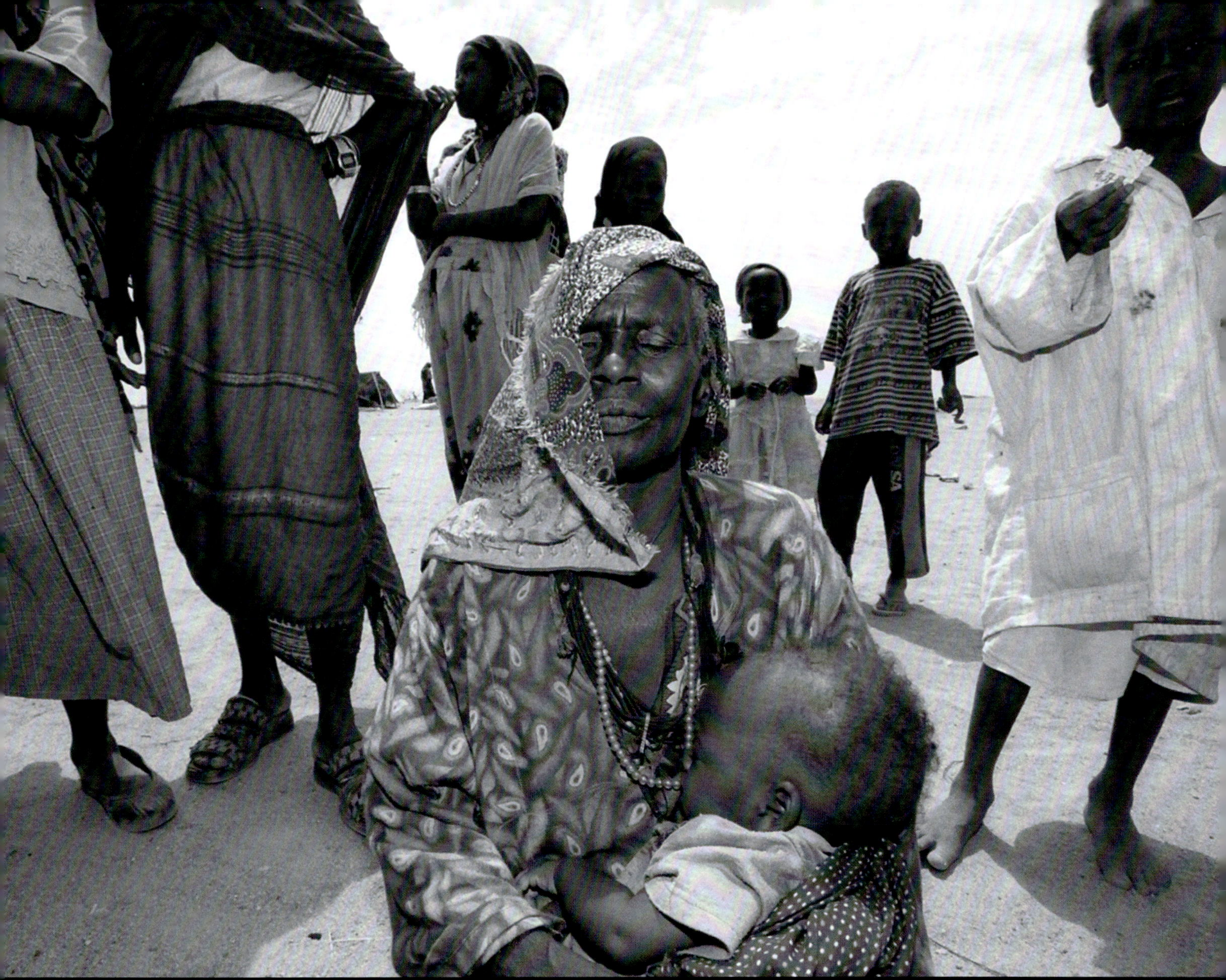

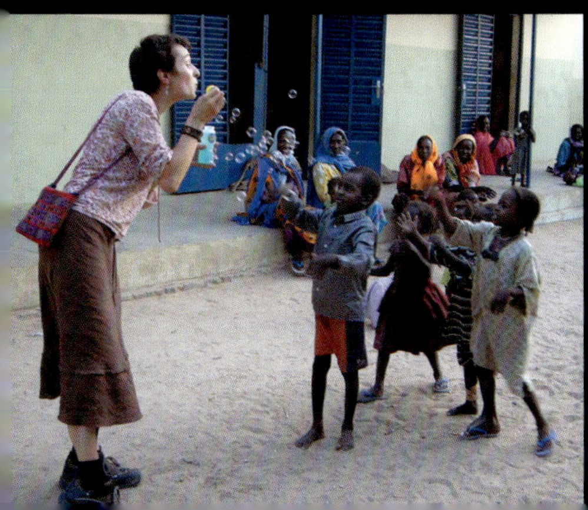

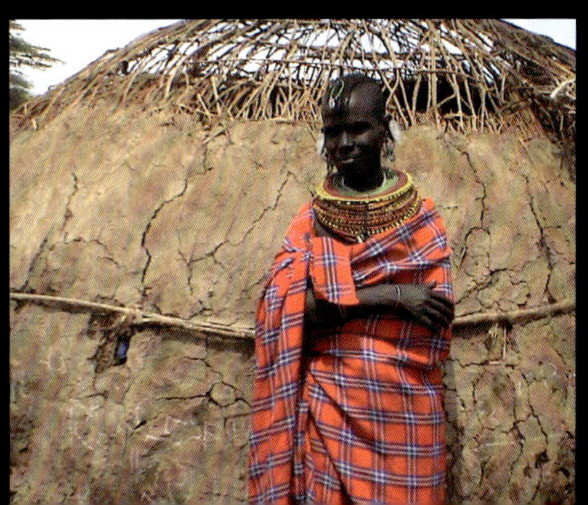

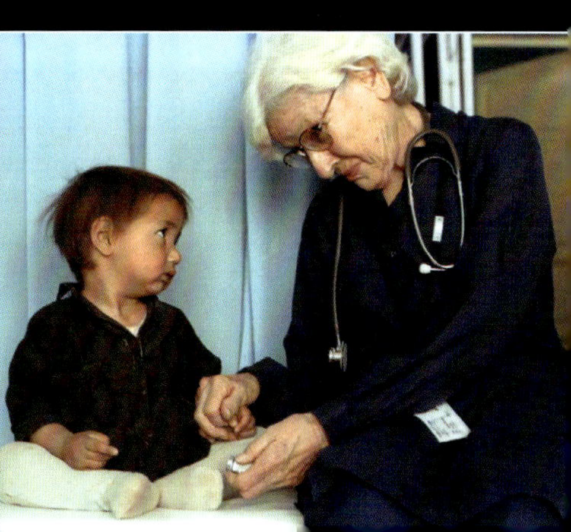

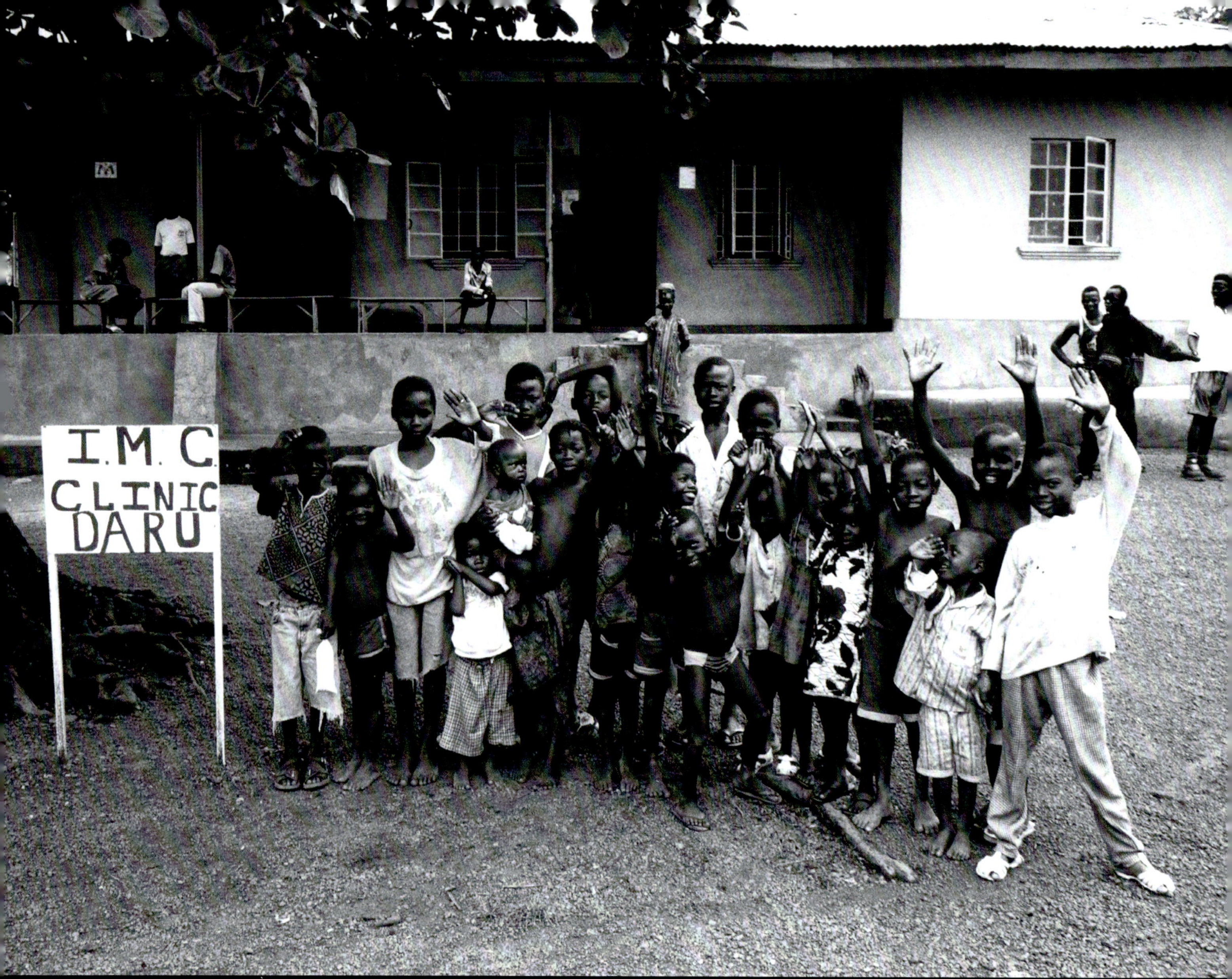

I.M.C
CLINIC
DARU

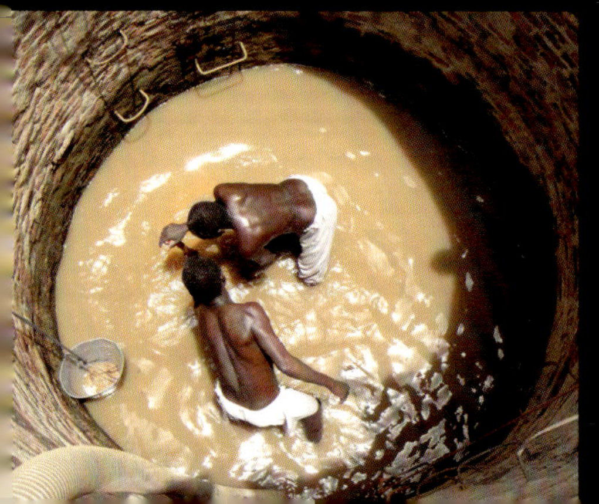

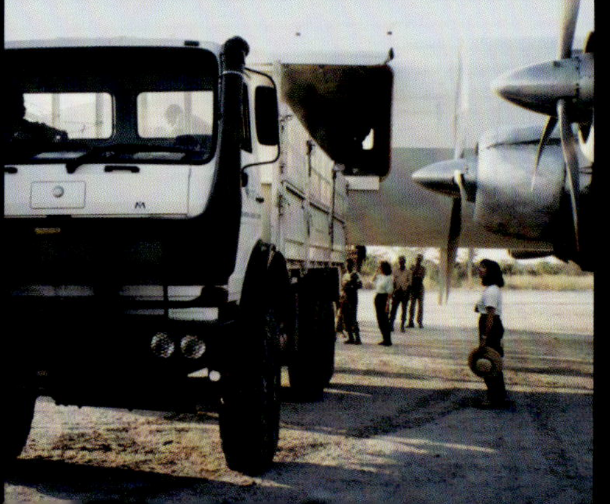

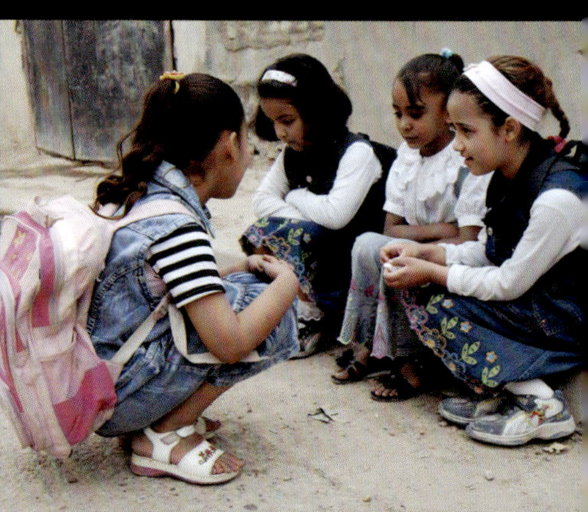

and saving lives. It tells a compelling story of the nonprofit organization's impressive dedication to humanitarian relief and training and of its commitment to helping civilians when their nation is overwhelmed by a natural disaster or when their government is not able or willing to provide for their health care. International Medical Corps' history is an inspiring one, and the photographs in this book celebrate that history.

BUT THE IMAGES IN THE BOOK ALSO tell another story: a troubling, 25-year chronicle of the impact of War. The premise upon which International Medical Corps was founded in Afghanistan was to aid civilian victims of war—all victims, regardless of the politics and no matter which side they were on. The fact is that violence and conflict often lie at the heart of many of the photos in this book. We have separated the book into six chapters—Global Health, War-Torn Nations, Refugee Relief, HIV/AIDS, Disaster Response and Food & Water—but many of the photos could just as accurately have been placed in the War-Torn Nations section. Conflict and war are often the reasons why humanitarian relief programs like those of International Medical Corps are needed.

This book's intention is not to glamorize the humanitarian response to war. Nor does this book mean to focus on the suffering of the poor, who may or may not have been poor and suffering before these conflicts began. Many of the civilian people International Medical Corps treats in the field have traveled far and lost everything in the process of escaping from war, famine and ethnic violence. They no longer look like the doctors, lawyers, students, professors, businesspeople, mothers, fathers, sons and daughters that they in fact are. Rather, these photos reveal how disastrous these conflicts have been to people around the globe—people who, a short while ago, in many ways may have been just like us.

FOR MANY PEOPLE WHO HAVE NOT YET gone—and others who never will go—to places like Sudan or Afghanistan, our only authentic connection to the people suffering there are the stories brought back by people like the International Medical Corps doctors, nurses and volunteers in the field. These stories show that the people International Medical Corps helps—those people who, but for their circumstances—are, indeed, just like us. These stories remind us of the need to support humanitarian work in dangerous places. And, perhaps most importantly, they reveal the common humanity that International Medical Corps staff witness around the world everyday.

TWENTY-FIVE YEARS of International Medical Corps stories are in these photographs…

… AND EVERY PHOTOGRAPH IN THIS BOOK SPEAKS A THOUSAND WORDS.

TABLE OF CONTENTS

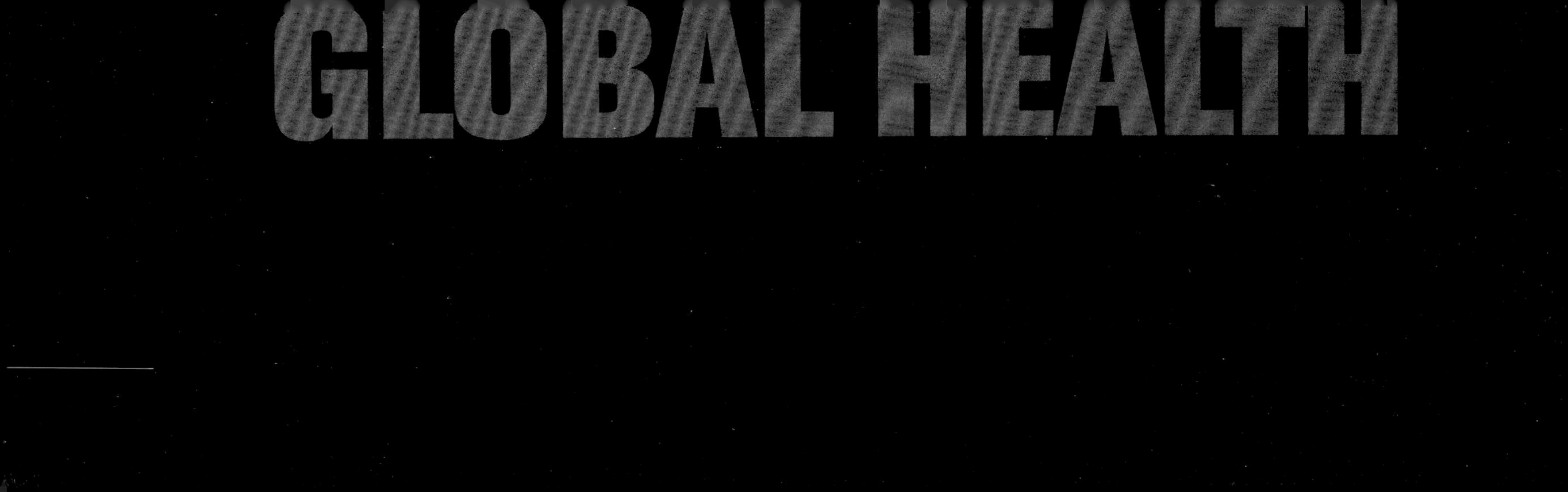
GLOBAL HEALTH

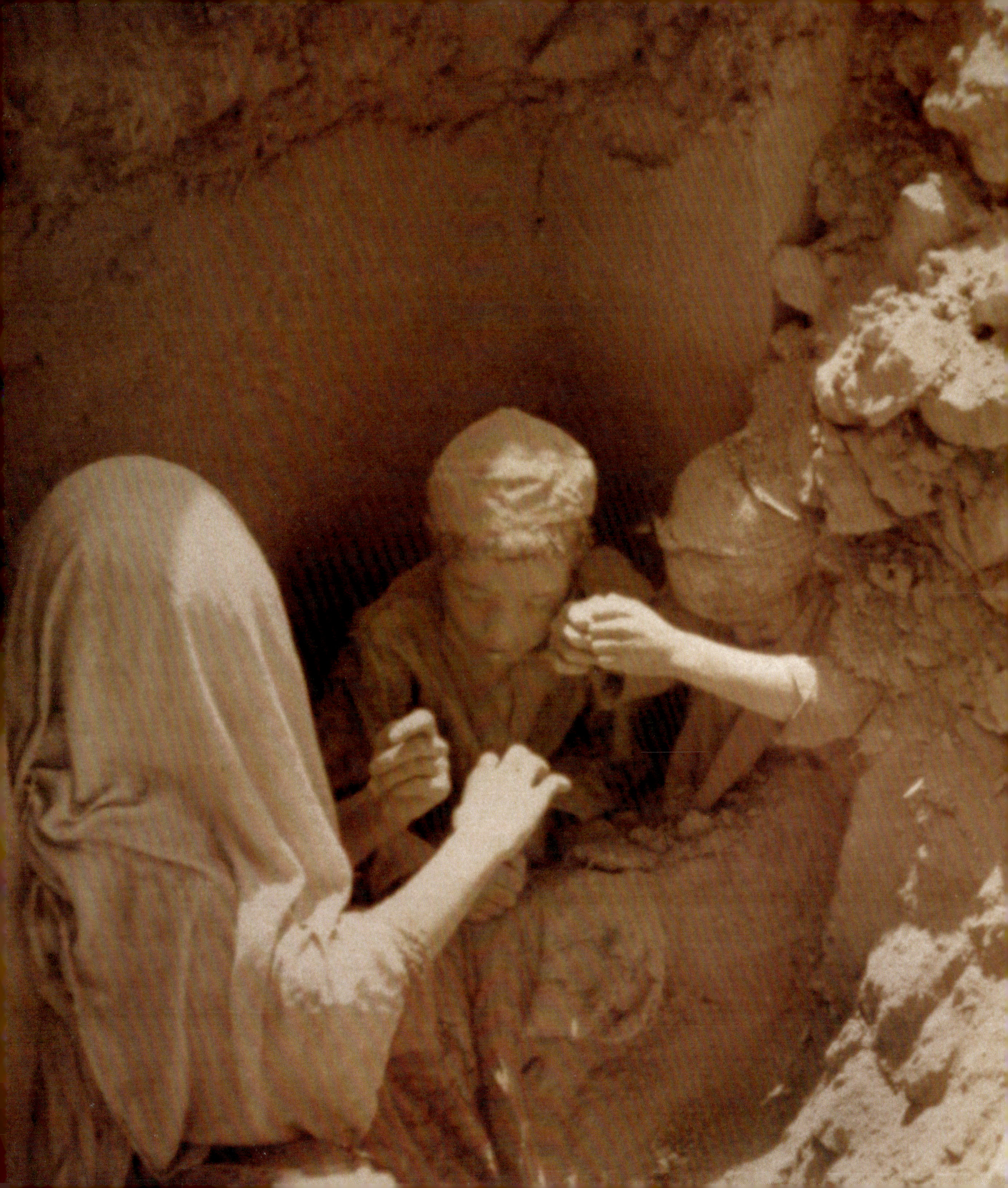

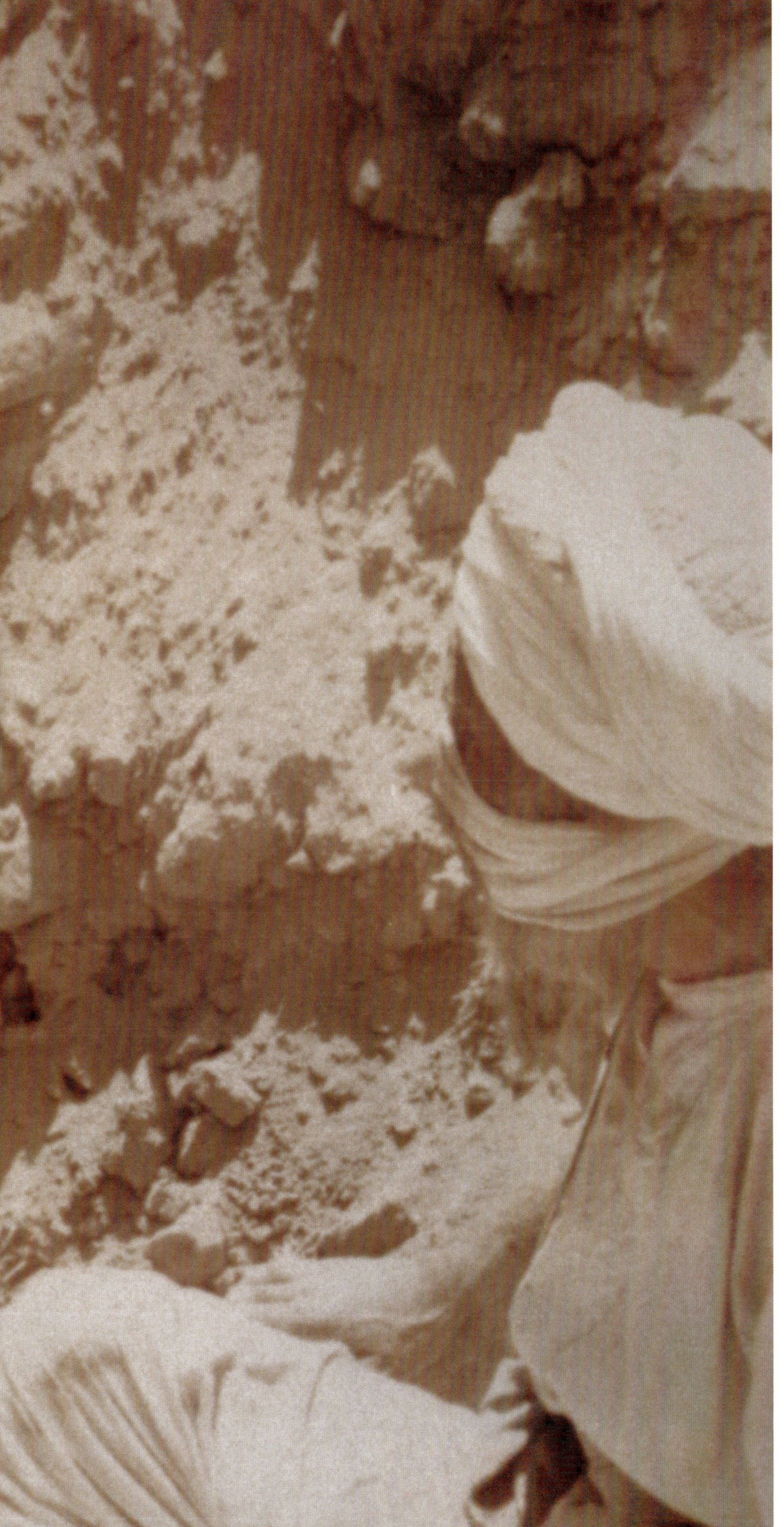

Afghanistan 1986
IMC staff

After a Soviet helicopter attack decimated an entire Afghan village, International Medical Corps entered to check for survivors. IMC doctors found this family frozen in time: two children reaching out to their mother as the building was struck by a missile and destroyed. Covered in the dust from the attack, all three were dead, and rigor mortis had set in, capturing their last desperate moments.

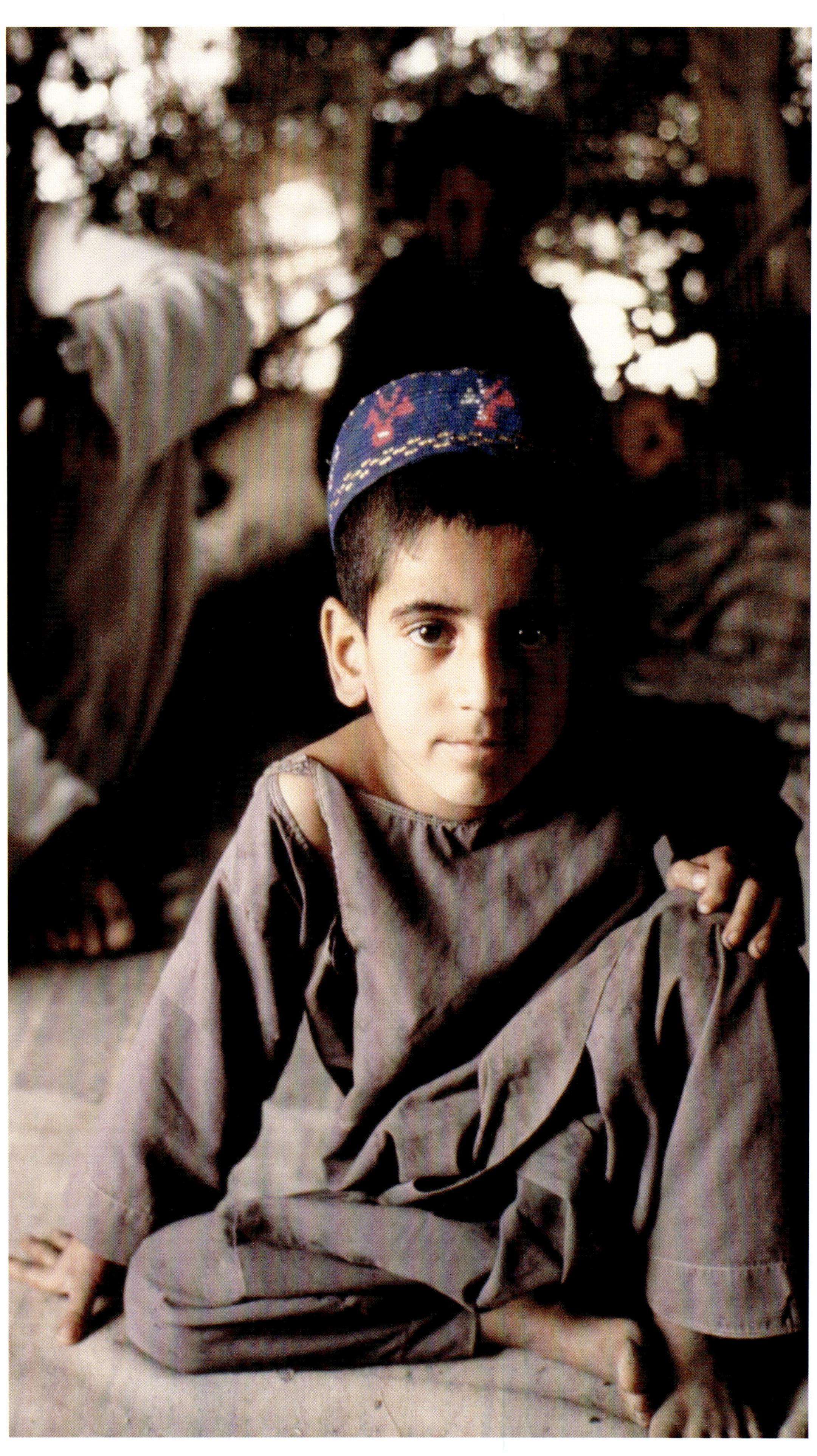

Afghanistan 1986
IMC staff (both pages)

Before the Soviet invasion, 1,500 doctors lived and worked in Afghanistan. By the time International Medical Corps arrived, more than 1,000 Afghan doctors had been imprisoned, killed or exiled, and most health care facilities were destroyed. Fewer than 100 physicians were left with limited health care options for people living in this war-torn region.

Opposite page: Afghan freedom fighters, the Mujahadeen, rode out on horseback to battle with Soviet tanks. Early on, IMC established contact with these freedom fighters and with them entered Afghanistan without government permission, carrying medications and setting up mountain clinics for sick and injured civilians.

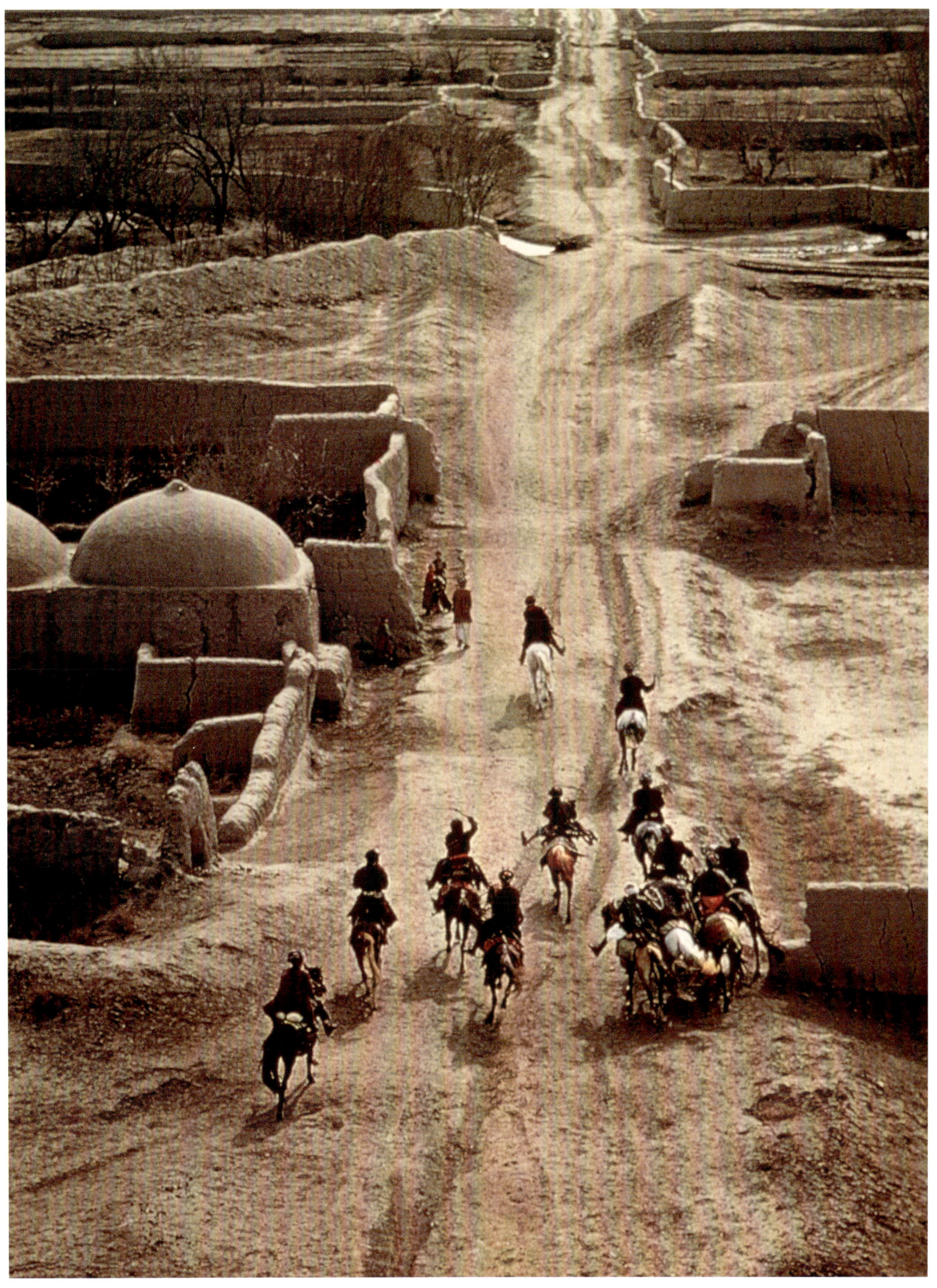

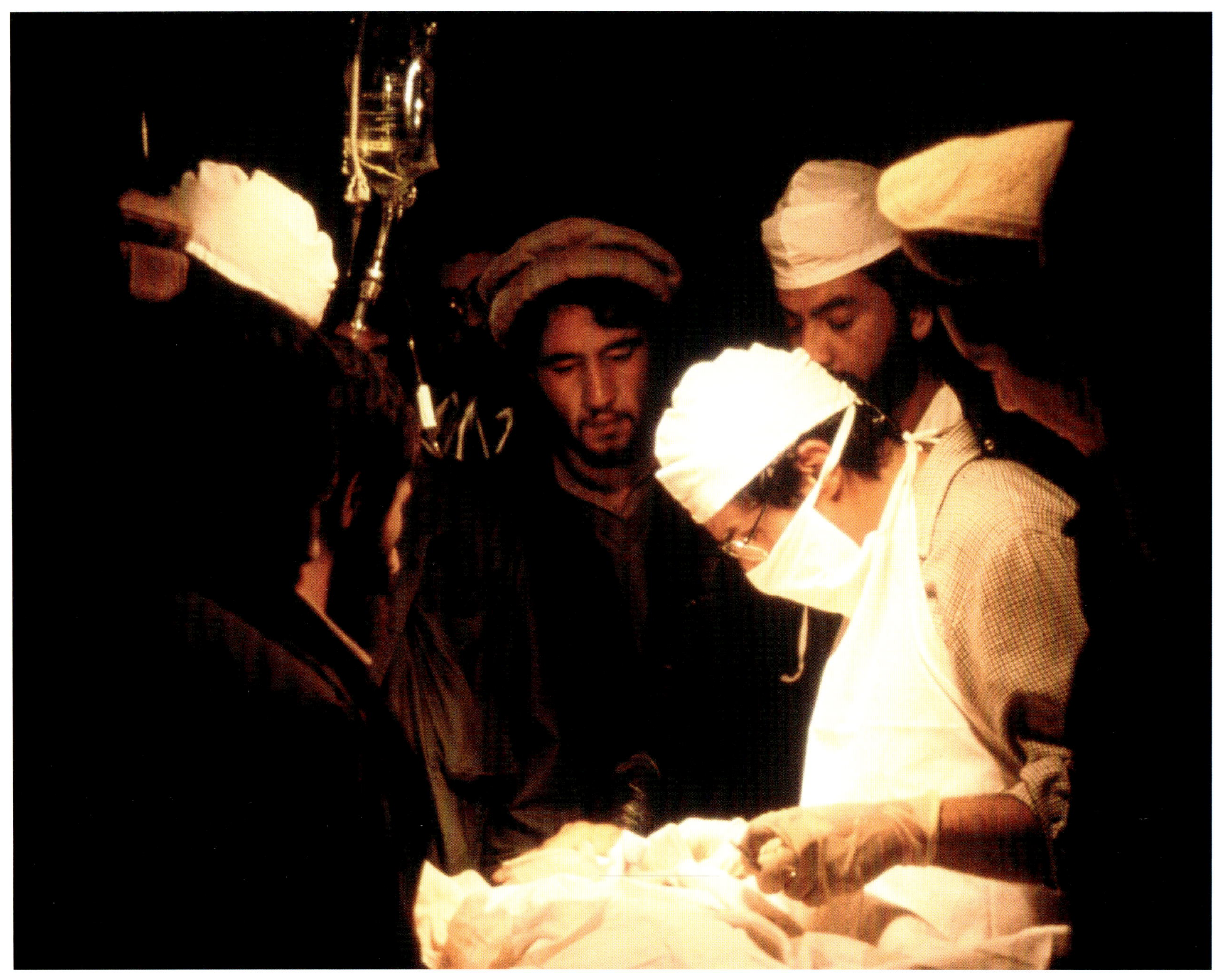

Afghanistan 1984
IMC staff

International Medical Corps founder Dr. Bob Simon traveled to Afghanistan to set up an emergency medical unit for Afghan civilians. With no intention of forming a humanitarian organization, Dr. Simon found the problems in Afghanistan were so pervasive and the need so great that he convinced other colleagues to join him. Thus, International Medical Corps was born. Here Dr. Simon teaches local Afghan medics in one of IMC's first tent clinics in Afghanistan.

Opposite page: International Medical Corps made an arrangement with 20 Mujahadeen commanders, each fighting in a different region in Afghanistan. Each commander individually agreed to send out two young fighters for IMC medical training. By the agreement, after schooling the medics would return to their regions with medications and necessary medical supplies to treat innocent civilians.

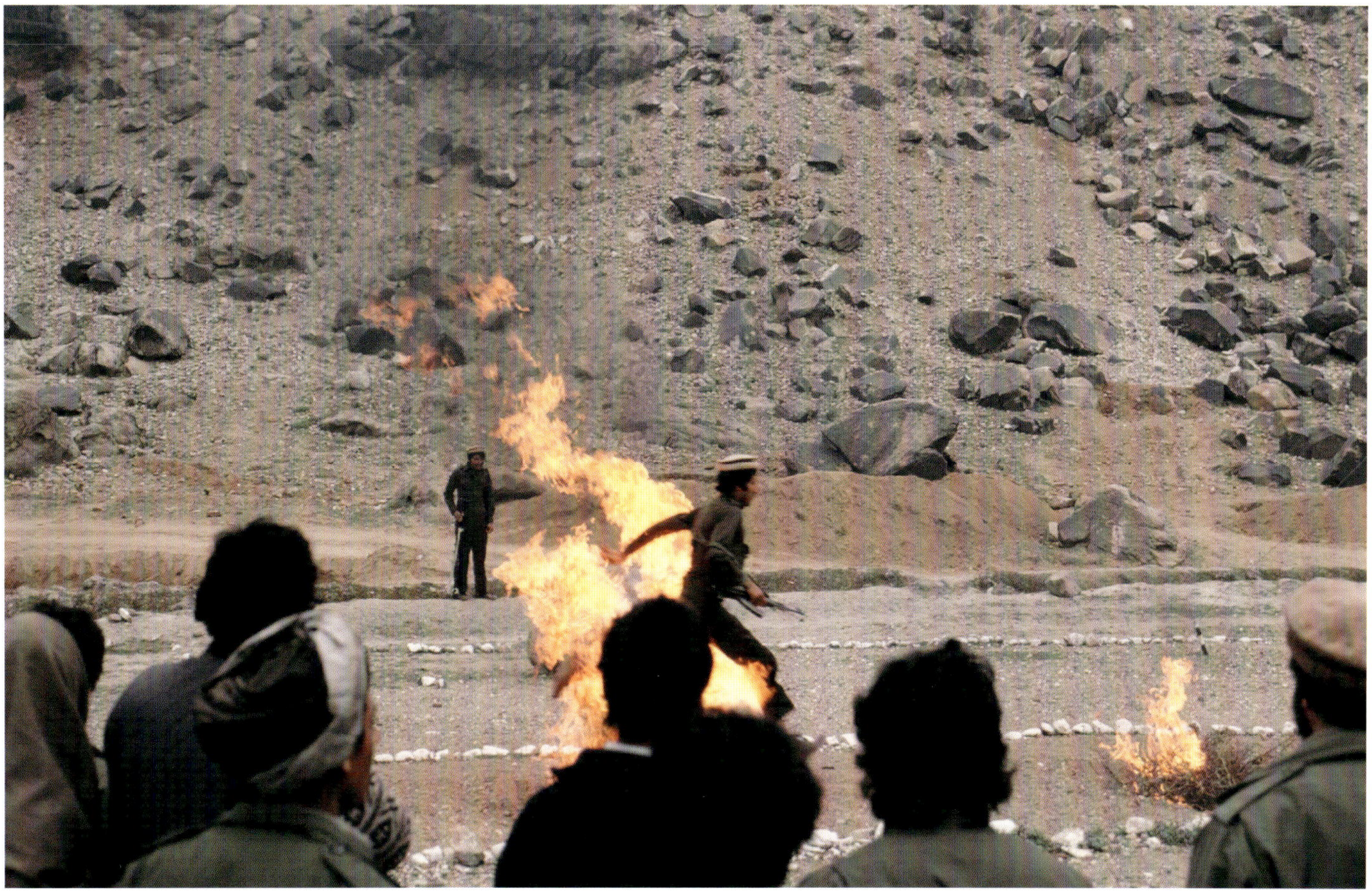

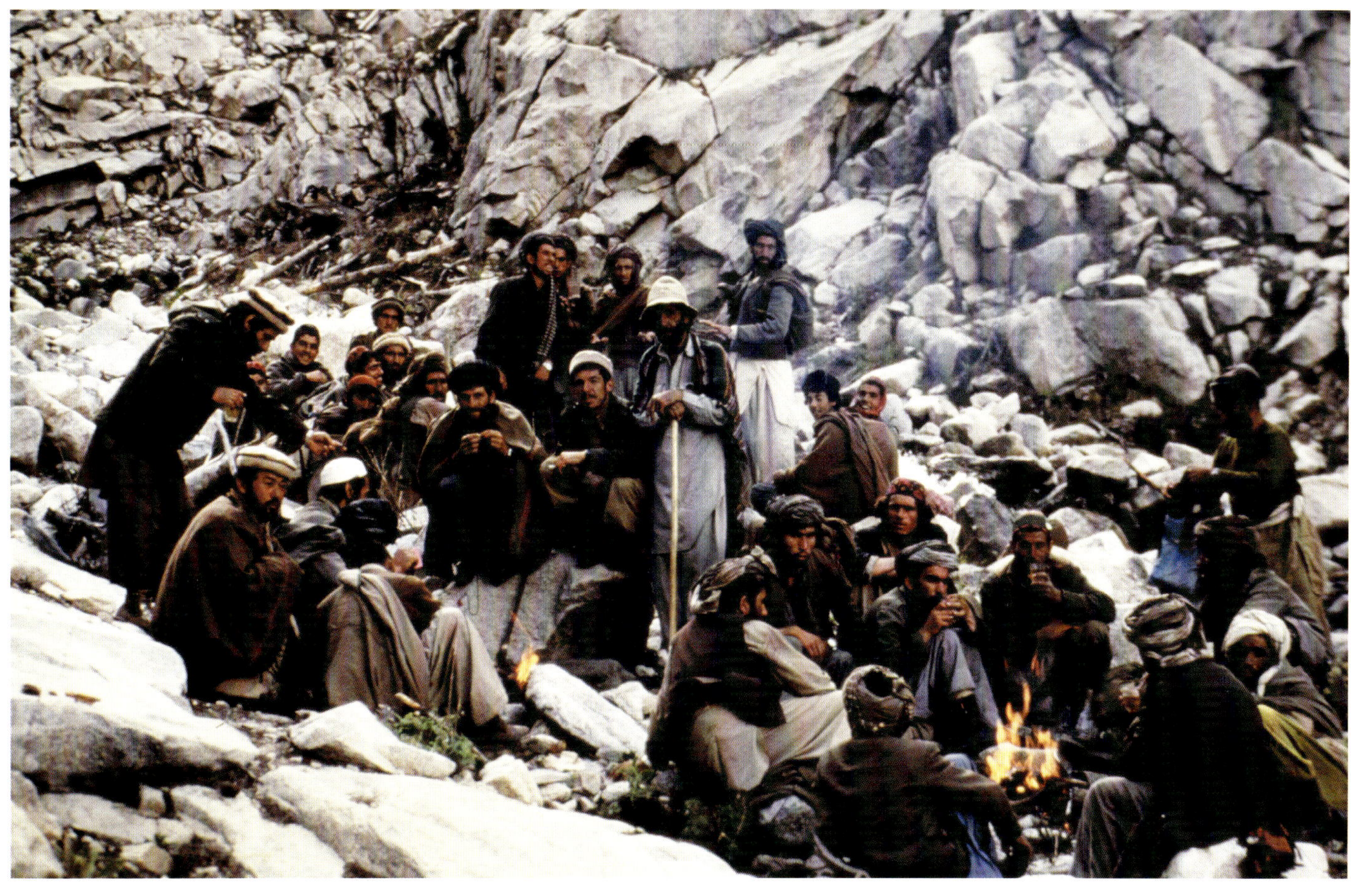

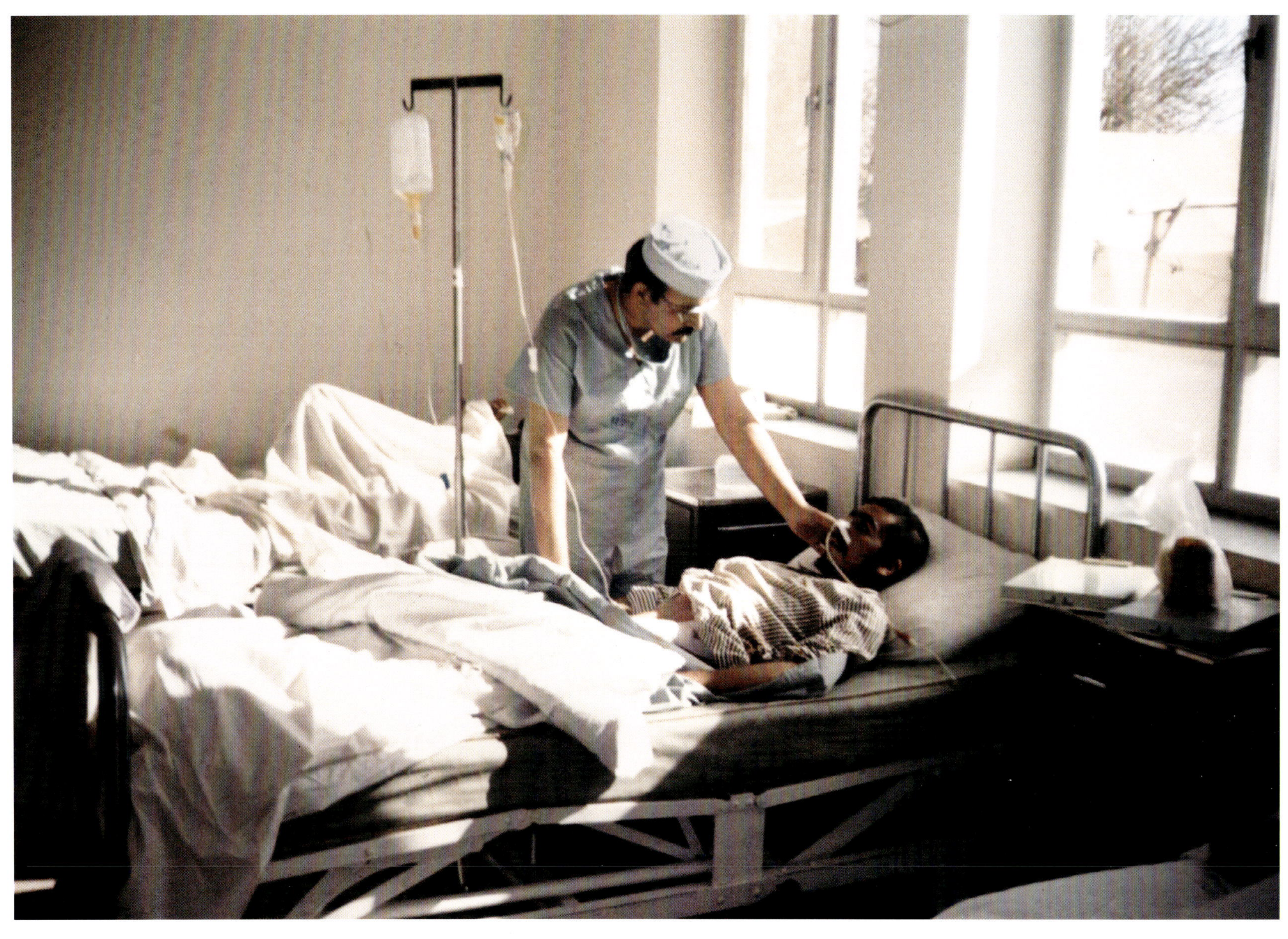

Afghanistan 1994
IMC staff (both photos)

International Medical Corps clinics in Afghanistan were set up to treat innocent civilians, many of whom traveled with weapons for their own protection. IMC health care workers would treat anyone who came to the clinics, as long as they disarmed before entering. International Medical Corps clinics have always enbraced this apolitical approach to global health.

Afghanistan 1984

Opposite page: A young man brought in to one of IMC's tent hospitals is successfully treated for extensive shrapnel wounds.

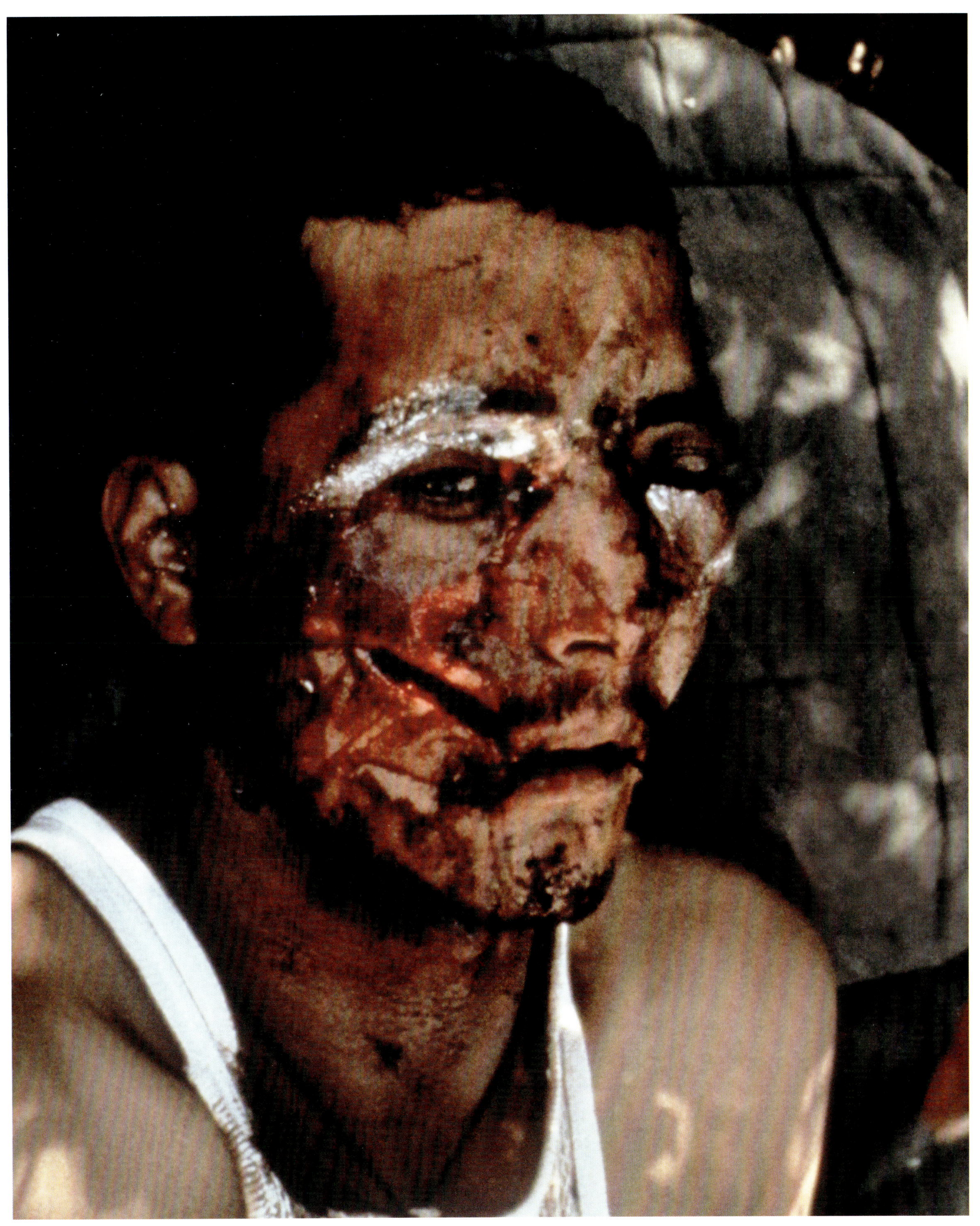

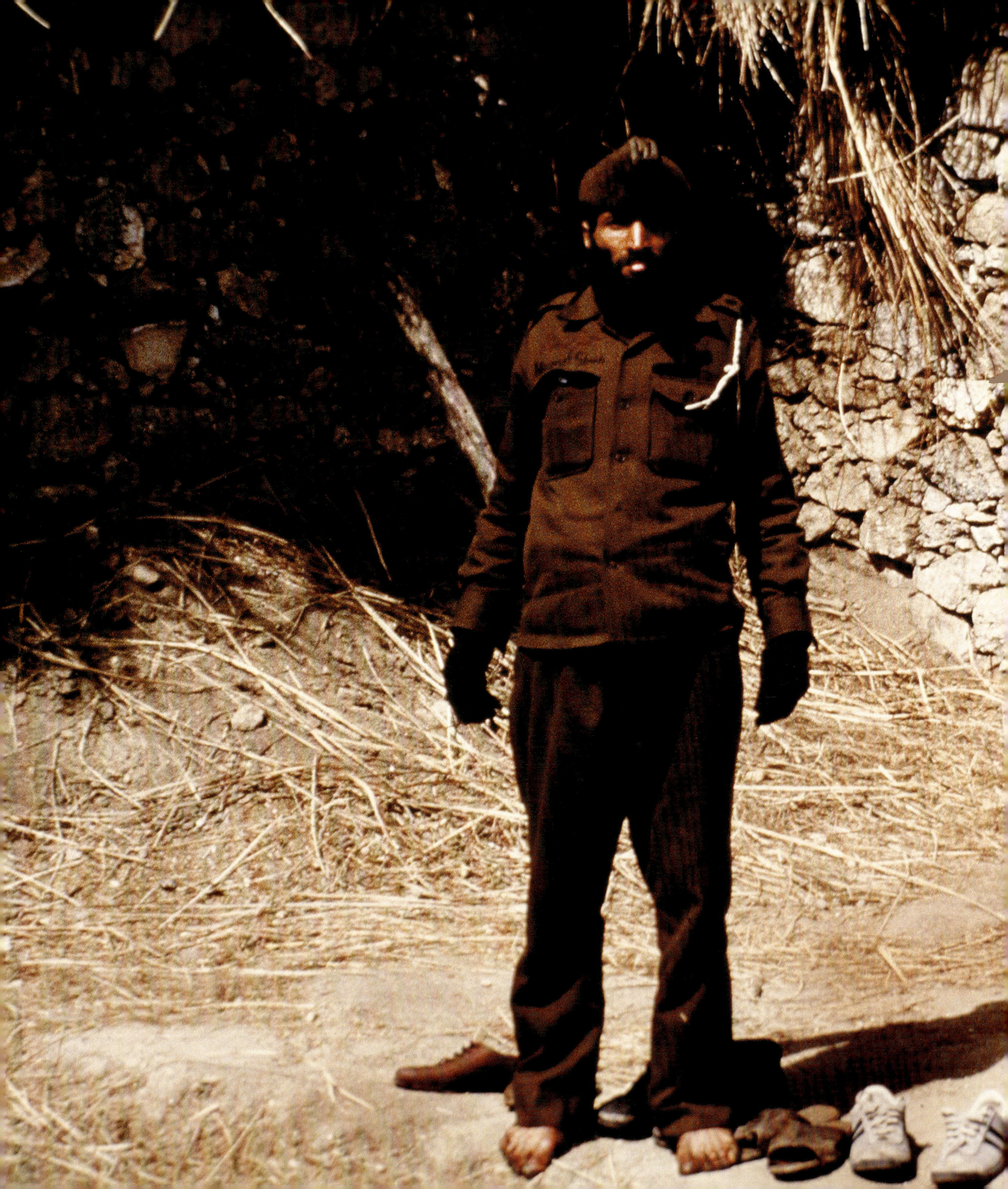

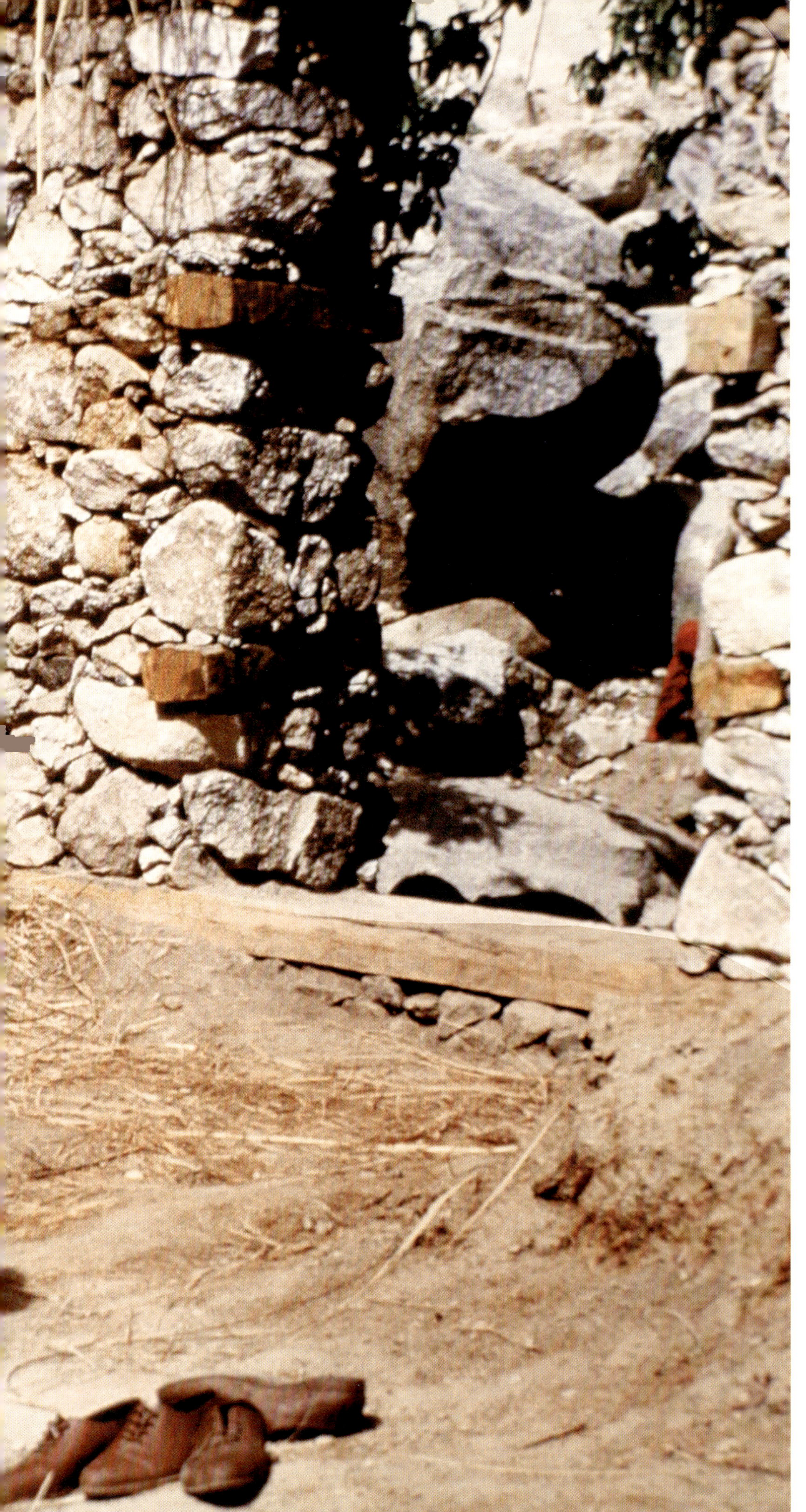

Afghanistan 1984
IMC staff

From the beginning, International Medical Corps believed that local people, carefully selected, could be trained in a matter of months to identify and treat 80% of the most common medical conditions in any population. Many of these local medics in Afghanistan were trained in IMC cave clinics like the one behind this trainee.

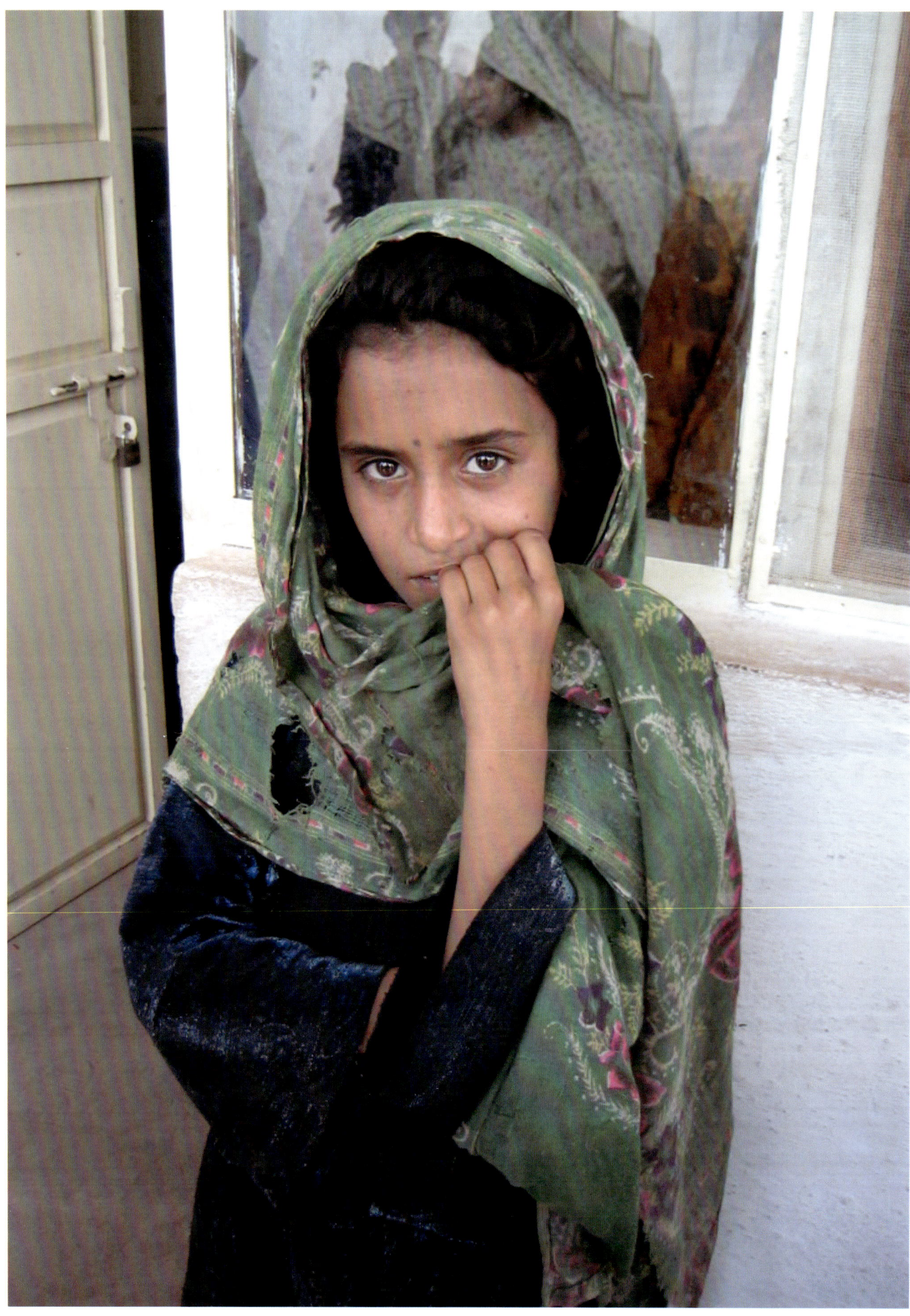

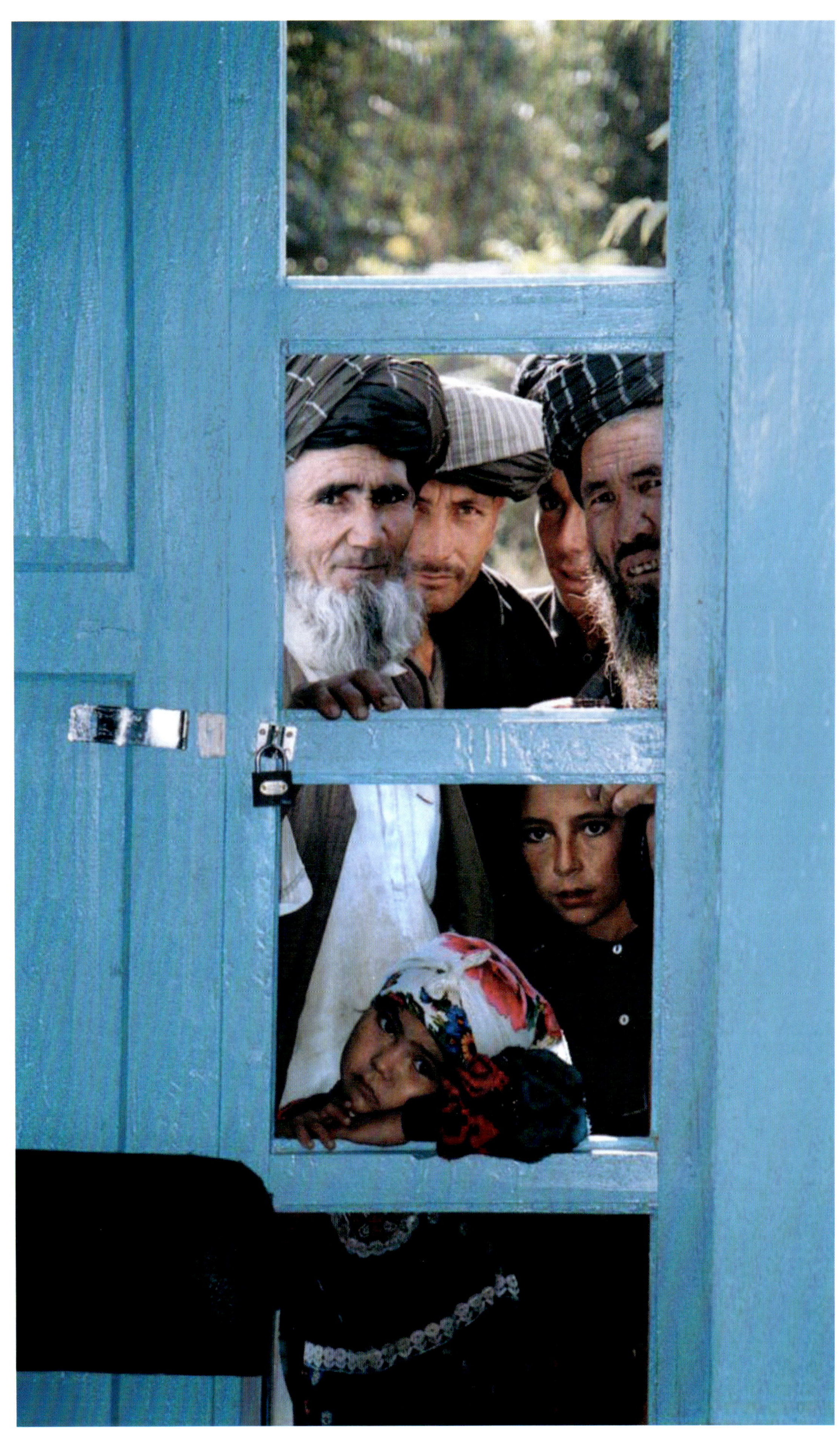

Afghanistan 2002
IMC staff (both photos)

By 1988, International Medical Corps was staffing 89 hidden clinics and hospitals inside Afghanistan and was actively immunizing children and women of childbearing age across the country. Today these IMC clinics continue to provide much-needed health care to Afghan people who are still affected by conflict in the region.

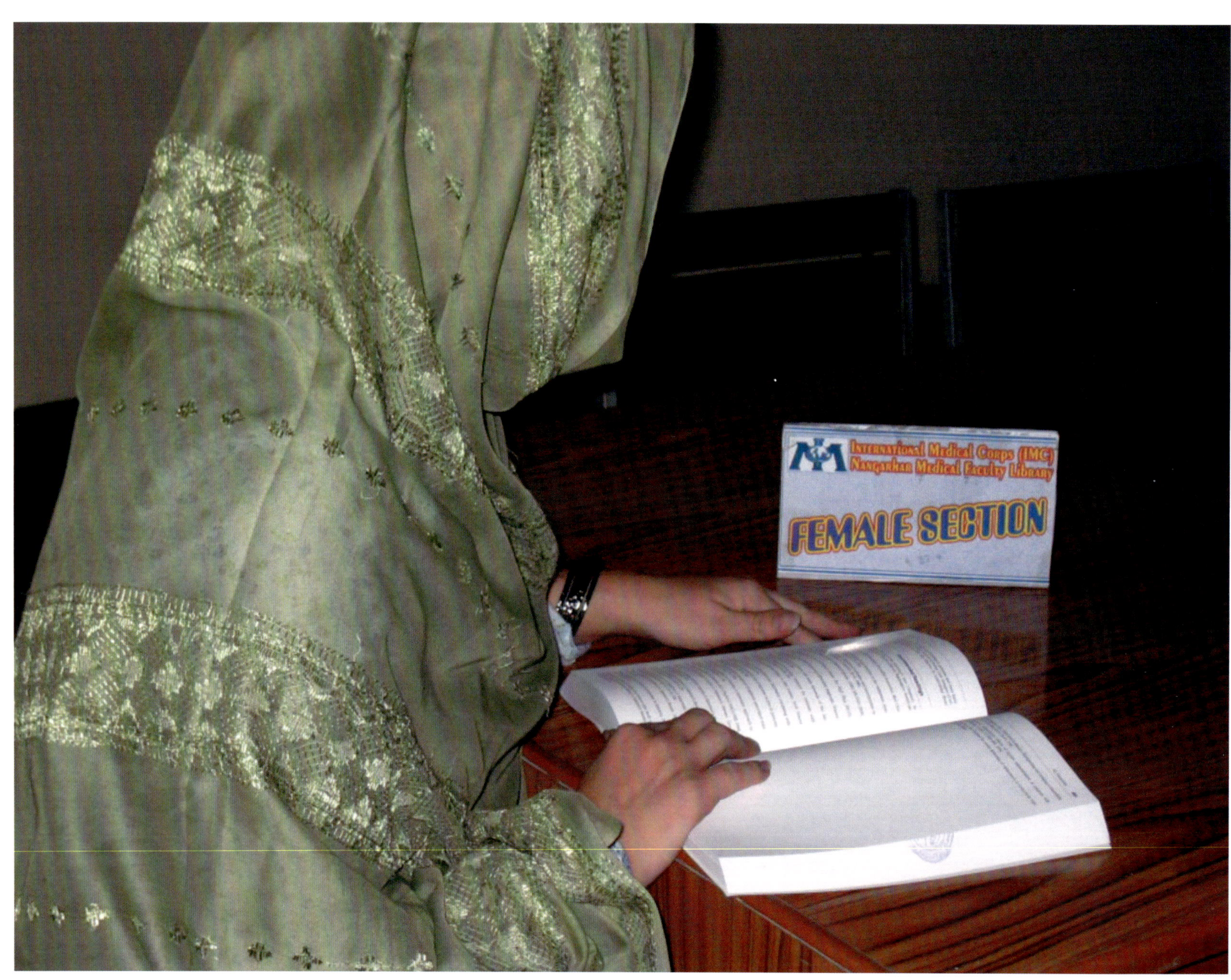

Afghanistan 2006
IMC staff

International Medical Corps was chosen to create a training program at Rabia Balkhi Women's Hospital. This hospital is Kabul's second busiest maternity hospital, with more than 15,000 babies born there each year.

Sara Terry

Opposite page: A new mother is taken by wheelchair to the front gate of the International Medical Corps hospital. Most Afghan women leave the hospital within a few hours of giving birth. The new mother is given a "feroza" (turquoise ring), which, according to local custom, she wears after delivery for 42 days to protect her and her child.

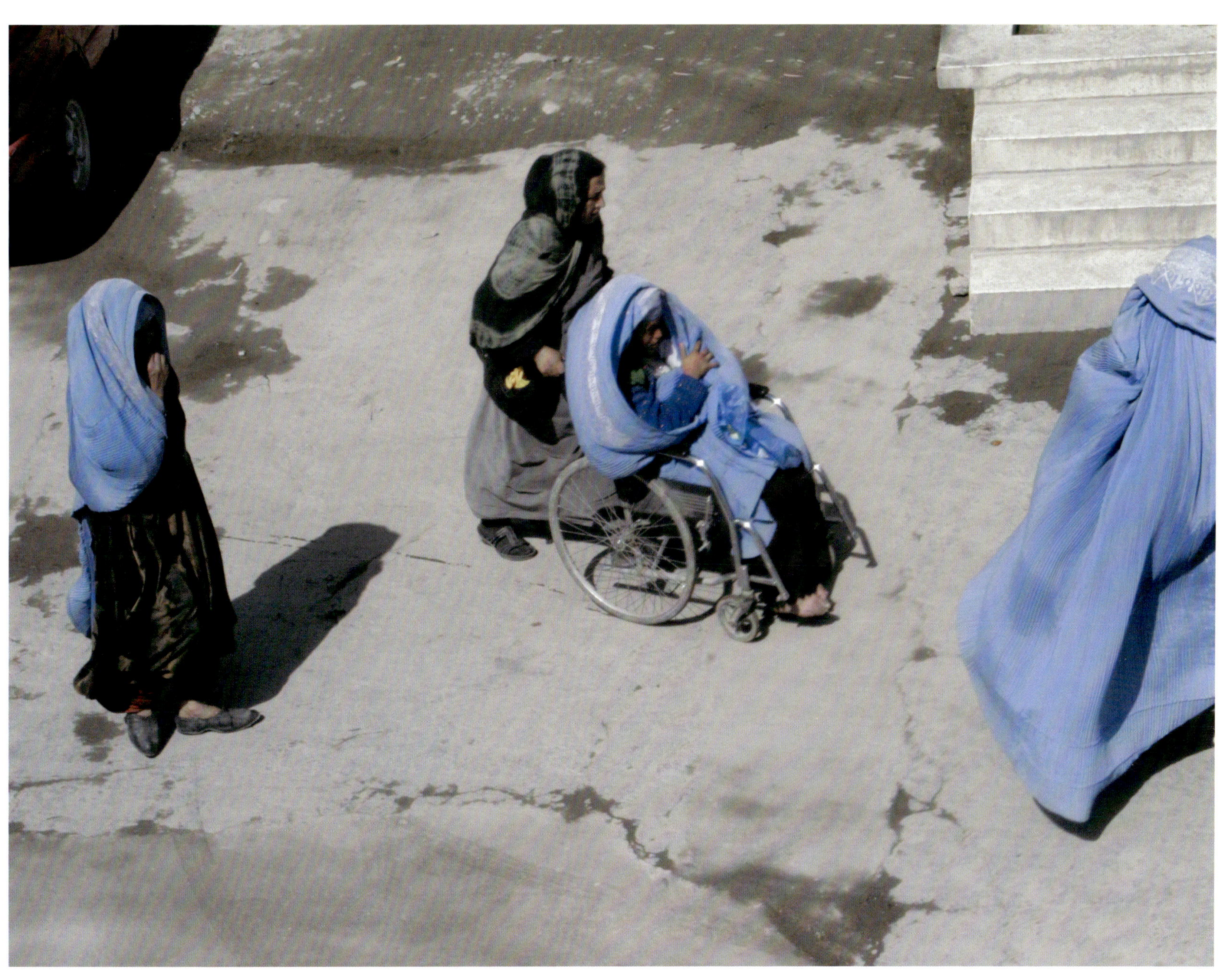

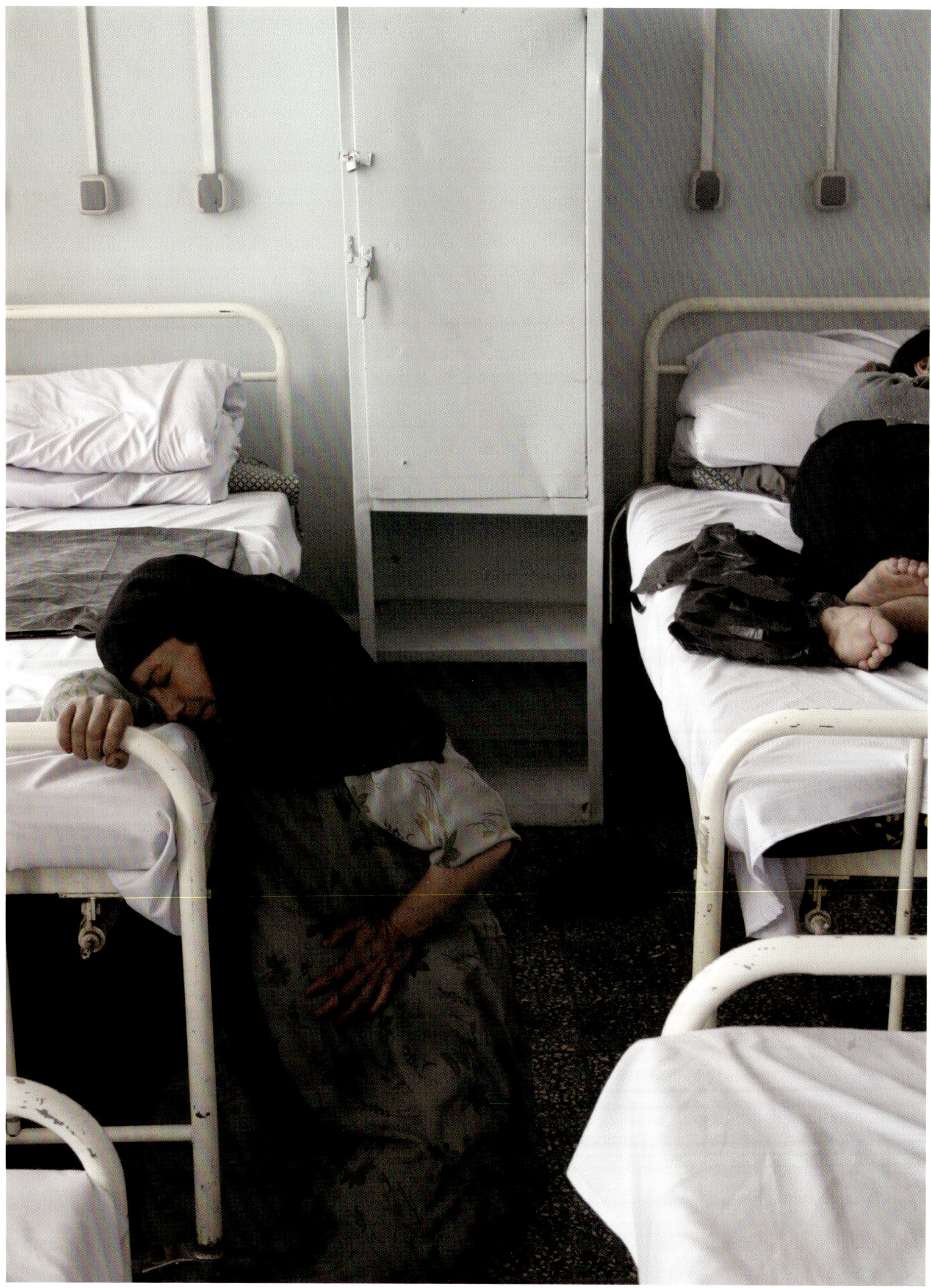

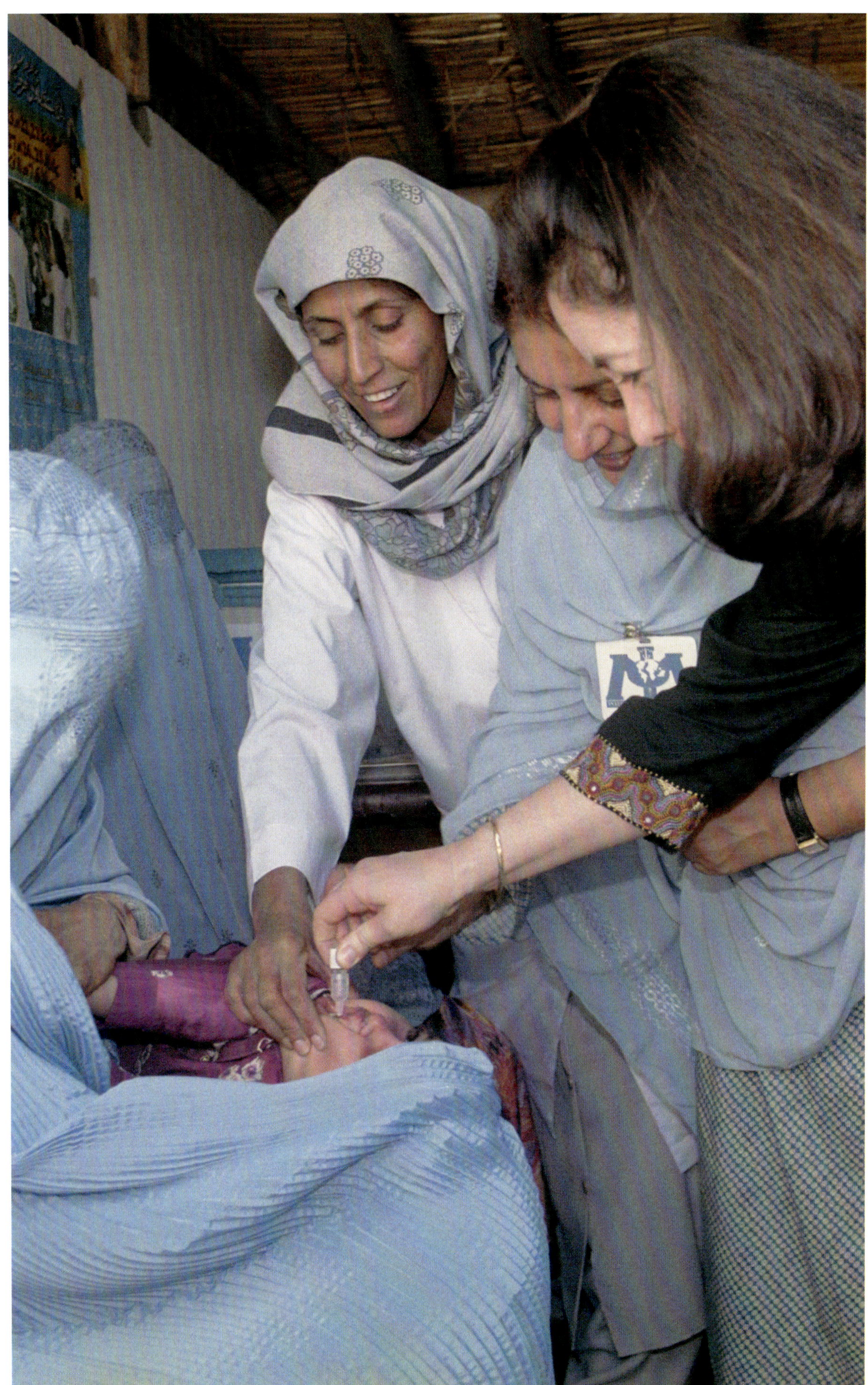

Pakistan 2001
IMC Staff
International Medical Corps CEO Nancy Aossey attends to an Afghan woman and her newborn child. In keeping with cultural and religious tradition in Afghanistan, female patients are examined by female health care workers. The Afghan women in this photo went back to Afghanistan after the fall of the Taliban and set up some of the first International Medical Corps women's clinics in Kabul.

Afghanistan 2006
Sara Terry
Opposite page: In the labor room, a woman is having contractions and is close to giving birth. The fertility rate among Afghan women is 6.6, two-and-a-half times higher than the world average. Almost half of the deaths of women in Afghanistan are due to problems in pregnancy or childbirth; it is estimated that 75 percent of those deaths are preventable.

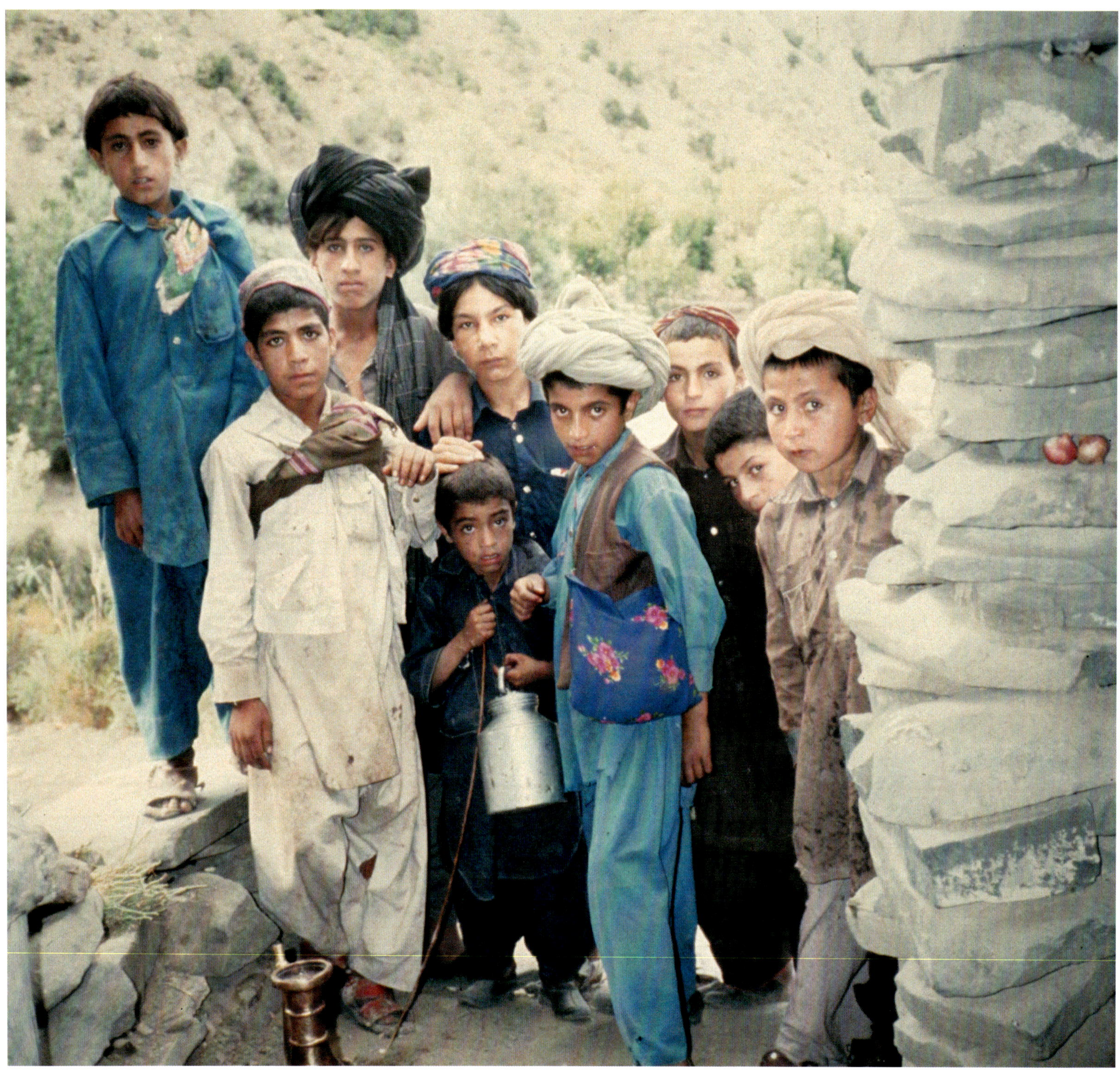

Afghanistan 1986
IMC staff

The rise of the Taliban has since made International Medical Corps clinics in Afghanistan even more necessary. Each day, hundreds of children are treated at IMC clinics and many risk their lives, walking for miles to reach the facility.

Afghanistan 2005
IMC staff

Opposite page: Dr. Lillian Rachlin, the first woman in the United States to serve as an orthopedic surgeon with the VA, was International Medical Corps' medical coordinator in the late '80s.

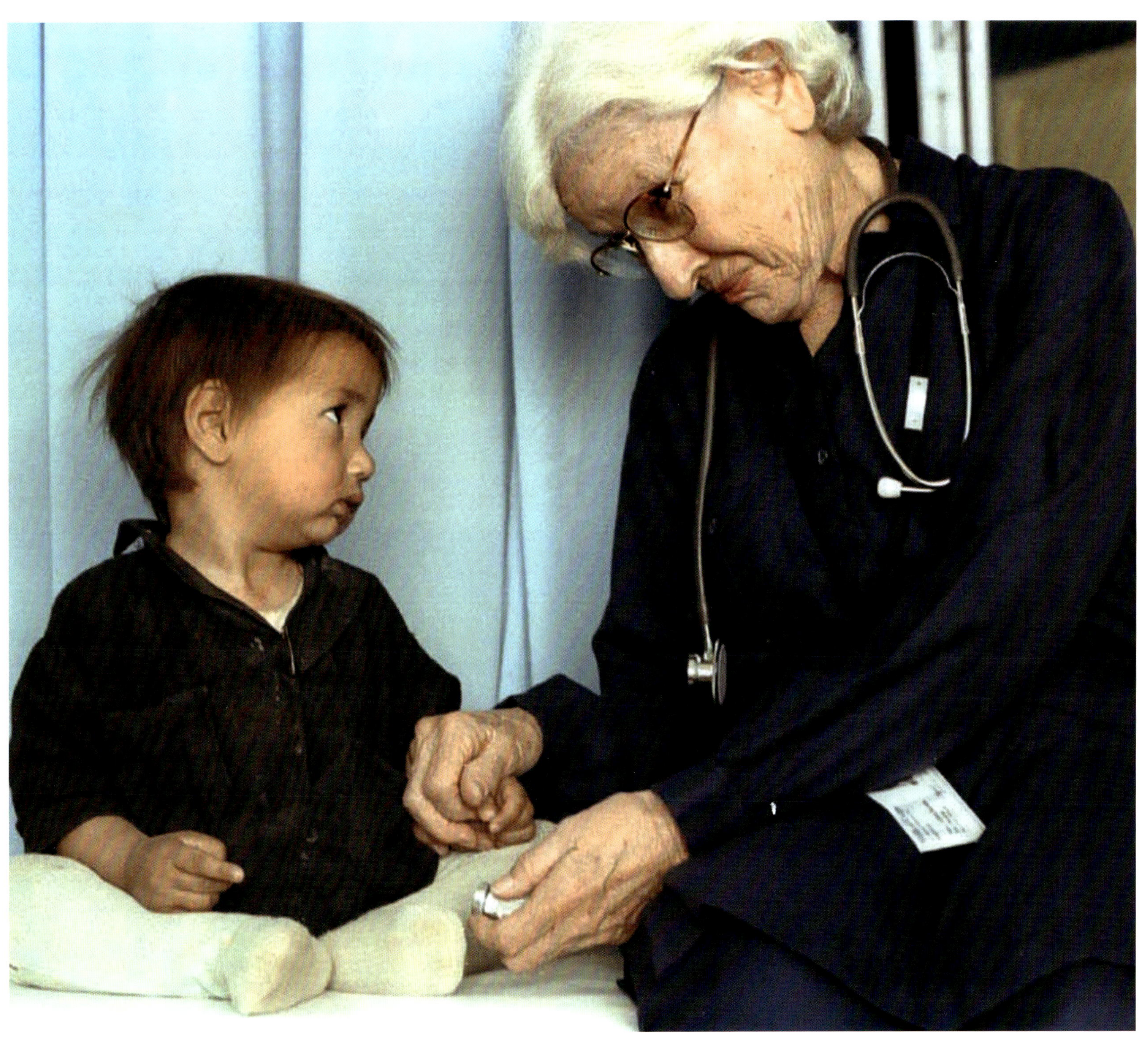

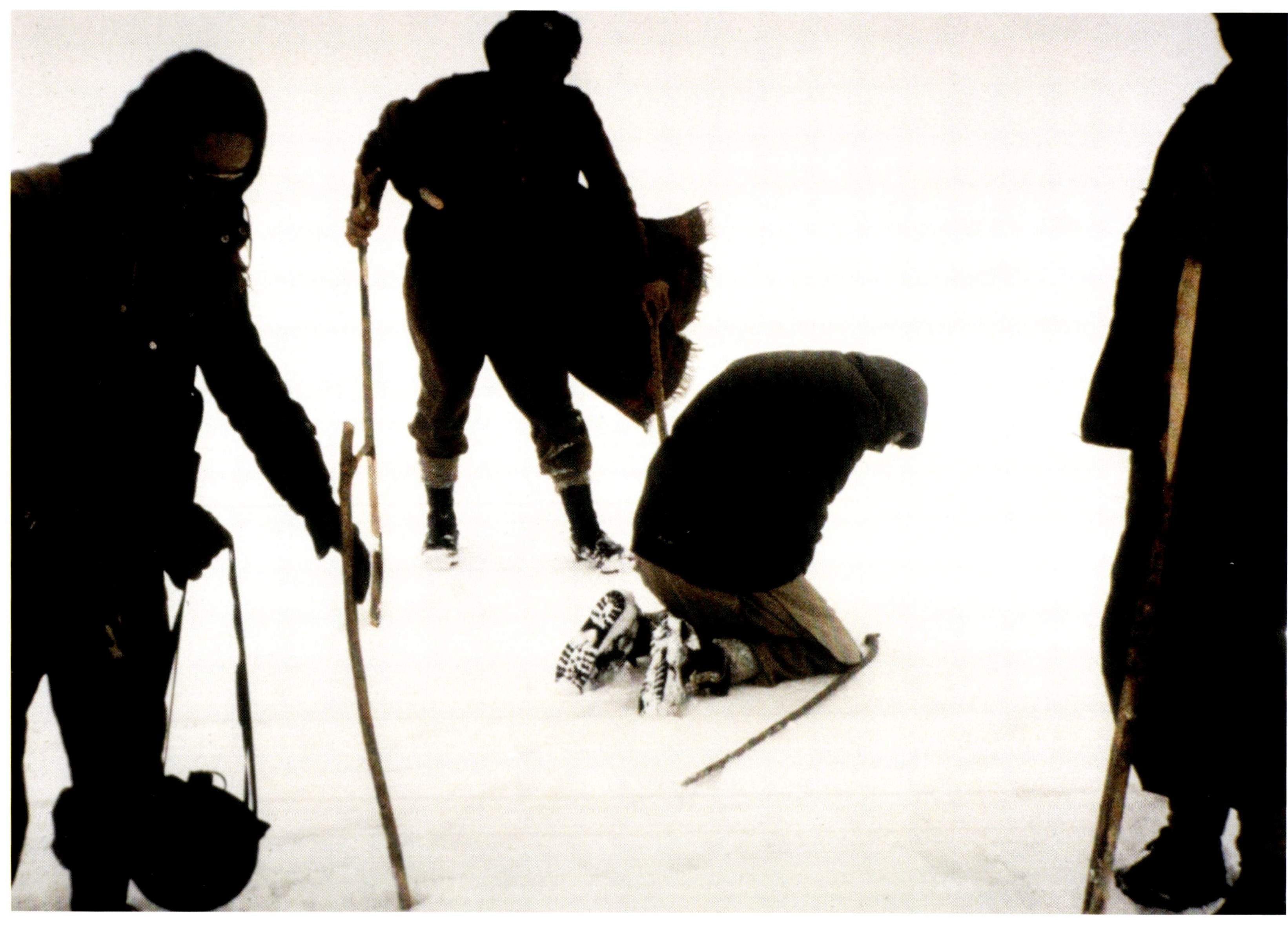

Pakistan 1986
IMC staff

The first two International Medical Corps teams traveled with the Mujahadeen and moved secretly from Peshawar, Pakistan into Afghanistan on short, six-week visits to treat many of the Afghan civilian victims. The third team entered Afghanistan accompanied by two reporters from Arizona and was discovered by Soviet forces while crossing the border. One of the journalists was killed; the rest of the team made it back safely into Pakistan. International Medical Corps was forced to move its training clinic to Pakistan, 11 miles from the Kyber Pass into Afghanistan. Afghan refugees are still being treated there today.

Pakistan 1986
IMC staff

Opposite, top: The founding philosophy of International Medical Corps was simply to provide assistance within a besieged nation. But when seven million Afghans (25% of the population) fled to Pakistan during the Soviet invasion, IMC began to care for thousands of Afghan child refugees in Pakistan. IMC treated several Afghan children disfigured by Soviet toy bombs.

Pakistan 2000
Marissa Roth

Opposite, bottom: Afghan girls cross the border to Pakistan with their mother to visit an International Medical Corps women's health clinic still operating there. For many Afghan women and girls, IMC is their only health care option.

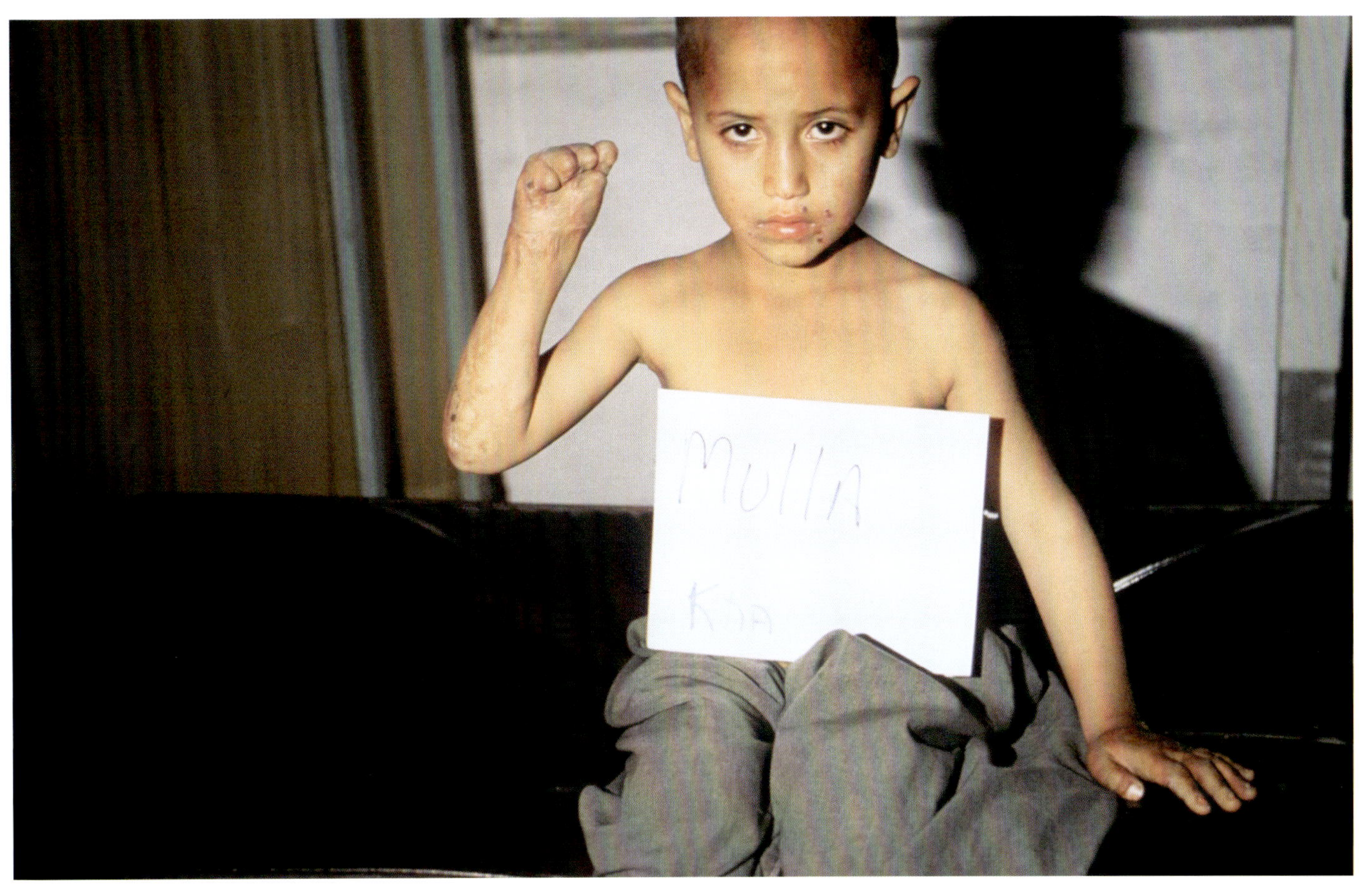
Mulla

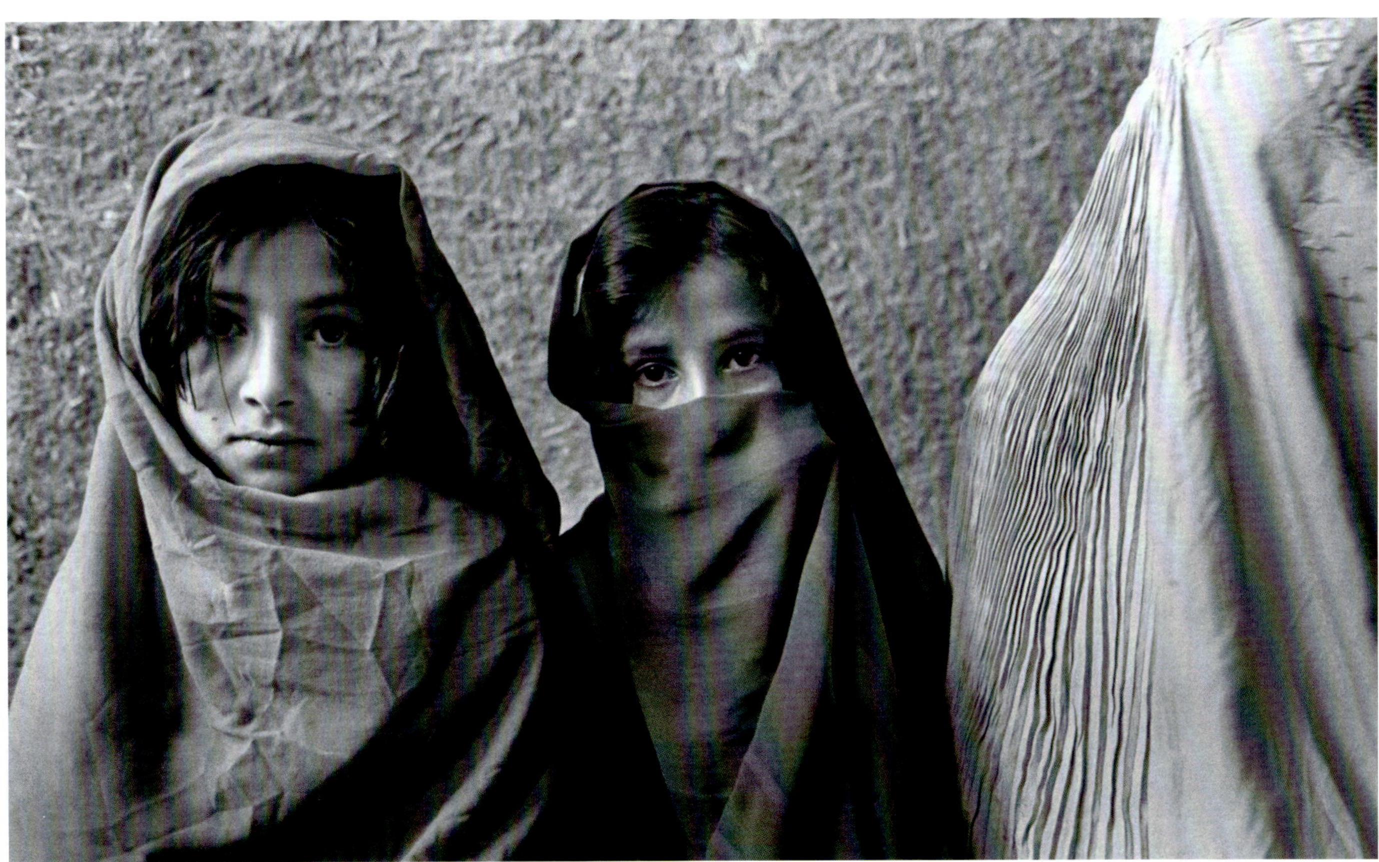

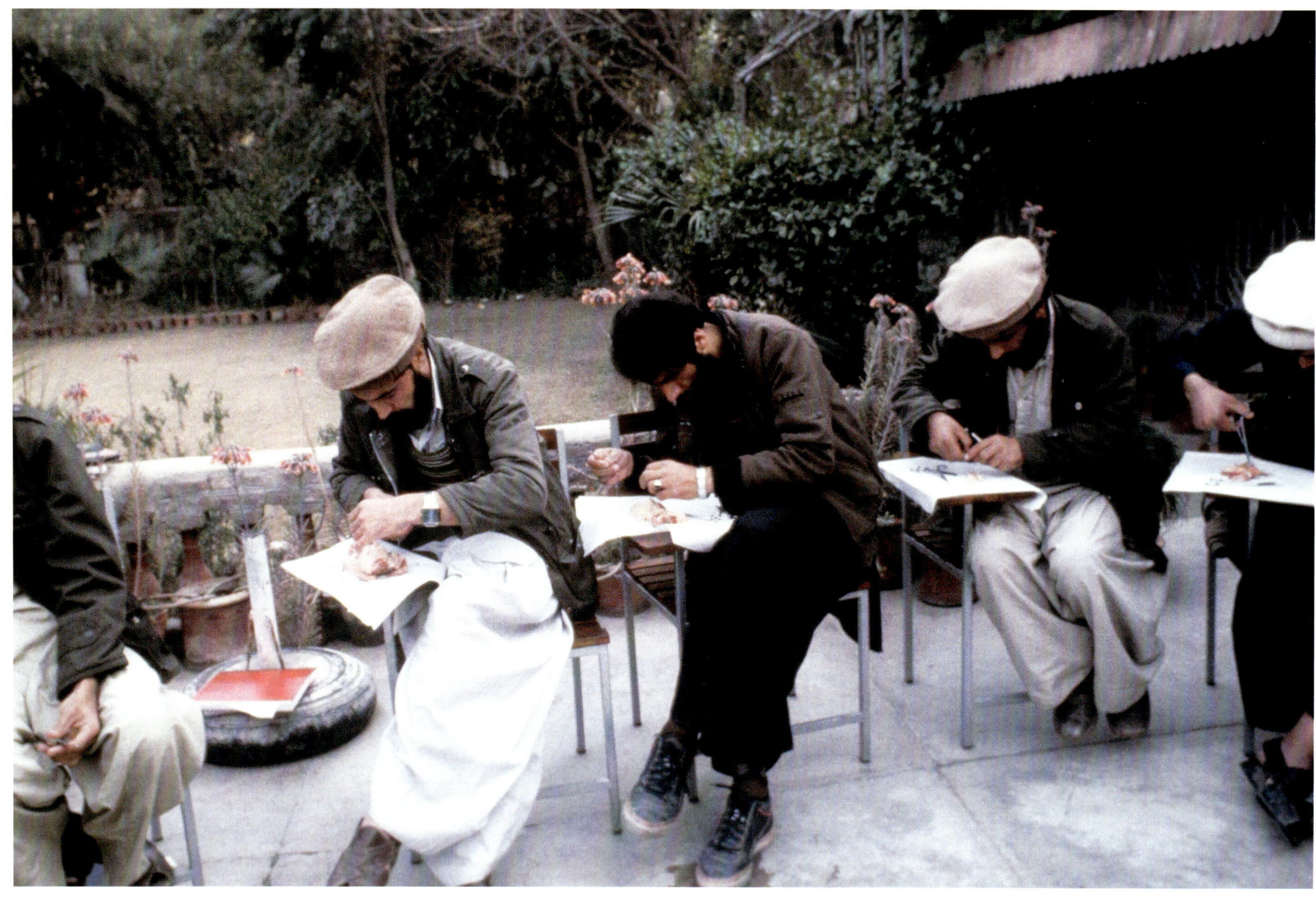

Pakistan 1986
IMC staff
International Medical Corps set up a medic-training school in Peshawar, Pakistan. There, Afghan medical trainees studied in outdoor classrooms where IMC doctors and nurses taught through translators recruited from the Afghan population.

IMC staff
Opposite page: An Afghan medic, trained by International Medical Corps, examines a child's ear in a local clinic. After their training, medics were sent back to Afghanistan to establish clinics in remote regions. Many of these medics continue to work to this day.

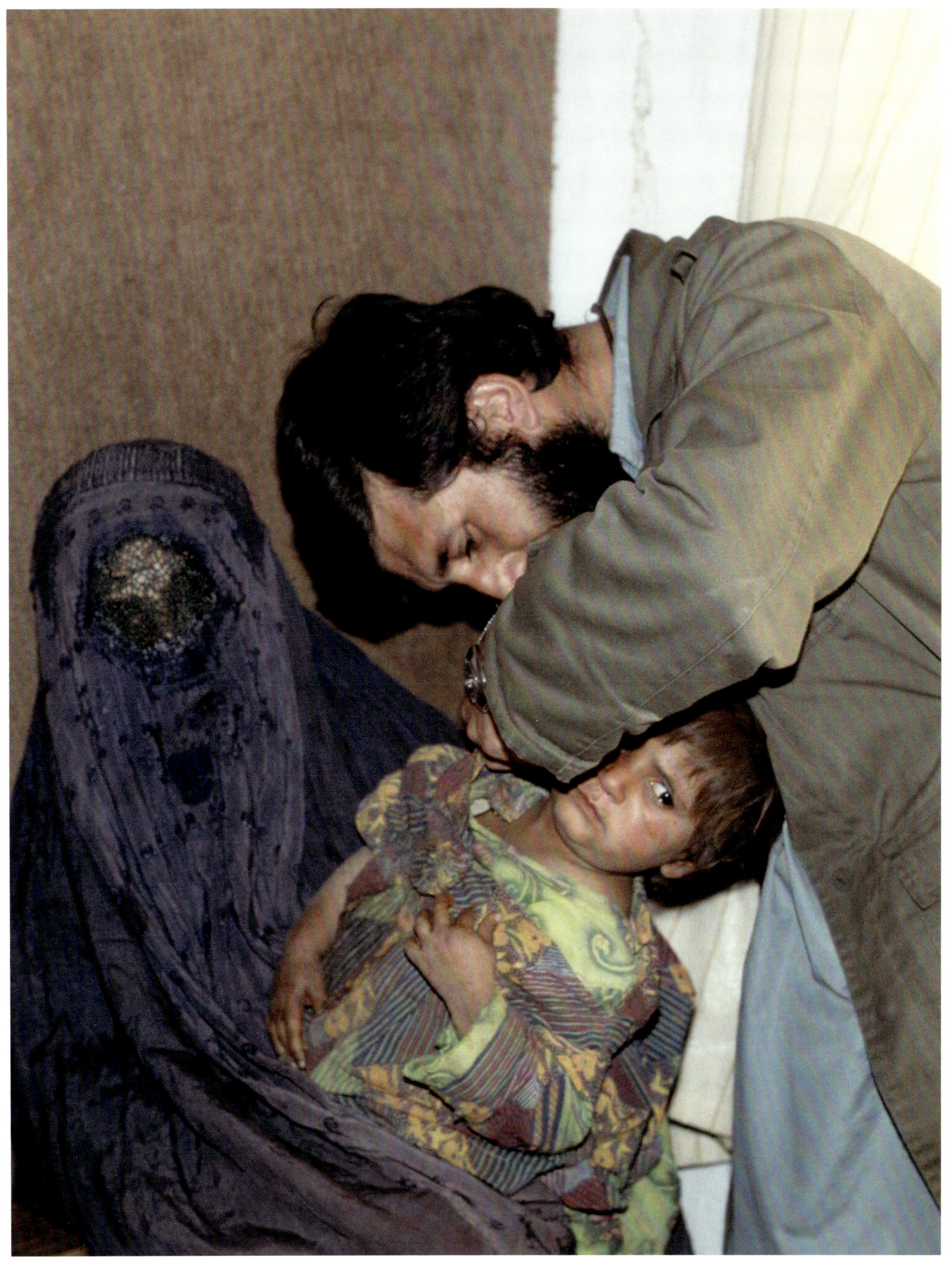

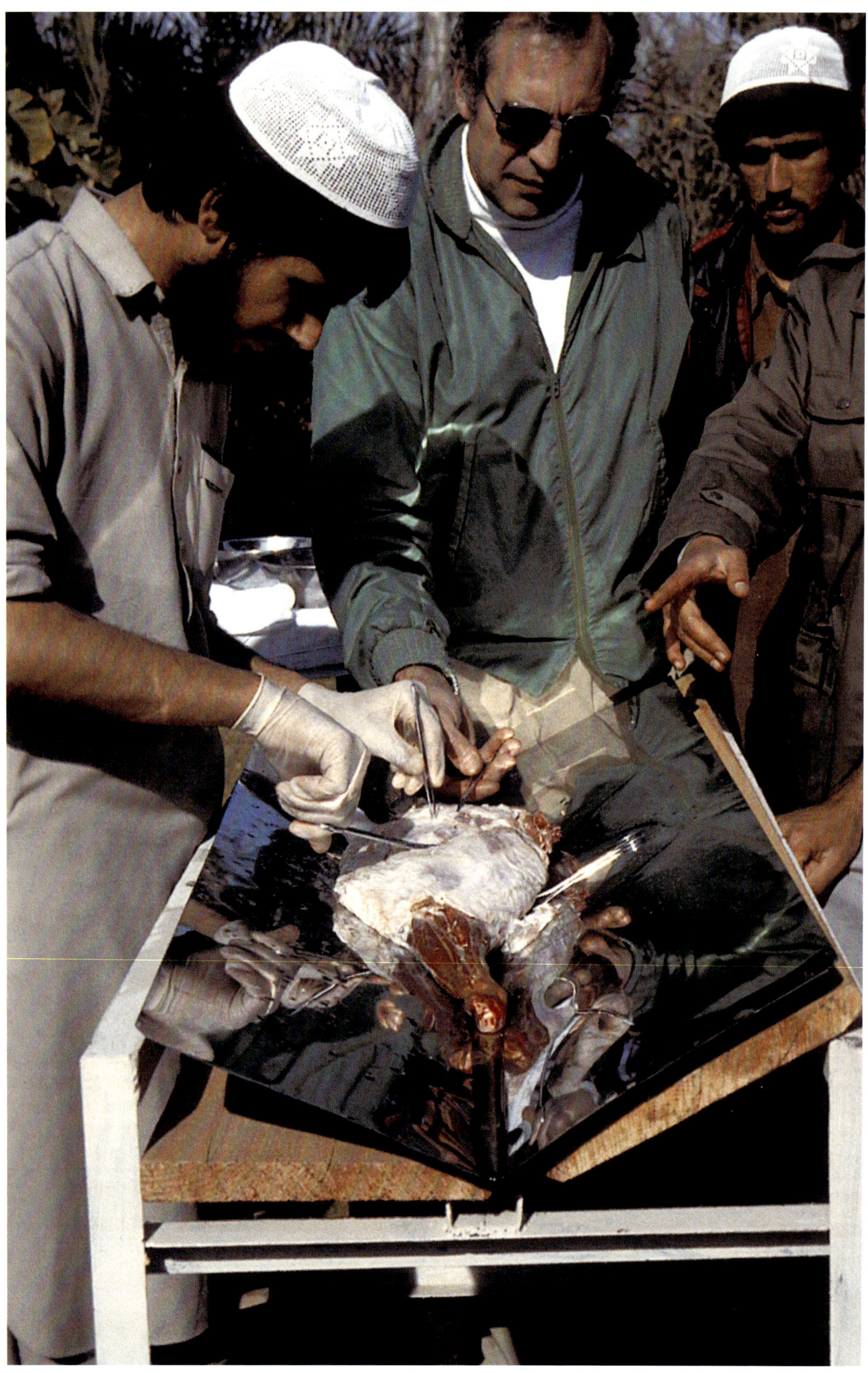

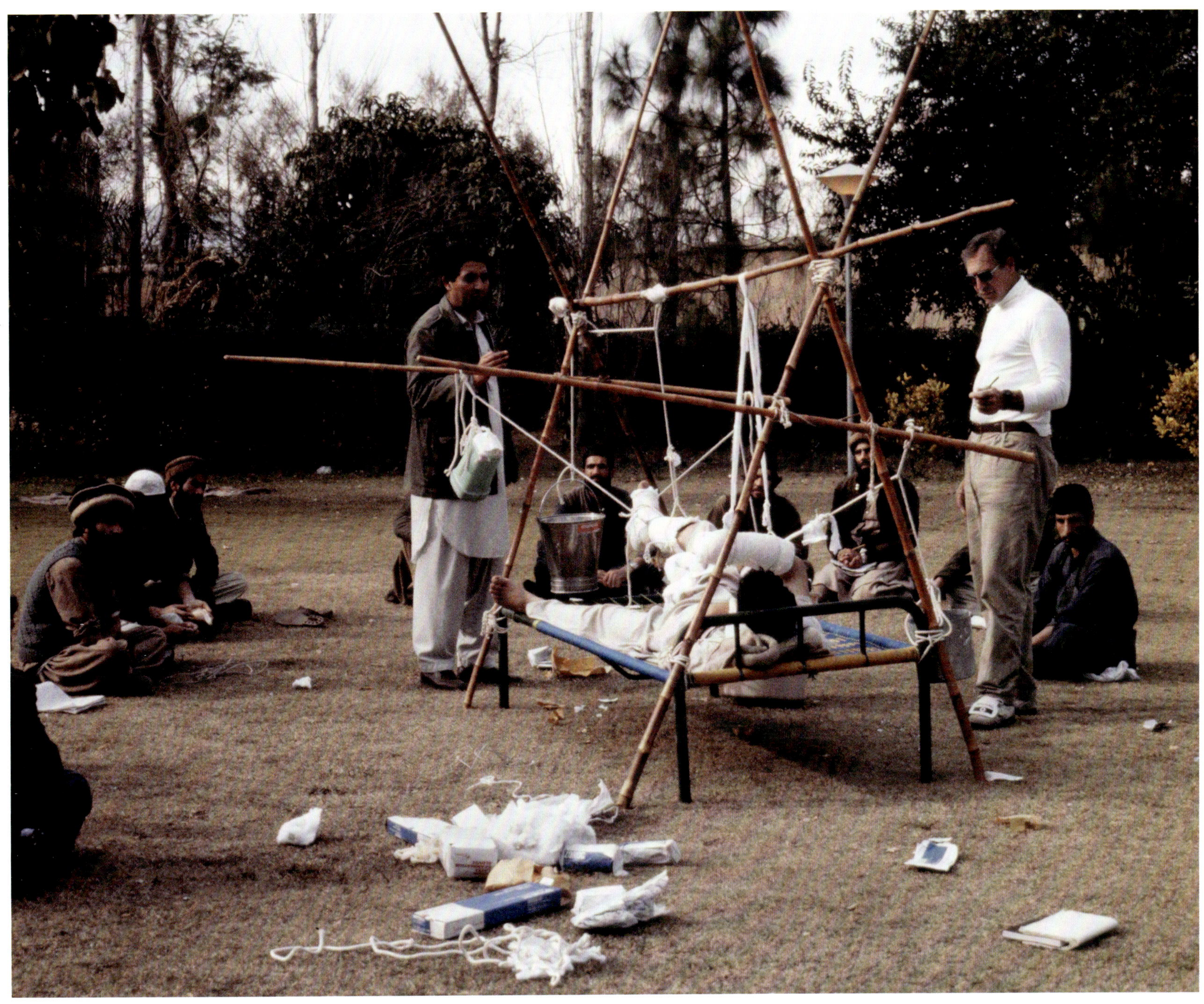

Pakistan 1986

IMC staff

International Medical Corps volunteer Dr. Henry Hood teaches Afghan medical trainees how to set up a traction device for a patient with multiple fractures. This portable orthopedic traction lab—the first of its kind—was made in the field from bamboo, gauze and rope, all lightweight and easy to transport across the border to Afghanistan.

IMC staff

Opposite page: International Medical Corps set up outdoor surgical labs at their training clinics, where anatomy and surgical tissue work was practiced on meat from the butcher shop. Each night, the practice meat was cooked for dinner.

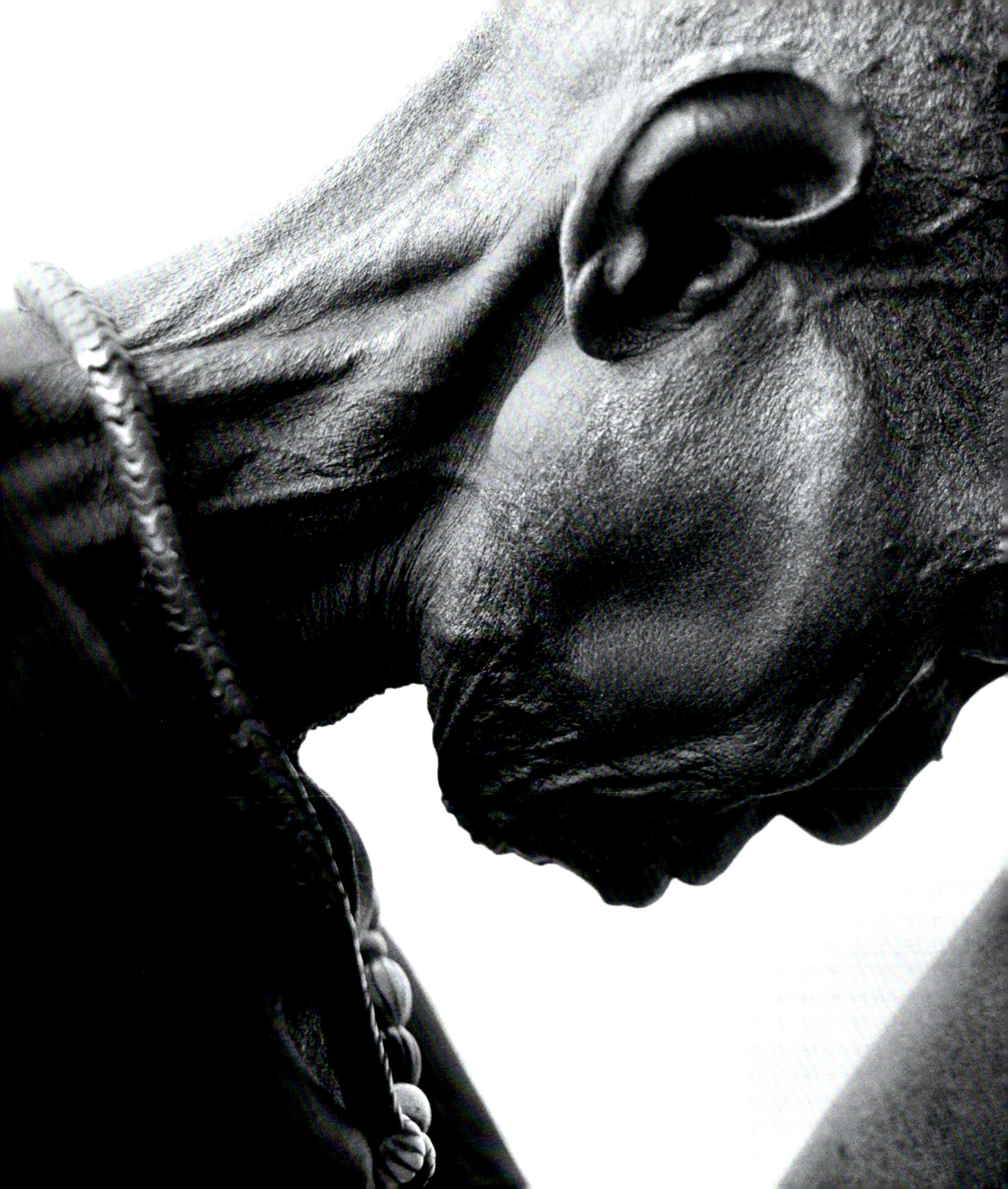

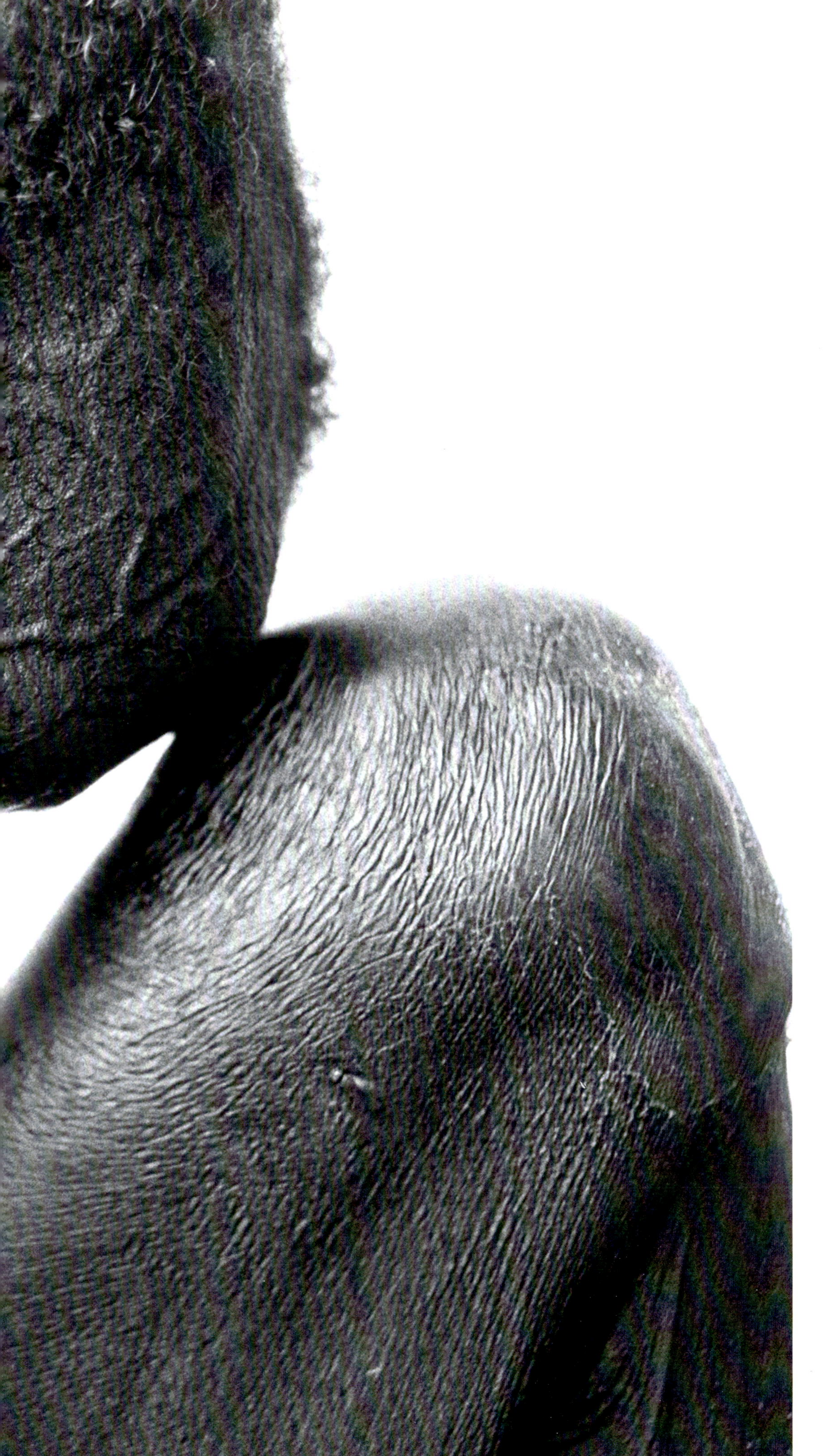

Darfur Sudan 1998
Colin Finlay

For years, the Darfur region of Sudan had been torn apart by a violent conflict that affected millions of Sudanese, killed tens of thousands, displaced more than two million people, and put an already fragile health care system into jeopardy. International Medical Corps had already been operating in Sudan for 10 years by the time it established official programs in war-torn Darfur in 2004.

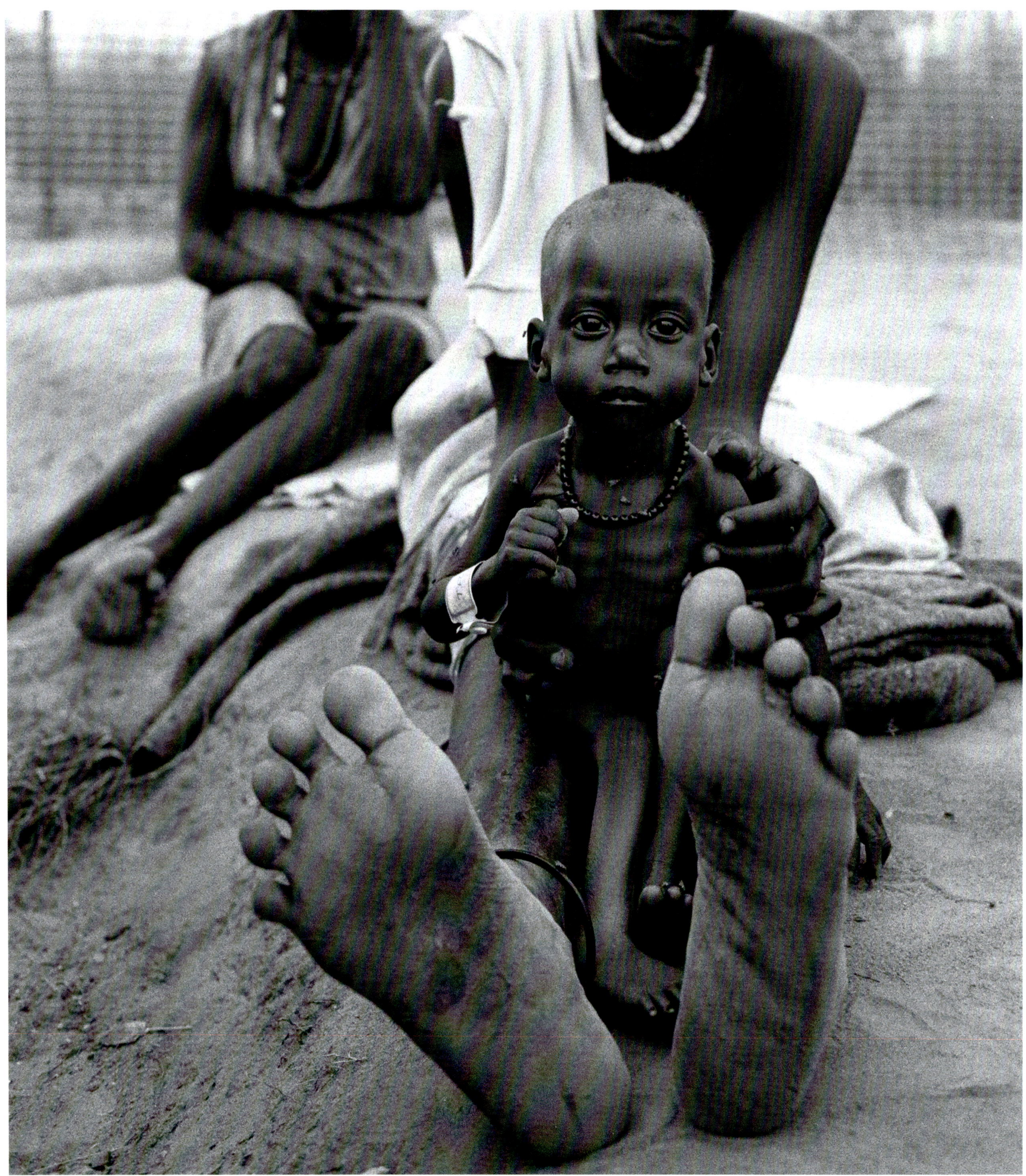

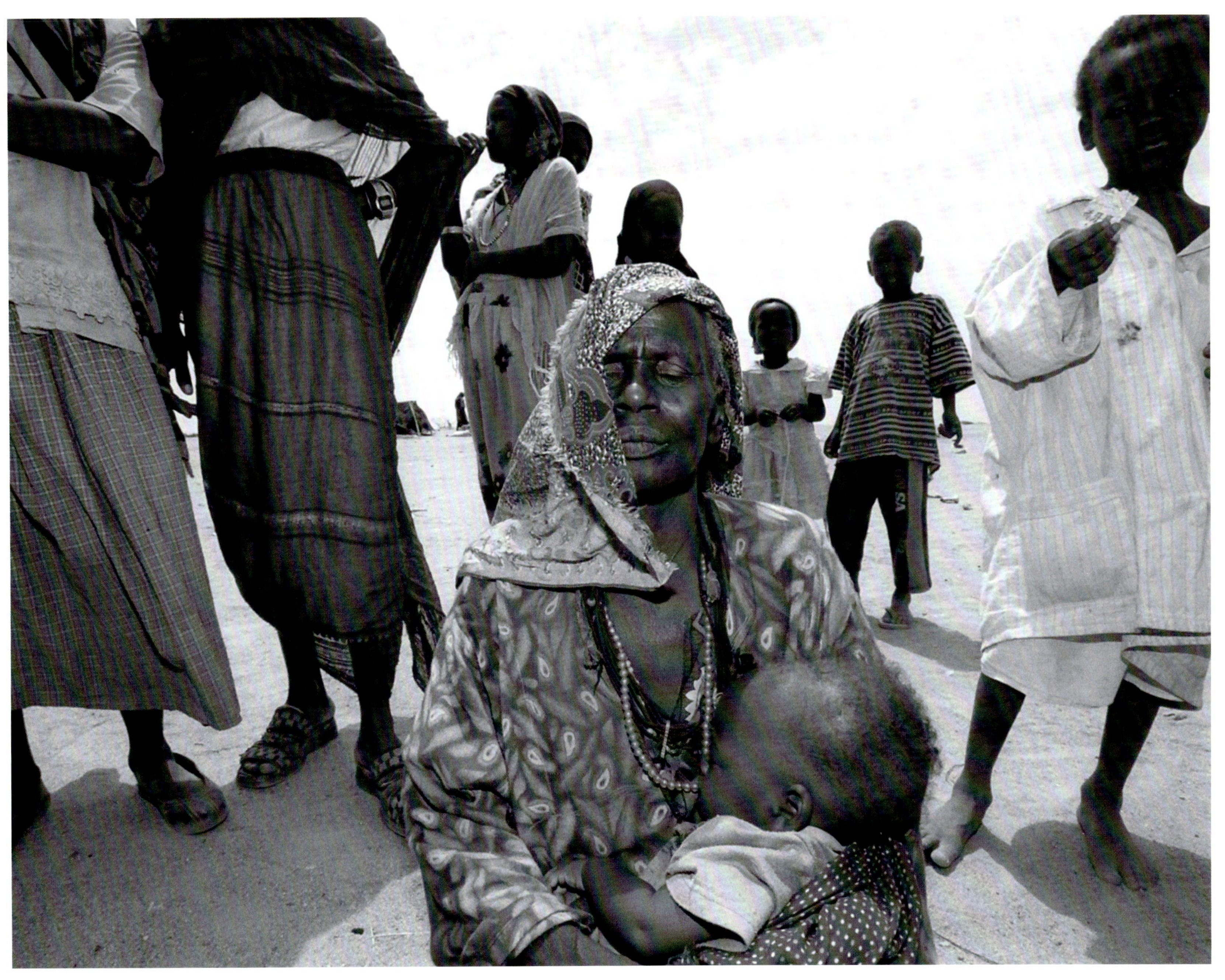

Darfur Sudan 2005
Tanya Habjouqa

An elderly woman—fleeing her village—traveled on foot, carrying her grandchild. With no idea if her other family members survived, she and her grandchild eventually found refuge at an International Medical Corps health clinic.

Darfur Sudan 1998
Colin Finlay

Opposite page: International Medical Corps implemented health, nutrition and water and sanitation programs for people living in West and South Darfur.

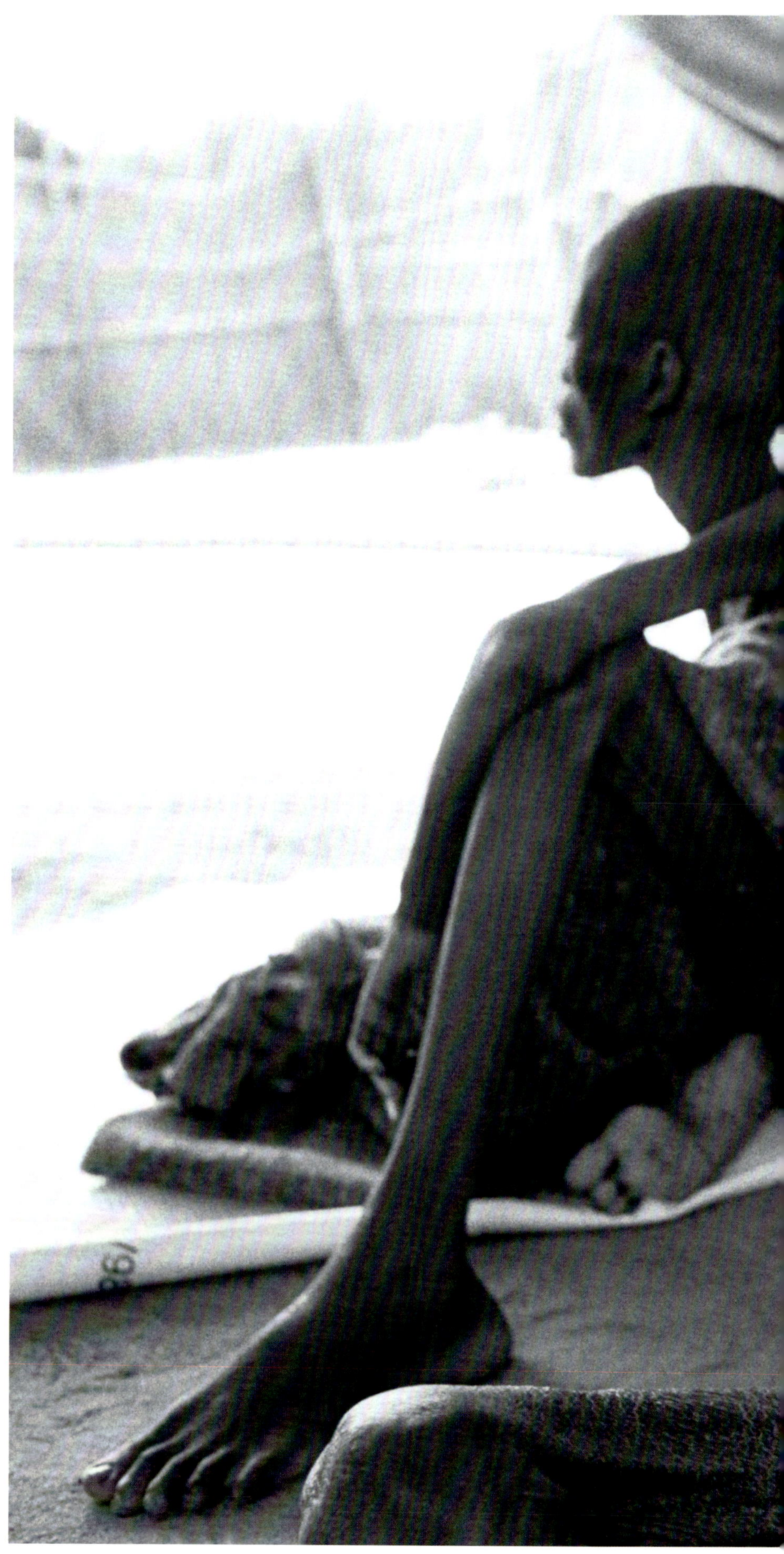

Darfur Sudan 1998
Colin Finlay

International Medical Corps is one of the few global humanitarian organizations to operate primary health care centers and mobile clinics within Darfur to provide both routine and emergency health care.

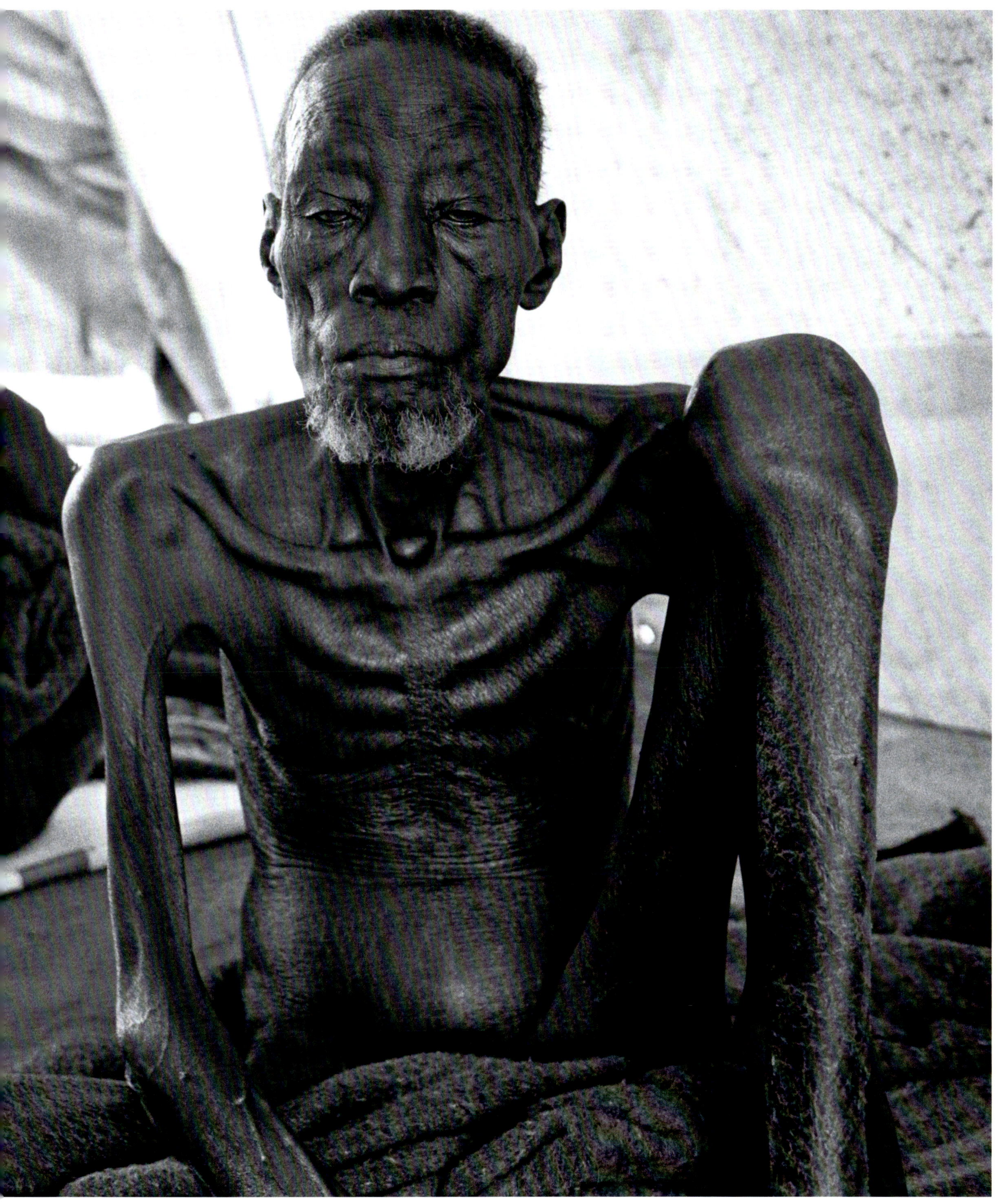

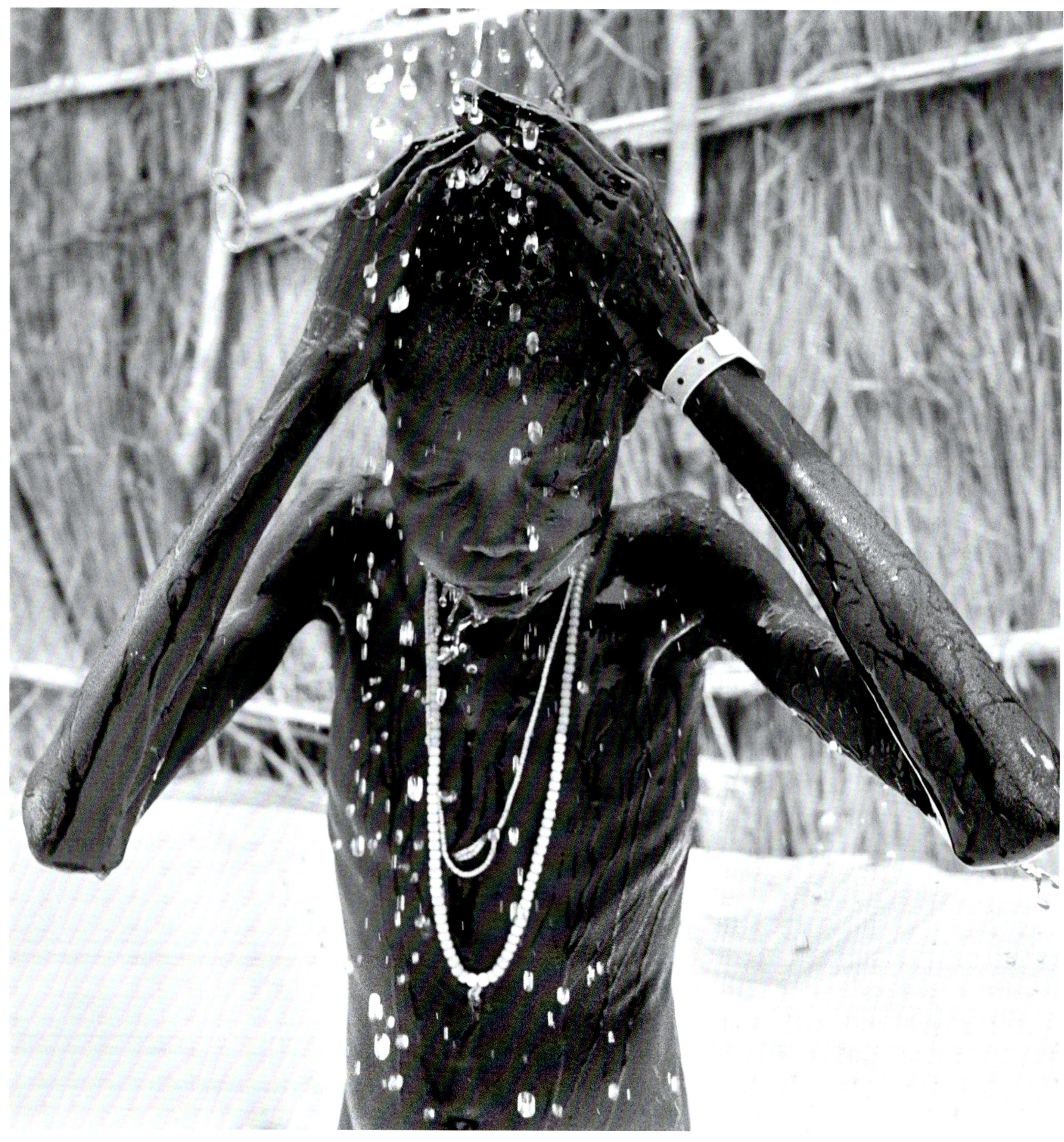

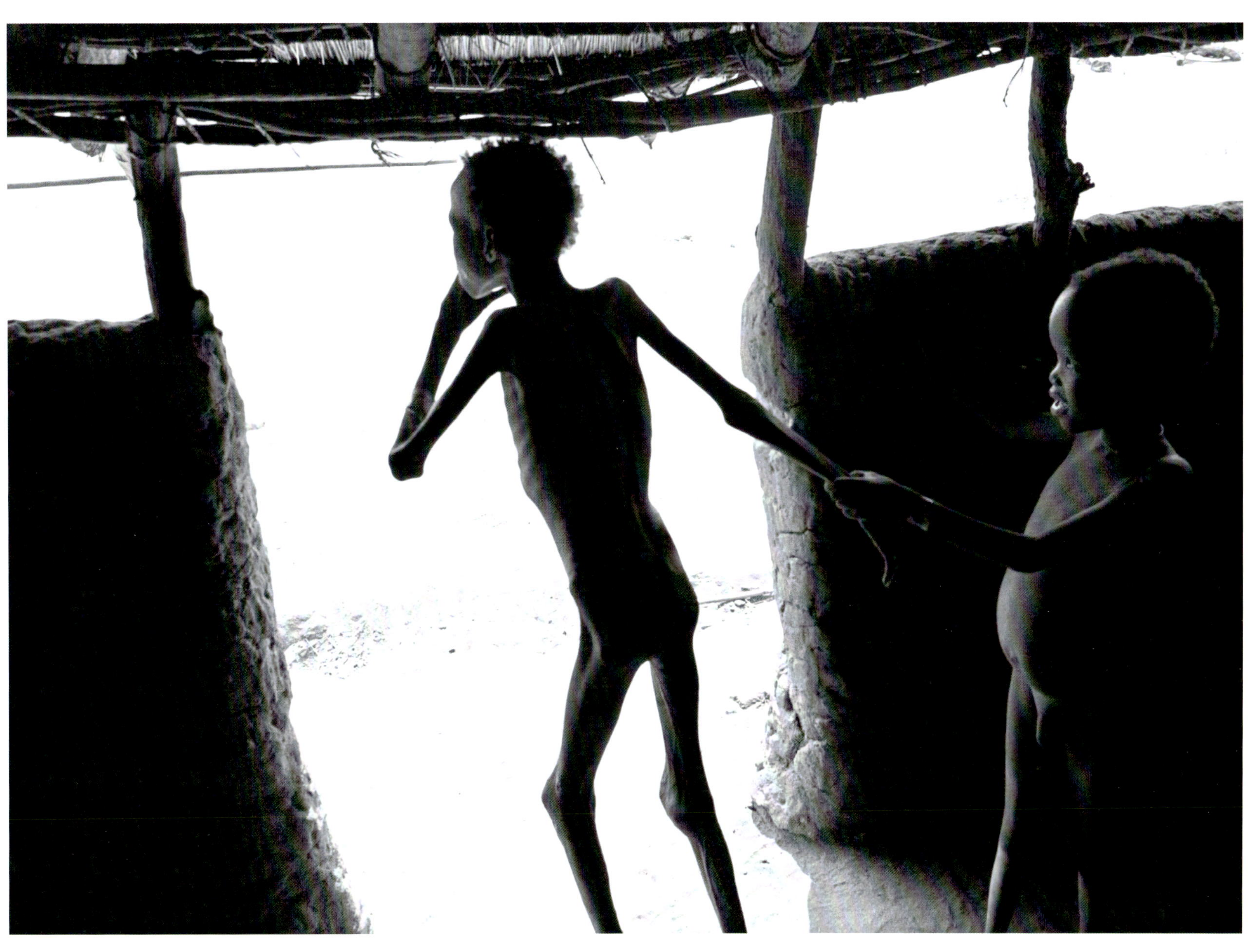

Darfur Sudan 1998
Colin Finlay (both pages)
Malnutrition rates were halved among those living near International Medical Corps health care clinics in Darfur. But continued fighting and precarious security conditions along supply routes left many thousands of Darfurians without food, clean water and basic medical supplies.

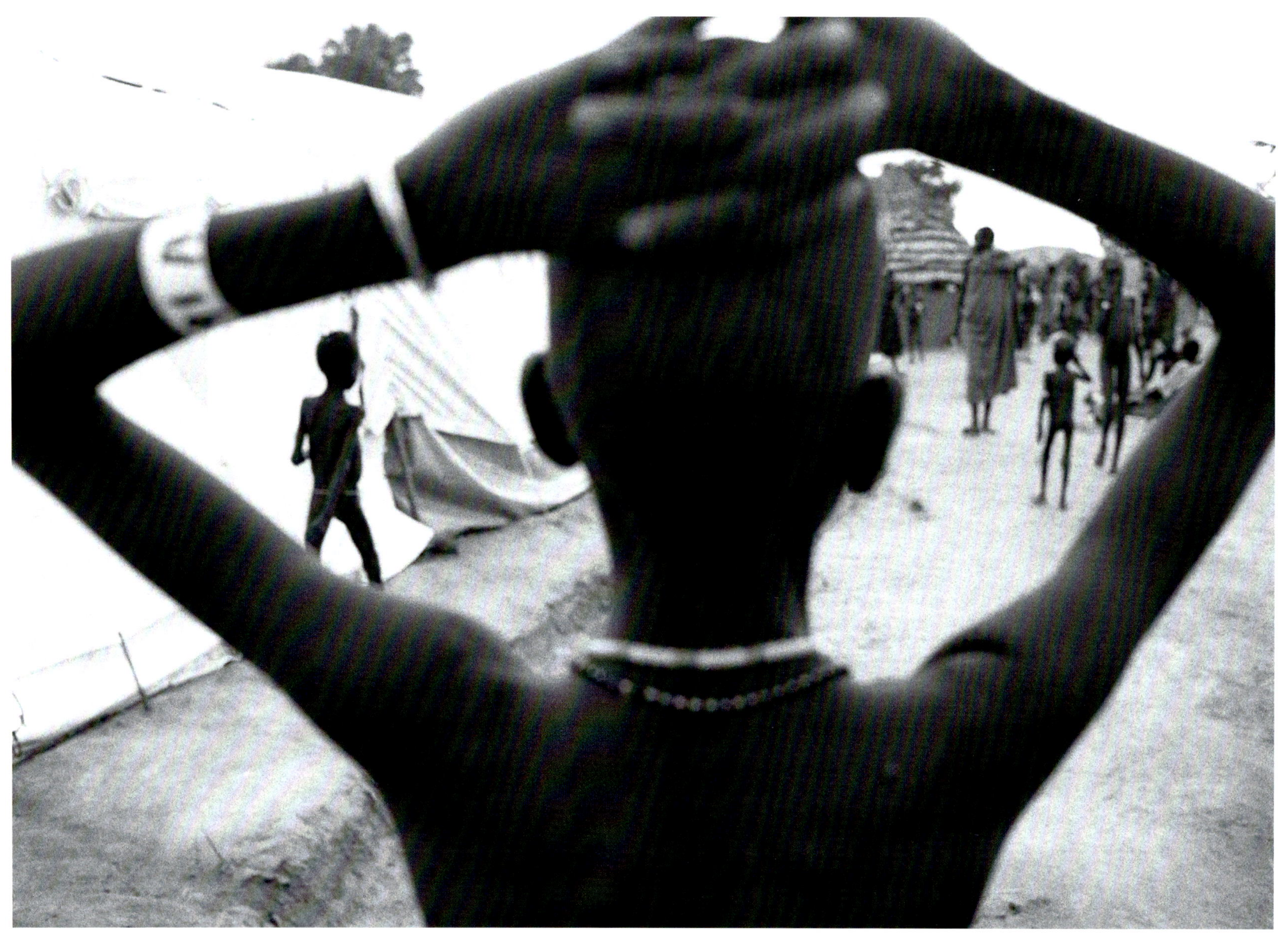

Darfur Sudan 1998
Colin Finlay (both pages)

Despite security challenges, International Medical Corps mobile clinic programs in Darfur have been successful, bringing health care and emergency medical supplies to some of the most dangerous and hard-to-reach areas in Darfur.

Darfur Sudan 1998

Opposite page: Despite efforts to provide emergency health care in Darfur, the violence and devastation were overwhelming. International Medical Corps often assisted victims of the conflict in Darfur with culturally sensitive, sanitary burials in accordance with the local customs of those who didn't survive the violent conflicts.

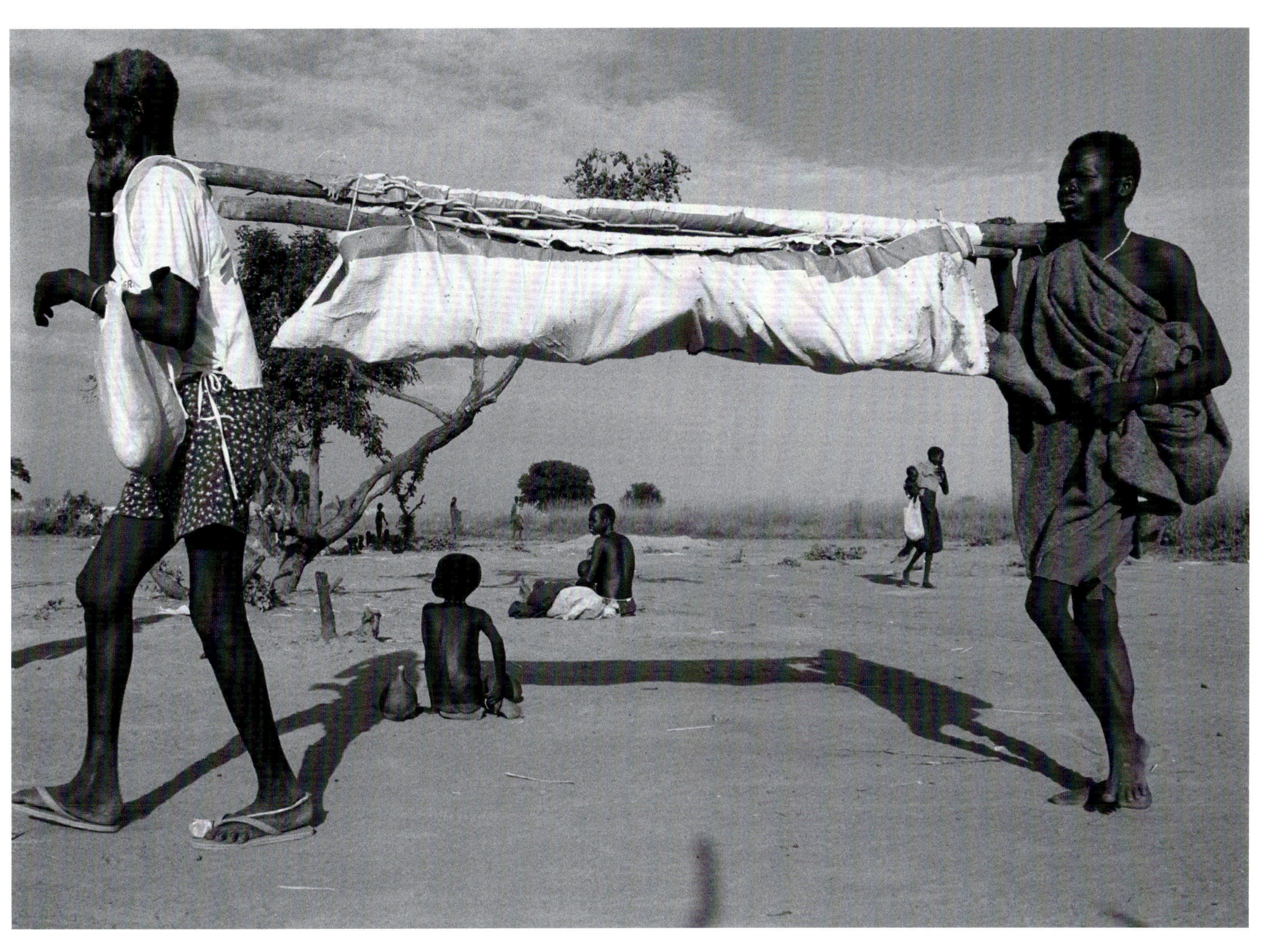

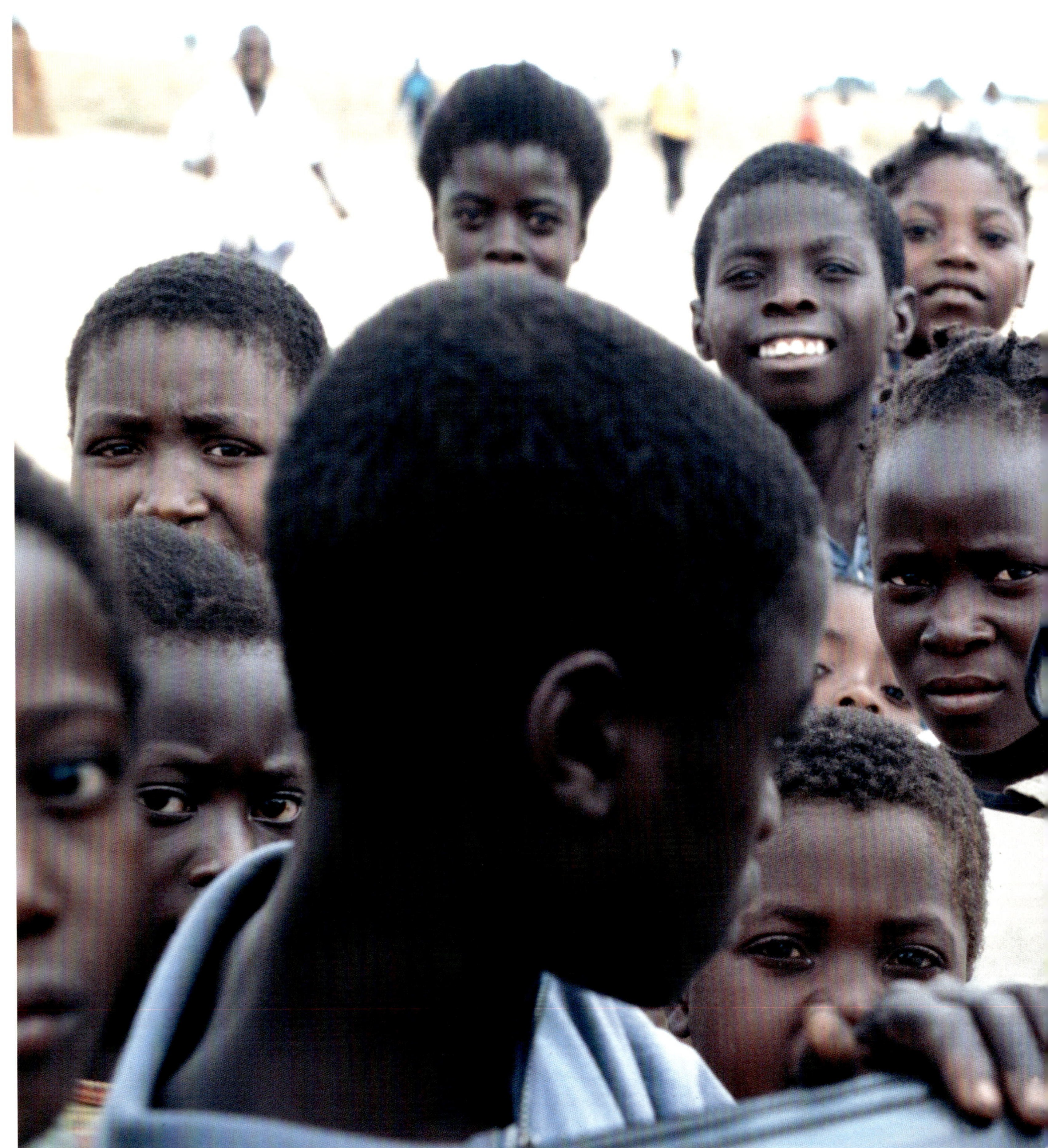

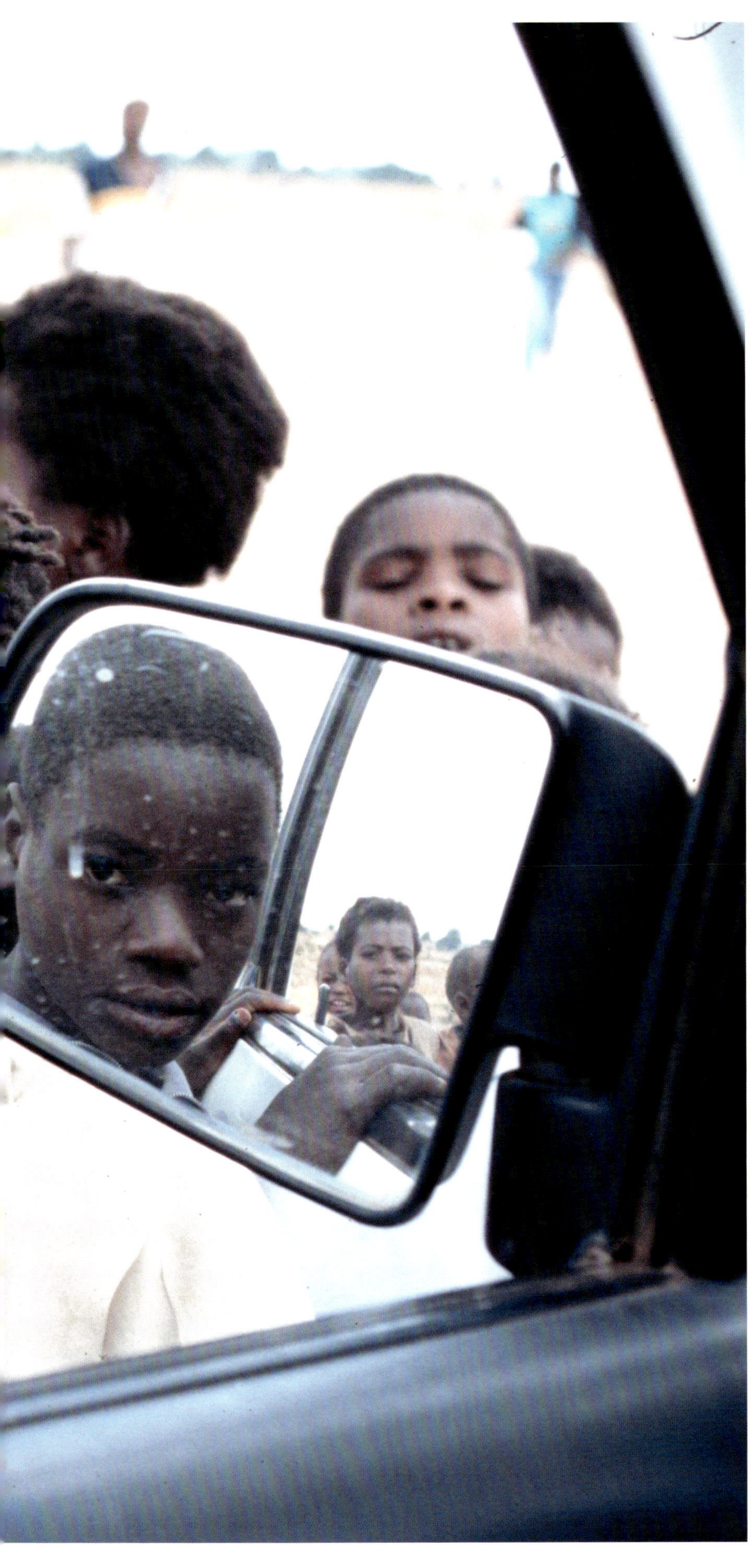

Angola 2002
Jenny Chu

Fifteen years of civil war combined with the worst Southern African drought of the 20th century had left Angola with one of the highest child mortality rates in the world. In 1990, International Medical Corps began its work in Angola by introducing therapeutic feeding programs and delivering emergency drug supplies.

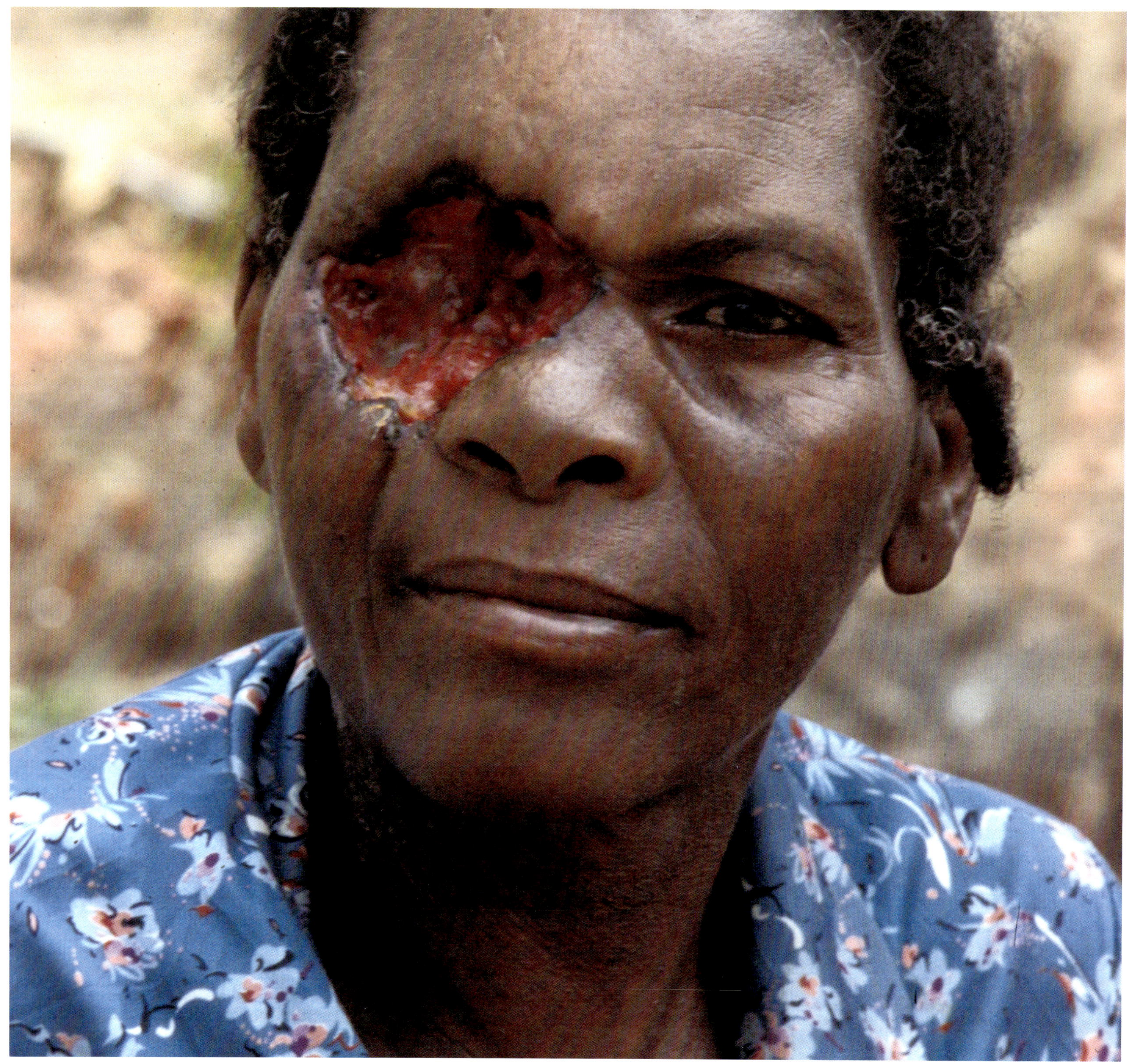

Angola 2002
Jenny Chu

By 1990, Angola had become one of the poorest and most dangerous countries in the world. International Medical Corps worked in partnership with the local people to help rebuild the health of the entire community.

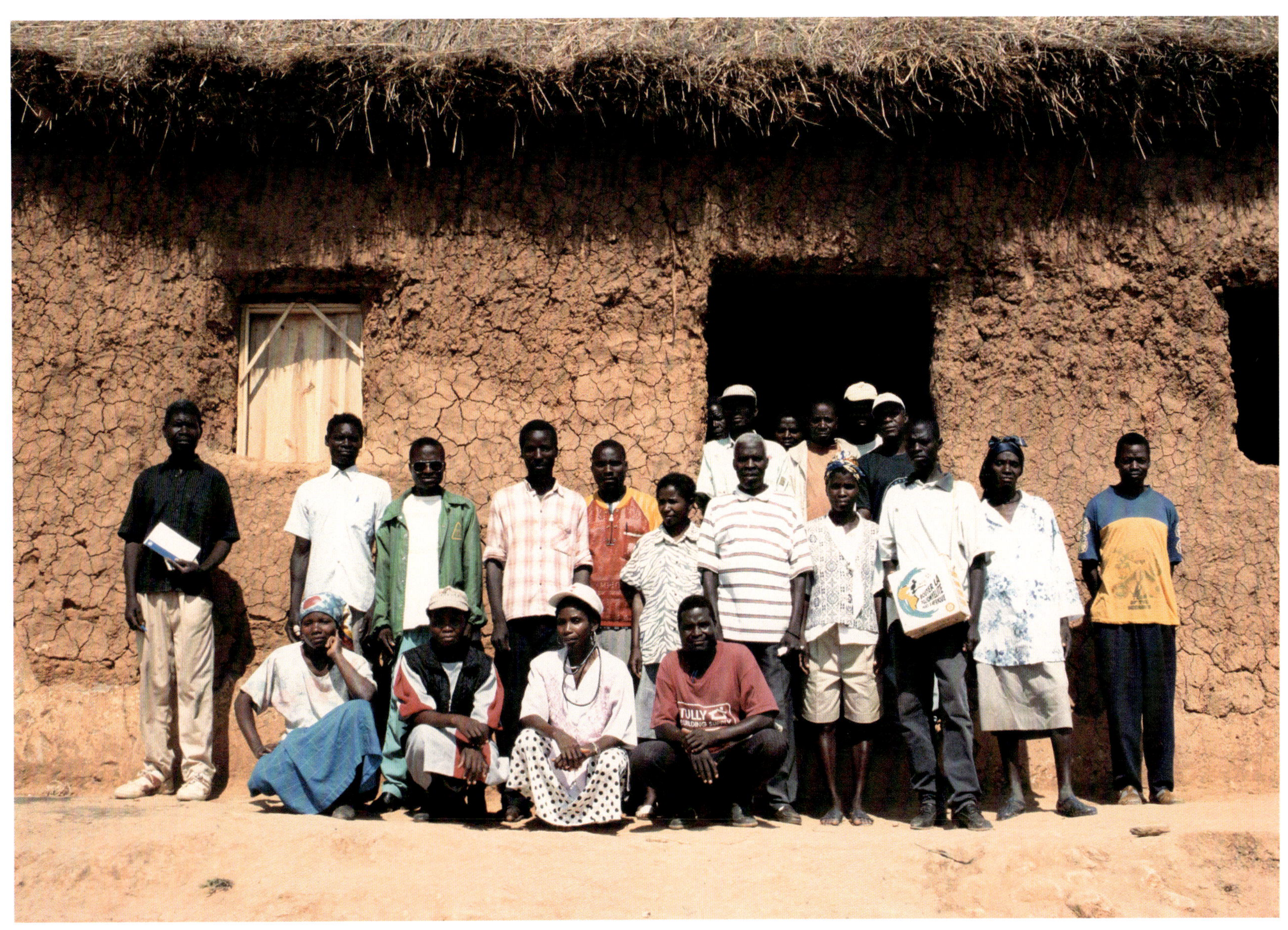

Angola 2002
Jenny Chu

In 1992, International Medical Corps began an extraordinary vaccination training program in Angola. The classroom was split evenly between supporters of the UNITA rebel group and loyalists to the Angolan government. Sitting on opposite sides of the room, they didn't look at each other, but they returned day after day. IMC training changed the way they viewed the war. It no longer mattered what tribe they belonged to; they were united in saving their children's lives.

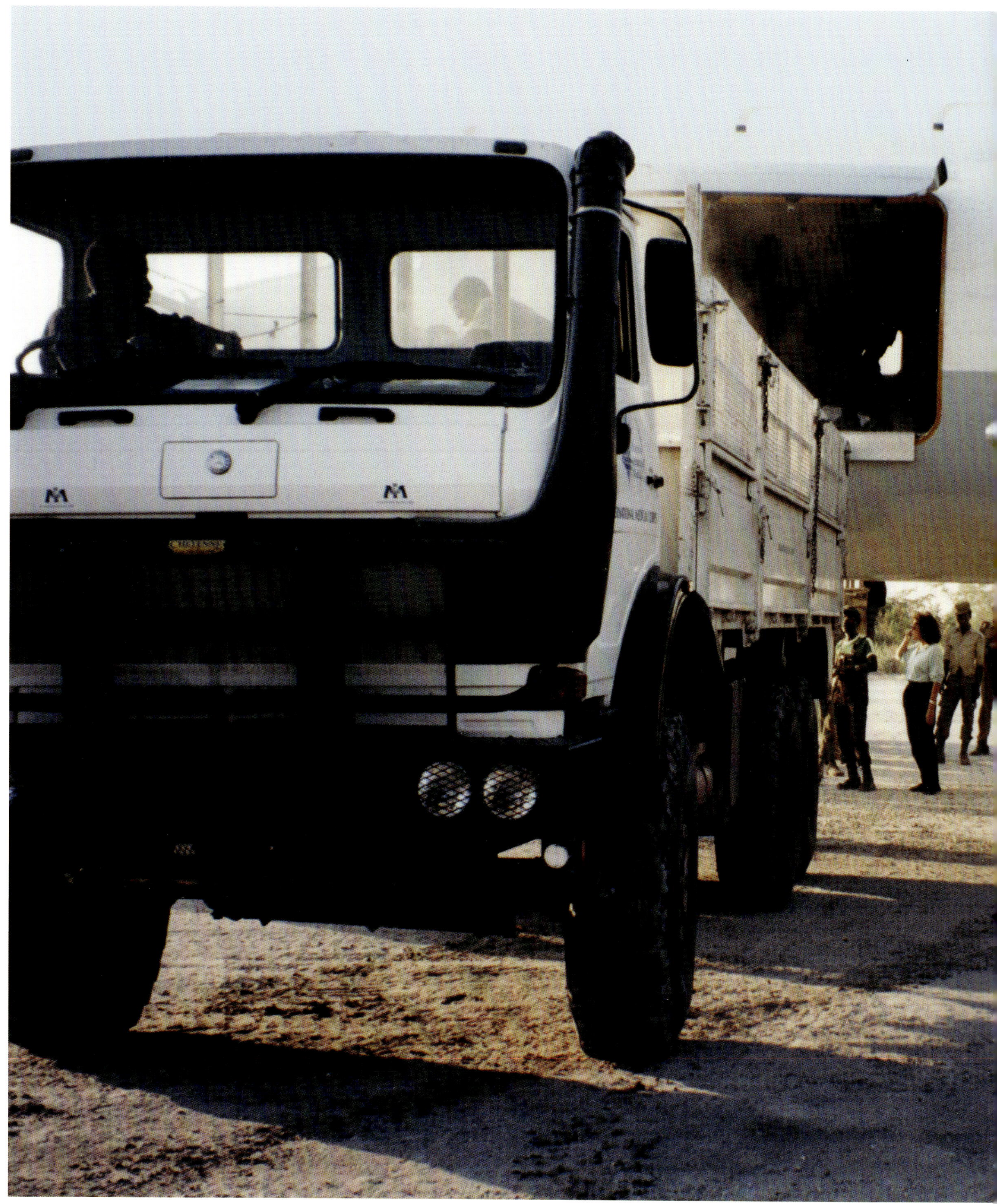

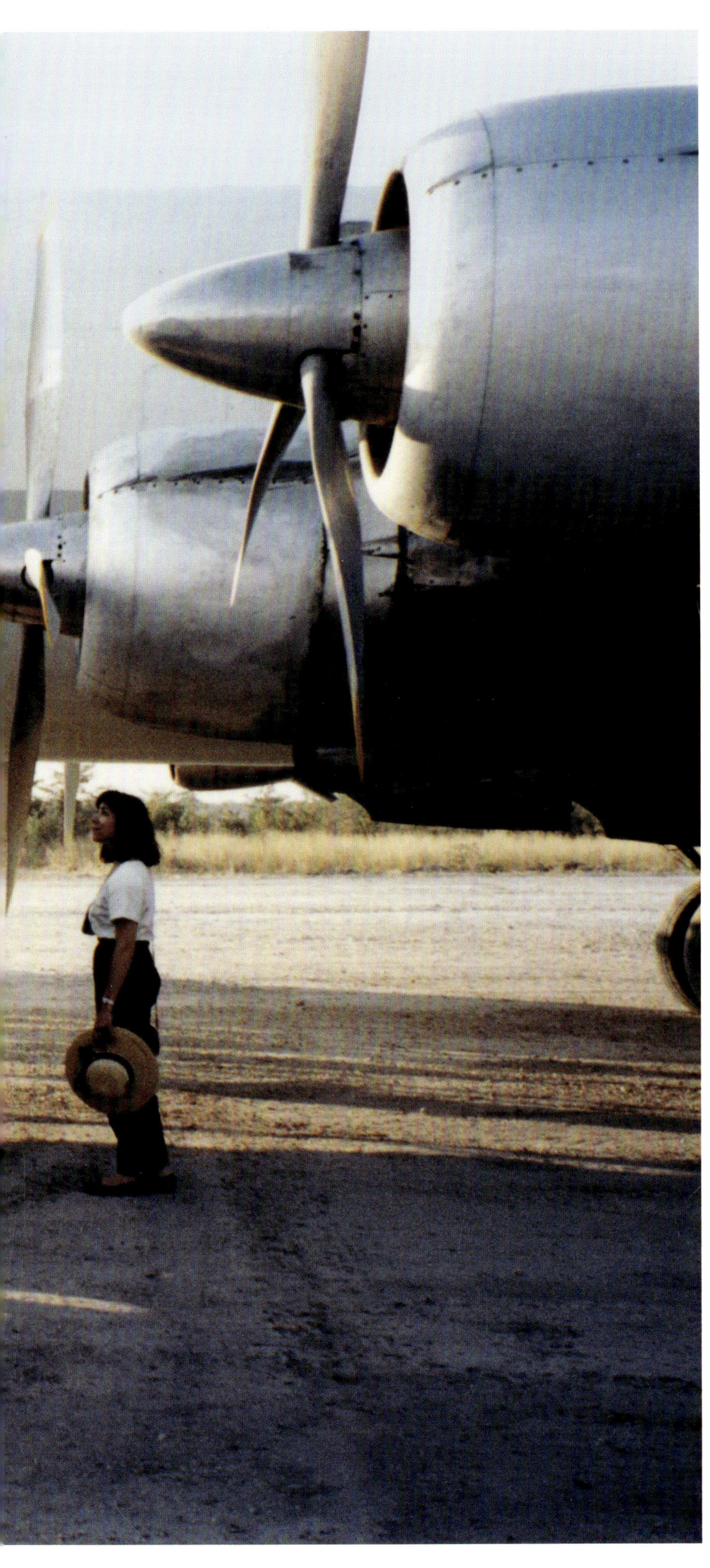

Angola 1991
IMC staff

Devastating drought and widespread famine hit Angola hard in 1991. International Medical Corps Logistics Teams coordinated one of the largest and most complicated airlifts in its history to deliver seeds, tools and supplies to jumpstart Angola's agricultural development and get Angolans planting again before the rains.

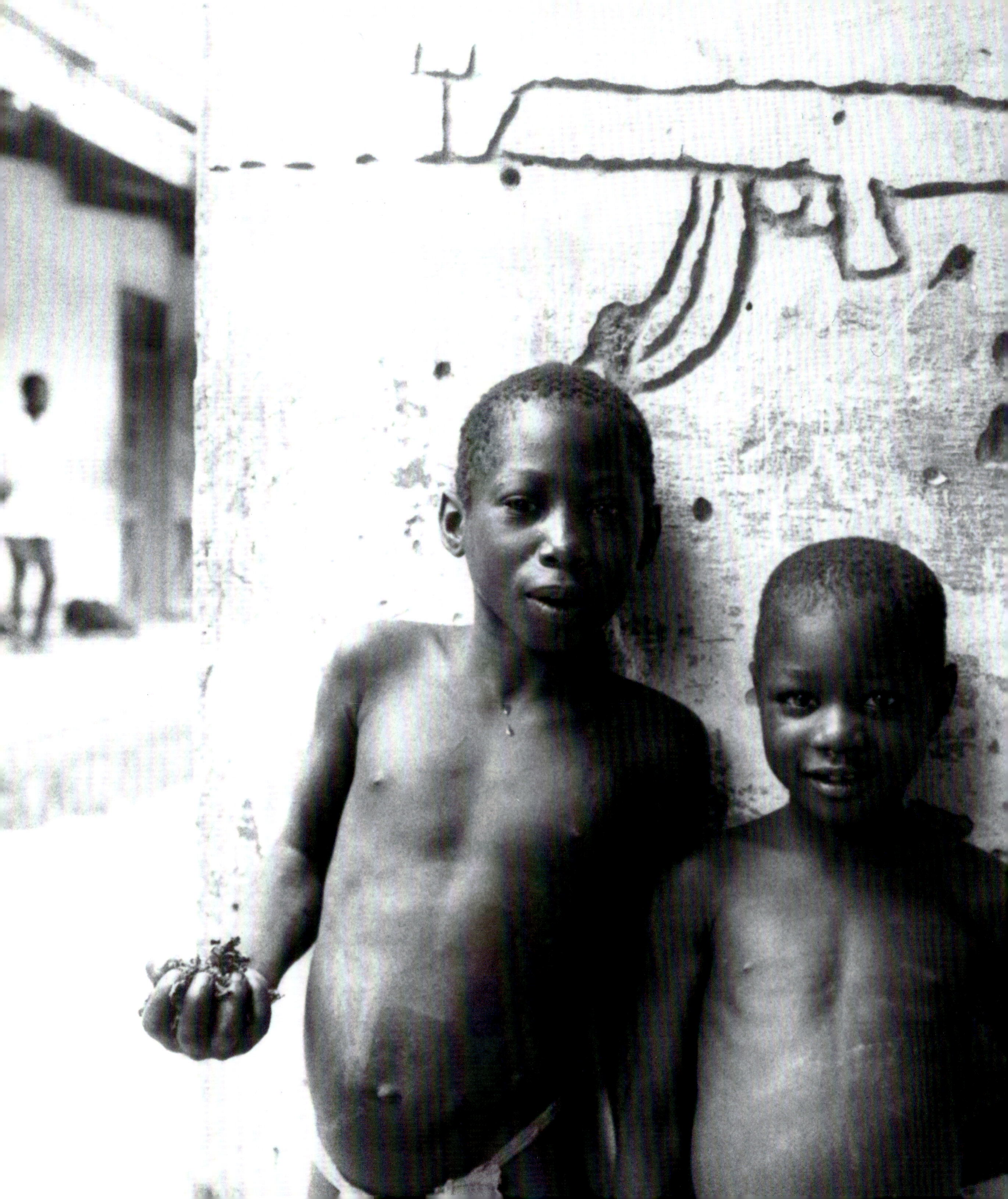

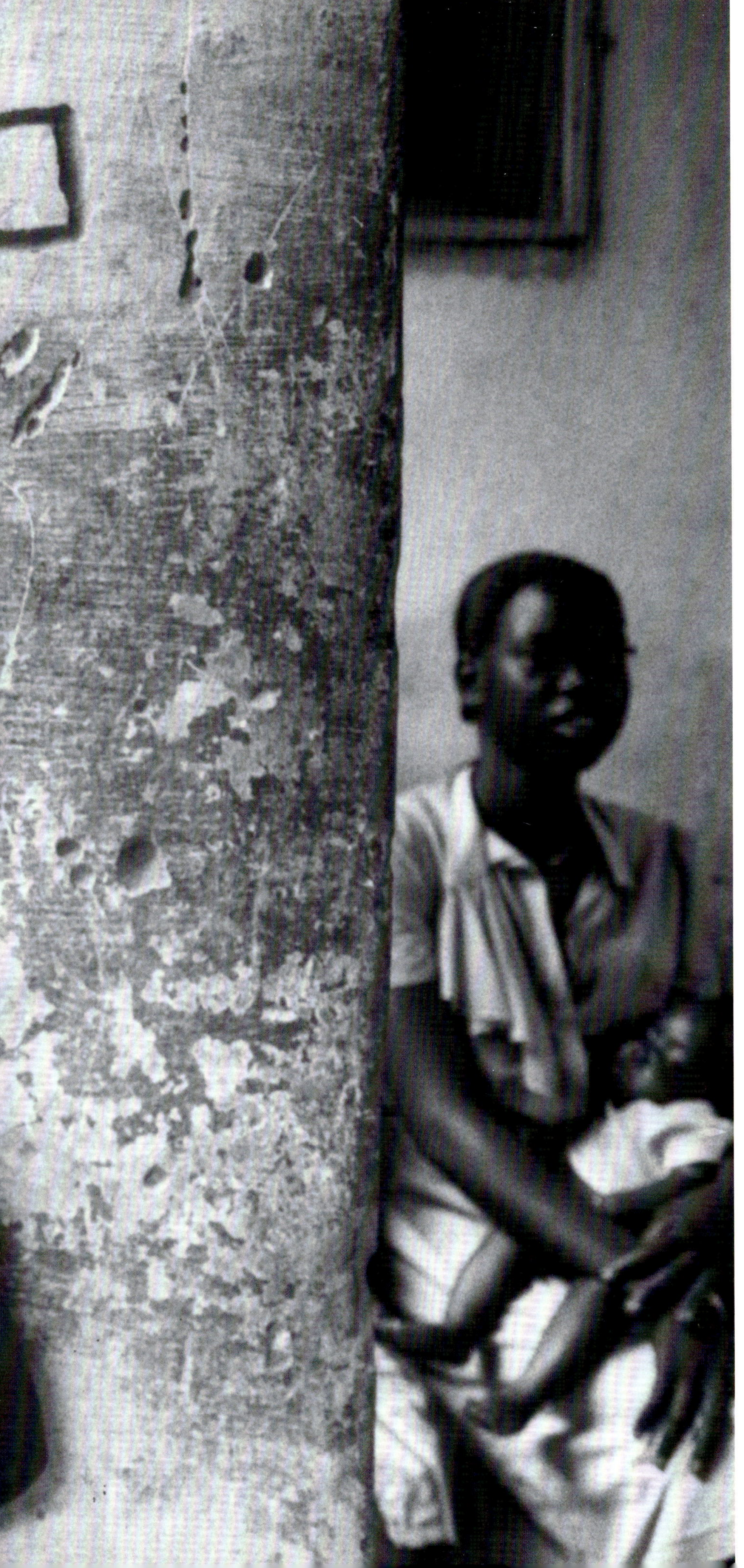

SOUTHERN SUDAN

Southern Sudan 1996
Yael Swerdlow

Since Sudan gained its independence in 1956, it has endured a nearly constant state of unrest. Even before the civil war, Southern Sudan lacked a well-developed health care infrastructure. International Medical Corps began working in Southern Sudan in 1994 to provide the most basic health needs that had not been met for decades.

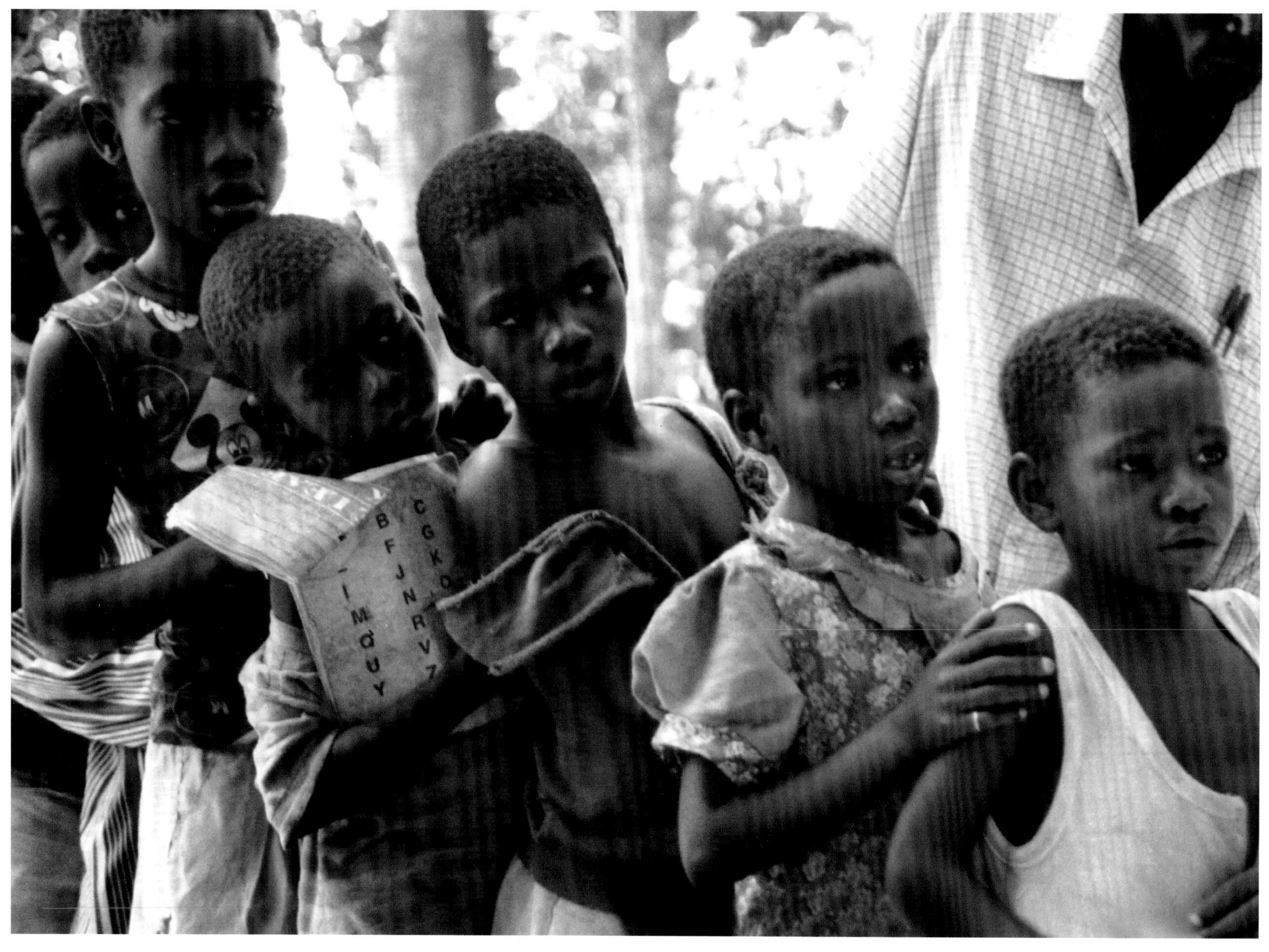

Southern Sudan 2000
Jennifer Rowland (both pages)

Sleeping sickness reemerged in Africa in the 1970s and in some places has reached epidemic proportions. International Medical Corps mobile teams traveled to villages to conduct blood screening tests. Often the entire village was screened because the lower the number of people carrying the parasite that causes the disease, the less likely it was to spread.

Opposite page: International Medical Corps' clinic in Southern Sudan treated patients with stage one sleeping sickness, which often caused headaches, itchy skin, joint pains and, in later stages, confusion, disorientation, dillusions and combativeness. Sufferers' wake cycle changed, causing them to sleep throughout the day and wake at night. IMC clinics in Southern Sudan worked around the clock to provide the care needed for this debilitating disease.

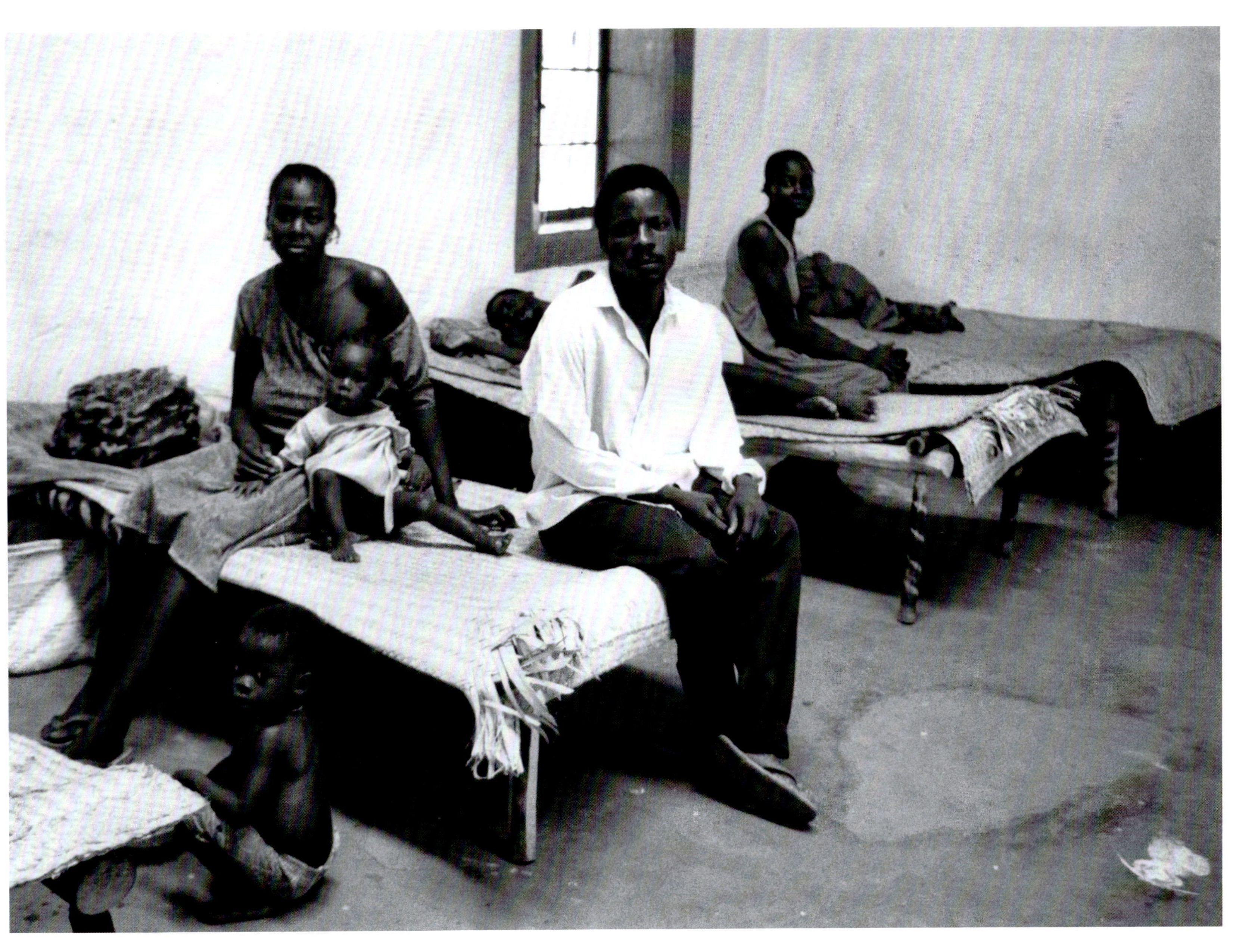

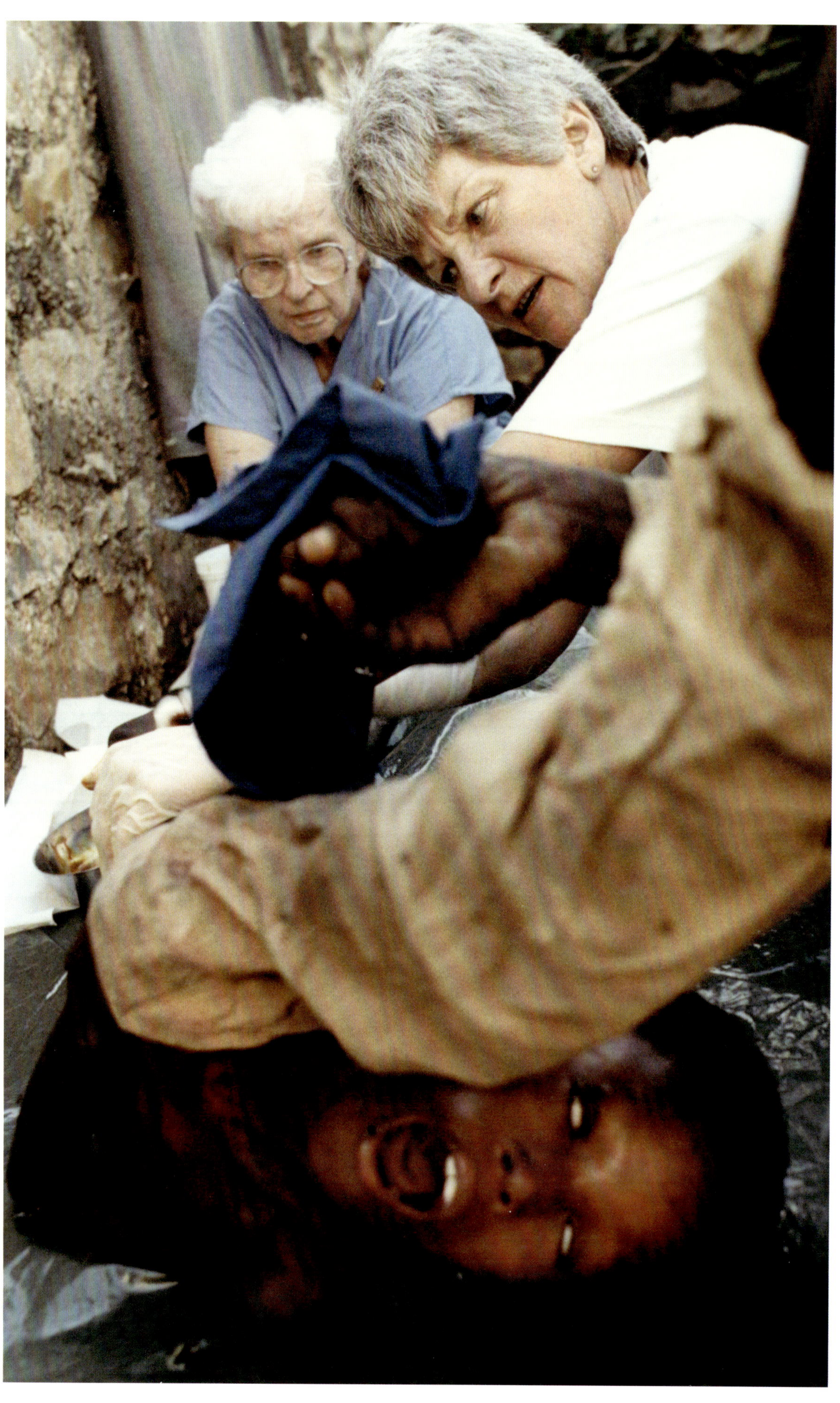

Southern Sudan 1998
Judy Walgreen-Dehaas

Those who test positive for sleeping sickness undergo a painful lumbar puncture test to determine whether or not they carry the parasite. International Medical Corps doctors must be absolutely certain as to whether or not the patient carries the parasite, because treatment is expensive and can be dangerous.

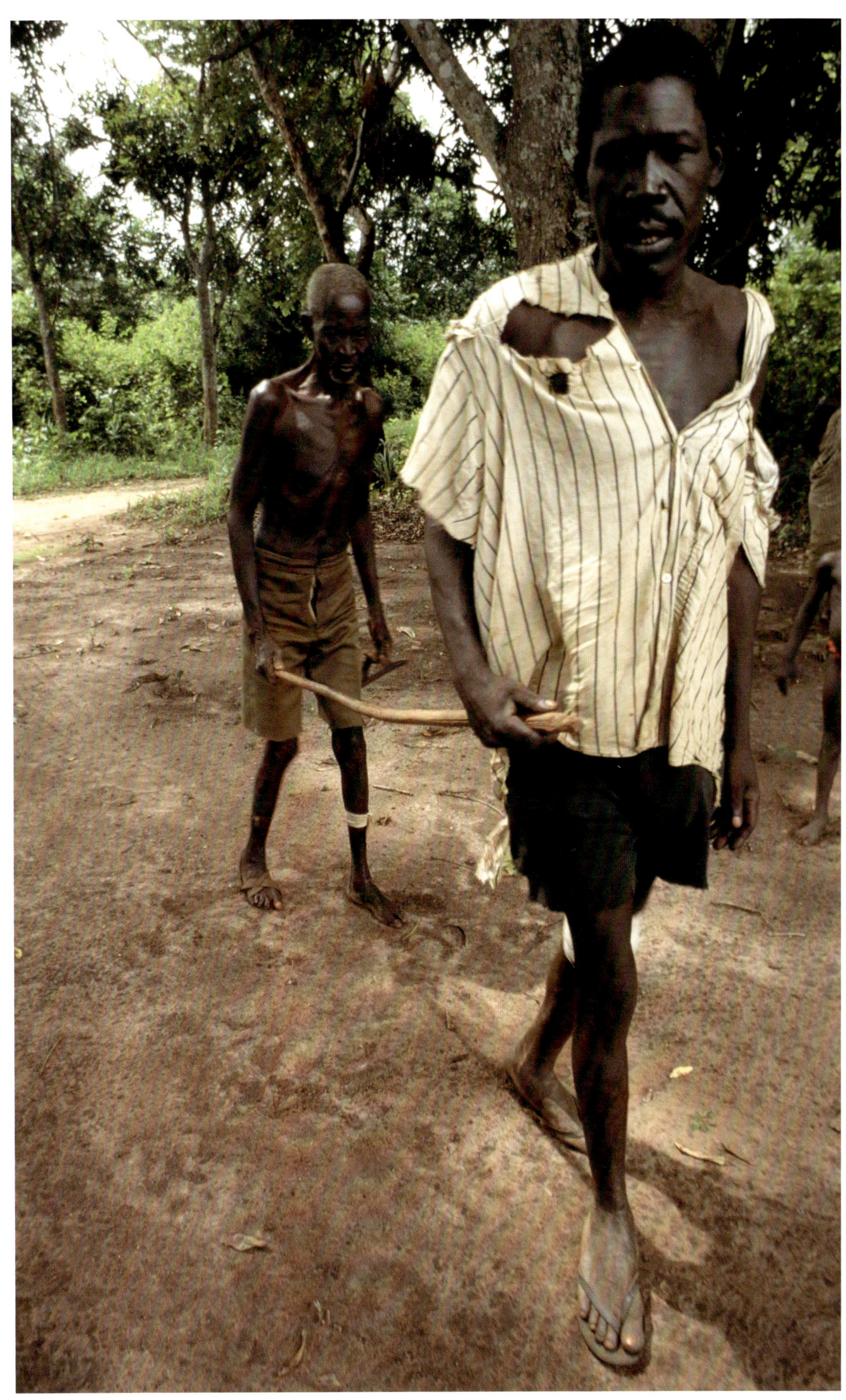

Southern Sudan 1996
Danny Hoffman

River blindness was rampant in Southern Sudan. The painful disease is caused by a parasitic worm transmitted from the bite of a common black fly. In 1994, International Medical Corps began working in Tambura County to eradicate river blindness and treated nearly 110,000 people in the region.

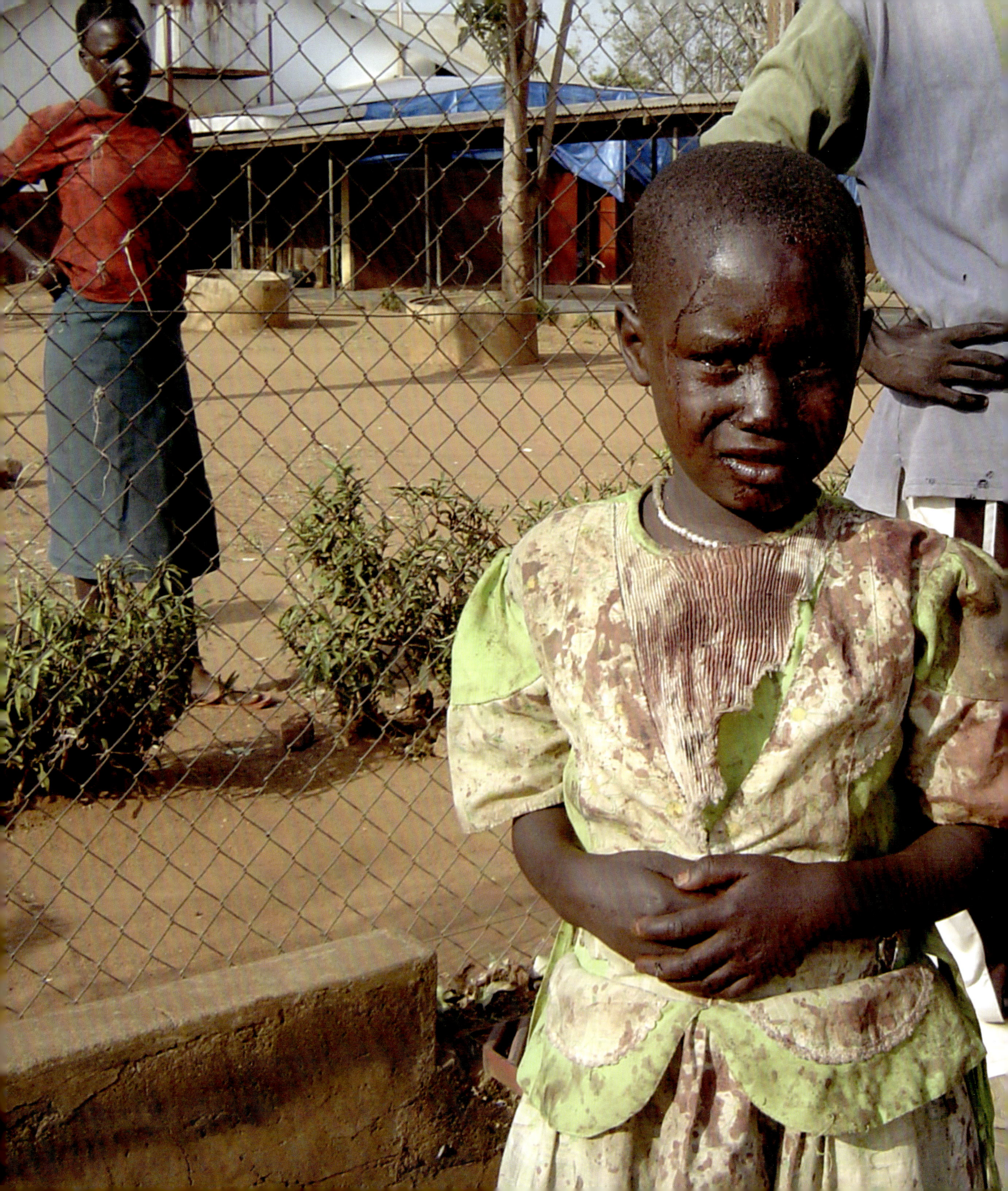

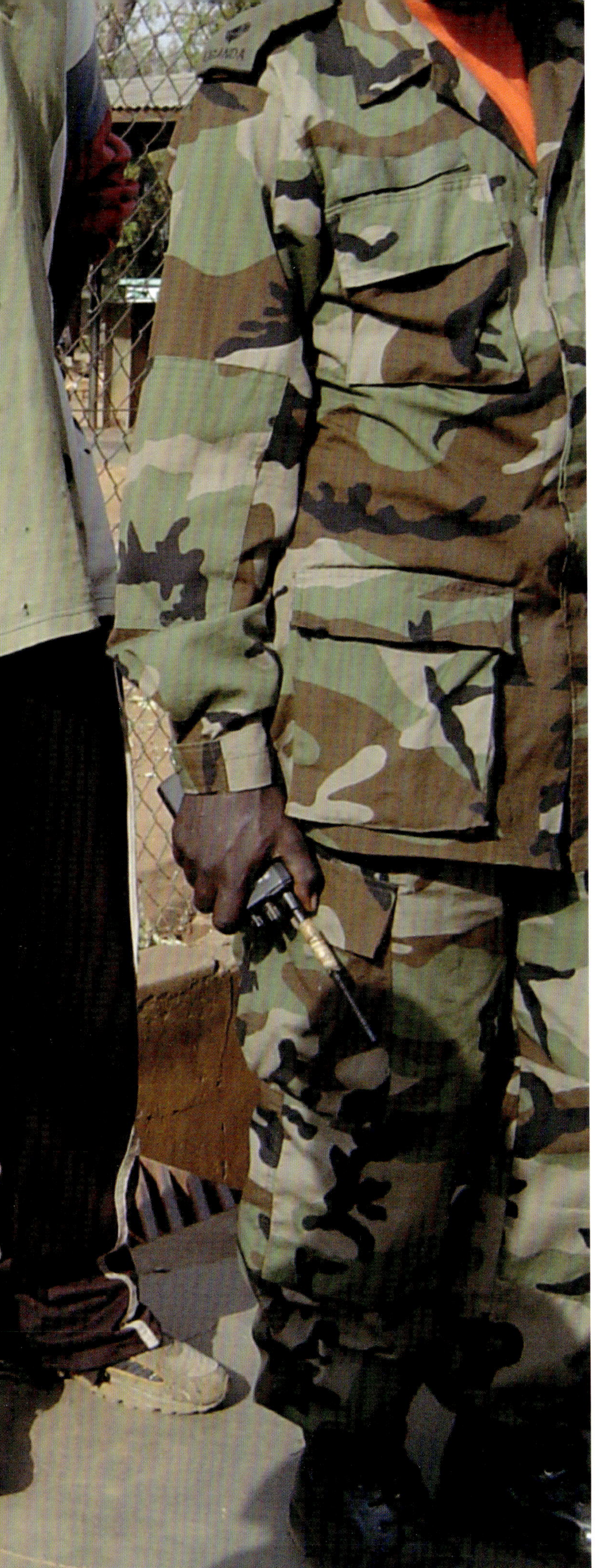

Uganda 2003
IMC Staff
International Medical Corps' work in Northern Uganda is a constant struggle for security due to a more than 20-year conflict between the Ugandan military and the Lord's Resistance Army. LRA rebel groups targeted children, more than 12,000 of whom have been abducted and forced into combat since the start of the conflict.

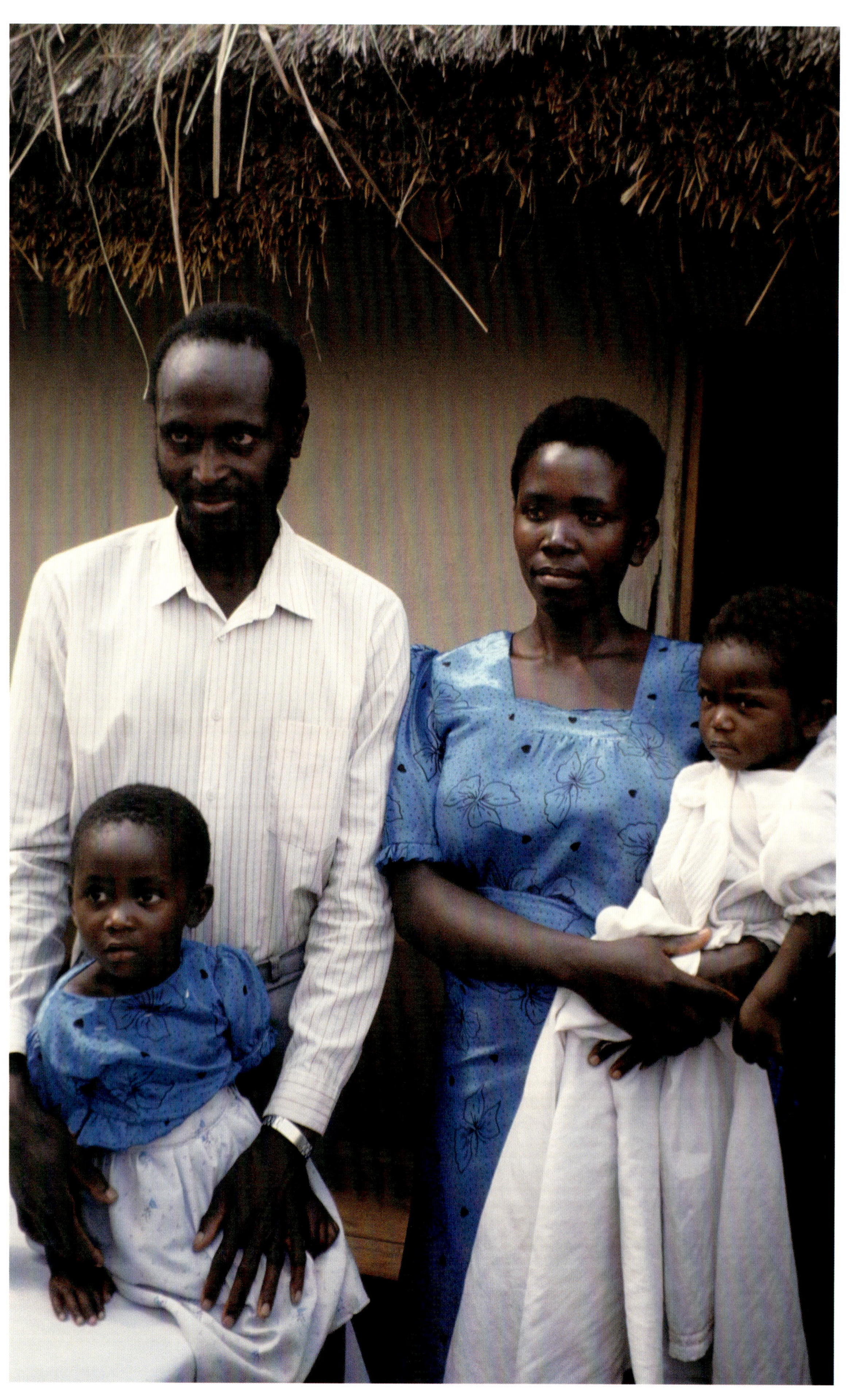

Uganda 2003
Tanya Habjouqa (both pages)
Health care in Northern Uganda is severely lacking. Only 20% of families live in proper homes, while the rest live in a chronic state of displacement and fear due to a more than 20-year guerrilla war. IMC mobile clinics reach more than 80 percent of the population in the north that has been displaced by the conflict.

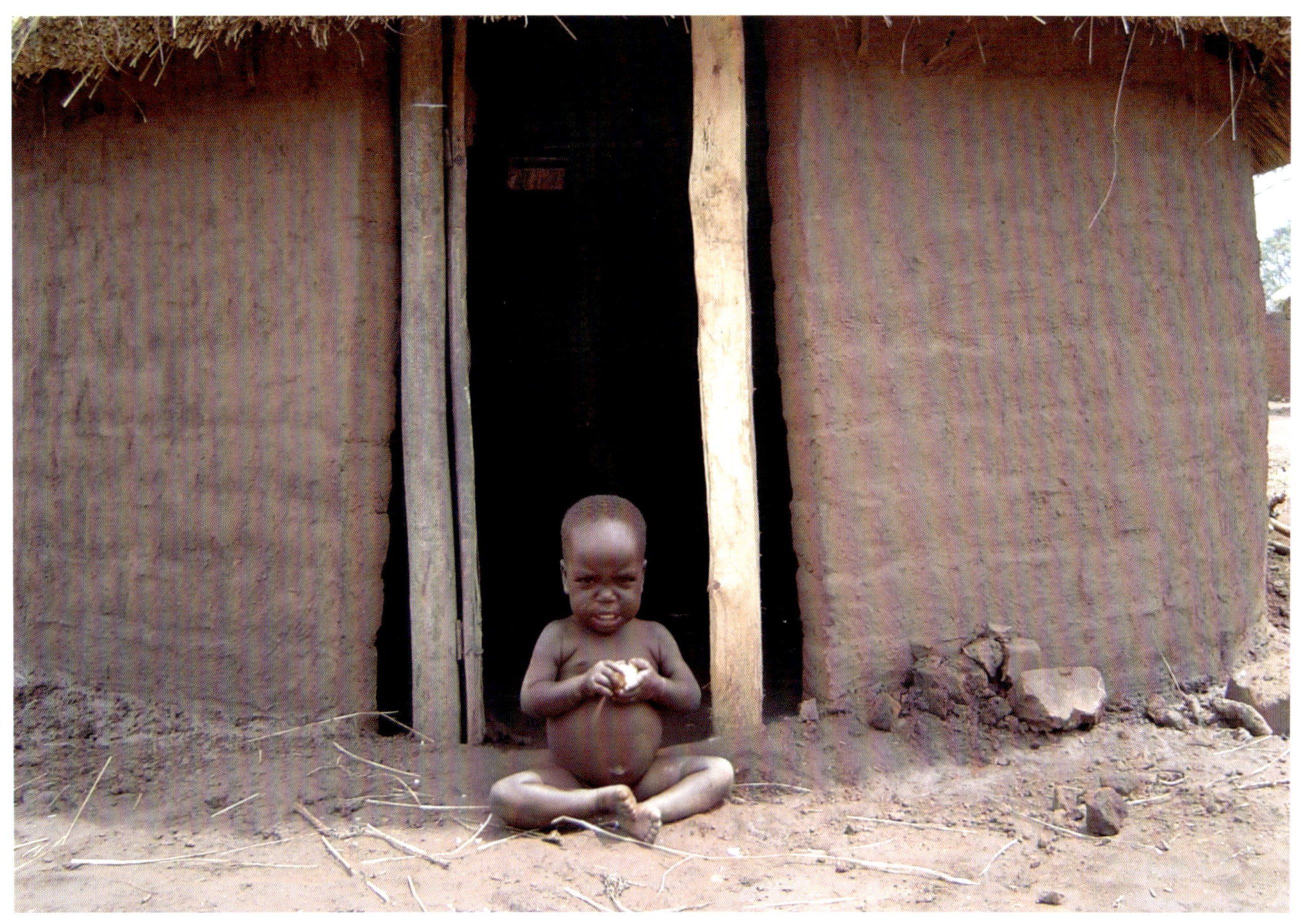

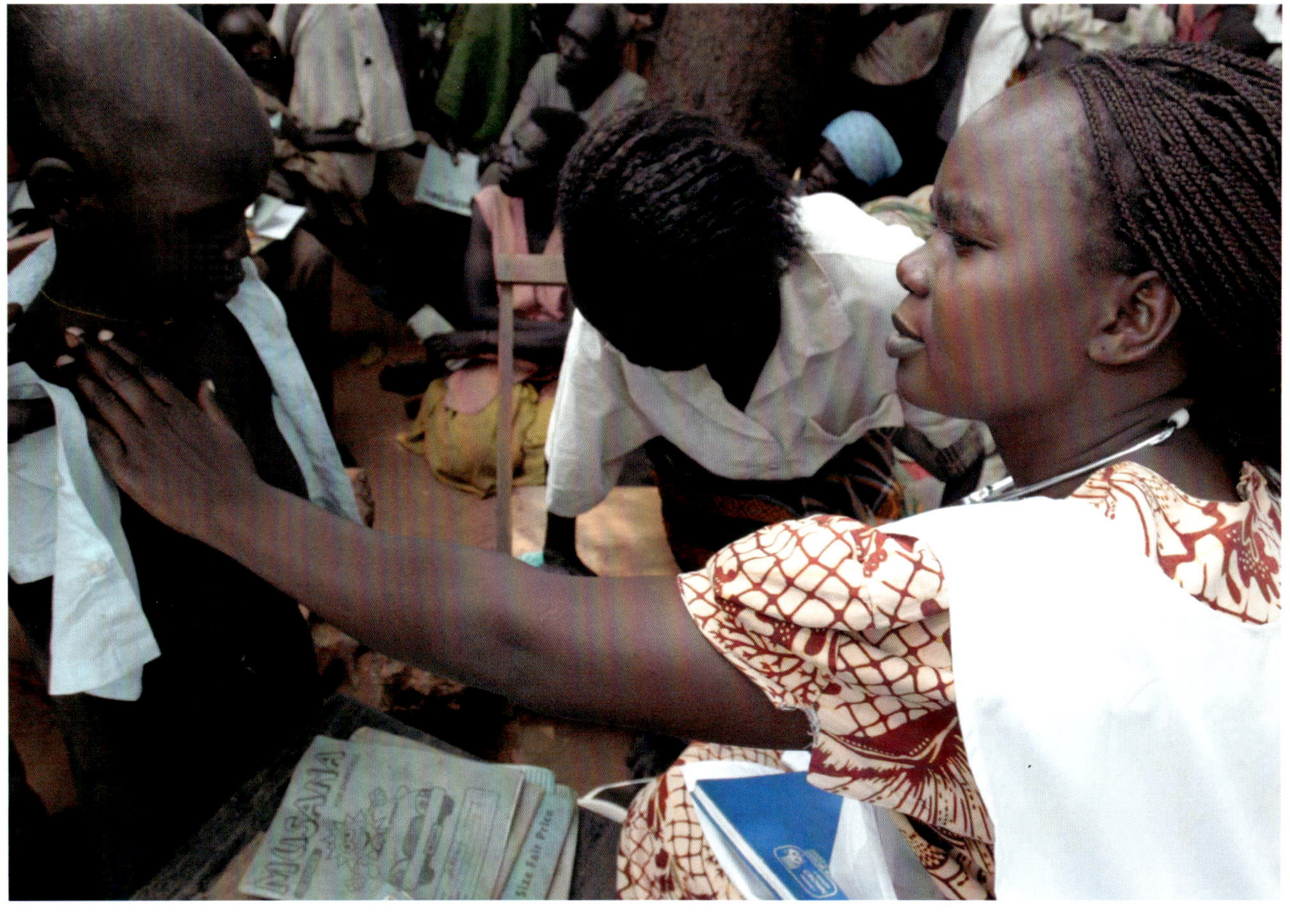

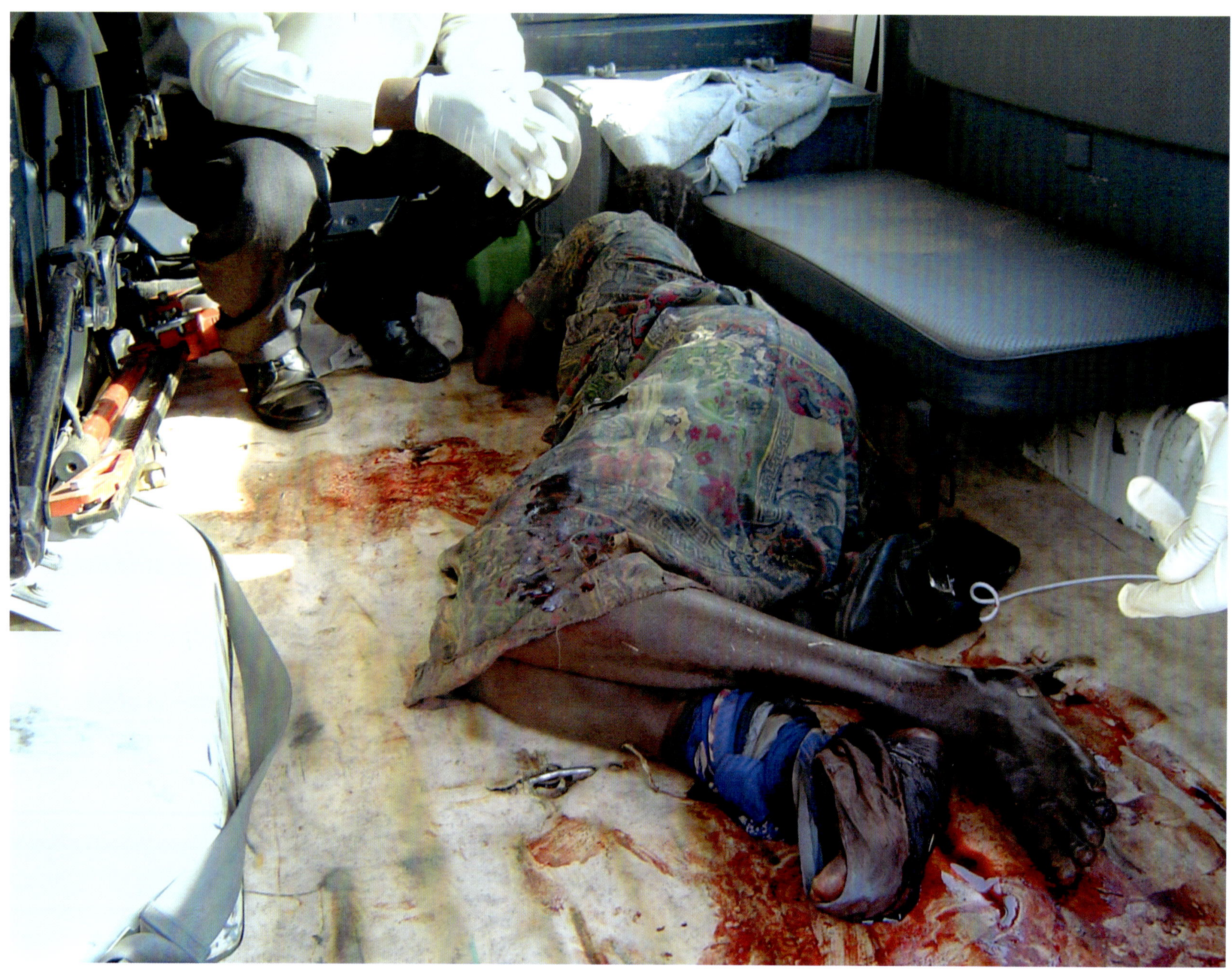

Uganda 2003
IMC Staff

Refugee camps for displaced populations normally provide a measure of safety from violence, but camps in Northern Uganda were actually magnets for rebel groups. International Medical Corps used mobile clinics to assist victims of an LRA ambush.

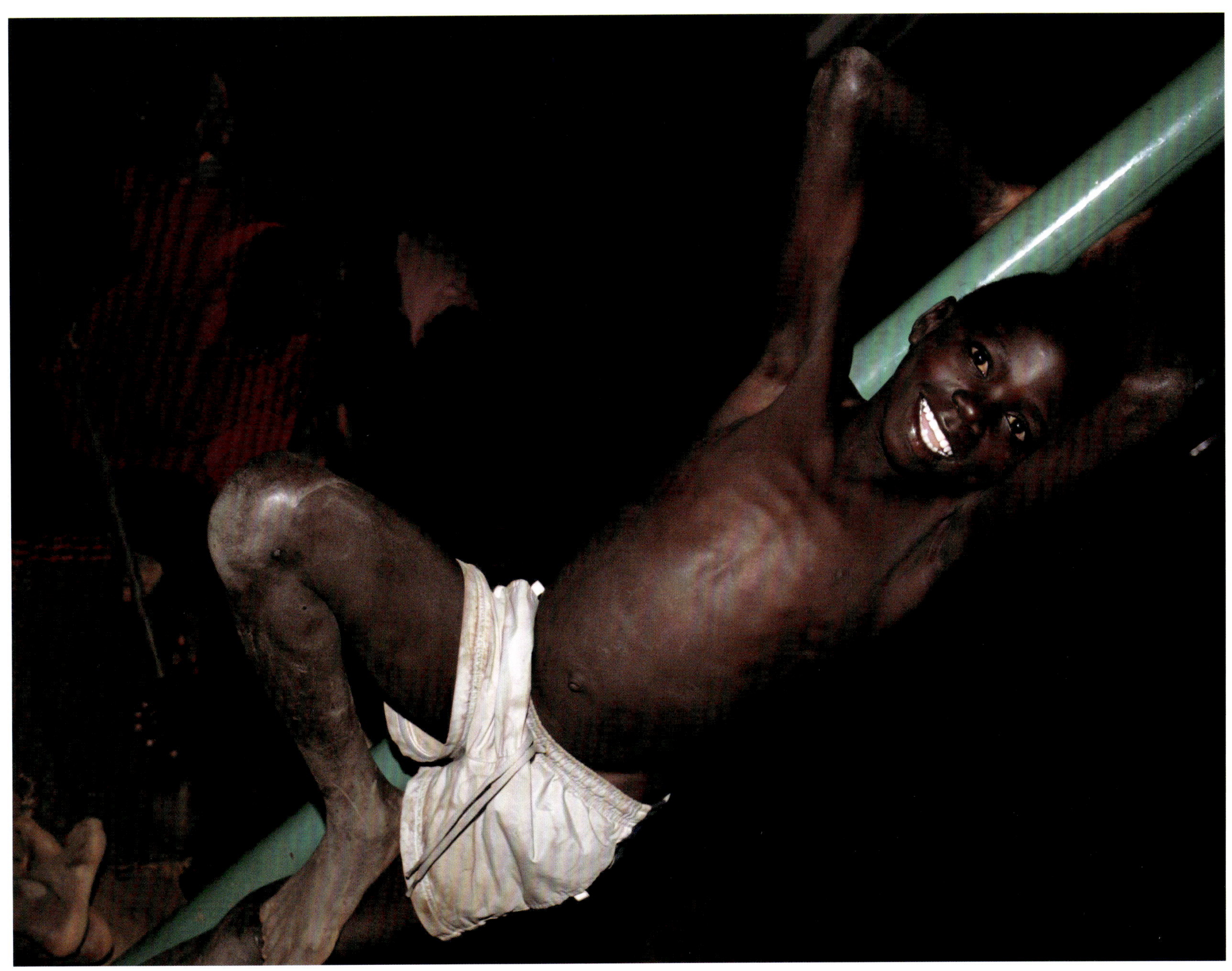

Uganda 2005
Tanya Habjouqa

As a result of rebel attacks on refugee camps, health facilities in the camps in Northern Uganda were chronically understaffed and undersupplied. International Medical Corps provided mobile health care services to the 300,000 families who visited the camps during the day but took refuge in towns at night. These refugees were known as night commuters.

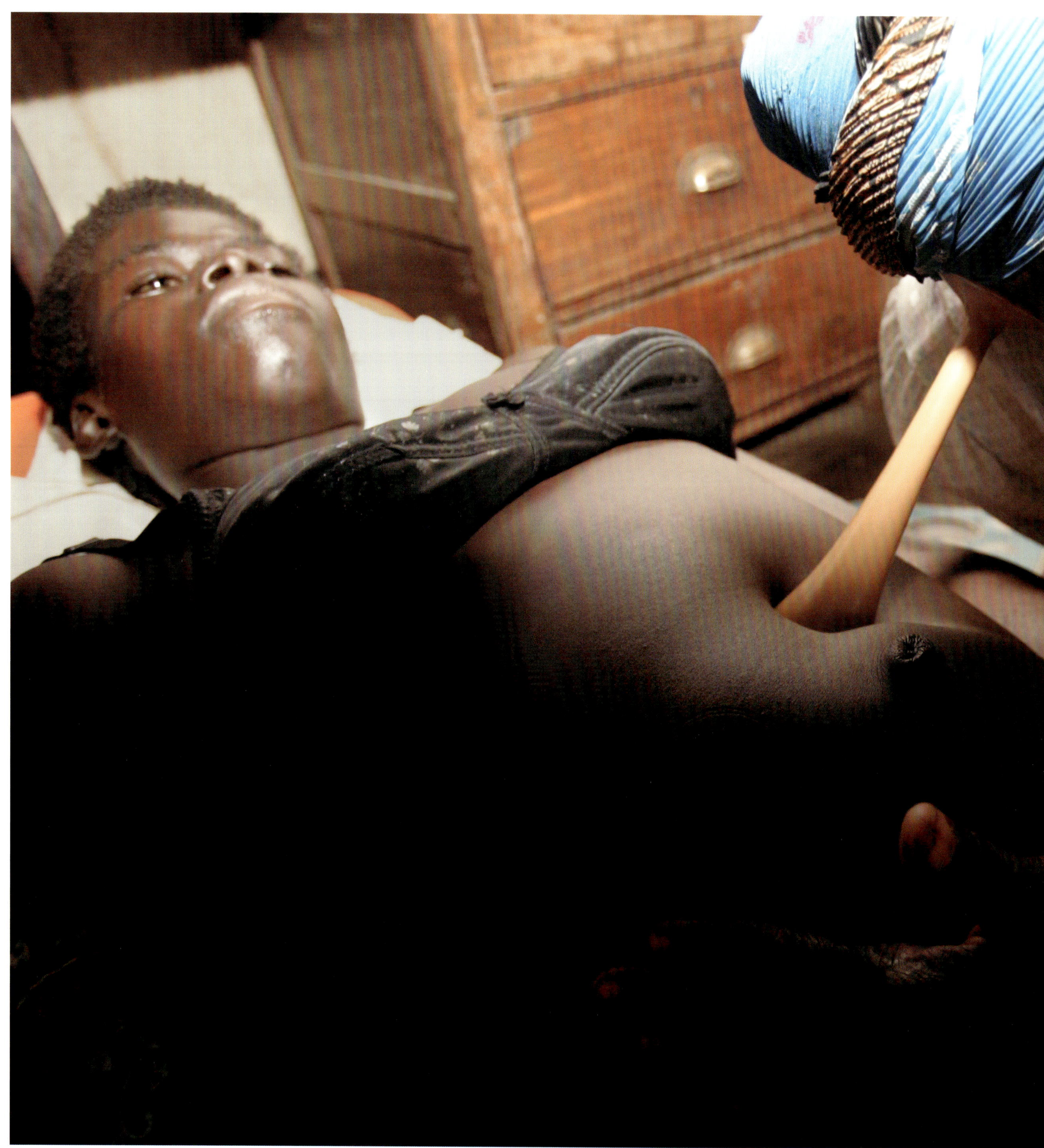

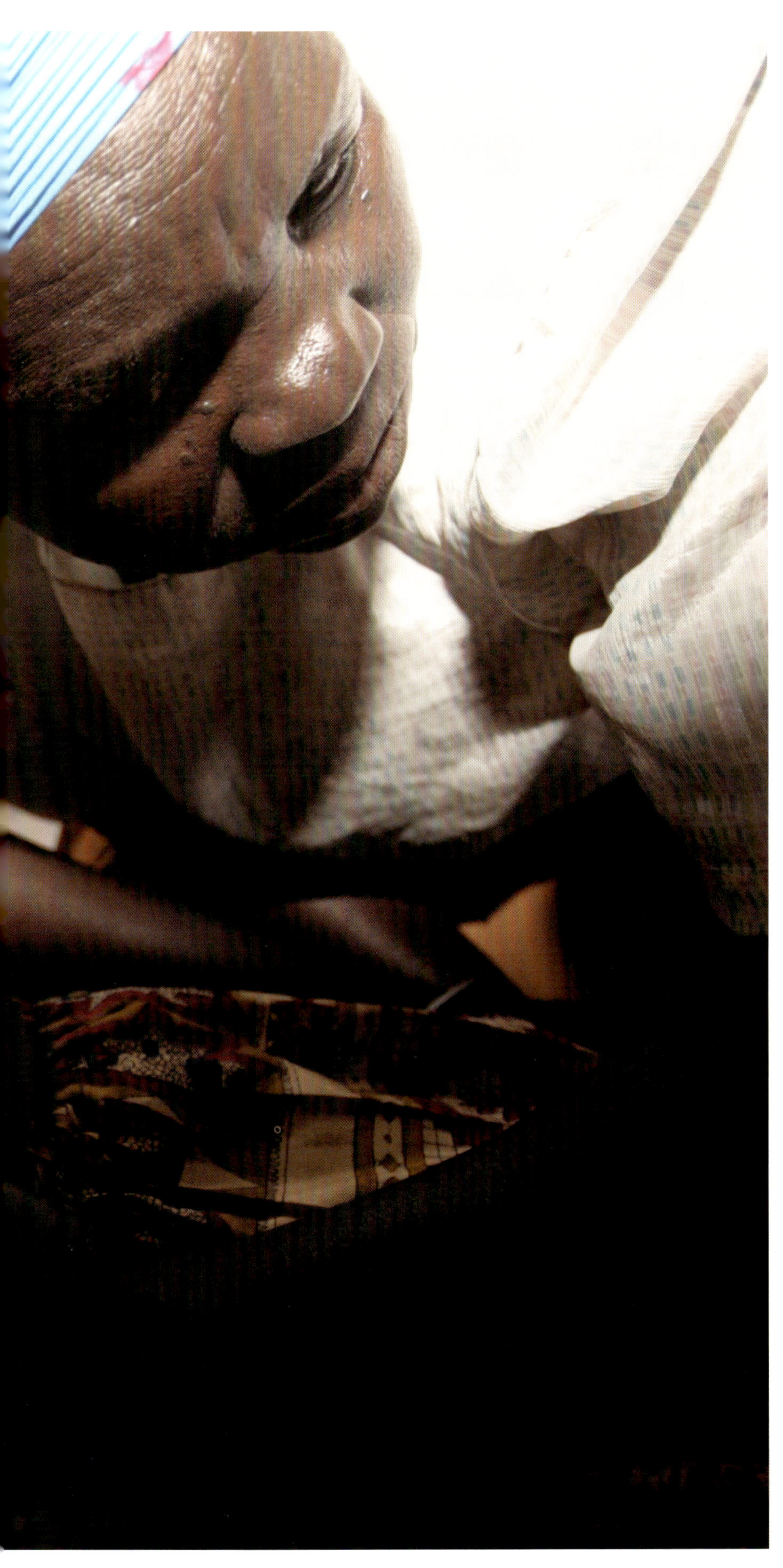

Uganda 2005
Tanya Habjouqa

In a matter of months, International Medical Corps trained 49 Ministry of Health workers and 114 traditional birth attendants in Uganda, where the number of births supervised by skilled health workers jumped from 20% to 50%.

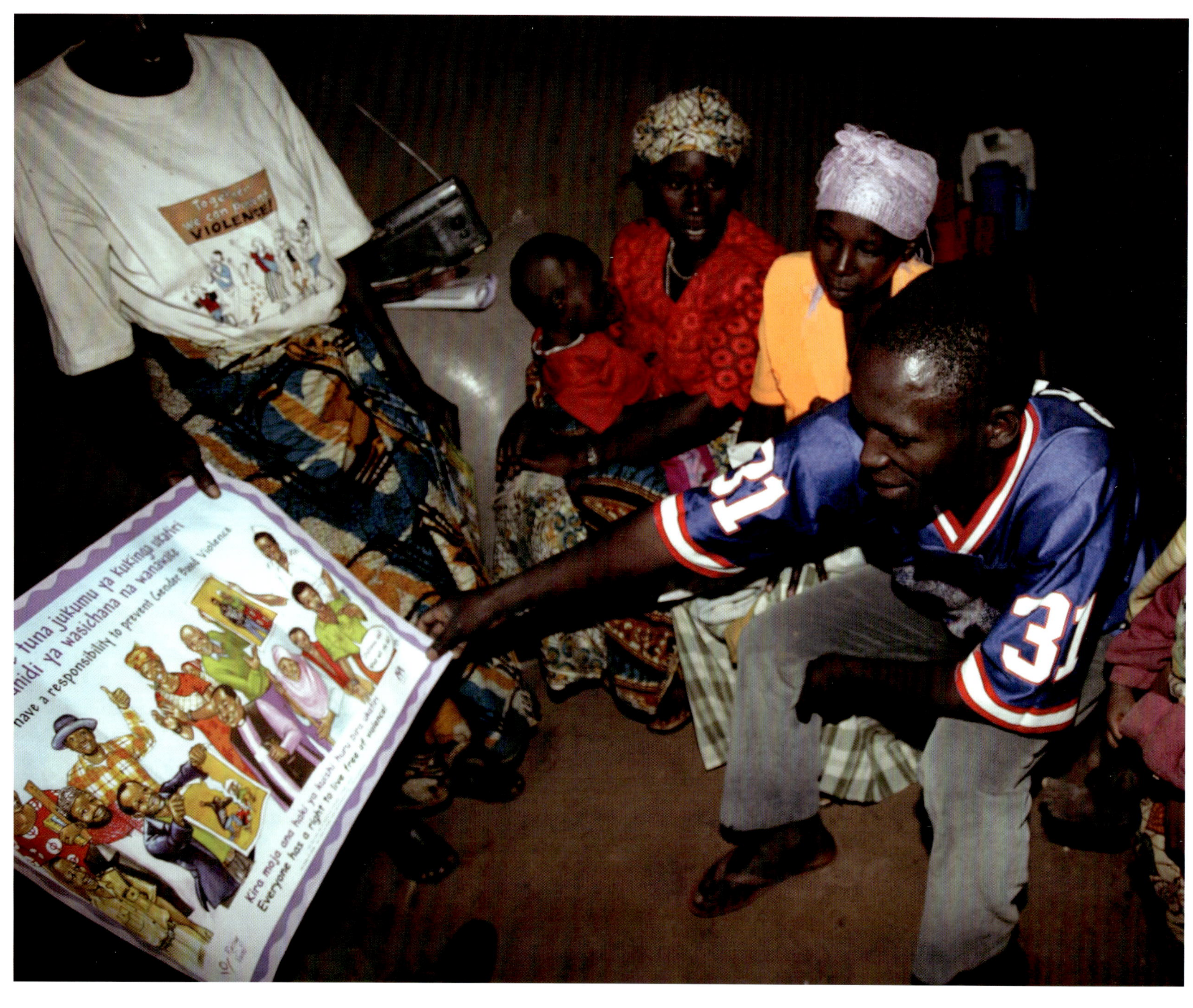

Uganda 2005
Tanya Habjouqa (both pages)

In 2003, International Medical Corps established a prevention and response program for sexual exploitation and gender-based violence (SGBV) in three Uganda refugee settlements in Hoima and Mbarara Districts. IMC trained 265 health workers and community leaders in medical management of rape survivors.

Opposite page: Working with local partners, International Medical Corps established community forums in Uganda to prevent and respond to sexual exploitation and gender-based violence through behavior-change campaigns like this one, in which two Ugandans act out a play about sexual violence.

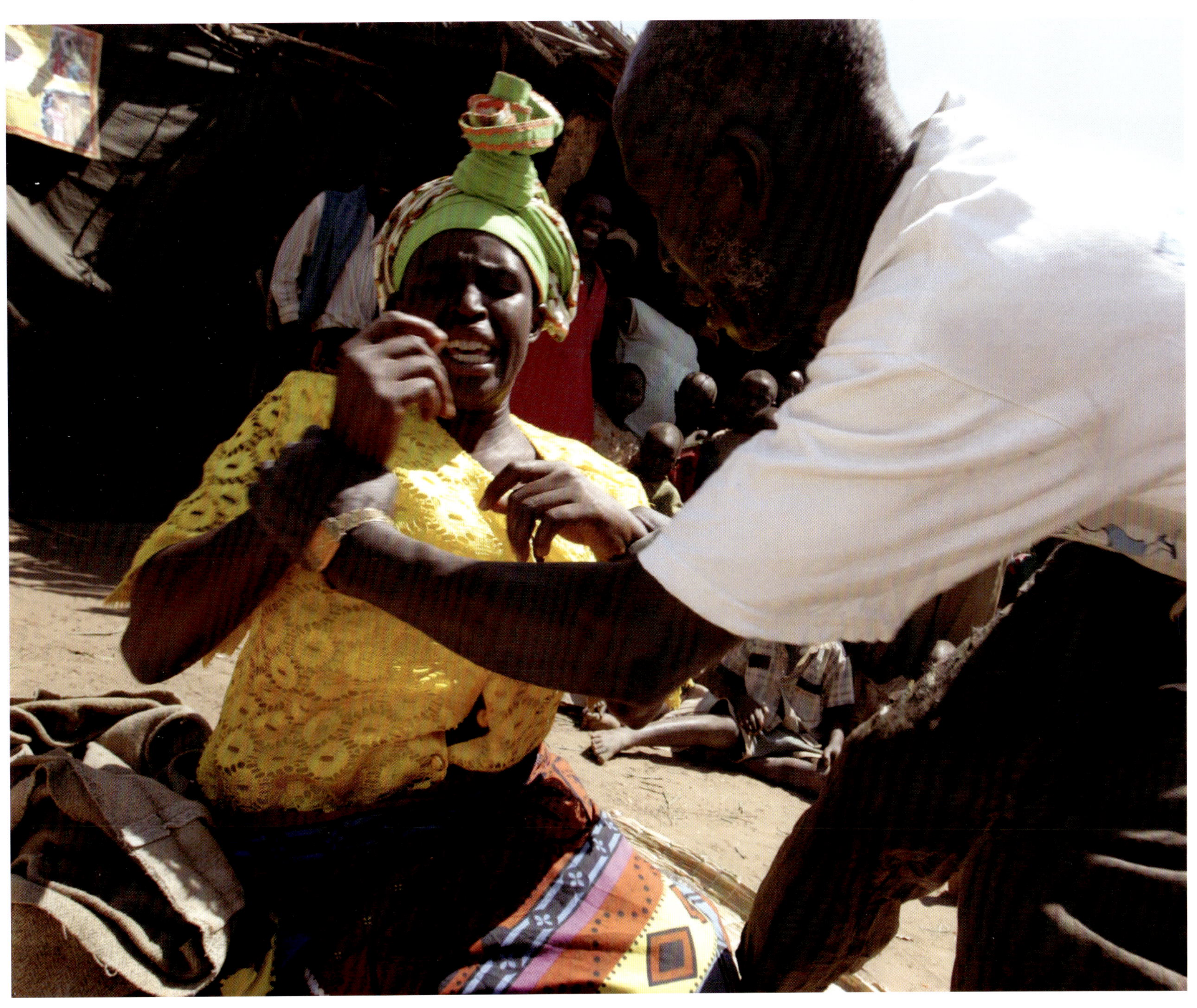

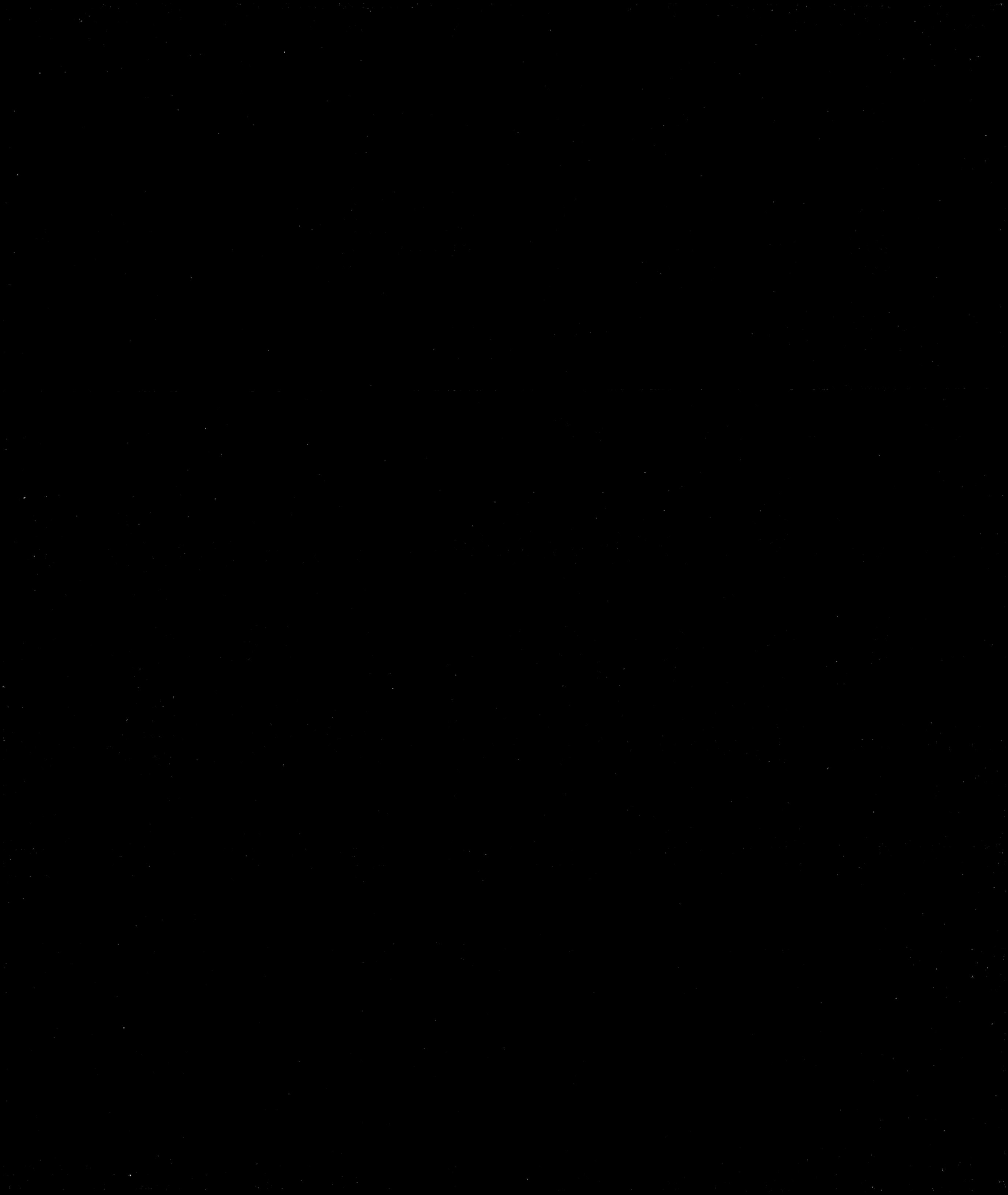

WAR-TORN NATIONS

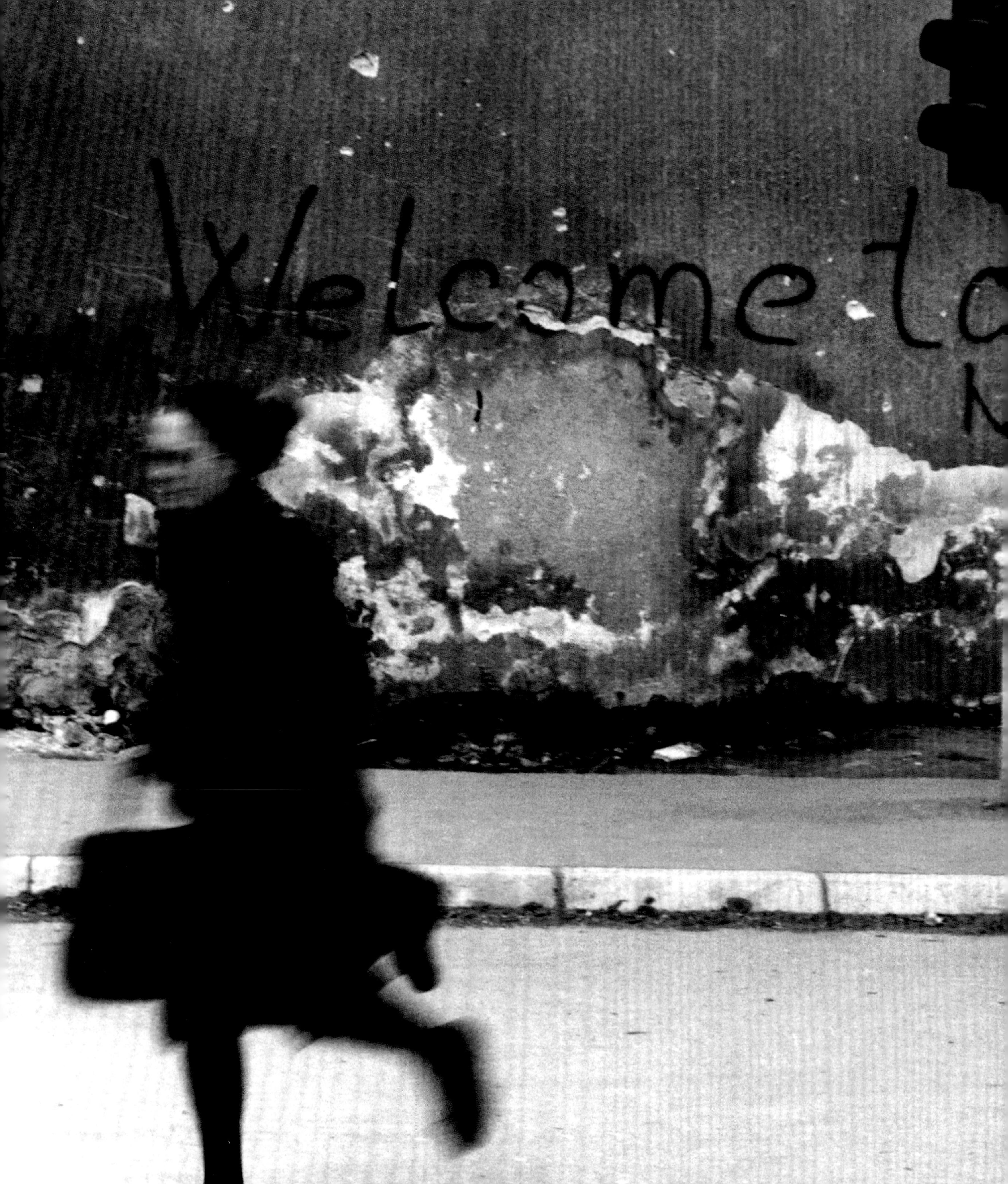
Welcome

BOSNIA

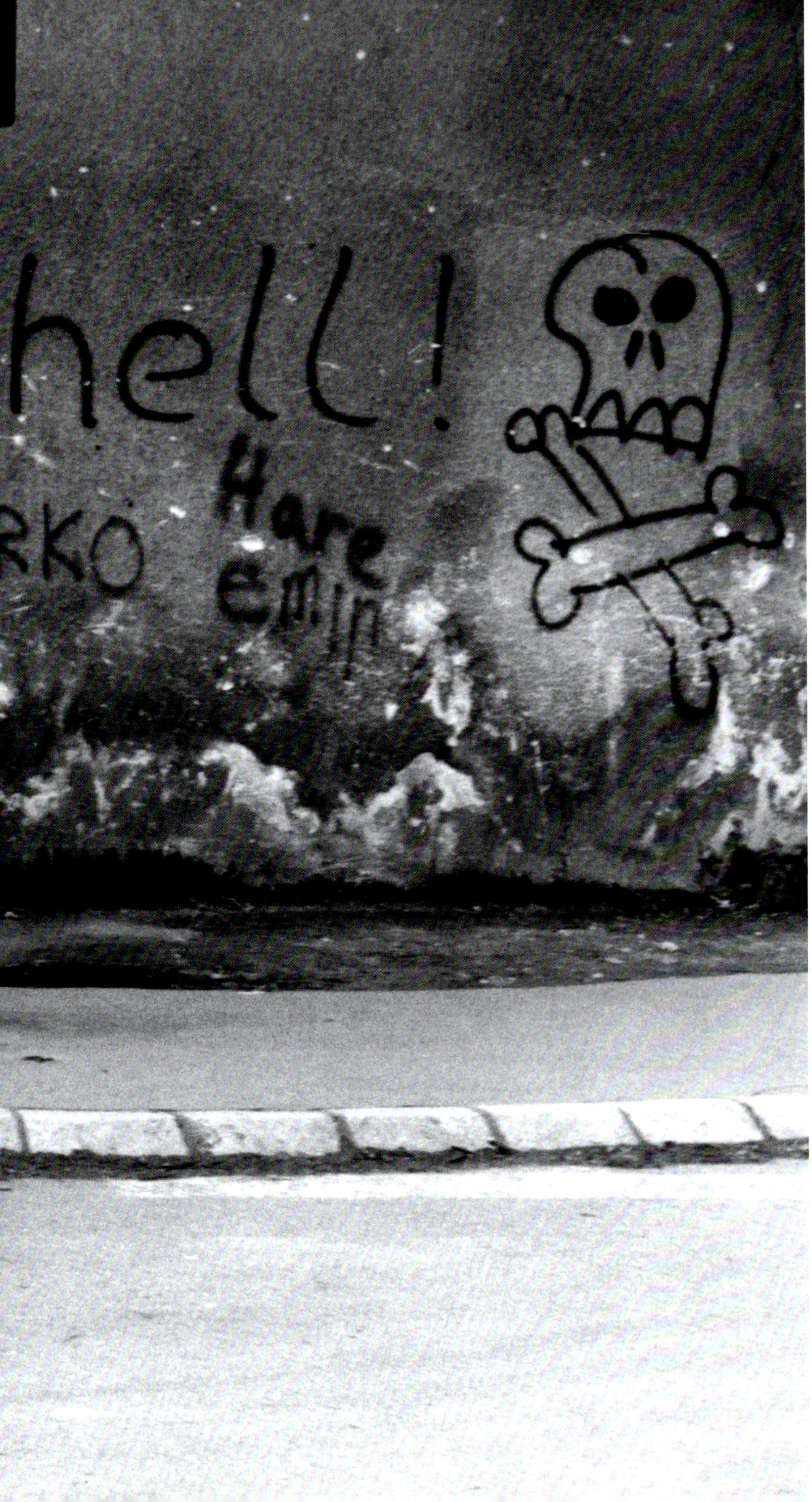

Bosnia 1993
Chris Rainier

When war broke out in Sarajevo in 1992, International Medical Corps deployed a group of doctors and nurses to the city to help with the sudden increase in gunshot and landmine injuries that overwhelmed local emergency response systems there.

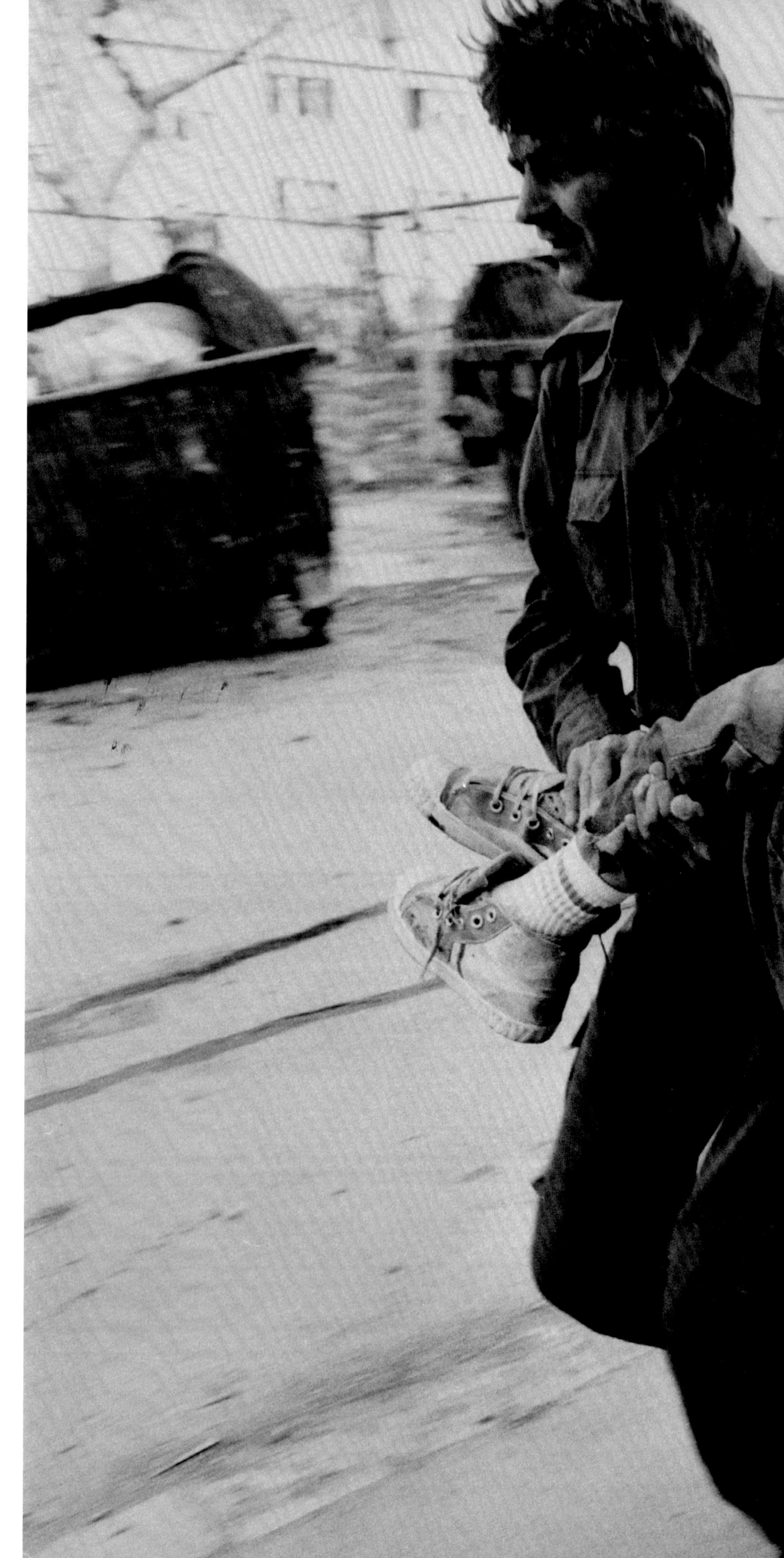

Bosnia 1993
Chris Rainier

When International Medical Corps came to Sarajevo, there were few ambulances or trained medics to provide pre-hospital transport and care. The sick and wounded were often carried to emergency rooms, and many people died or were permanently injured en route to the hospitals.

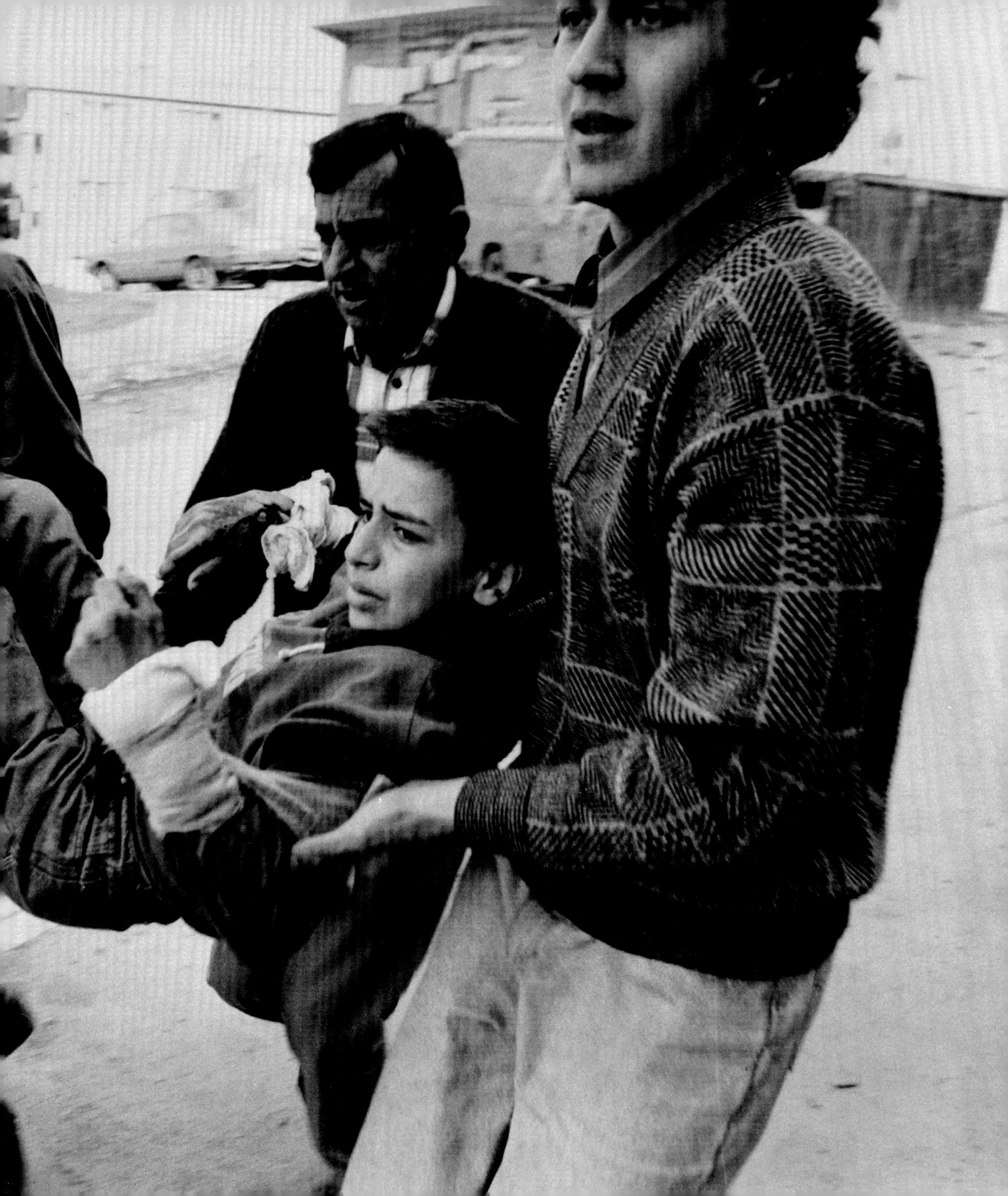

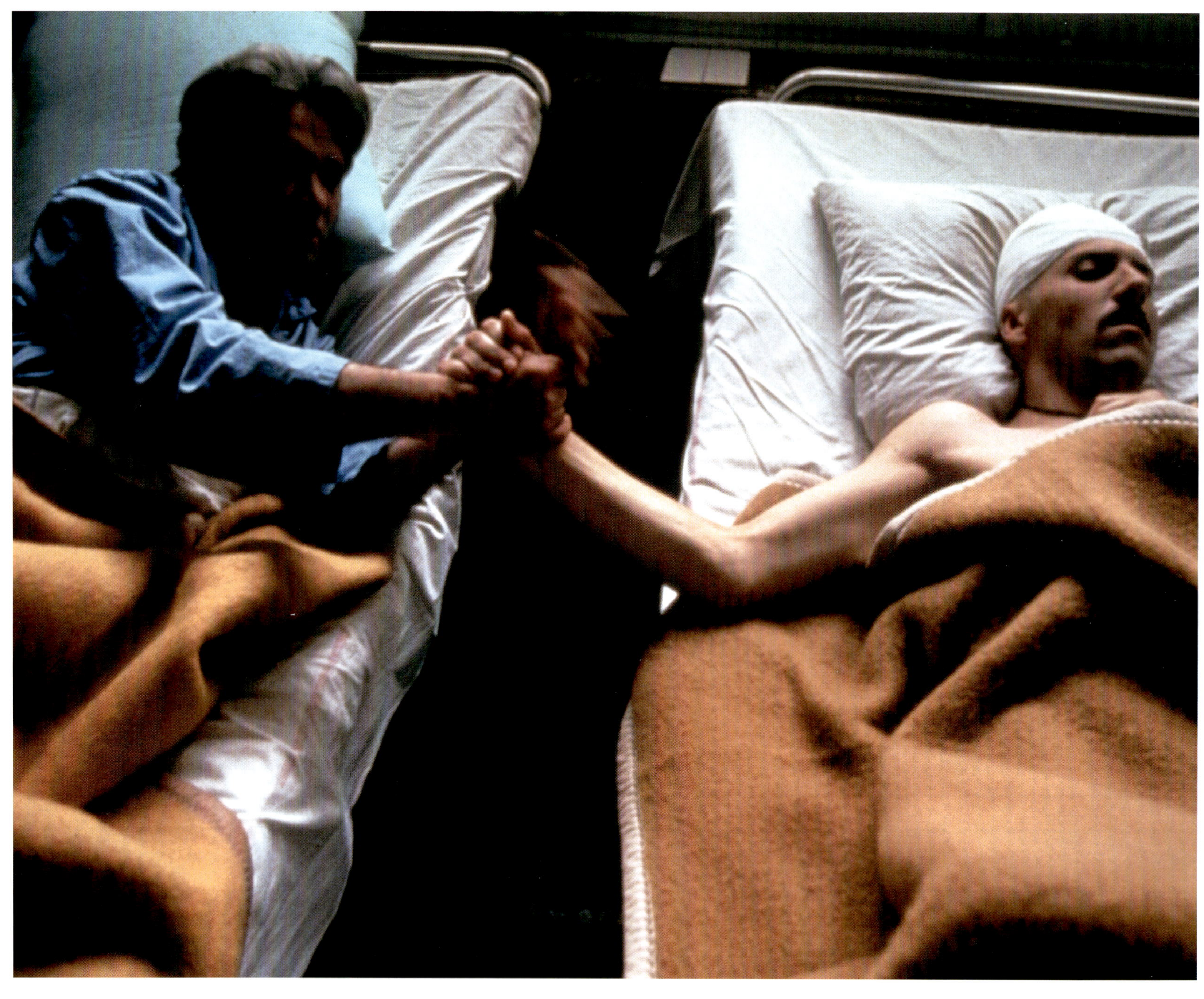

Bosnia 1993
Chris Rainier (both pages)

By the early 1990s, the combination of a centralized health care system and a relatively poor medical education system had hindered the development of Bosnia-Herzegovina's emergency response capacity. When the war broke out, hospitals were overwhelmed, and most local physicians had no formal training in basic life support. Many Bosnians died in crowded receiving areas because there were no emergency rooms. International Medical Corps set up emergency room capabilities in several hospitals.

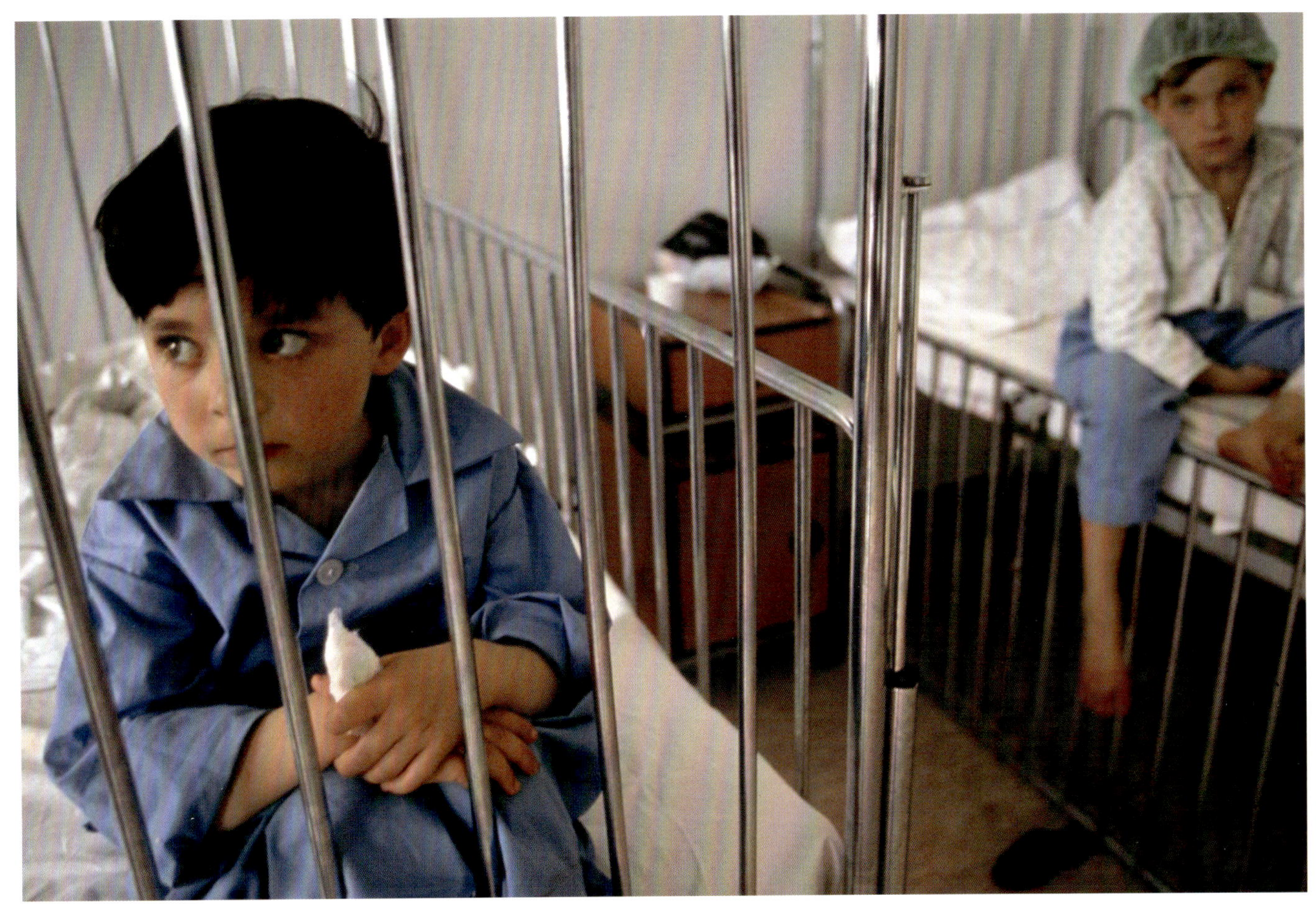

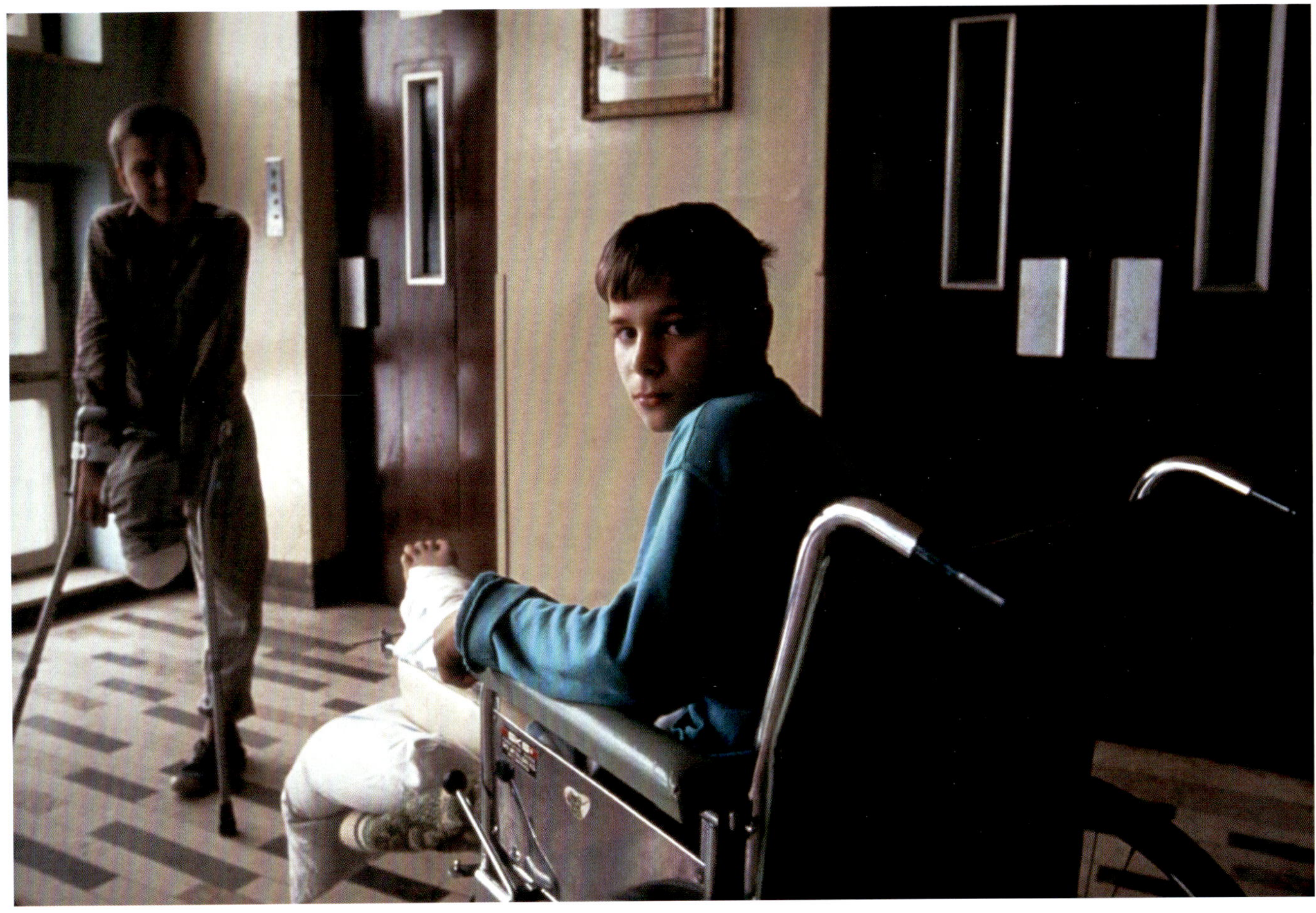

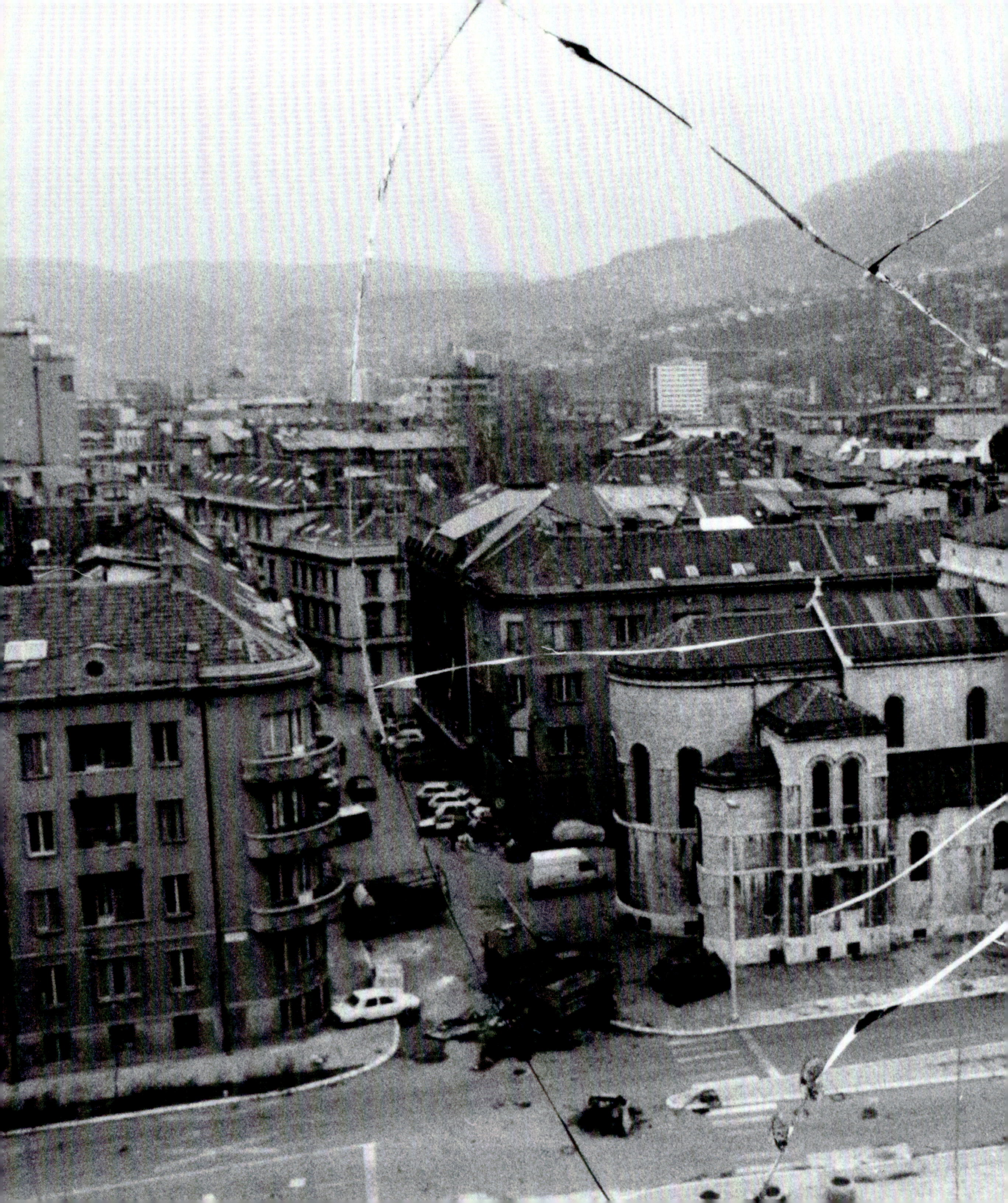

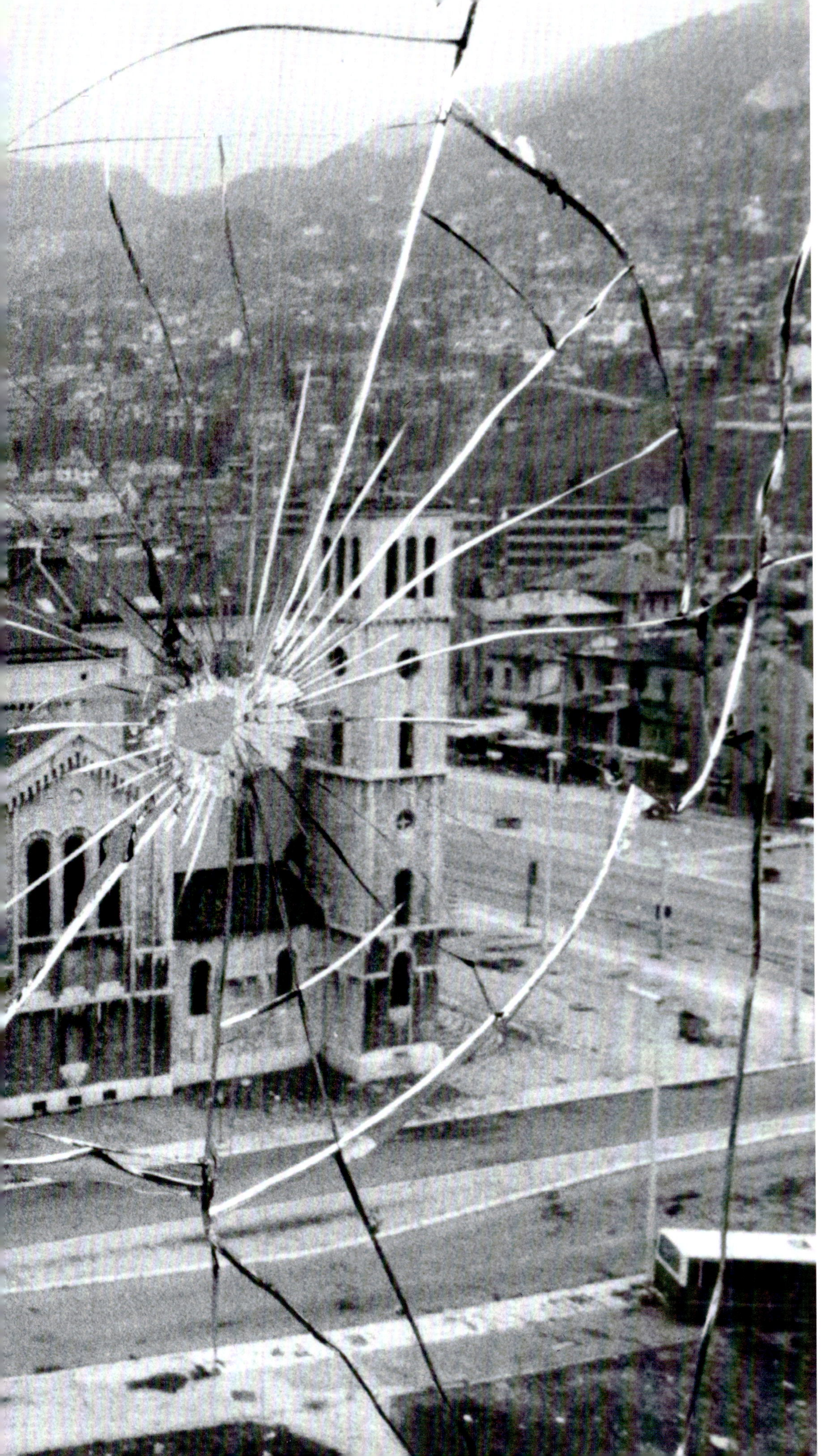

Bosnia 1993
Chris Rainier

From inside their hotel room in Sarajevo, International Medical Corps doctors and nurses were often caught in the crossfire of conflict. Many IMC health workers risked their own lives to work in this war-torn city.

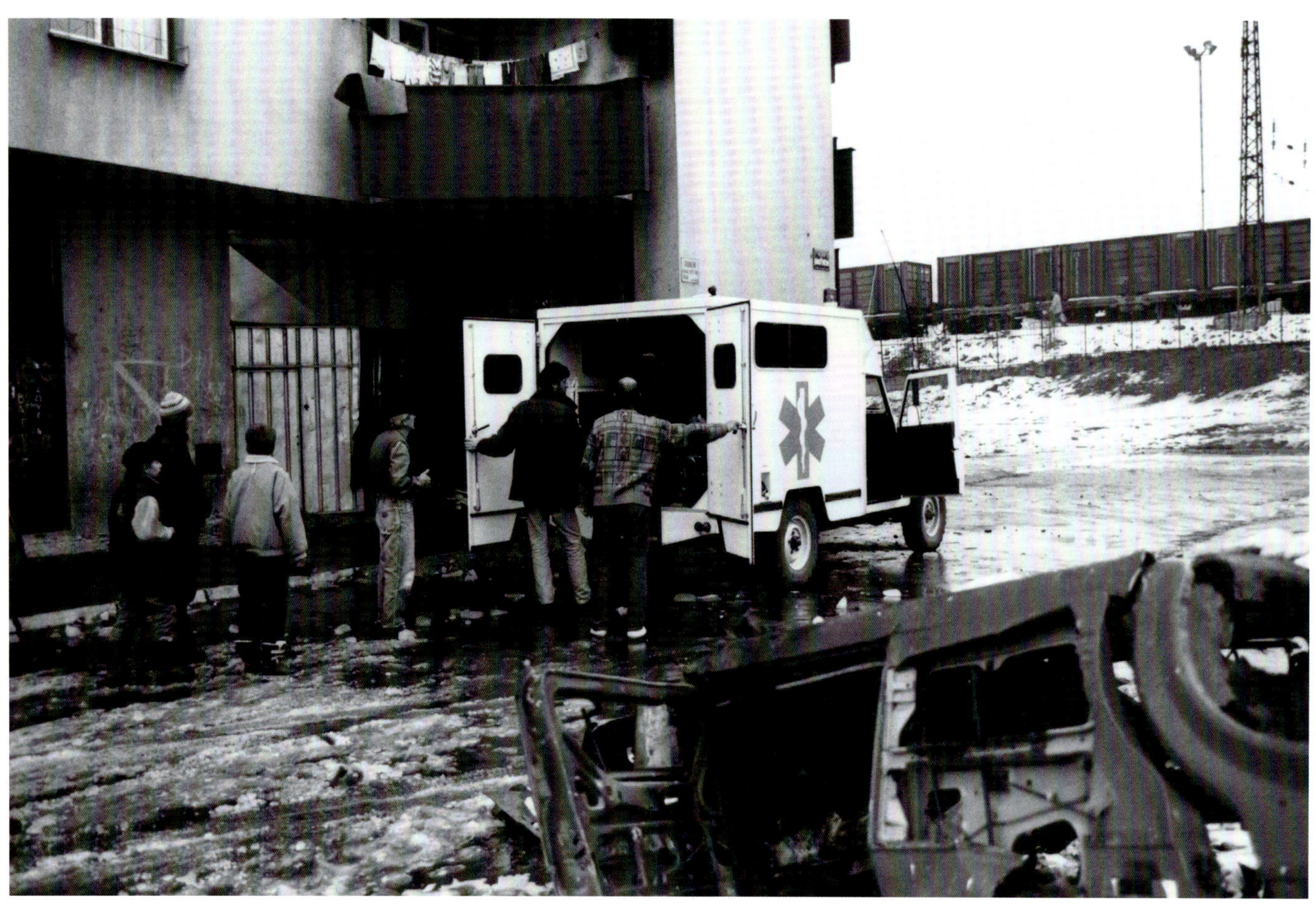

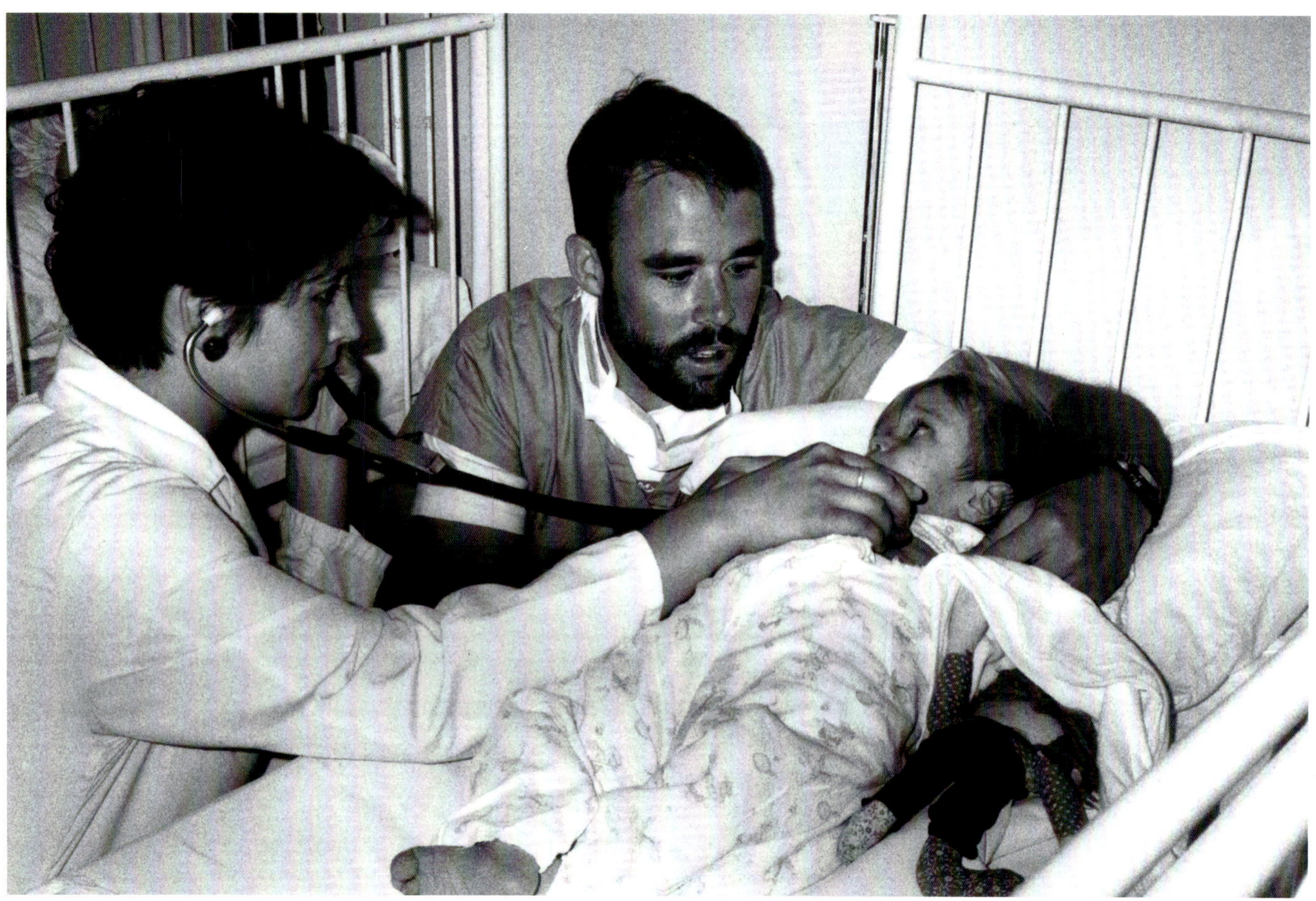

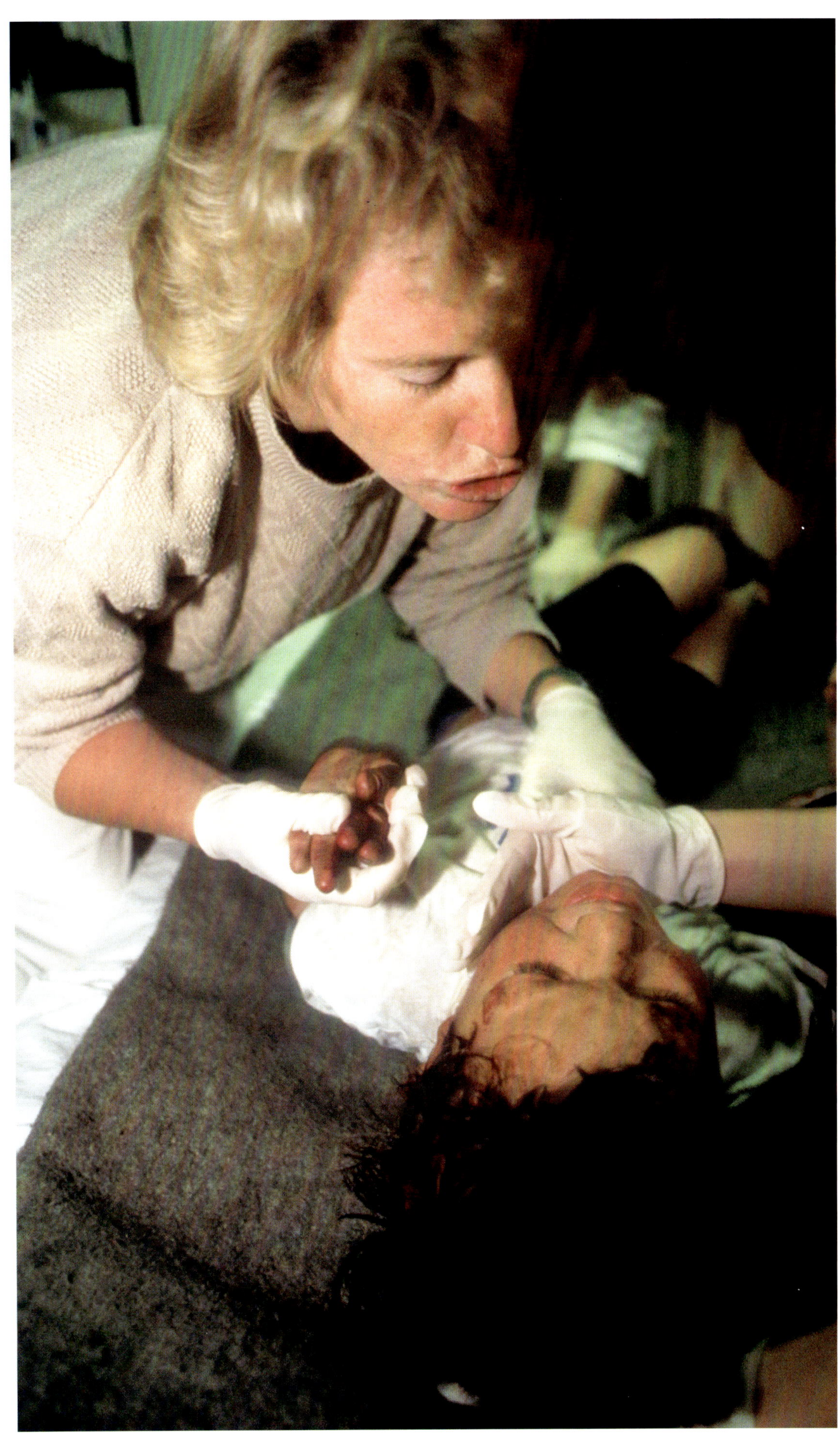

Bosnia 1994
IMC staff (both pages)

Opposite, top: International Medical Corps built Bosnia-Herzegovina's first emergency response system, which included a modern emergency transport ambulance system.

This page and opposite, bottom: International Medical Corps trained Bosnian, Croatian and Serbian health care workers side-by-side to treat the victims of war—many of whom were children. Their work together to save children was in stark contrast to what was happening on the battlefield.

RWANDA

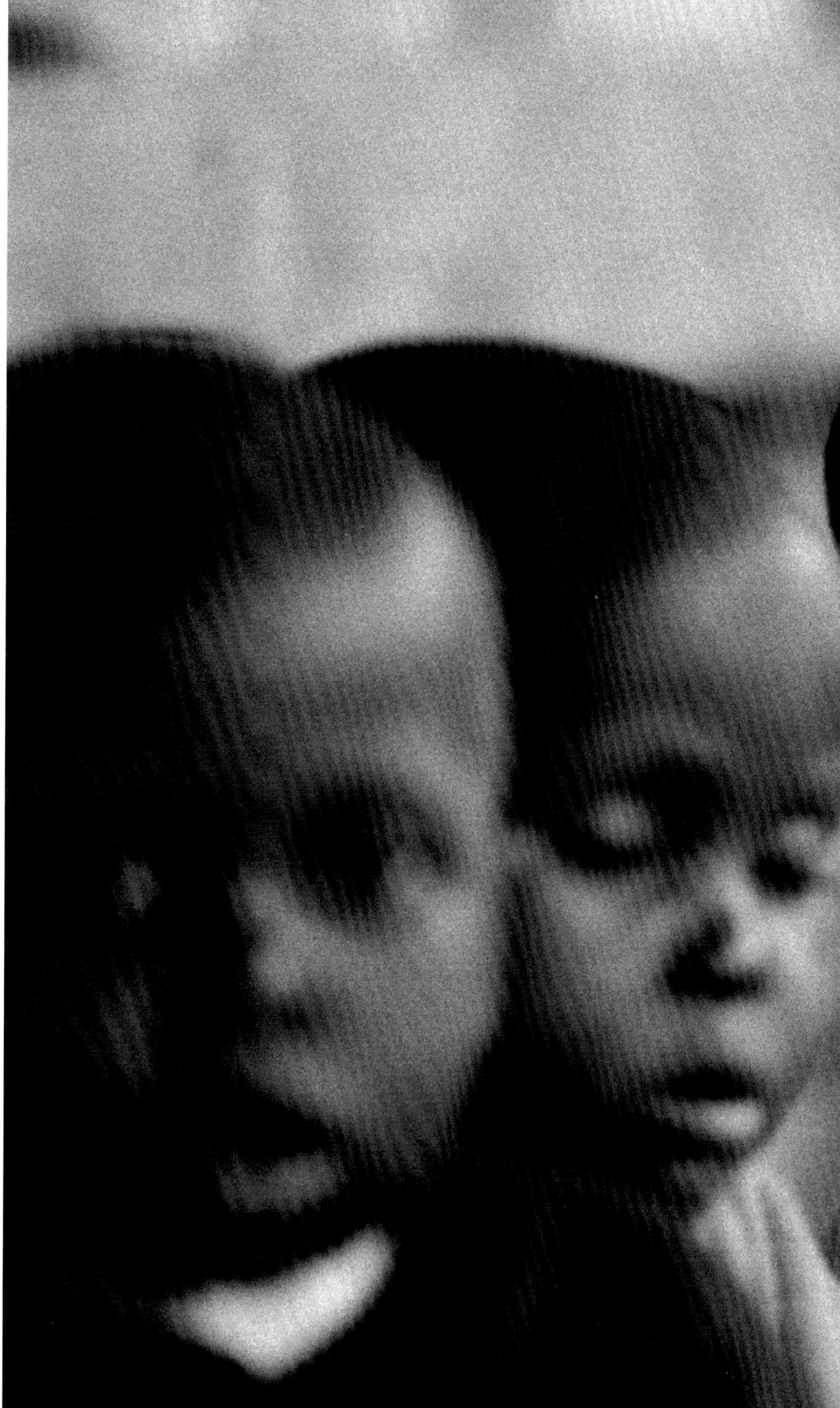

Rwanda 1994
Colin Finlay

Between April and June 1994, an estimated 800,000 Rwandans were brutally killed in a genocide lasting 100 days. The scale and speed of the slaughter left the country and its health care system in disarray. International Medical Corps immediately deployed an emergency response team into Rwanda to meet the needs of the survivors of this genocide.

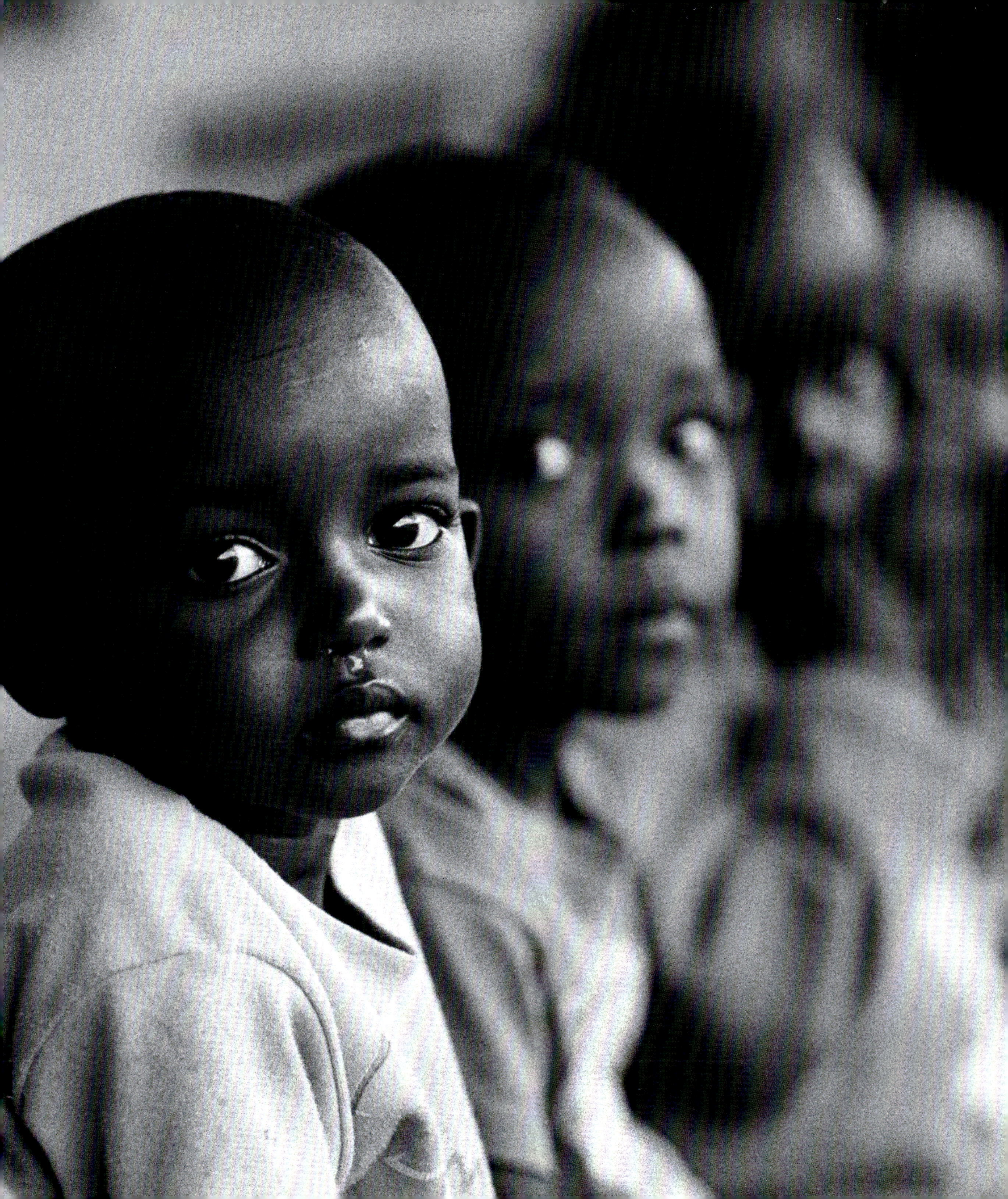

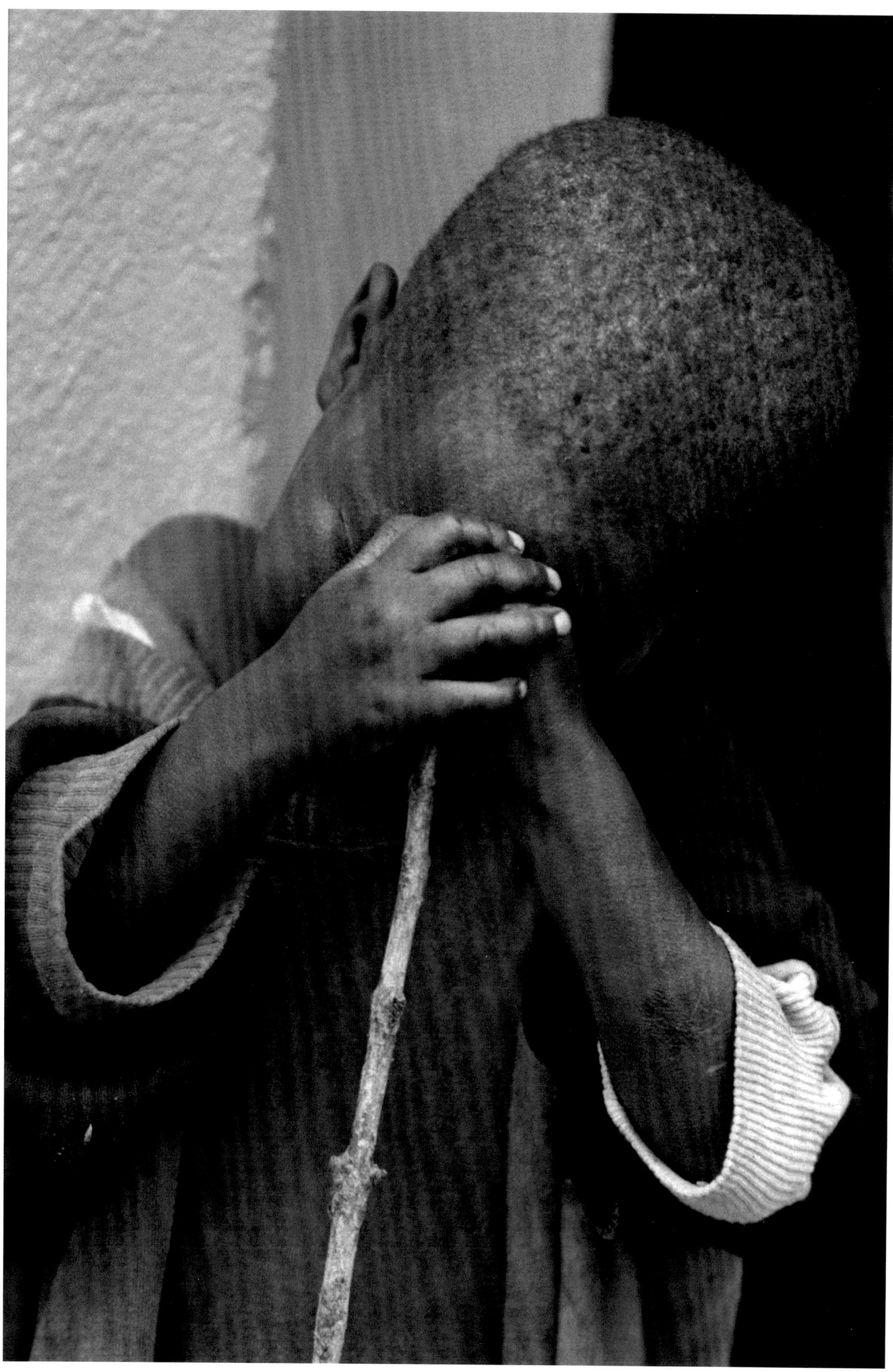

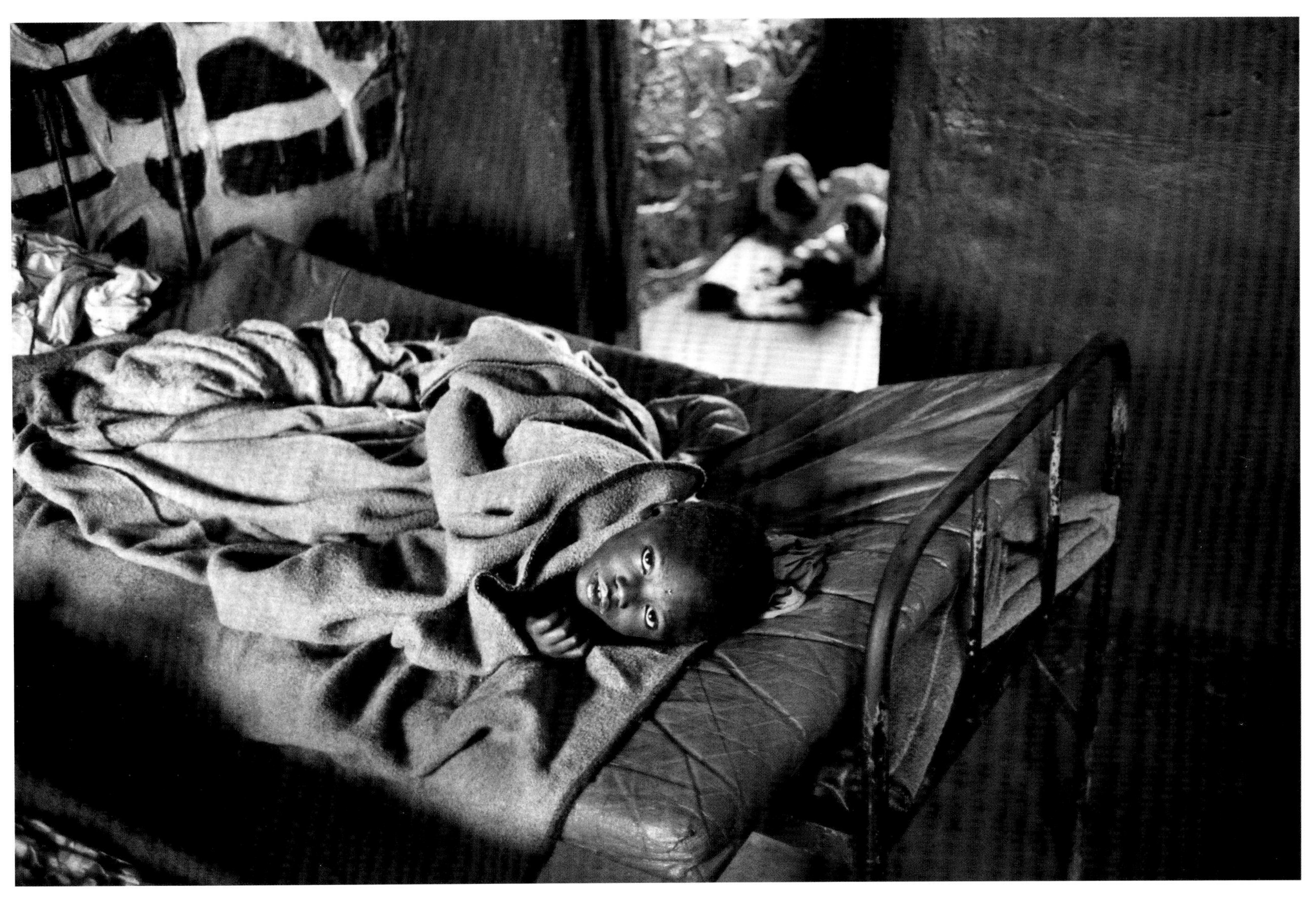

Rwanda 1994
Colin Finlay (both pages)

When International Medical Corps' emergency response team arrived in Kibungo Hospital in Rwanda in the midst of the 1994 genocide, it found a situation unlike any it had encountered before. The hospital was a ghastly murder scene, ransacked and looted, covered in blood and filled with bodies. Children were left unattended and dying while more still kept coming. The IMC team got to work administering triage, cleaning rooms and assembling makeshift beds.

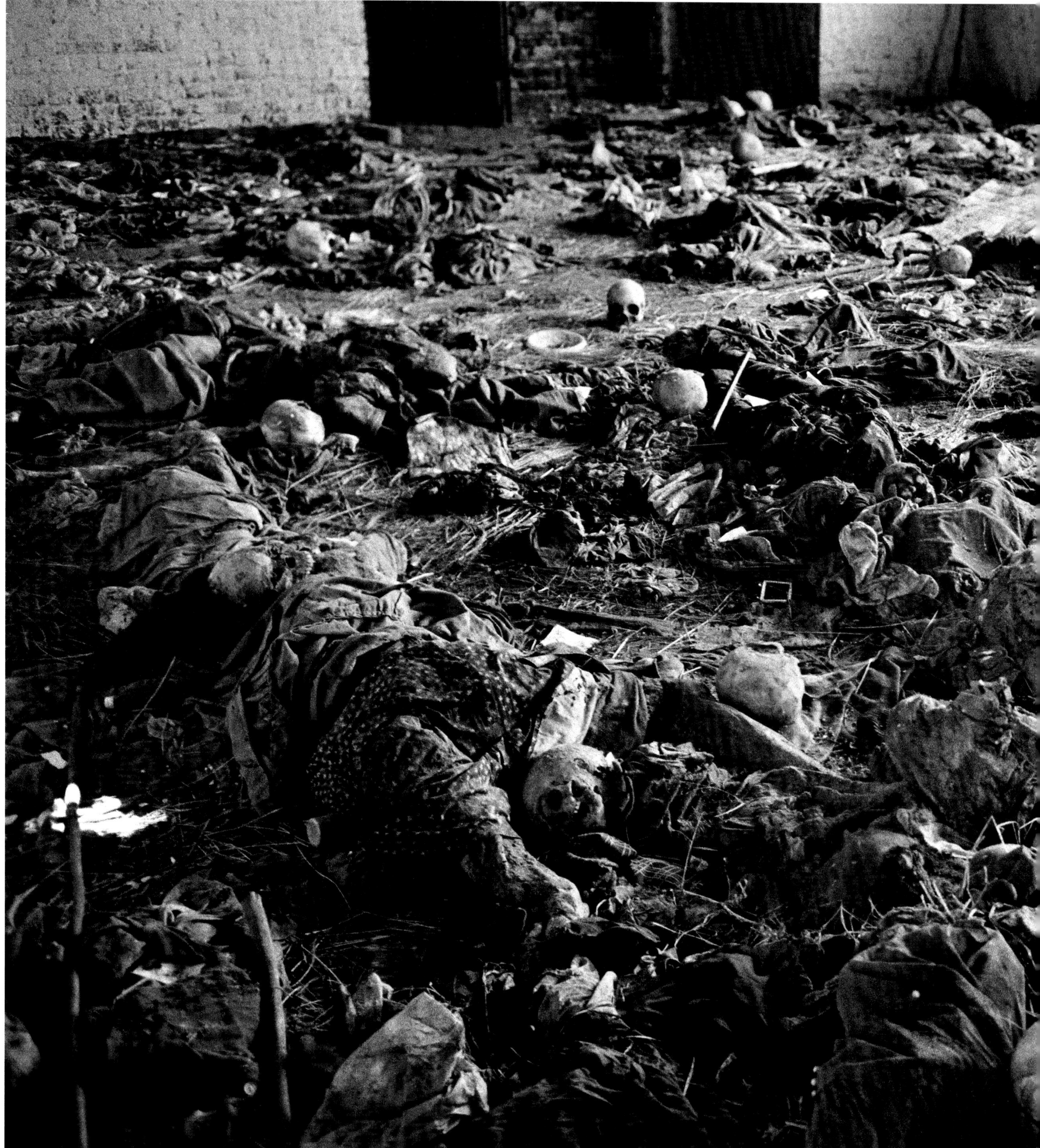

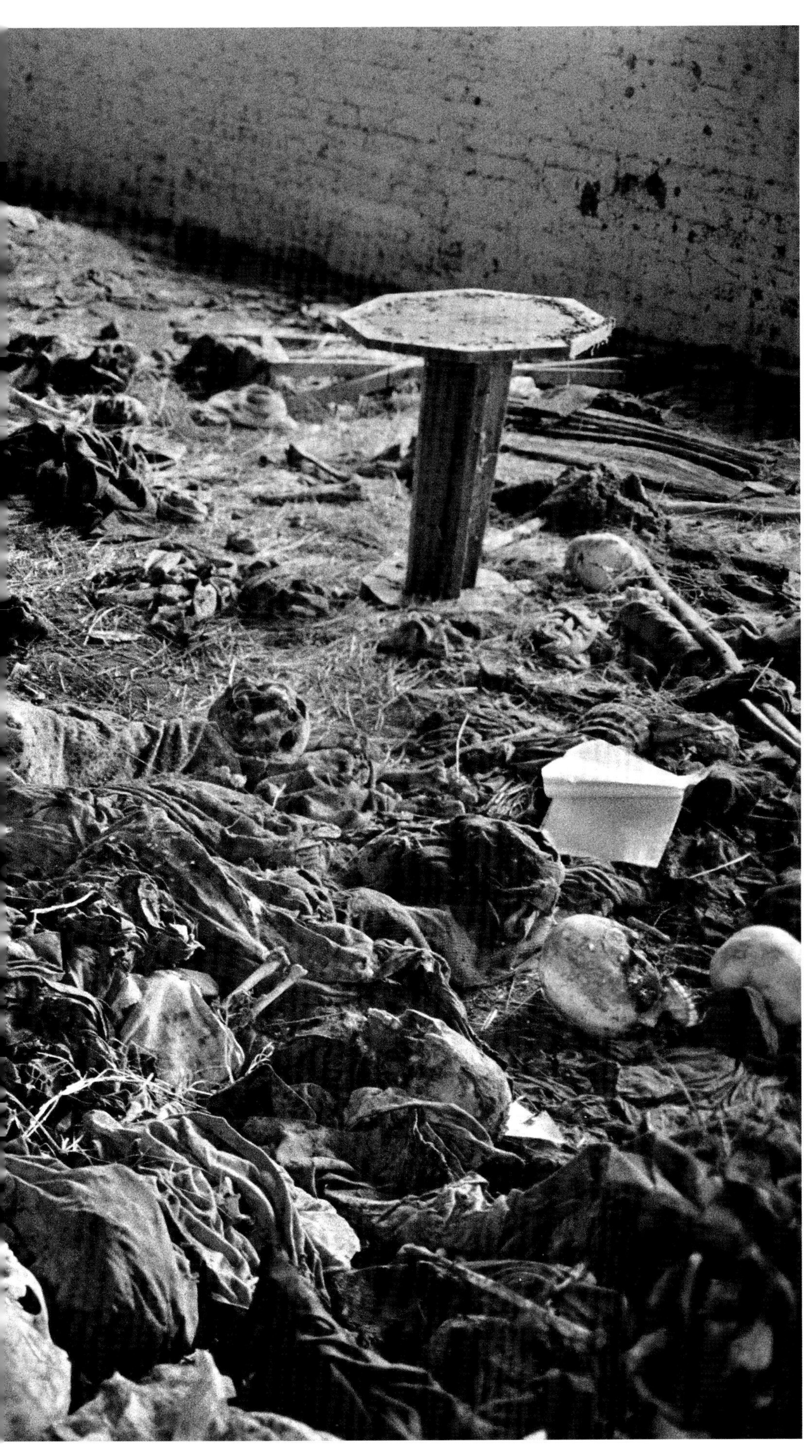

Rwanda 1994
Colin Finlay

The scale and swiftness of the killing was staggering, and the "genocidaires" had taken little time to dispose of their victims. Bodies were piled everywhere—in churches, schools and hospitals. The first task of International Medical Corps' rapid response teams in Kibungo, Rwanda, was to bury dozens of fallen Rwandan doctors and nurses found in the courtyard of the local hospital.

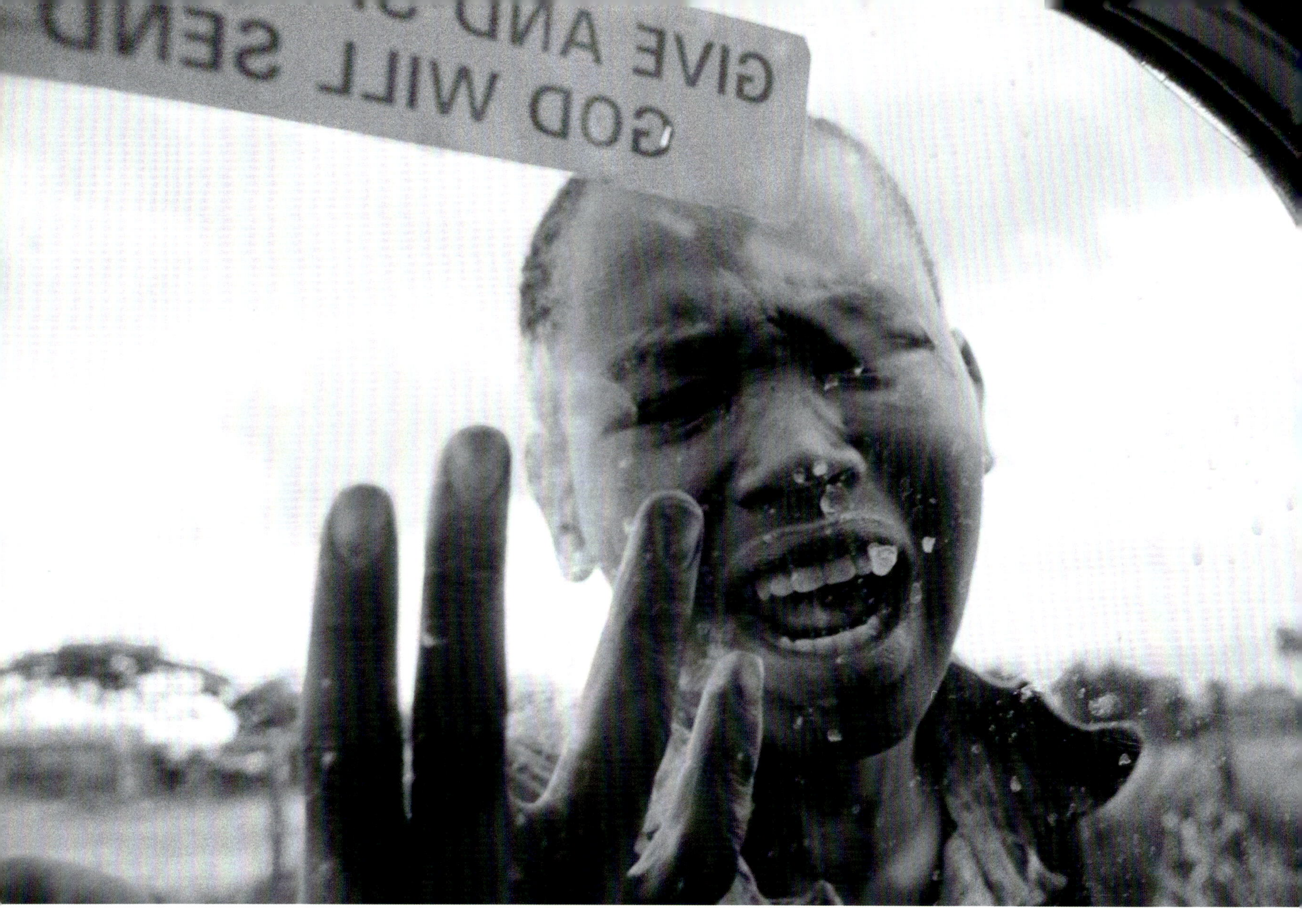
GIVE AND
GOD WILL SEND

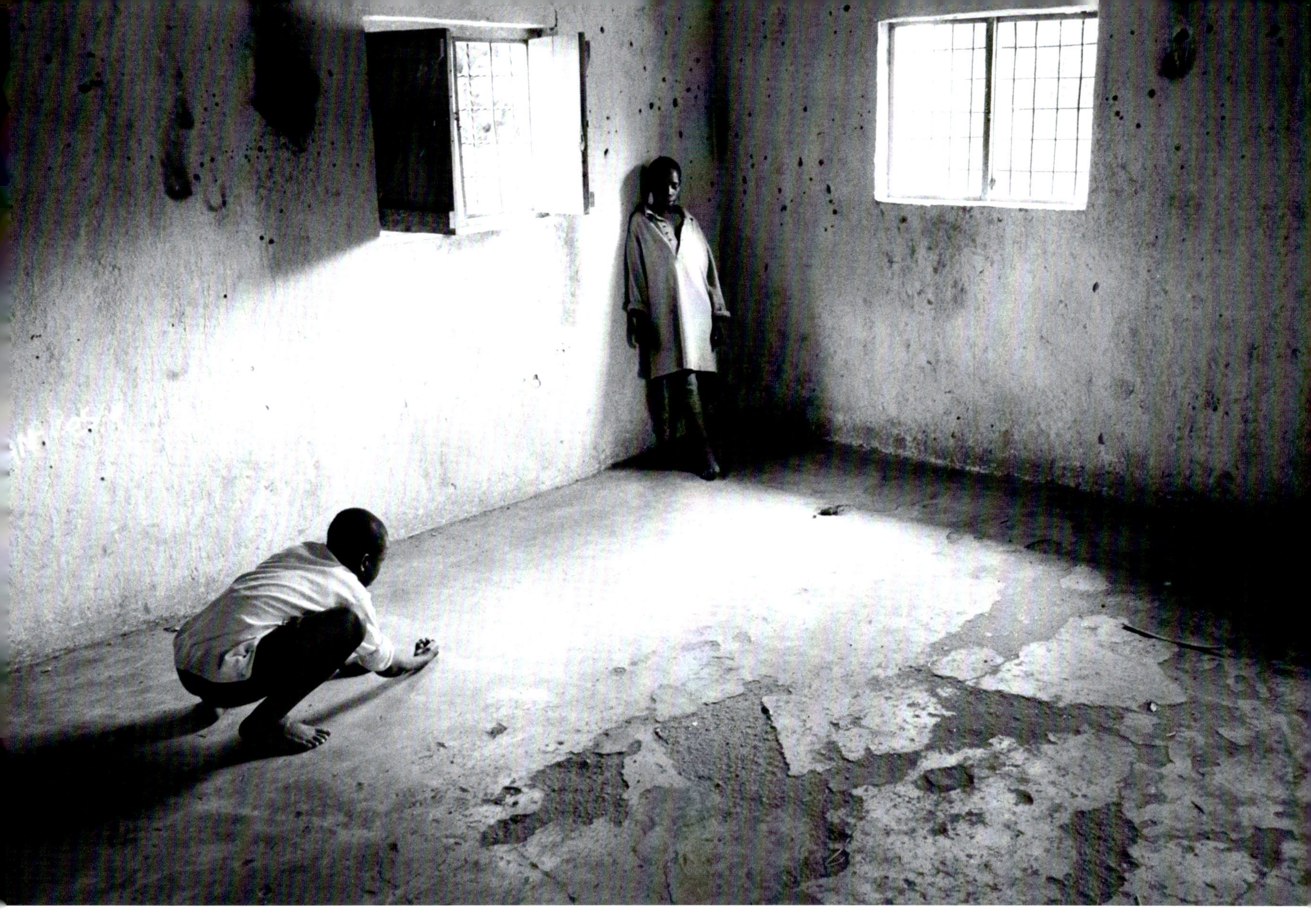

Rwanda 1994
Colin Finlay (both pages)

The situation International Medical Corps encountered in Rwanda was devastating. Thousands of Rwandans looked to IMC for help. Tutsis had made up the majority of Rwanda's health professionals before the genocide, leaving virtually no doctors and nurses afterward.

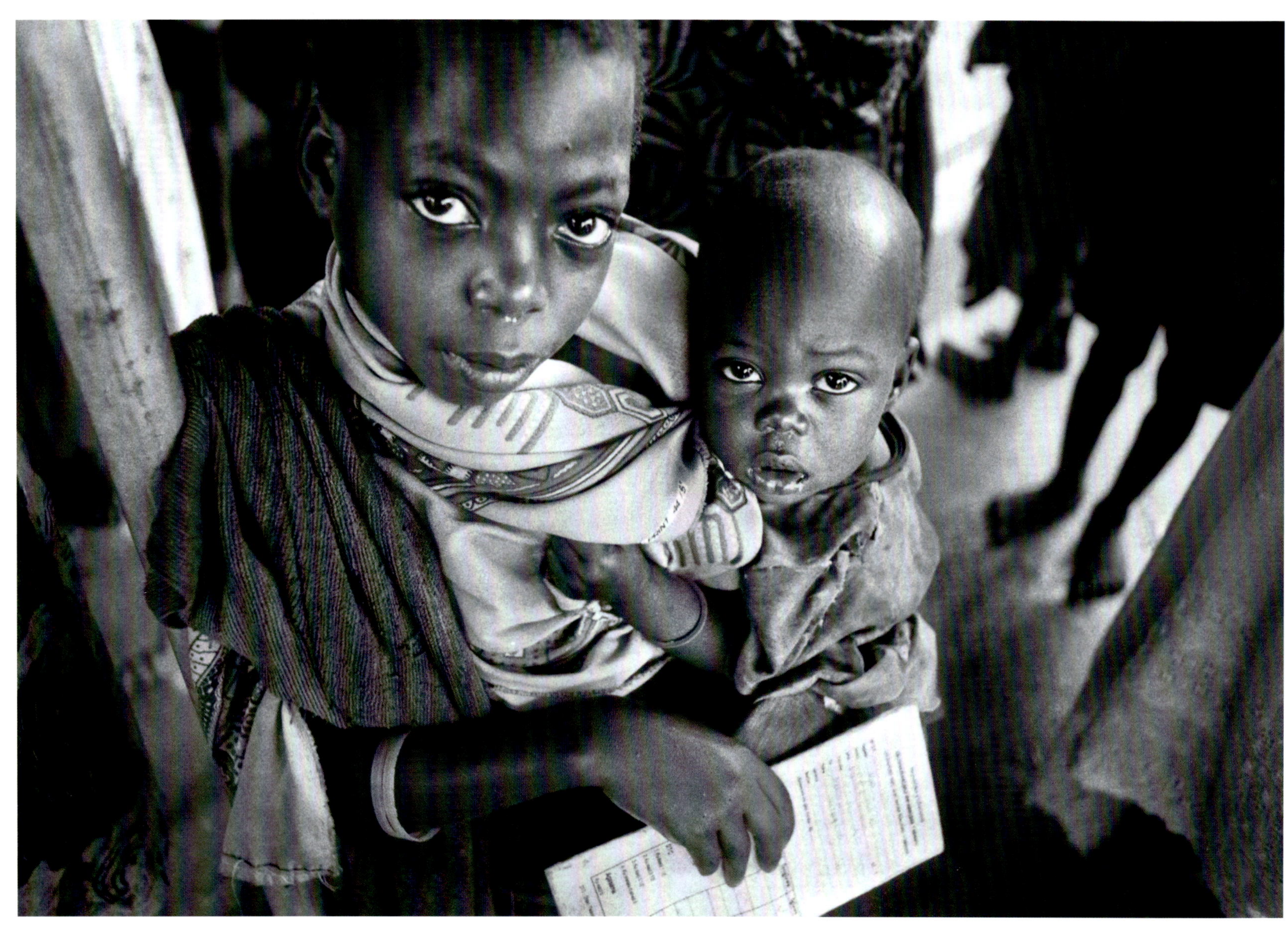

Rwanda 1994
Colin Finlay (both pages)

International Medical Corps provided much-needed medicine, vaccines and surgical care for victims of the violence in Rwanda. At one point, an IMC volunteer doctor was the only surgeon in all of Southern Rwanda.

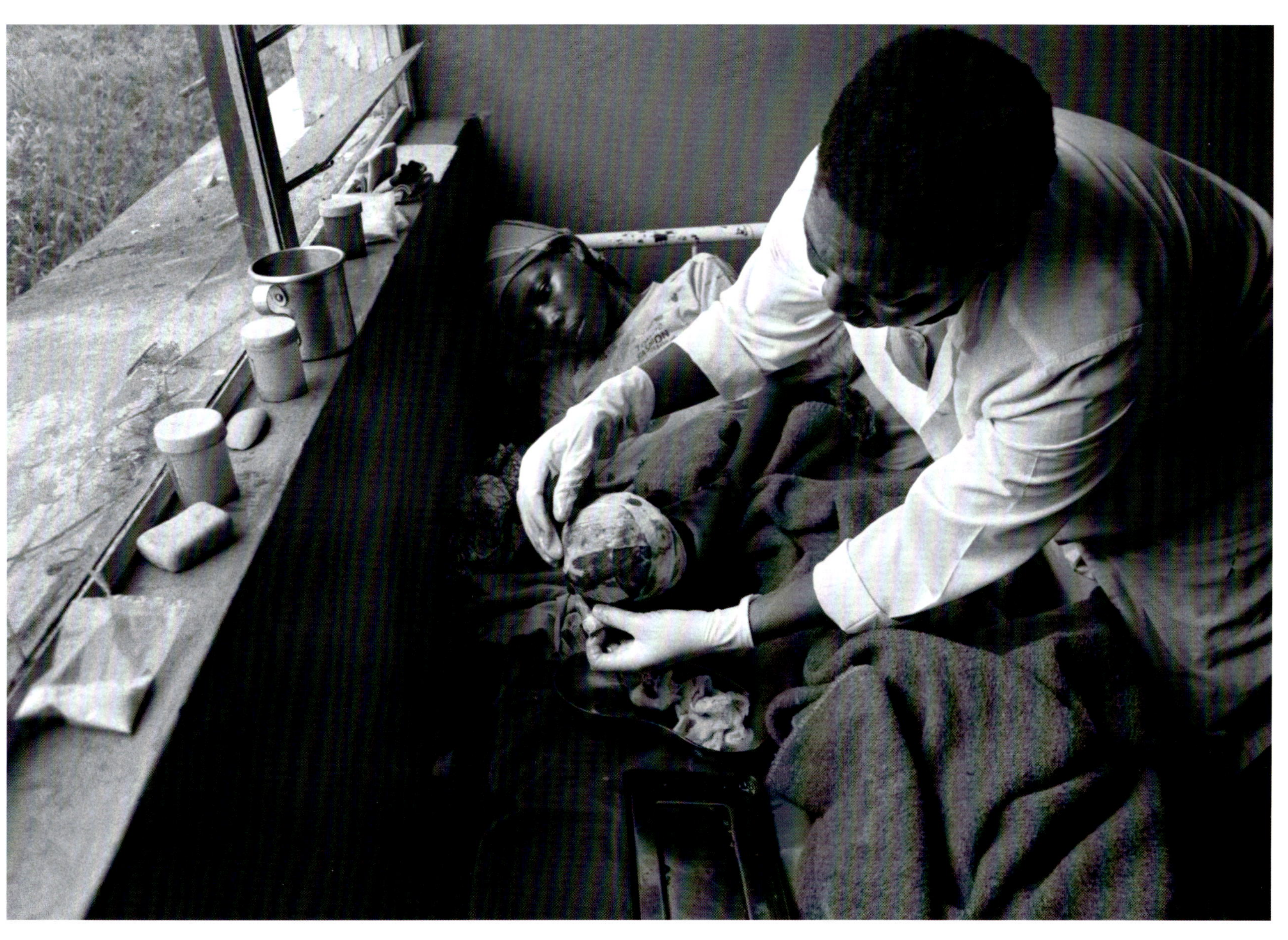

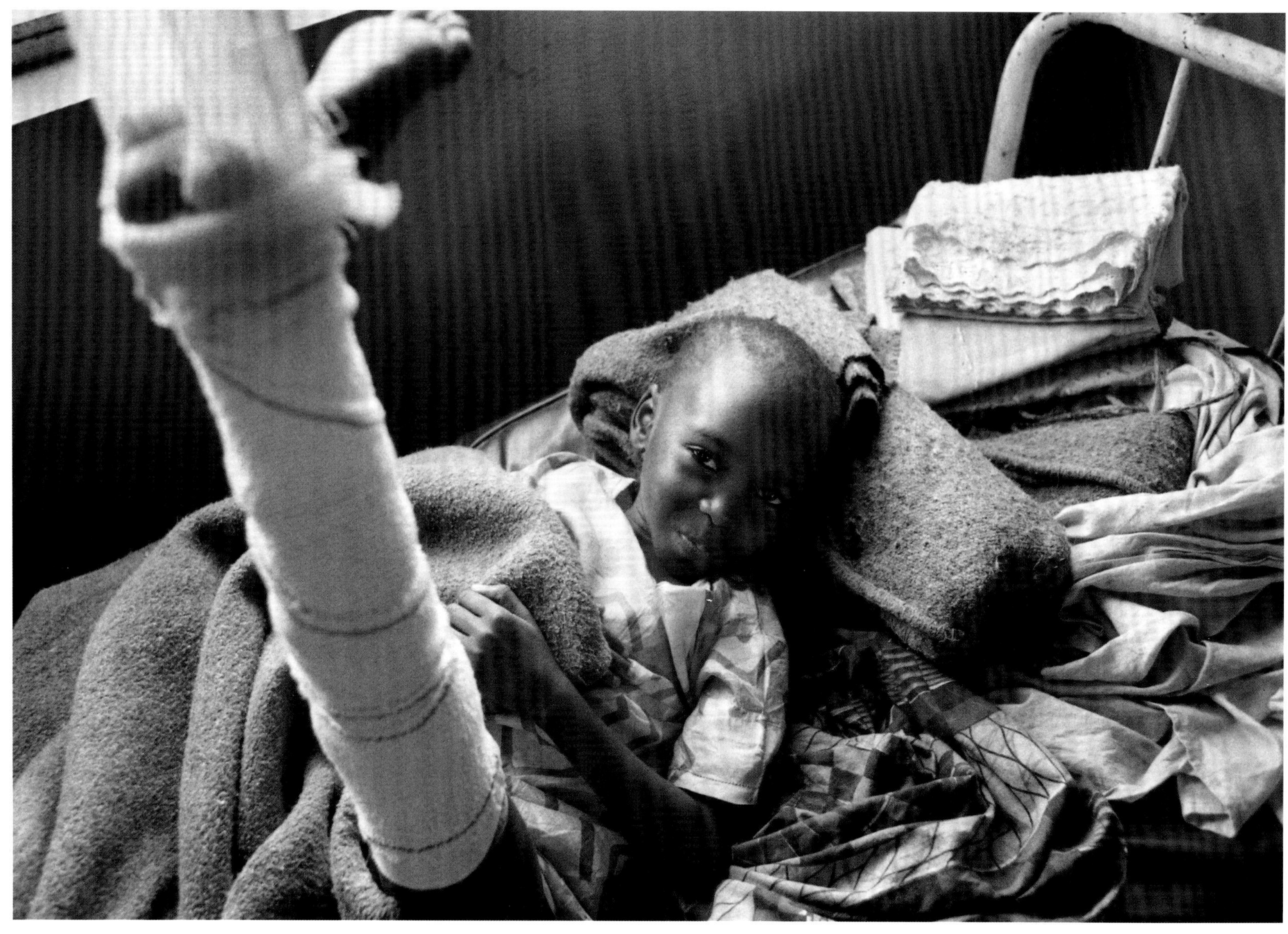

Rwanda 1994
Colin Finlay (both pages)

Against insurmountable odds, Rwanda is now considered a success story for International Medical Corps. By fully integrating Rwandans, IMC returned the responsibility of the country's health care back to its people. Providing Rwandans the opportunity to get their country back in order, IMC helped turn several hospitals that were totally ruined into functioning hospitals doing eight to ten surgeries a day—once again, run by Rwandans. Always concerned with re-establishing a community to self-reliance, IMC turned over its operations to local health care authorities in Rwanda in 1996.

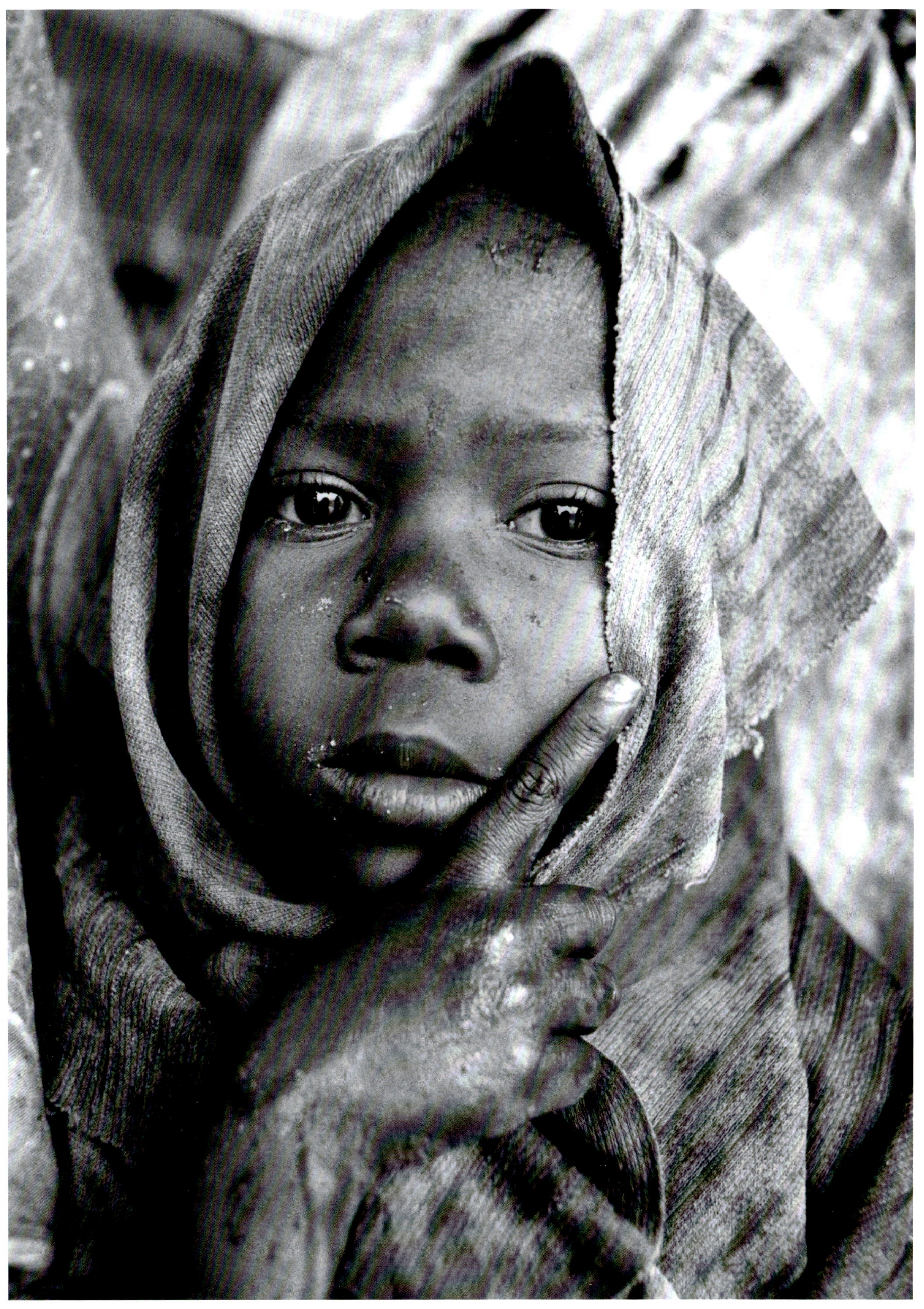

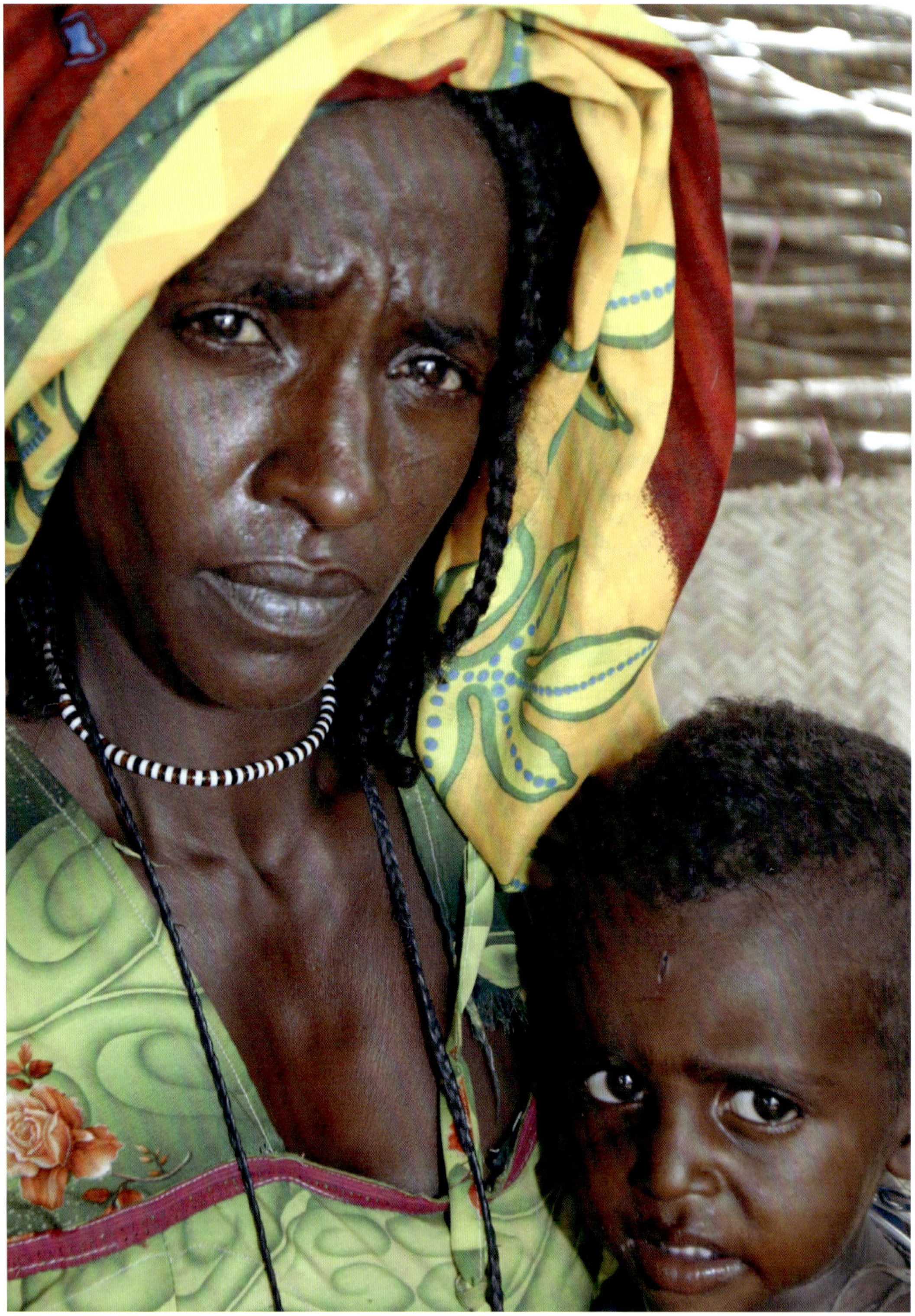

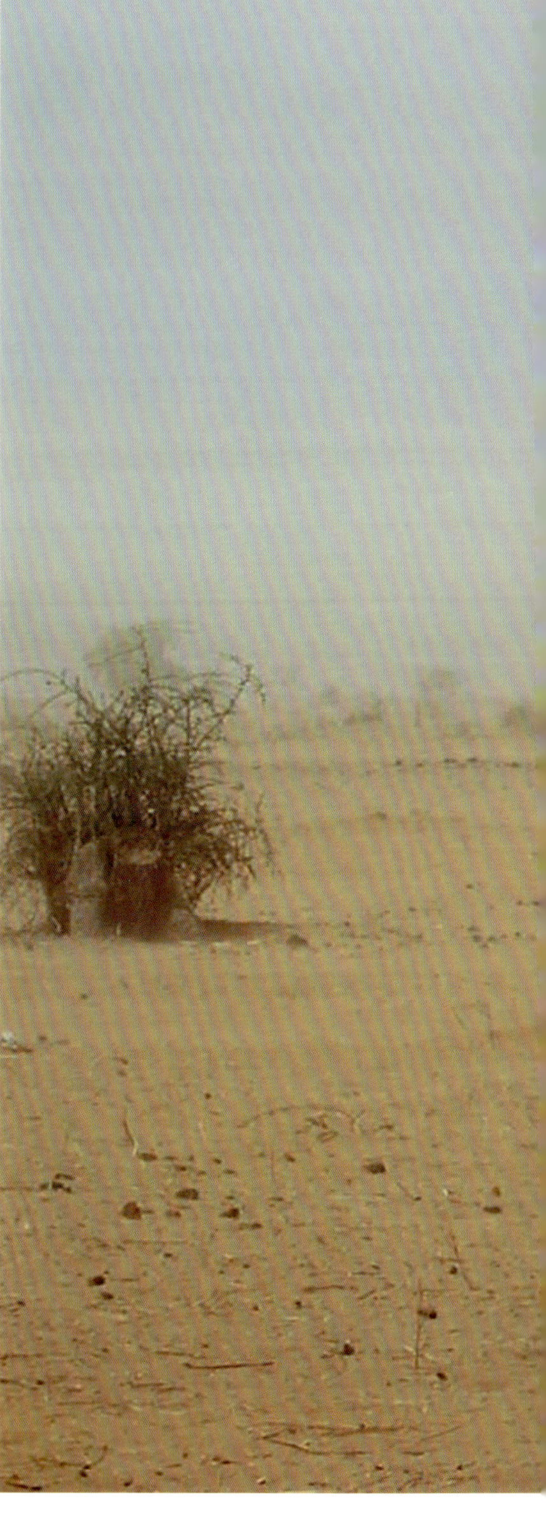

Darfur Sudan 2006
Tanya Habjouqa

Since 2004, International Medical Corps has worked in Darfur, Sudan, where violent conflict has killed tens of thousands of people and displaced millions more.

IMC Staff

Opposite page: After fleeing their attackers, women often still don't find a safe place. Some walk for miles to find shelter at one of International Medical Corps' seven mobile clinics.

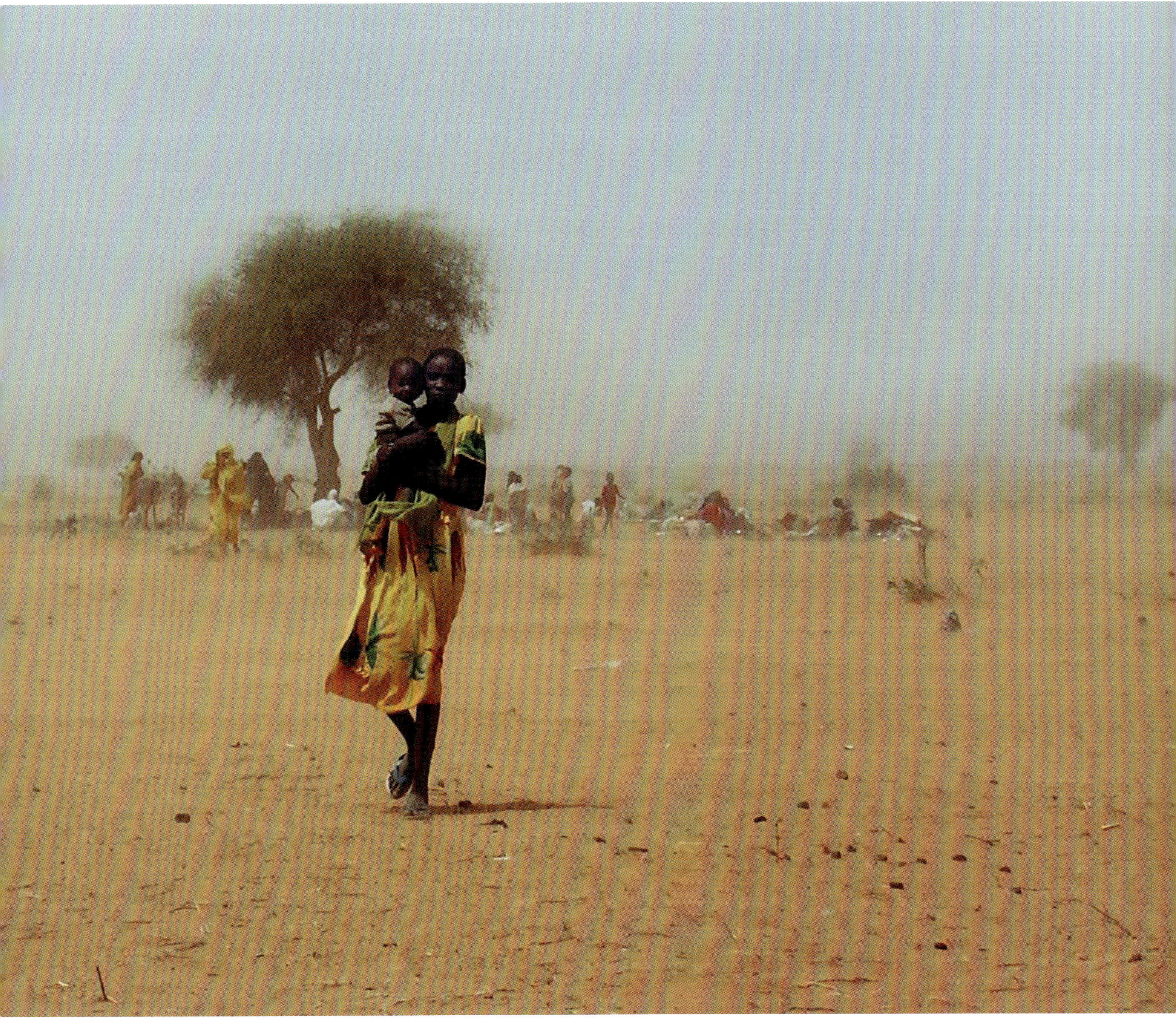

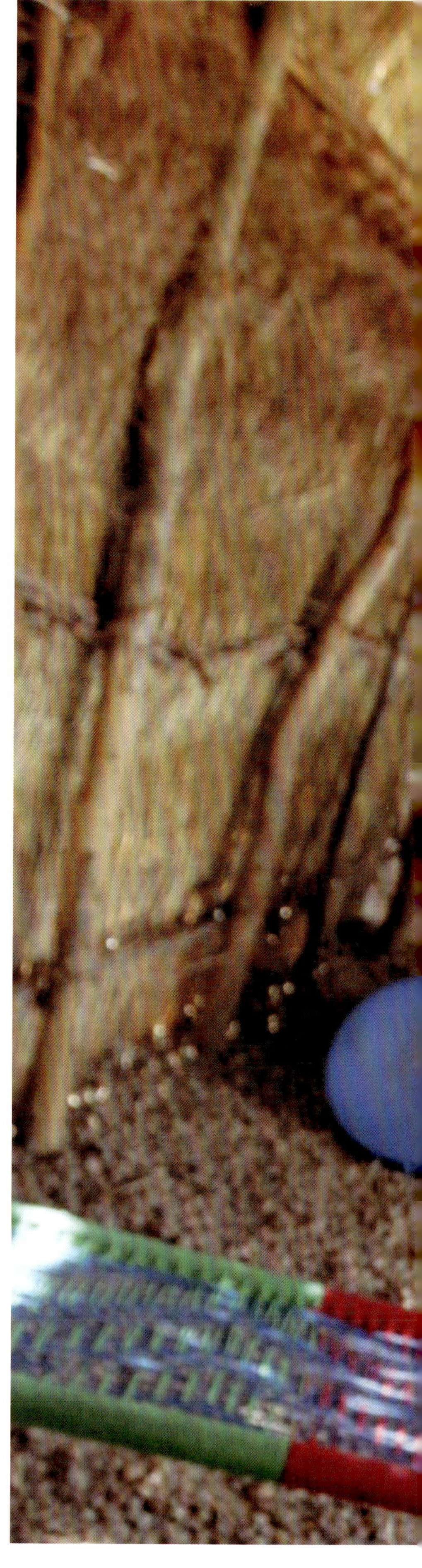

Darfur Sudan 2006
Tanya Habjouqa
A mother and her son at an International Medical Corps health clinic, where services included primary health care, maternal health care, immunizations, growth monitoring and a full range of nutritional care.

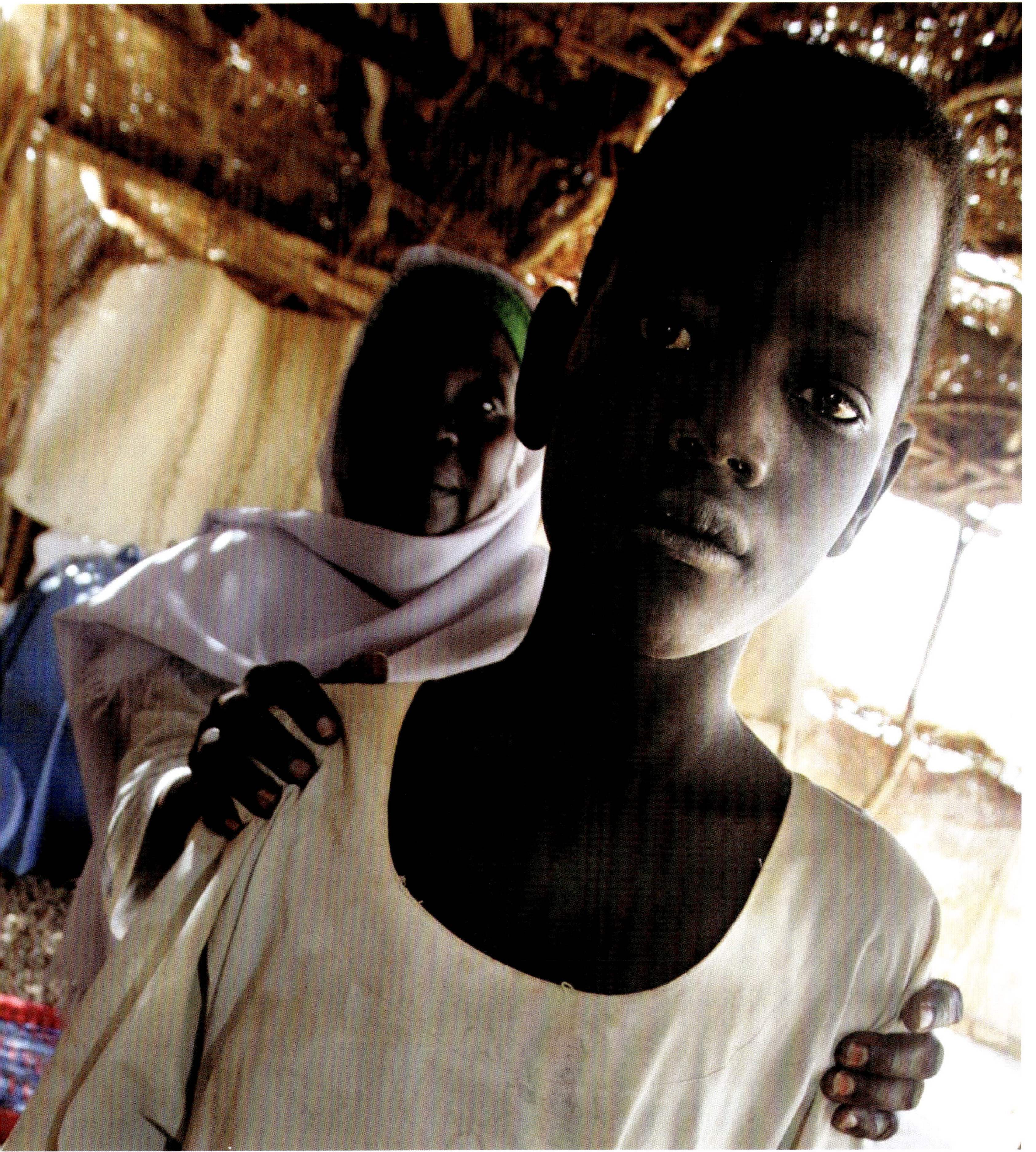

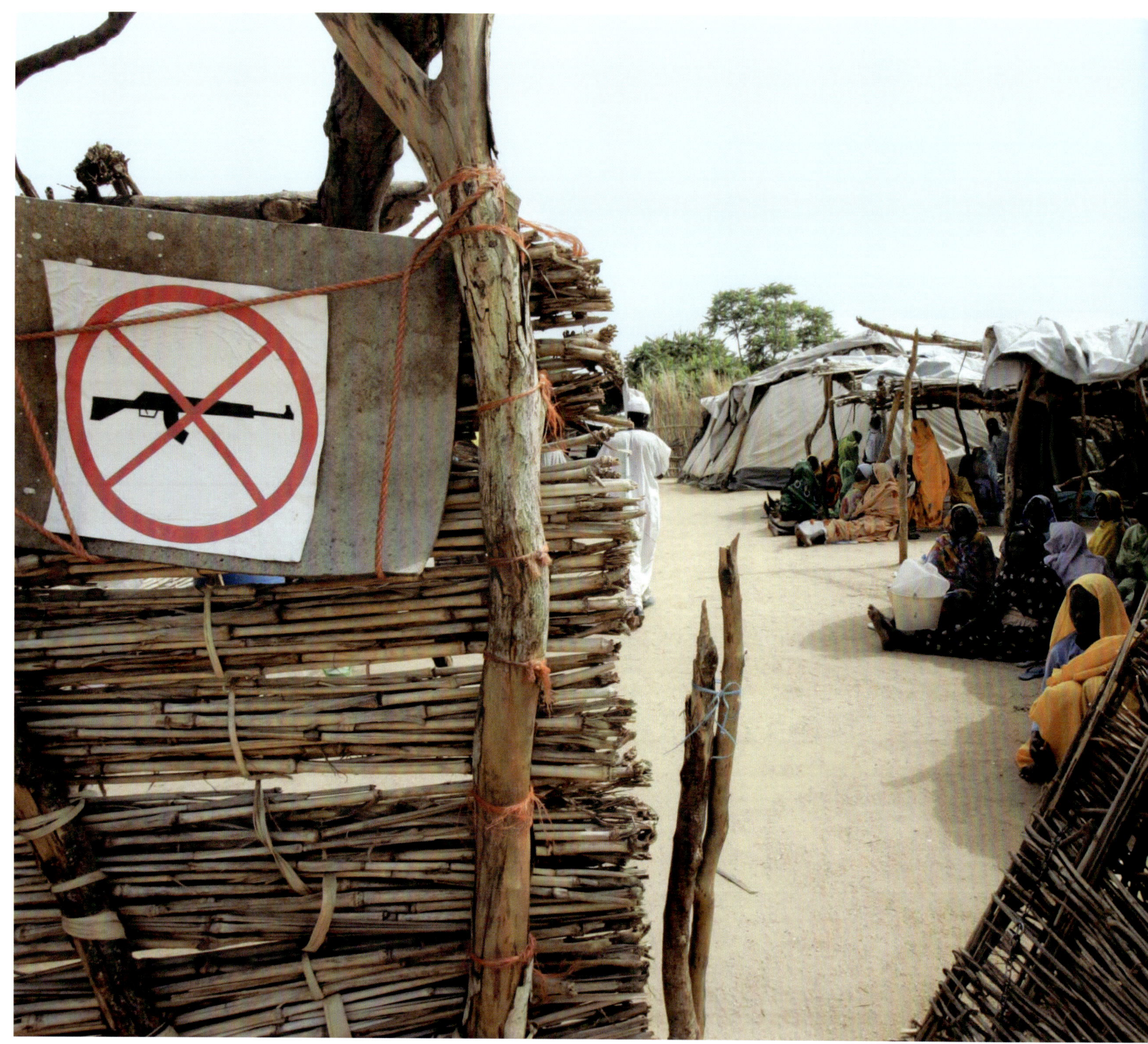

Darfur Sudan 2006
IMC staff

International Medical Corps' Al Jir Camp outside Nyala in South Darfur before it was attacked by rebels. In the early morning hours, armed forces surrounded the camp, forced residents out, and bulldozed rows of huts. Men were beaten, mothers and children separated and IMC's clinic tear-gassed.

Tanya Habjouqa

Opposite page: International Medical Corps logistics teams work in challenging and precarious security conditions to navigate and coordinate supply routes to reach thousands of Darfurians with mobile clinics that provide food, clean water and medical supplies.

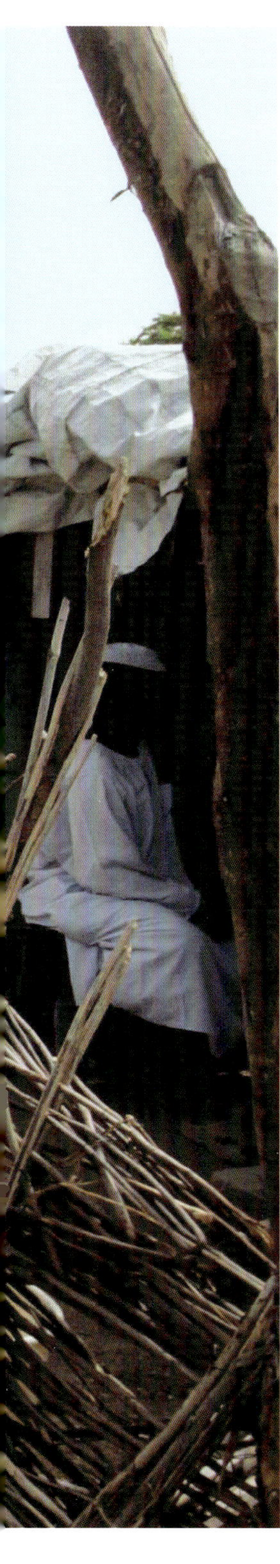

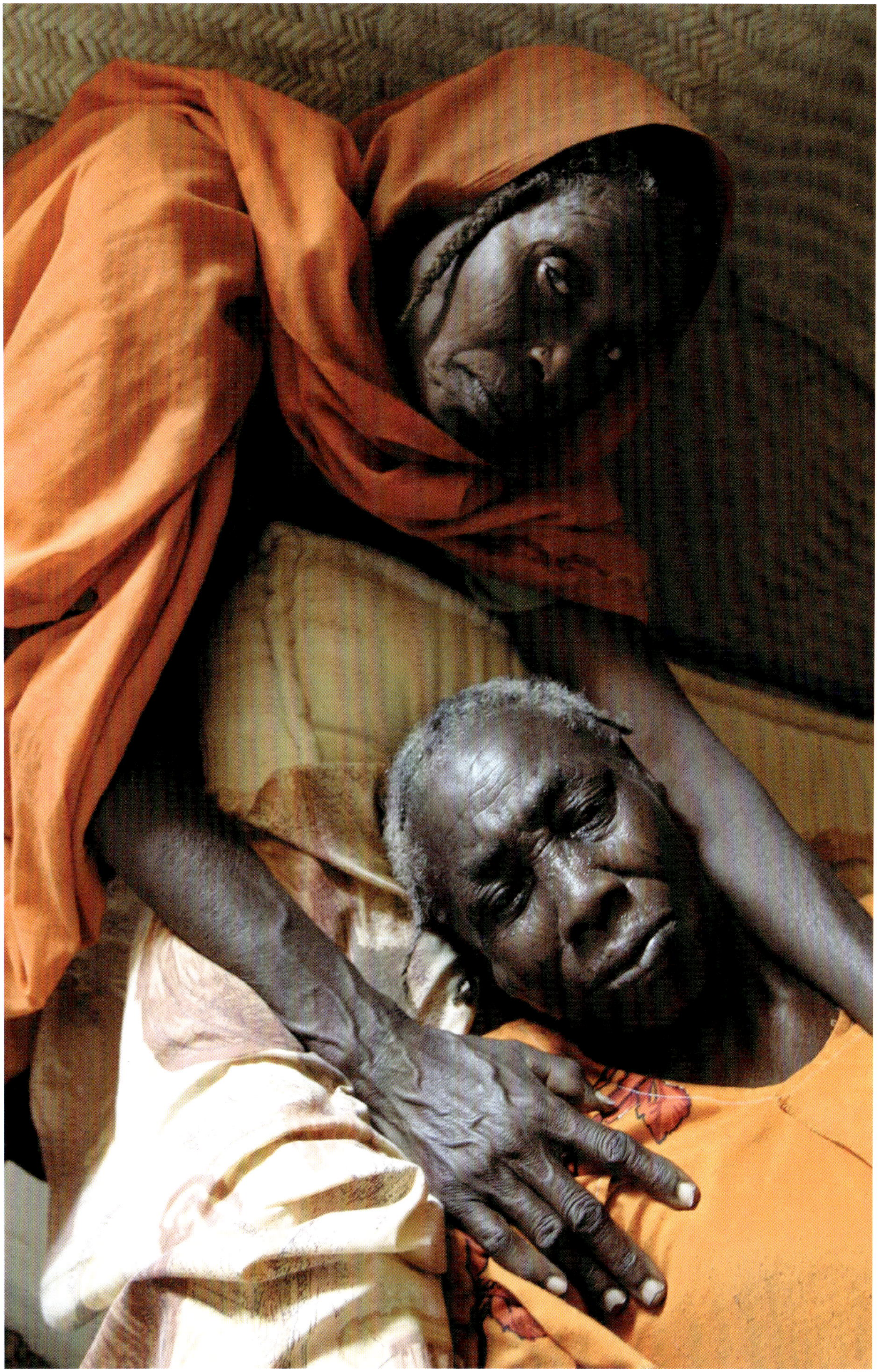

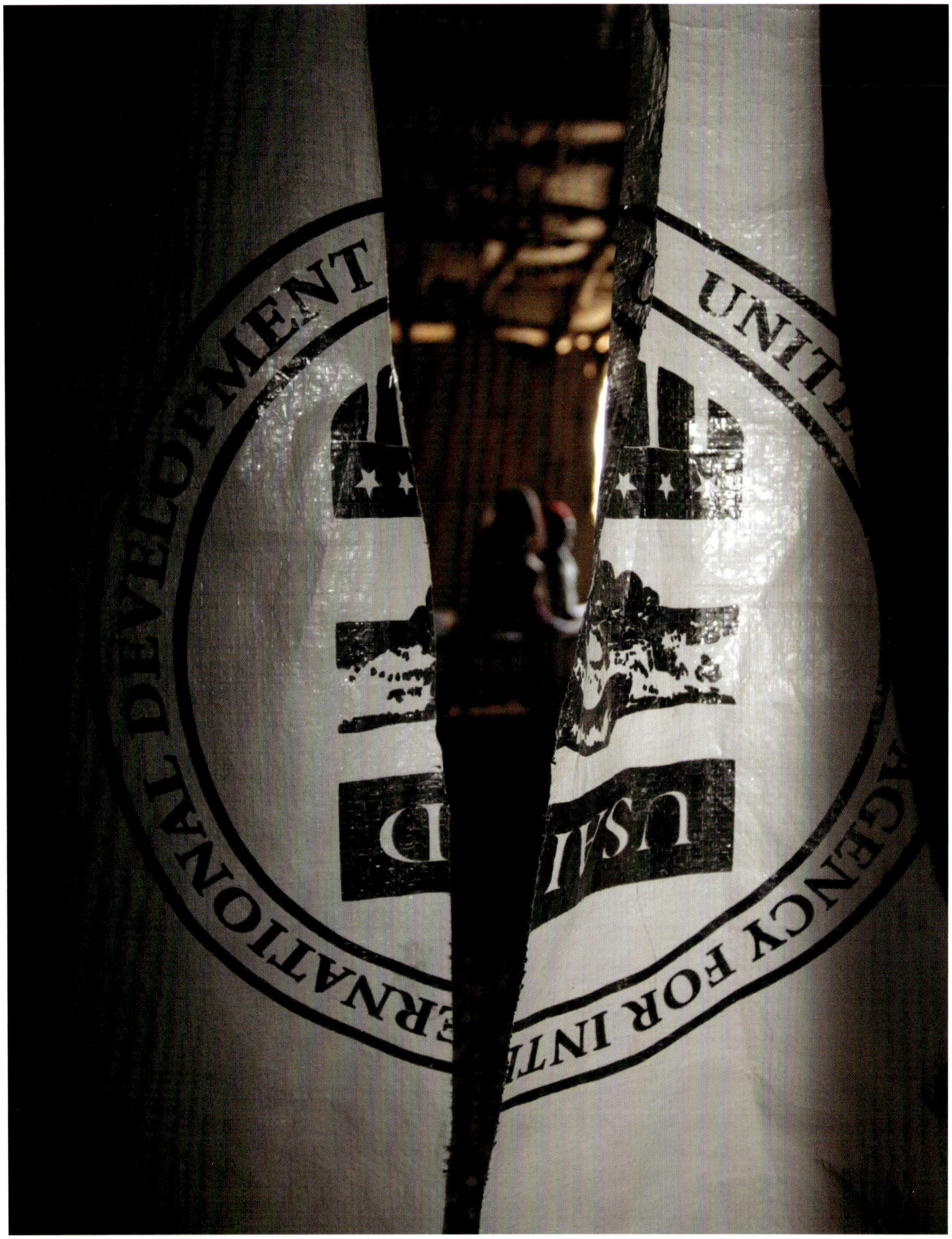

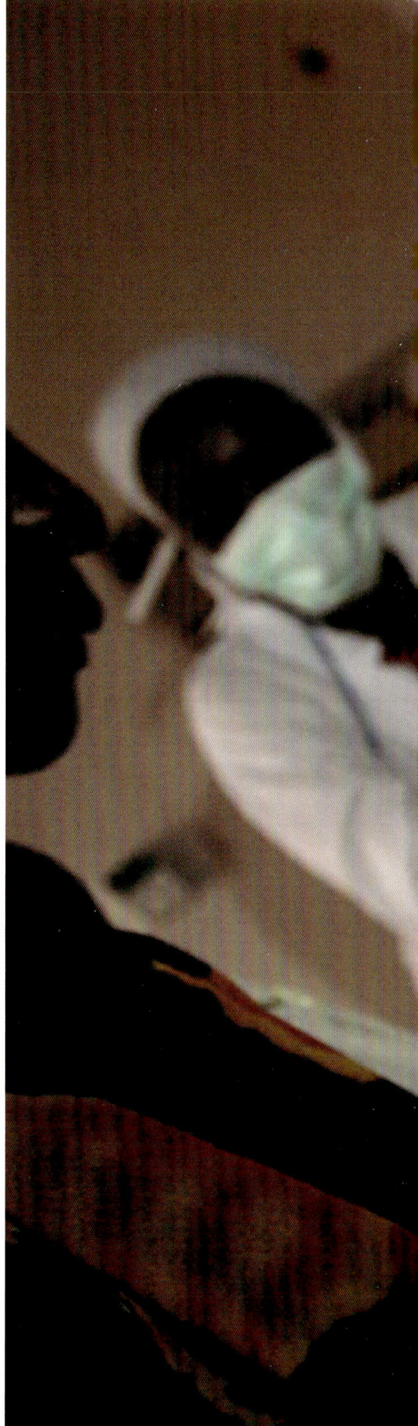

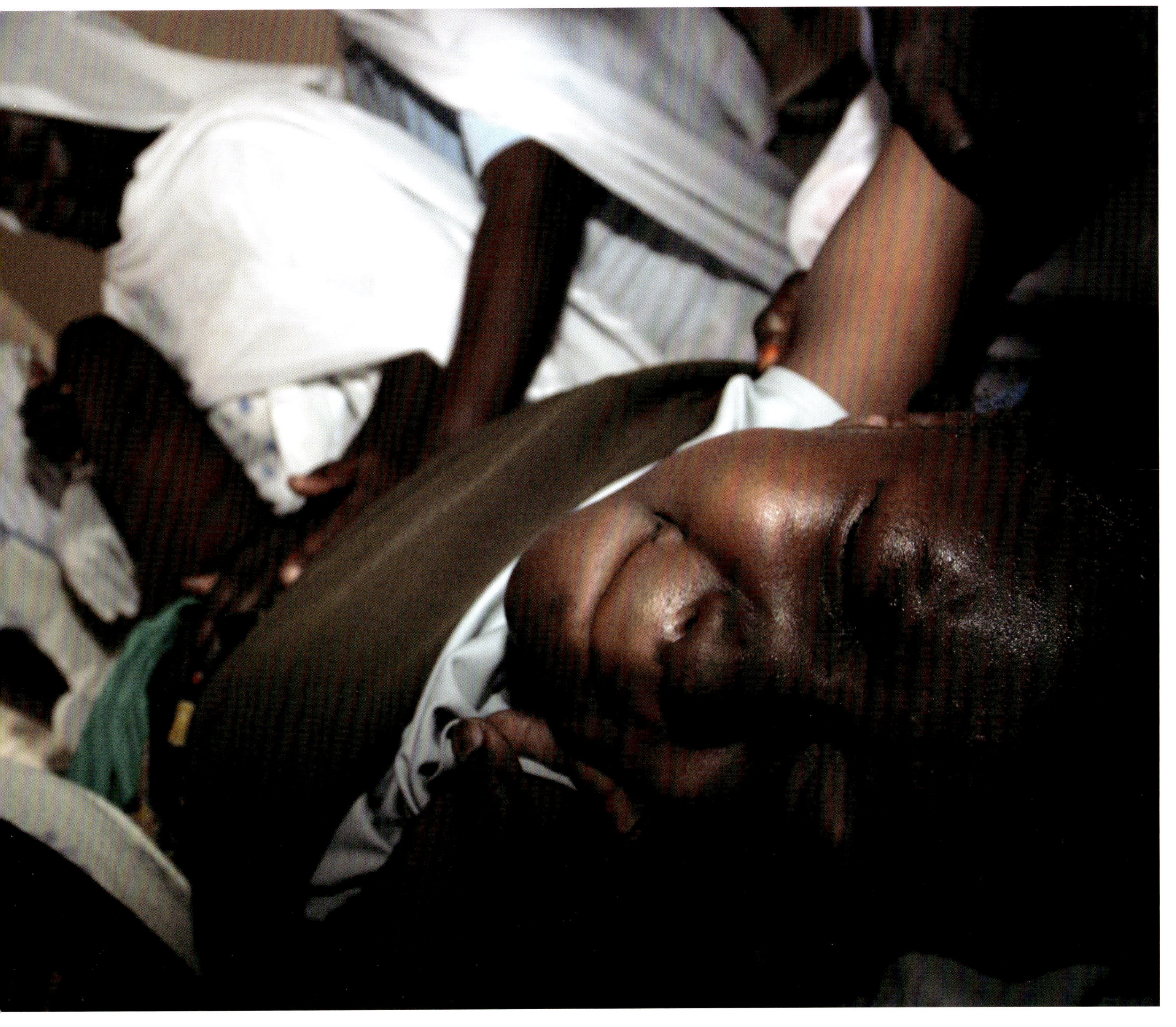

Darfur Sudan 2006
IMC staff (above)
Tanya Habjouqa (opposite page)

International Medical Corps' mobile teams provide prenatal care to pregnant women on a weekly basis and train midwives and community health workers in villages where maternal and child health care was almost nonexistent. A Darfurian woman—attended by IMC-trained midwives—gives birth at International Medical Corps' Nyala Al Jir clinic.

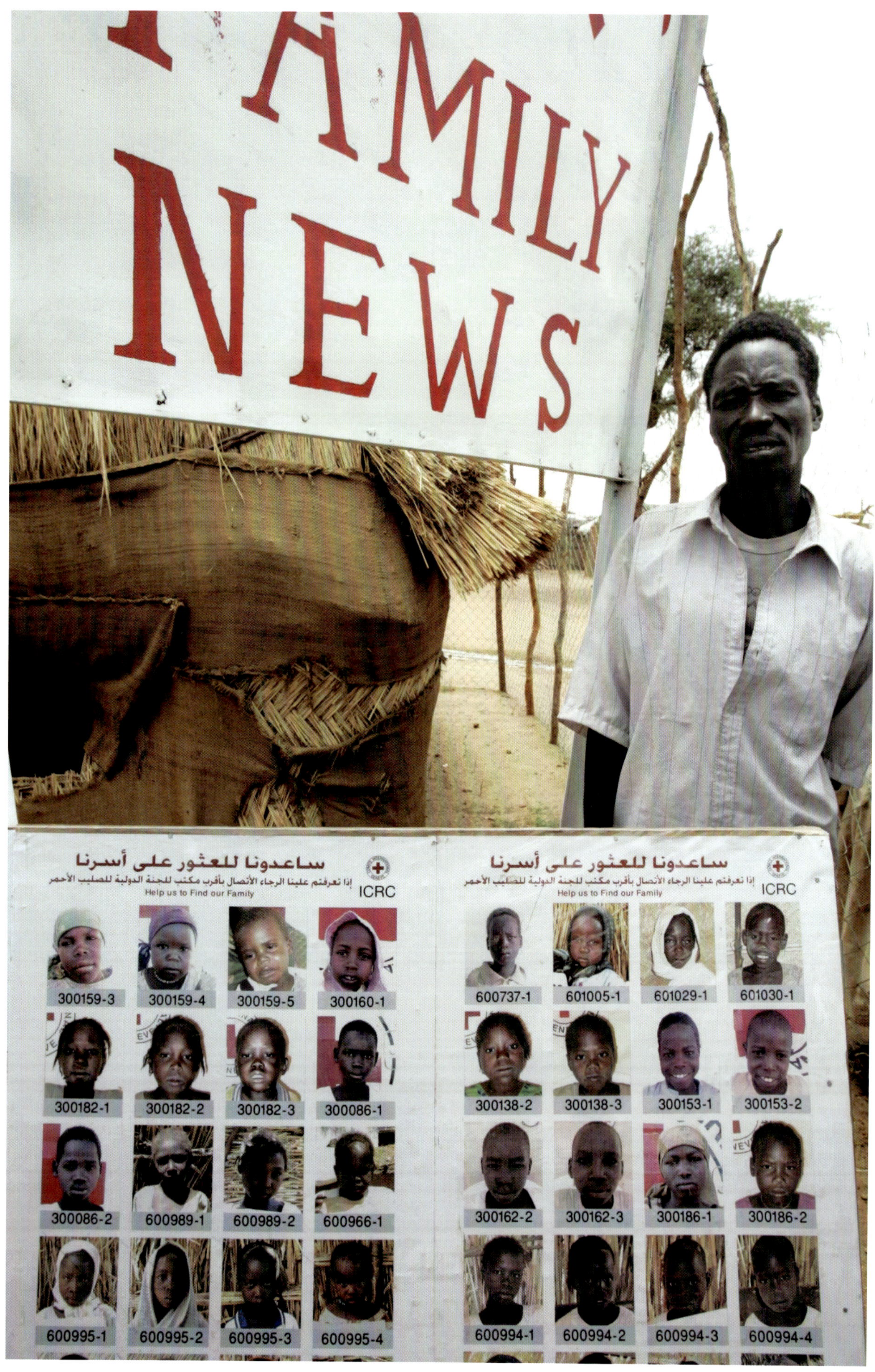
AMILY
NEWS
ساعدونا للعثور على أسرنا
إذا تعرفتم علينا الرجاء الأتصال بأقرب مكتب للجنة الدولية للصليب الأحمر
Help us to Find our Family
ICRC
300159-3 300159-4 300159-5 300160-1
300182-1 300182-2 300182-3 300086-1
300086-2 600989-1 600989-2 600966-1
600995-1 600995-2 600995-3 600995-4
ساعدونا للعثور على أسرنا
إذا تعرفتم علينا الرجاء الأتصال بأقرب مكتب للجنة الدولية للصليب الأحمر
Help us to Find our Family
ICRC
600737-1 601005-1 601029-1 601030-1
300138-2 300138-3 300153-1 300153-2
300162-2 300162-3 300186-1 300186-2
600994-1 600994-2 600994-3 600994-4

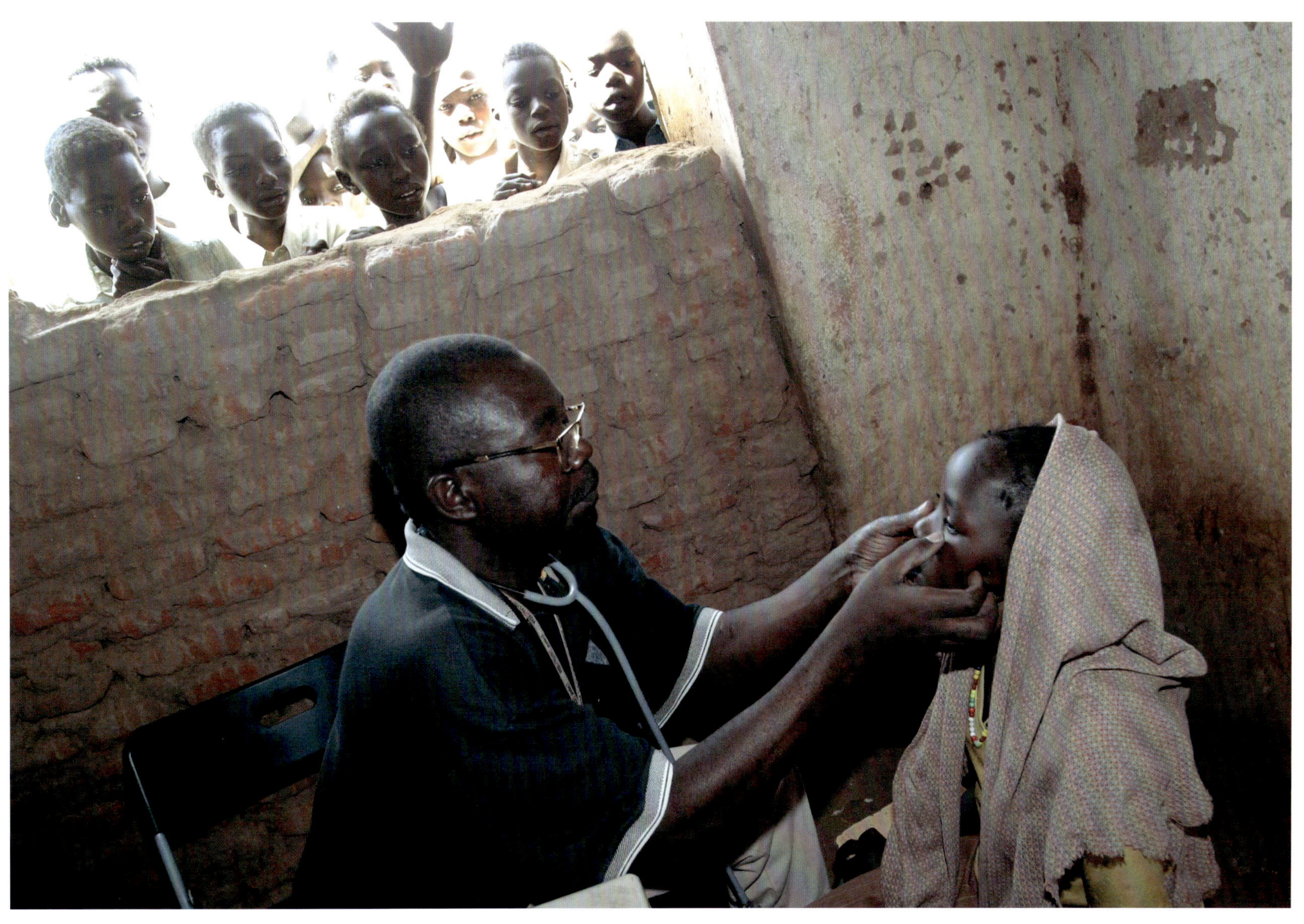

Darfur Sudan 2006
Tanya Habjouqa
An International Medical Corps doctor examines a child while her friends look on at IMC's Zalingi Urokom mobile clinic.

IMC staff
Opposite page: IMC's mobile clinics also served as displacement camps and offered a central point for food, water, health care, and information about missing loved ones.

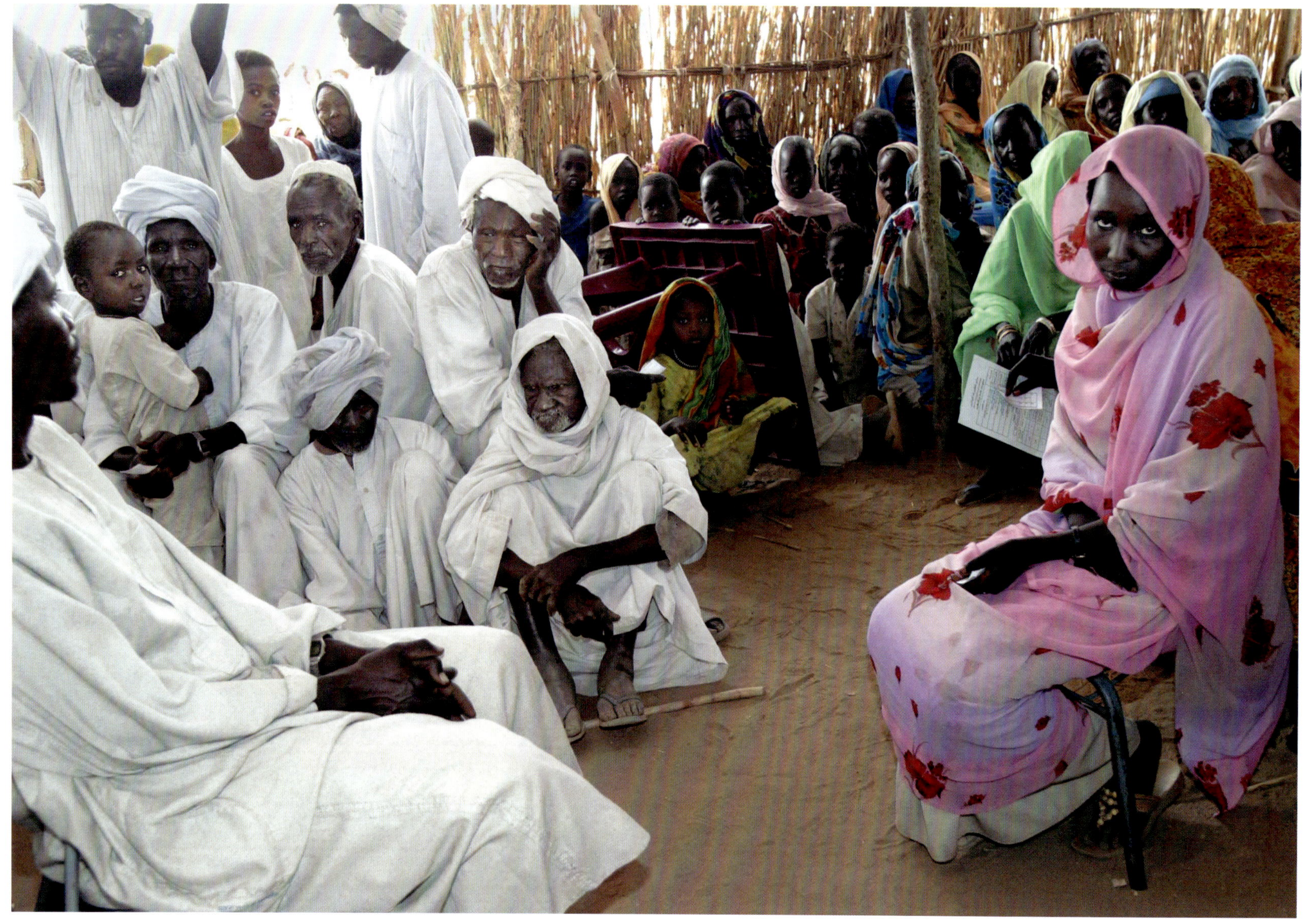

Darfur Sudan 2006
Tanya Habjouqa (both pages)

International Medical Corps recruited and trained nearly 200 local Sudanese health workers—including vaccinators, midwives, health educators and water chlorinators—who became responsible for the health care needs of thousands of their own displaced people.

Opposite page: Locally trained International Medical Corps midwives attend to a woman in labor at an IMC clinic.

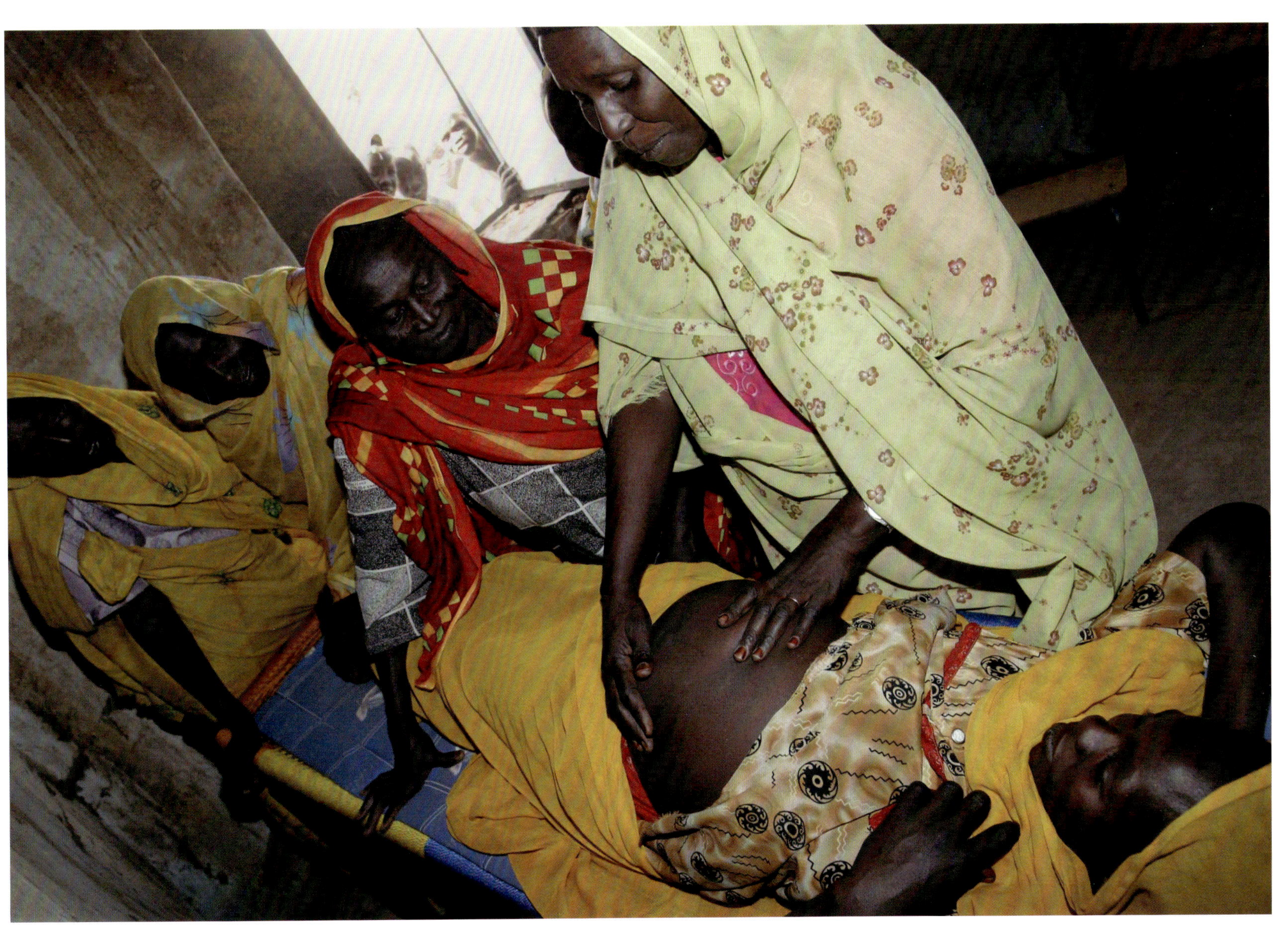

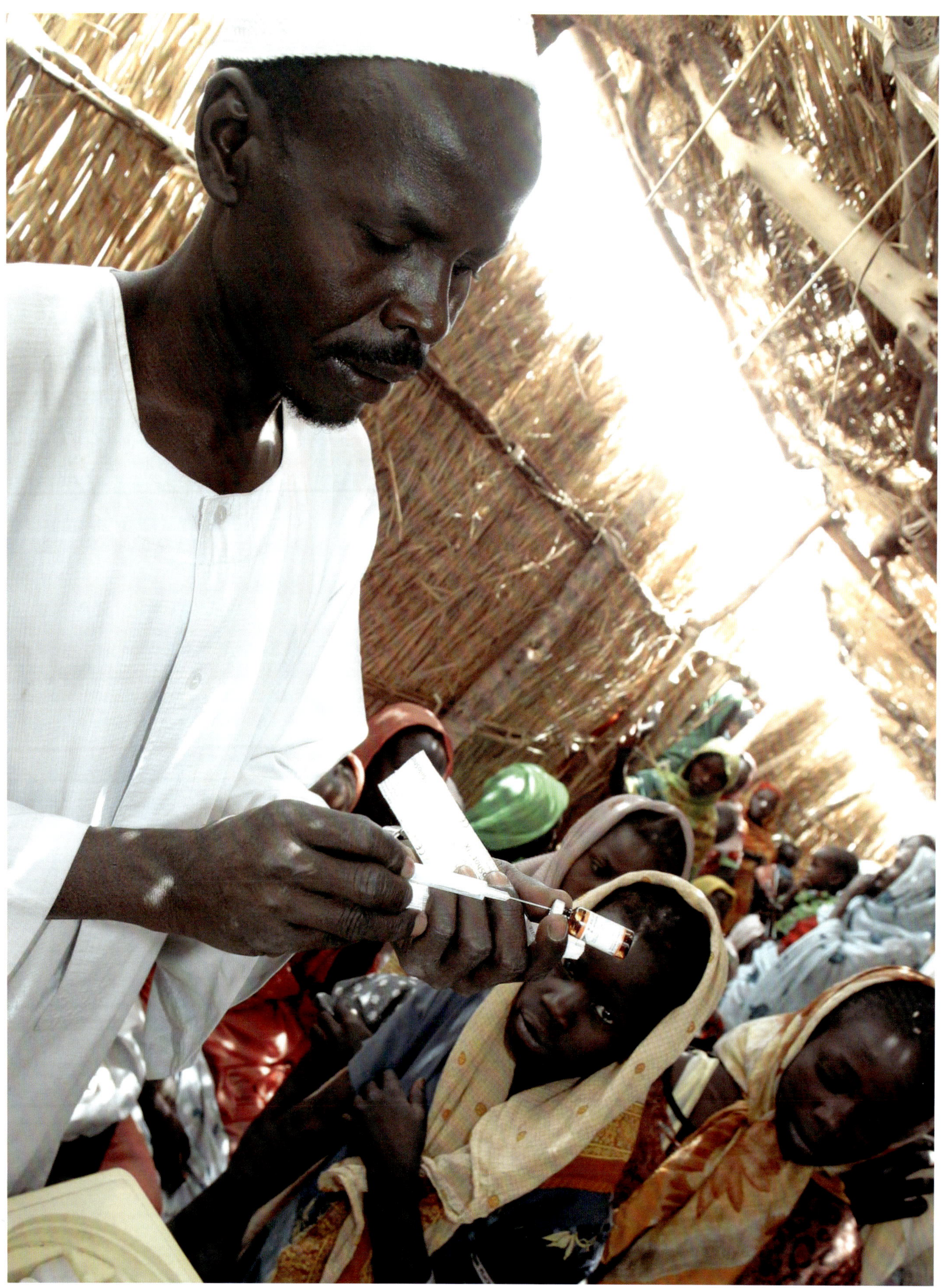

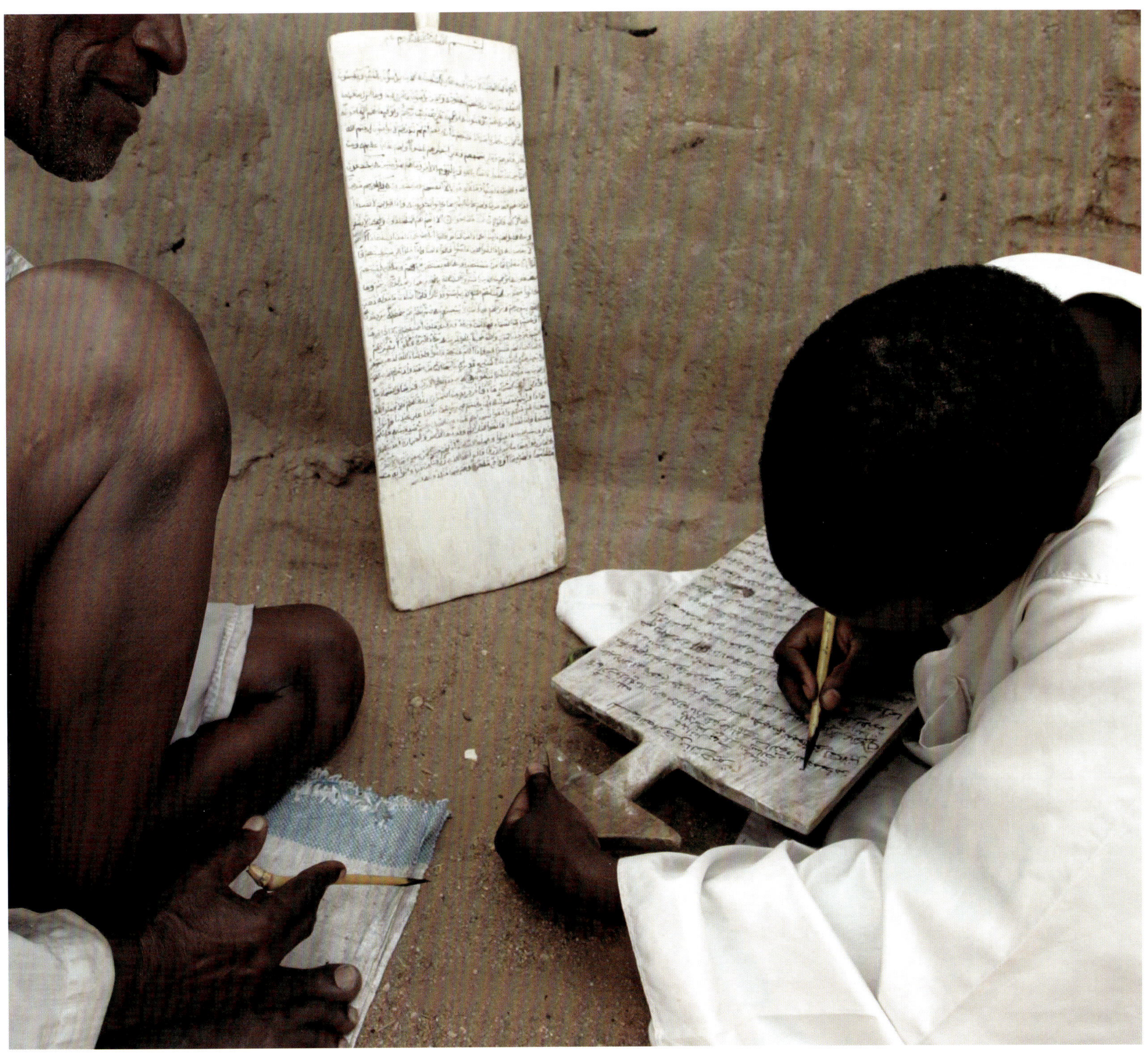

Darfur Sudan 2006
IMC staff (above)

Amid violent conflict and difficult conditions, International Medical Corps staff is undaunted by the harsh realities of working in Darfur. If anything, the conditions strengthened their resolve and dedication to a culture torn apart by conflict.

Tanya Habjouqa

Opposite page: An International Medical Corps health care worker administers vaccines at IMC's Zalingi Urokom mobile clinic.

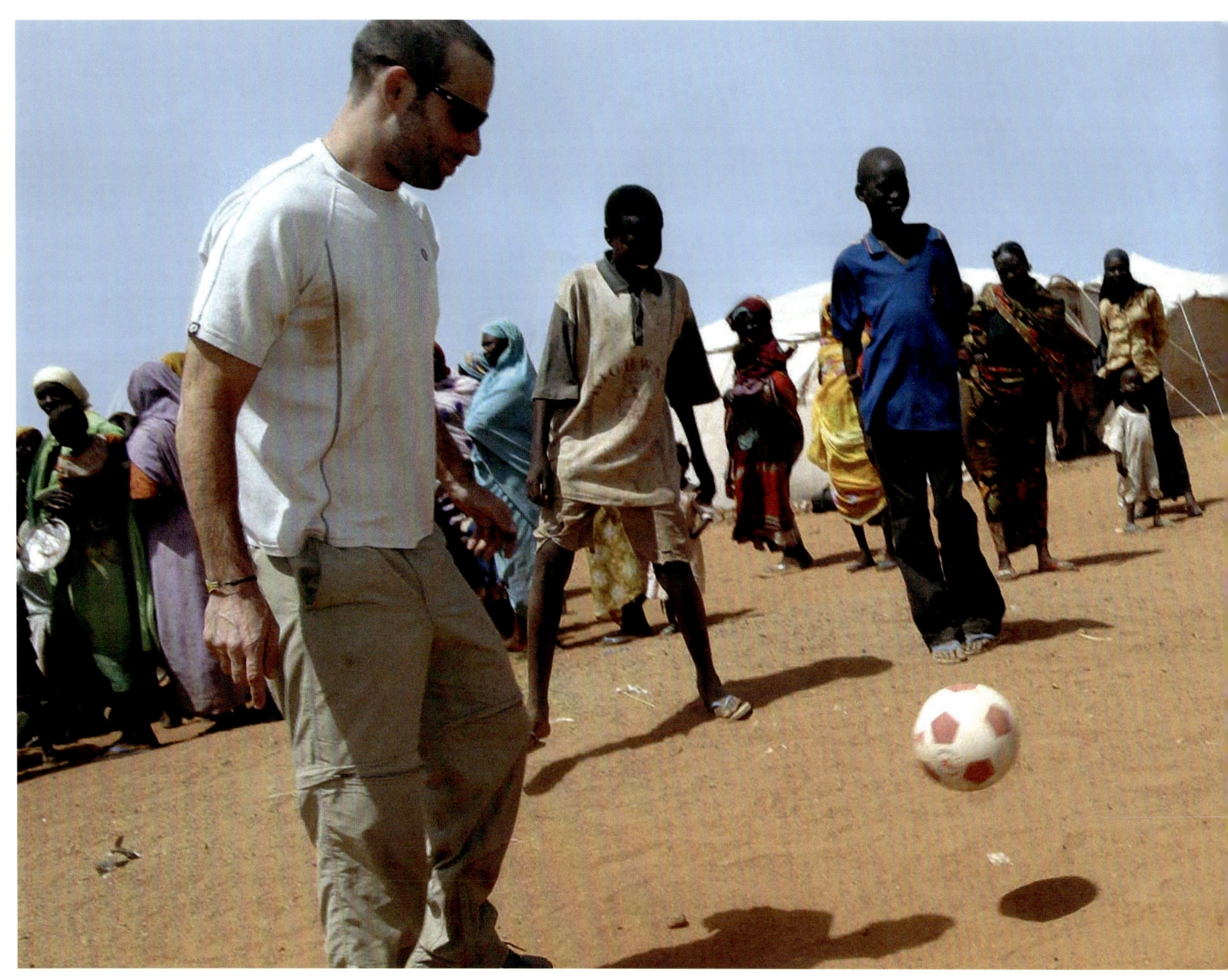

Darfur Sudan 2005
Tanya Habjouqa

In 2004, International Medical Corps began implementing mental health programs in Darfur to address the needs of displaced populations and those affected by the psychological violence of the war, particularly children suffering from trauma. An IMC health worker plays soccer with local boys getting treatment at one of IMC's clinics.

Darfur Sudan 2006
IMC staff

Opposite page: The International Medical Corps clinic in Zalingi Hamedia—with its tidy paths and freshly painted huts—offers a glimmer of hope for tens of thousands of internally displaced people in South Darfur.

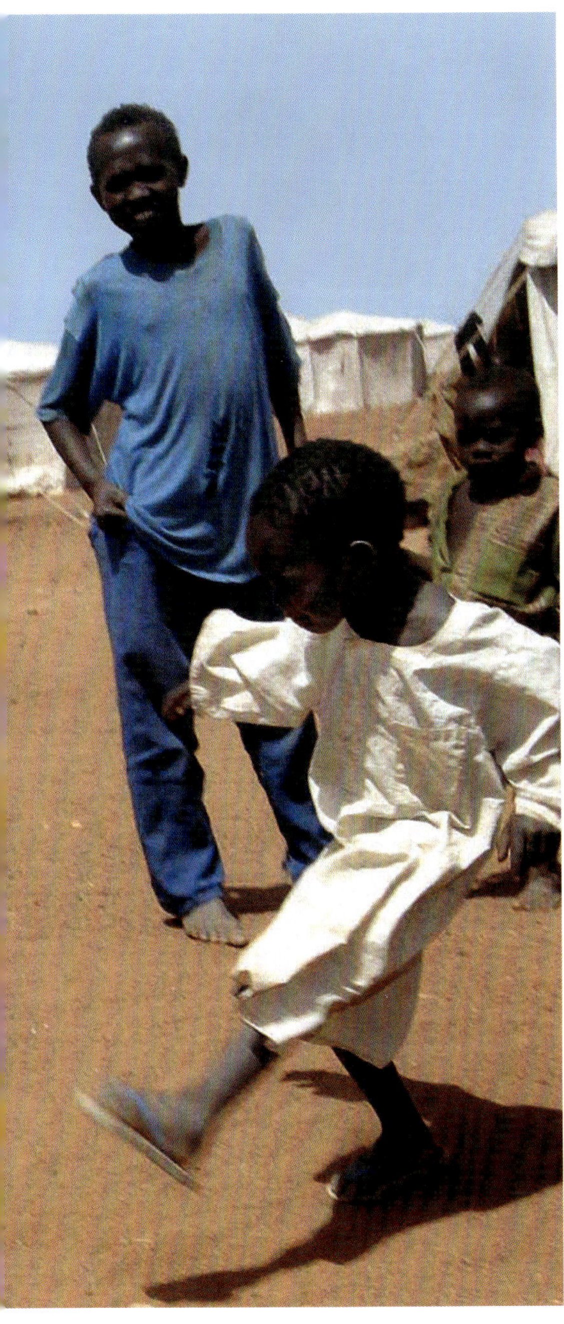

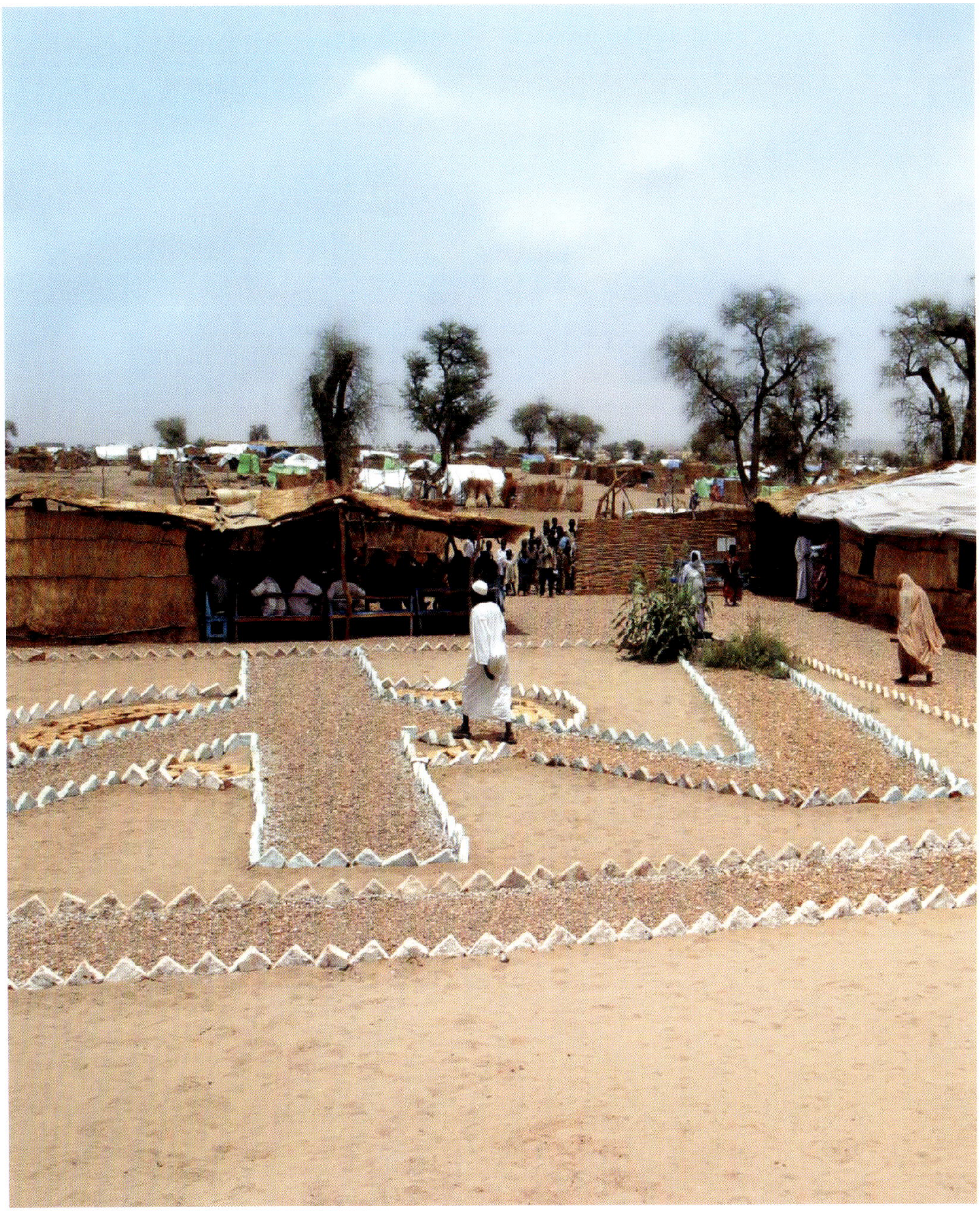

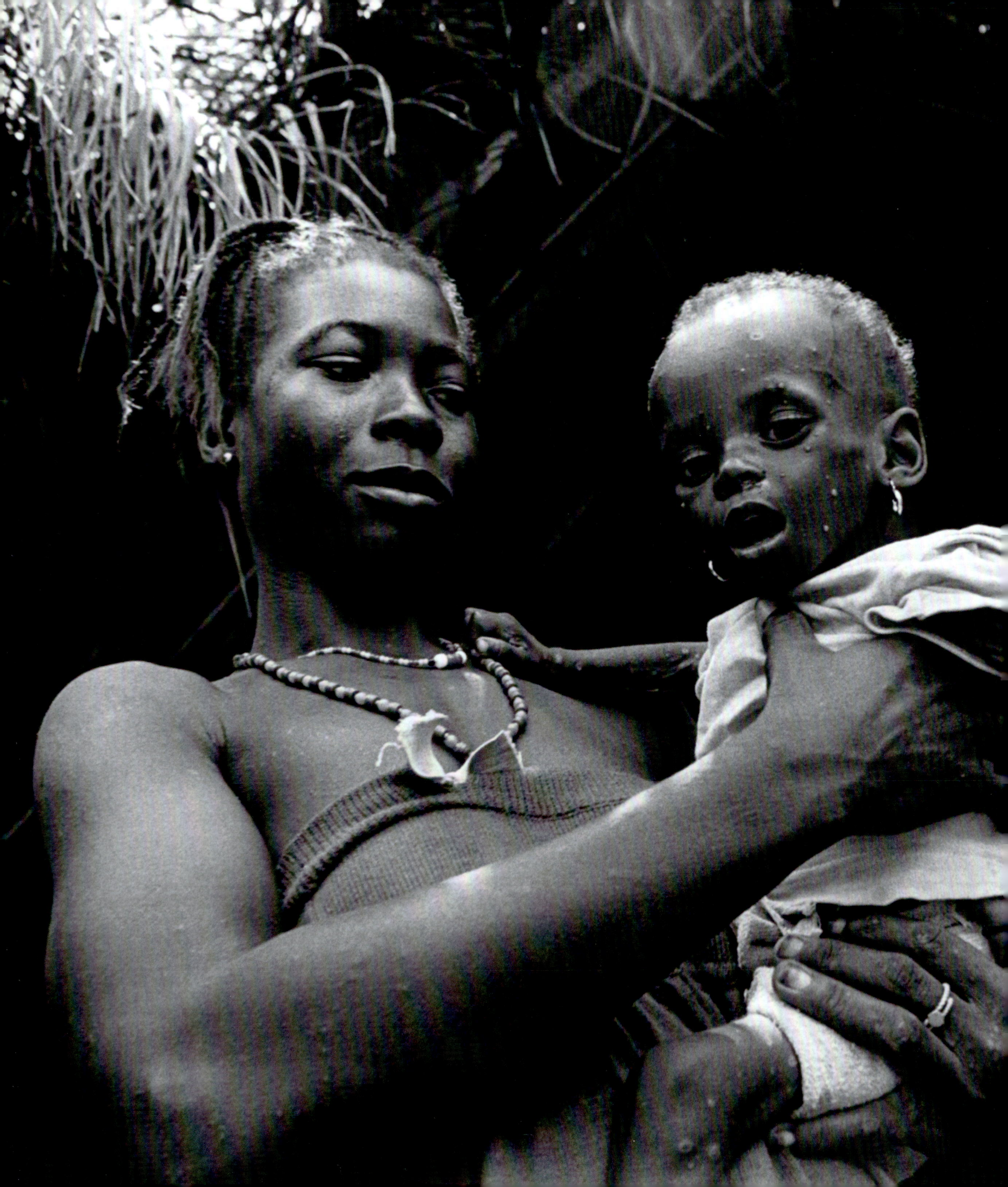

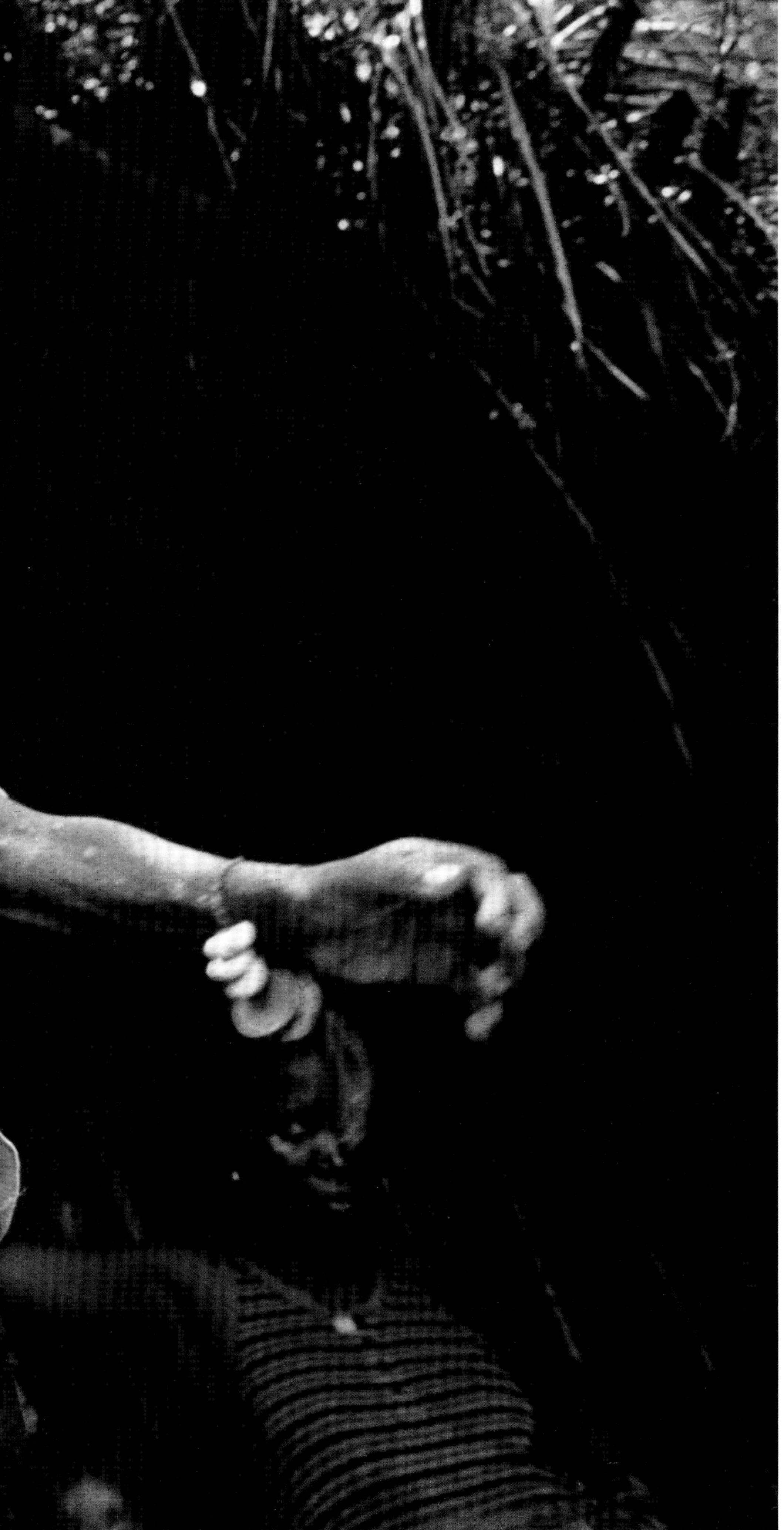

SIERRA LEONE

Sierra Leone 2000
Robert Knoth

International Medical Corps began working in Sierra Leone in 1999, three years before the 11-year civil war ended. The country was in ruins, hospitals and health clinics were destroyed and abandoned, fields had not been farmed in years, and nearly half the population was displaced.

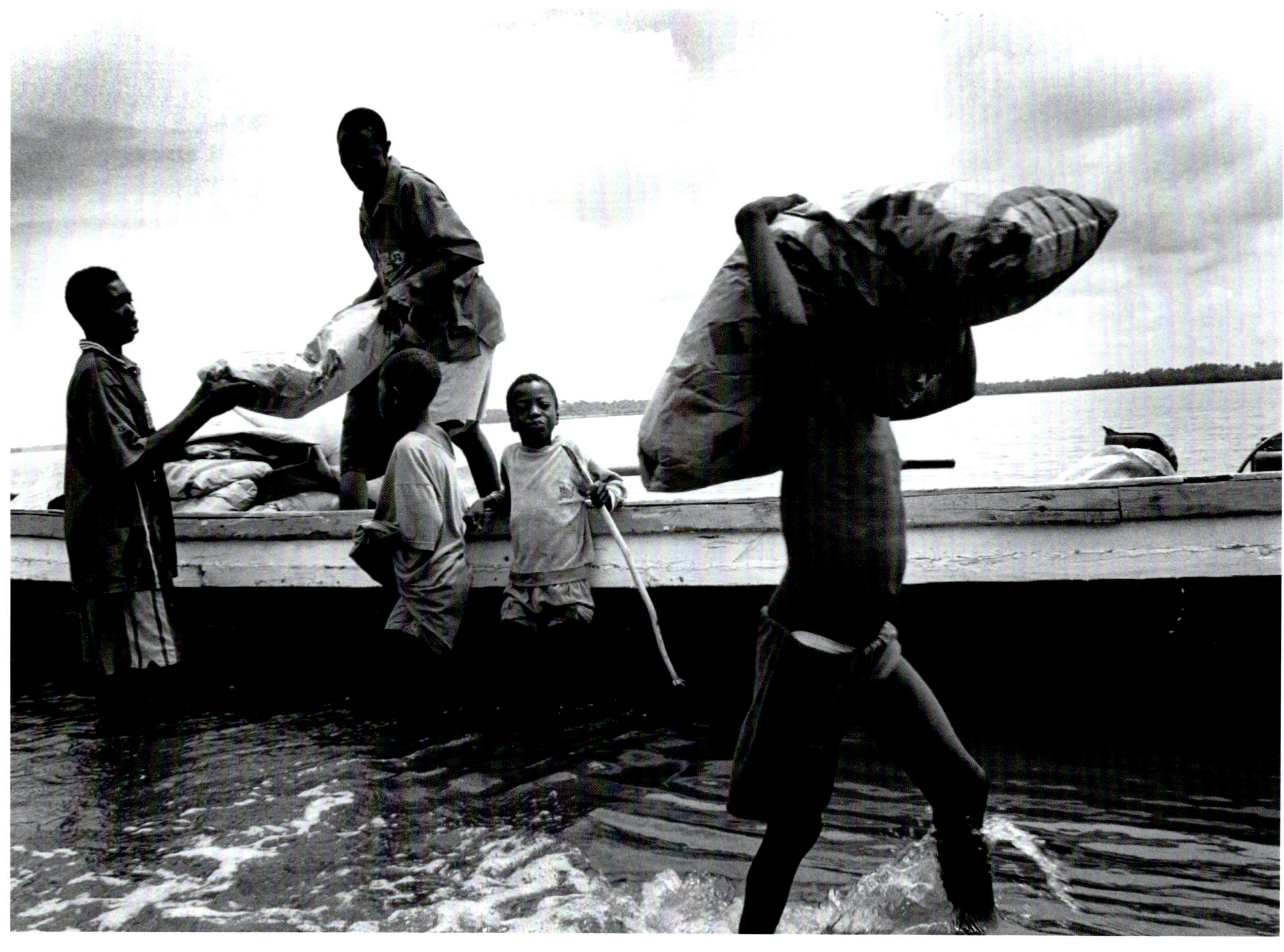

Sierra Leone 2000
Robert Knoth
During the end of the civil war, International Medical Corps doctors and nurses working in Sierra Leone were caught in the crossfire of at least four different militias, which would stage attacks on each other and then retreat across the borders. IMC brought much-needed food and medical supplies to those trapped by the conflict.

Sierra Leone 2006
Sara Terry
Opposite page: Kailahun is a Northeast town on the opposite side of the country from the capital, Freetown, and was once a thriving agricultural center. When International Medical Corps relief workers arrived there, they found a virtual wasteland, with many sick and injured left trapped and helpless.

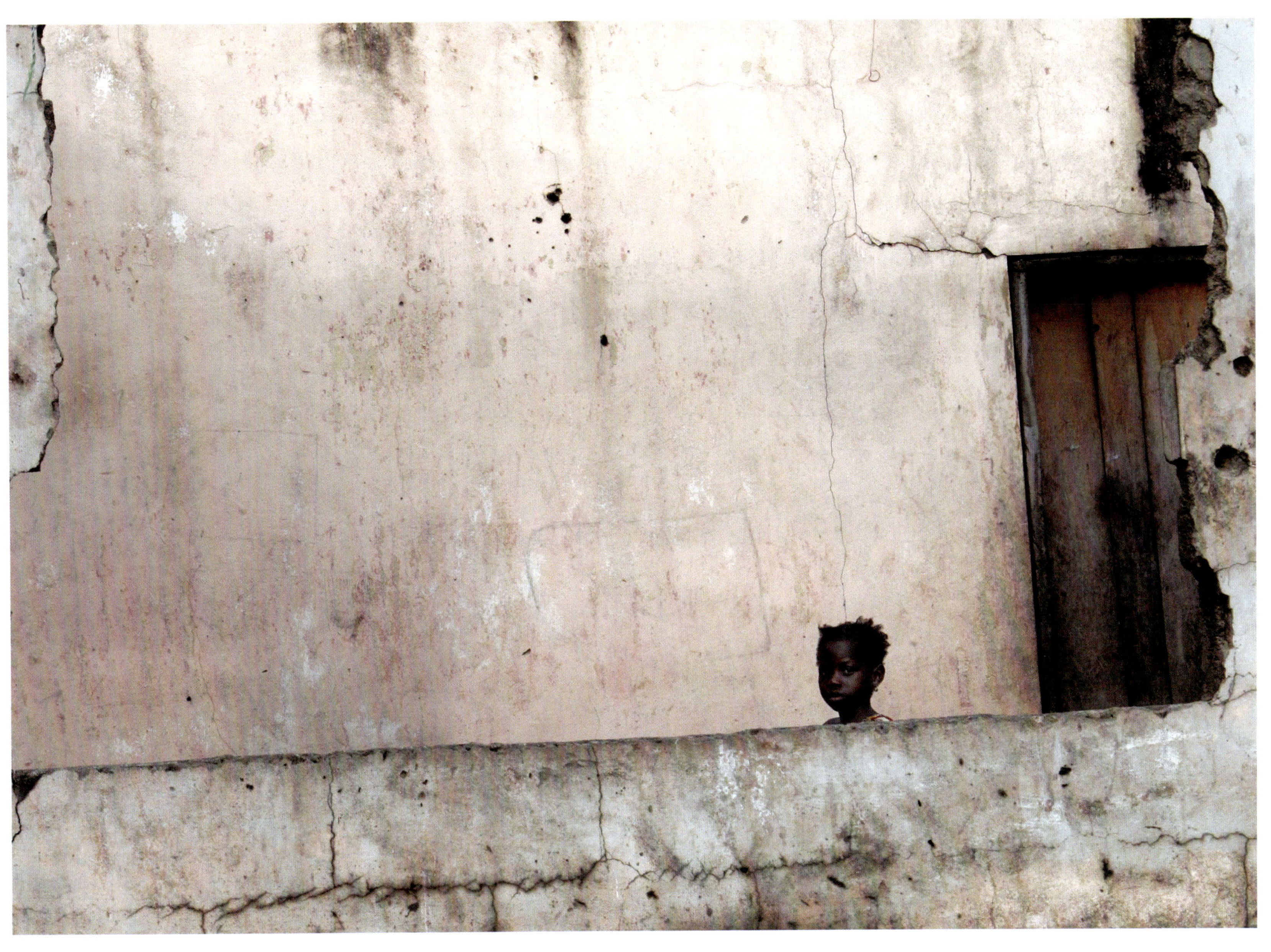

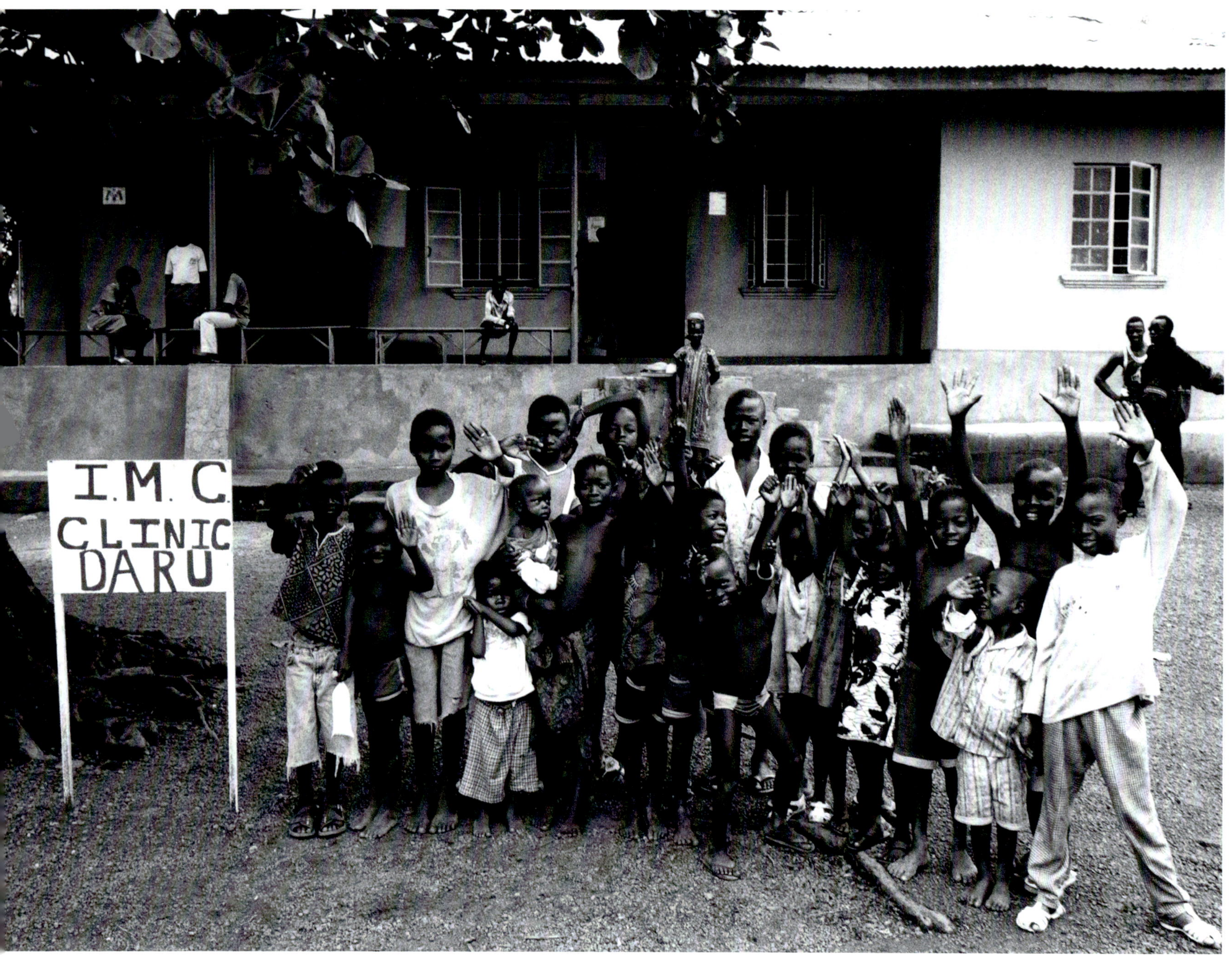

Sierra Leone 2000
Tim Hetherington

For years during the conflict, there was not a single health worker in Kailahun or the surrounding area, and many health facilities were looted and destroyed. International Medical Corps opened several clinics like this one in Daru, providing primary health care, maternal and child services, and mental health assistance.

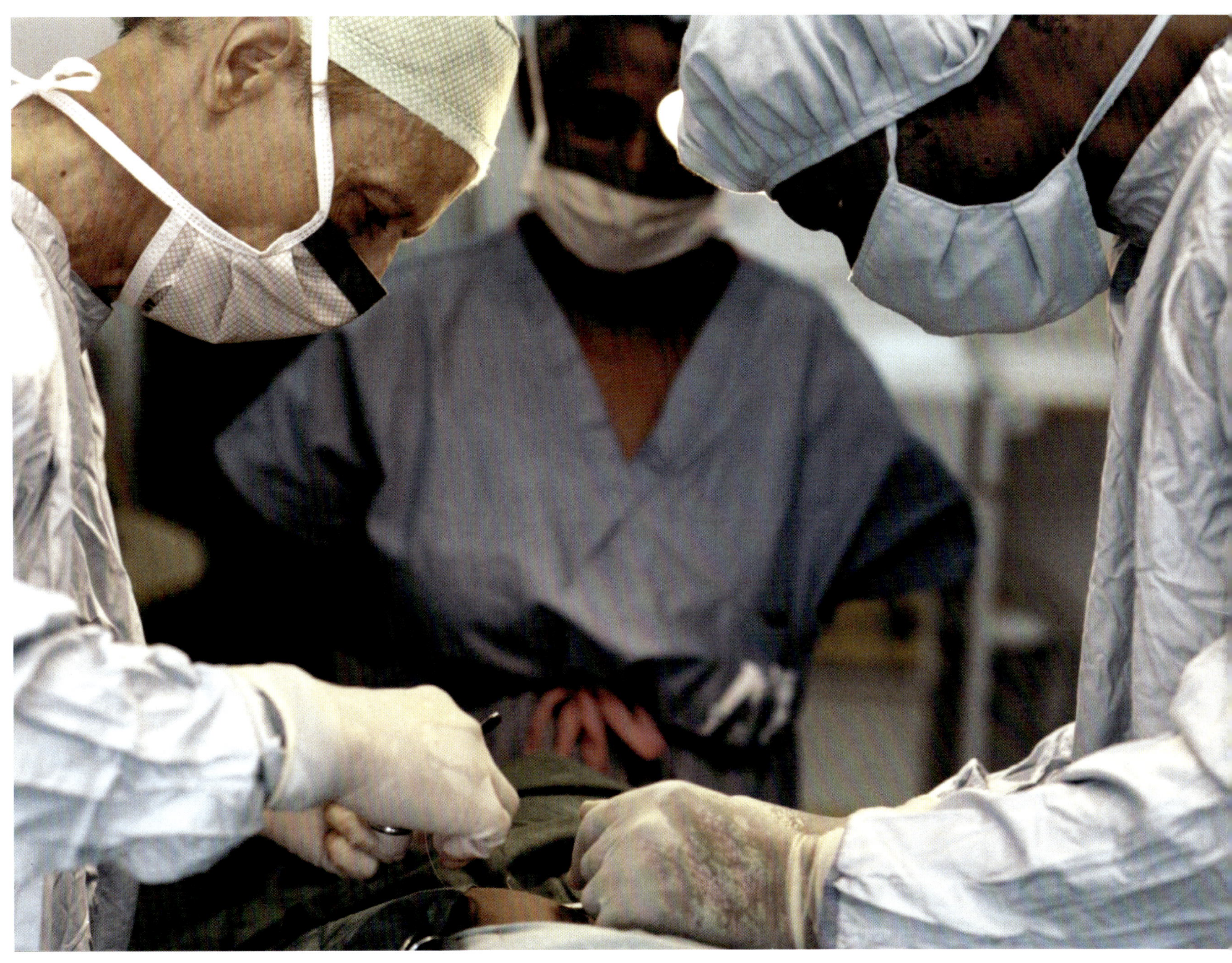

Sierra Leone 2001
Danny Hoffman

International Medical Corps volunteers worked side-by-side with local volunteers in surgery and medical training clinics in Sierra Leone. Here an IMC doctor and a local doctor work together to remove a war-brand scar from a man's chest.

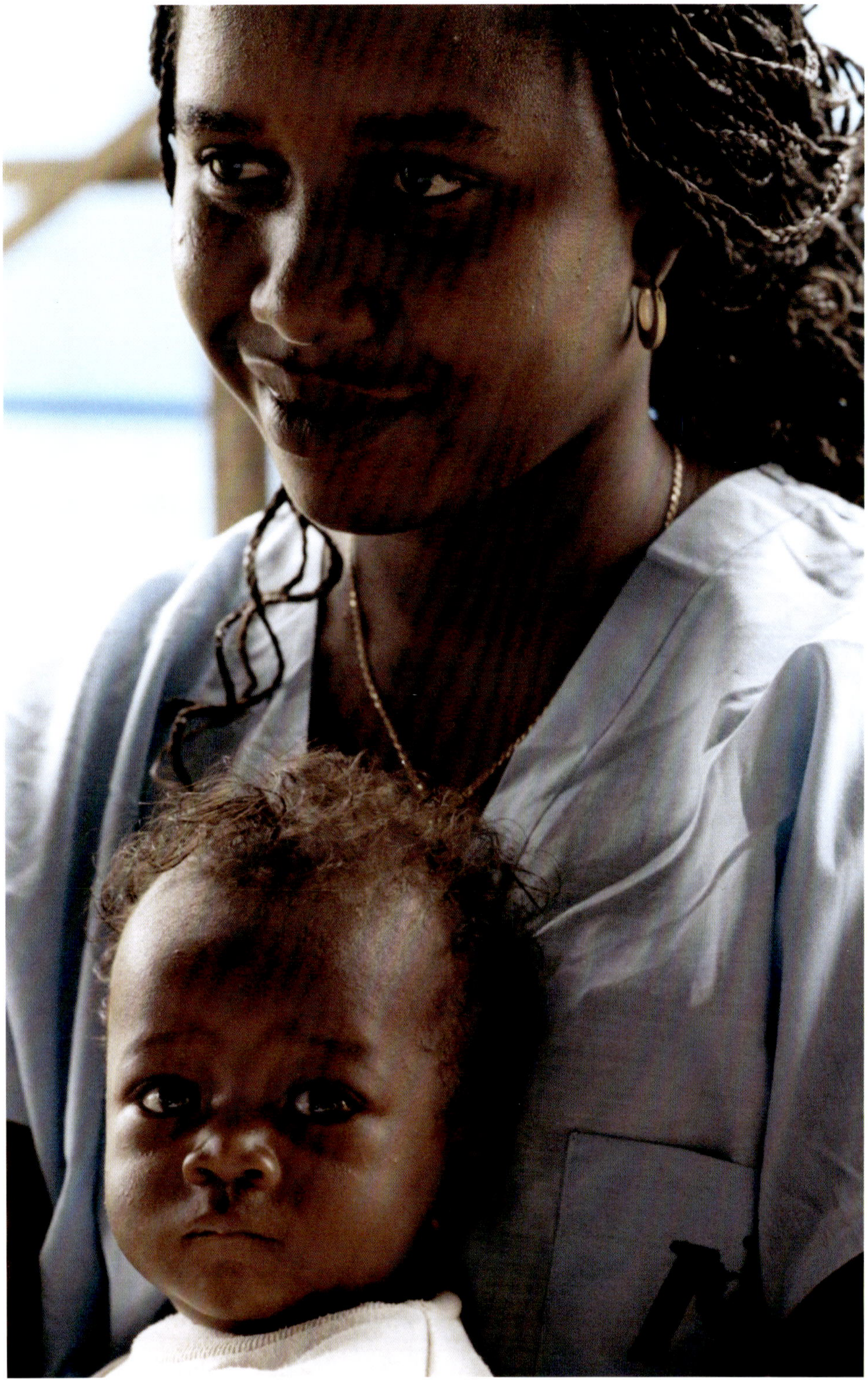

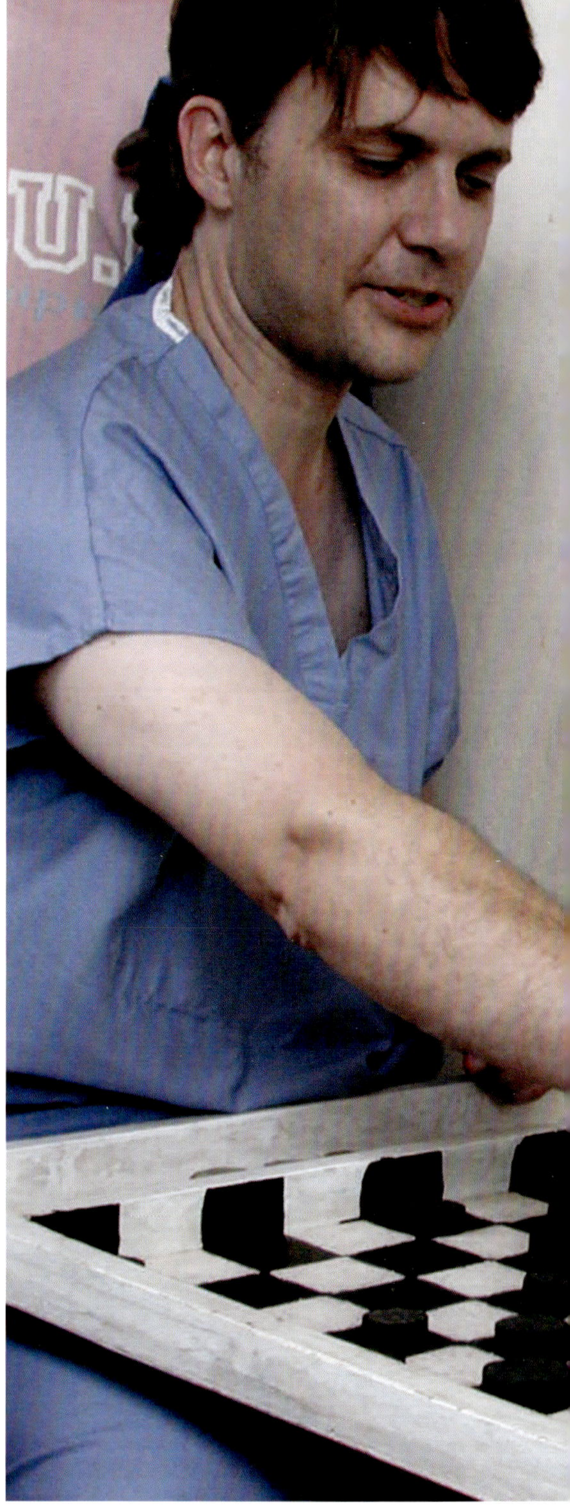

Sierra Leone 2001
Danny Hoffman

International Medical Corps was the first relief agency to enter rebel-held territory in Sierra Leone with a mobile clinic that would drive five hours each way to deliver medicines and health care to those at the heart of the conflict.

IMC Staff

Opposite page: International Medical Corps' volunteer plastic surgeon, Dr. Jeff Colyer, plays chess with his patient, who is recovering from surgery after Dr. Colyer removed a war-brand scar from his chest.

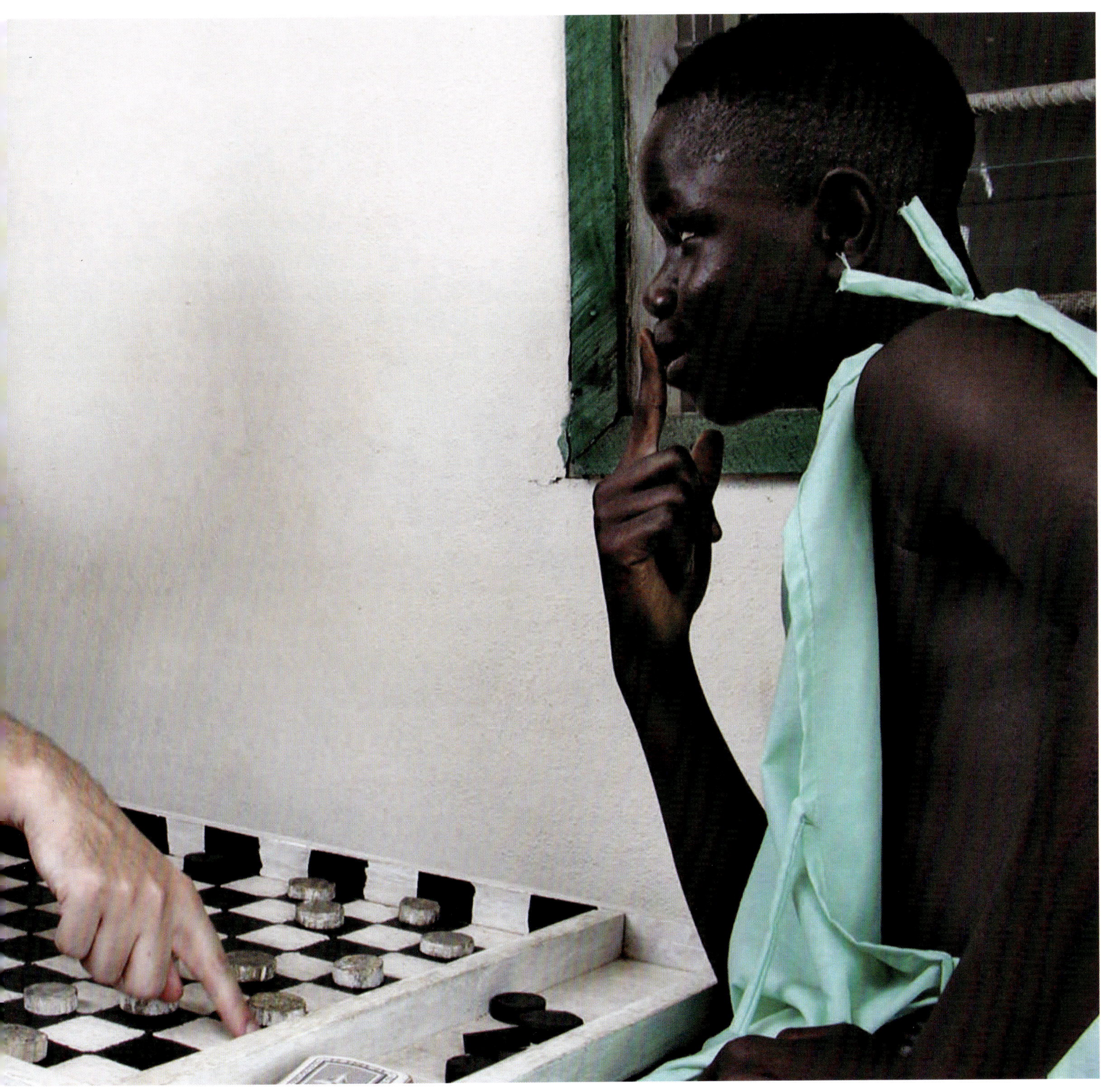

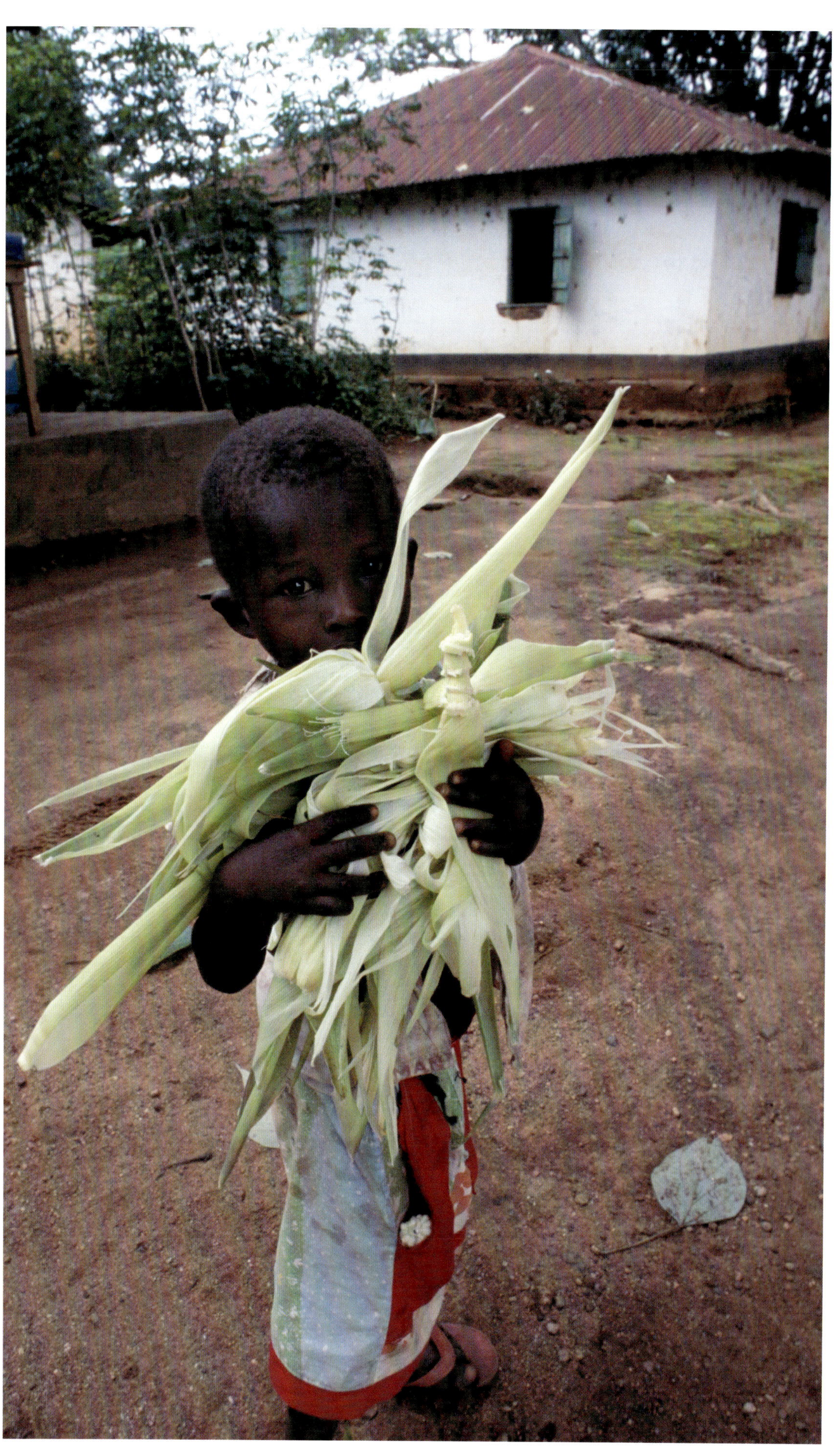

Sierra Leone 2002
Jenny Chu

A child gathers corn in Eastern Sierra Leone. An 11-year civil war displaced millions of people and destroyed most of the country's agriculture, but after the 2002 peace agreement, International Medical Corps helped communities rebuild.

Sierra Leone 2002/2006
Sara Terry (opposite, top)
Jenny Chu (opposite, bottom)

Opposite page: At the end of the war in 2002, IMC worked with local contractors and community laborers—including former combatants and returned refugees—to completely rehabilitate Kailahun Government Hospital.

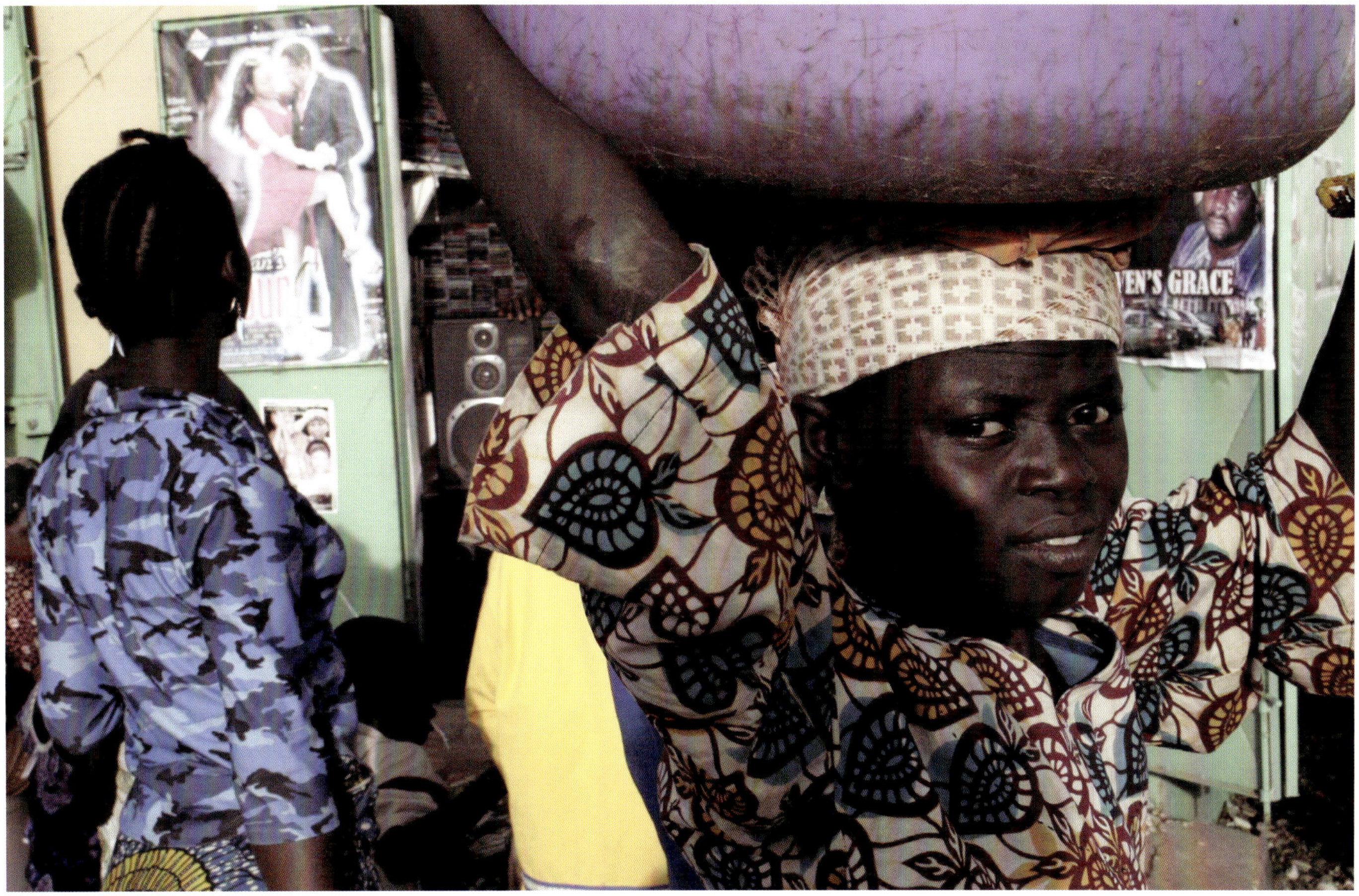

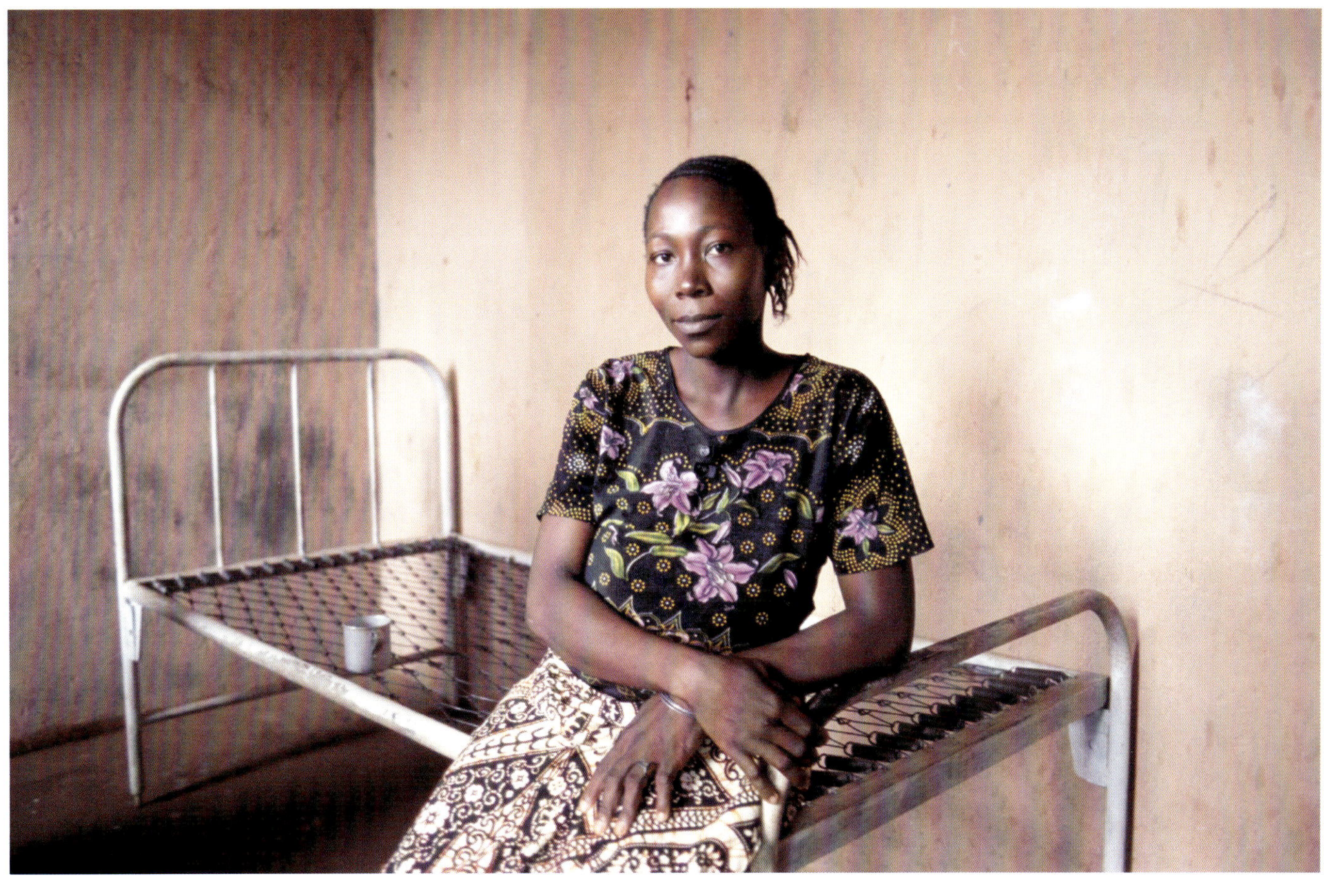

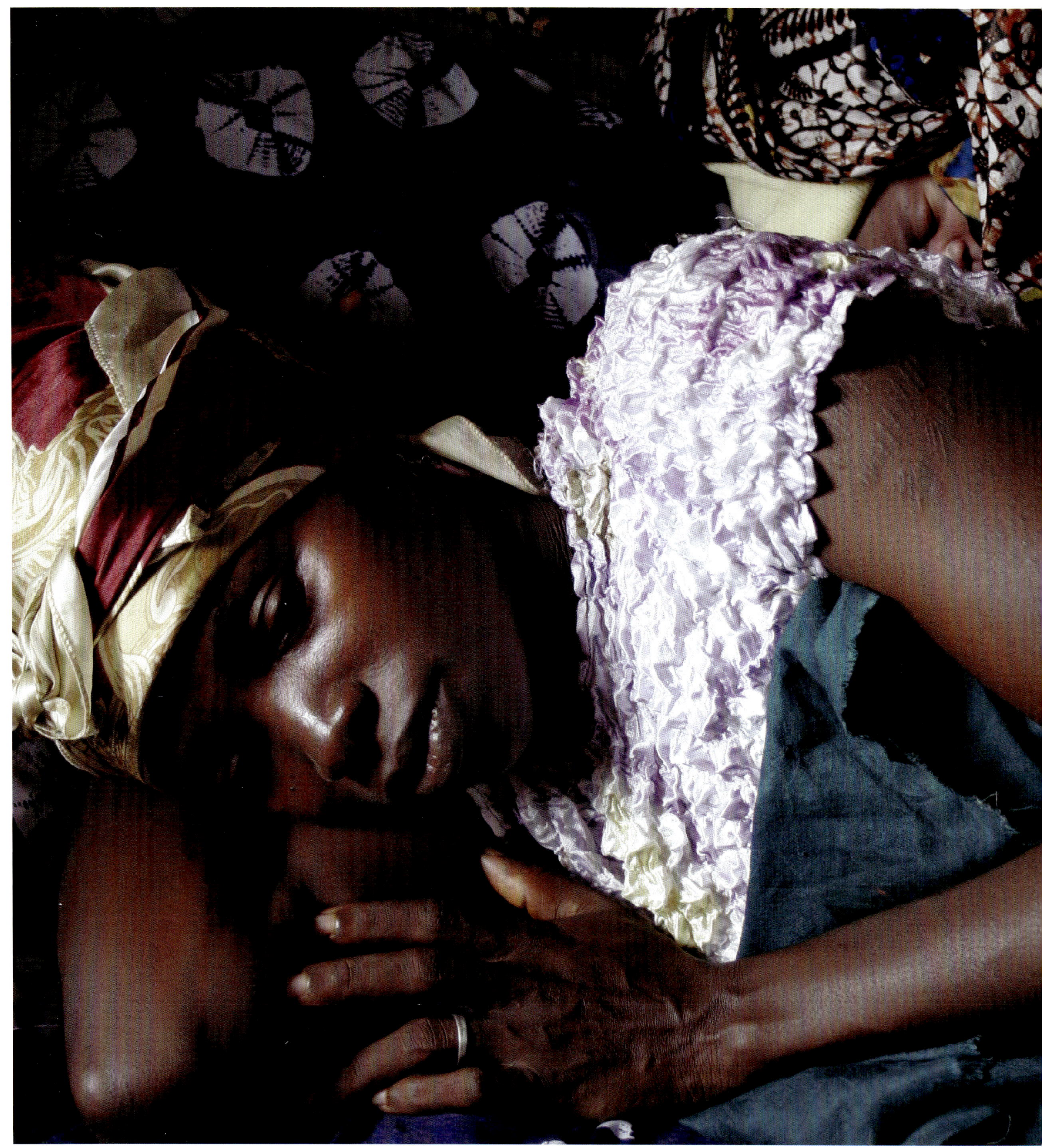

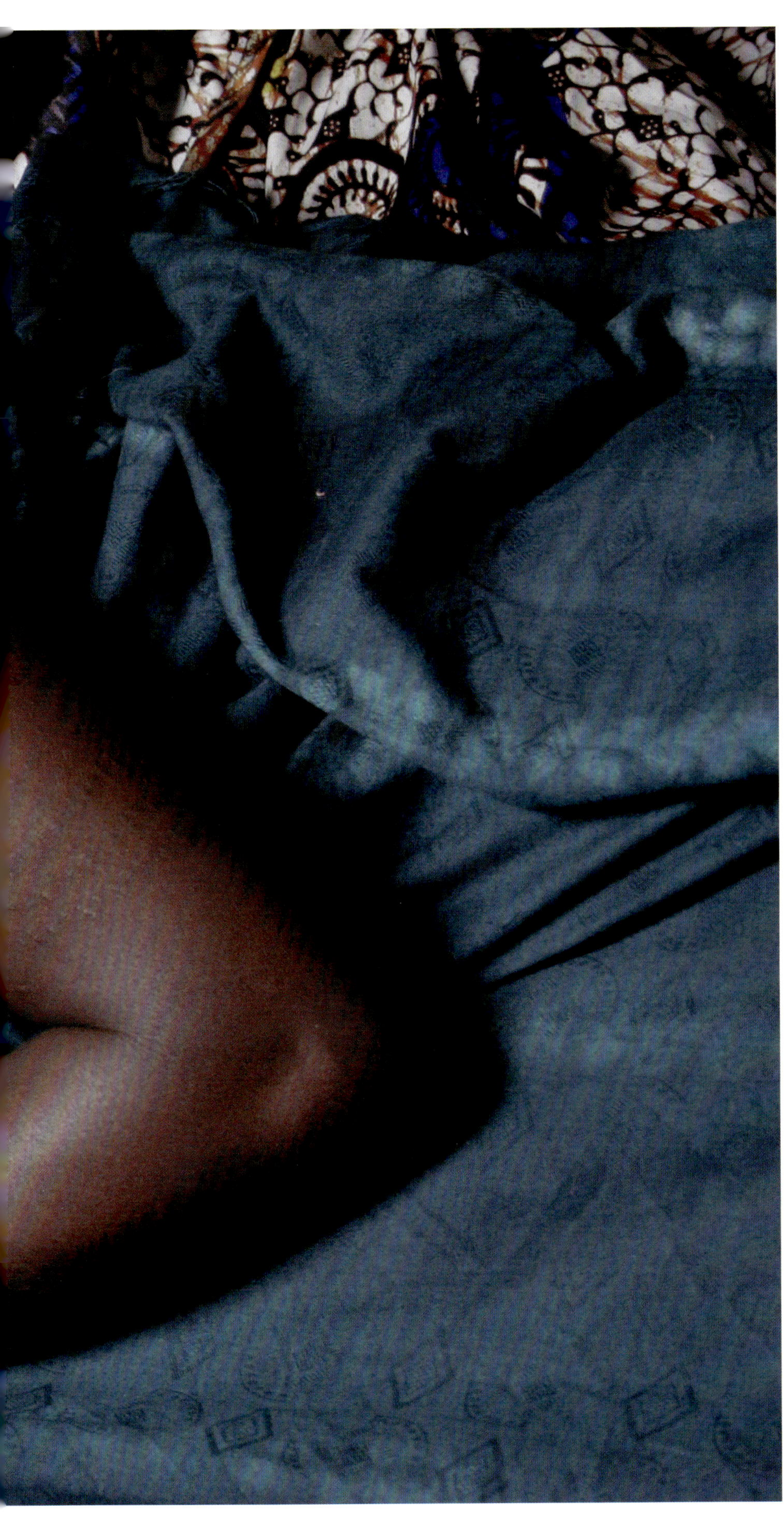

Sierra Leone 2006
Sara Terry

At the Largo camp and clinic, a mother and her newborn baby rest in one of International Medical Corps' new pediatric wards. IMC rehabilitated eight primary health care clinics, constructed six new clinics, and trained the local support staff.

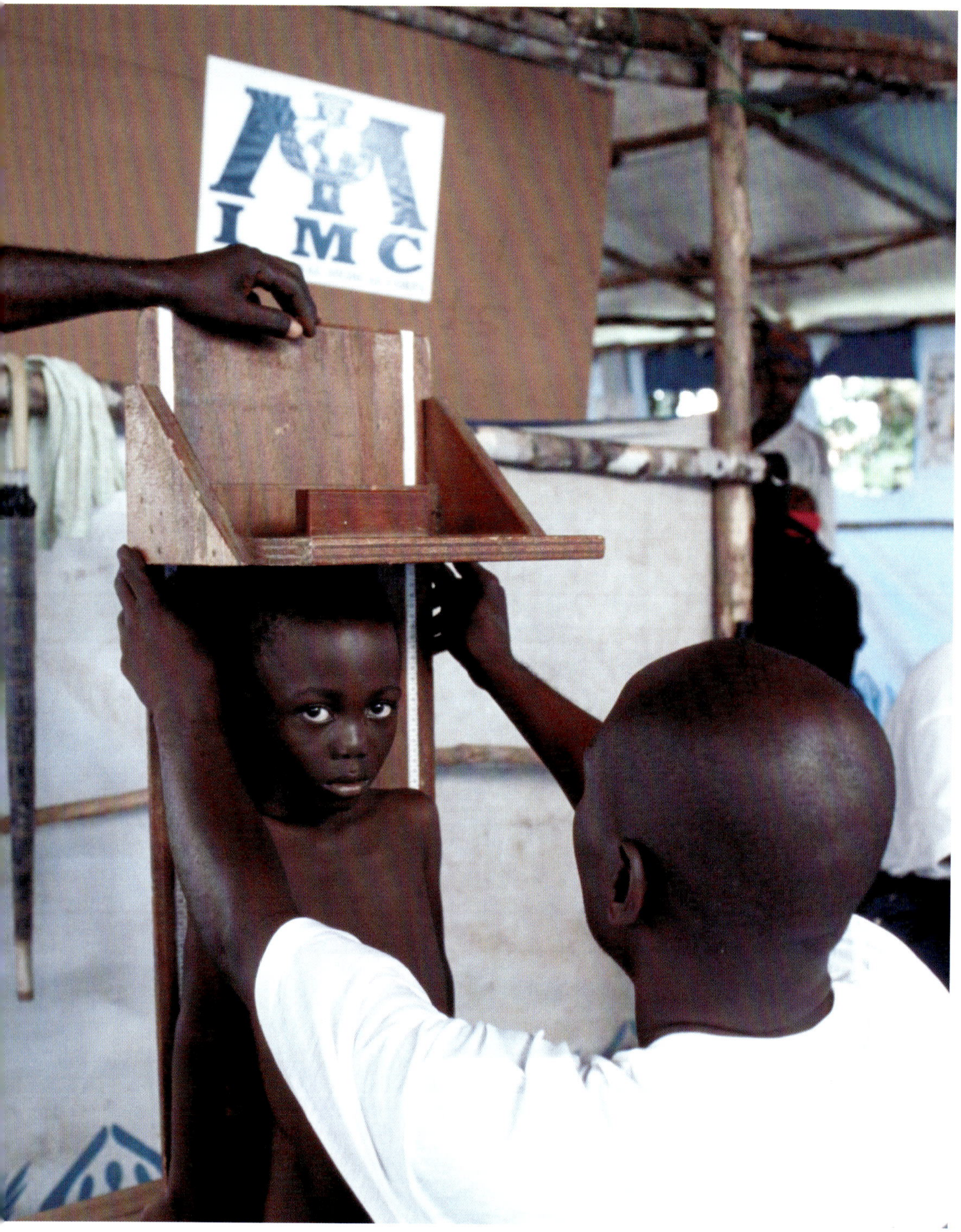

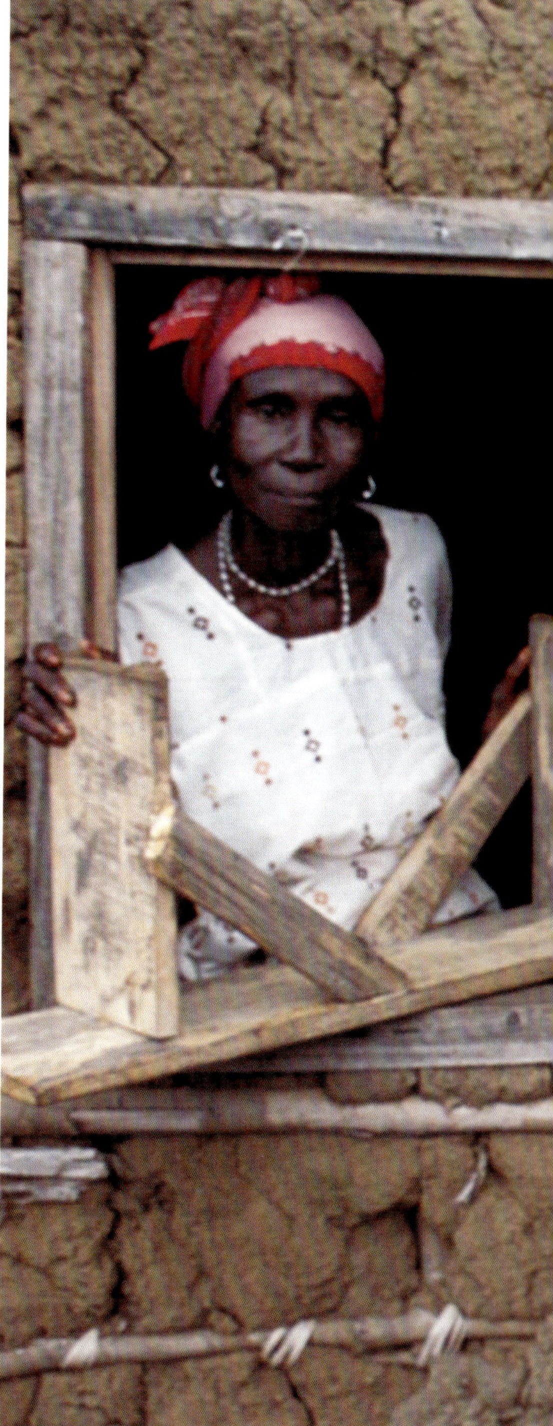

Sierra Leone 2002
Jenny Chu (both pages)

At the site from which the rebel movement was launched in 1991, International Medical Corps' work in Kailahun was particularly important. The reopening of Kailahun Government Hospital signaled not just the restoration of access to medical care in the district, but also the reestablishment of government and civil order for people living in a country devastated by war.

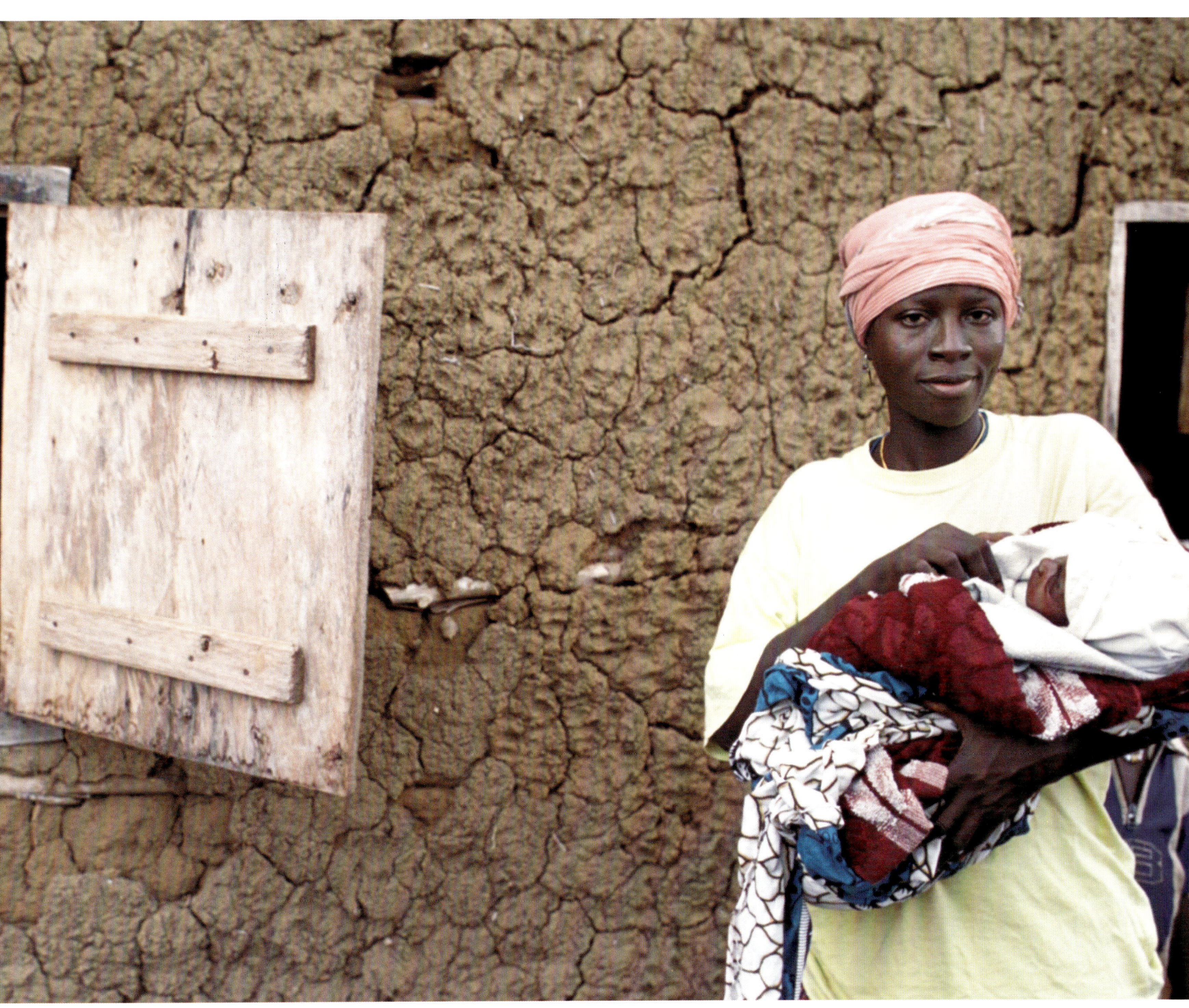

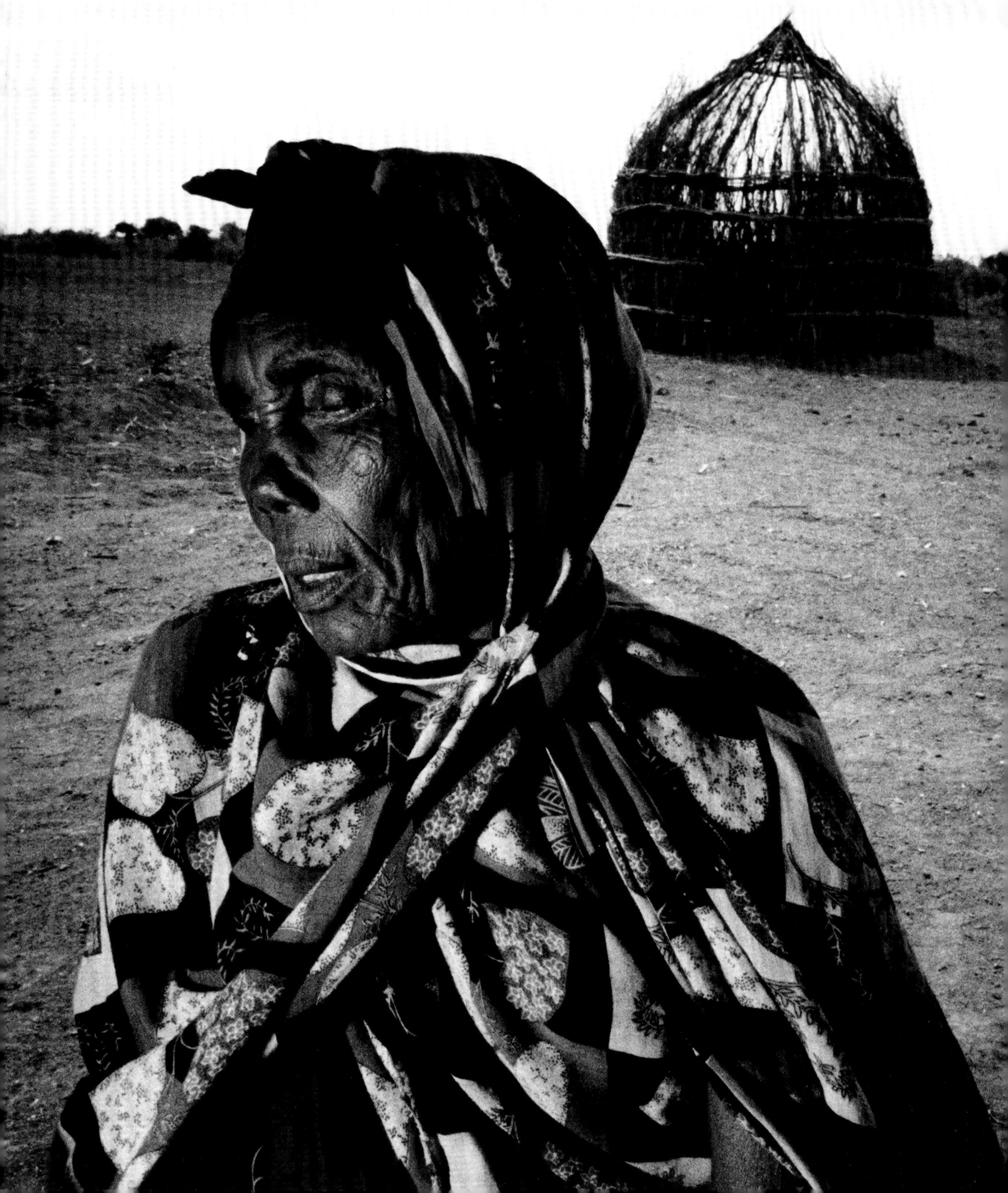

SOMALIA

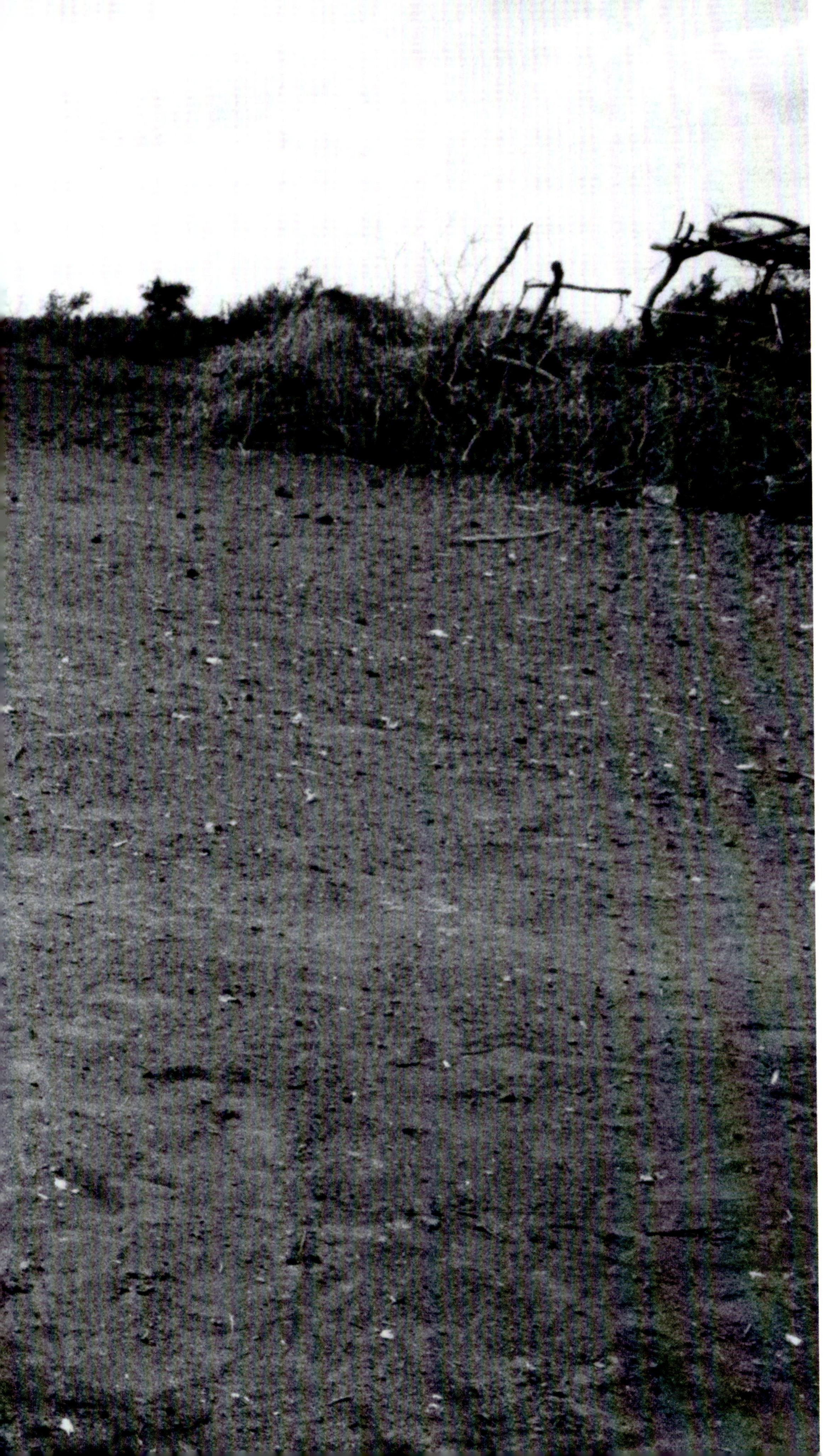

Somalia 1992
Chris Rainier
International Medical Corps' commitment to the people of Somalia began in 1991, when it was the first American non-governmental organization to arrive in war-torn Mogadishu following the overthrow of President Siad Barre.

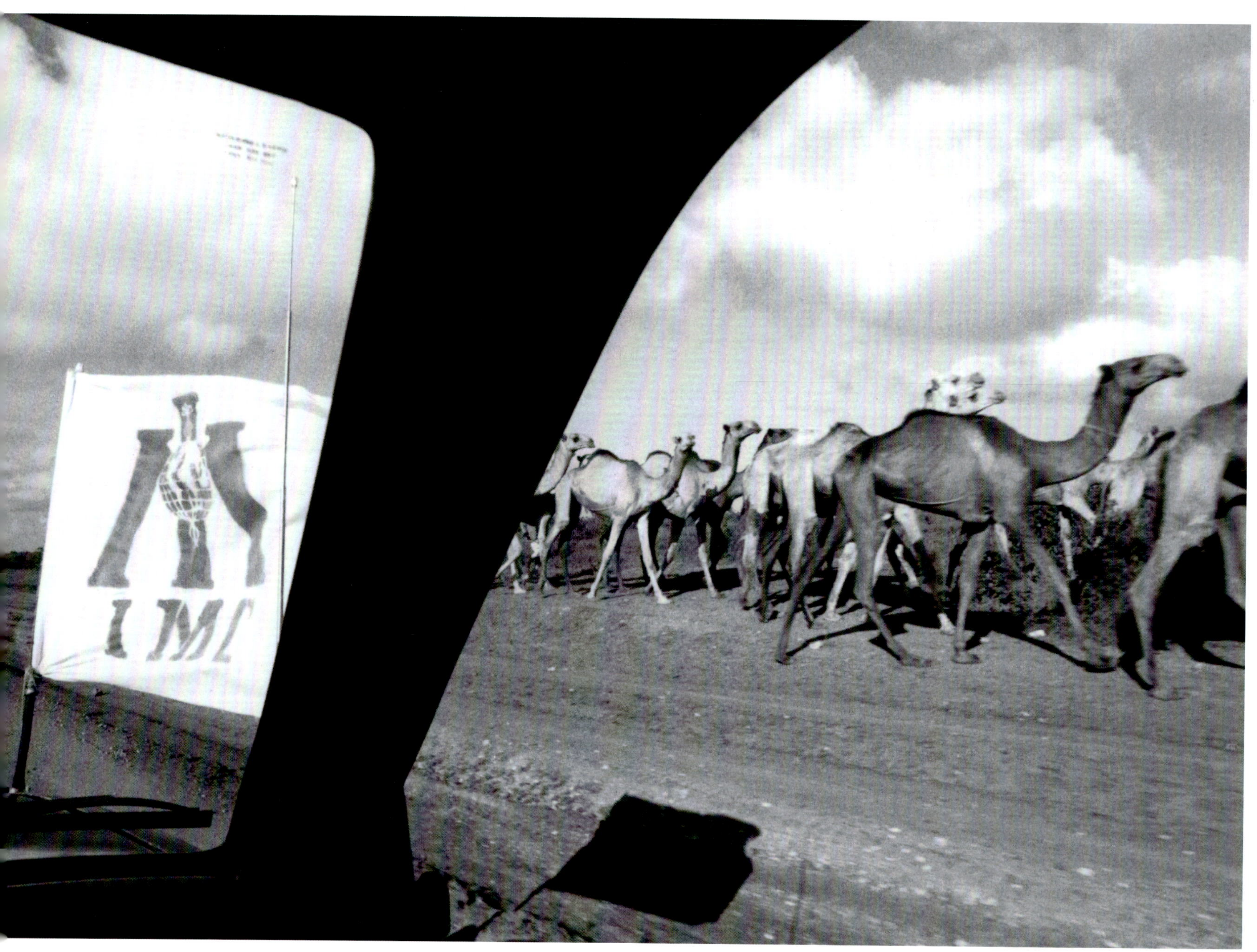

Somalia 1992

Chris Rainier (both photos)

In 1991, International Medical Corps became the principal provider of community-based primary health care in the dangerous, war-torn region of South-Central Somalia.

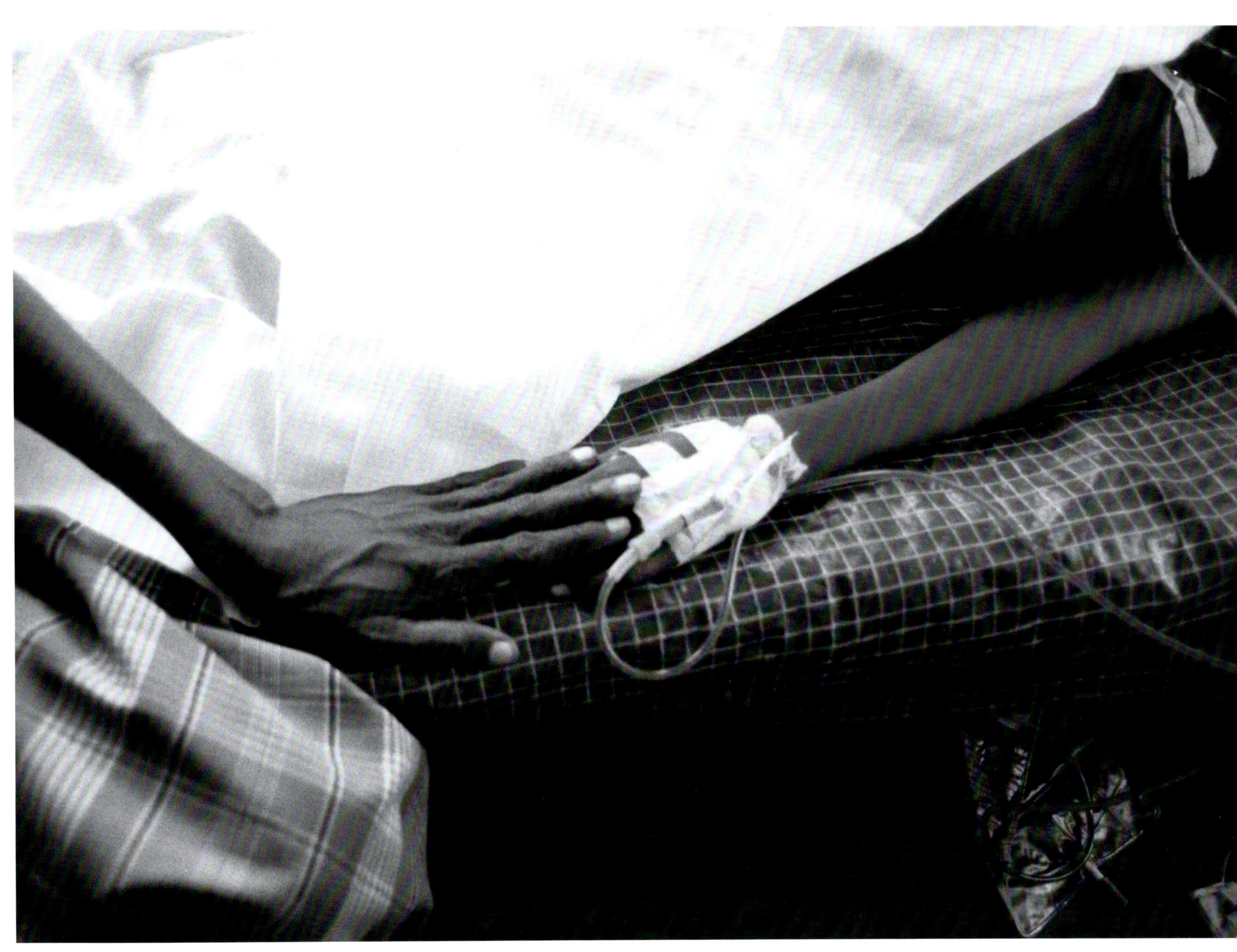

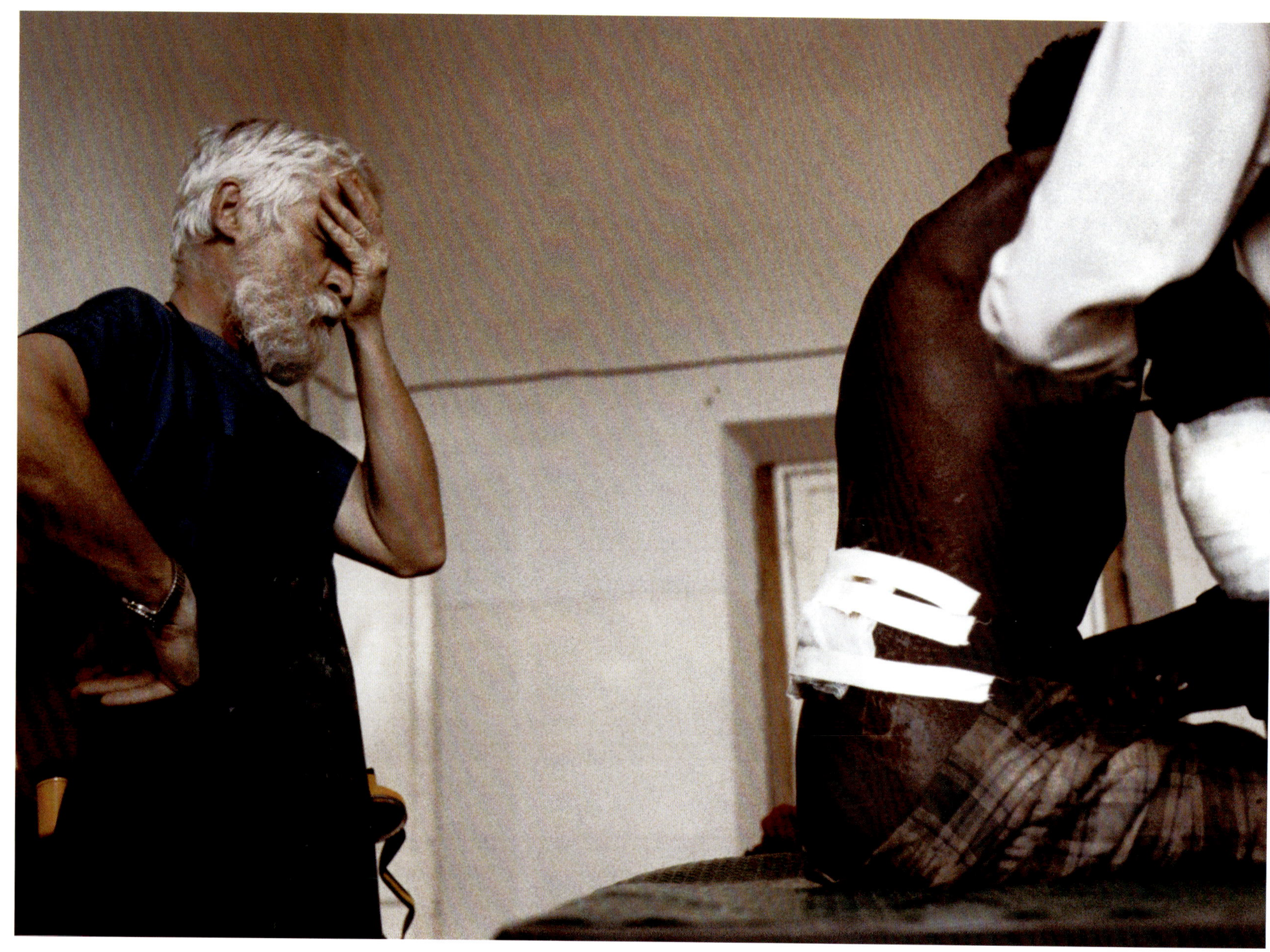

Somalia 1992
Judy Walgreen-Dehaas
Mogadishu hospitals overflowed with injured civilians, most of whom were victims of stray bullets nicknamed "yusefs" for the sound they made as they whizzed by. Many people, totally dispossessed, would line up outside International Medical Corps offices every day, begging for help of any kind.

Peter Menzel
Opposite page: Hargeisa, Somaliland was bombed and looted heavily during the civil war. A 50-year-old woman who stepped on a landmine while herding cattle waits at an IMC clinic to be fitted for a prosthetic leg.

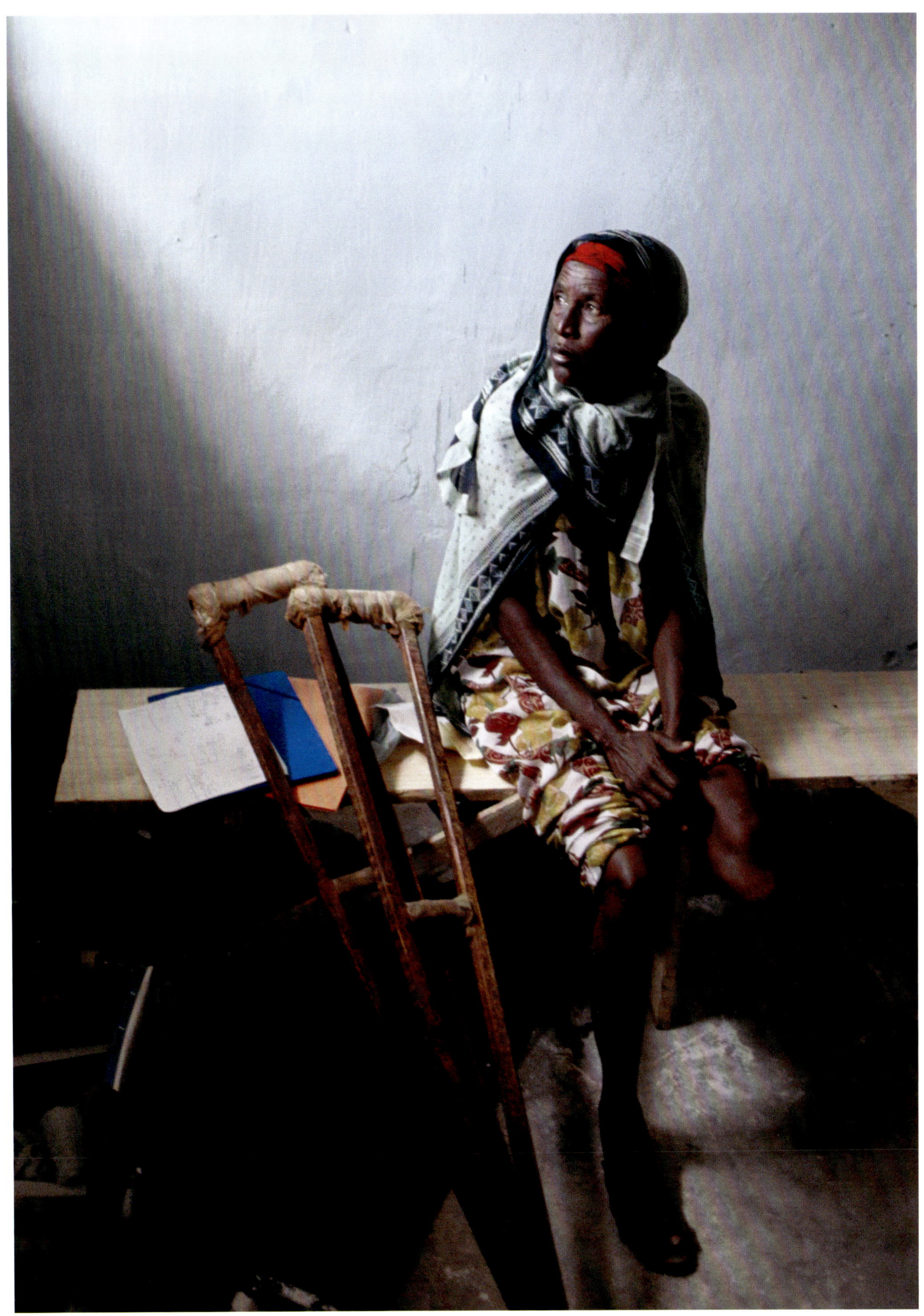

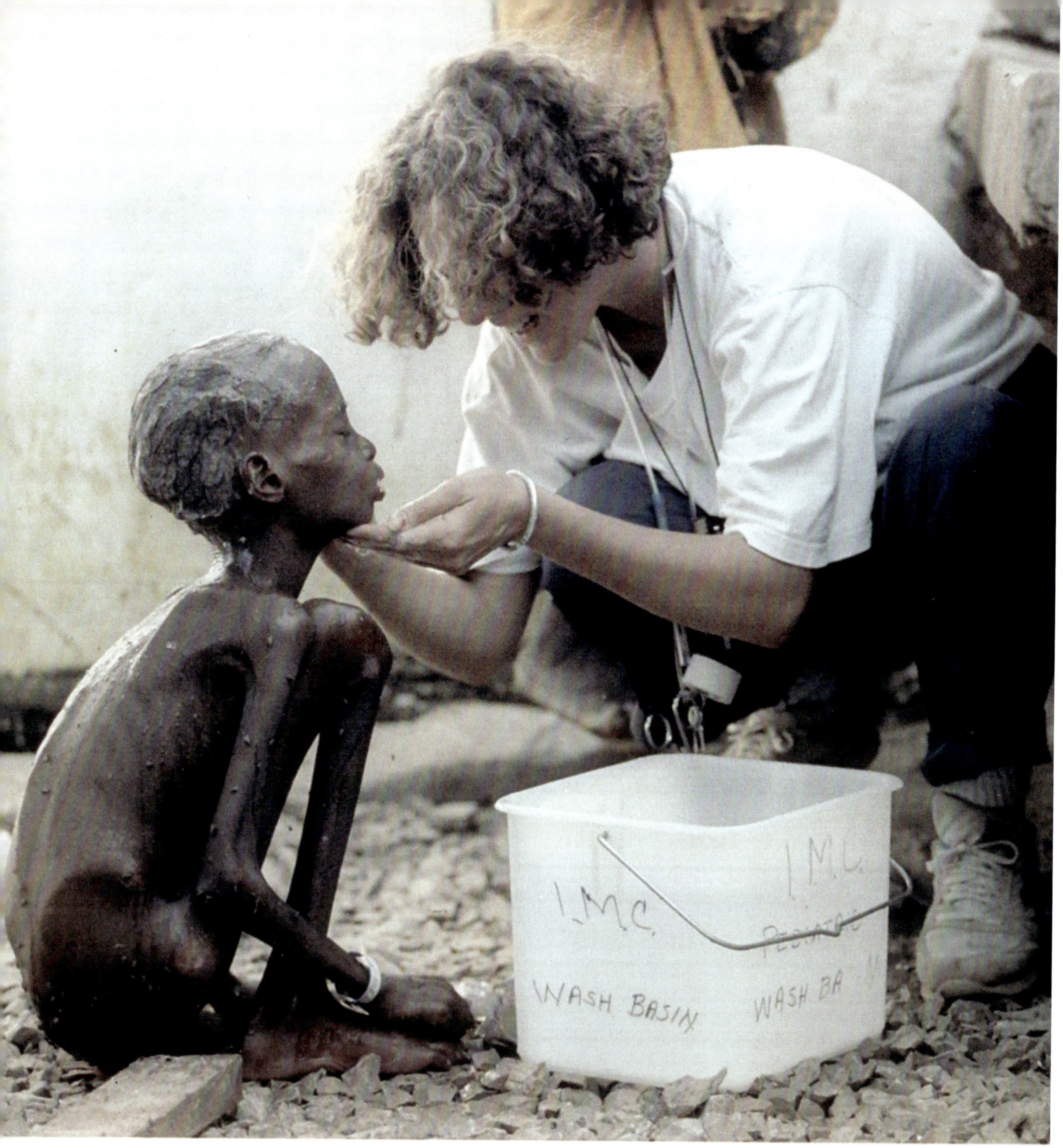

Somalia 1992
Benny Sieu (above)
Chris Rainier (opposite page)

Eight hundred people were dying of starvation each day in Baidoa, but providing food relief had become dangerous because of the anarchy. Since both central and local governments had crumbled in Somalia, so had the rule of law. Local health workers discovered, however, that operating under the umbrella of International Medical Corps afforded them the safety they needed to do their jobs. Above: An IMC nurse helps wash a severely malnourished child at one of IMC's therapeutic feeding clinics in Baidoa. Opposite page: International Medical Corps Dr. Mickey Richer examines a malnourished man in one of IMC's primary health care centers.

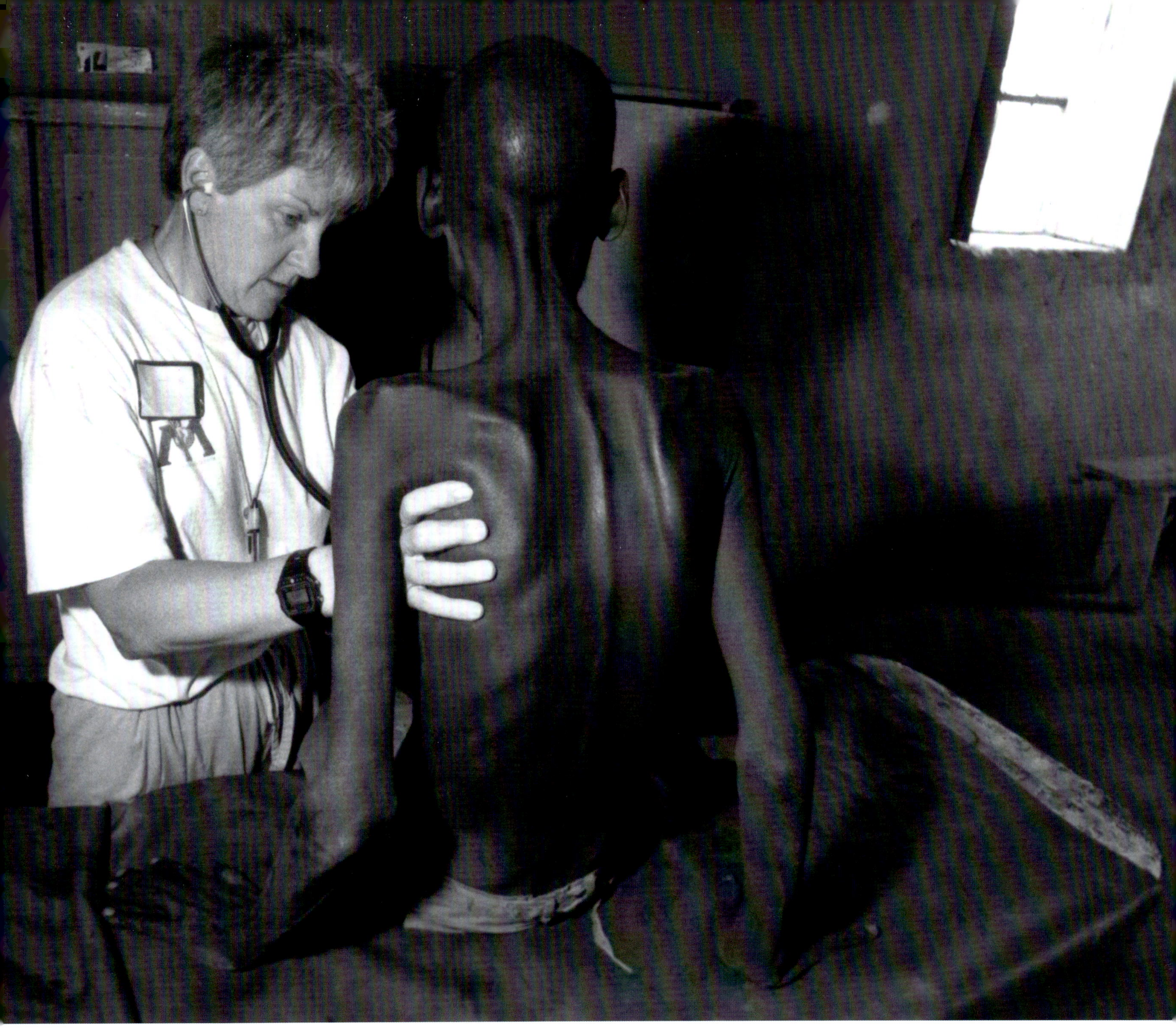

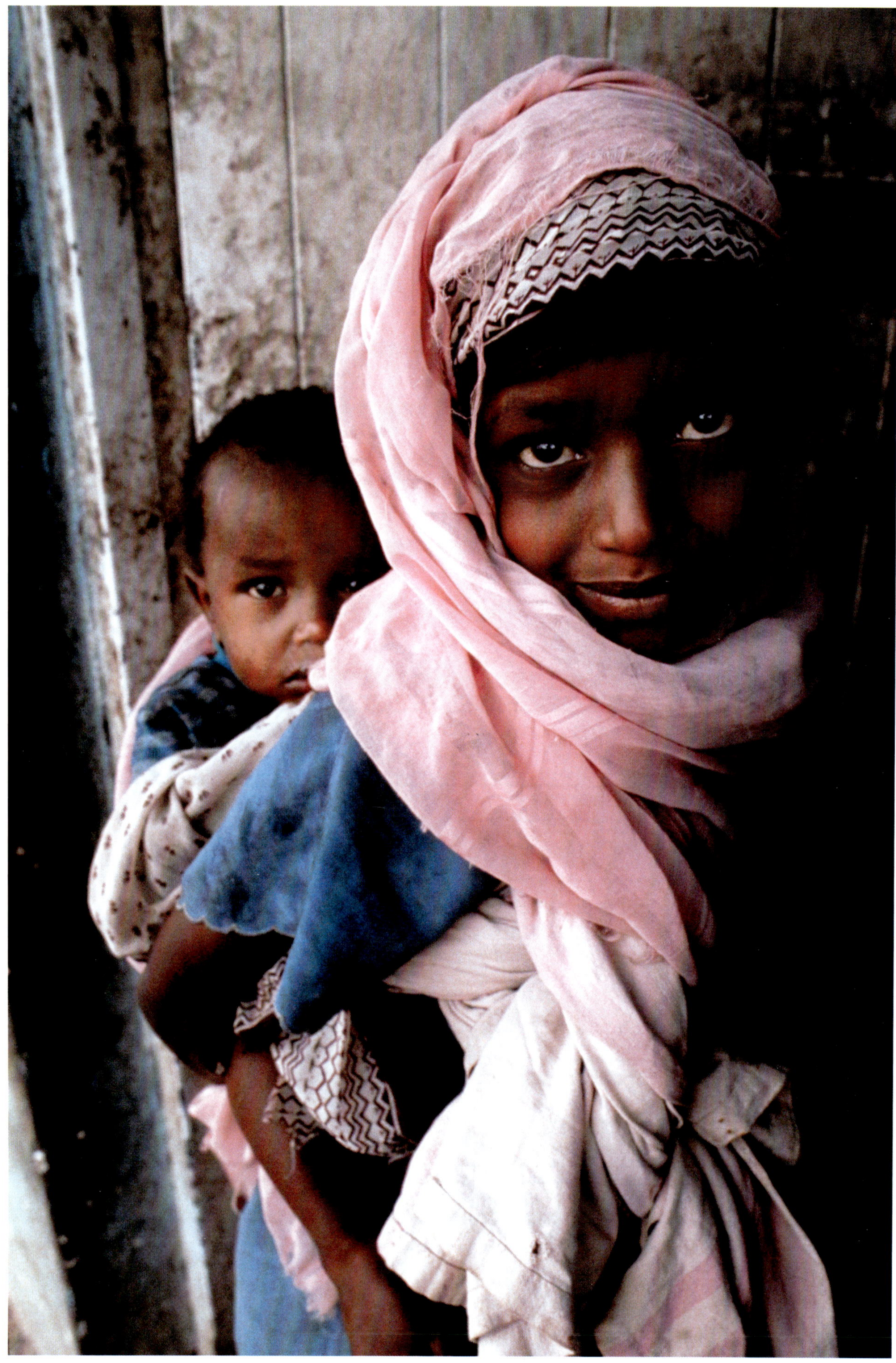

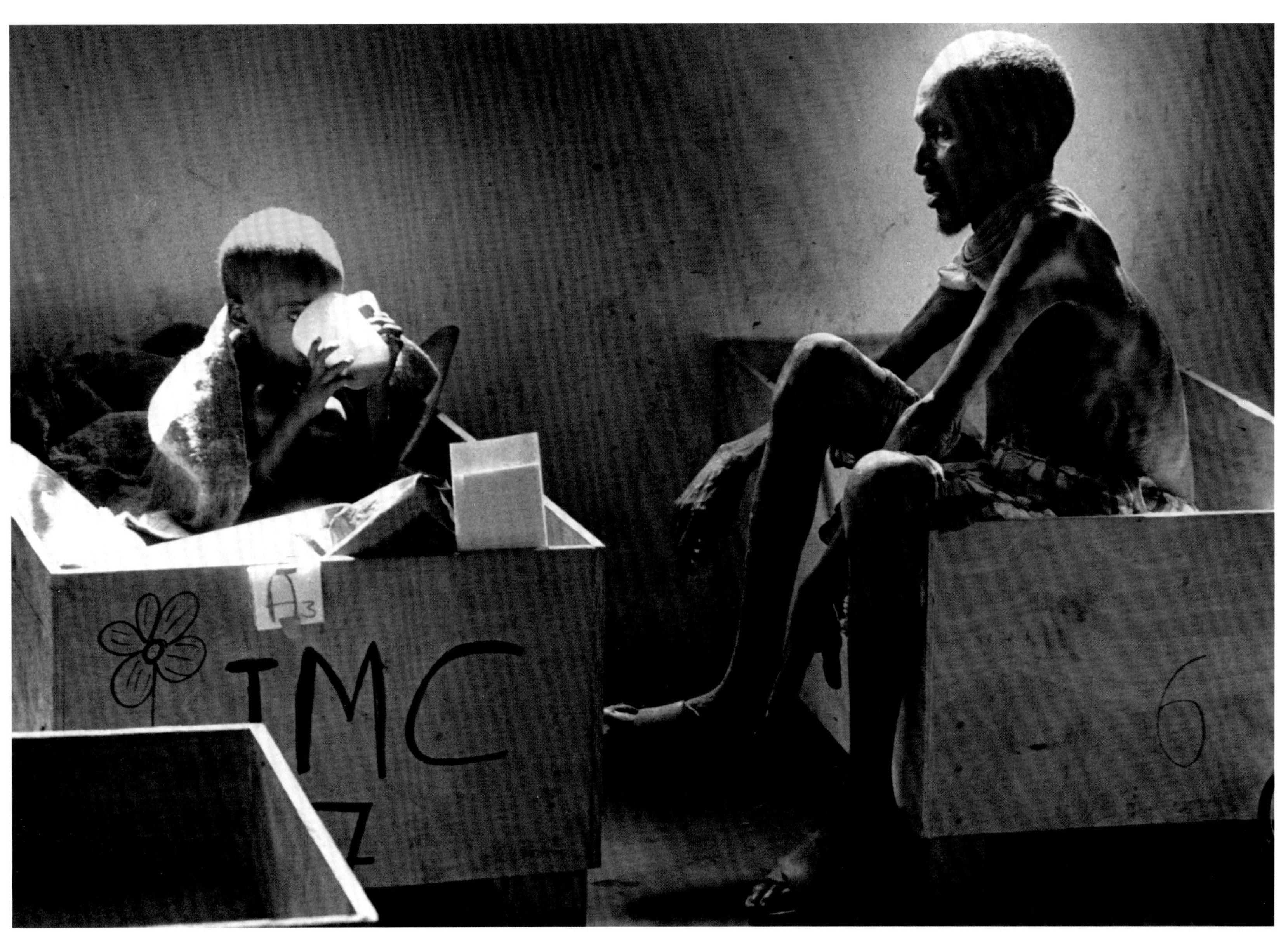

Somalia 1992
Benny Sieu (above)
Peter Menzel (opposite)

In Baidoa, Somalia, International Medical Corps workers constructed cribs from available materials to create a pediatric ward to treat thousands of wounded and starving infants and children. A grandfather is treated for malnutrition alongside his grandson. Both slept in the cribs.

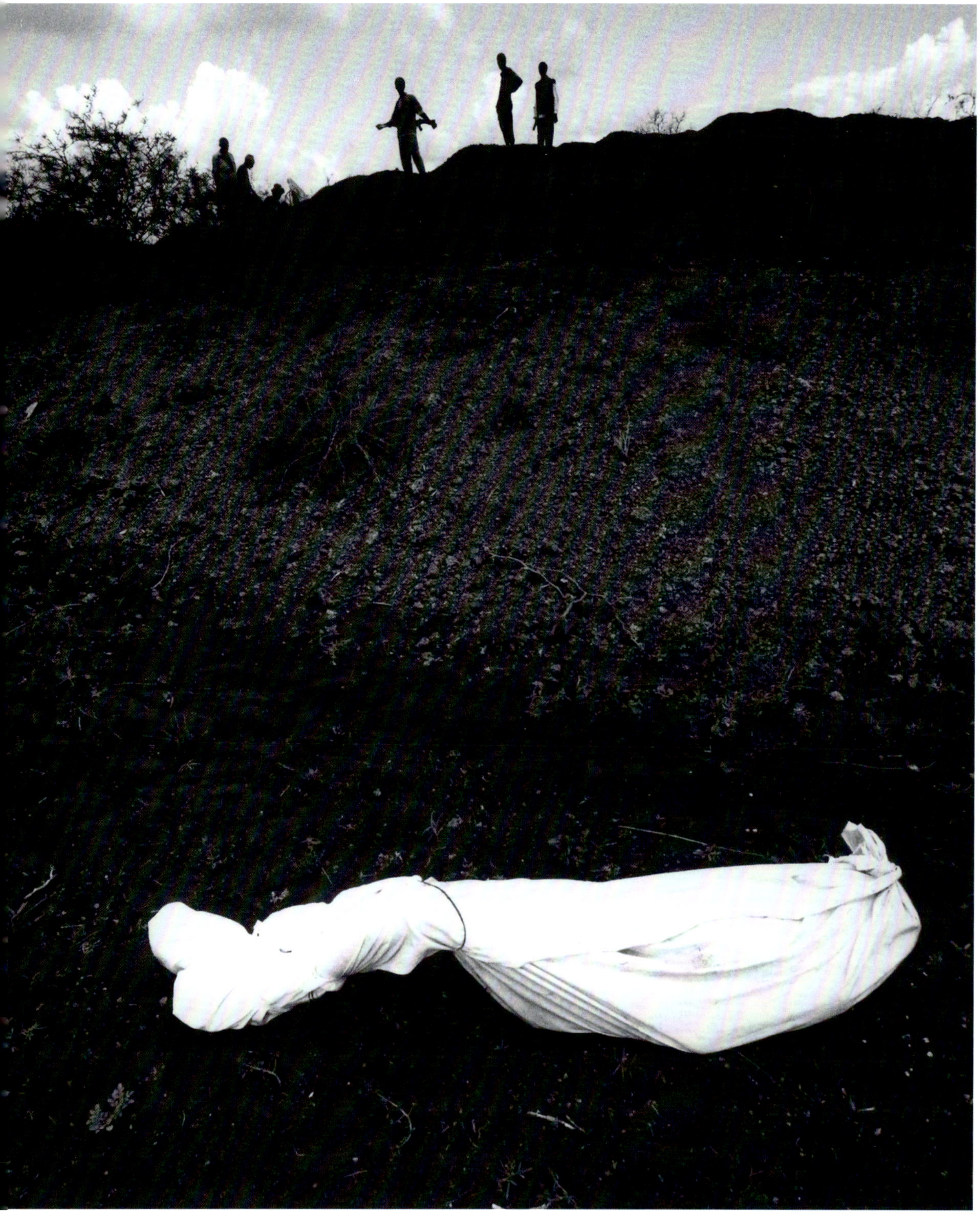

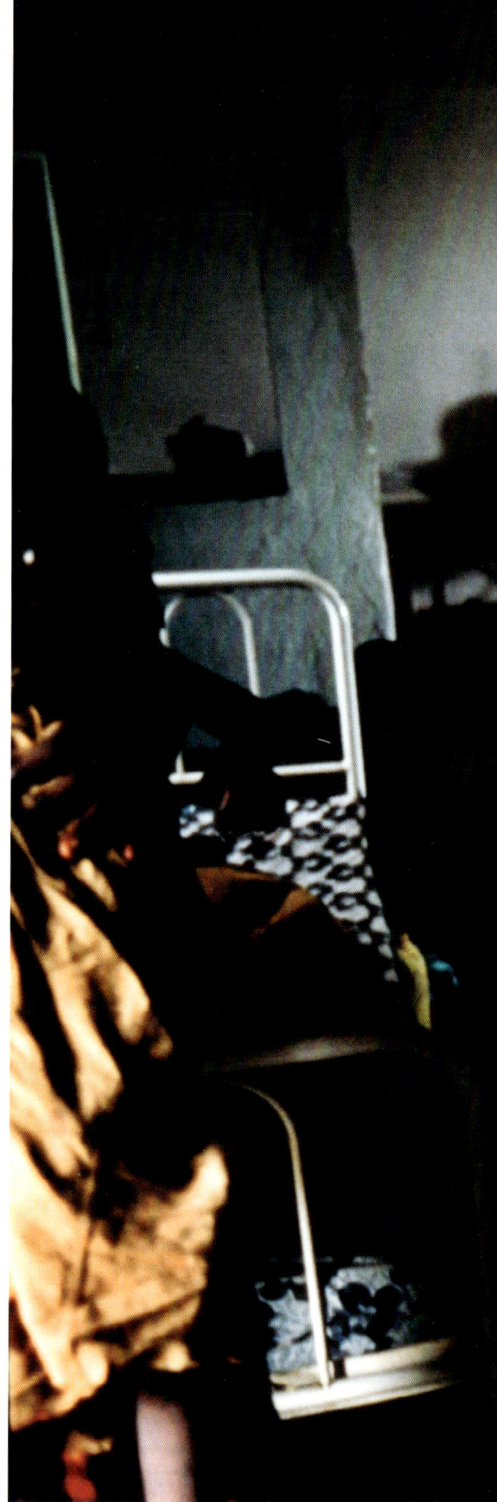

Somalia 1992
Chris Rainier

As the clans fought, civil war and anarchy intensified, and warring tribes lived off land and grain stores stolen from villagers in Baidoa. Food became a valuable commodity—a source of wealth and power. For this reason, food relief became a dangerous business in Somalia.

Somalia 1993
John Trotter

Opposite page: An International Medical Corps health worker comforts a baby in one of IMC's therapeutic feeding centers in Somalia.

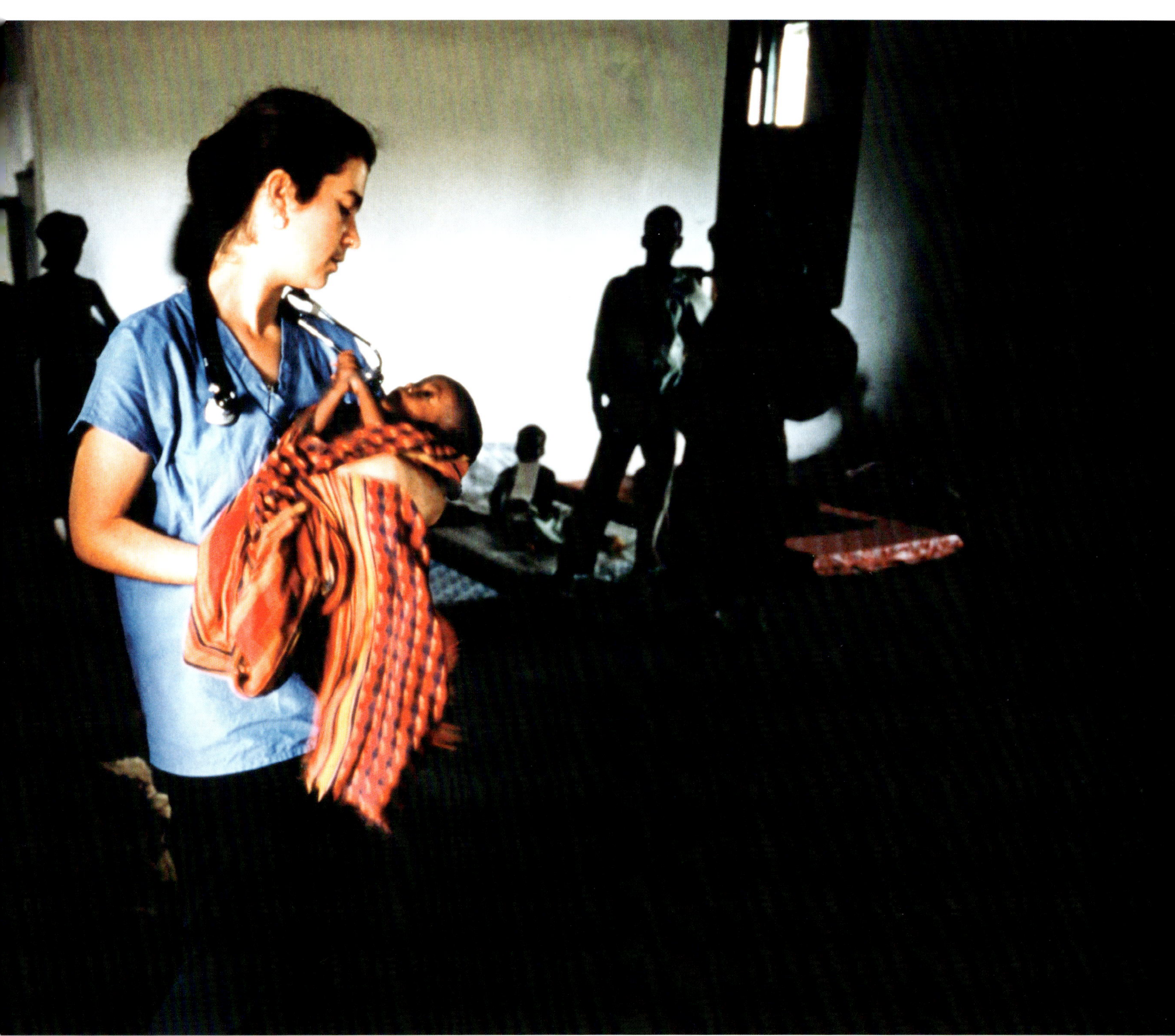

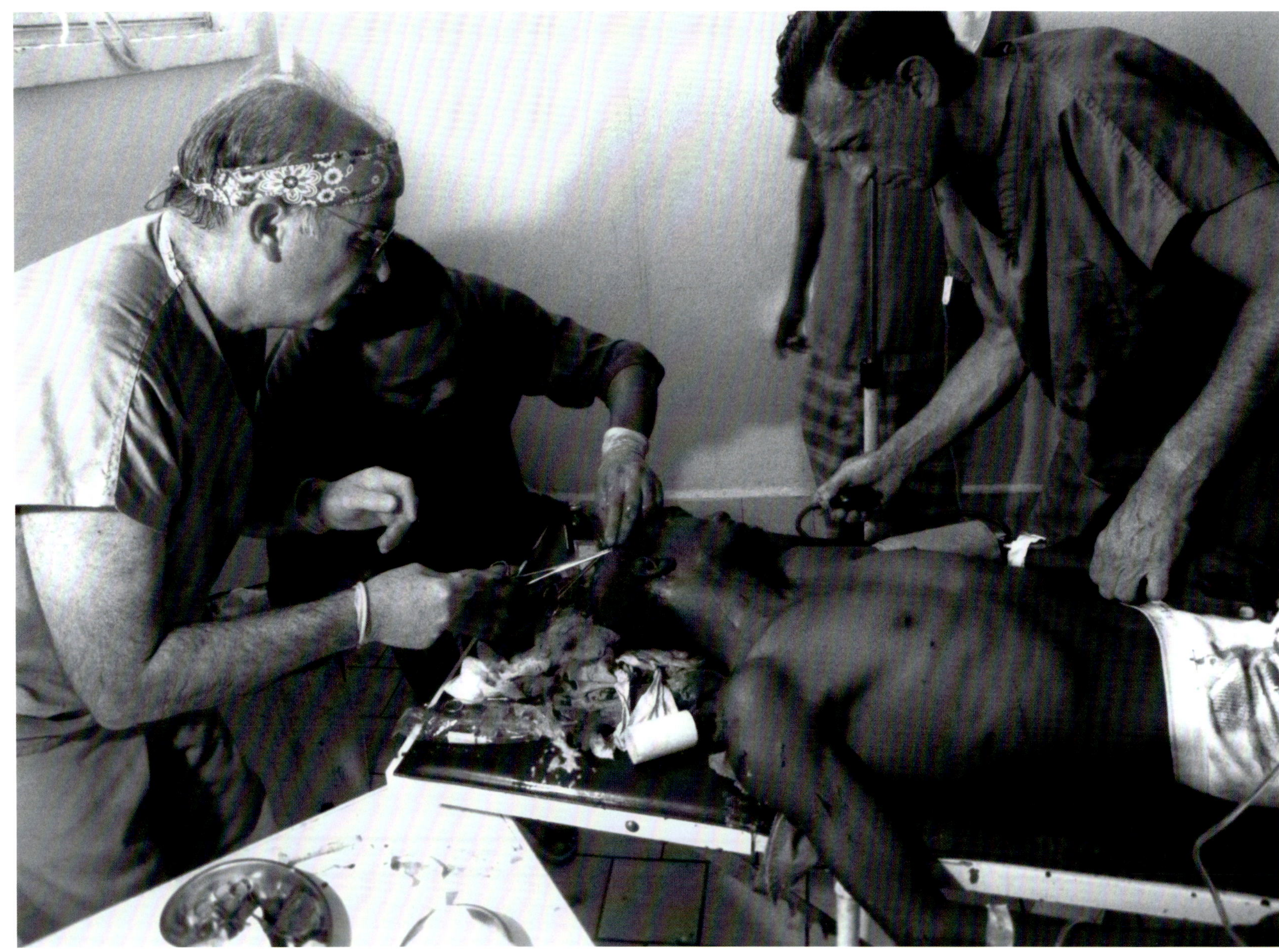

Somalia 1992
Chris Rainier

Often working in appalling conditions, International Medical Corps doctors operated without equipment, blood or operating tables. In a make-shift hospital in Modagishu, IMC doctors remove a bullet from a victim's head.

Chris Rainier

Opposite page: Many of the hospitals in Somalia were overrun, and many patients' beds were stolen. It was not uncommon for patients to be found on the floors of rooms splattered with the blood of war, like this woman with her child at an IMC clinic.

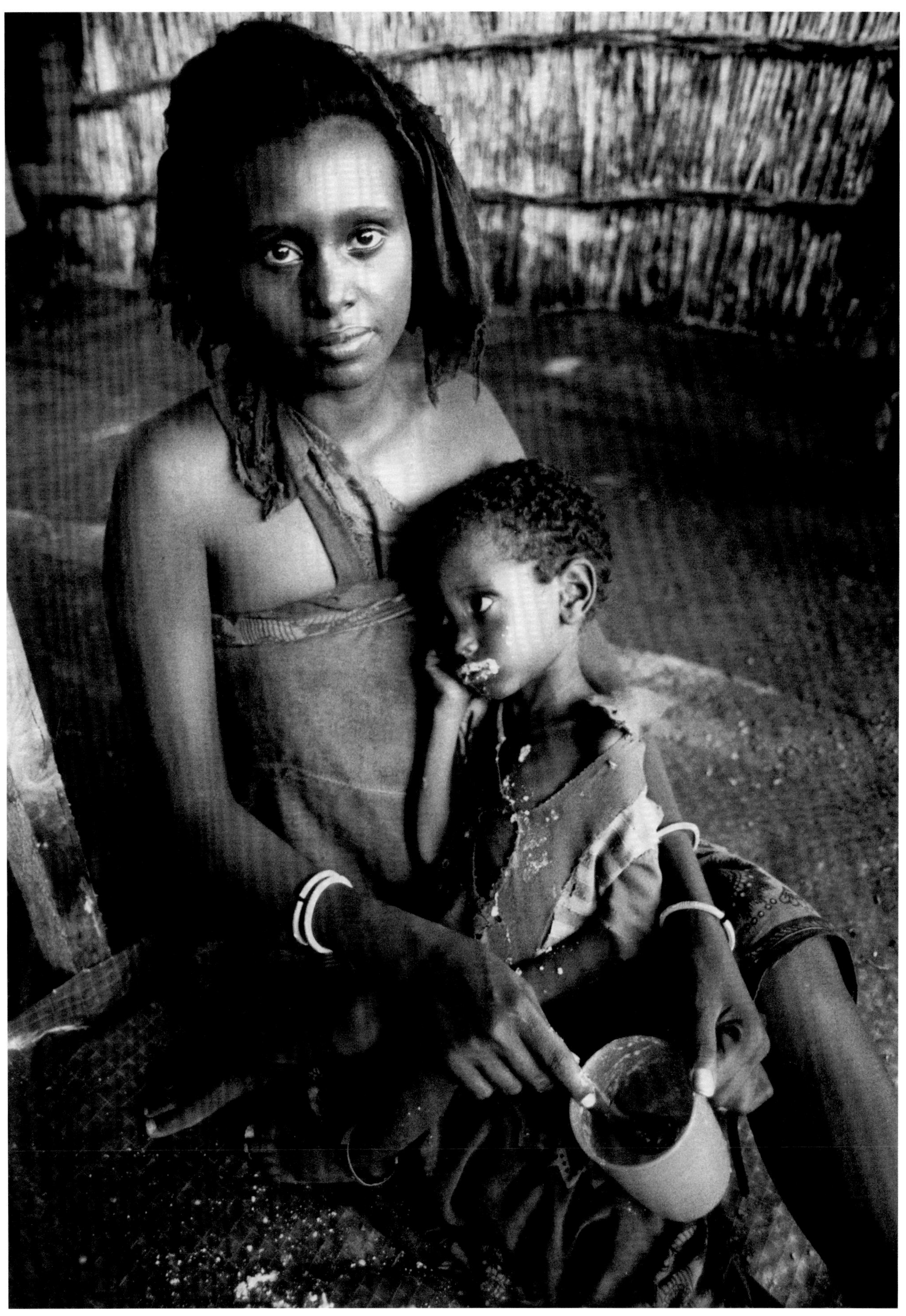

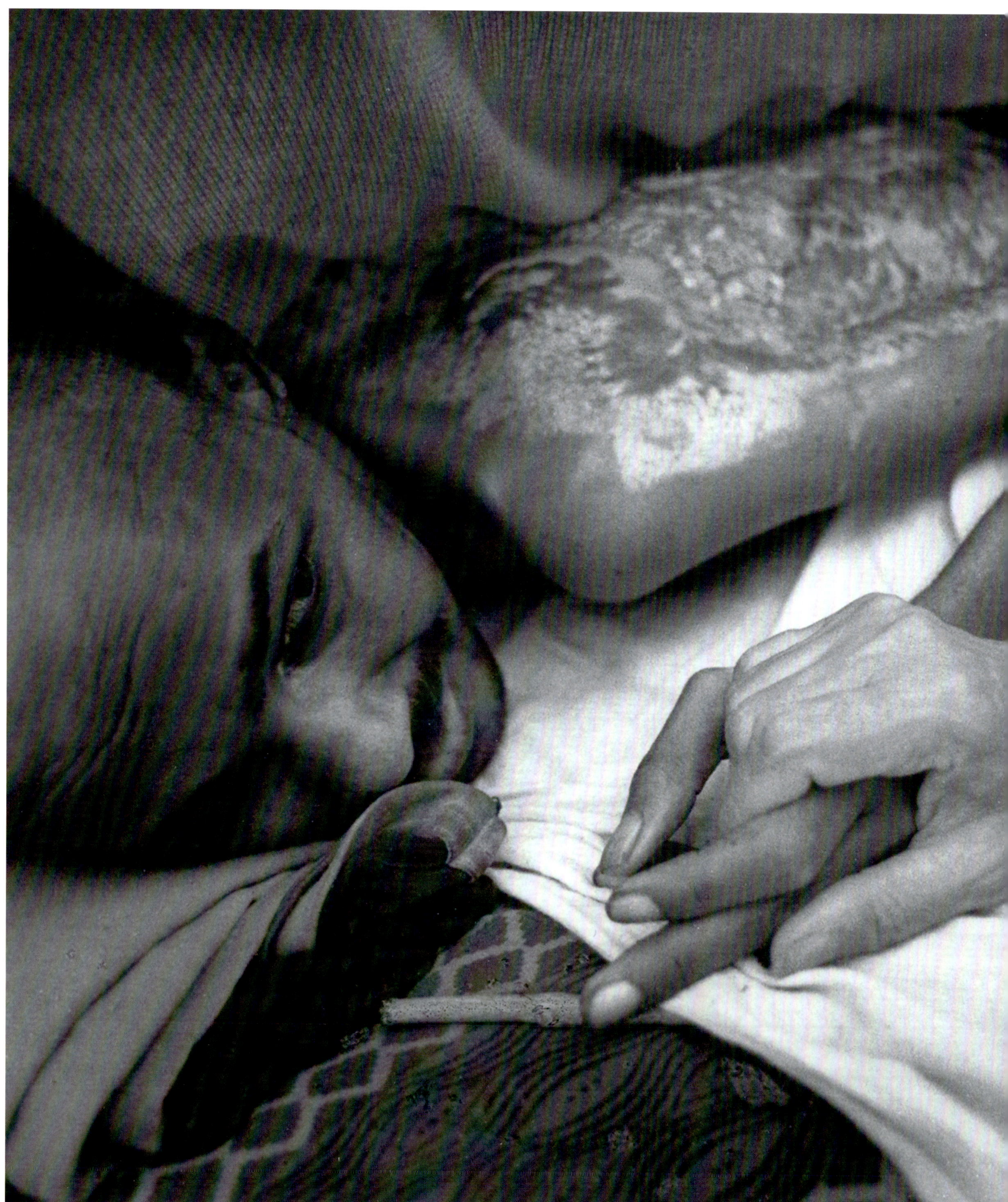

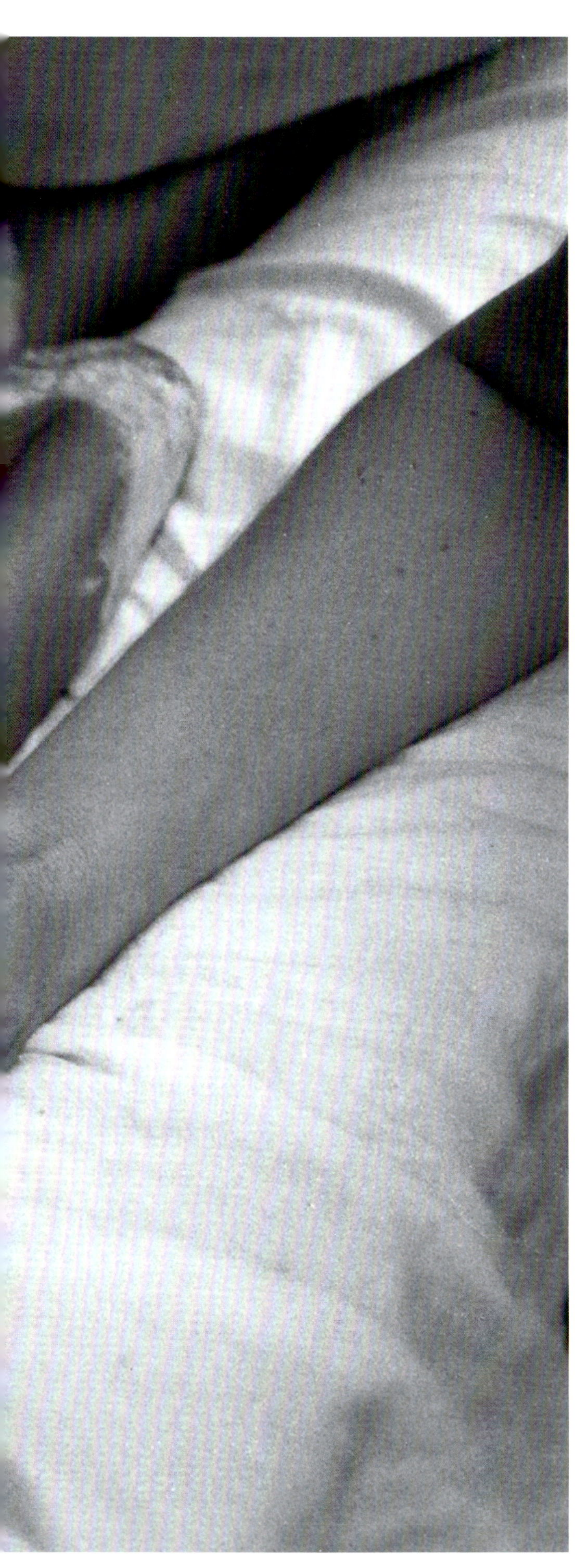

Somalia 1992
Chris Rainier

Comforting a badly burned victim, an International Medical Corps nurse holds the hand of a man as he dies. Often patients died due to the lack of blood or simply because there were not enough doctors to operate.

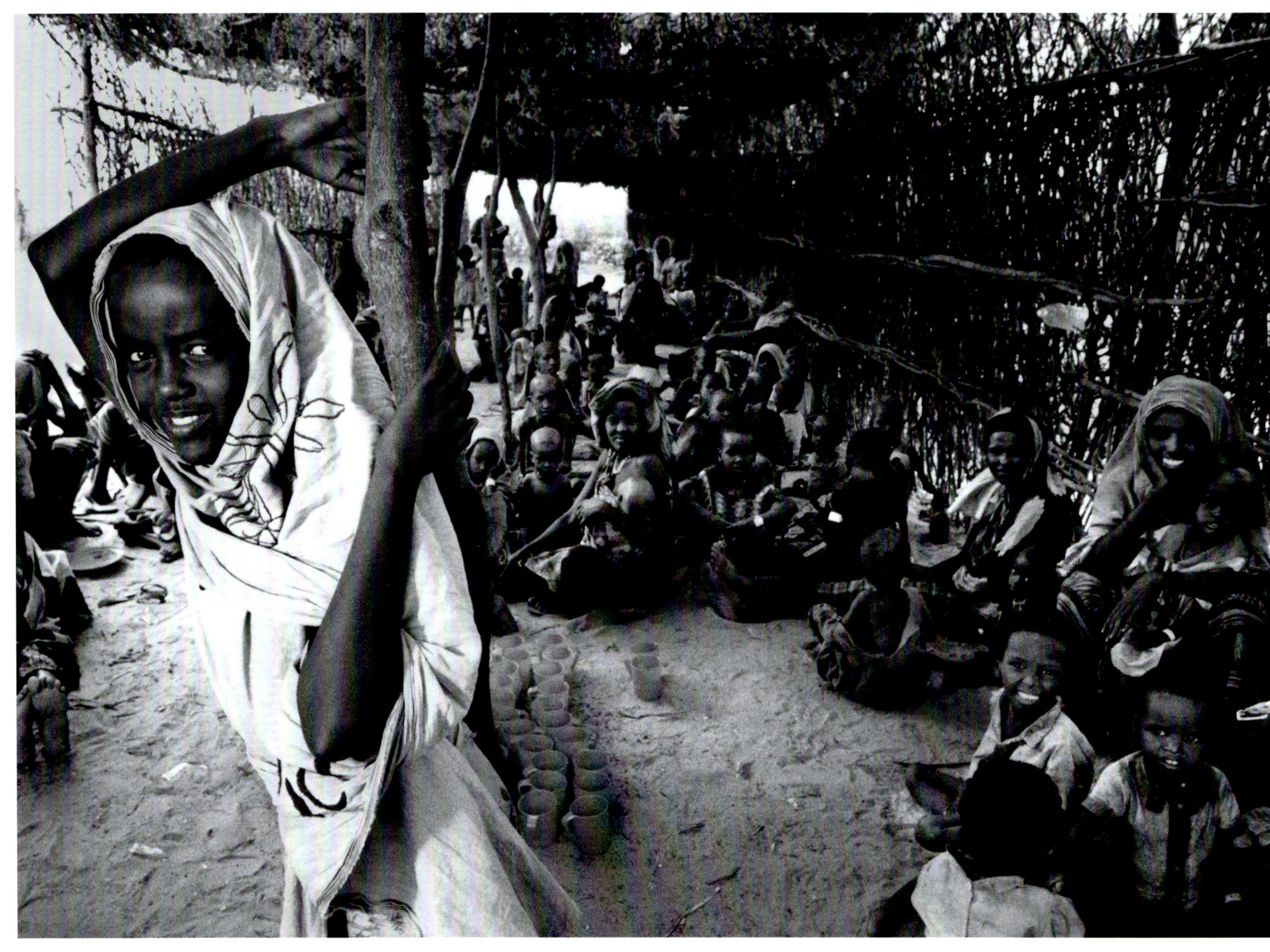

Somalia 1992

Chris Rainier

While droughts and disease outbreaks are predictable, most Somalis were powerless to prevent them from becoming health crises. As a result, Somalia's health indicators were among the worst in the world: Life expectancy was just 47 years, and almost one quarter of all children died before the age of 5.

Chris Rainier

Opposite page: International Medical Corps doctors, nurses and volunteers were often caught in the crossfire of Somalia's violent civil war. In one incident, while loading people and supplies onto a relief flight at Mogadishu airport, a man assigned to protect International Medical Corps workers was shot and killed.

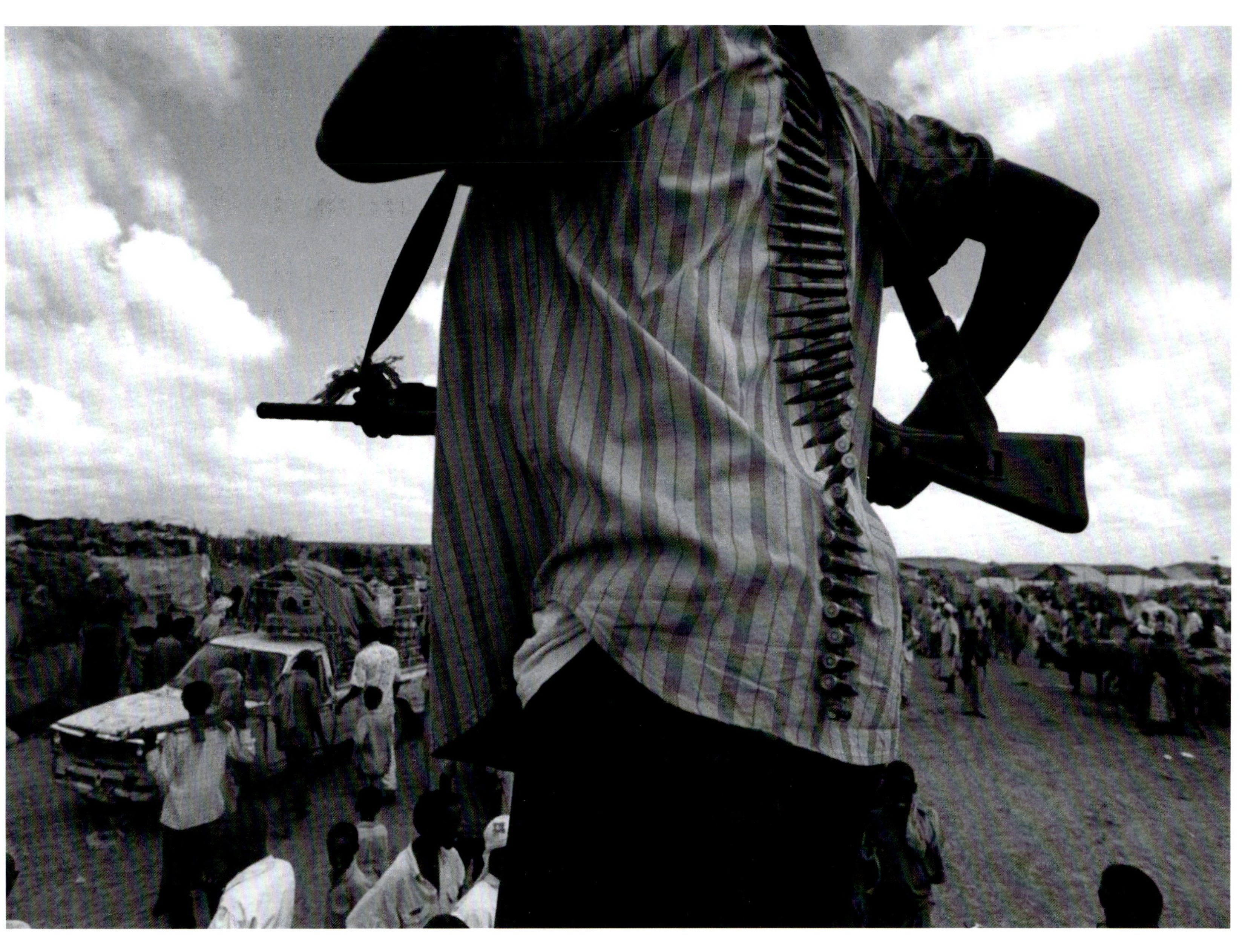

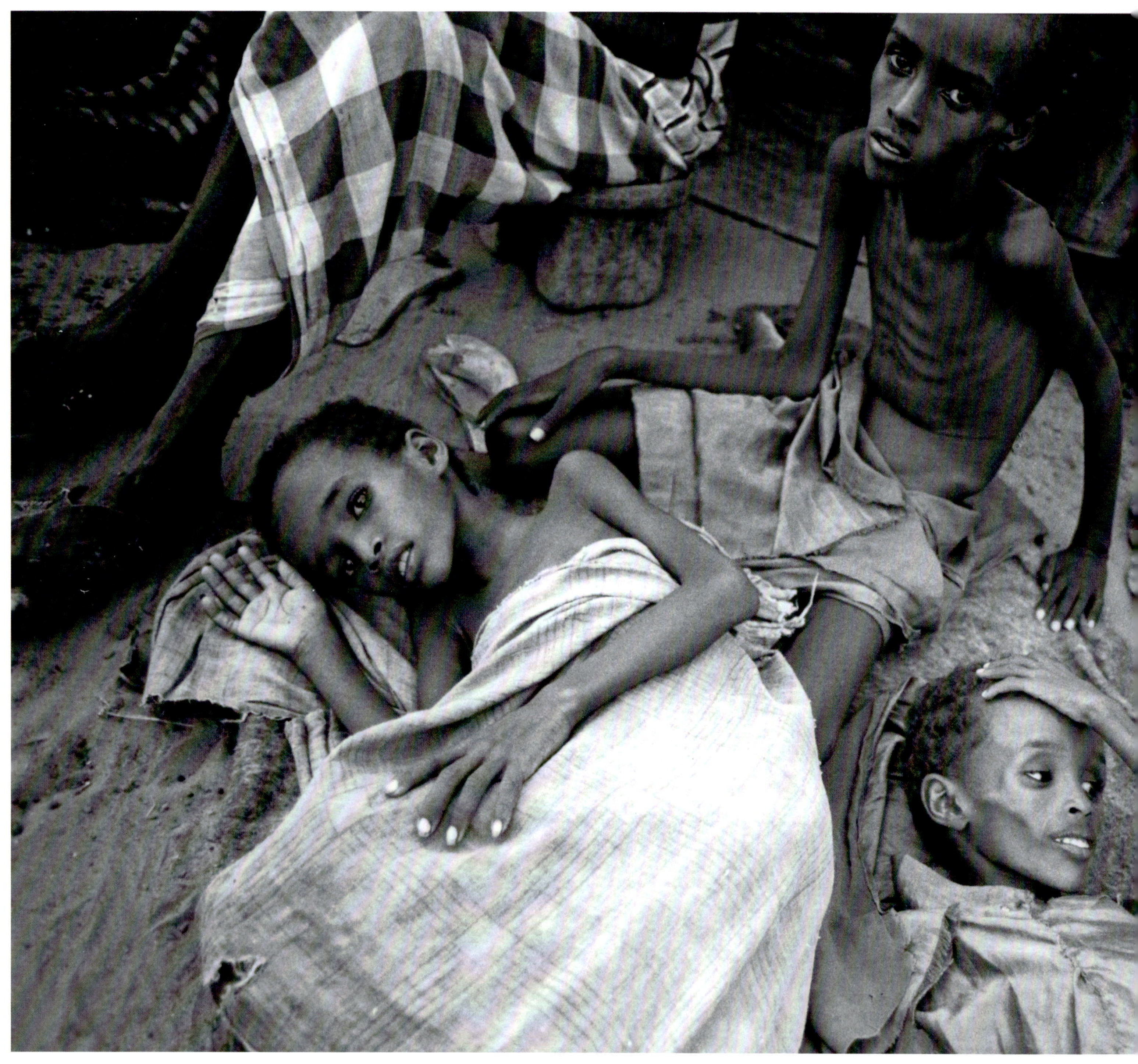

Somalia 1992
Chris Rainier
Benny Sieu (opposite)

For thousands of vulnerable Somalis, International Medical Corps was their only hope. IMC provided supplementary feeding and care for malnourished children and their families as well as training of local health staff to care for the devastated victims of the famine brought on by the country's civil war.

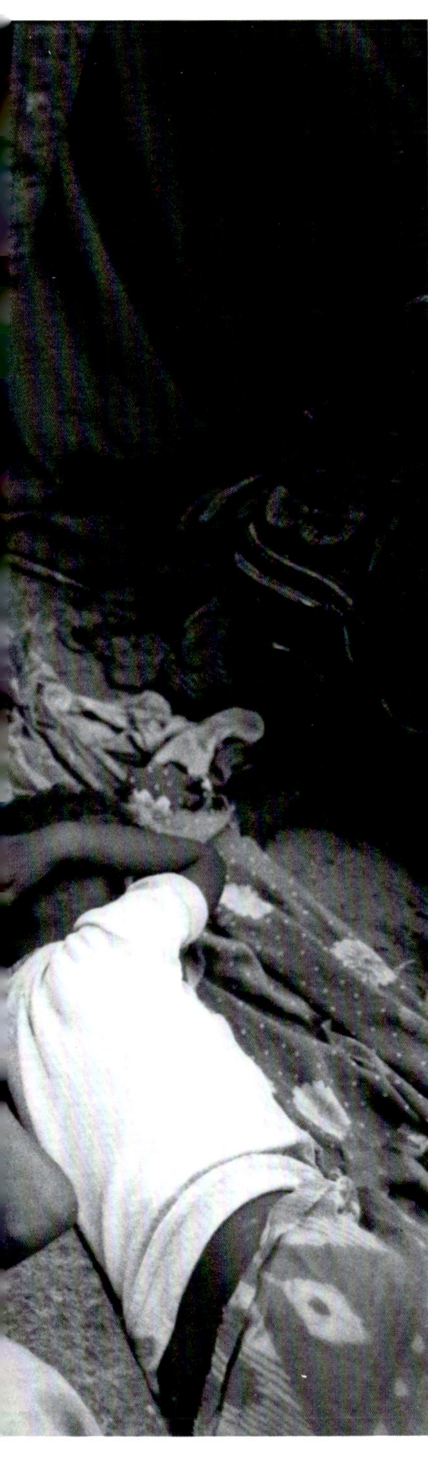

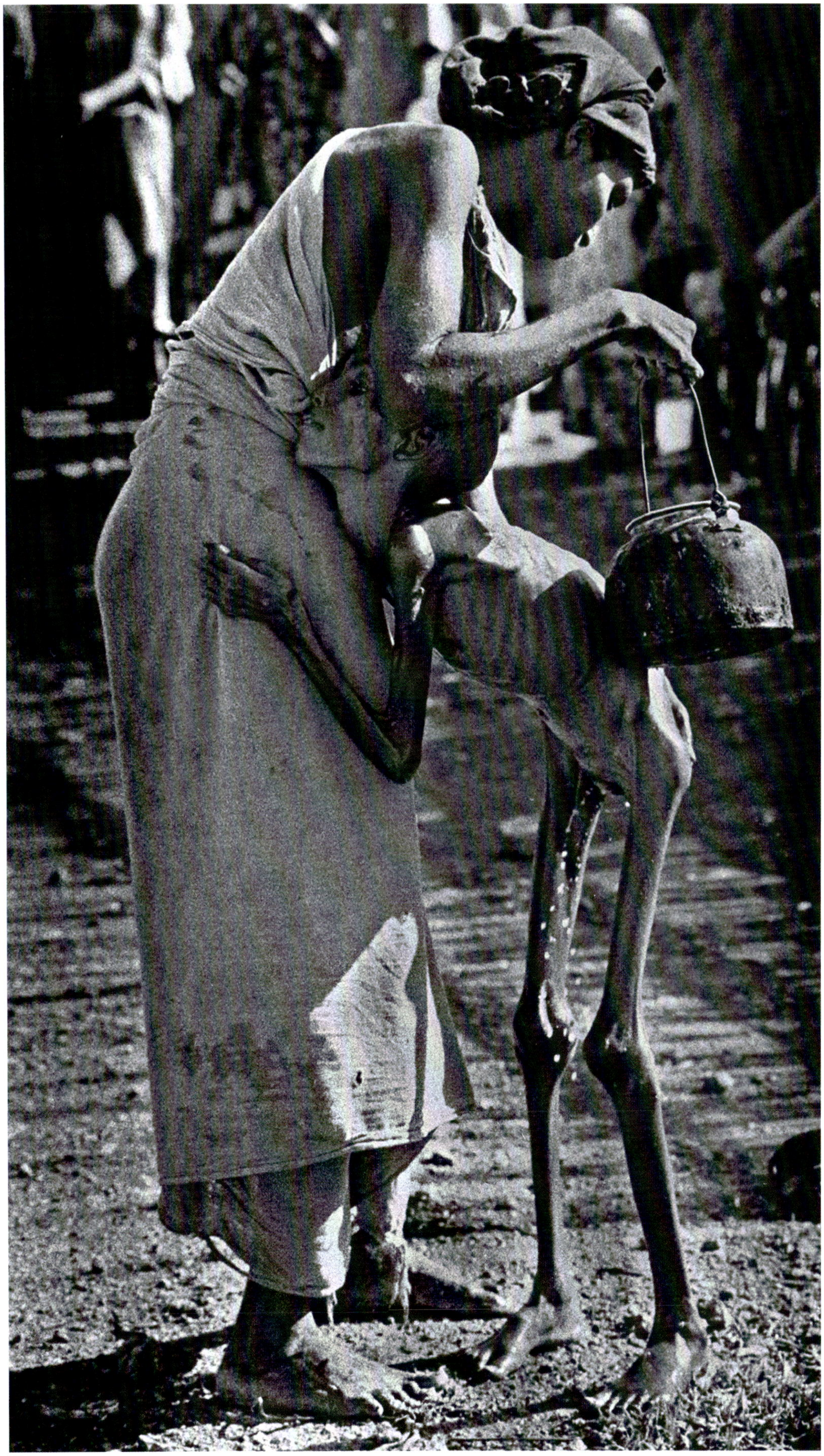

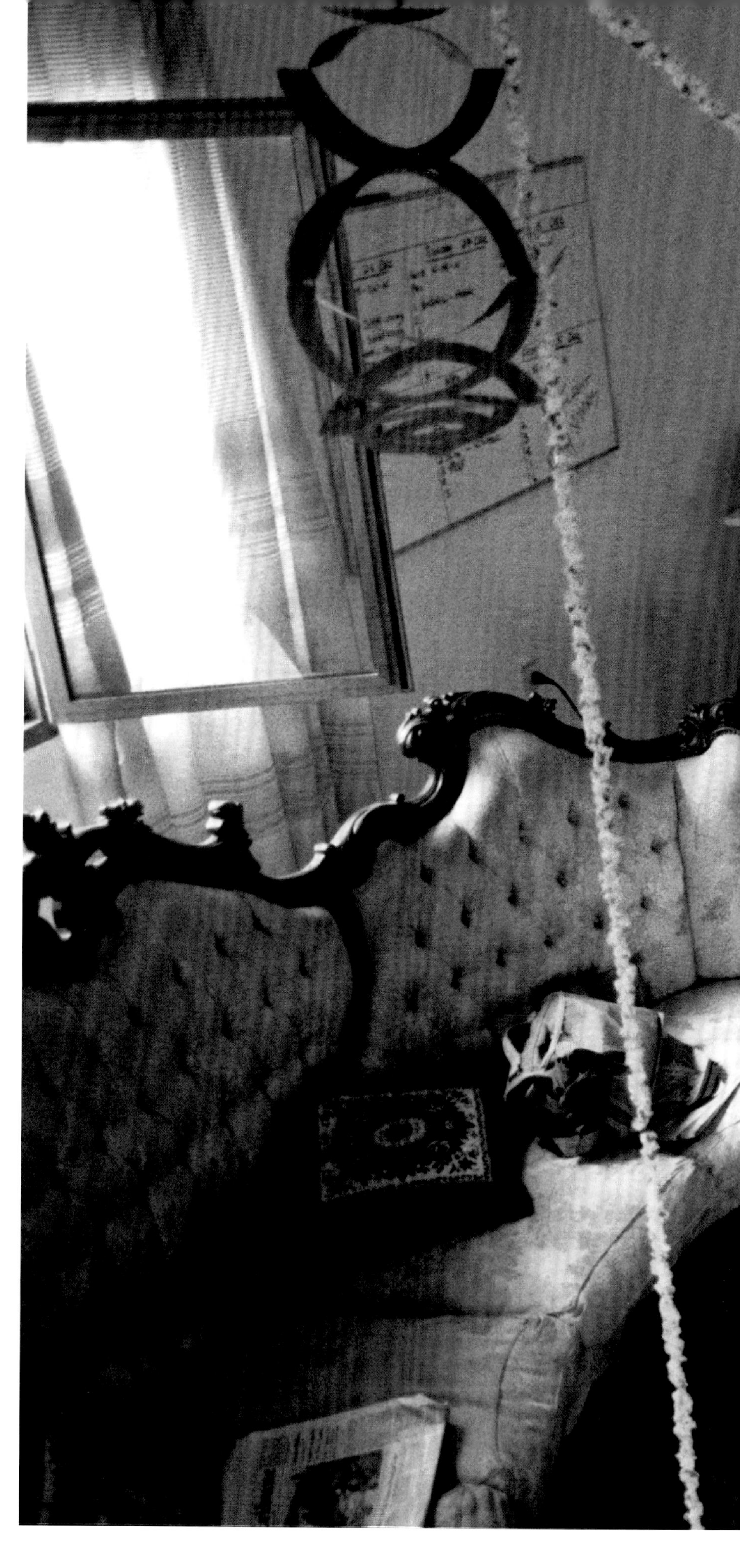

Tim Reese

A volunteer decorates a clinic in Somalia for International Medical Corps doctors and nurses who chose to stay in Somalia and work during the holidays.

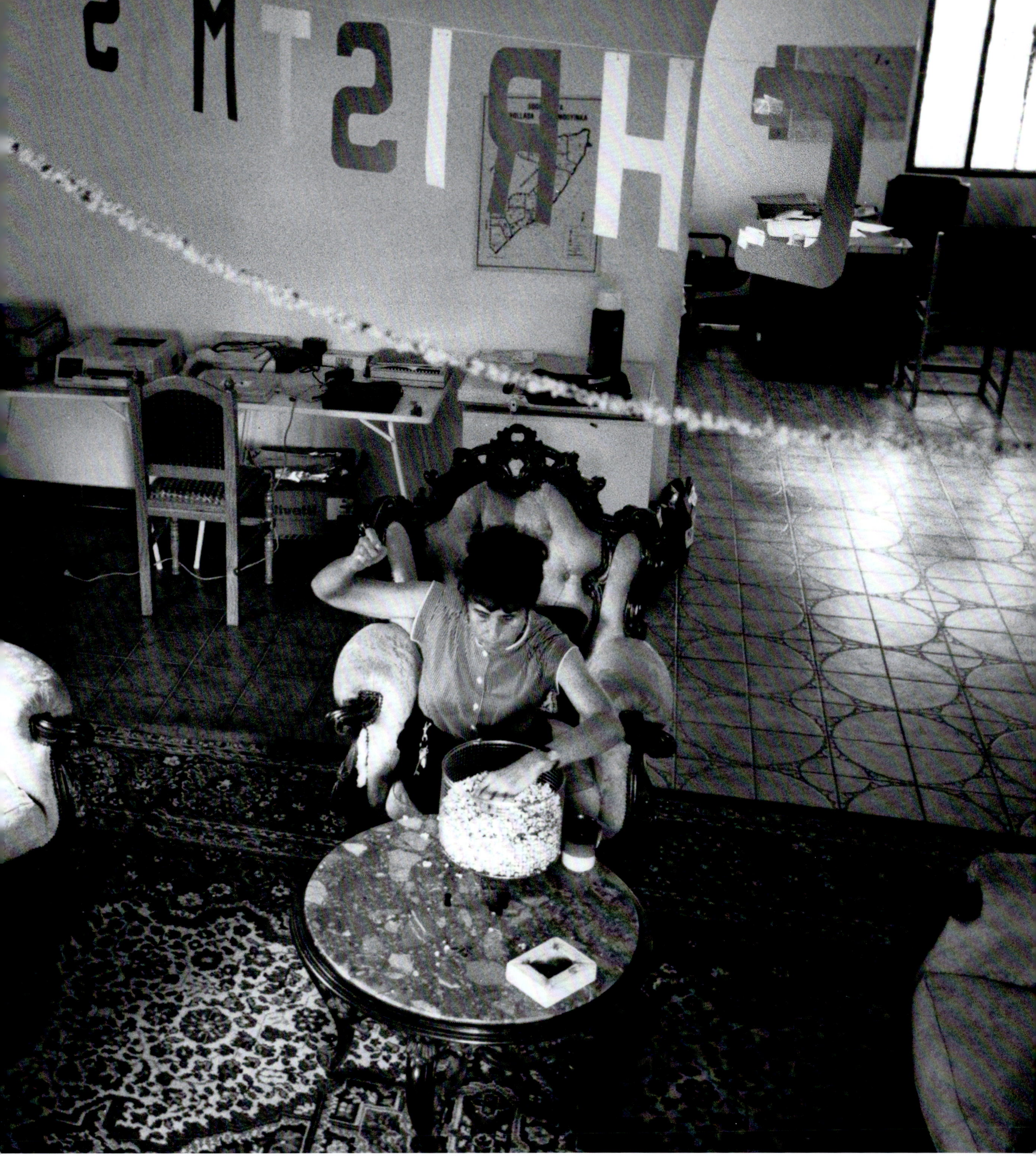

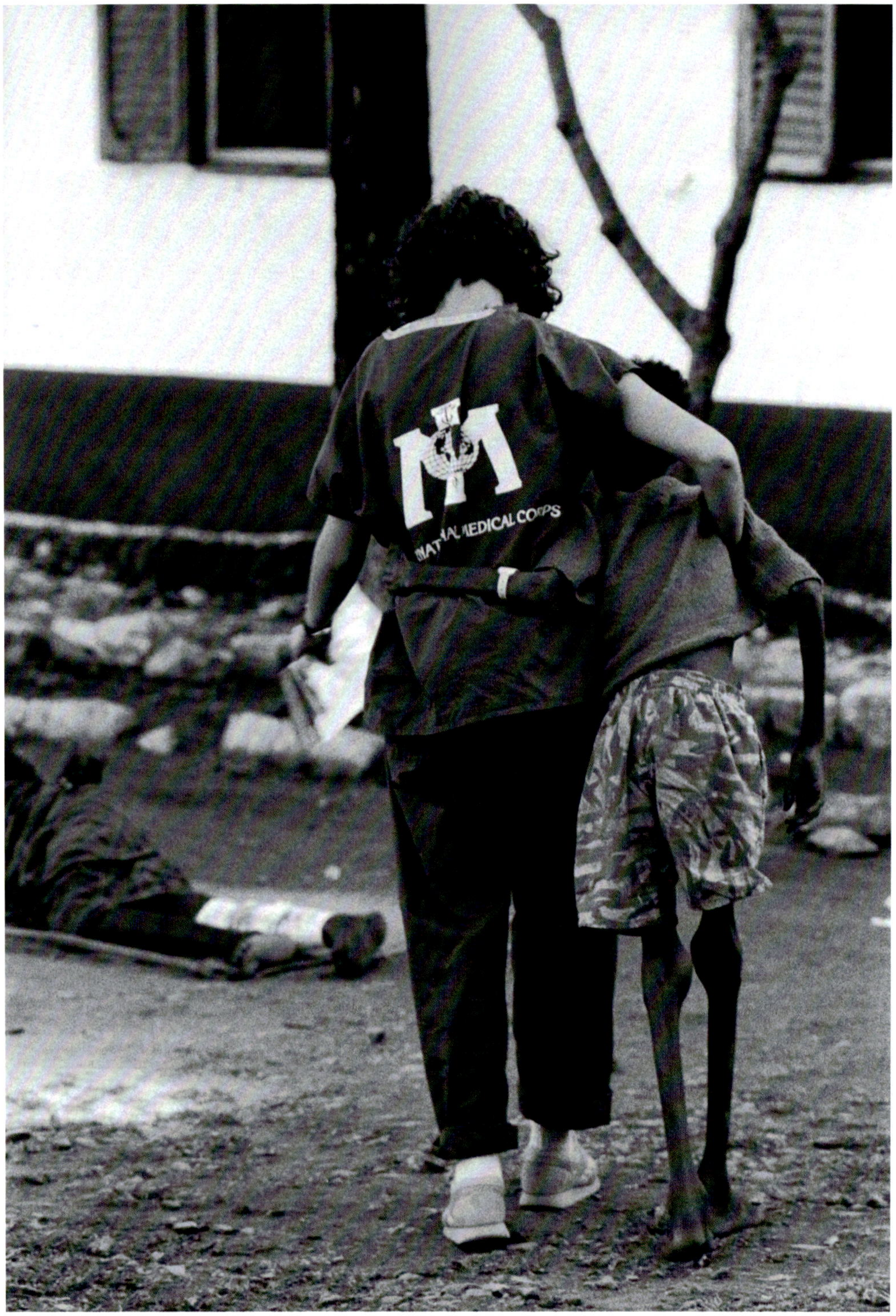

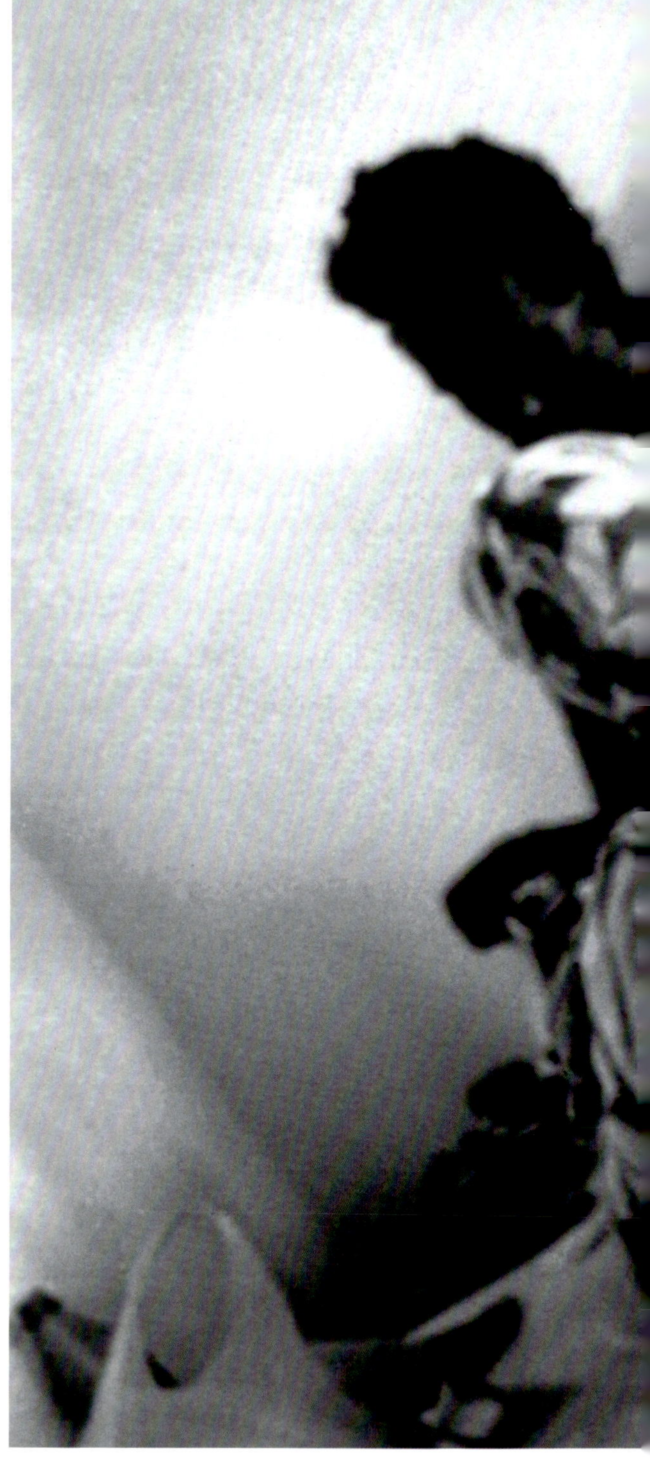

Somalia 1992
Chris Rainier (both photos)

Long after other international agencies pulled out of Somalia, International Medical Corps' community-based health care clinics still functioned as the sole local health provider in many parts of Somalia—regions still haunted by the devastating affects of famine and war.

Opposite page: In Somalia, International Medical Corps opened 103 health posts and six maternal and child health centers targeting nearly 800,000 people—almost 10% of the national population. IMC nurse Theresa Hinkle comforts a young patient in one of those centers.

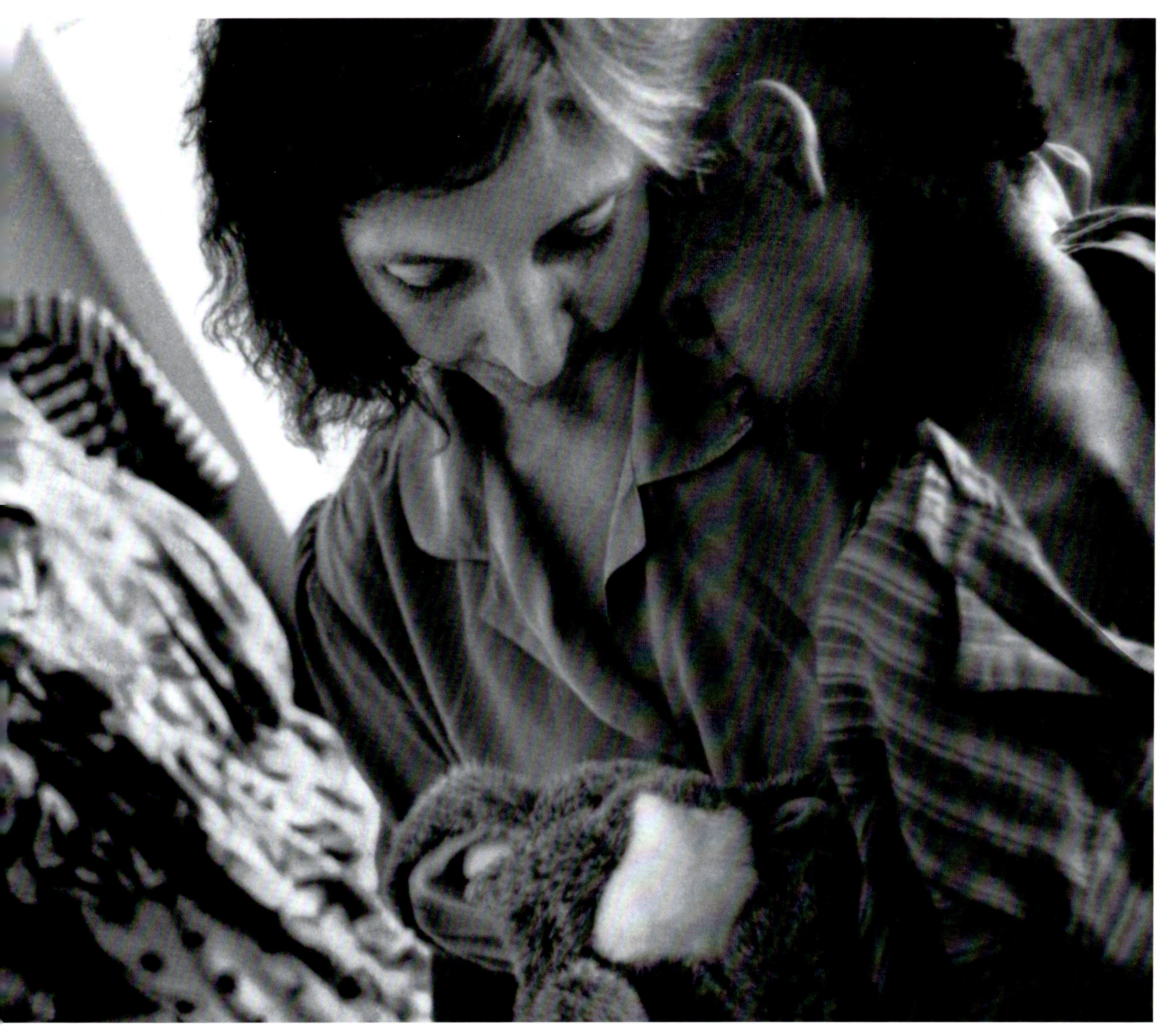

REFUGEE RELIEF

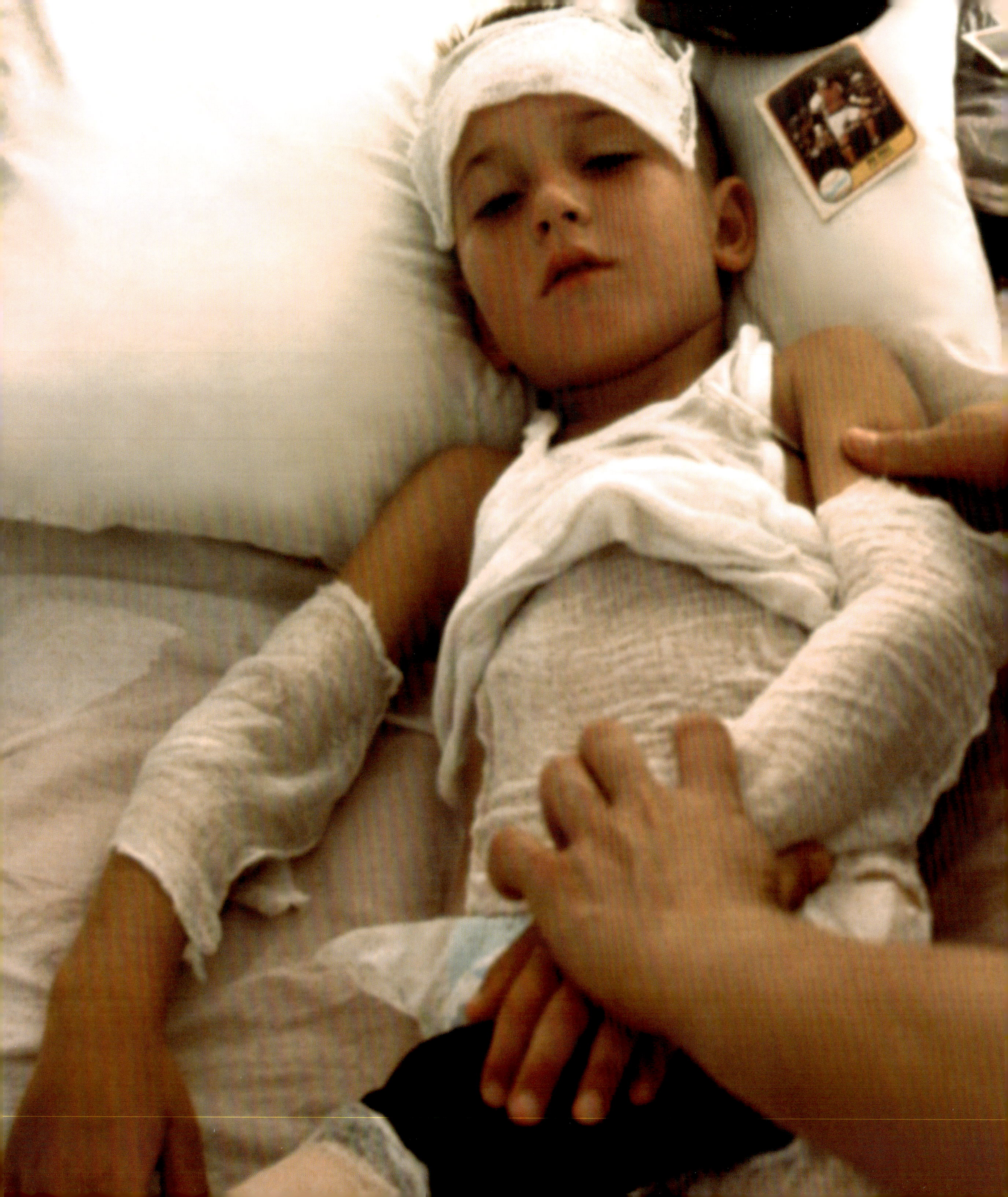

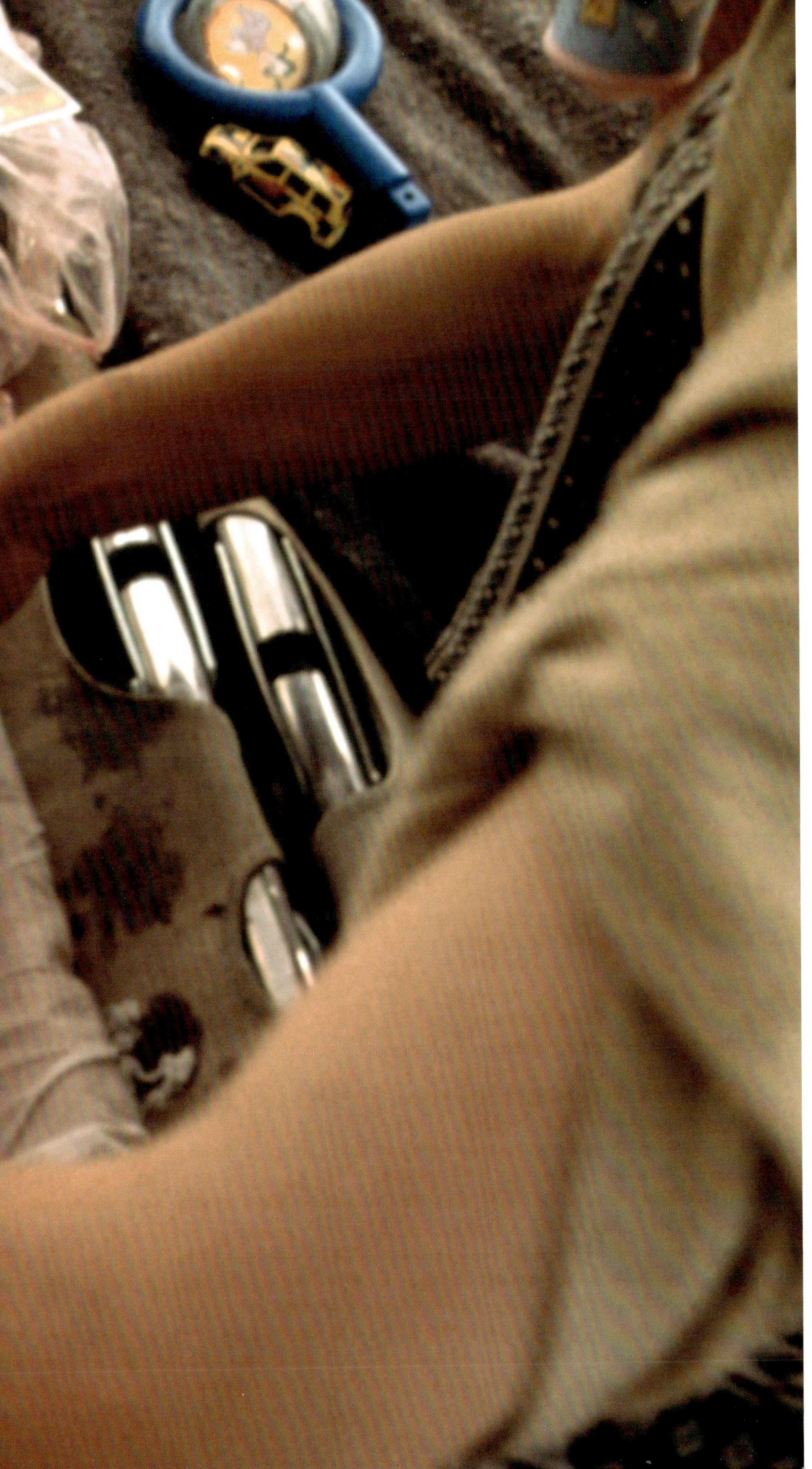

Albania 1999
Danny Hoffman

At International Medical Corps' clinic, a Kosovar boy is treated for severe burns. In 1998 and 1999, more than 2,000 people were killed by violent conflict between Serbian military and Kosovar Albanian resistance forces. International Medical Corps focused on providing medical support and emergency surgery to victims of shootings by Serb forces as well as transporting refugees to safety.

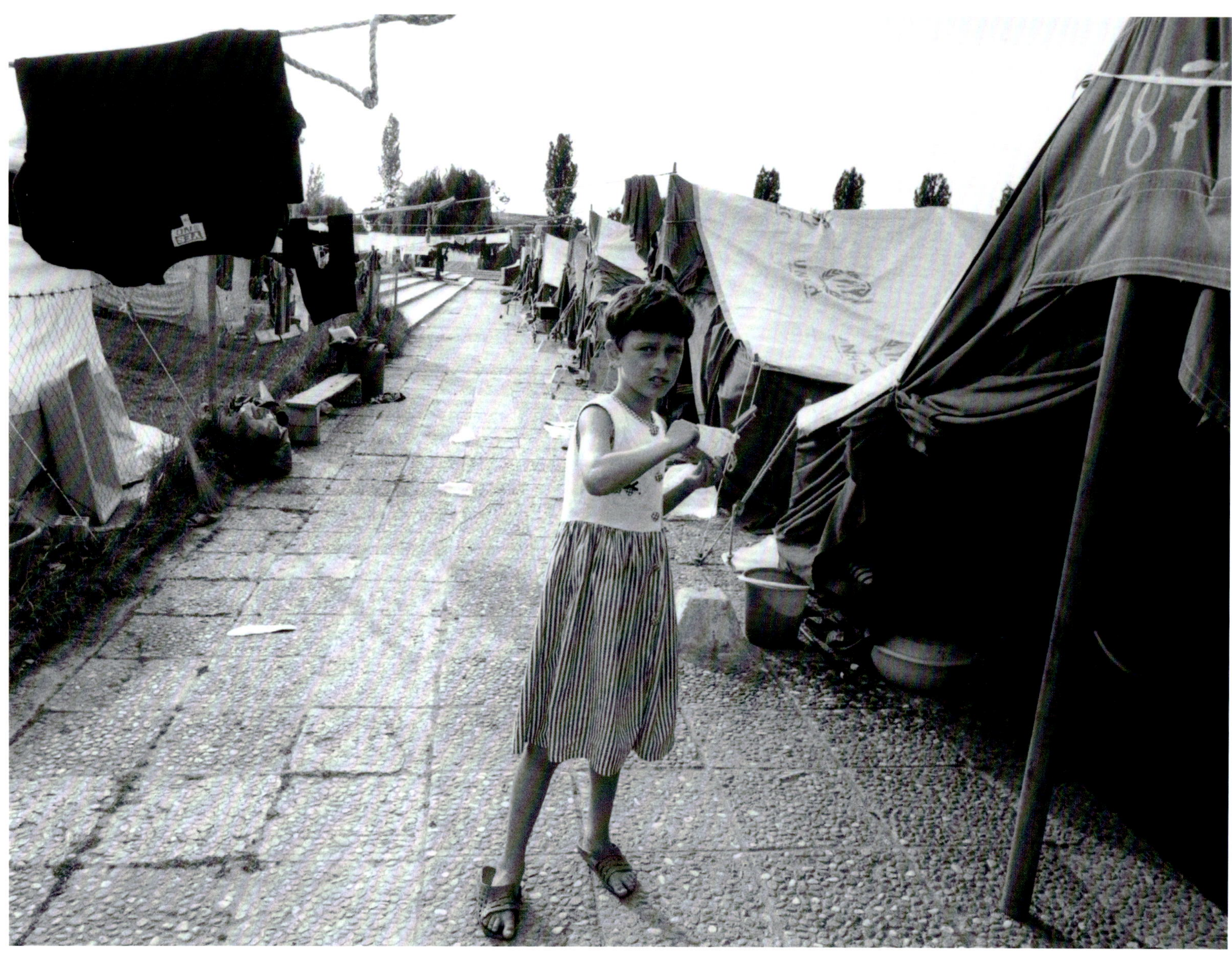

Albania 1999
Marissa Roth (both photos)
A child living with her family in a refugee camp in Tirana, Albania, known as "The Pools" because it was set up in a large park area with a number of abandoned swimming pools. More than 5,000 Kosovar refugees were cared for by various humanitarian organizations, including International Medical Corps.

Opposite page: By mid 1999, 90% of Kosovo's peoples had been expelled from their homes. More than 225,000 Kosovar men were believed to be missing, and at least 5,000 Kosovars had been executed. A Kosovar Albanian refugee waits with her child in front of an embassy, hoping to get a visa to leave Tirana, Albania.

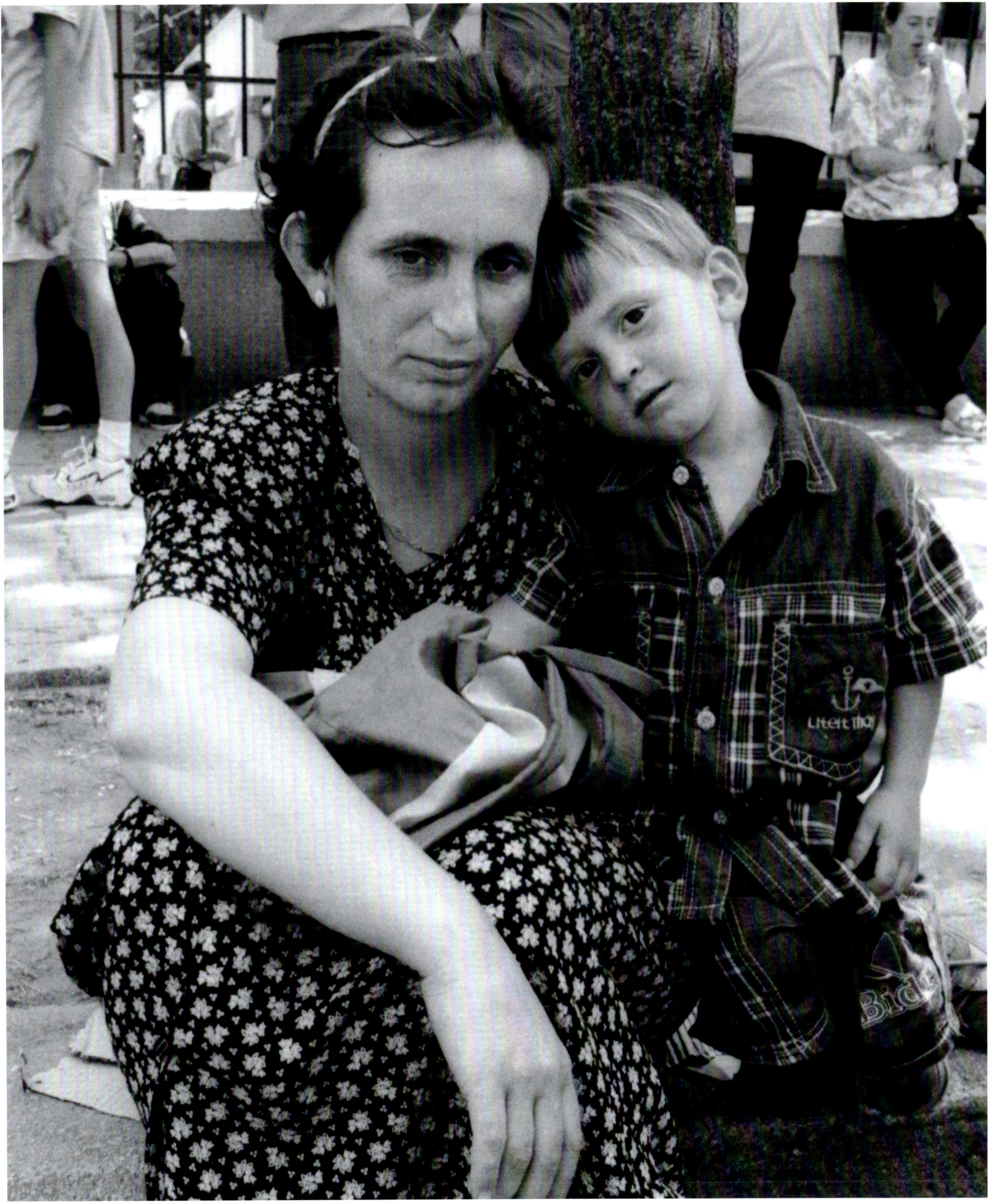

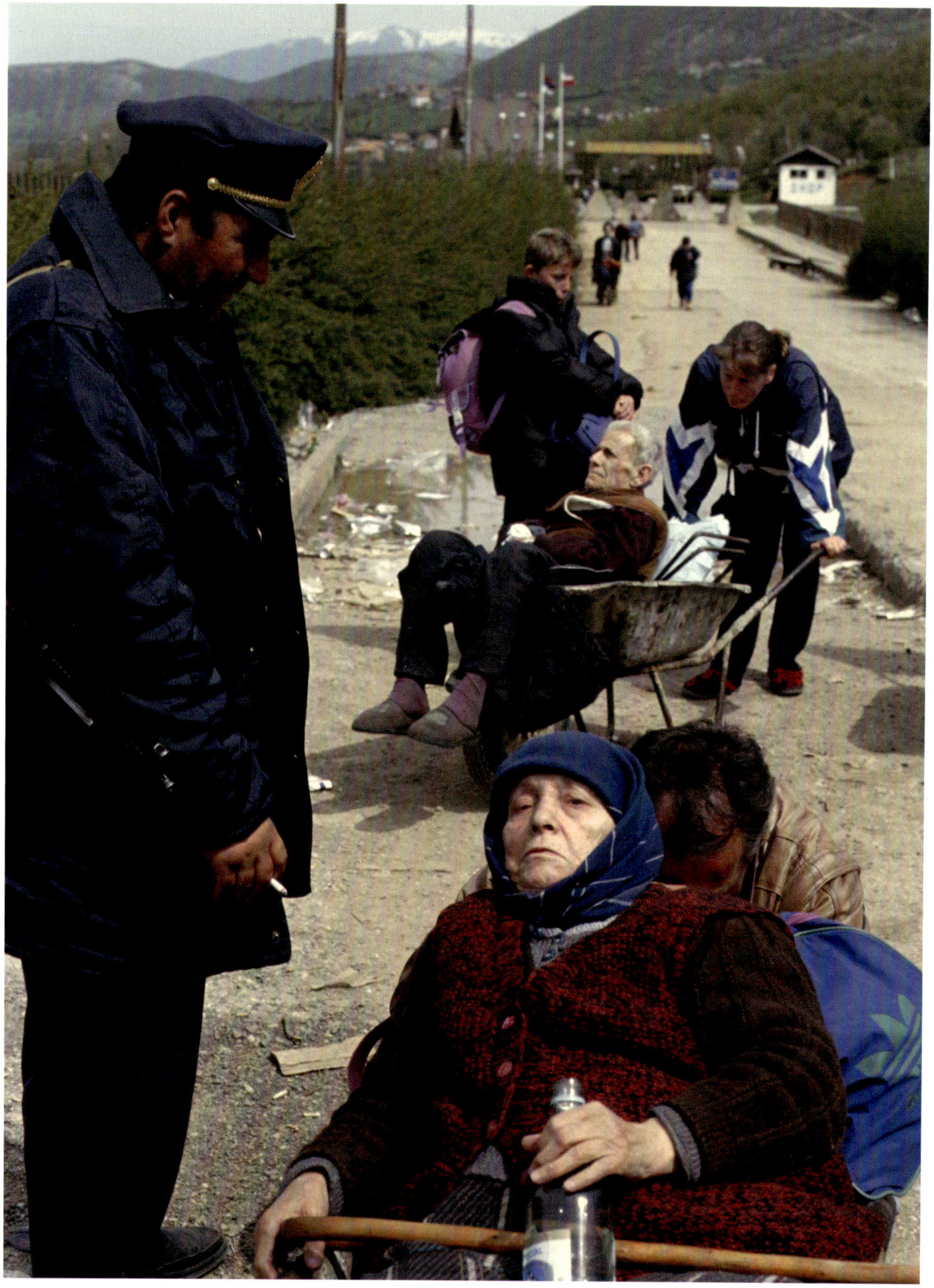

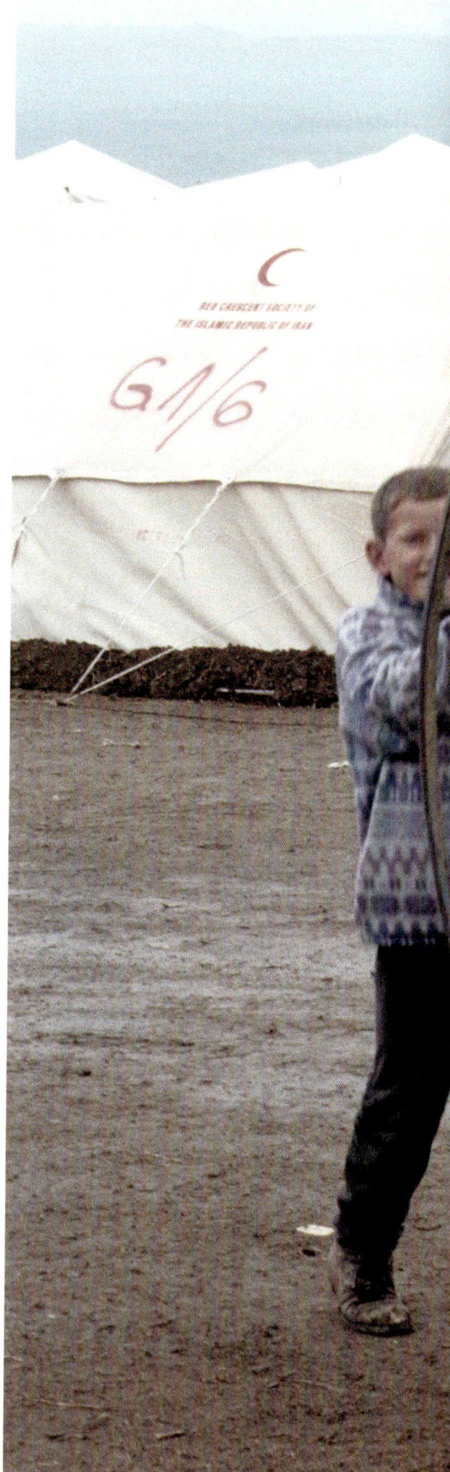

Albania 1999
IMC staff (both photos)

In 1998, when their houses, villages and crops were destroyed by the violence, almost half a million Kosovar Albanians were forced from their homes and into the International Medical Corps displaced persons camp in Albania.

Above: As Albanian families fled their homes, the migration on foot was difficult. Many elderly family members were transported across the treacherous terrain in wheelbarrows.

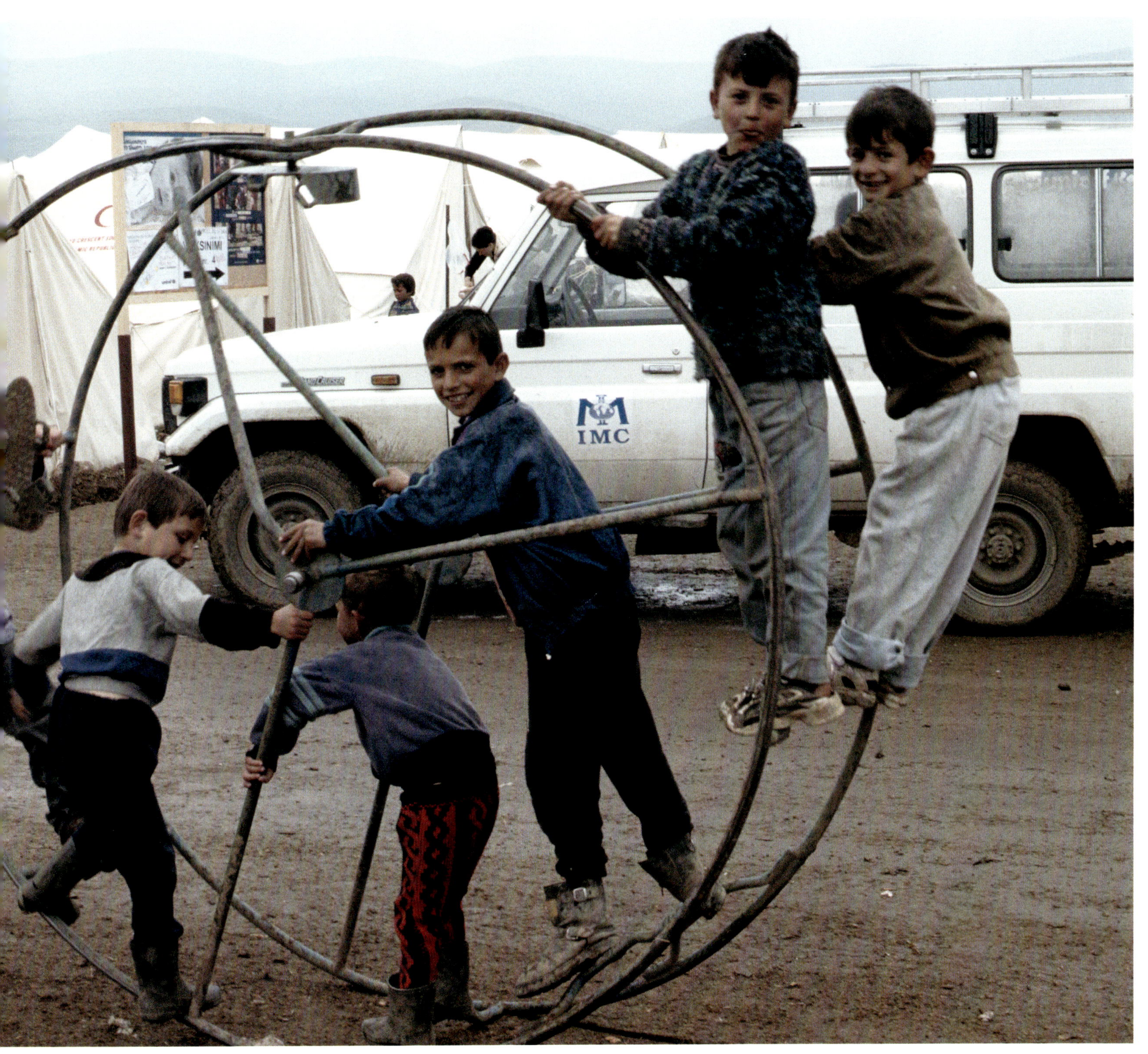
IMC

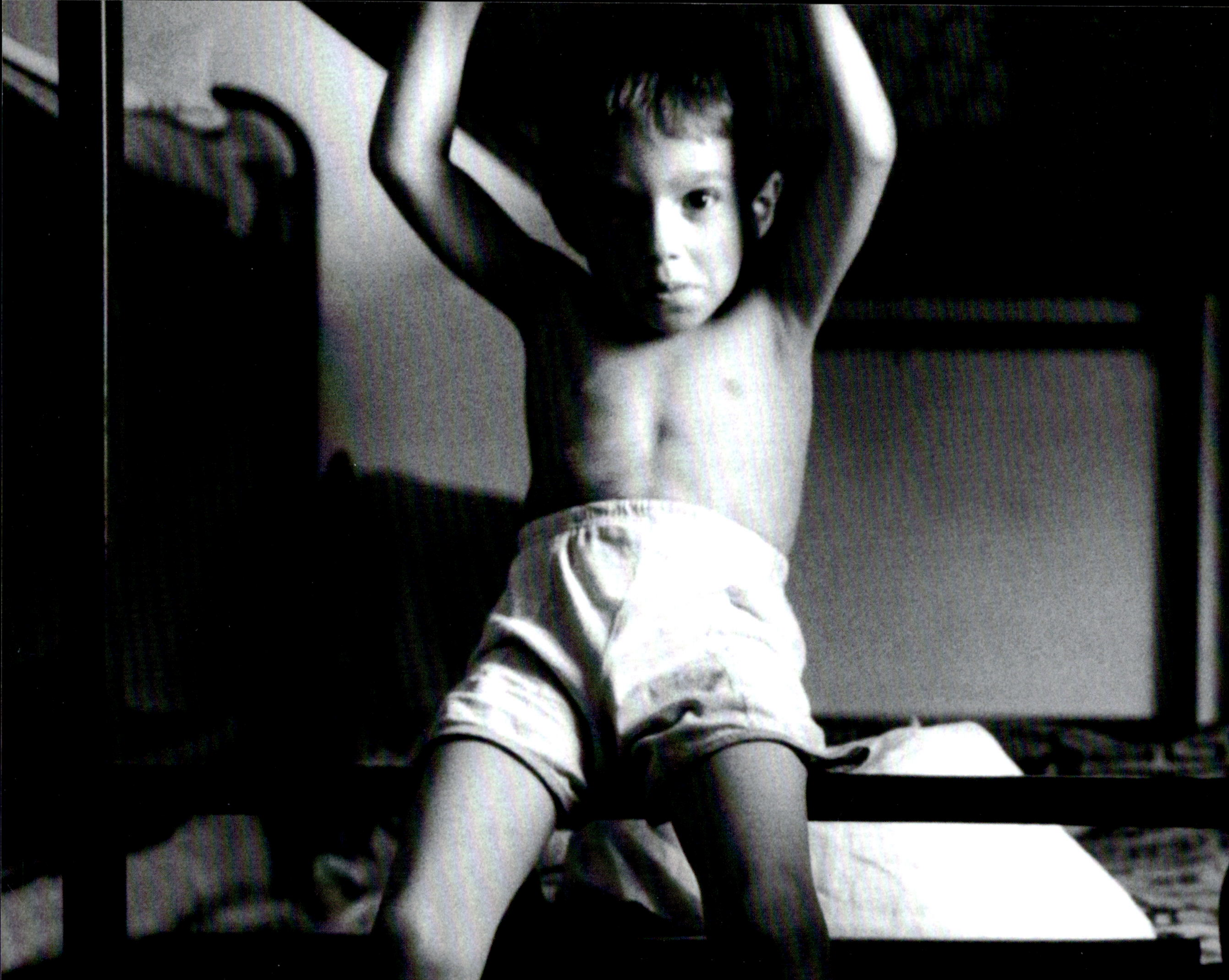

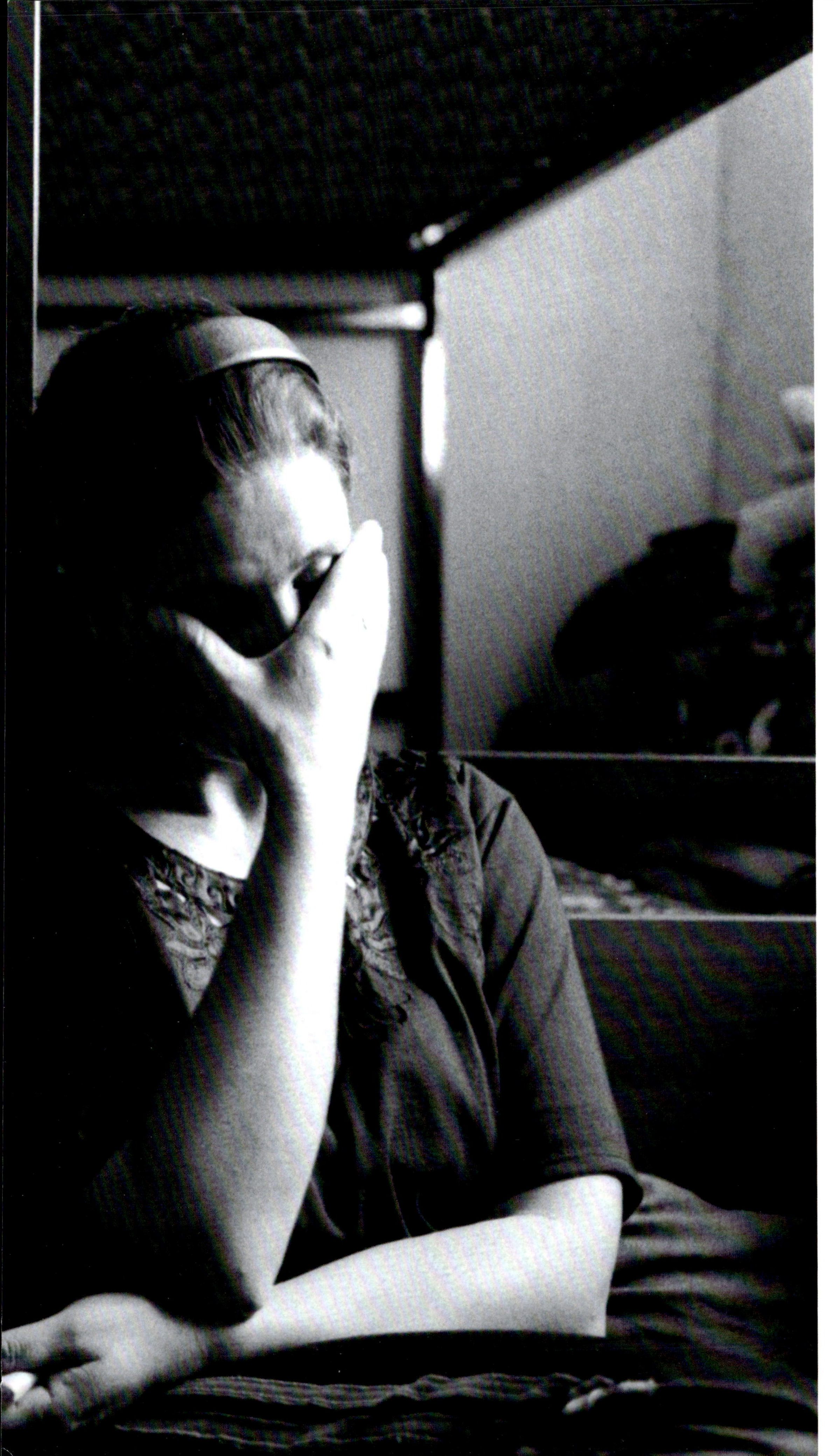

Albania 1999
Marissa Roth

In a warehouse in Tirana, Albania where refugees were being housed, a 29-year-old woman, who lost her three children and all five of her nieces and nephews in the bombing of her home, sits at the edge of her bunk. The boy to her left is the child of other refugees.

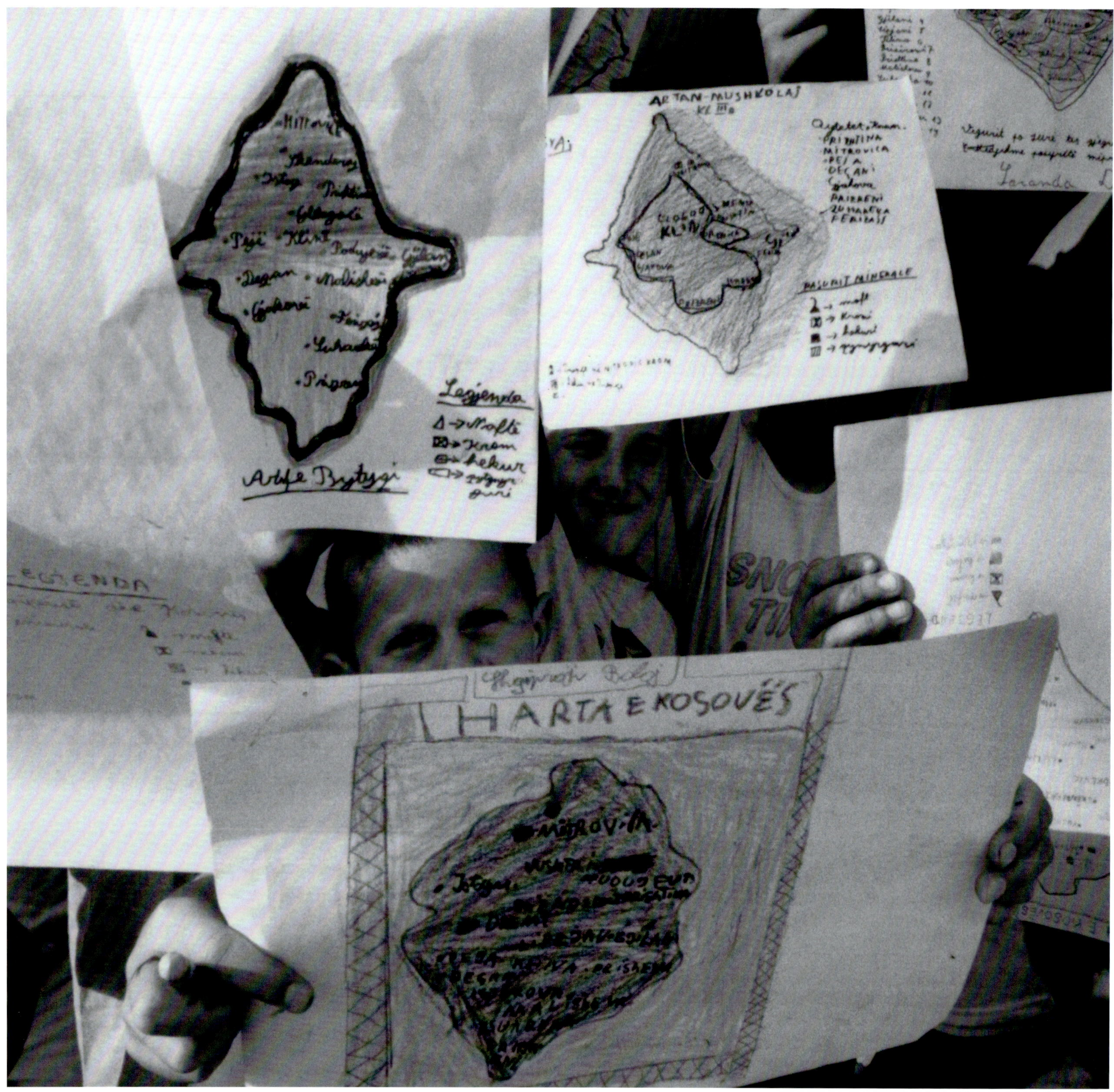

Albania 1999
Marissa Roth (both photos)

At an International Medical Corps clinic in a refugee camp in Tirana, Albania, children in a makeshift camp classroom display maps they drew of Kosovo.

Opposite page: The refugee camp in Tirana, Albania was known as "The Pools" because it was set up in a large park area with a number of abandoned swimming pools. About 5,000 Kosovar refugees lived at The Pools.

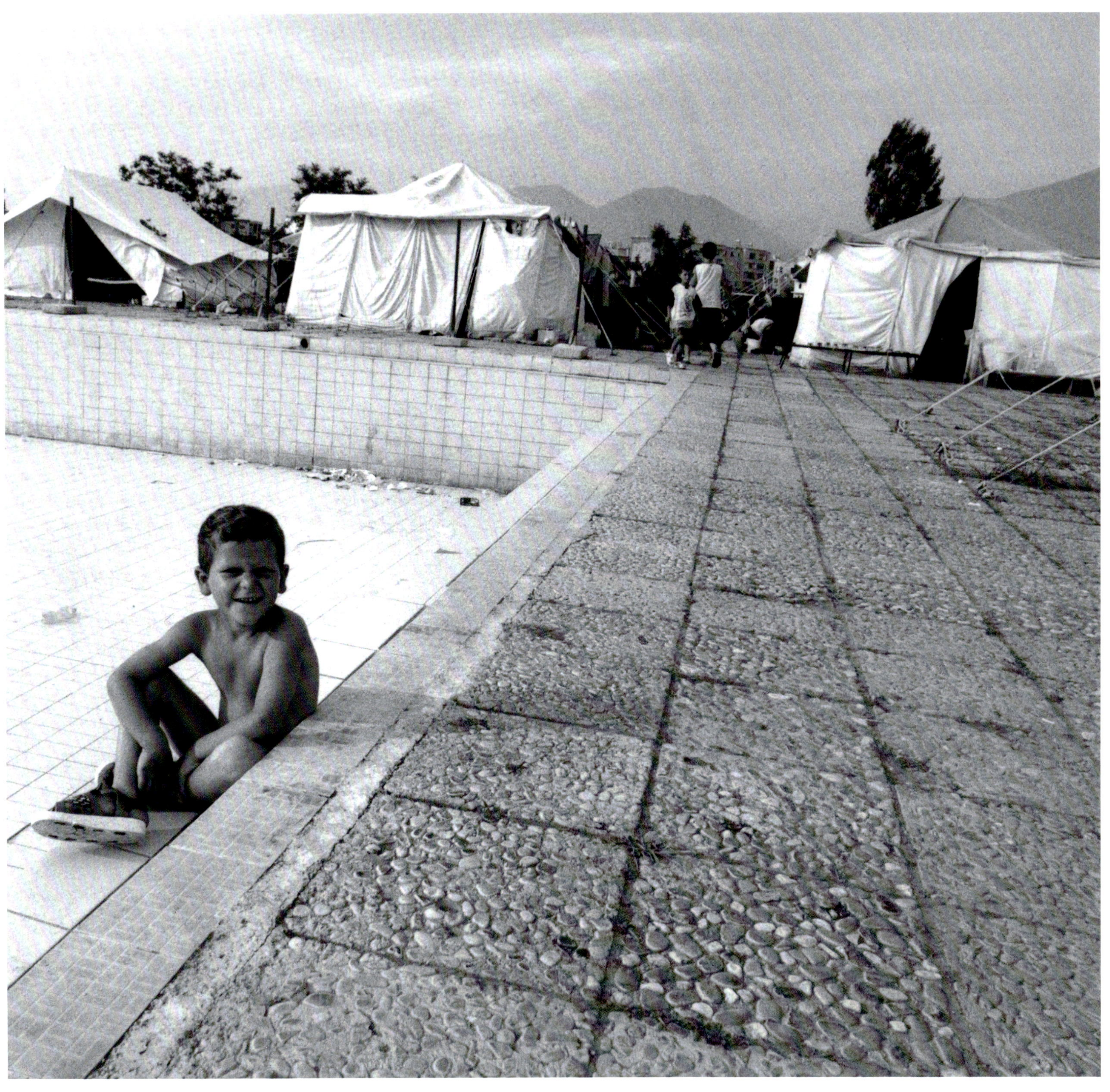

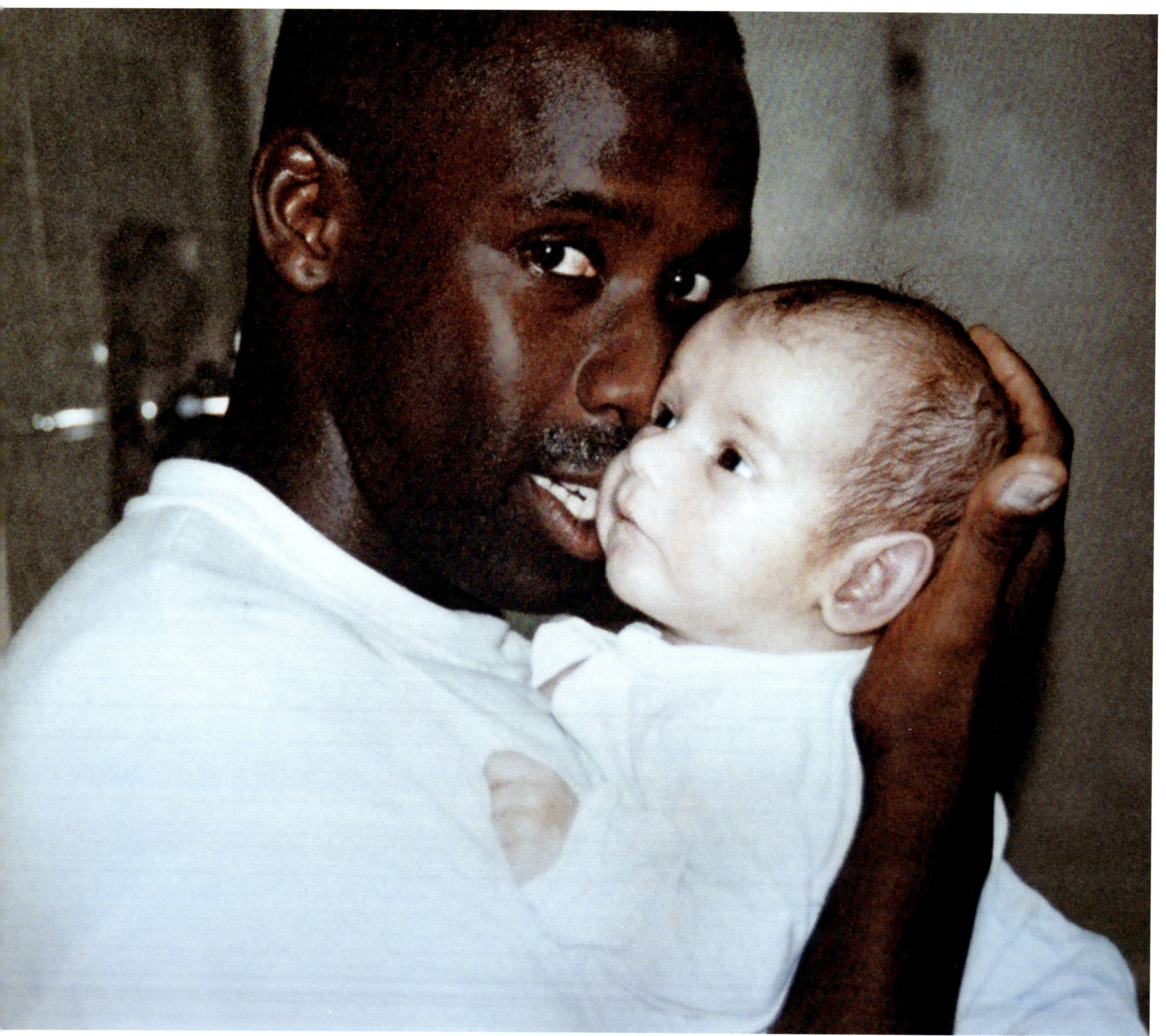

Albania 1998
IMC staff

International Medical Corps had already been working in pre-war Albania before the ethnic cleansing and violence began in 1999. Maternal and child health services were the main priorities of the IMC clinics before the war. An IMC volunteer holds a newborn baby born in the Albanian IMC clinic.

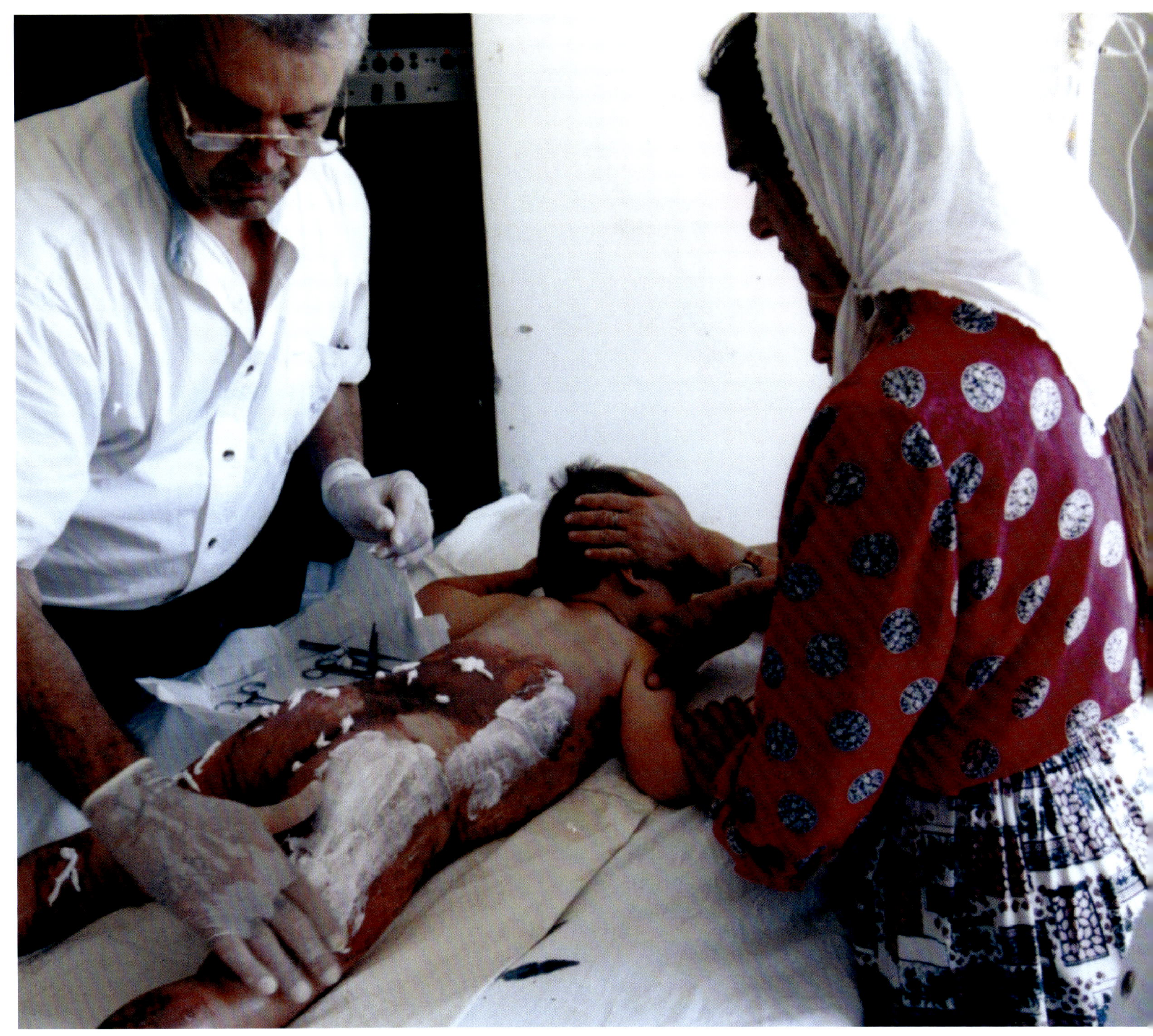

Albania 1999
IMC staff

Because International Medical Corps was already present in Albania, it was quick to respond to the medical needs of victims of the violence early on in the conflict. Many children were treated for burns and gunshot wounds in IMC clinics already operating there.

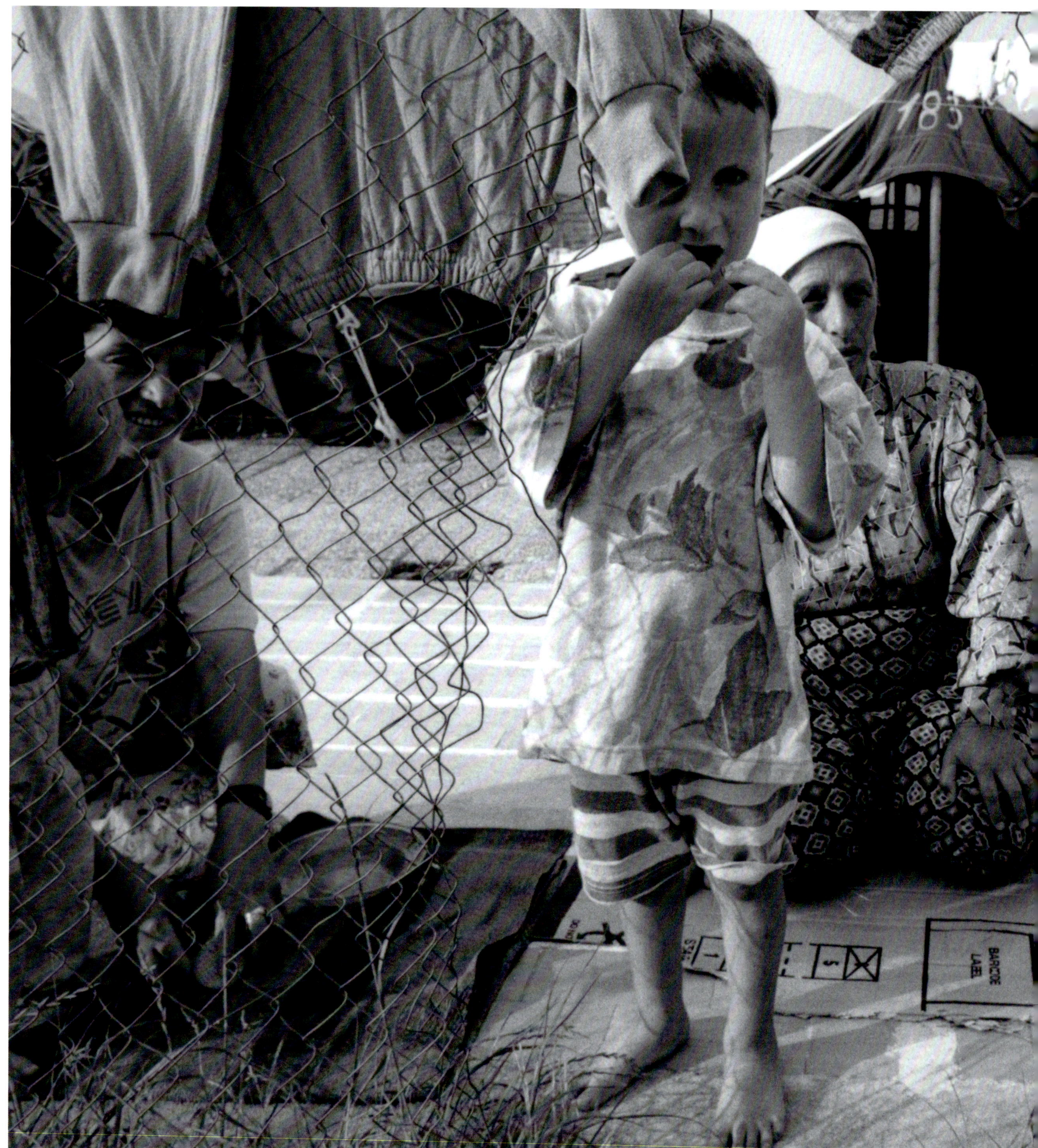

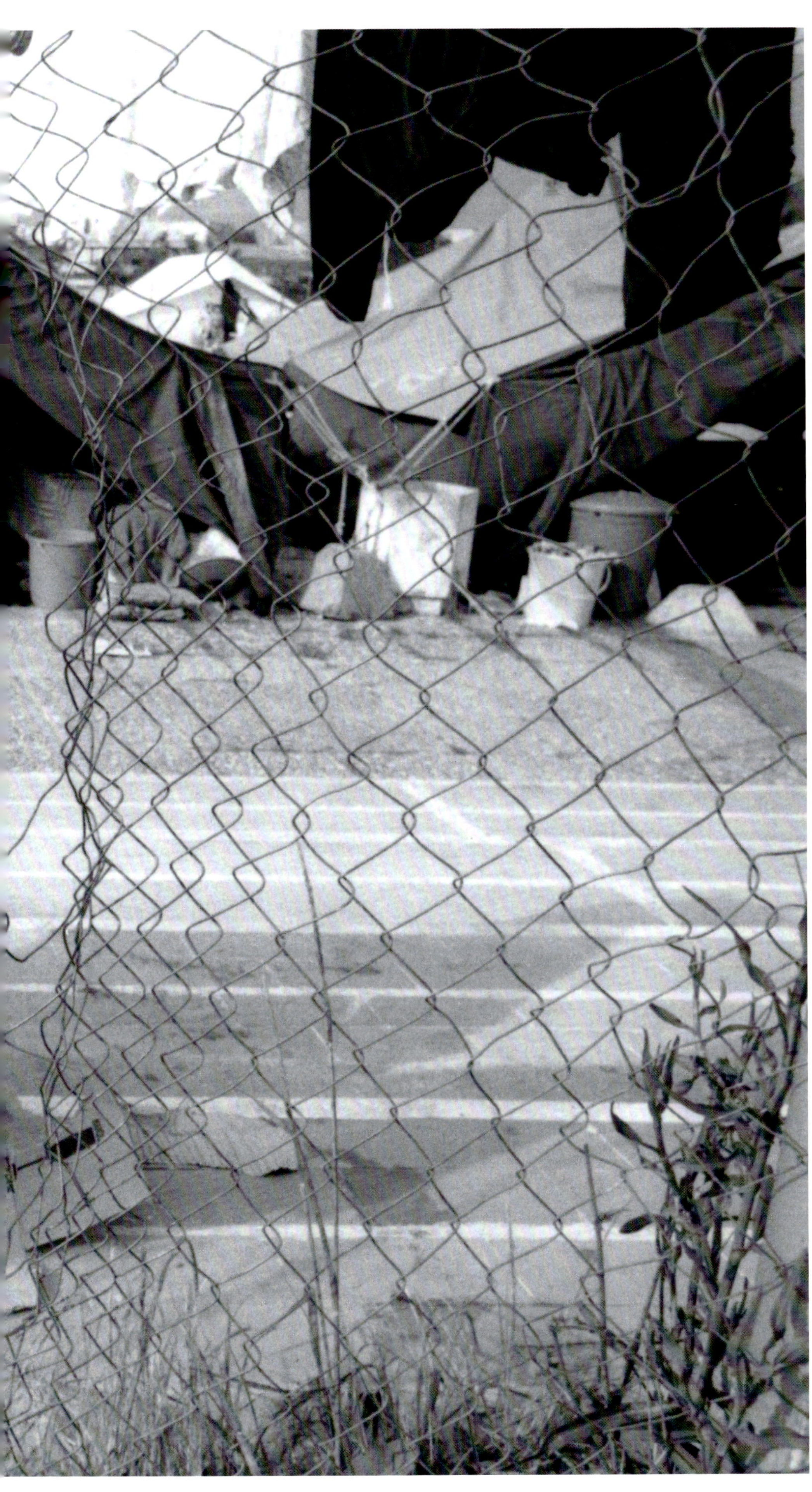

Albania 1999
Marissa Roth
International Medical Corps camps for displaced people housed thousands of children and provided food, water and medical services to families living there.

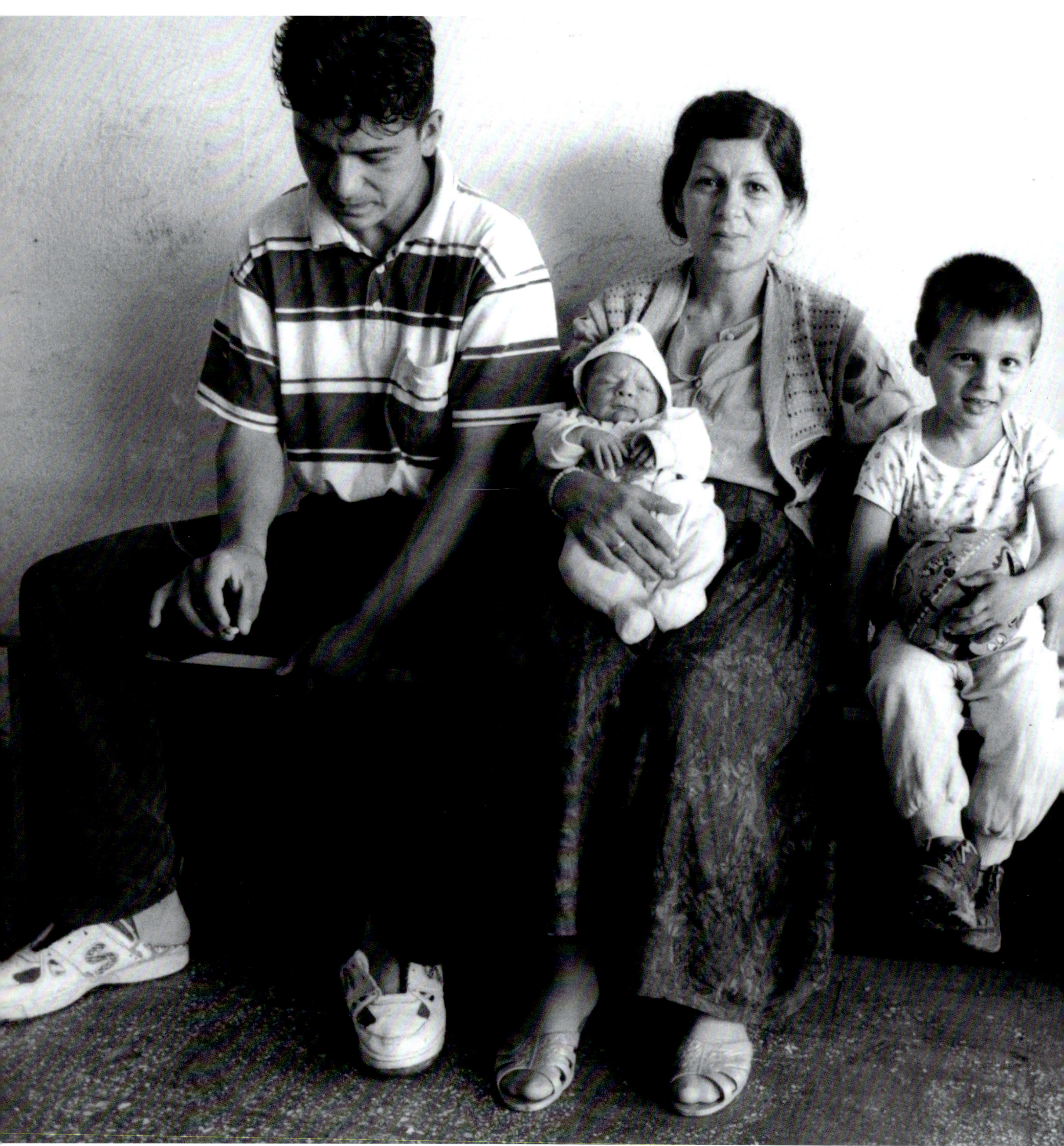

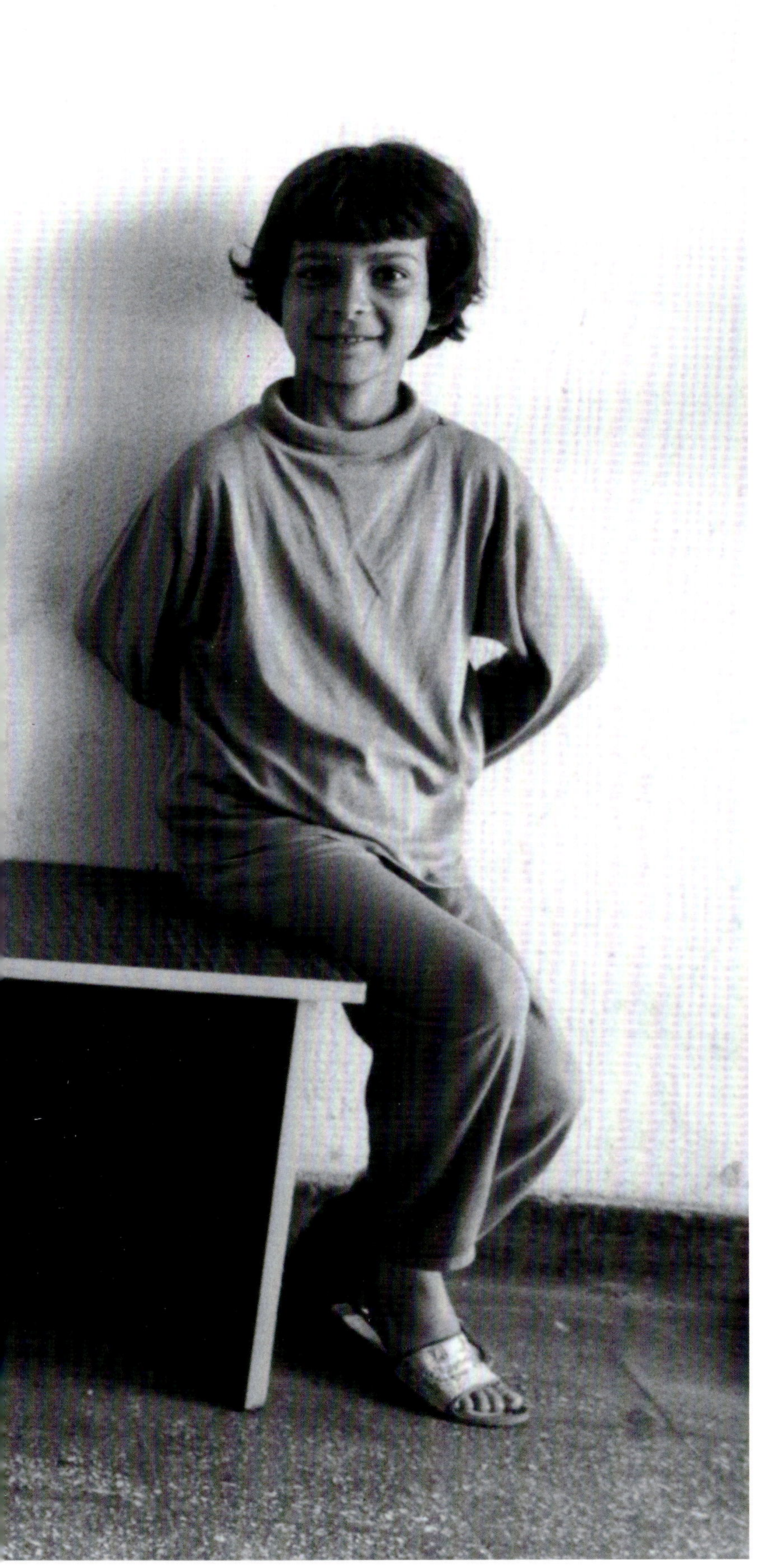

Albania 1999
Marissa Roth

Refugees from Peja, a small city in Kosovo, were sheltered in an abandoned warehouse in Tirana, Albania. A mother sits with her two children and her baby, who was born in the International Medical Corps camp. The man on the left is not related to them.

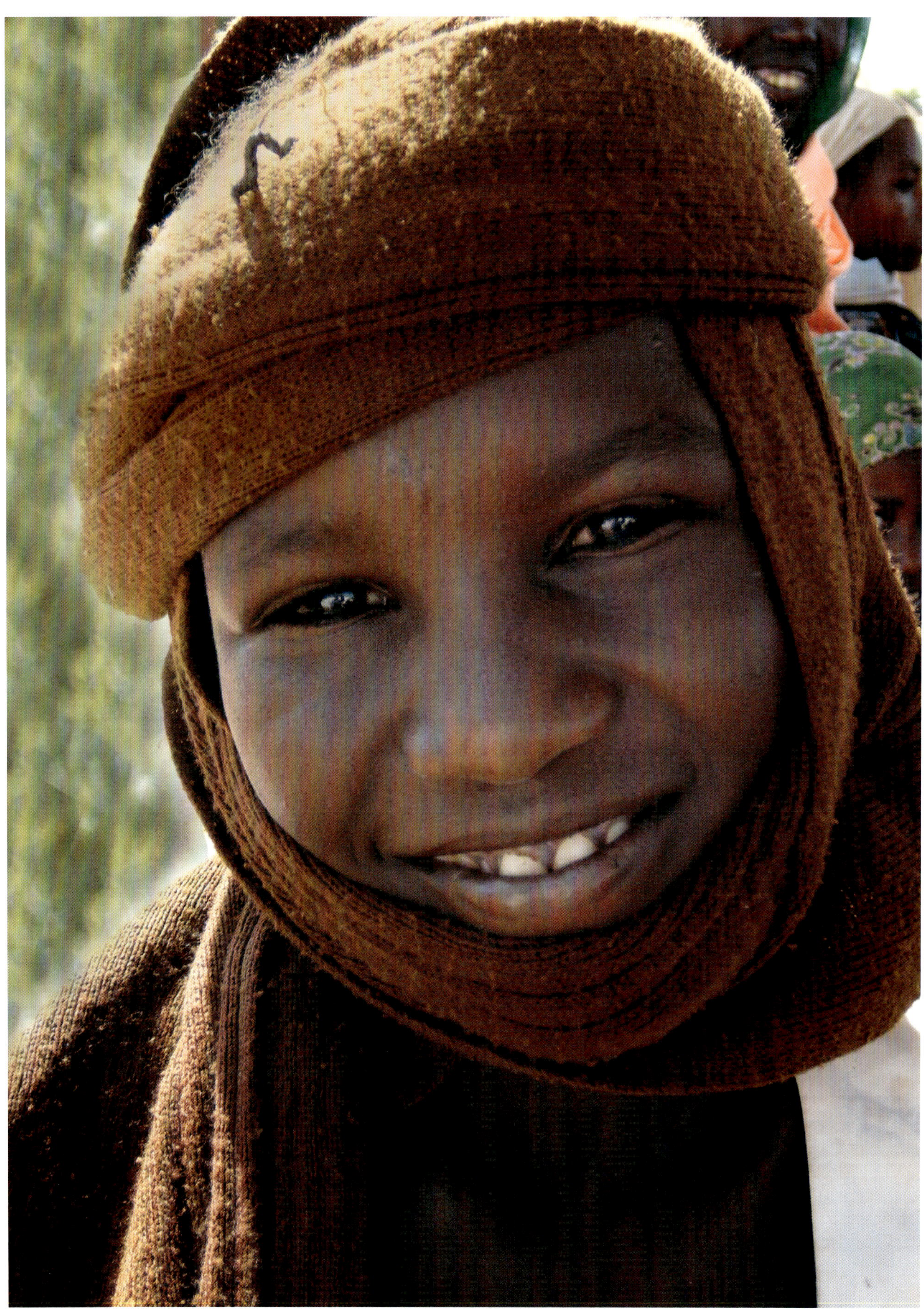

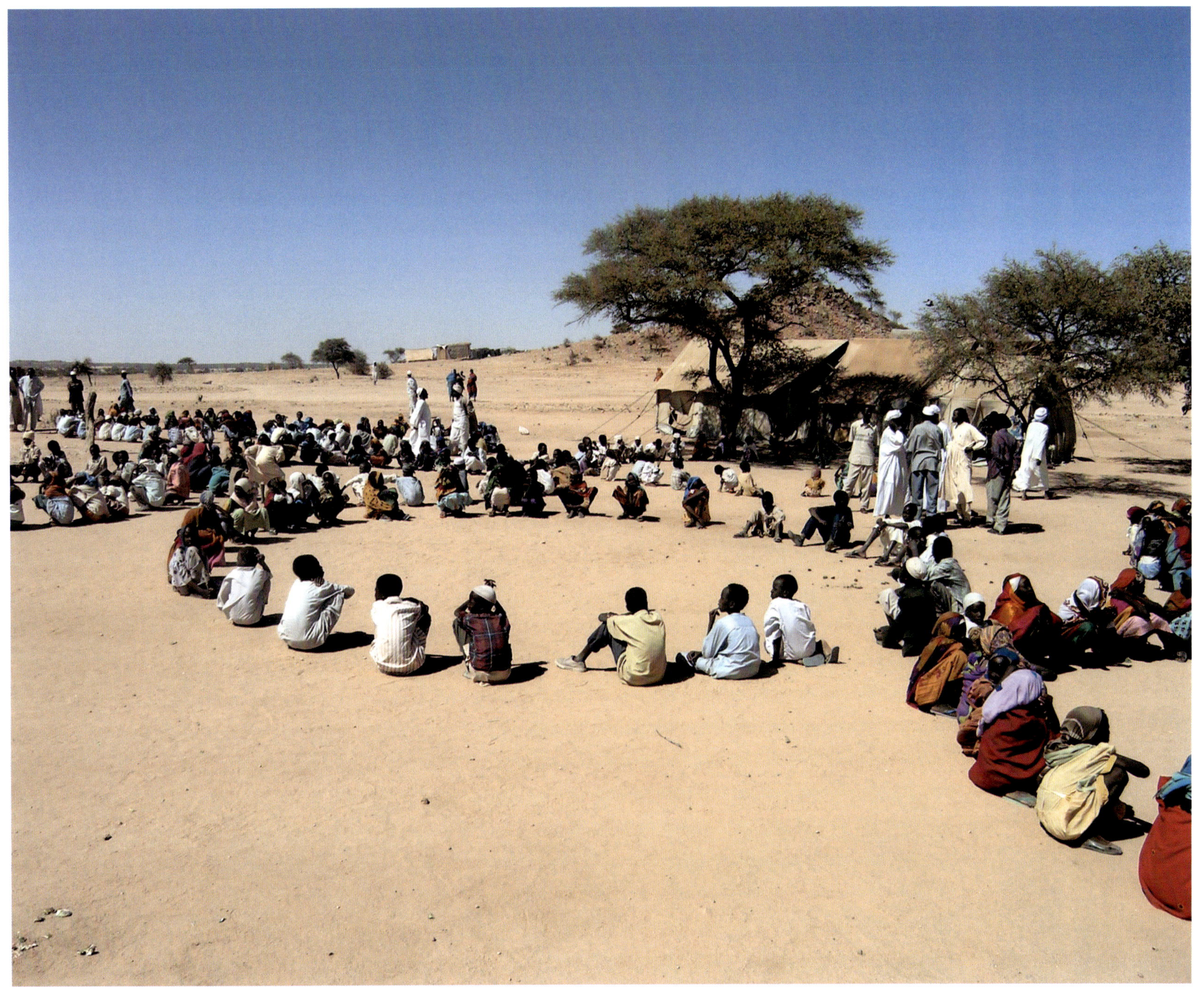

Chad 2005
IMC Staff (both photos)

In 2005, more than 200,000 Sudanese refugees lived in Eastern Chad. Most had lost nearly everything and had endured the journey into one of the most resource-poor environments in the world. Their influx severely strained the host populations' natural and social resources and challenged International Medical Corps' capacity to treat the people of the region.

Opposite page: International Medical Corps began providing health care to Sudanese refugees and local Chadian communities in 2004, shortly after intense fighting forced hundreds of thousands of people to flee the Darfur region of Sudan and cross the border into Chad.

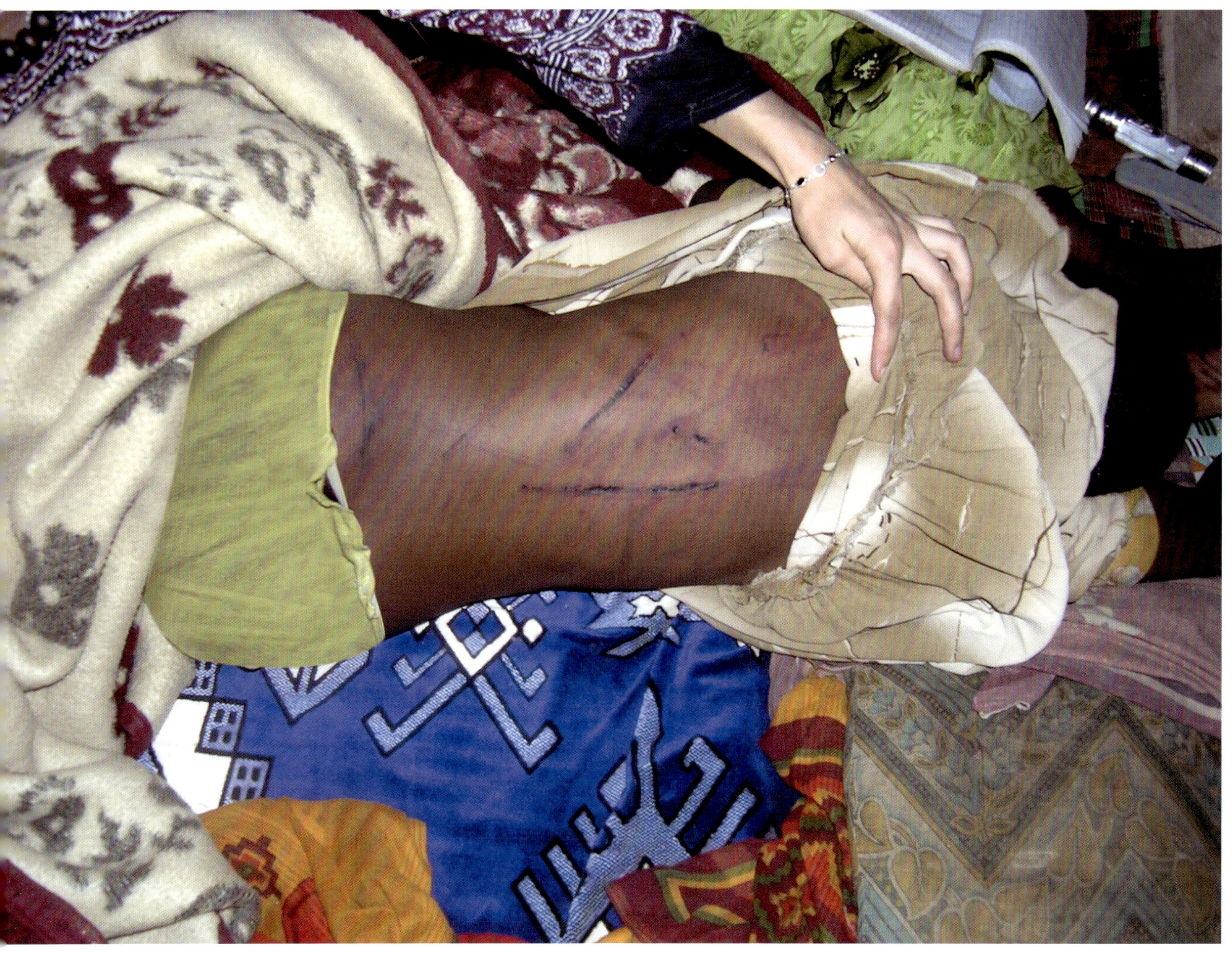

Chad 2005
IMC staff (all photos)

When a scarcity of wood for cooking, a lack of water for animals, and overgrazing began to manifest itself in random attacks between Sudanese and Chadian communities, and when Chadians started posing as refugees at Sudanese refugee camps in an effort to receive health care, International Medical Corps recognized the need for outreach directed at the Chadian host population as well as Sudanese refugees.

Opposite page: Sharing their meager means with refugees since 2003, Chadians became just as vulnerable to malnutrition and disease as the Sudanese refugees. IMC administered a broad range of health care services to the estimated 80% of people in Chad that live below the poverty line.

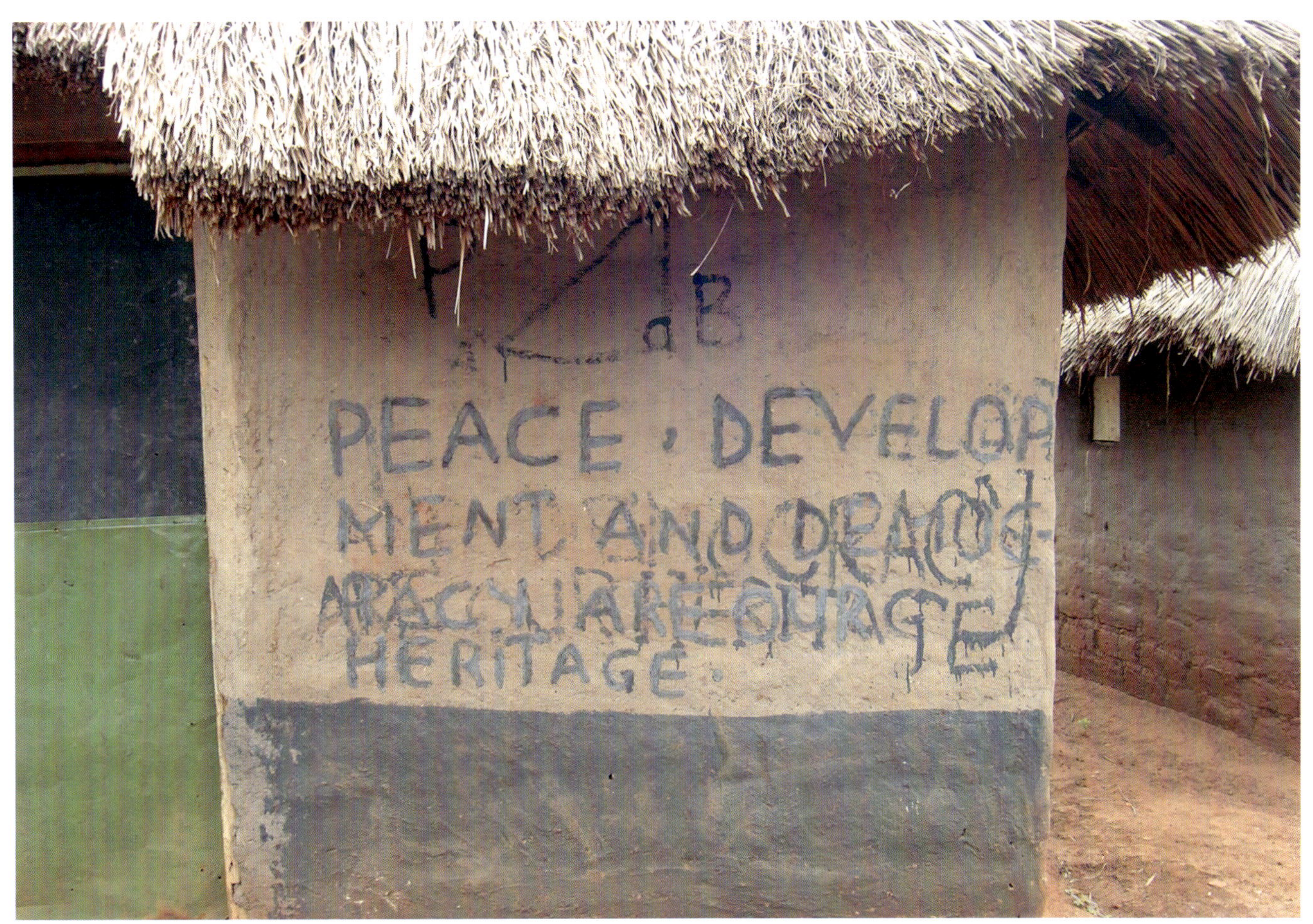
PEACE , DEVELOP
MENT AND
HERITAGE.

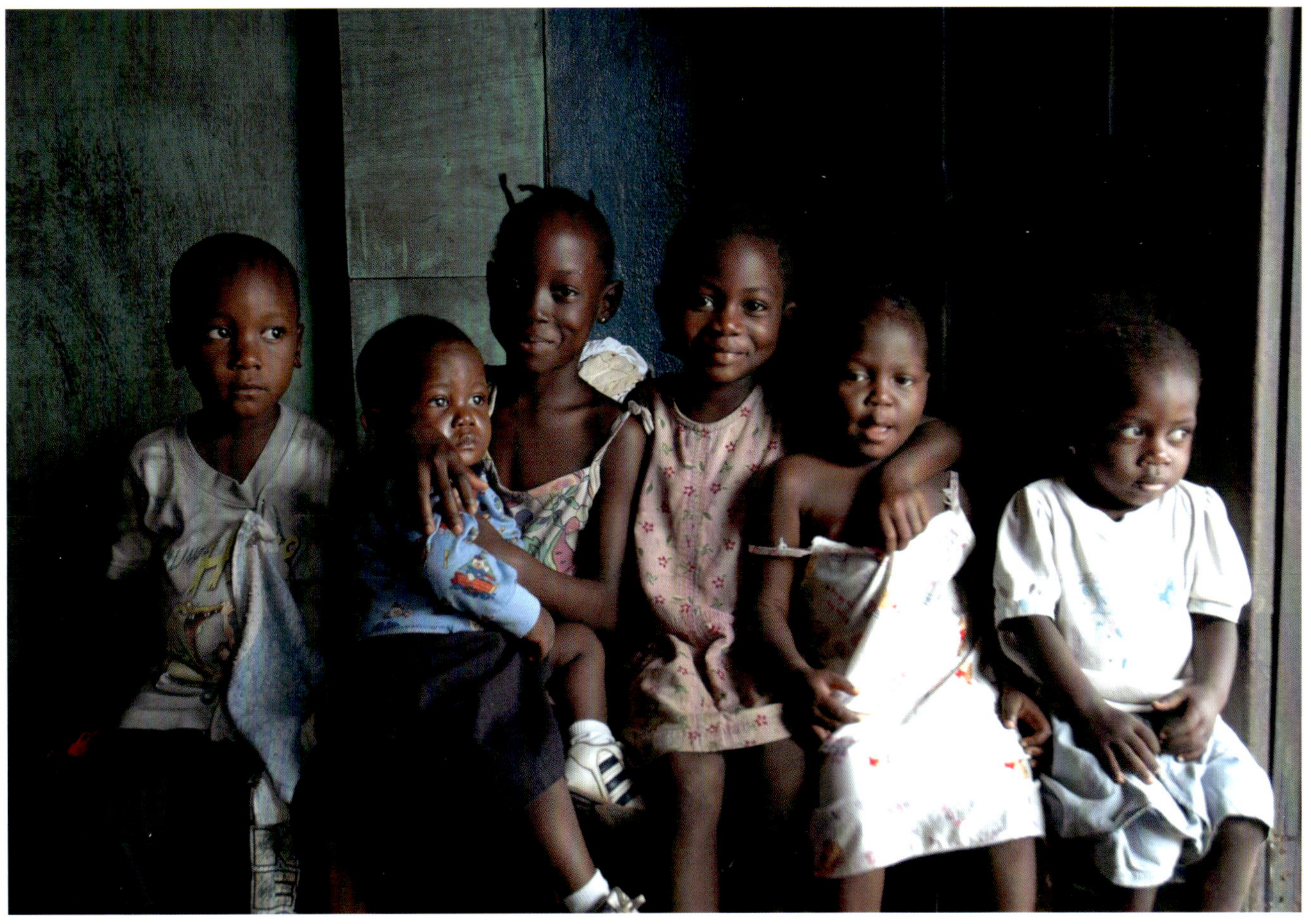

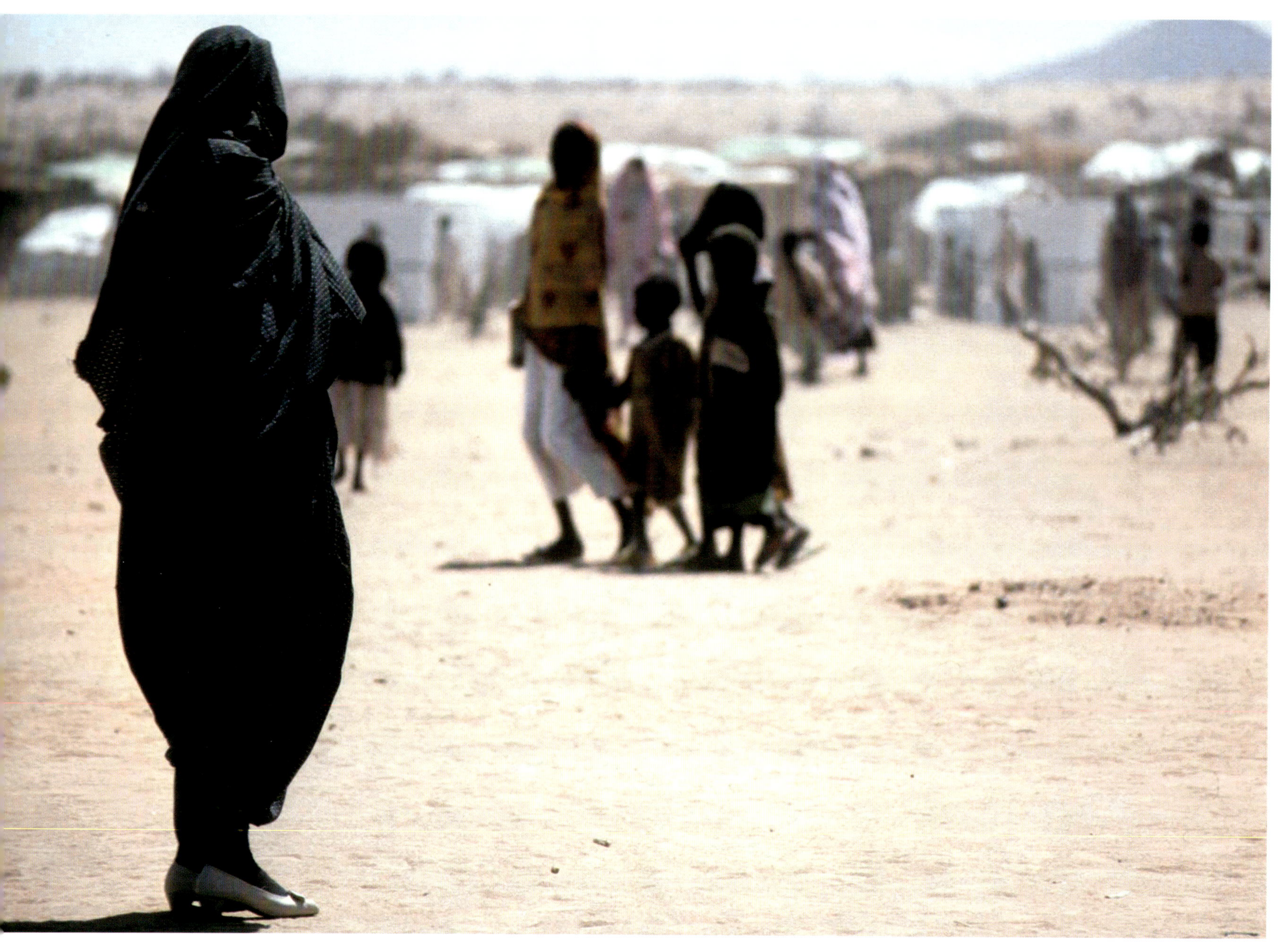

Chad 2005
IMC staff (both photos)

Despite security challenges, the International Medical Corps mobile clinic program in Chad has been successful. International Medical Corps' presence has eased tensions between Chadians and Sudanese as both groups welcomed health care, medicine and nutritional services. IMC is visibly helping to bridge gaps among different groups who gather at the same mobile clinic sites. It is now common to see women of different tribal affiliations interacting with one another as they wait for the clinic caravans to arrive.

Opposite page: Due to dangers facing those traveling on roads, International Medical Corps logistics teams coordinated the complicated delivery of services directly into targeted communities with mobile medical vans and airplanes filled with medicine, supplies and experienced doctors, nurses and midwives.

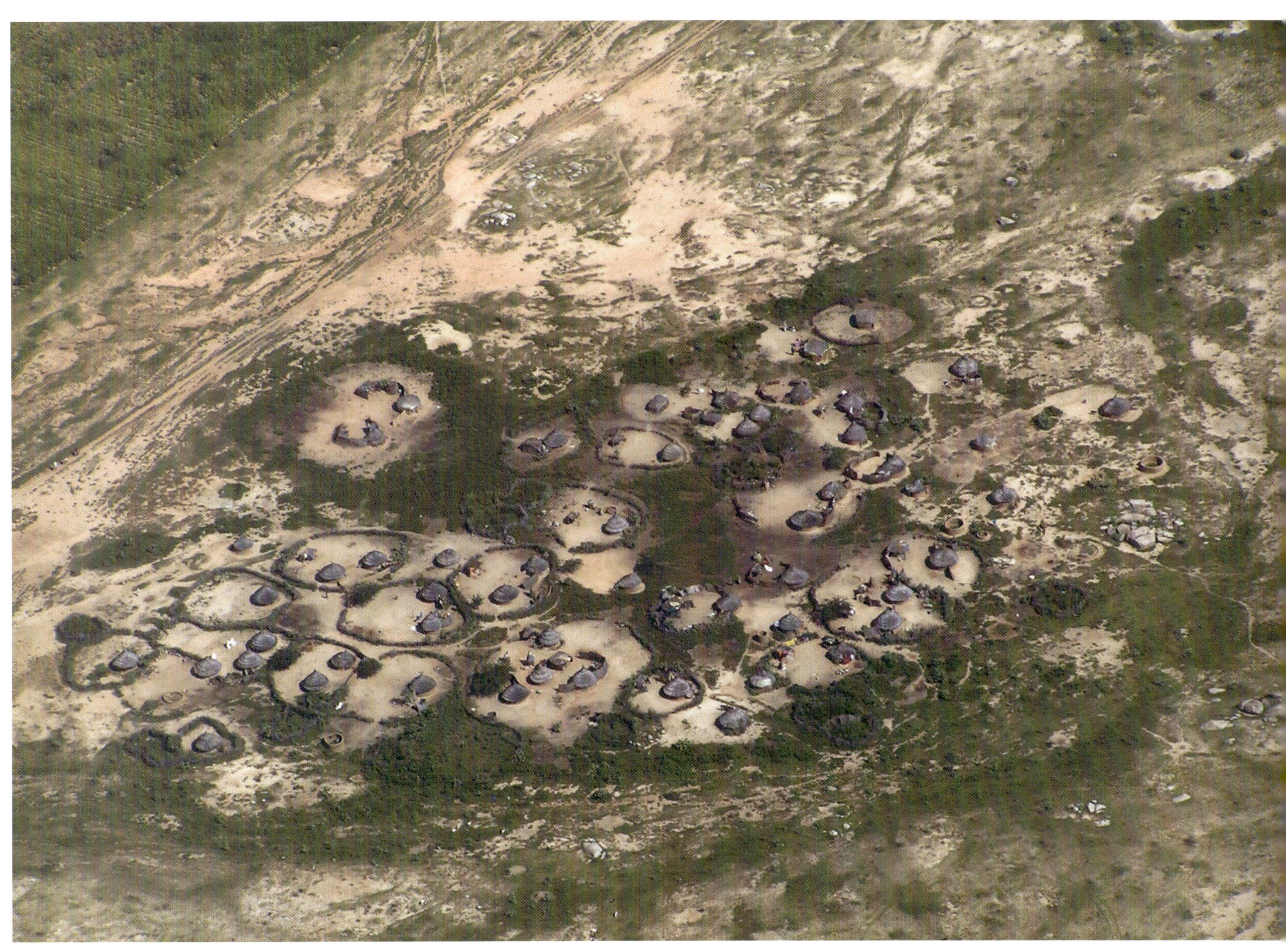

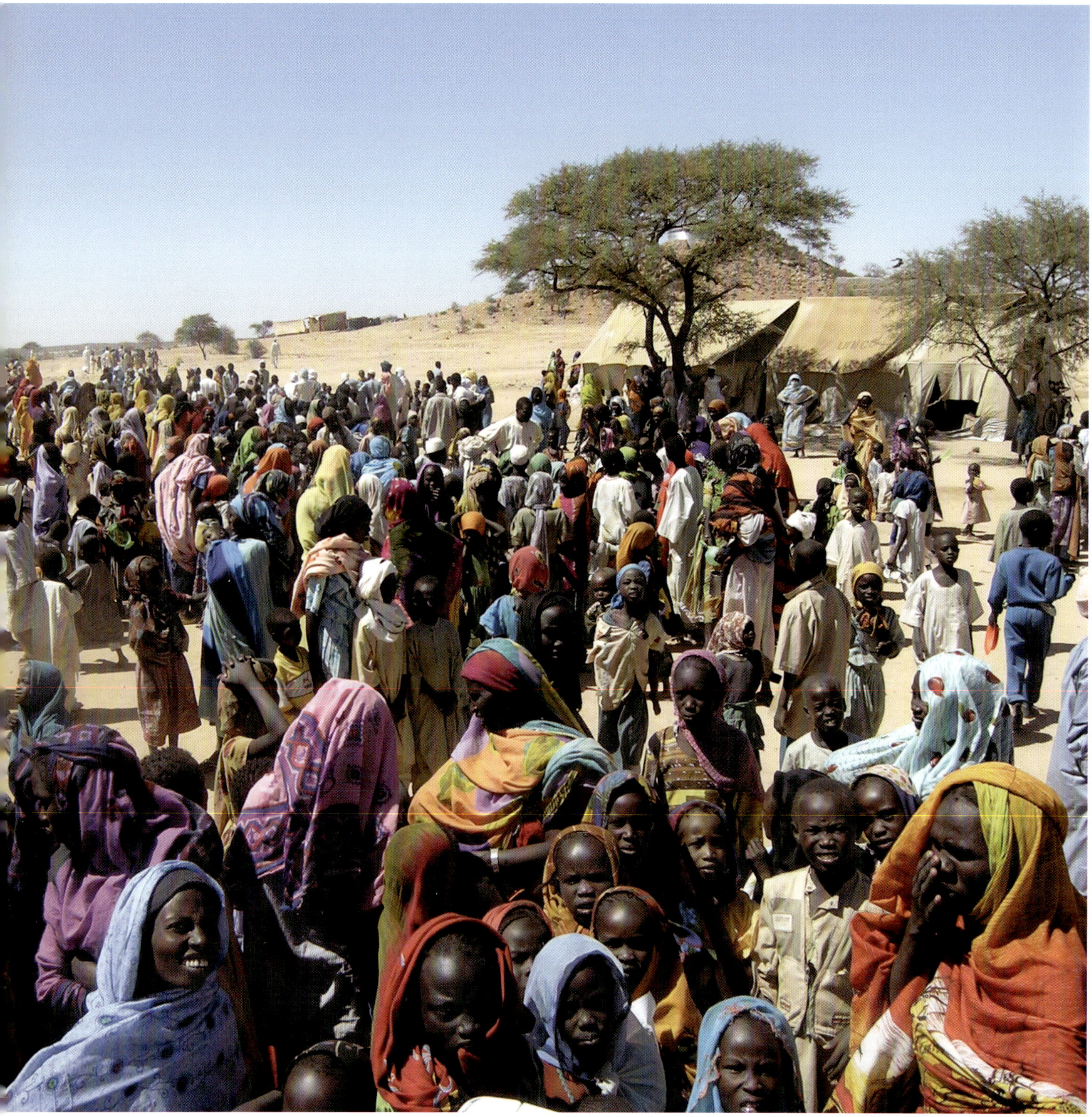

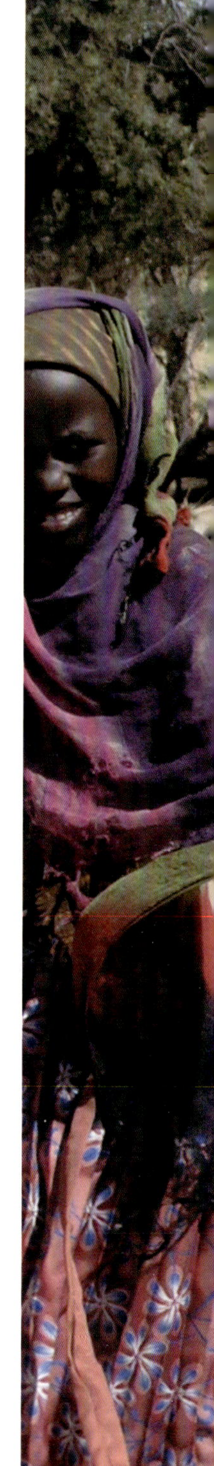

Chad 2005
IMC staff (both photos)

Due to a dearth of midwives, many villages in Chad had a complete void of maternal and child health care. International Medical Corps started a mobile women's and children's health care program for eight communities near refugee camps in Eastern Chad, where it already offered services.

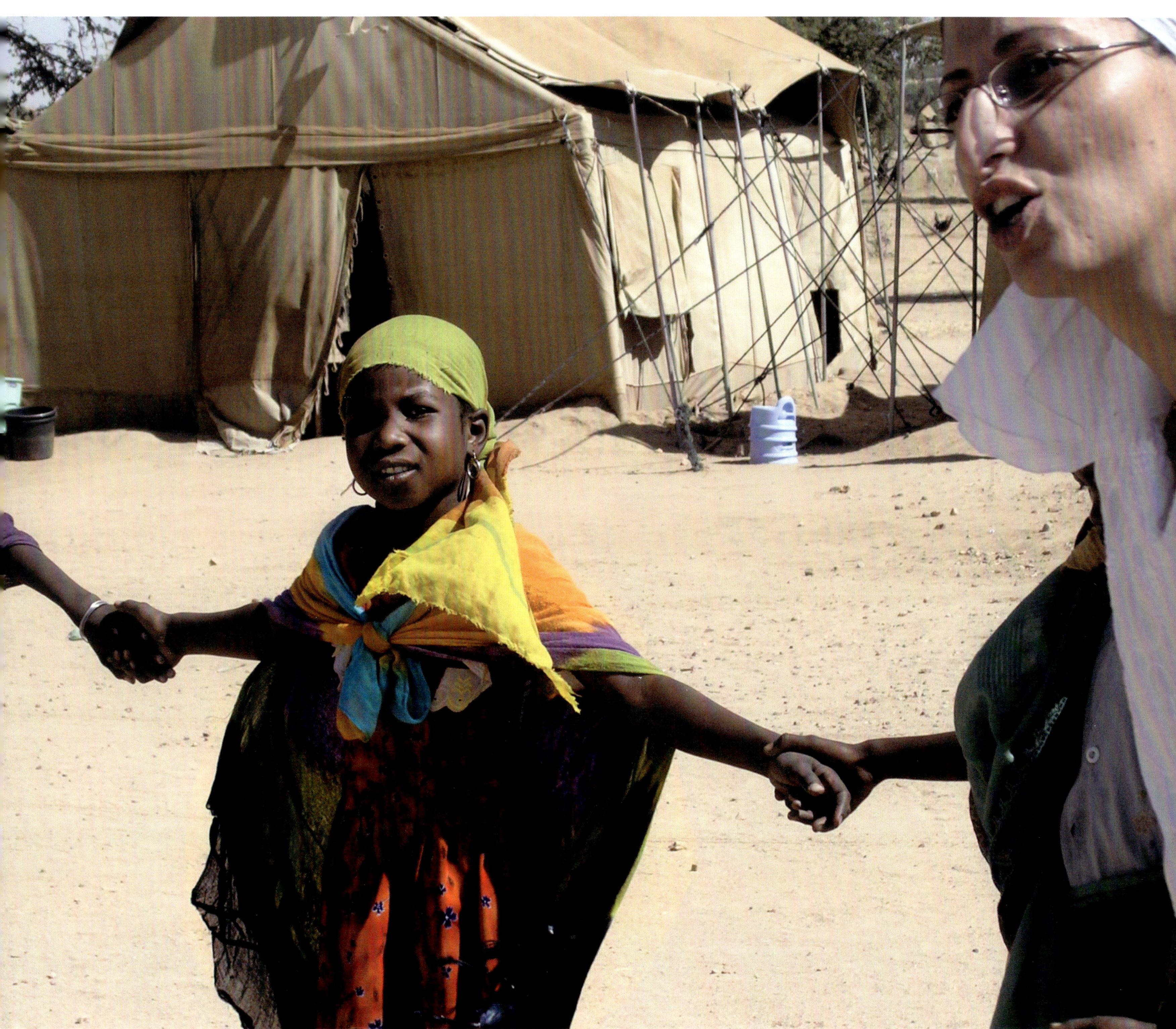

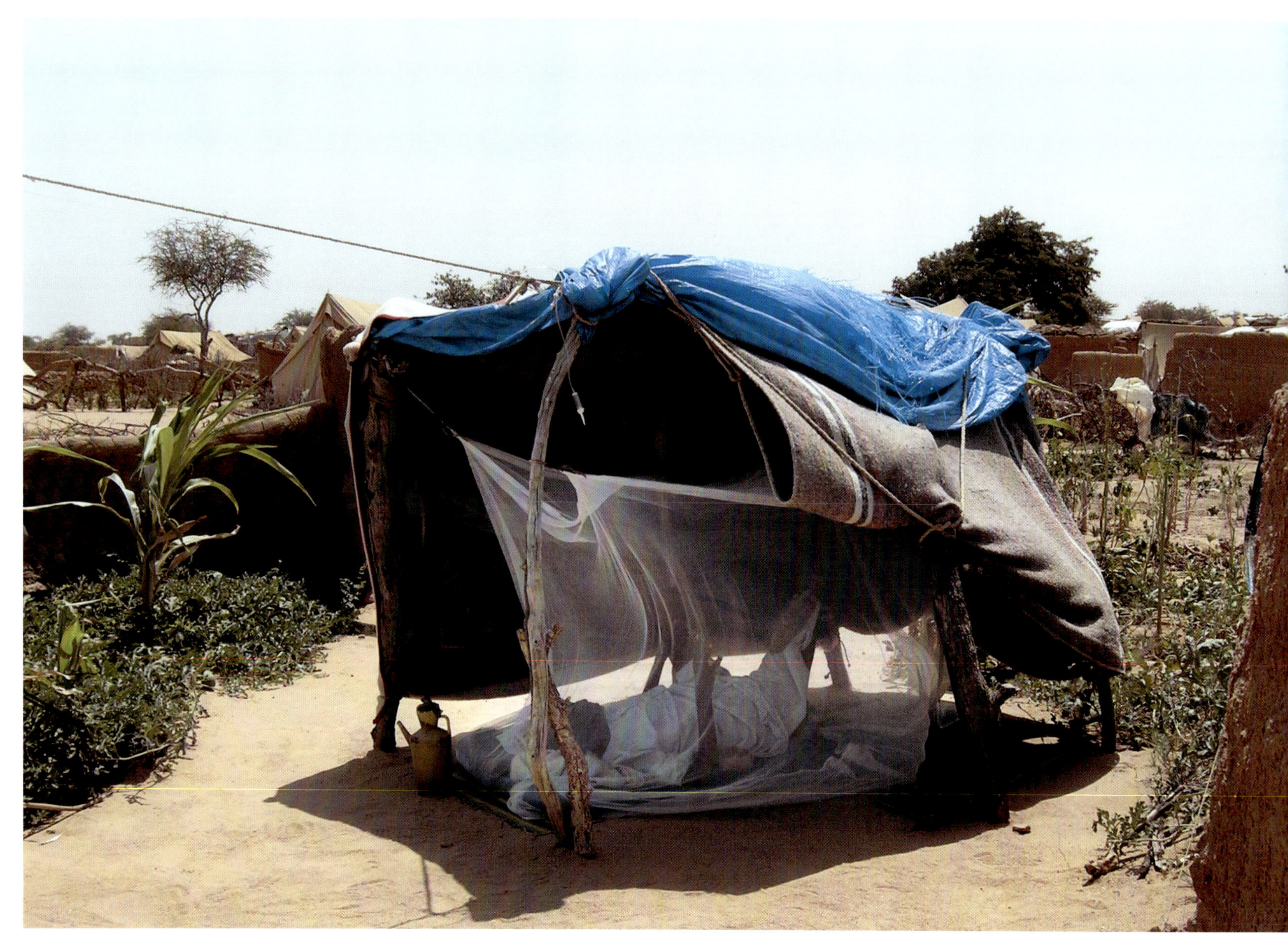

Chad 2005
IMC staff (both photos)

Throughout 2005, International Medical Corps operated primary health care centers and mobile clinics to provide both routine and emergency care to those who fled the conflict in Darfur. A man recovers in a tent after minor surgery at an IMC clinic.

Opposite page: IMC provided care for communities suffering from malnutrition and built wells and water systems to provide clean water to thousands living in camps and villages throughout Darfur and Eastern Chad.

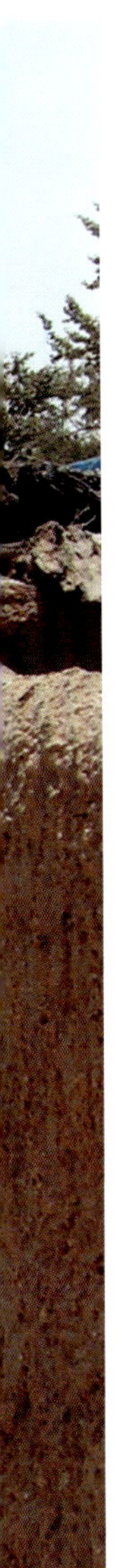

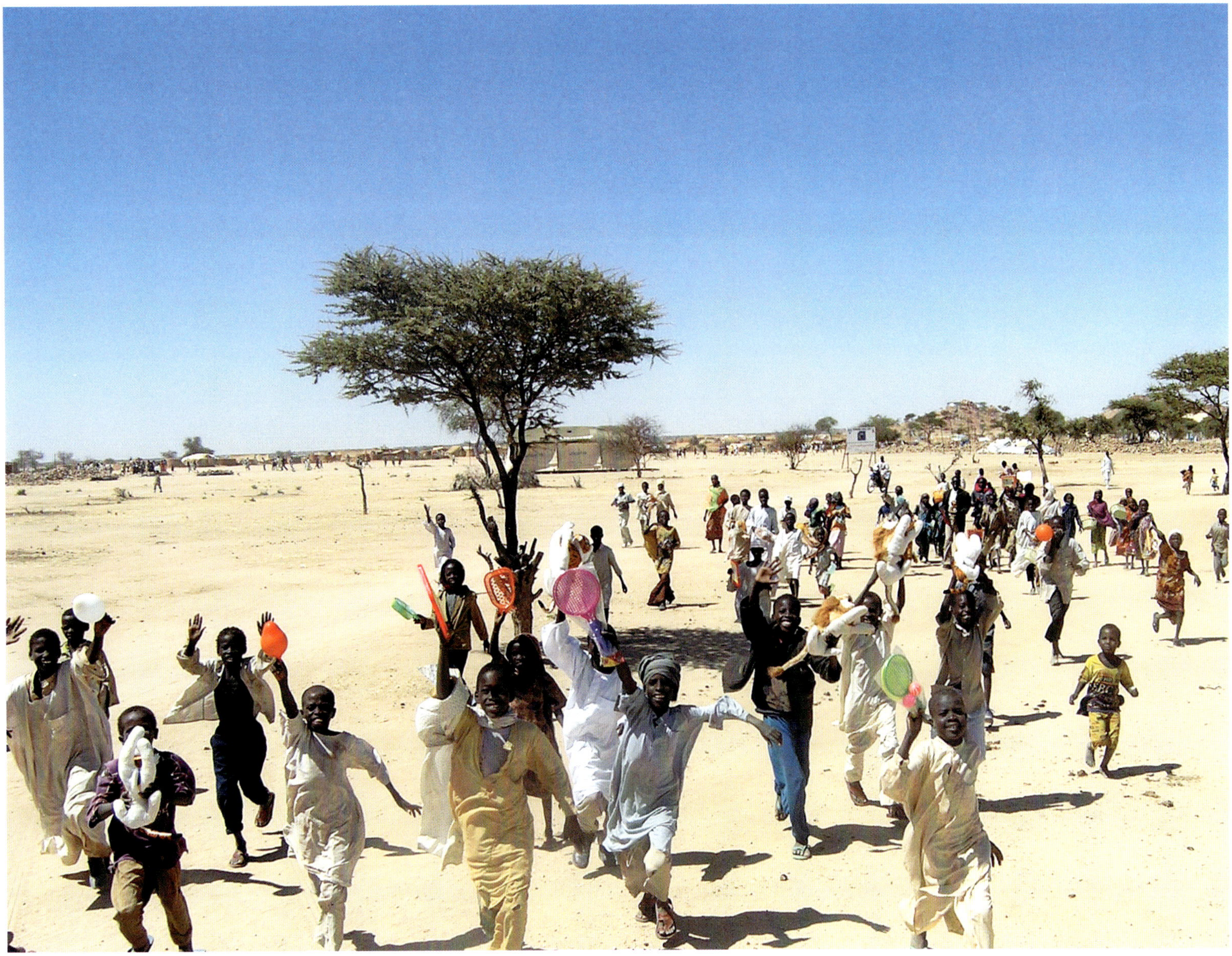

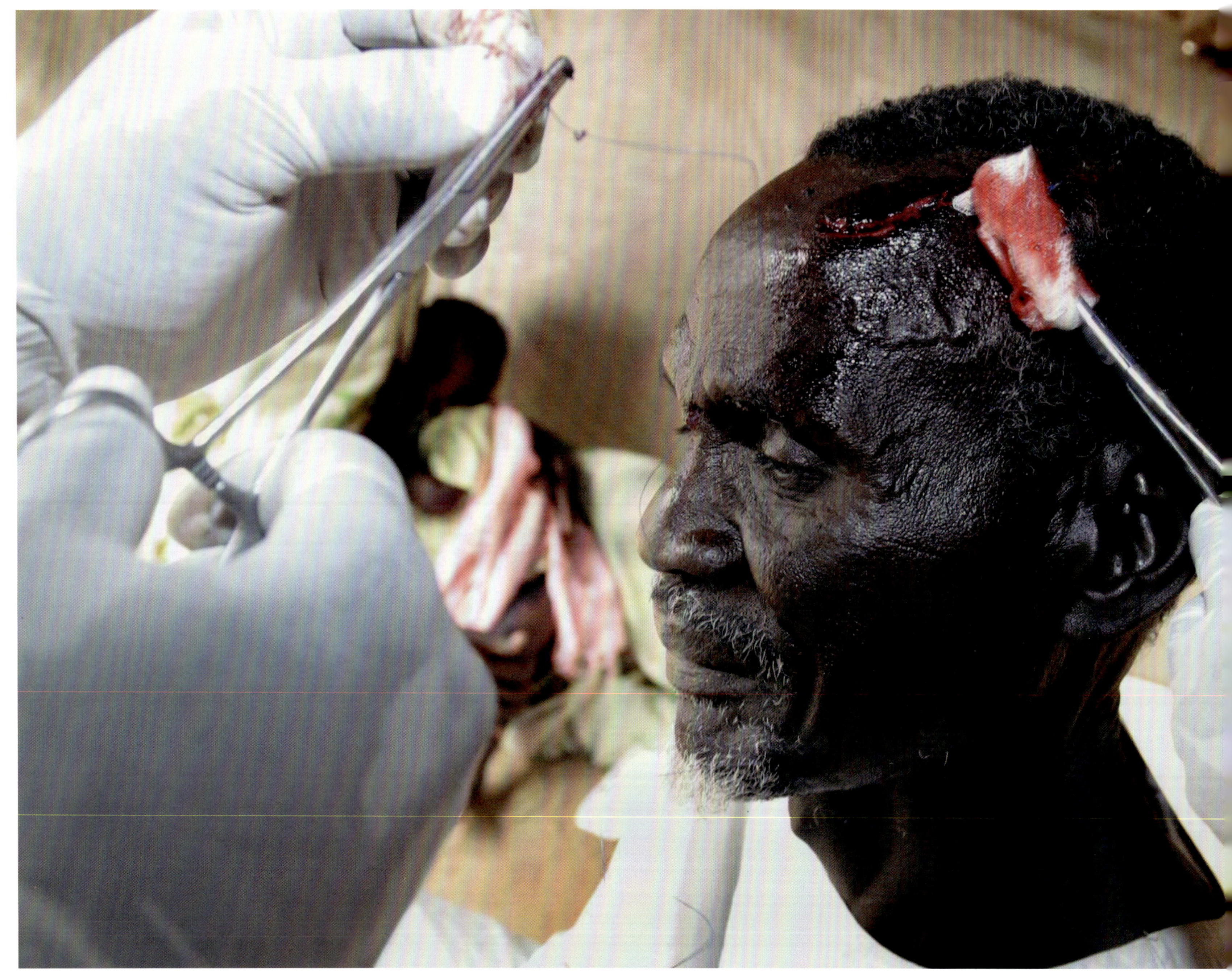

Chad 2005
IMC staff (both photos)

Eastern Chad was desperately short on nearly every resource, from food and water to fuel and building materials. But when confronted with 200,000 refugees fleeing the Darfur crisis in 2004, another of the region's shortages became frighteningly apparent: There were almost no qualified health workers. Training local staff has always been a key component of International Medical Corps' interventions, but, given the circumstances, it became an urgent priority for IMC in Eastern Chad.

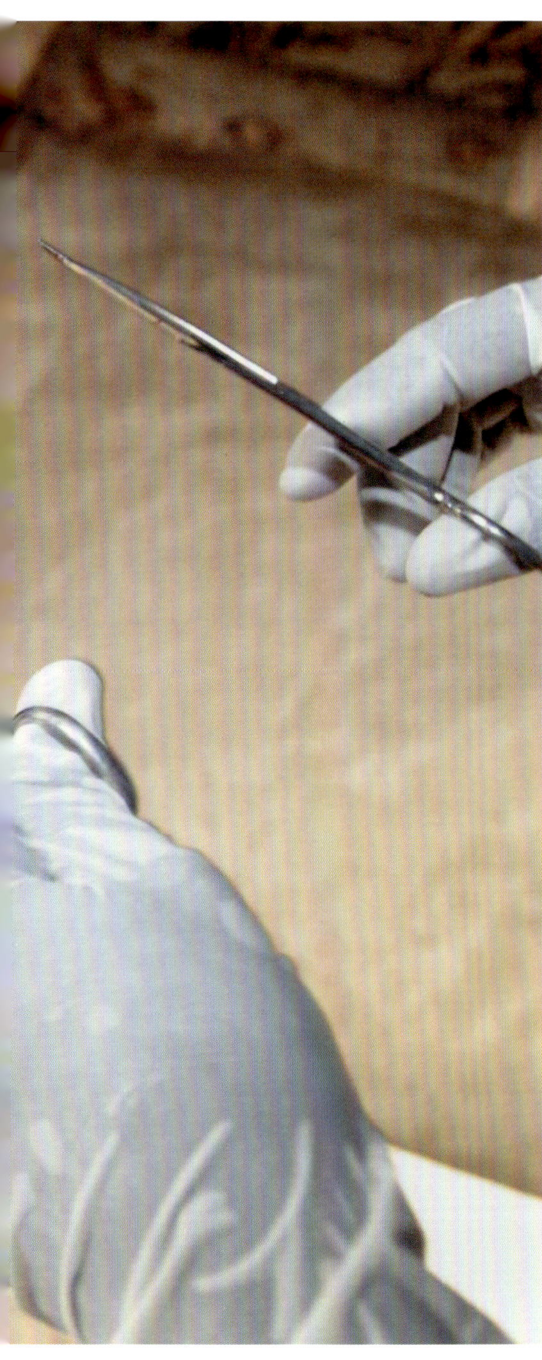

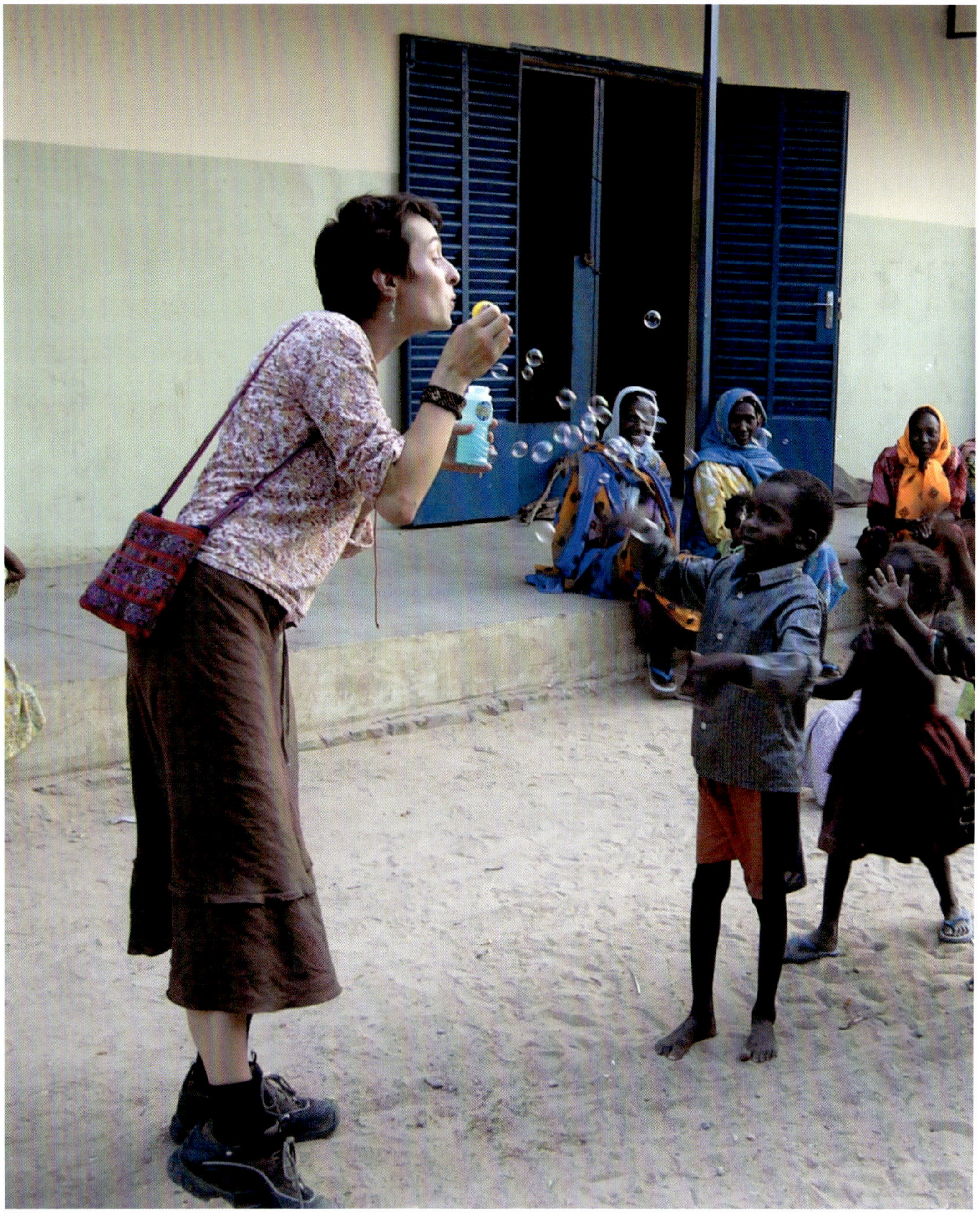

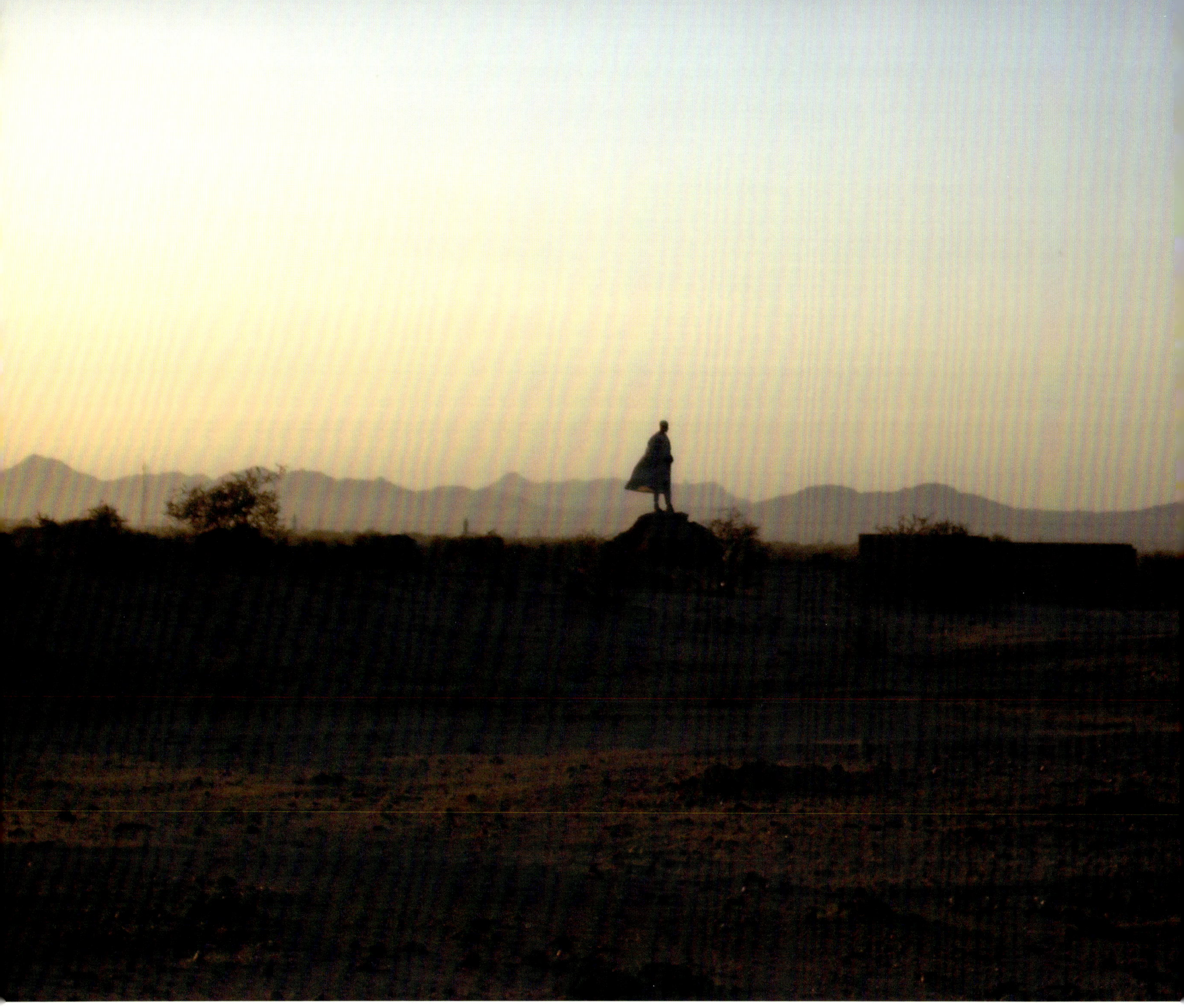

Chad 2005
IMC staff (both photos)

Comprehensive mental health services were fully integrated into International Medical Corps' programs for Sudanese refugees in Chad. This included culturally-sensitive mental health and psychosocial services, support groups for women, and therapy for youth in refugee camps.

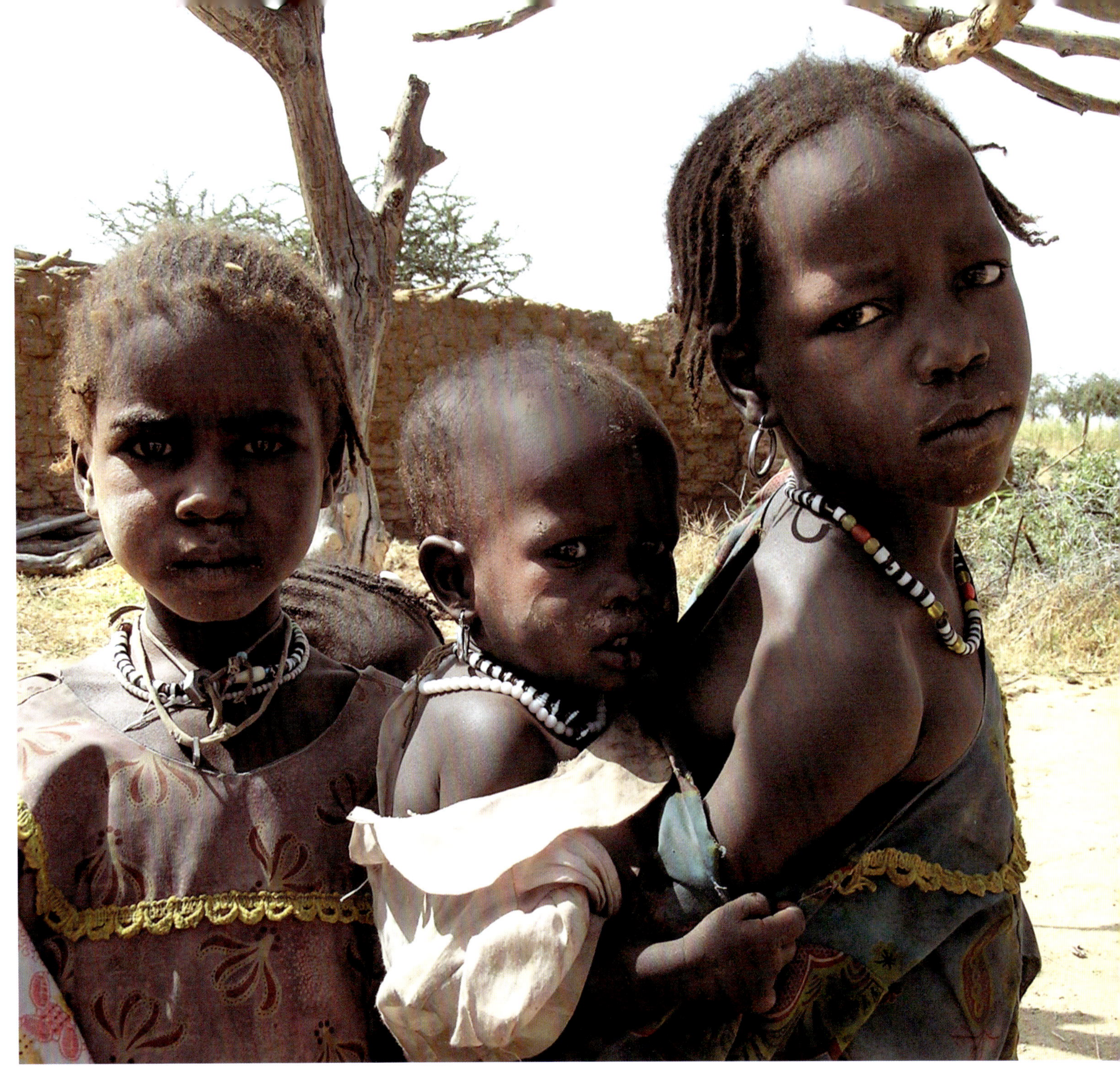

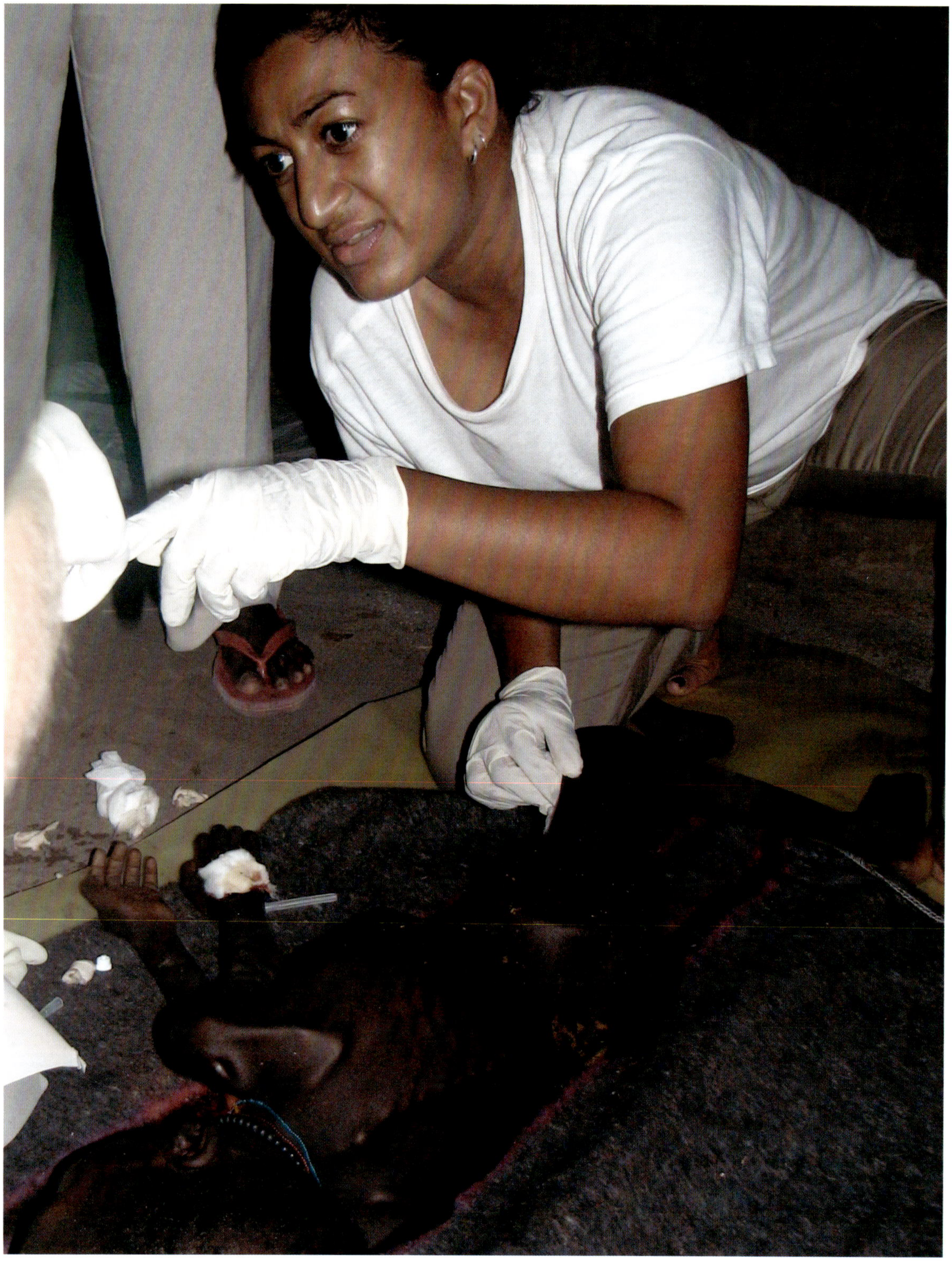

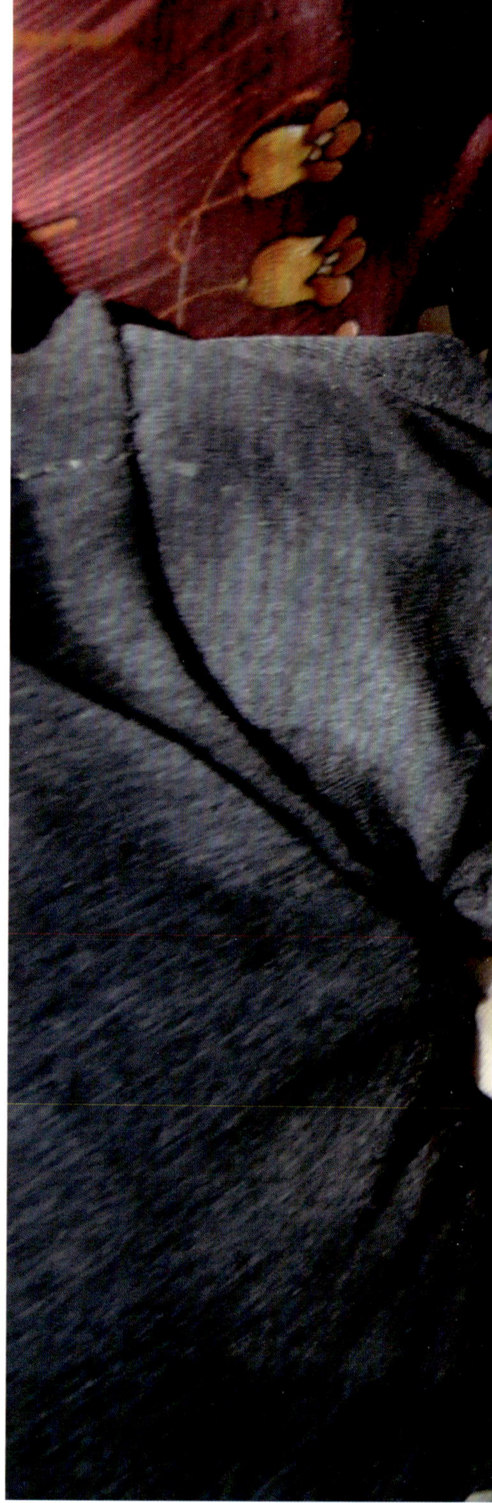

Chad 2005
IMC staff (both photos)

International Medical Corps Dr. Jill John-Kall examines a young malnourished patient in one of IMC's children's nutrition centers in Chad. Most of the photographs in this section were taken by Dr. Jill as she worked with Sudanese refugees in an IMC clinic in Chad.

Opposite page: In 2005, International Medical Corps was the sole health care and nutrition provider for refugees in Chad, providing health care to nearly 20% of the Sudanese refugee population in three camps, as well as 41,000 local Chadians. International Medical Corps is one of the few humanitarian relief agencies still there today.

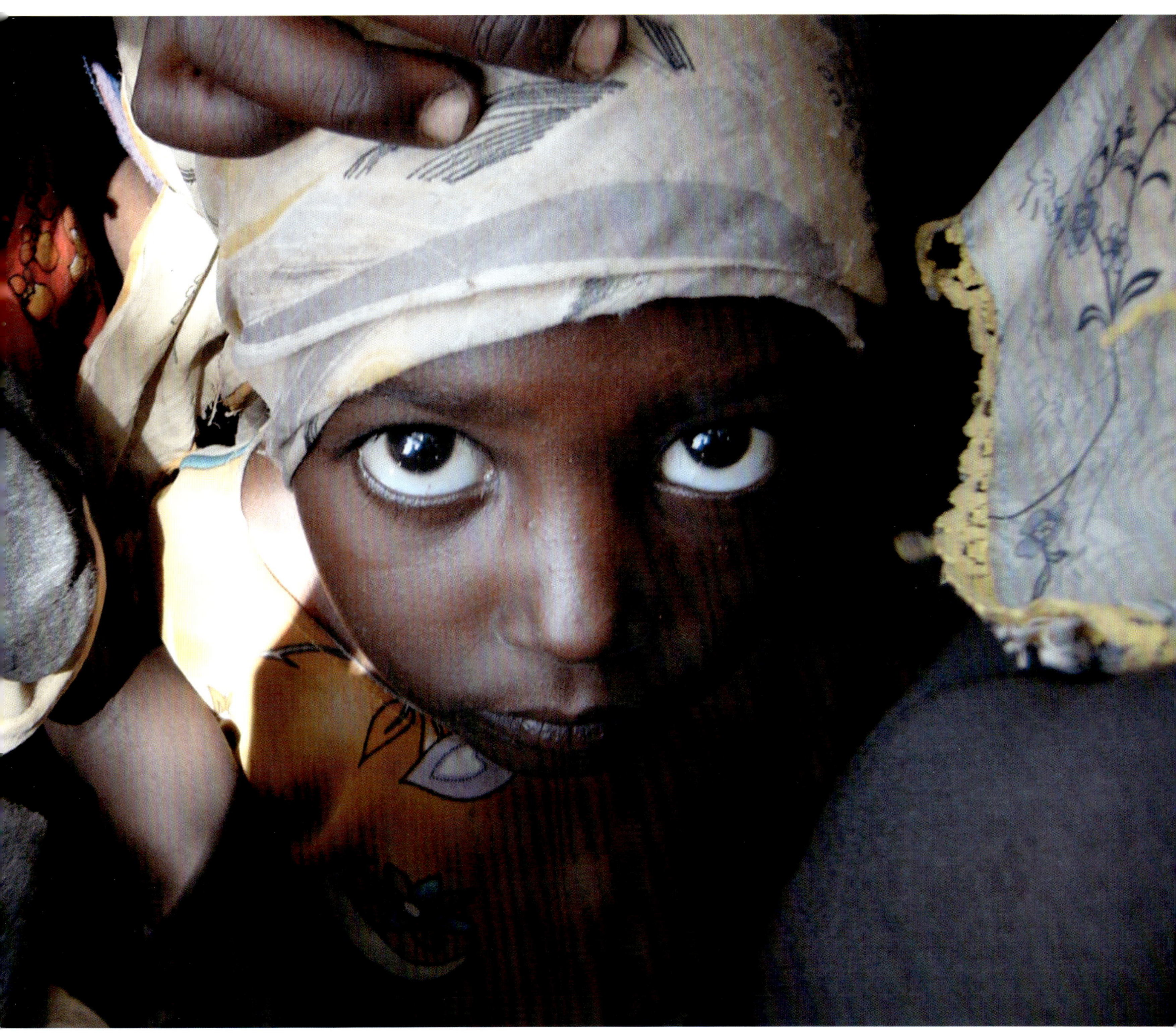

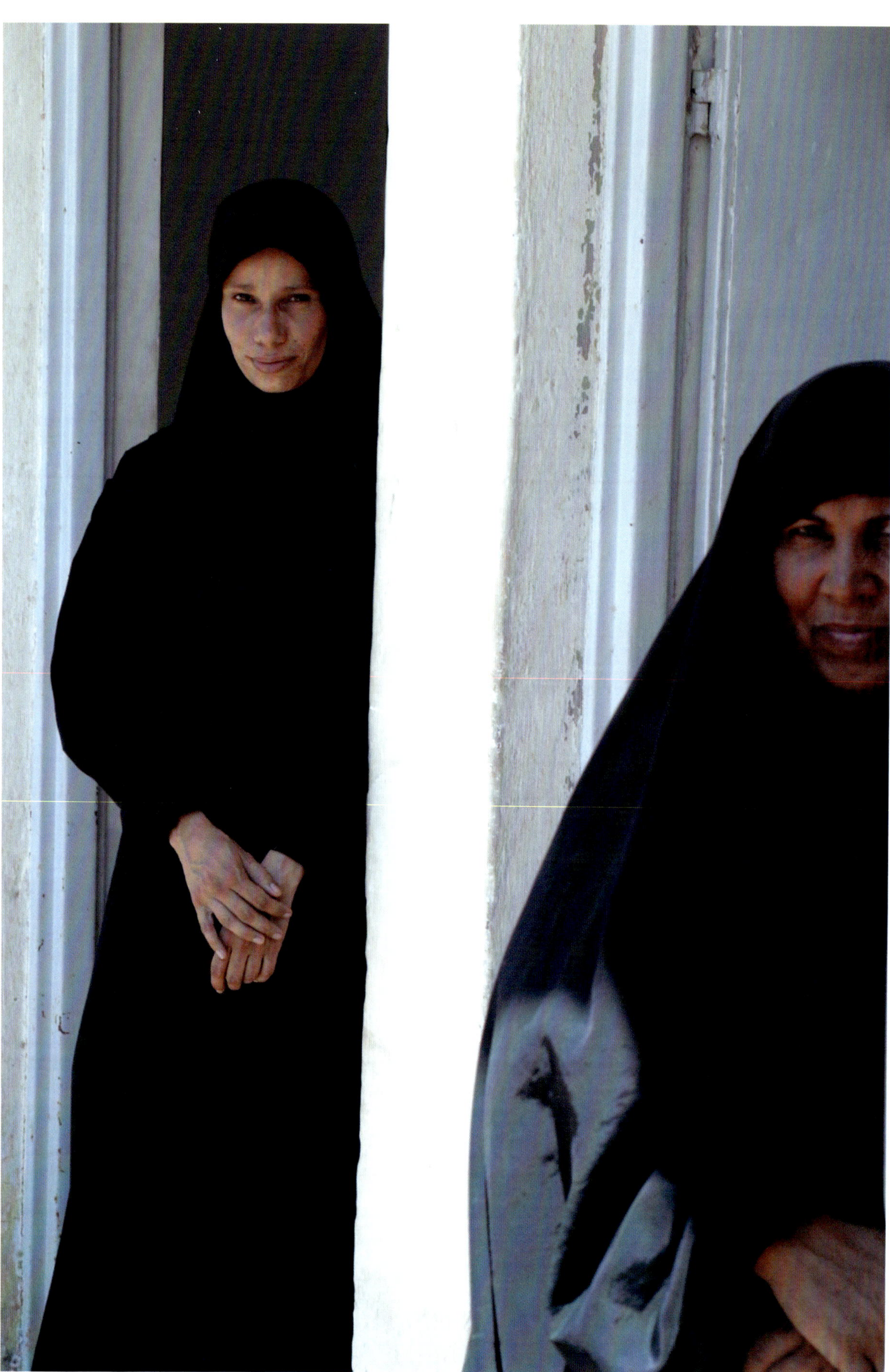

Iraq 2004
IMC staff
(both photos)

International Medical Corps was the first non-governmental organization to enter Southern Iraq in 2003 (before fighting had ceased) and to enter Baghdad after its fall. IMC began assisting Iraqi displaced people in this emergency situation, in a place where many other humanitarian organizations were unable or unwilling to venture.

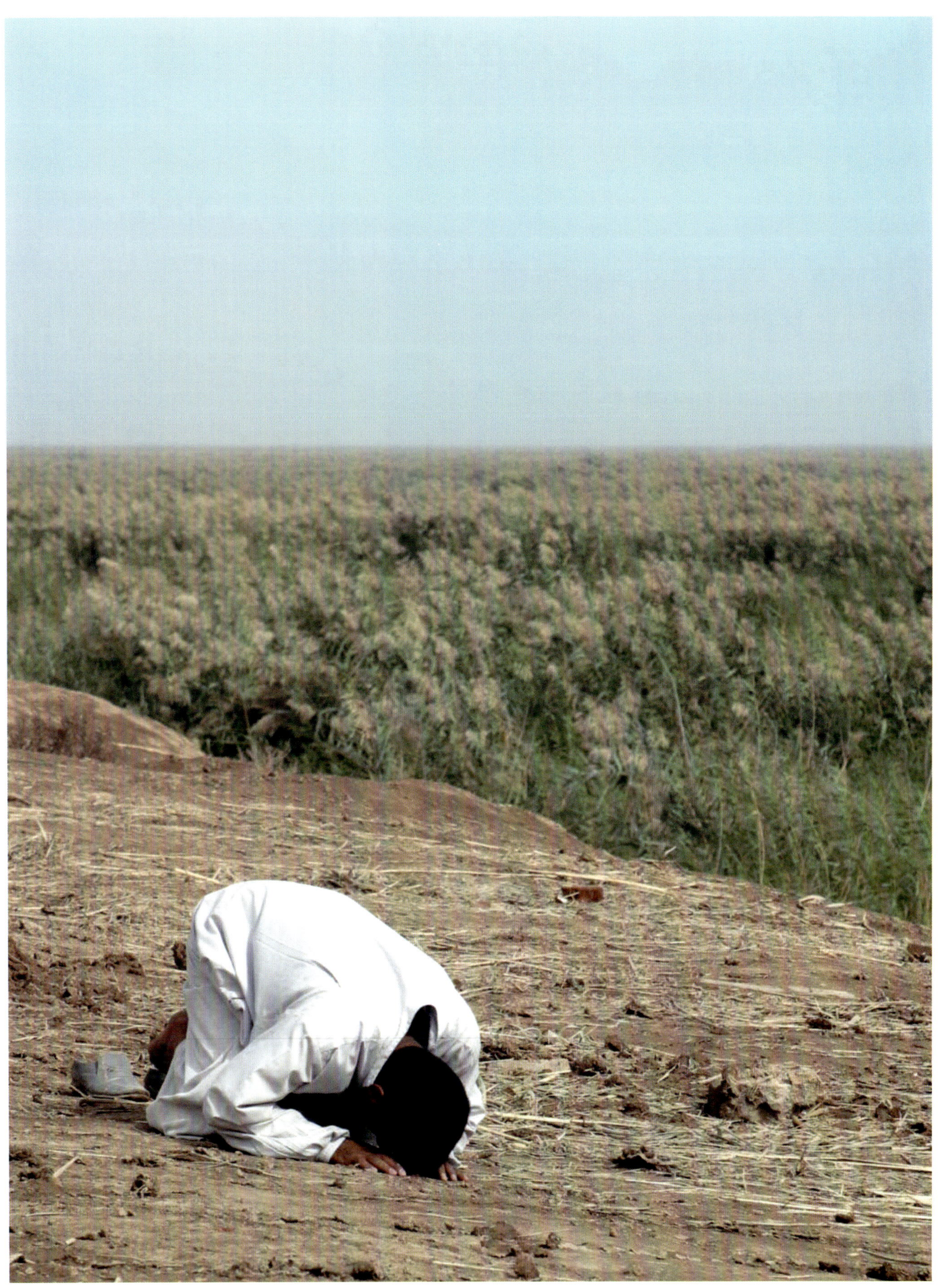

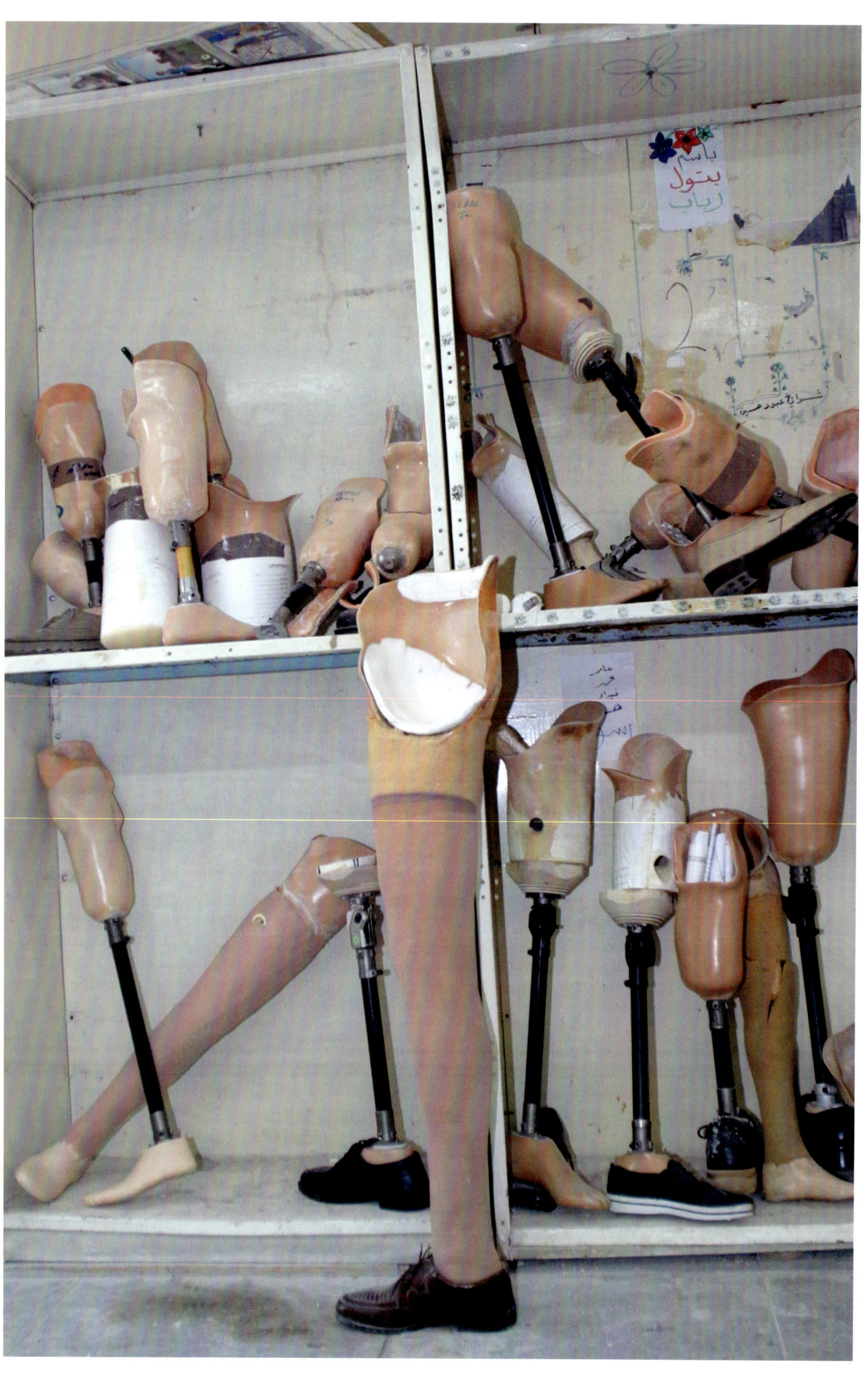

Iraq 2004
IMC staff (both pages)

Brought to a complete halt by severe looting just as people were falling prey to the perils of cluster bombs and post-war chaos, International Medical Corps was the first NGO on the scene at the Baghdad Medical Rehabilitation and Arthritis Center, providing specialized care to patients suffering from paralysis and arthritis, as well as many victims who required prosthetics.

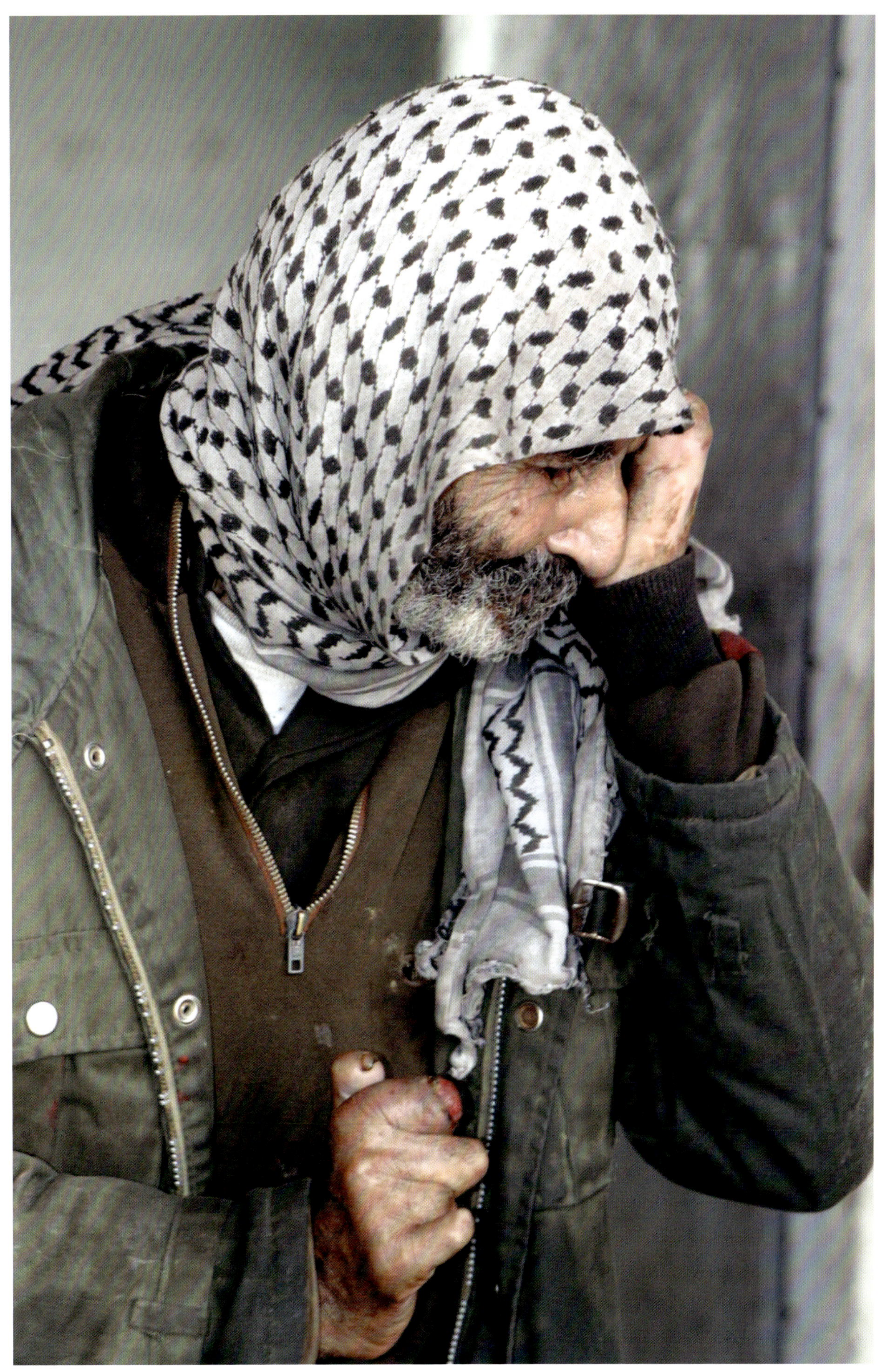

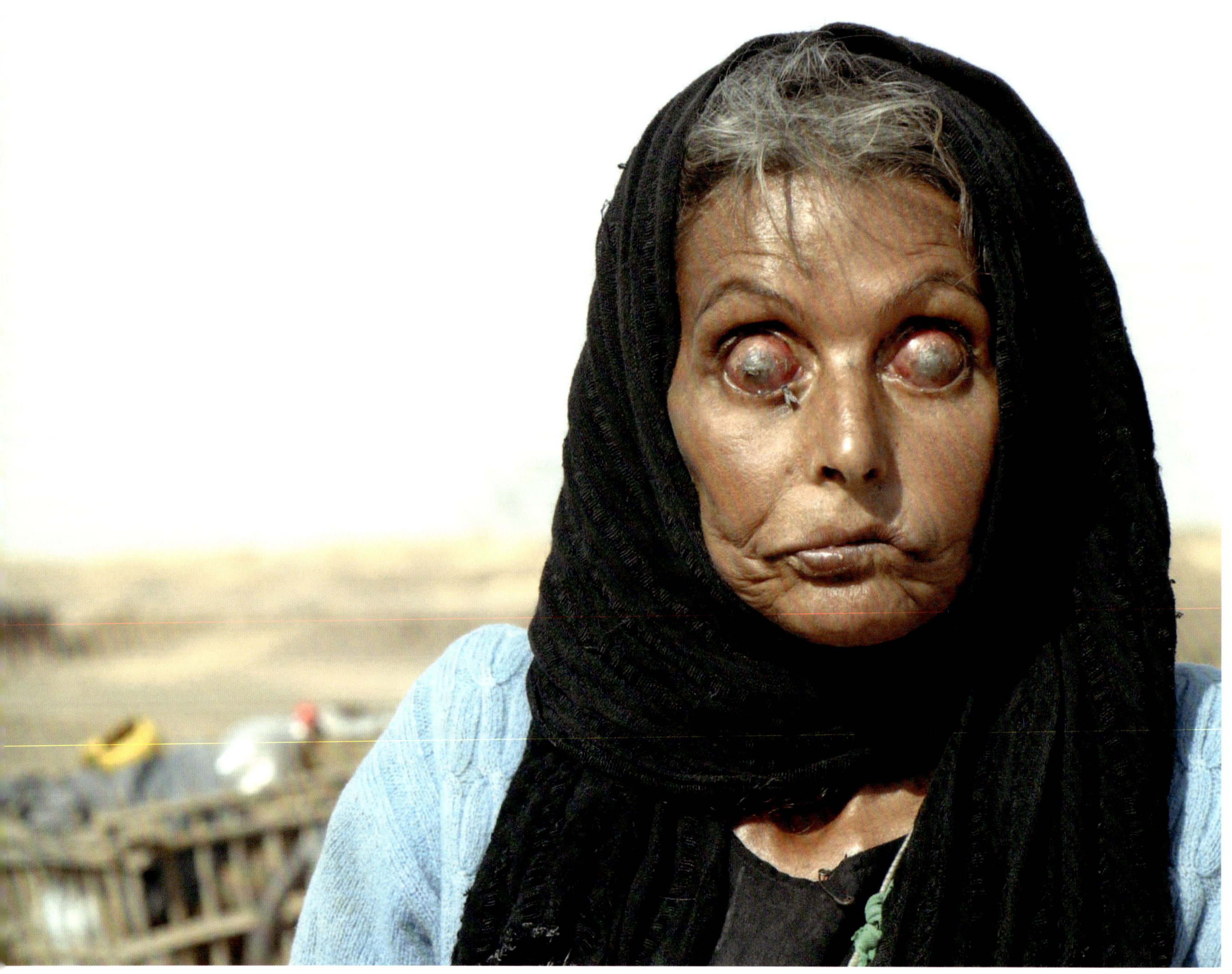

Iraq 2004/2003
IMC staff (both photos)

As one of the few humanitarian medical agencies working in Iraq, International Medical Corps is dedicated to the health care needs of Iraqi people in their country and in exile. IMC treats a blind woman at the Amarah Leper Colony in Iraq.

Opposite page: Even though supplies were flooding into Iraq, the bureaucratic vacuum severely limited the capacity of the central drug warehouse in Baghdad to distribute to district-level warehouses. In many cases and under dangerous conditions, International Medical Corps logistic teams facilitated the transportation of drugs and equipment directly to Iraqi civilians and refugees.

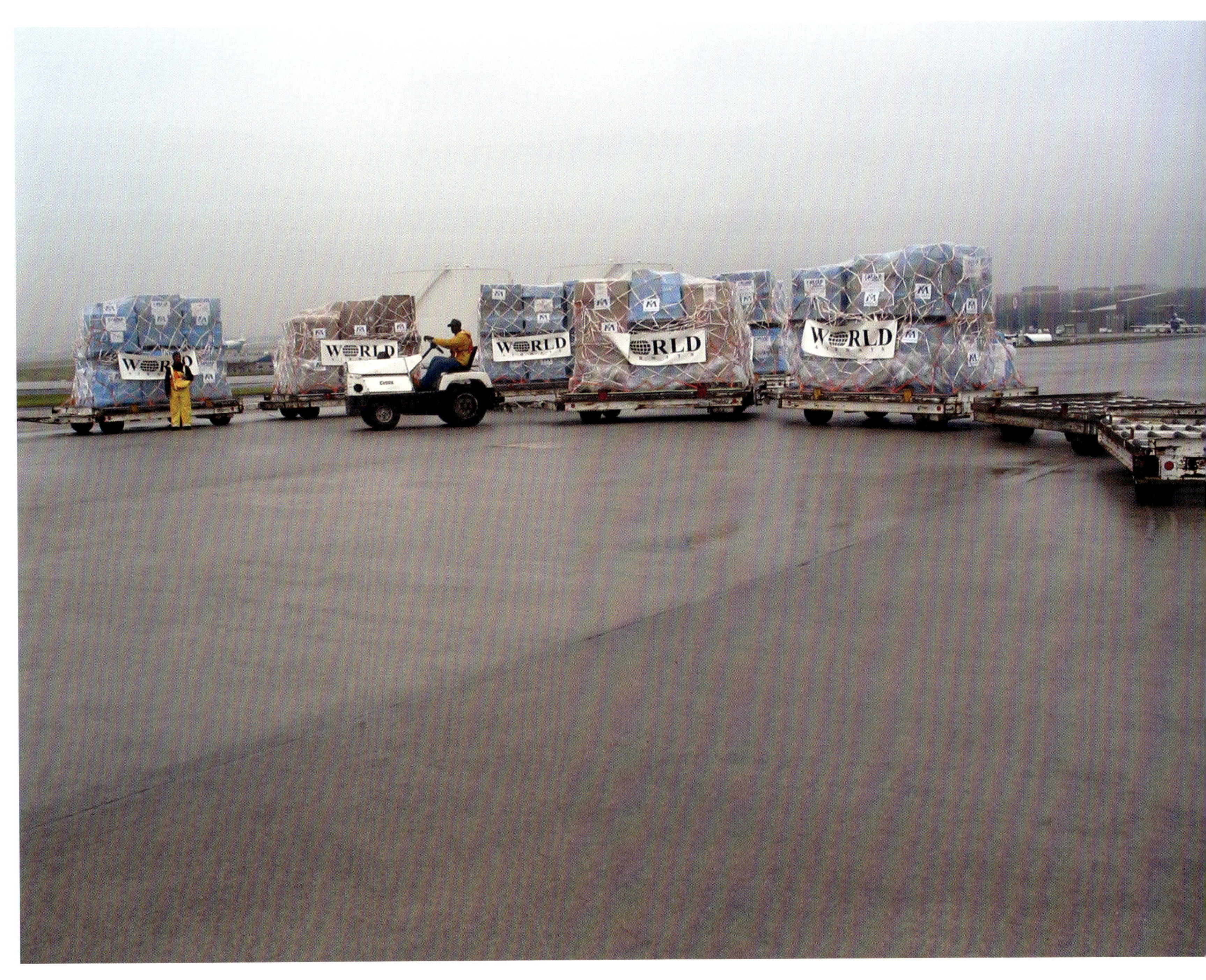
WORLD
WORLD
WORLD
WORLD

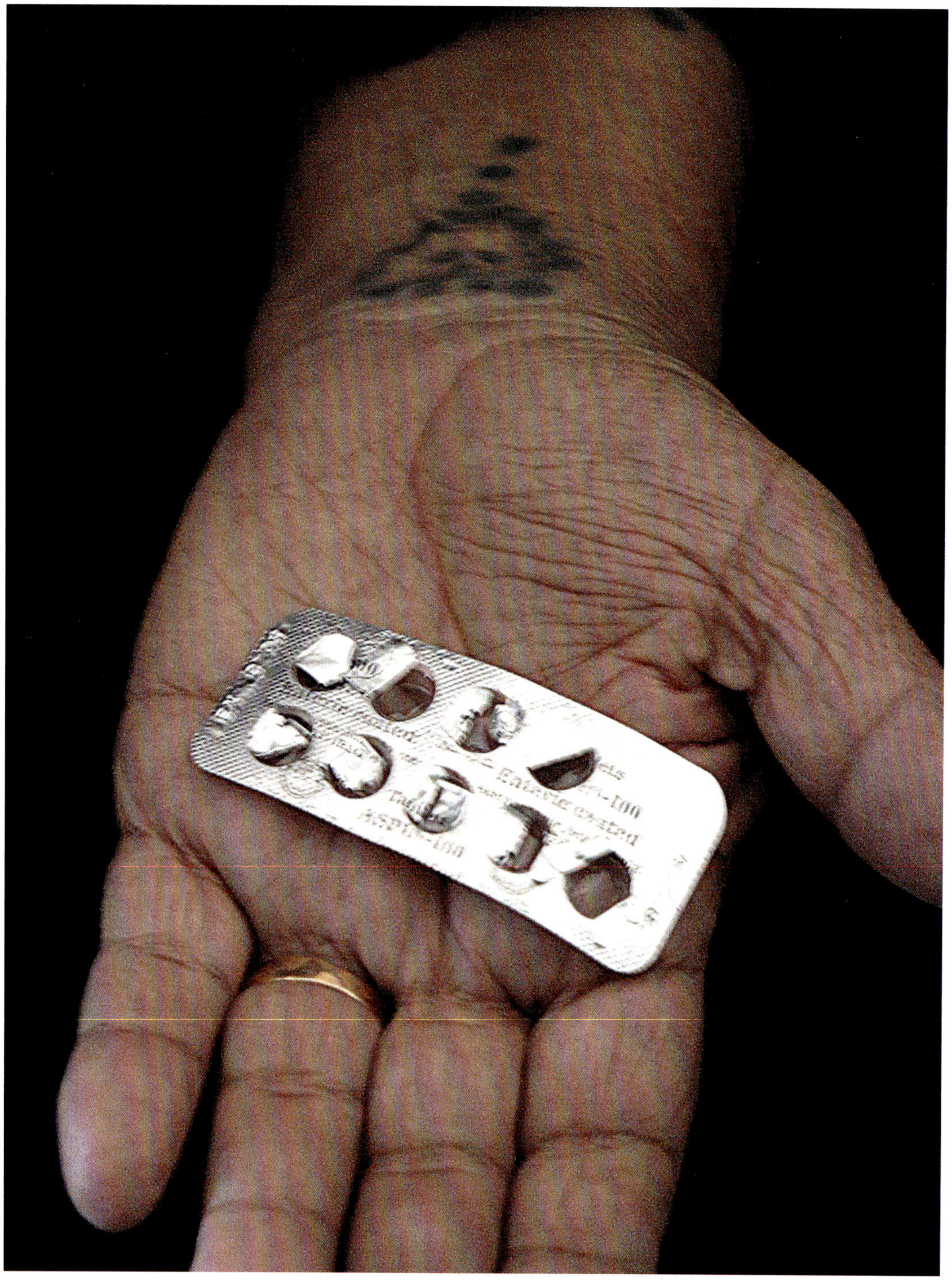

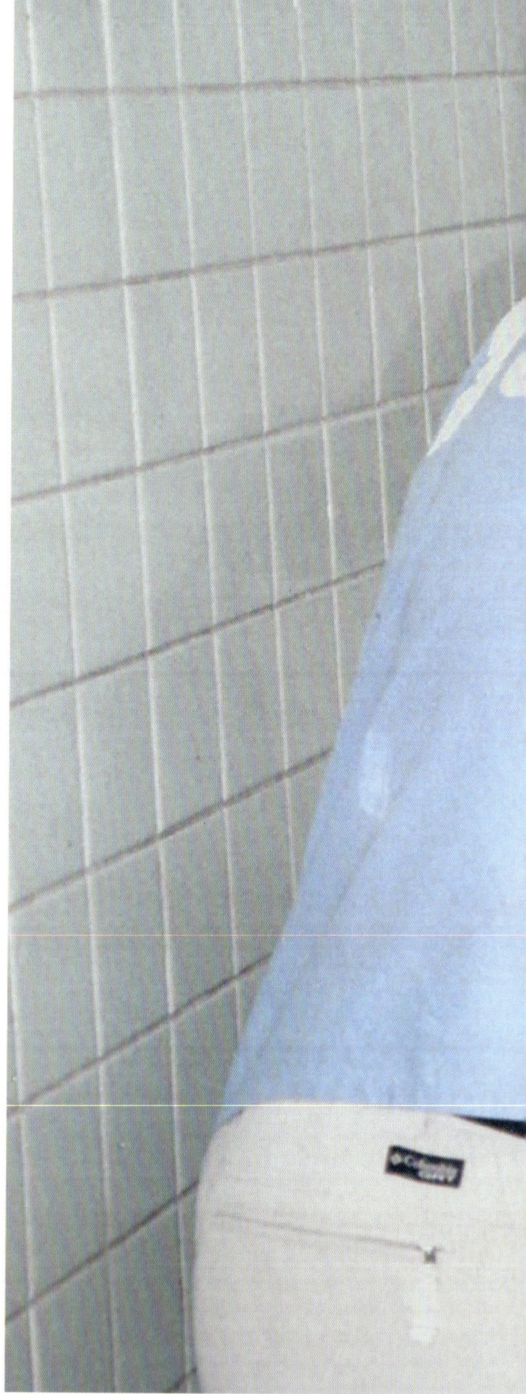

Iraq 2003
IMC staff (both photos)

As temperatures swelled and hospital teams tried desperately to care for the growing number of Iraqis seeking medical attention at looted hospitals and clinics, International Medical Corps worked to strengthen existing Iraqi health care systems by reconnecting supply routes, training local health workers and distributing much-needed medicine.

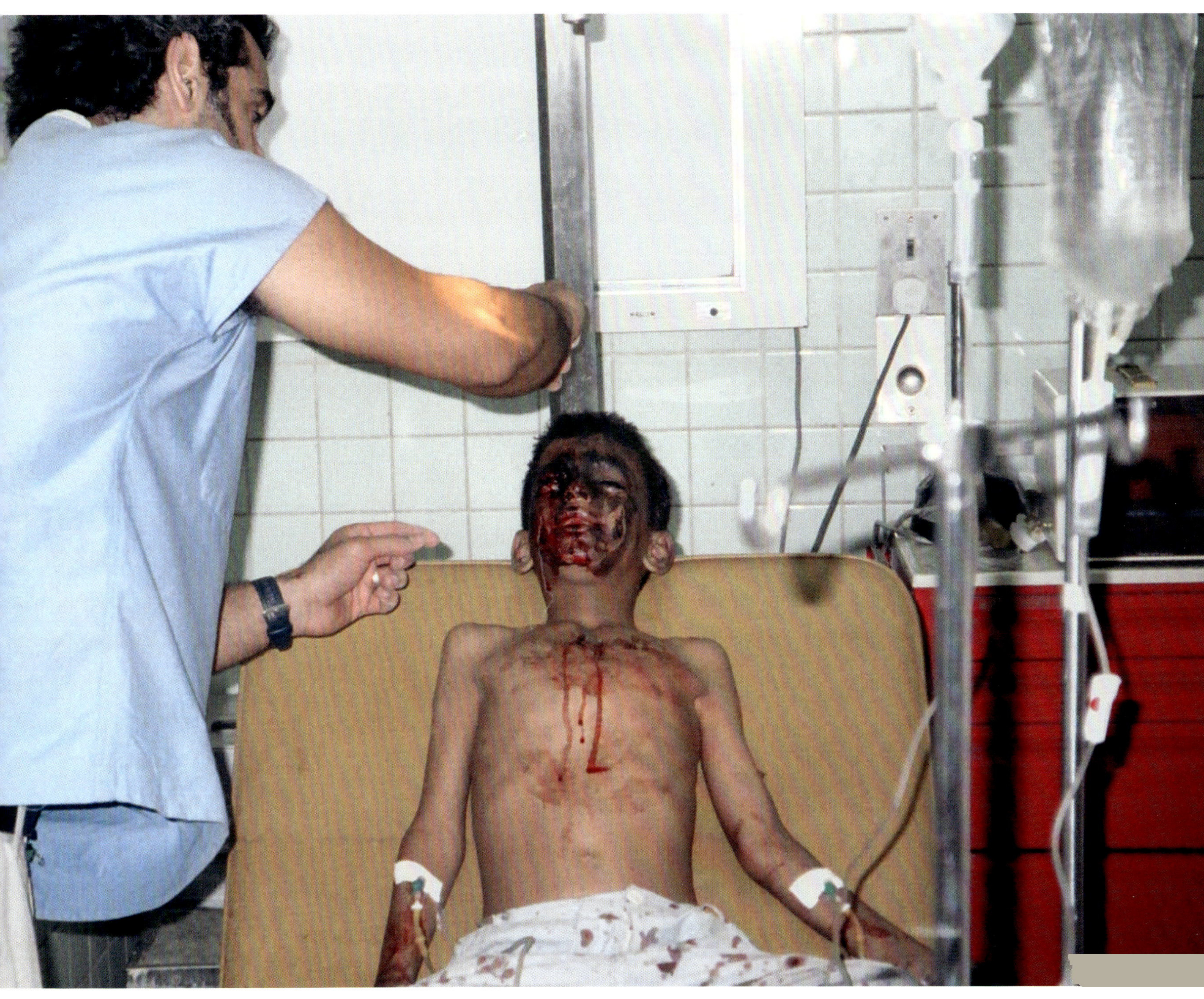

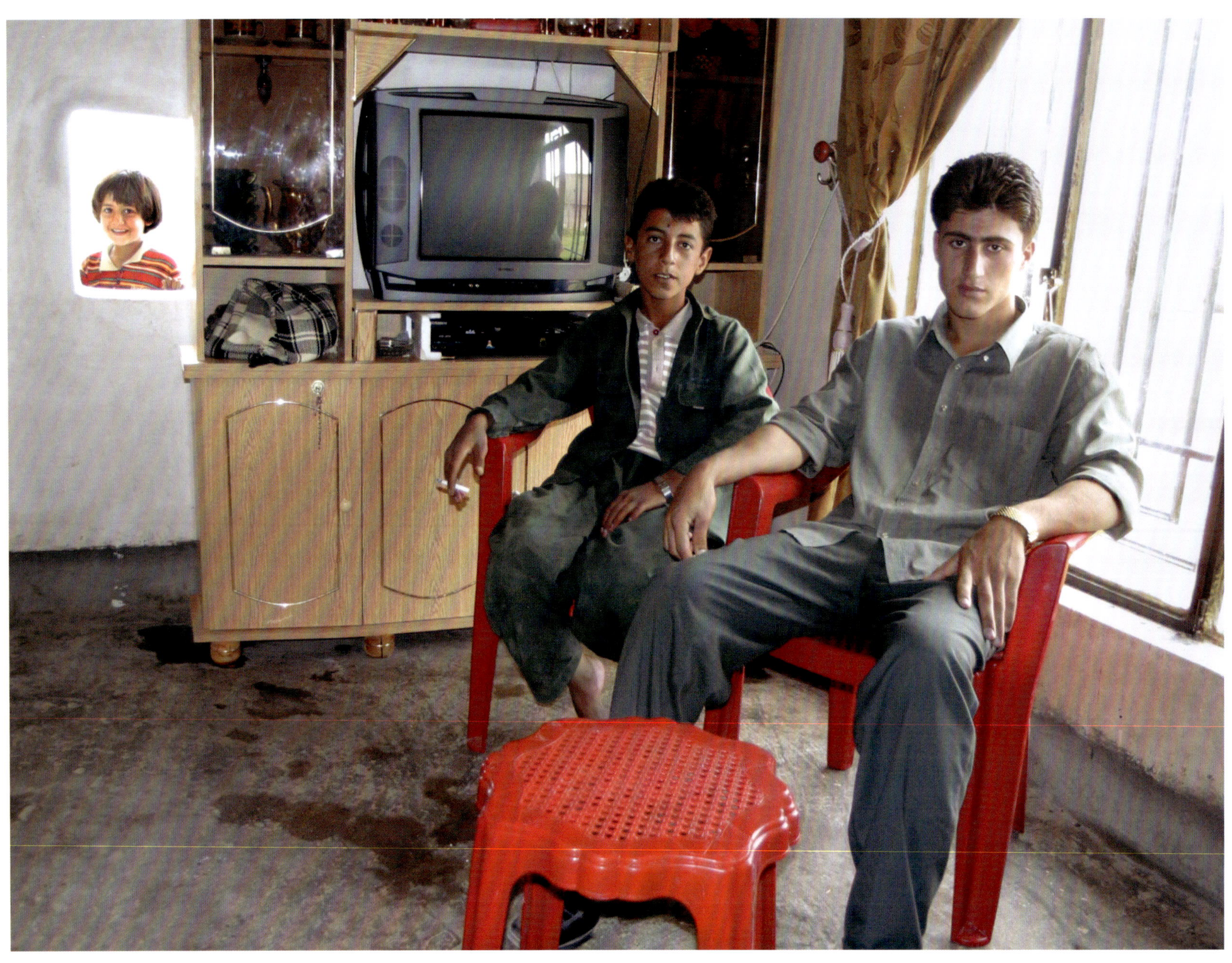

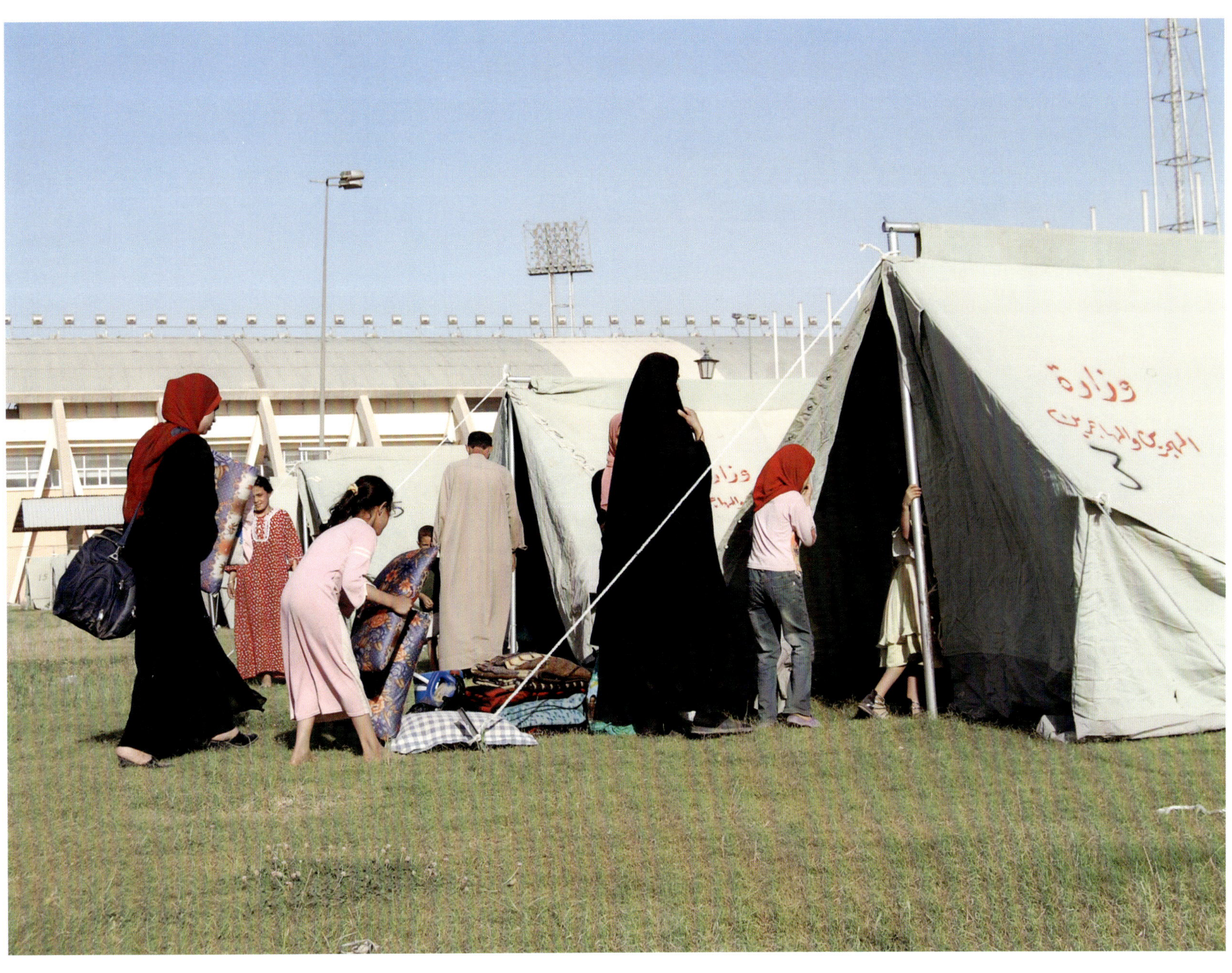

Iraq 2004 (opposite)
Iraq 2008 (above)
IMC staff

After the beginning of the invasion in Iraq, sectarian violence and ongoing insecurity had produced one of the largest refugee movements in the world since 1948. More than two million Iraqis left their stable homes and jobs behind to live in squalid conditions or in refugee camps with limited access to health care and education. Newly arrived refugees move into tents set up by IMC workers in a local stadium.

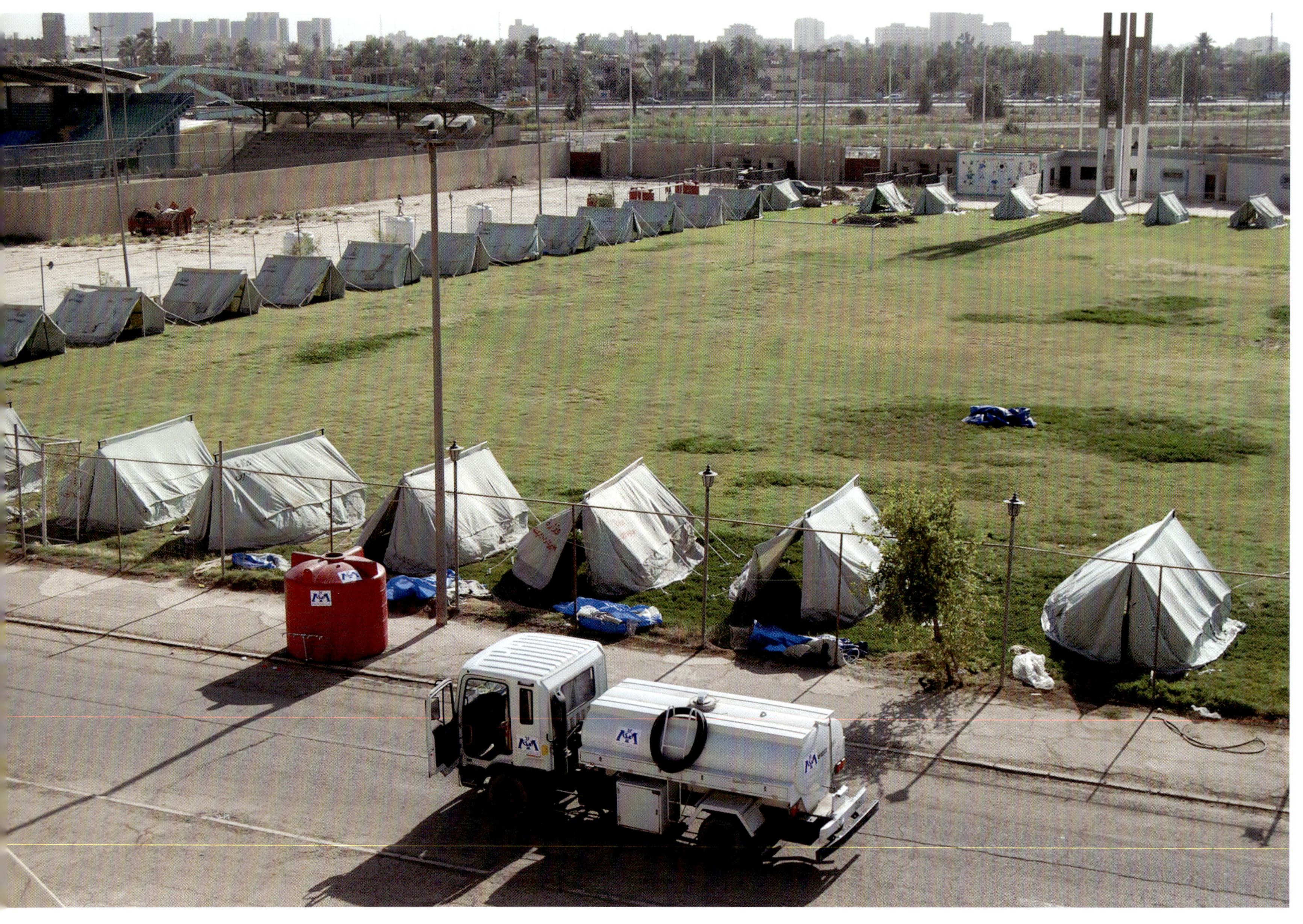

Iraq 2008
IMC staff (both photos)

International Medical Corps was often the only health care option for many of these unlikely refugees. Refugee camps were set up in local stadiums to provide shelter, food and water to thousands of internally displaced persons in many cities in Iraq.

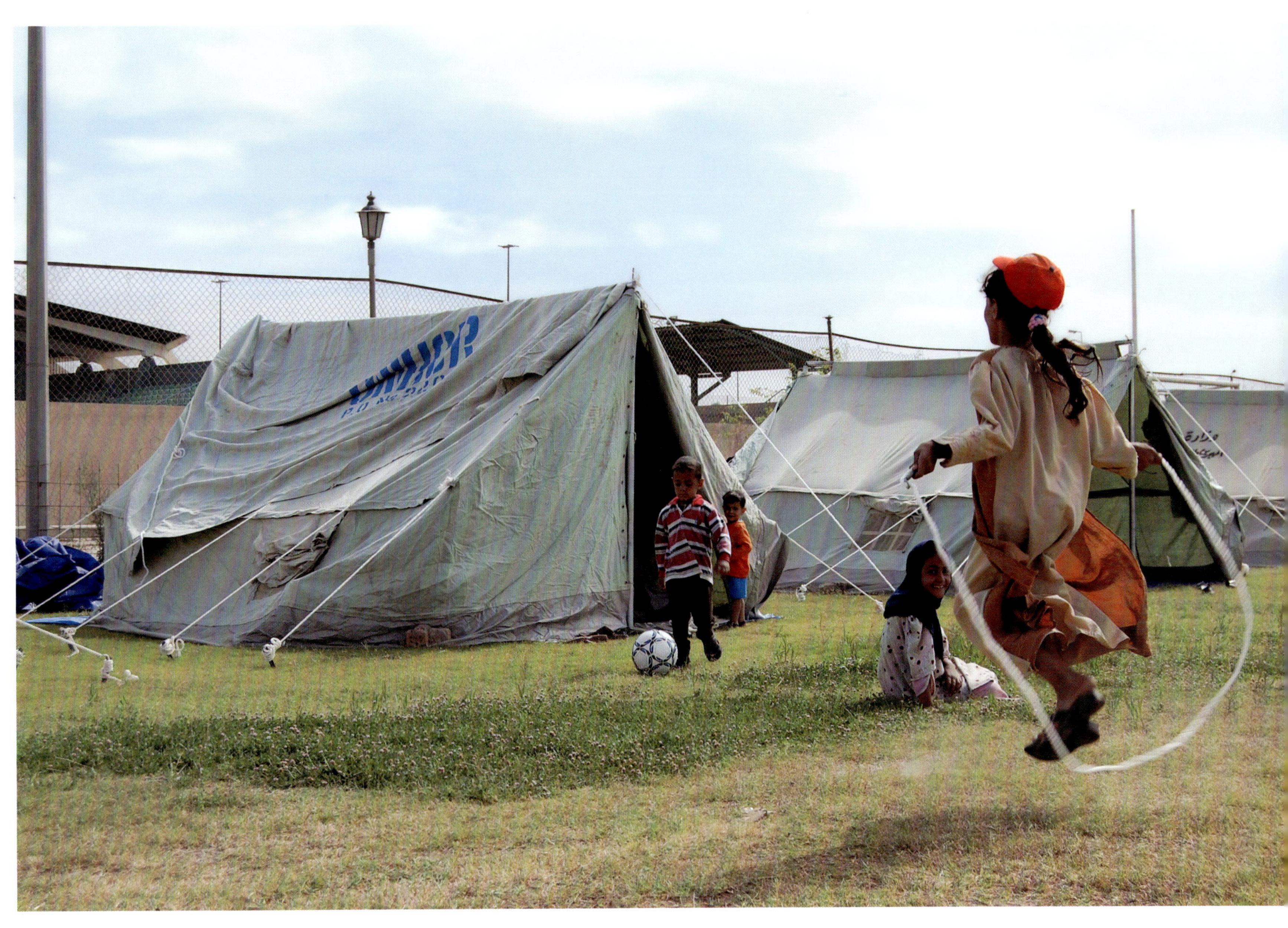

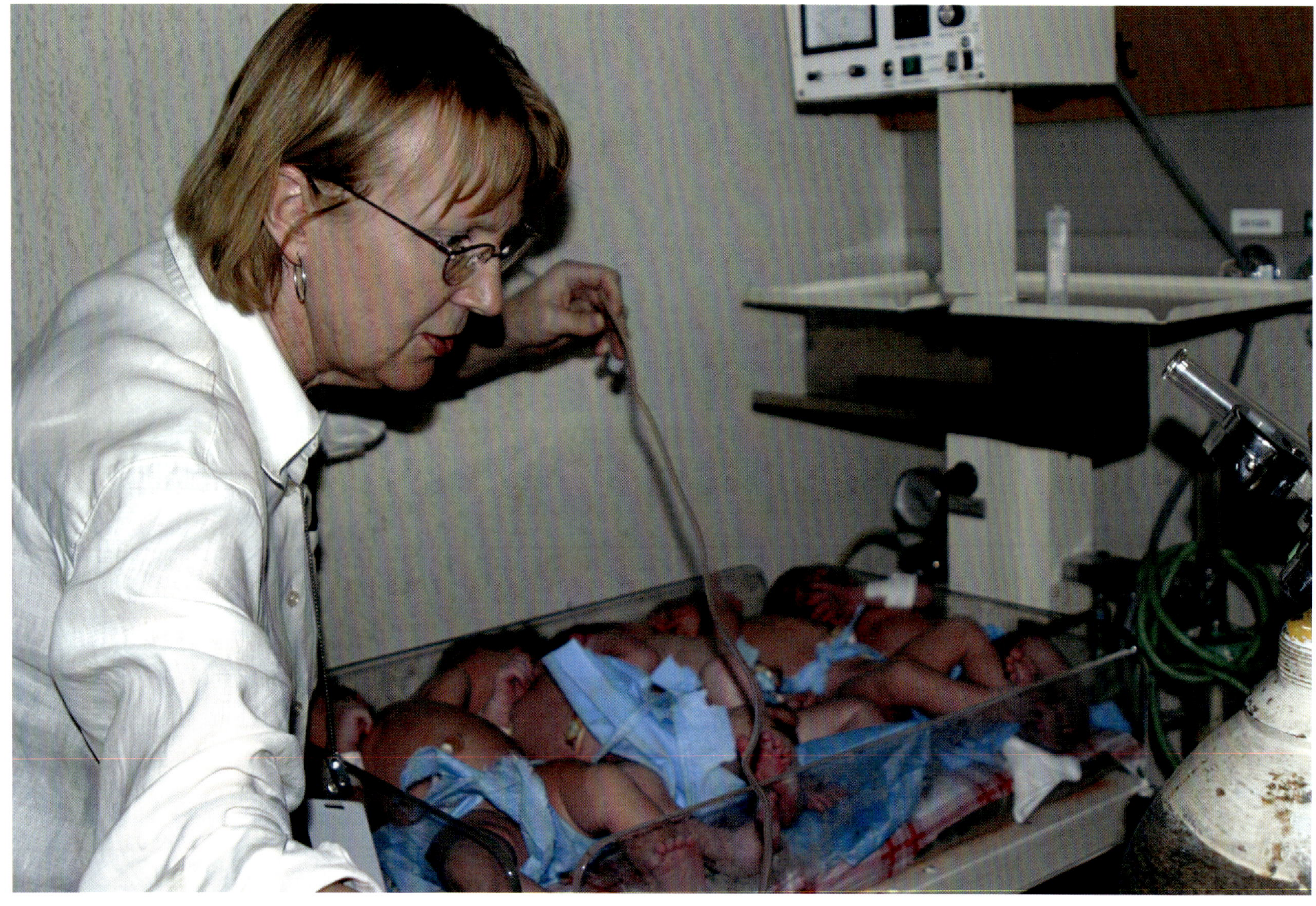

Iraq 2004
IMC Staff

Because roads were unsafe and fuel was scarce, Iraqi nurses had difficulty getting to the hospitals that so desperately needed their help. To remedy this challenging situation, IMC hired nine 50-seat buses to regularly take 400 to 500 nurses to Medical City, a 2-mile area in Baghdad that contains five hospitals and two teaching facilities. Helping the nurses get to work every day was a critical first step in the reactivation of the health care system in Iraq.

Opposite page: International Medical Corps rehabilitated the emergency department of one of Southern Iraq's busiest hospitals, Nassariyah General Hospital. Iraqi women in black abayas slipped silently into the hospital corridors to bring their children for treatment. The hospital's ER unit now has a triage system, 14 active emergency beds, a rehabilitated minor surgery room, and a resuscitation room, allowing the hospital to service more than 1,000 patients a day, many of whom are children.

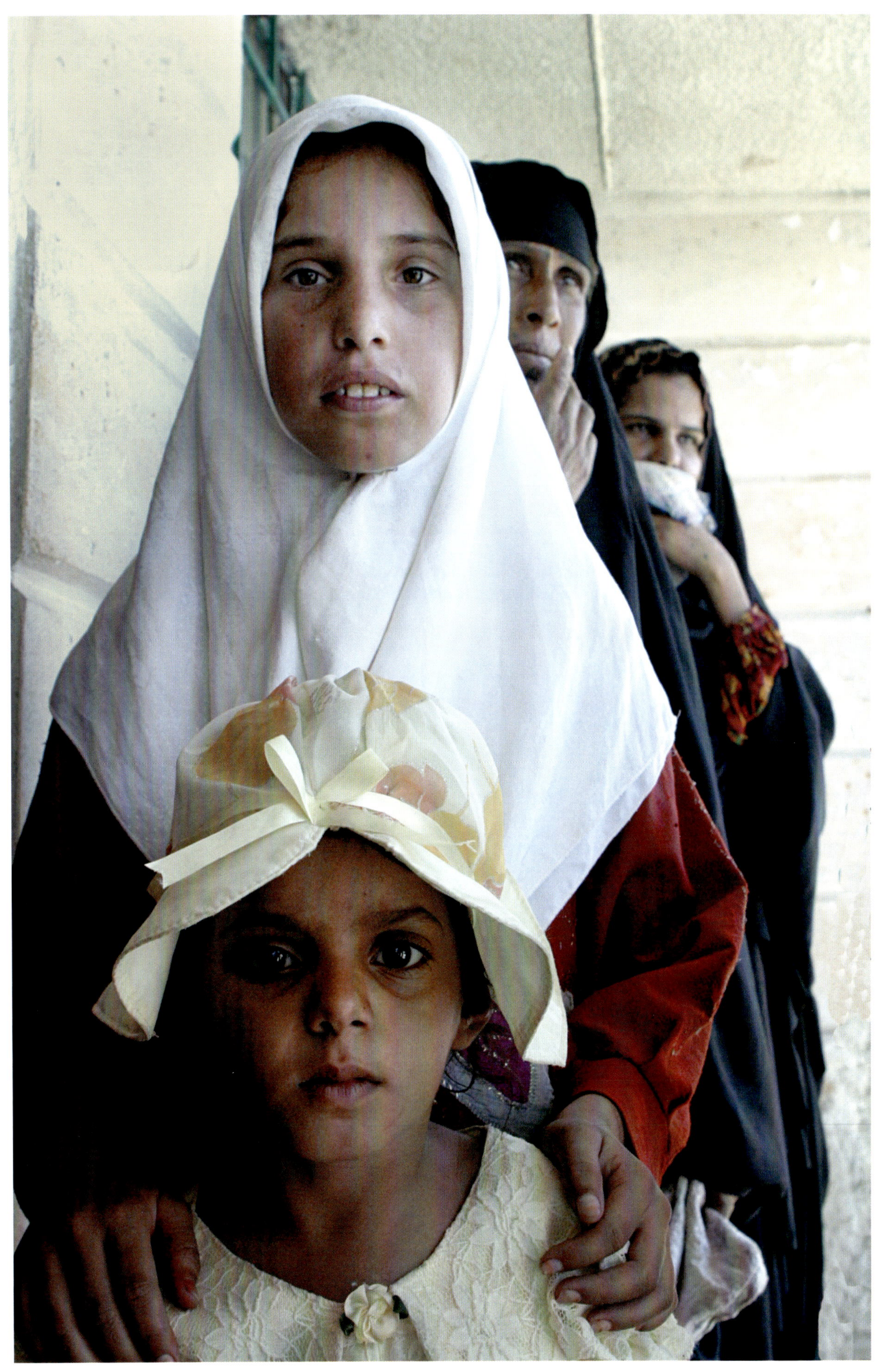

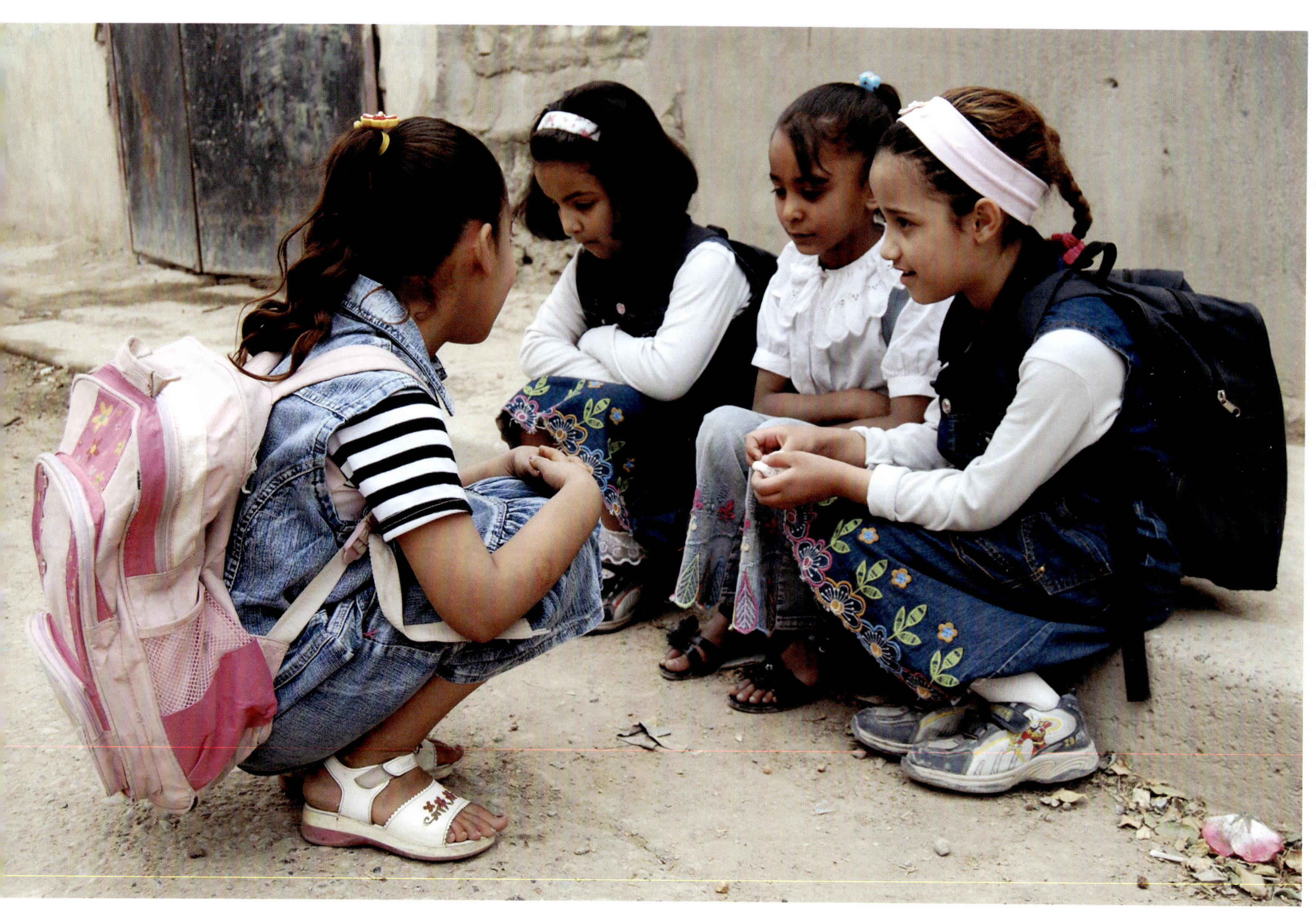

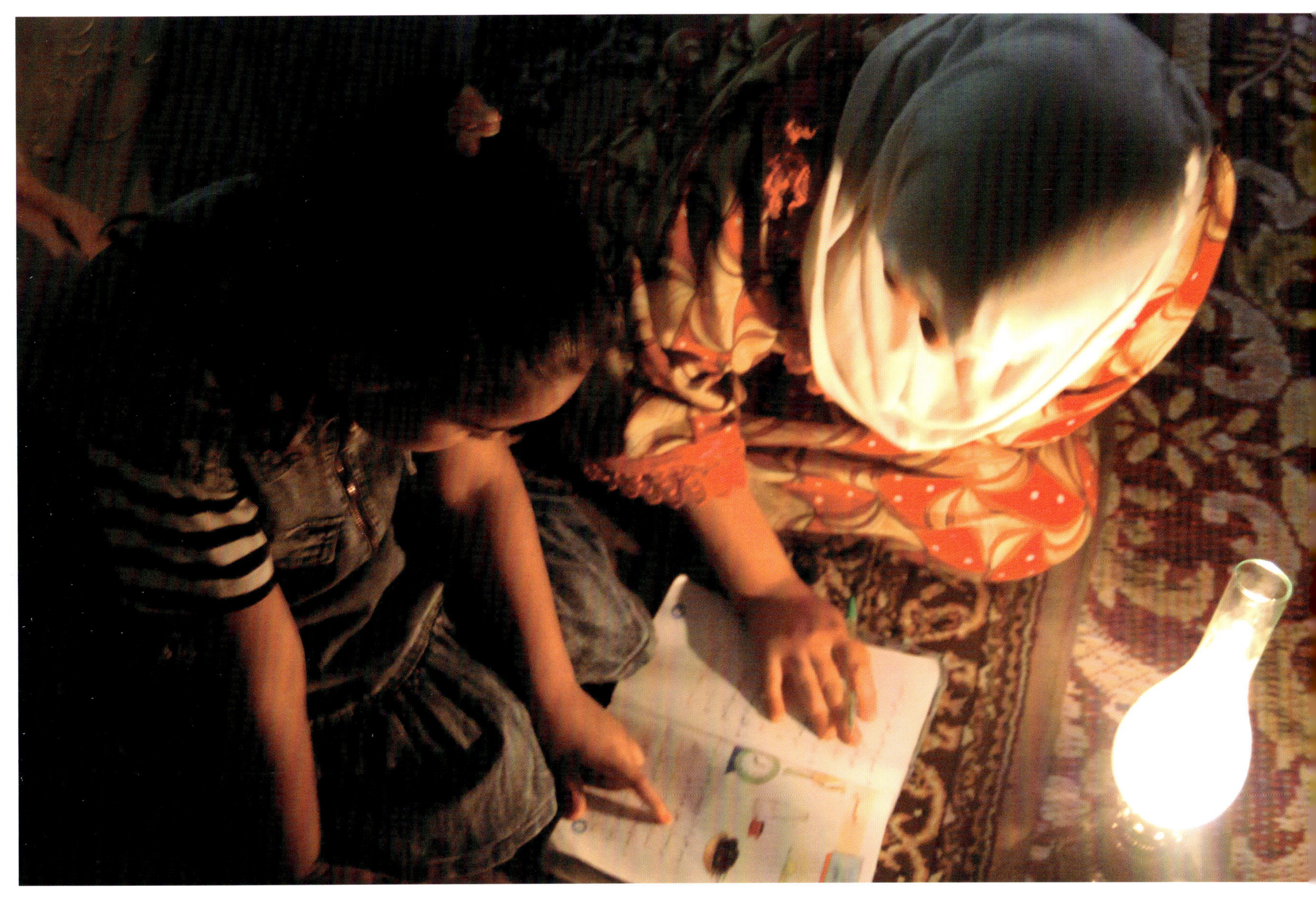

Iraq 2008
IMC staff (both photos)

More than two million Iraqis fled their country for safety in Lebanon, Syria and Jordan. Host countries were overwhelmed by the influx of refugee families. International Medical Corps found many Iraqi refugee children not only lacking proper health care, but also education.

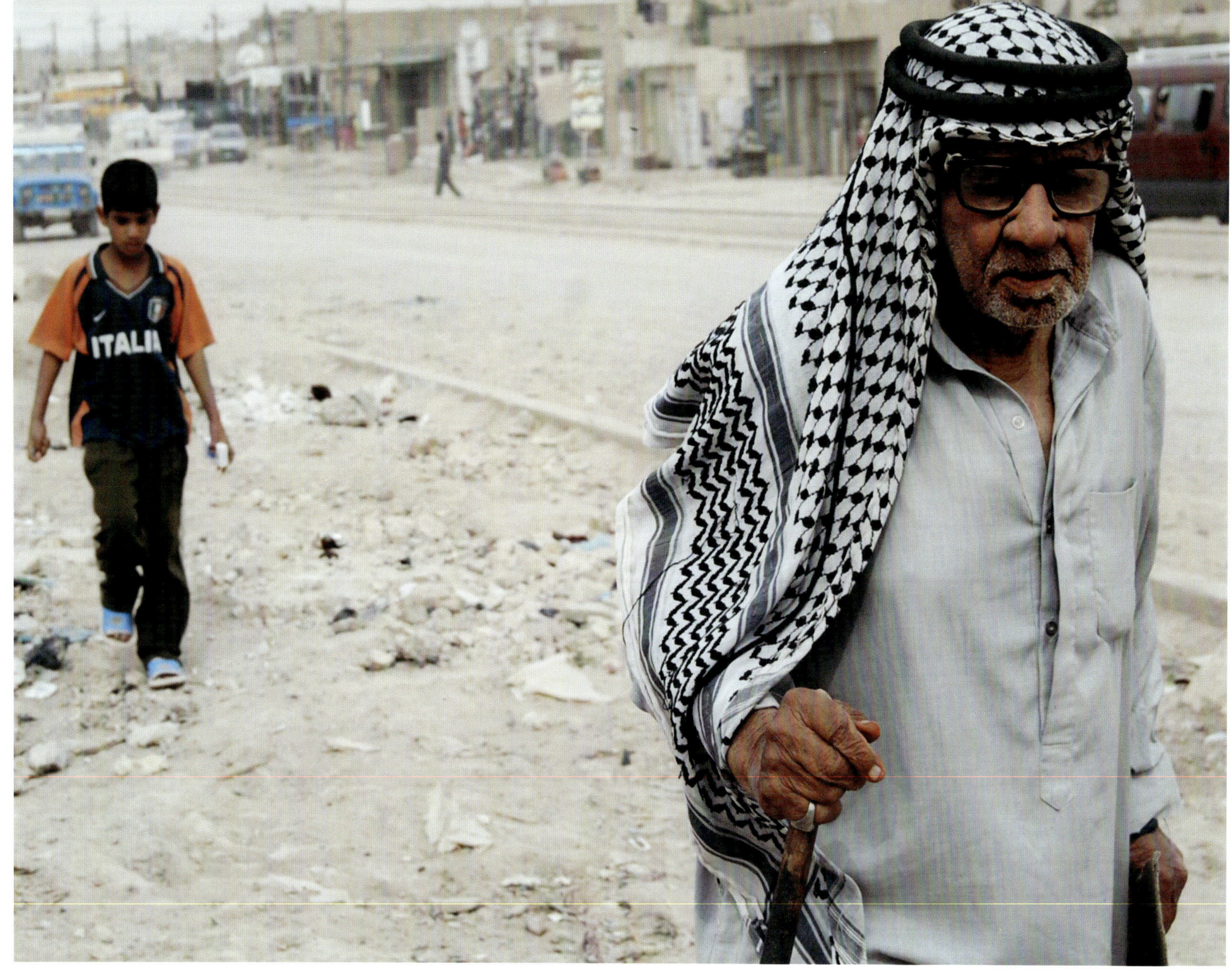

Iraq 2008
IMC staff (both photos)

As one of the few fully operational, independent humanitarian organizations in Iraq, International Medical Corps has a deep understanding of the problems Iraqis face, both in their country and in exile. Establishing clinics and improving existing primary health care facilities through technical assistance and trained personnel, IMC often is the only resource for the health of many Iraqi refugees.

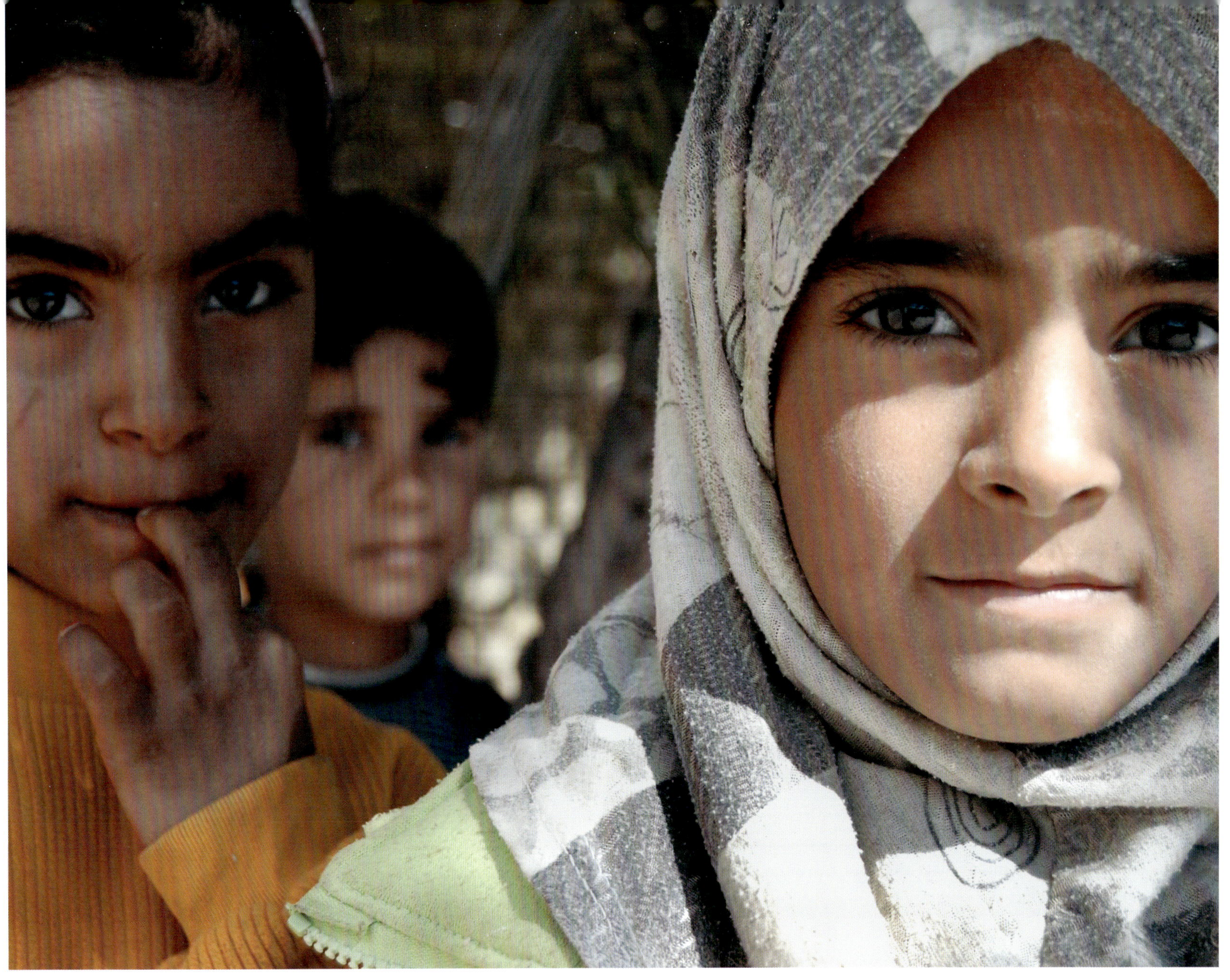

DISASTER RESPONSE

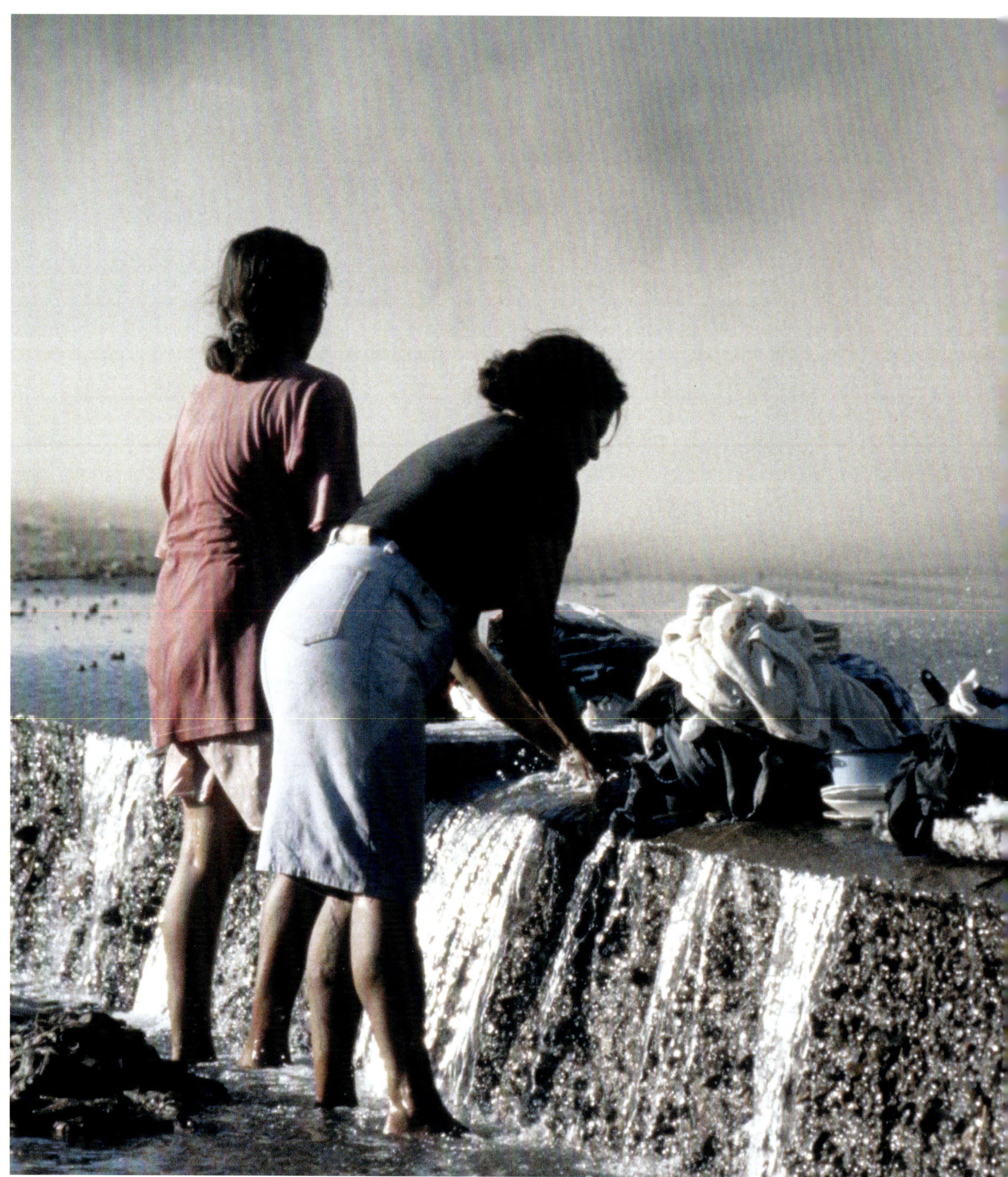

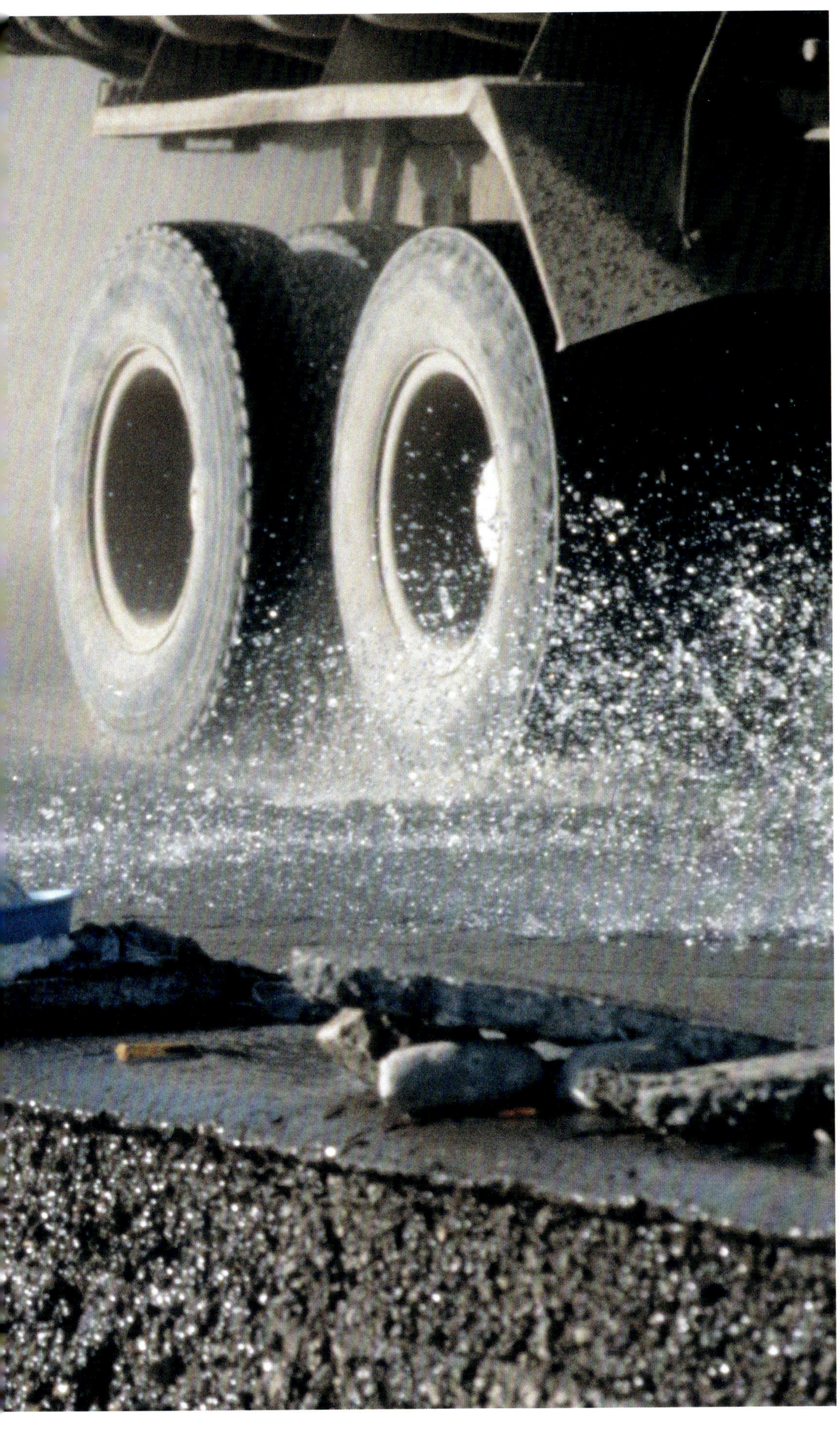

Honduras 1998
IMC staff

In the aftermath of Hurricane Mitch, which devastated many rural communities in Honduras, International Medical Corps' world-renowned rapid-response teams provided health care to the most devasted areas.

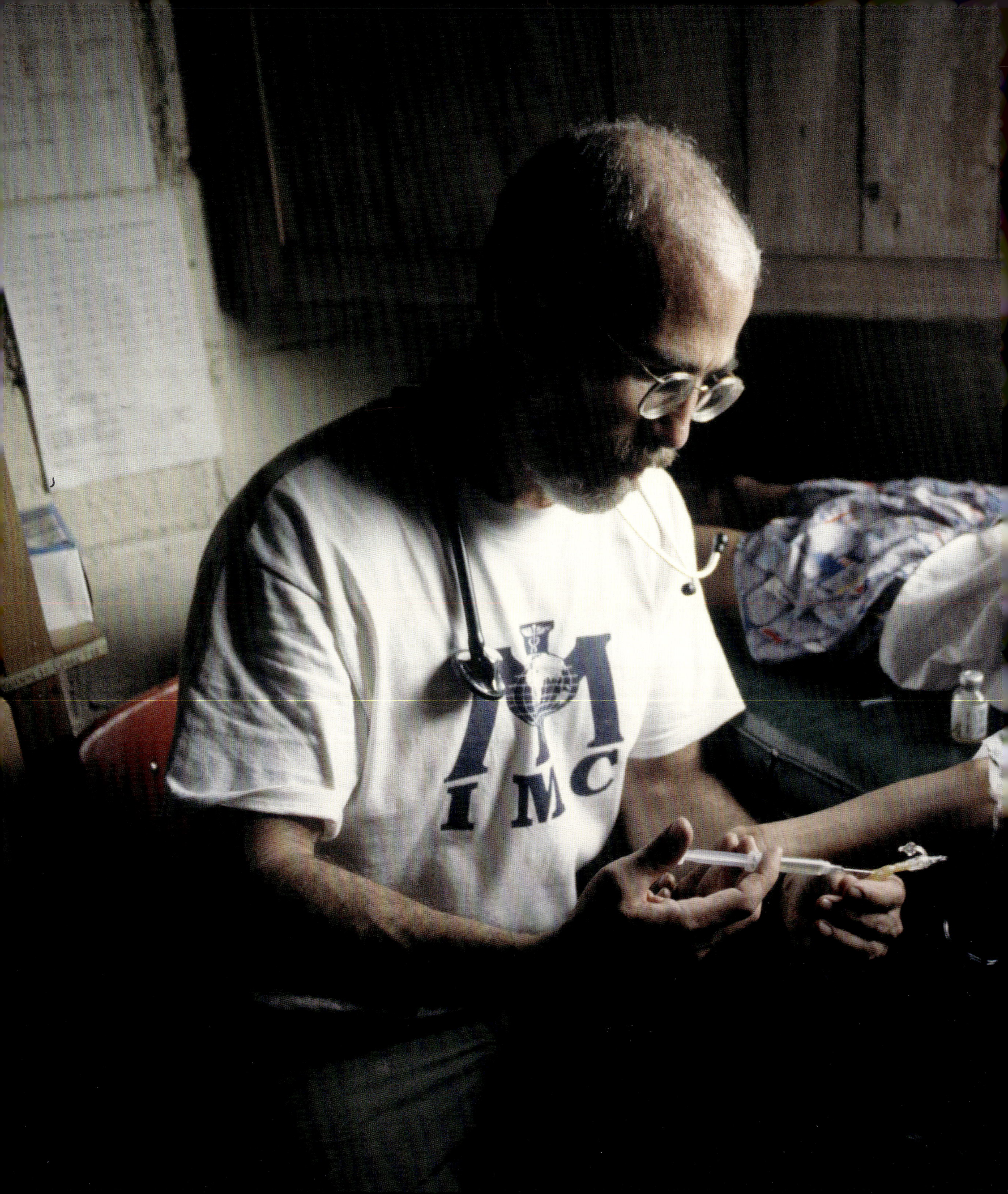
IMC

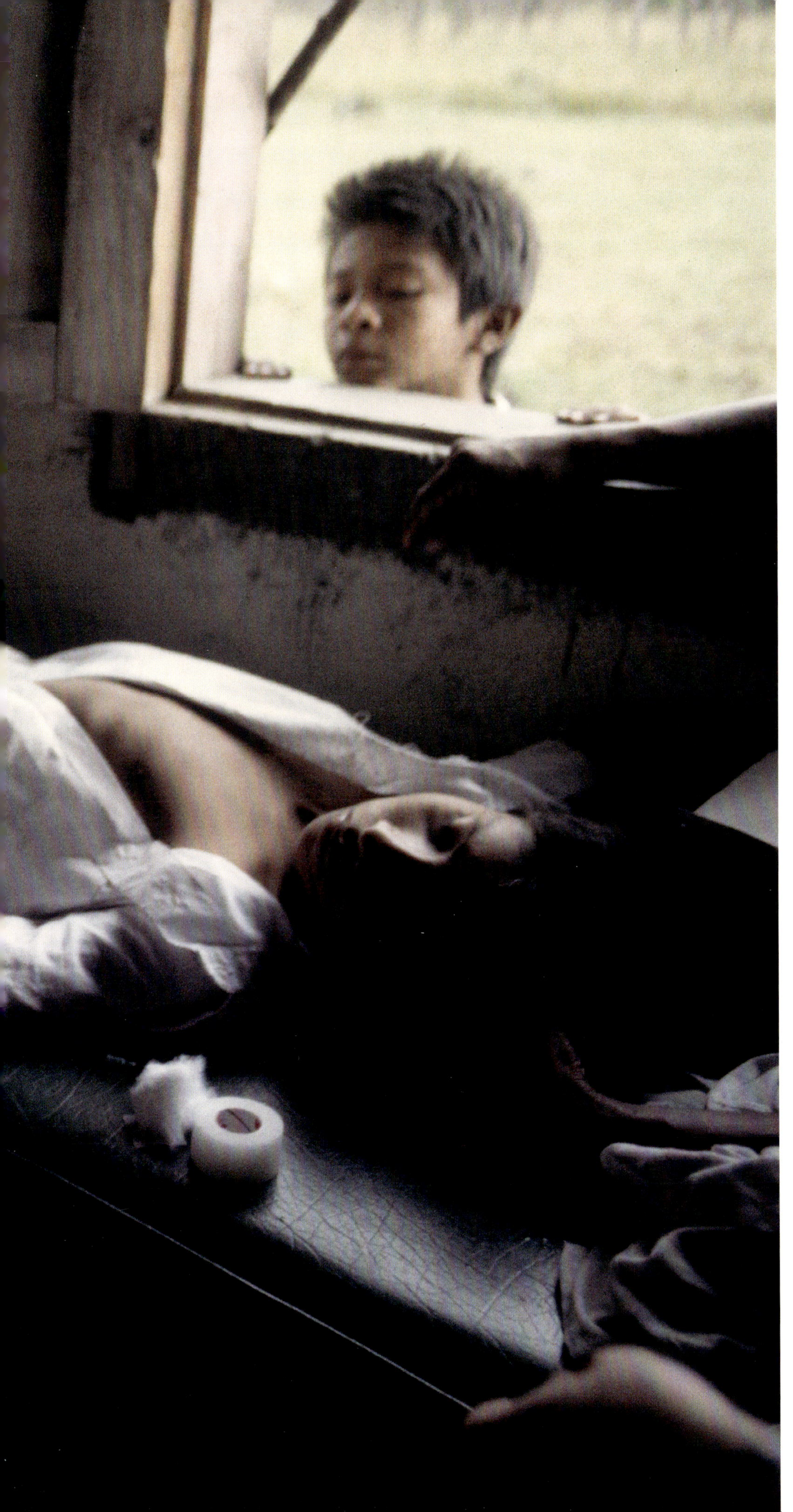

Honduras 1998
IMC staff

An International Medical Corps doctor administers life-saving immunizations to prevent diseases common in the aftermath of natural disasters when water, sanitation and other community services are compromised.

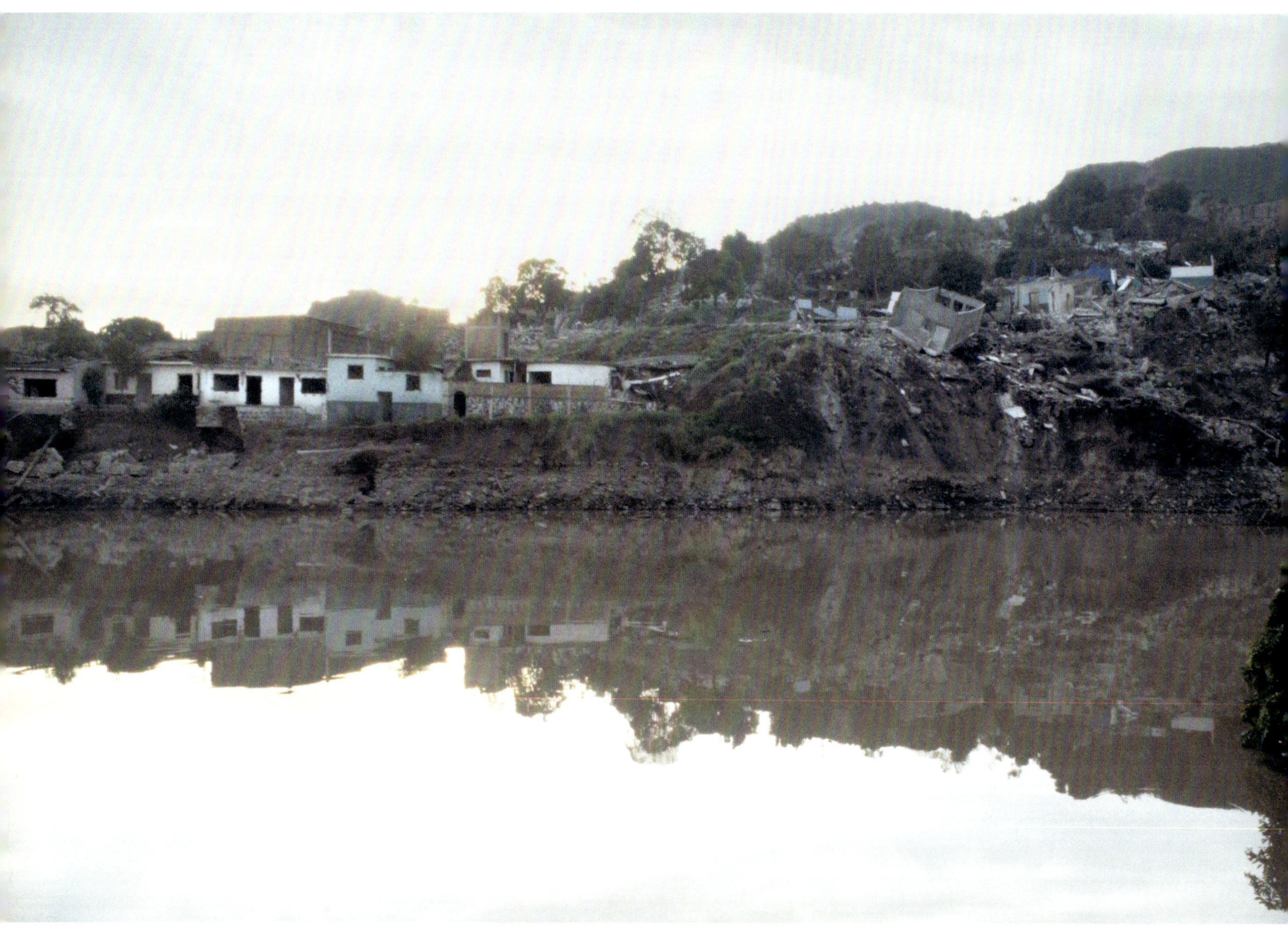

Honduras 1998
IMC staff

Hurricane Mitch leveled many communities in Honduras that were already overcrowded—and where tetanus, measles and polio were still common. International Medical Corps' disaster-response teams provided feeding programs to malnourished children as well as support to local health care systems that had collapsed.

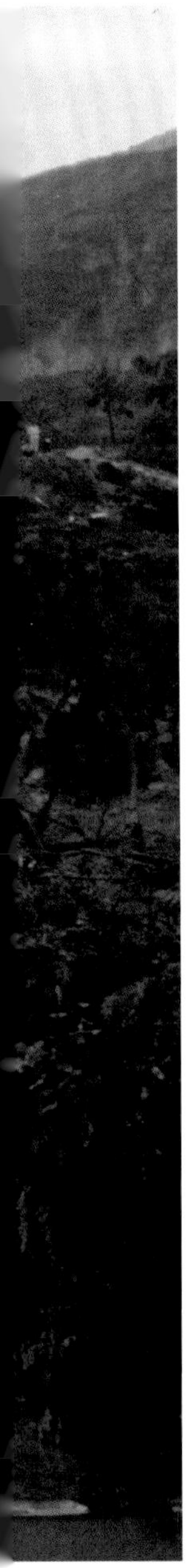

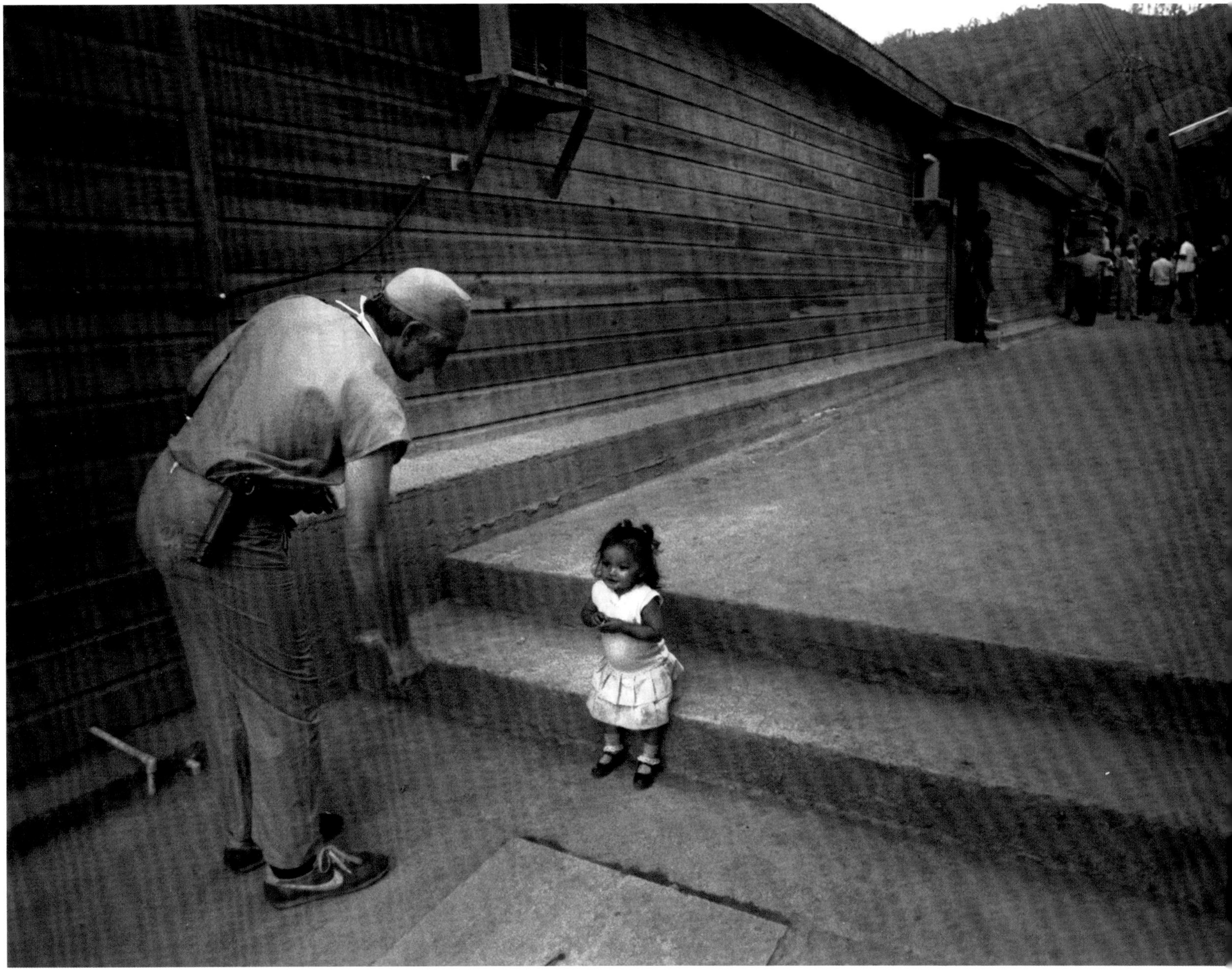

Honduras 1989
IMC staff

In a local hospital on the border of Nicaragua, an International Medical Corps doctor befriends a young patient. IMC had provided health care training programs in Honduras 10 years before the hurricane hit.

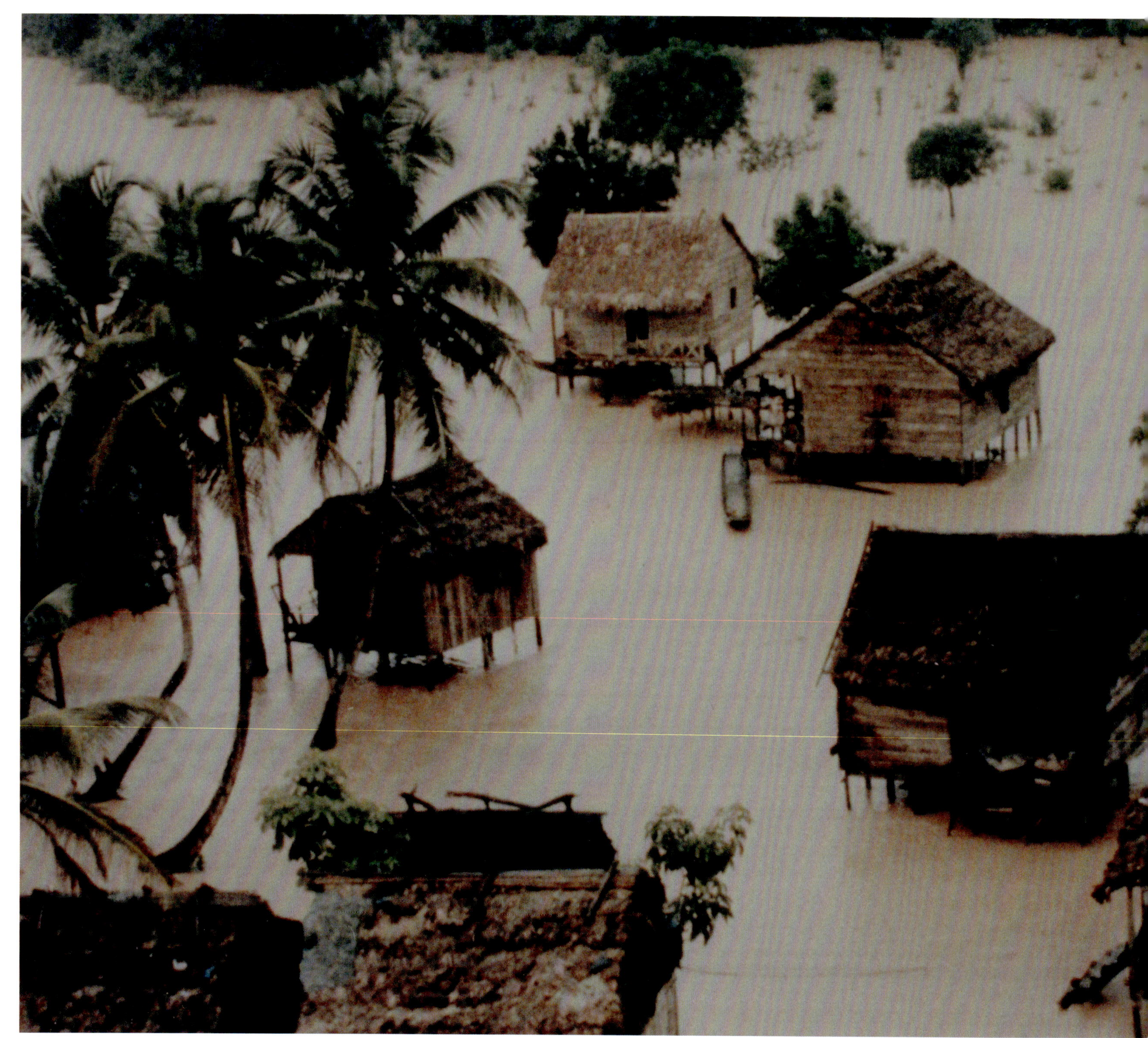

Honduras 1998
IMC staff (both photos)

In Honduras, International Medical Corps' water and sanitation teams provided potable water supplies to displaced populations and dealt with waste and sewage management to prevent the spread of disease.

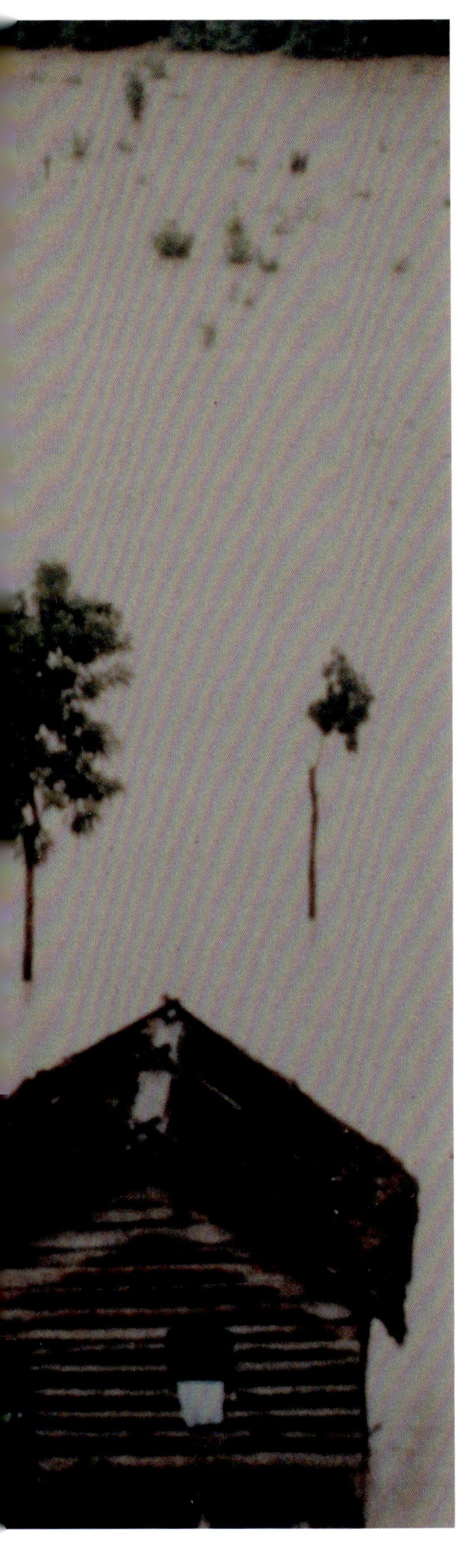

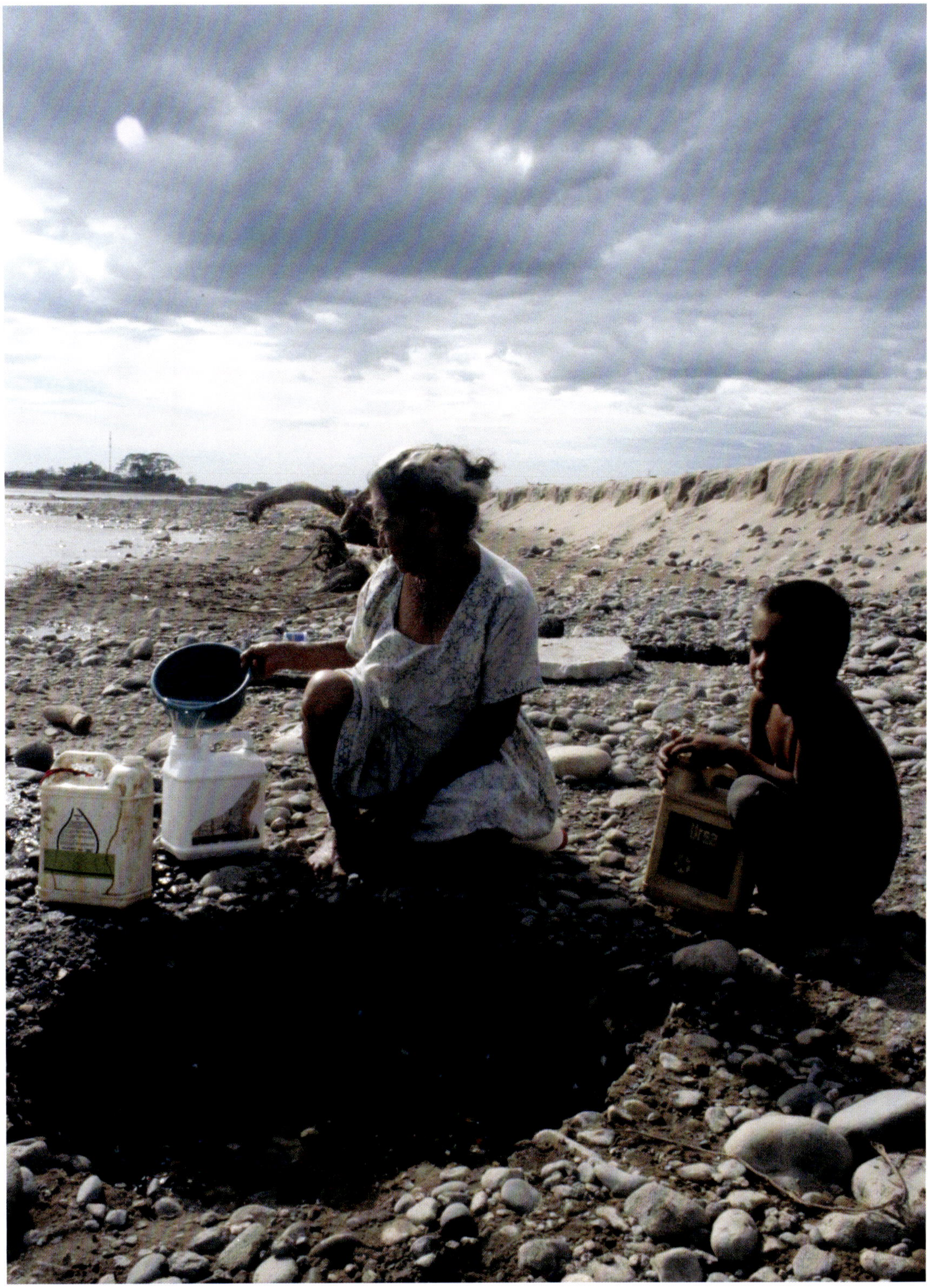

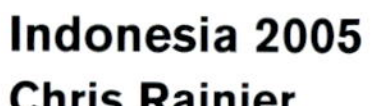

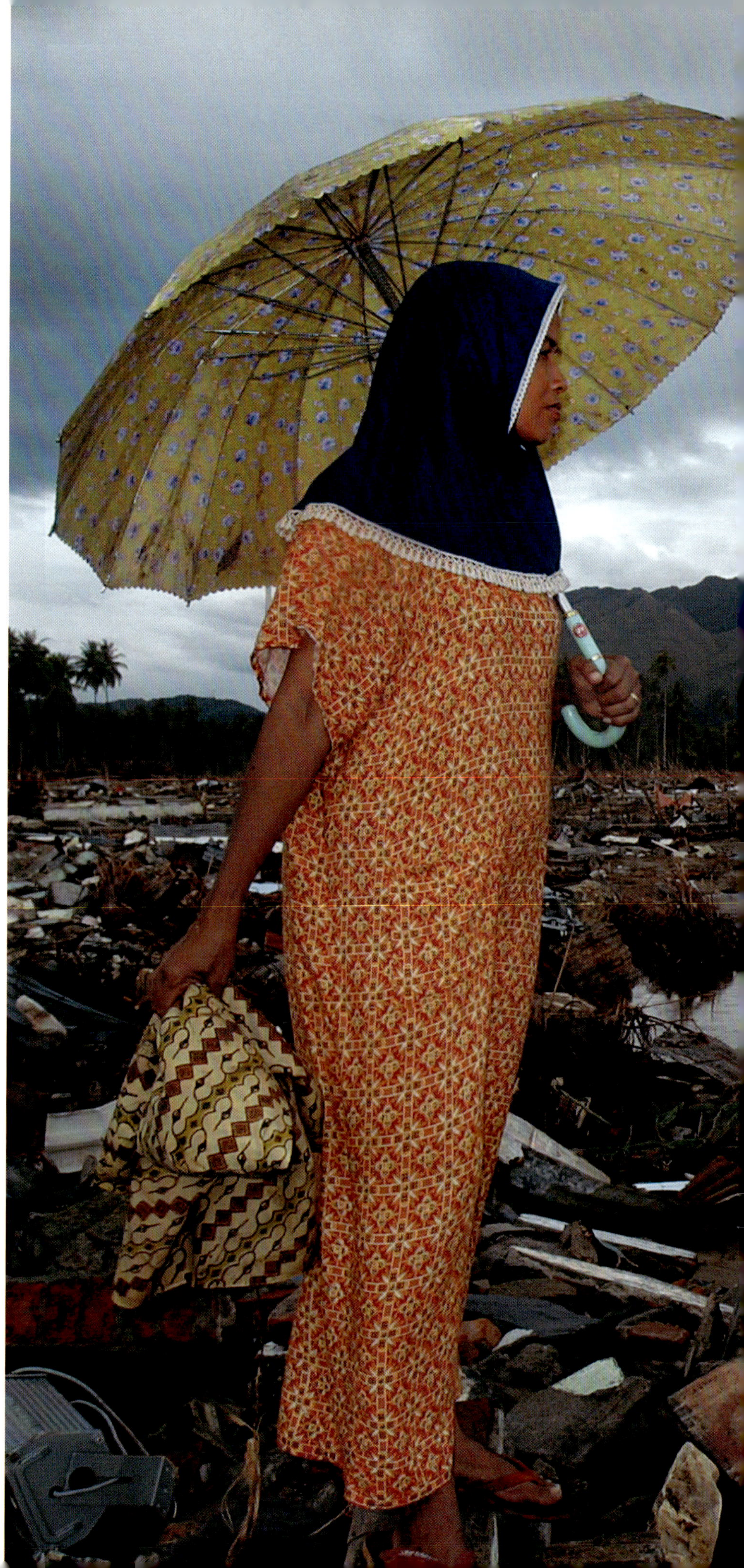

Indonesia 2005
Chris Rainier

An Indonesian woman surveys the damage in Aceh the day after the tsunami destroyed virtually everything in its wake. International Medical Corps doctors and nurses already working in Indonesia were deployed as emergency rapid-response teams to the most remote areas. IMC was one of the first organizations to reach hardest-hit Banda Aceh.

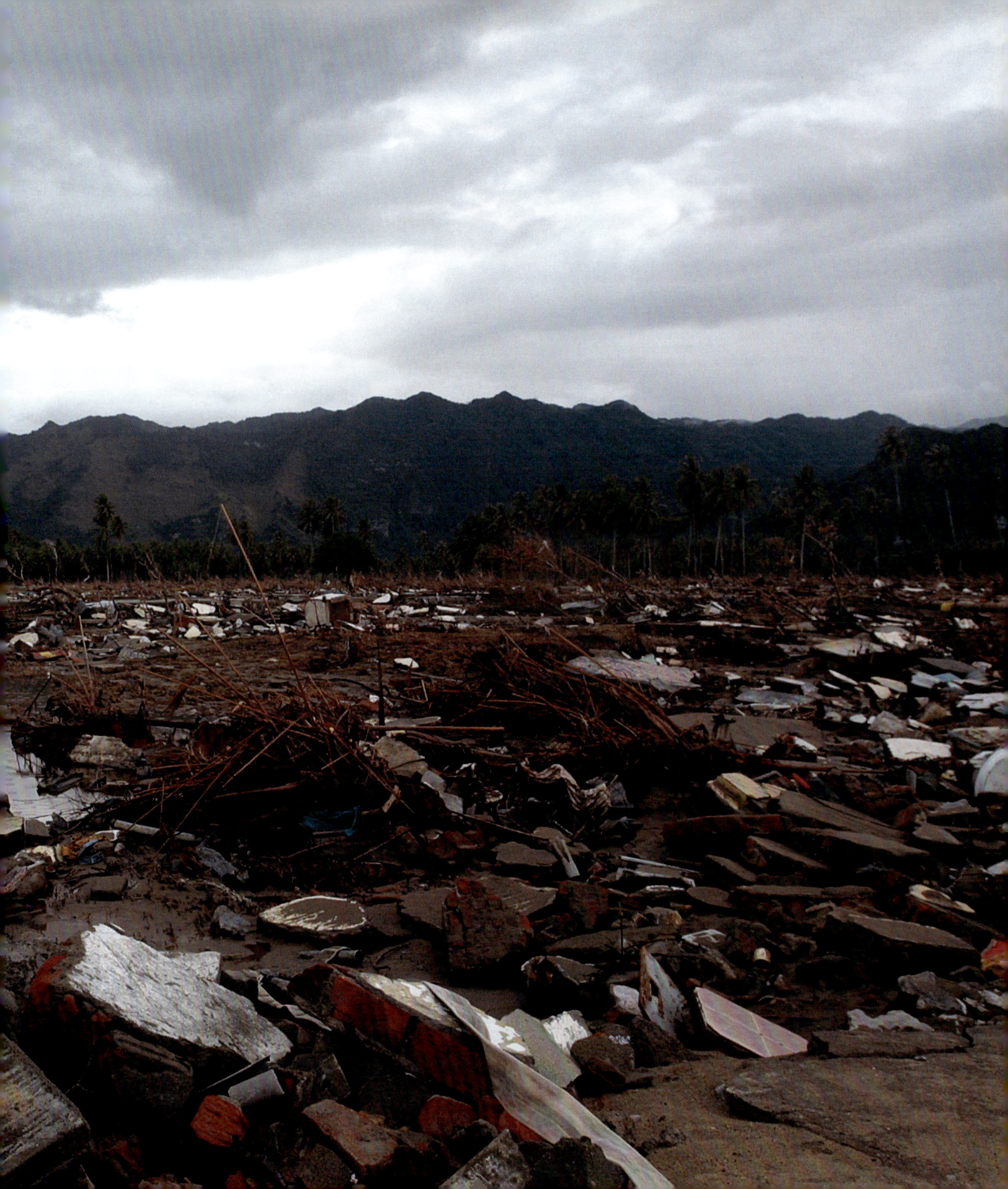

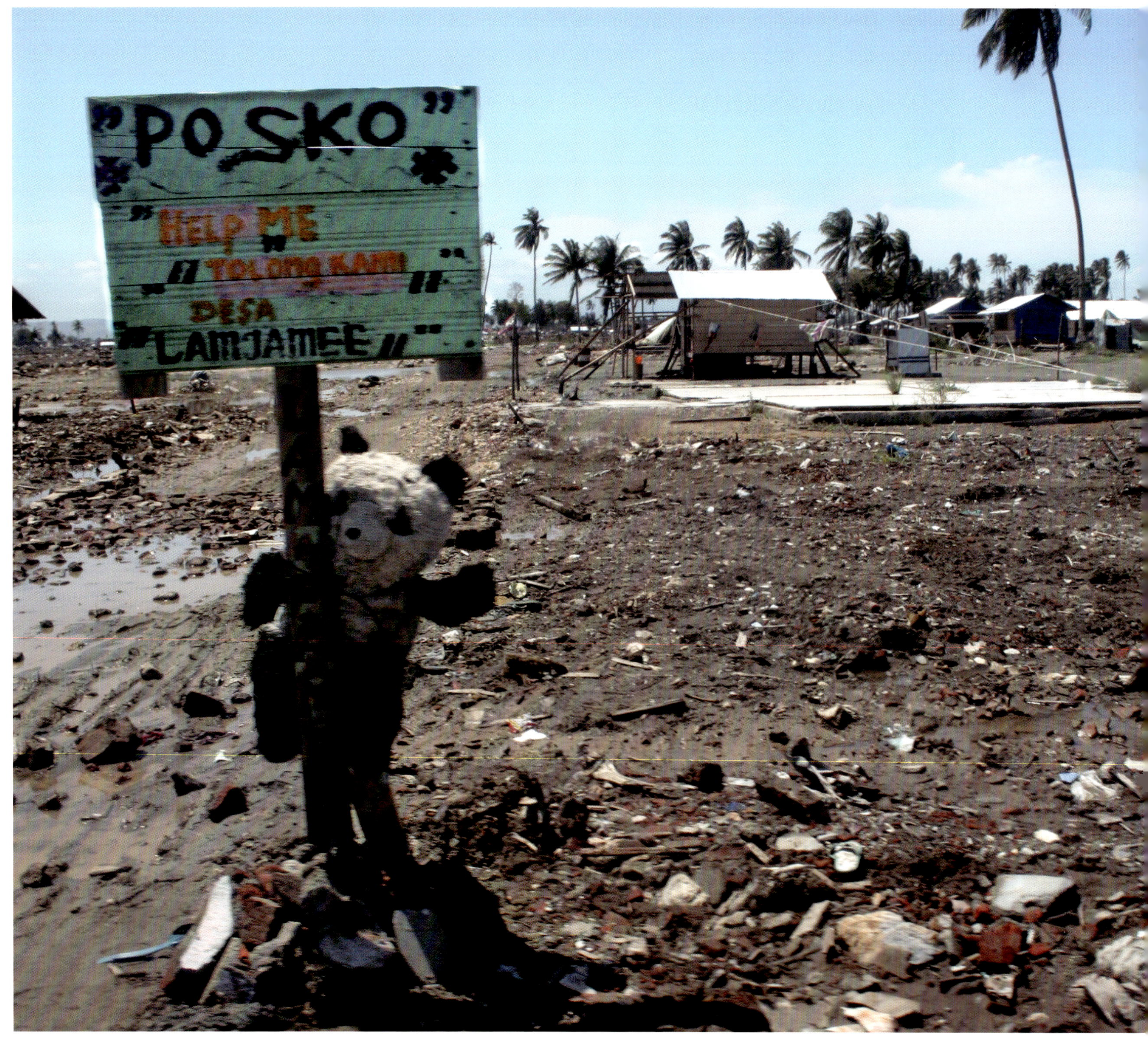

Indonesia 2005

Sara Terry

International Medical Corps was one of the first humanitarian organizations on the ground in Southeast Asia in the aftermath of the massive December 26, 2004 tsunami that killed nearly 200,000, injured as many, and left vital health care systems in ruins.

Chris Rainier

Opposite page: Finding survivors in hard-to-reach areas was central to International Medical Corps' relief efforts in Indonesia.

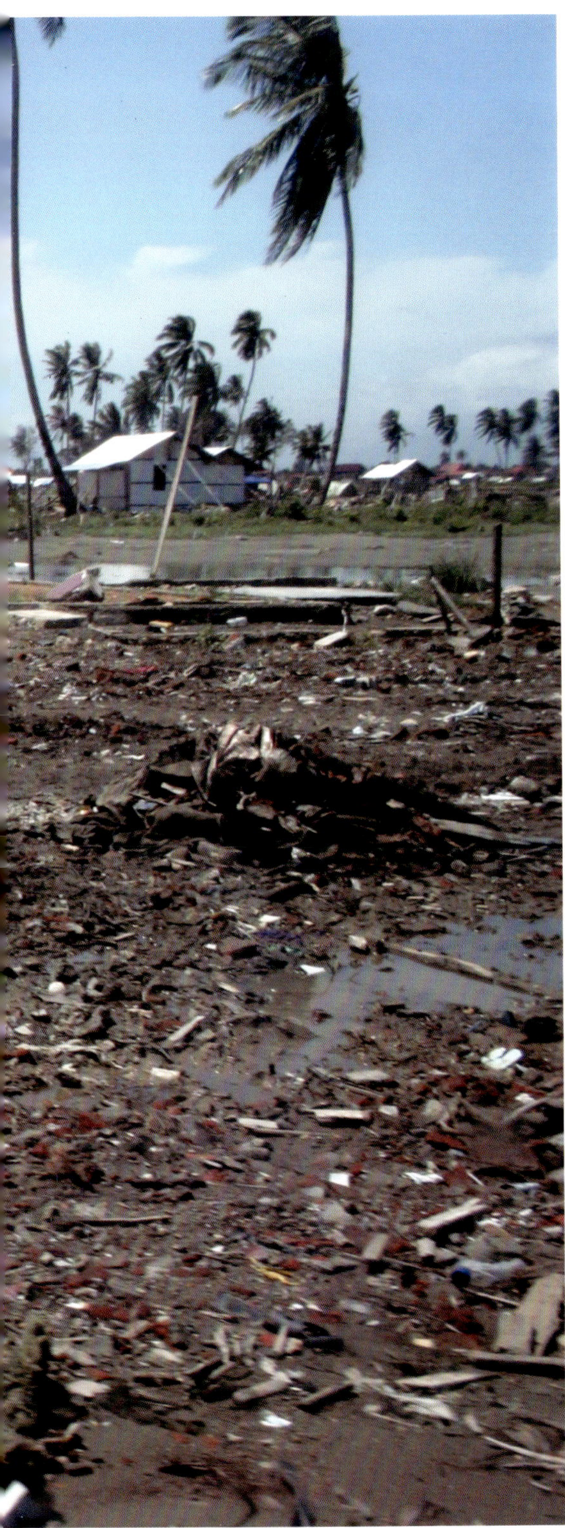

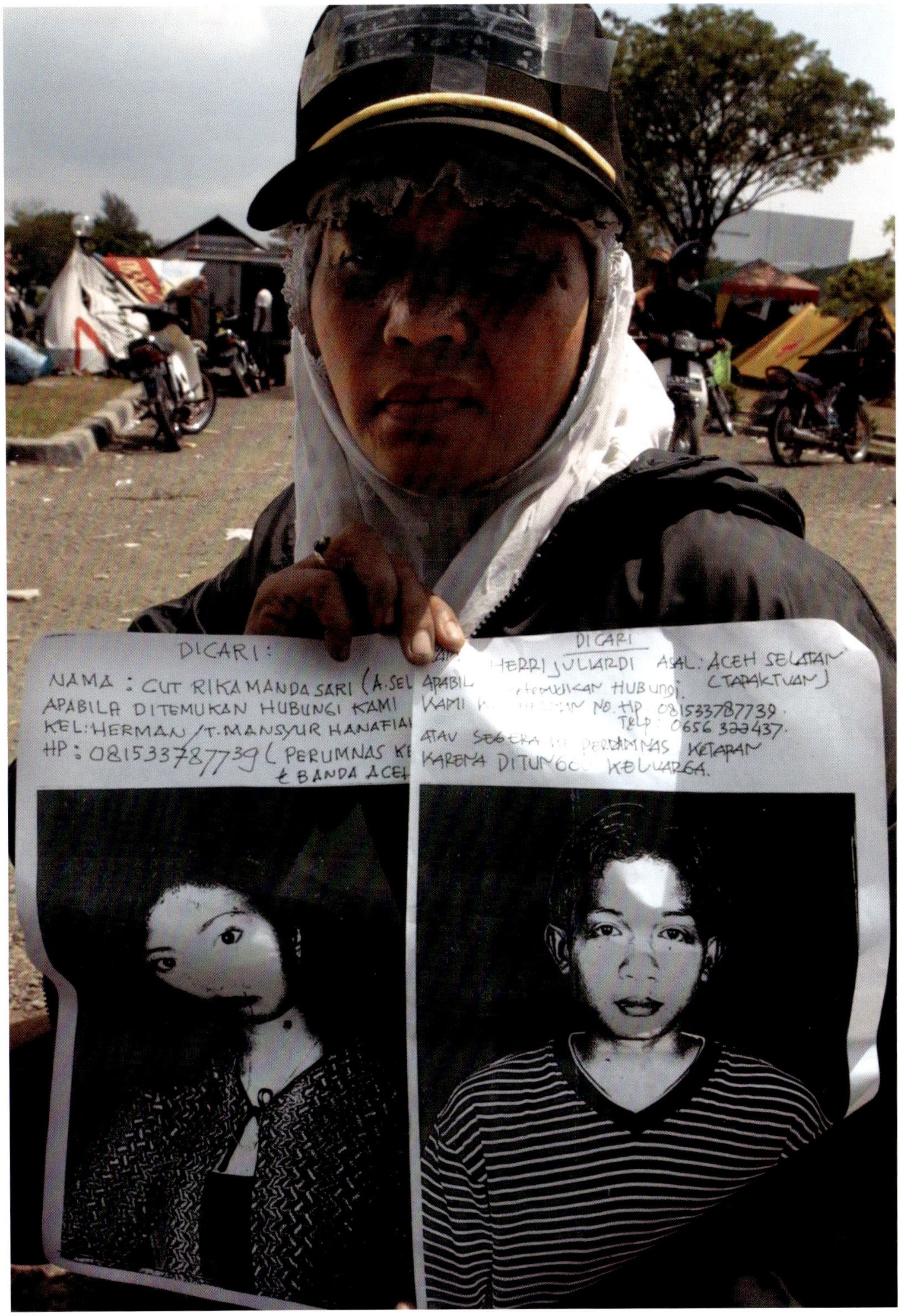

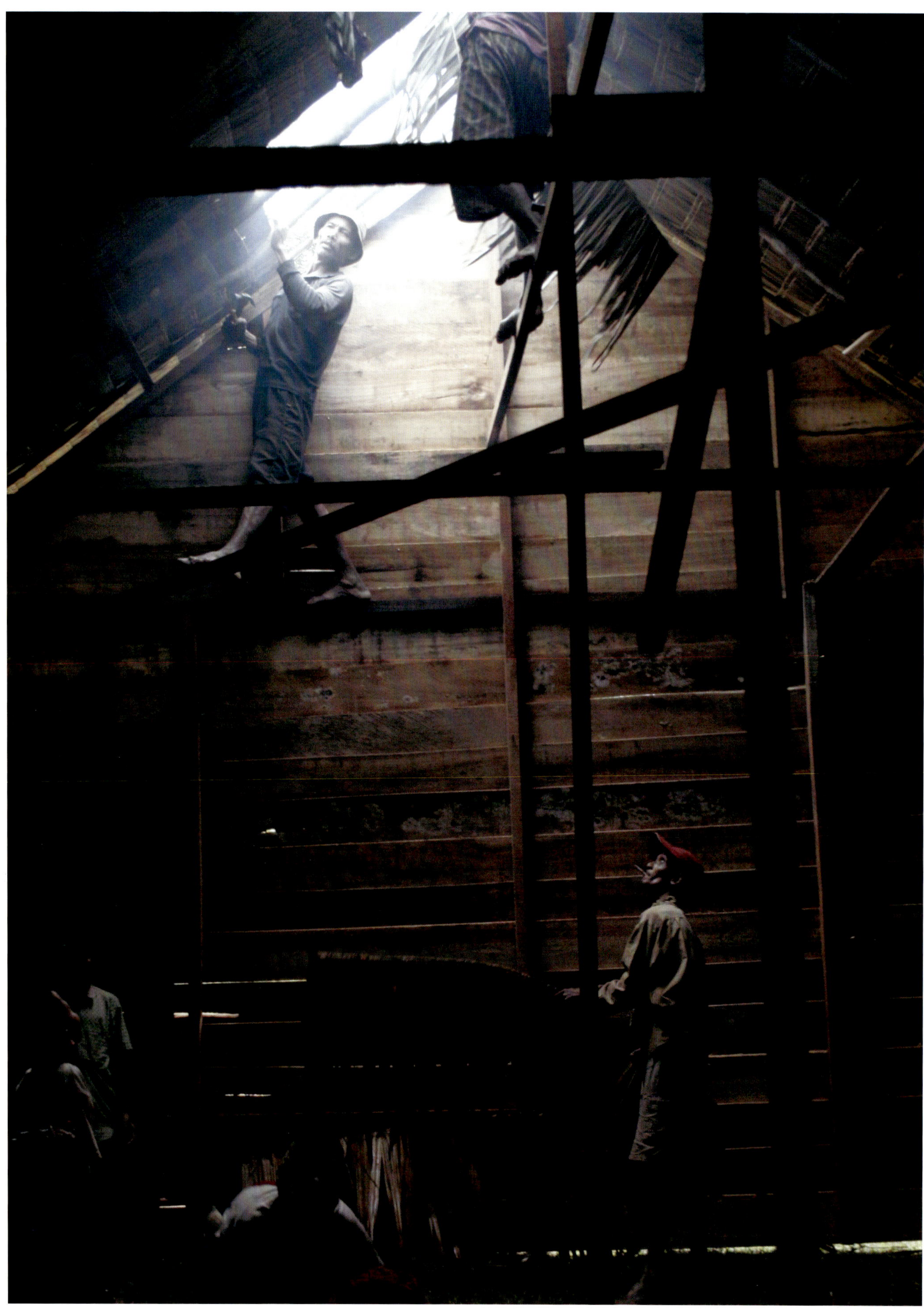

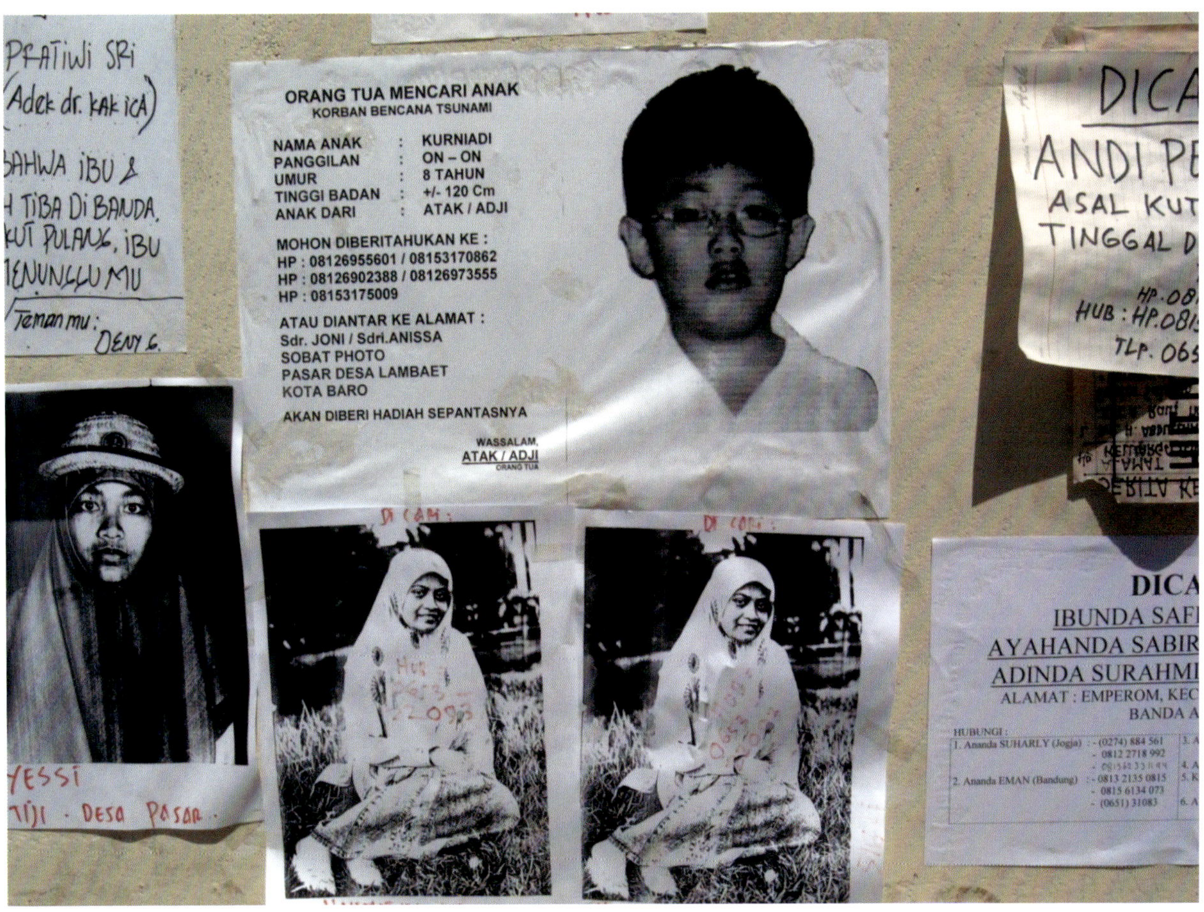

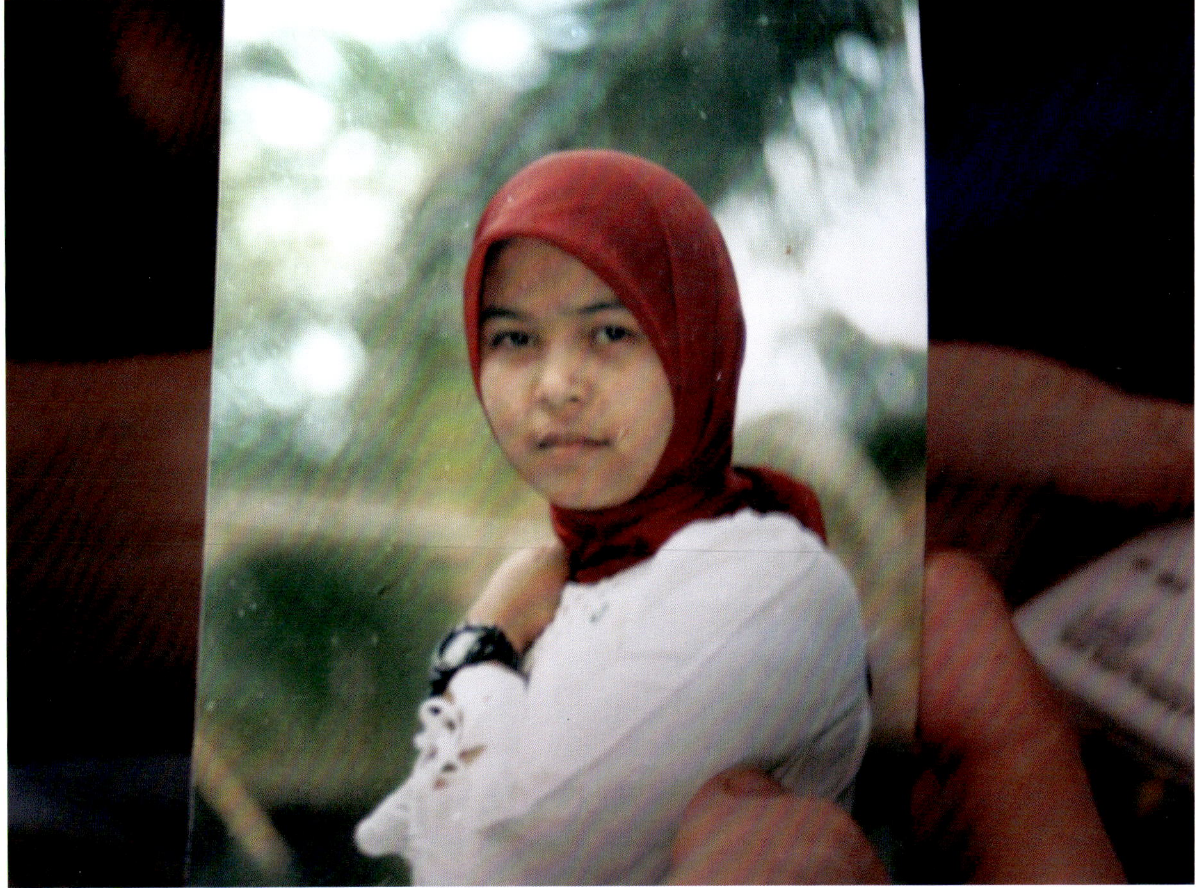

Indonesia 2005
Sara Terry (opposite)
Chris Rainier (this page, top)
Sara Terry (this page, bottom)

When the tsunami hit on December 26, 2004, International Medical Corps immediately began providing relief and recovery assistance to victims. Because of its pre-existing local presence, IMC was able to provide the first response so critical to saving lives after devastating natural disasters.

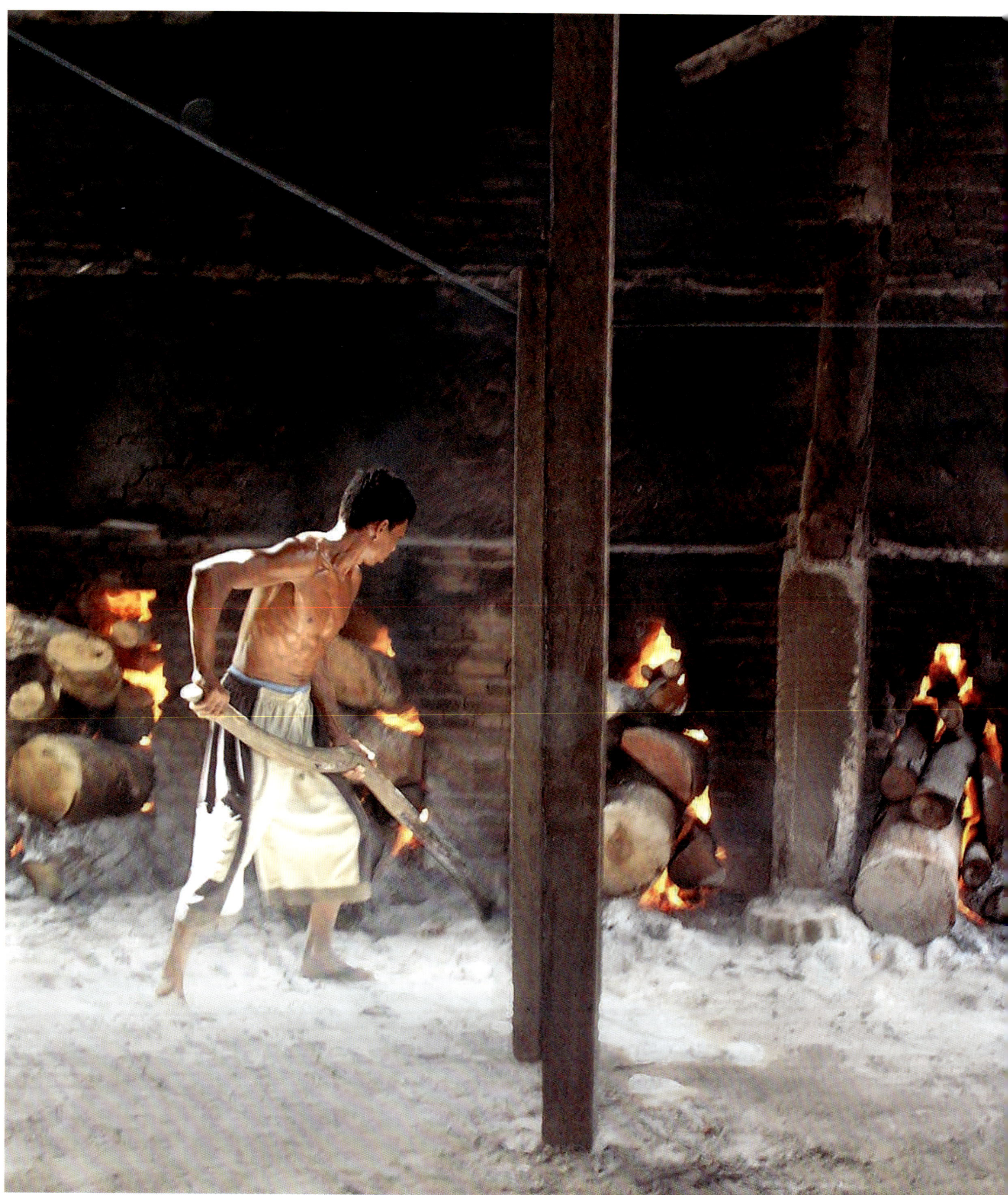

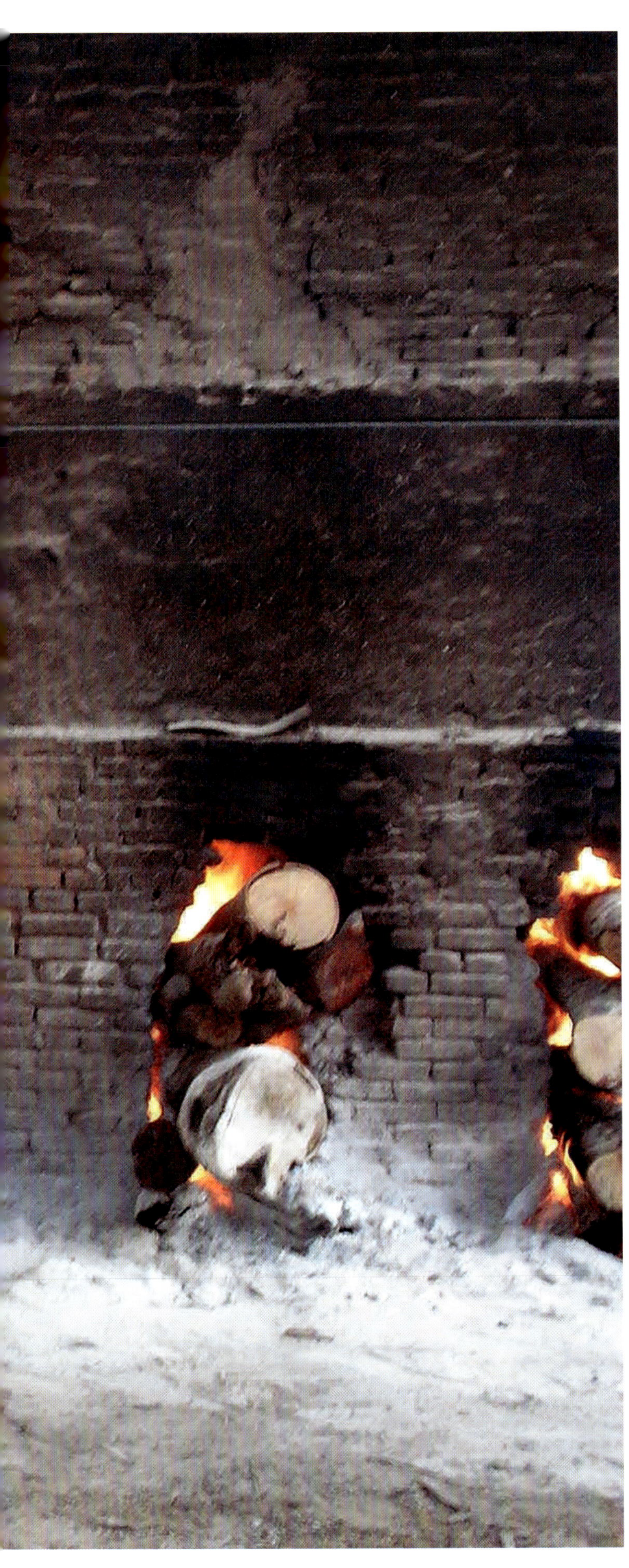

Indonesia 2005
Sara Terry

In 2005, International Medical Corps focused on helping tsunami-affected communities rebuild and return to self-reliance through livelihood projects like brick-making. One year after the tsunami devasted Southeast Asia, IMC programs had benefited 1.7 million survivors in Indonesia alone.

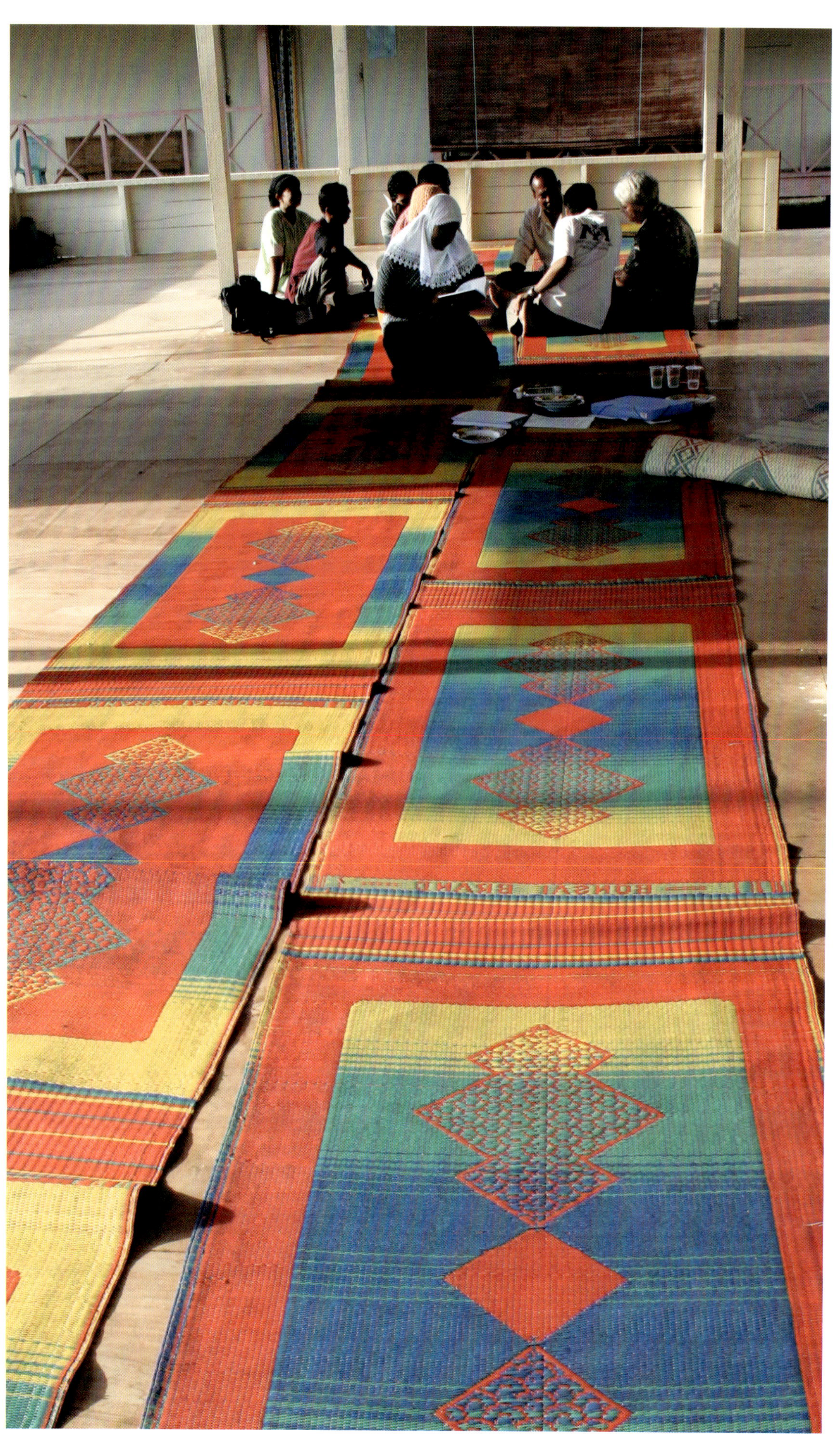

Indonesia 2005
Sara Terry (both photos)

During the emergency phase of the tsunami aftermath, IMC focused on saving lives. By 2005, IMC health care teams had gradually shifted their focus to supportive roles, reinforcing Ministry of Health staffs, training local health care workers and helping to restore the health systems of Indonesia.

Opposite page: International Medical Corps provided mental health assistance through health clinics, schools and home visits, with more than 2,000 consultations in 2005 alone. An IMC psychiatrist uses art therapy to help a child cope with the loss of her family as a result of the tsunami.

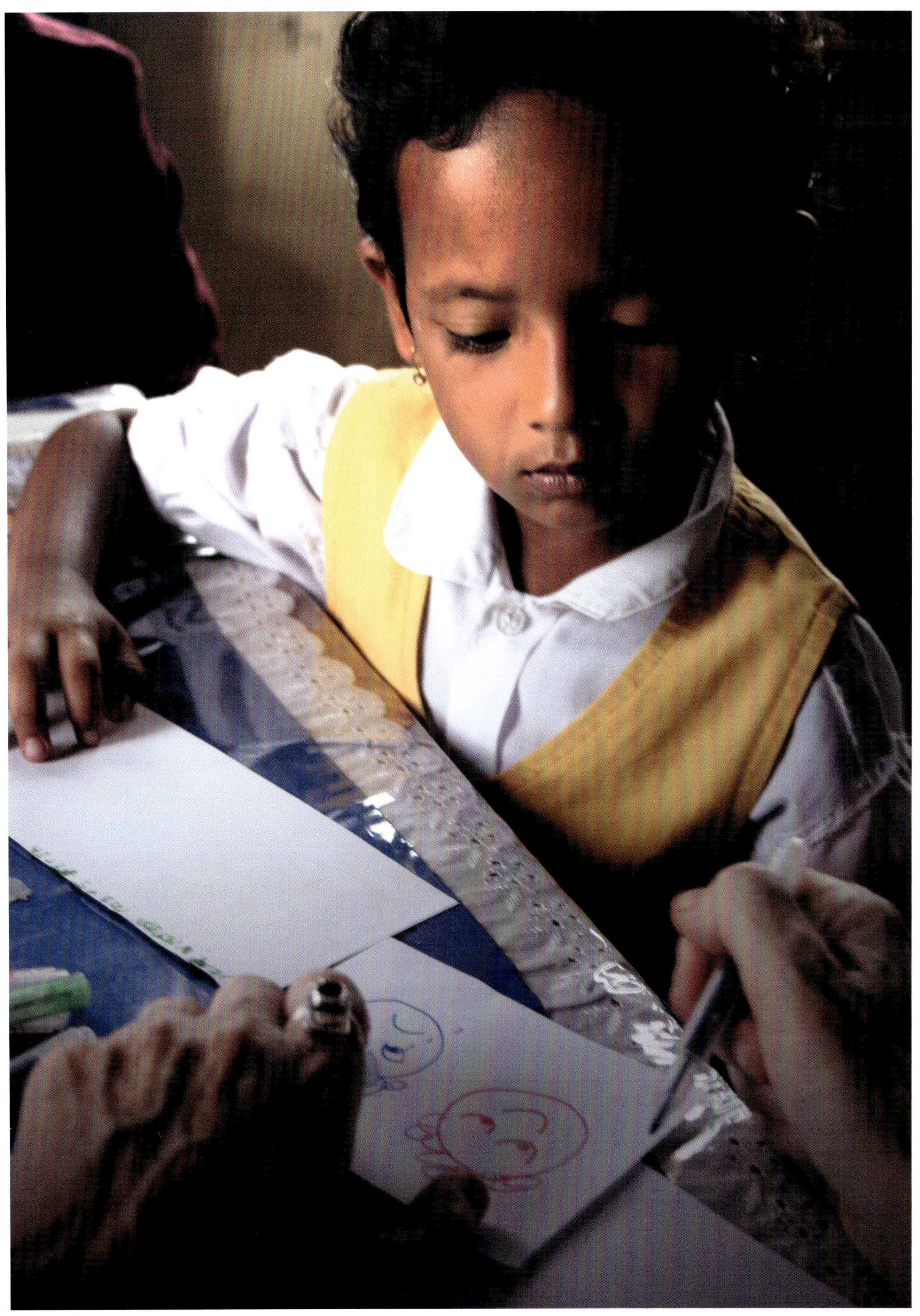

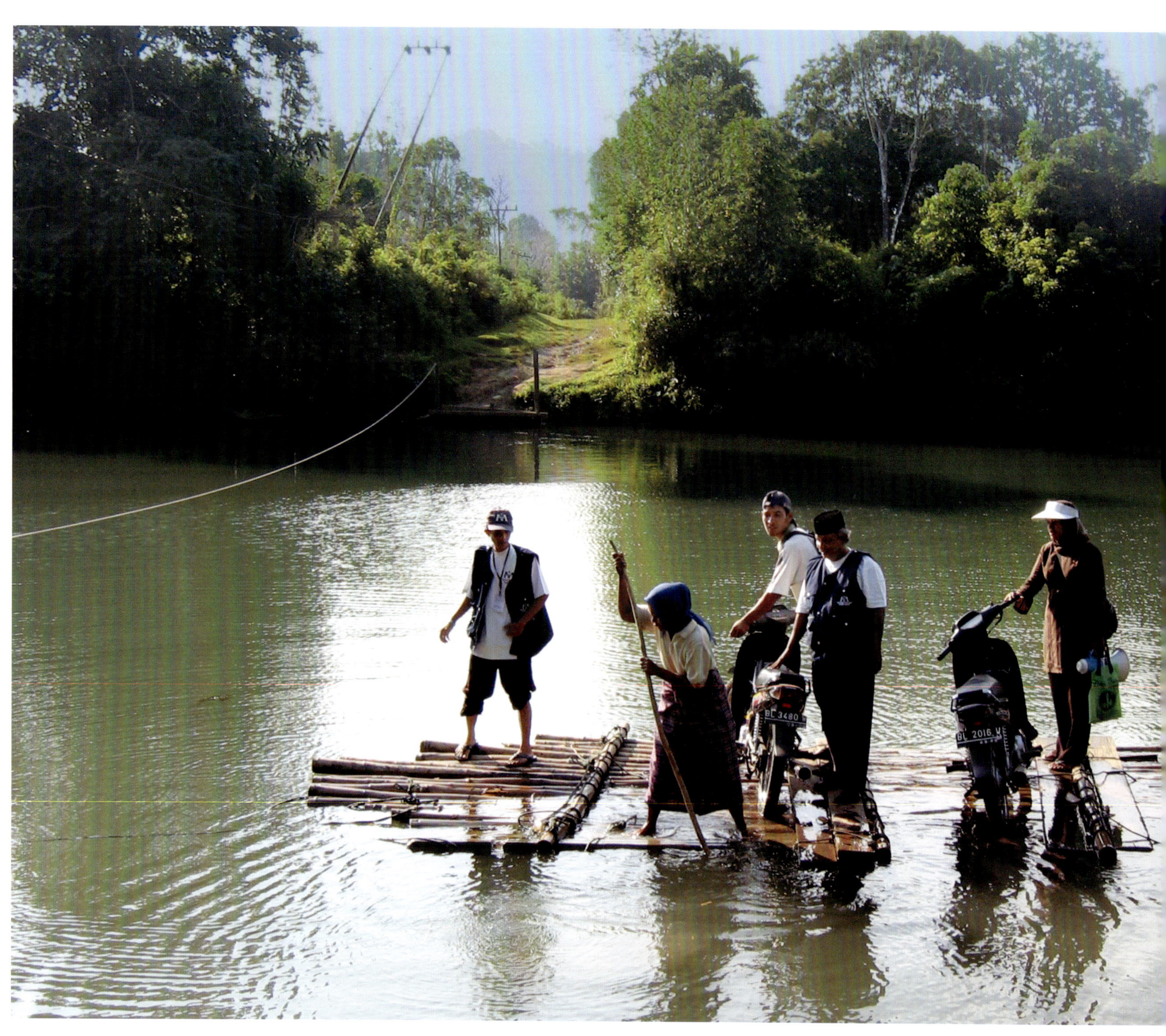
BL 3480
BL 2016 V

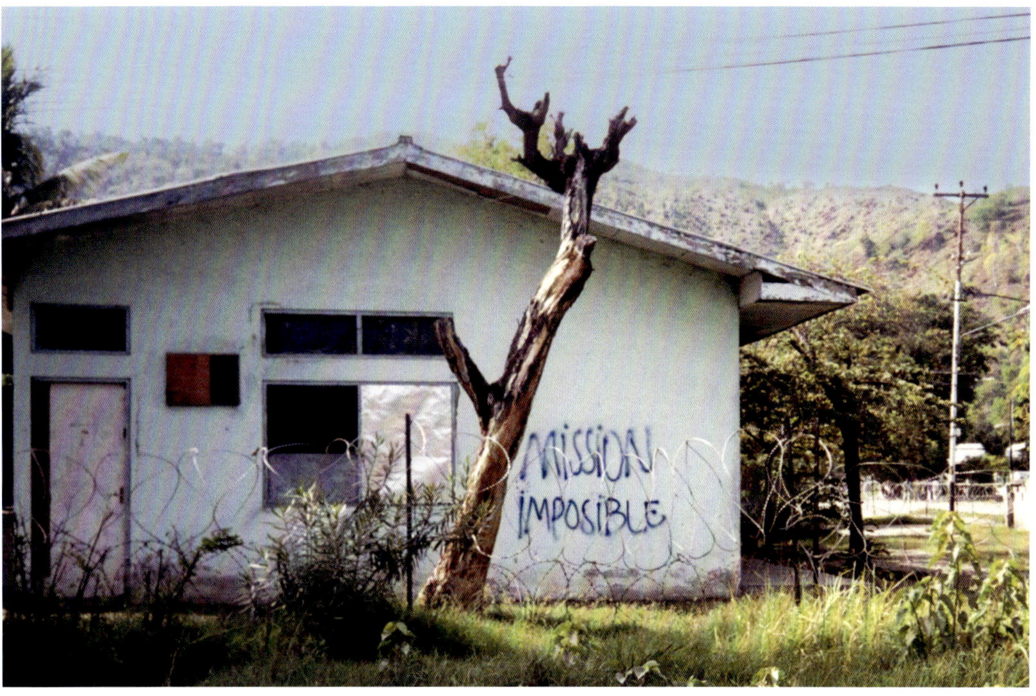

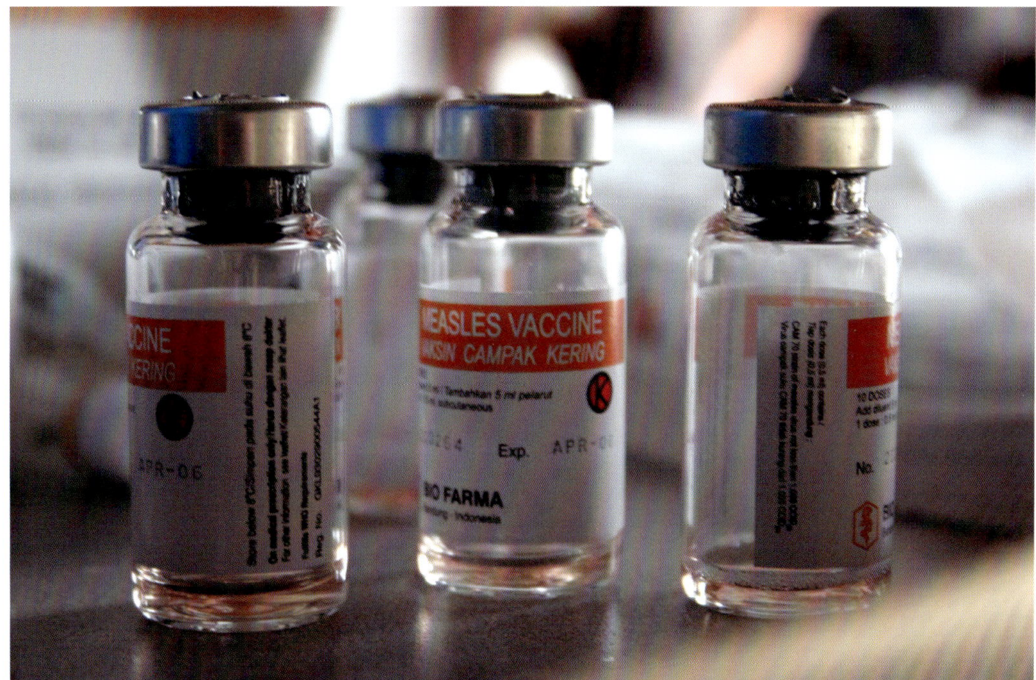

Indonesia 2005
IMC staff (both pages)

Roads leading to many towns were either washed out or made impassable by debris. Many Indonesians did not think assistance would ever reach them after the tsunami. IMC focused its disaster-response efforts on these hard-to-reach communities, bringing lifesaving medicine and emergency assistance.

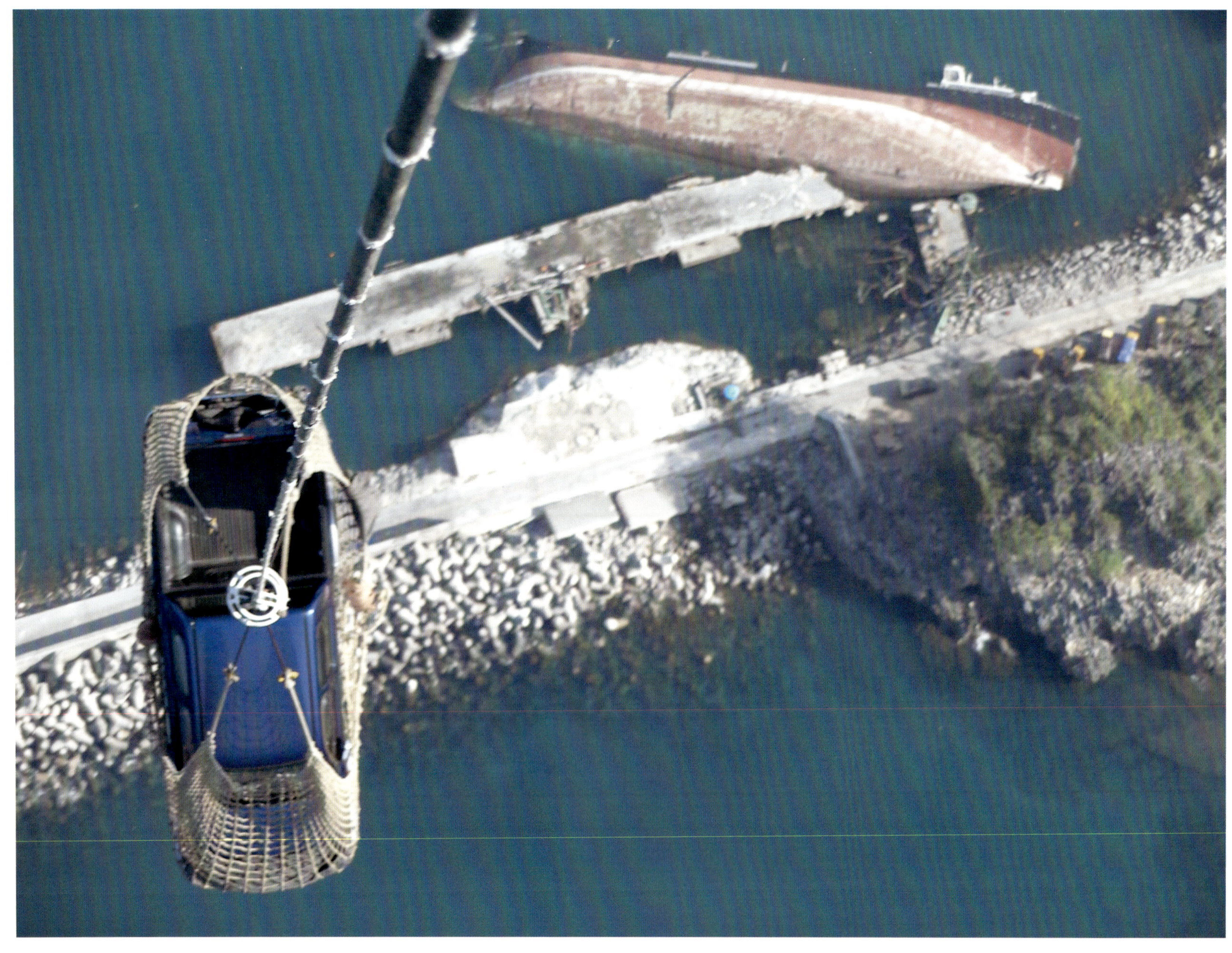

Indonesia 2005
IMC staff (top)
Chris Rainier (opposite page)

International Medical Corps' existing infrastructure, built up by a six-year presence in Indonesia, enabled it to immediately deploy relief teams by boat and helicopter to remote communities otherwise left to cope with overwhelming losses on their own and without resources.

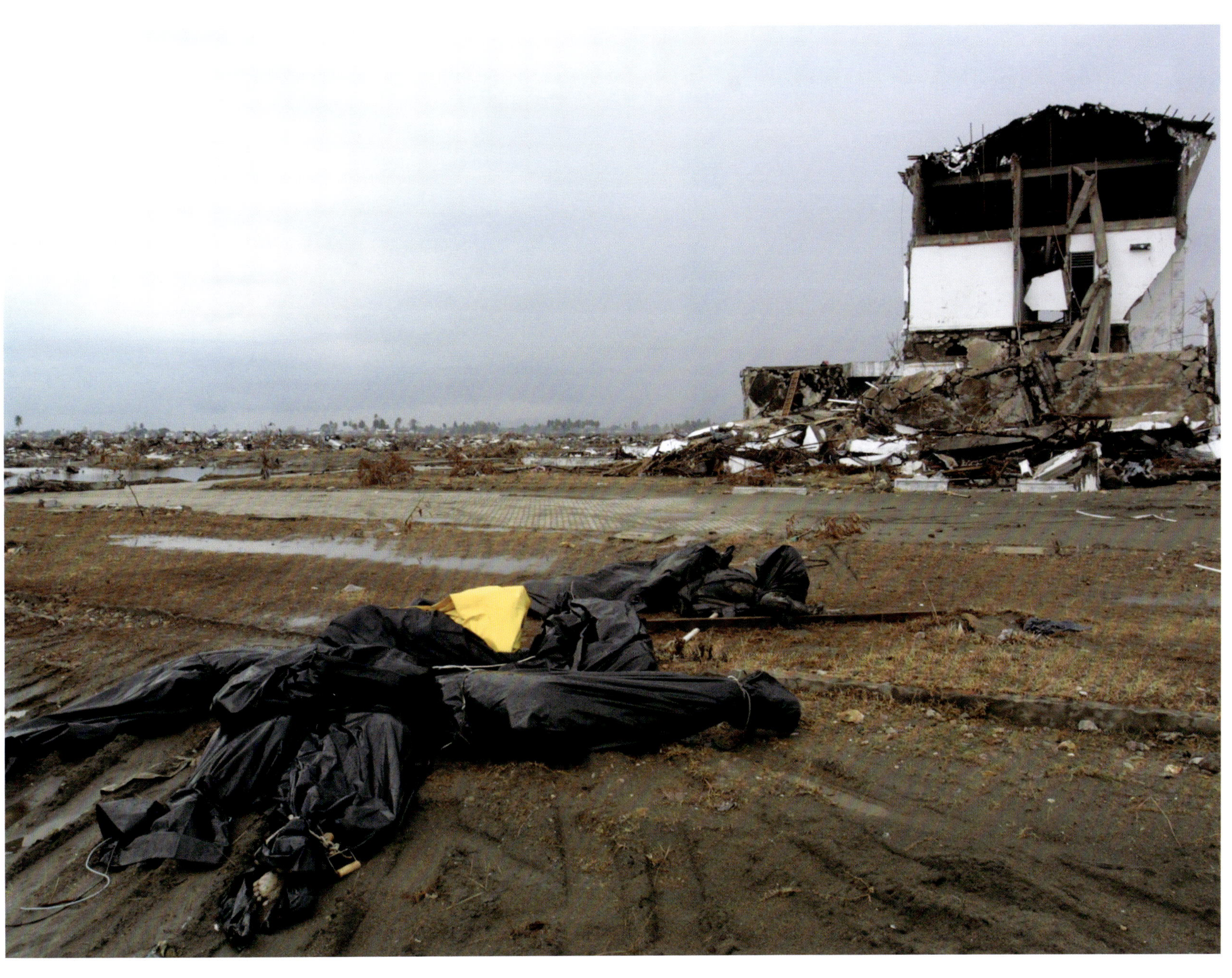

PAKISTAN

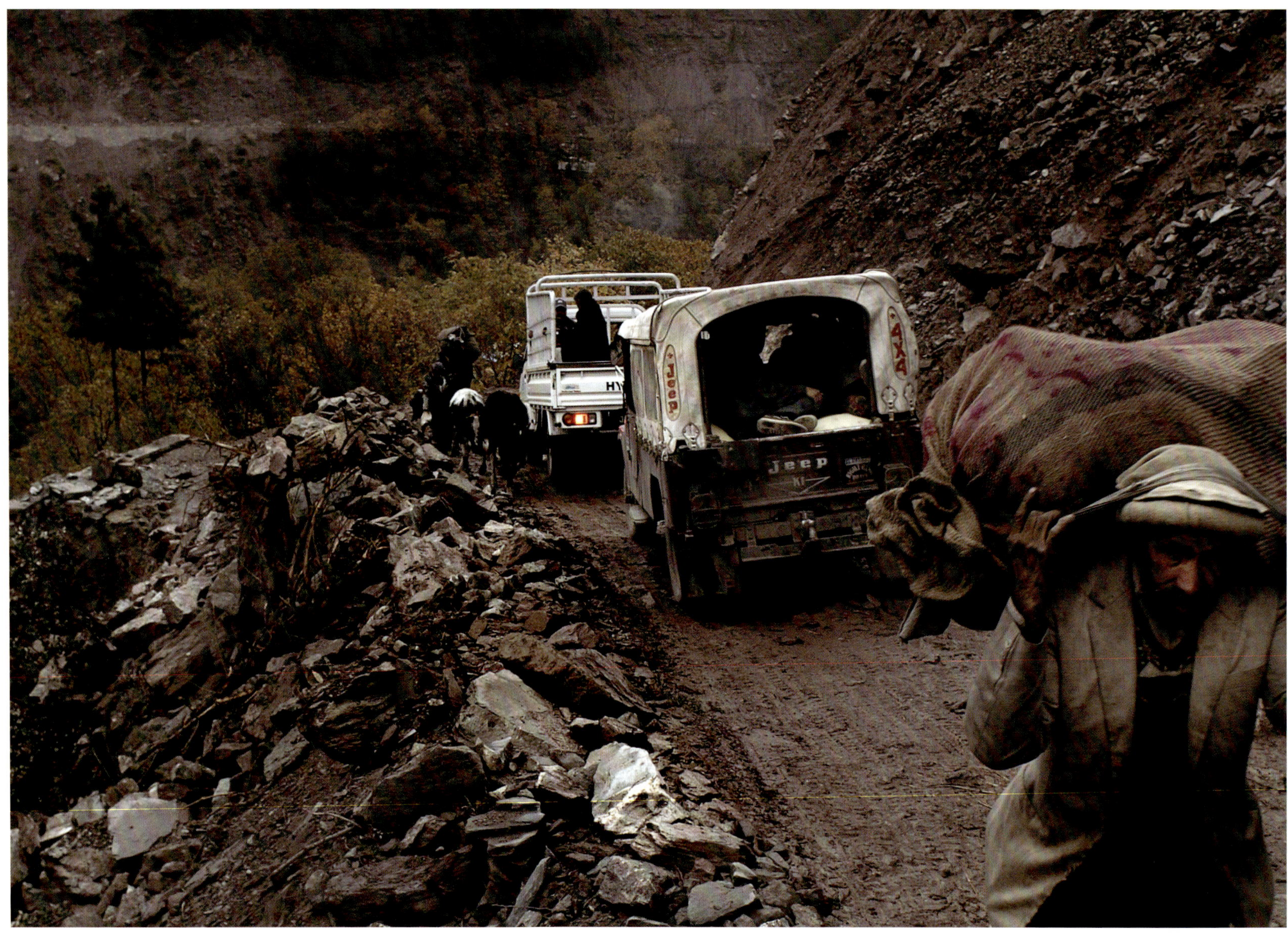

Pakistan 2005
Asim Rafiqui

On October 8, 2005, Northwest Frontier Province and Kashmir were hit by a 7.6-magnitude earthquake. International Medical Corps mobilized five rapid-response medical teams within 12 hours of the quake, providing emergency care to the most affected regions. Despite the near destruction of transportation infrastructure, IMC staff made their way—by car, helicopter, mule and foot—to remote, hard-hit villages to provide vital care.

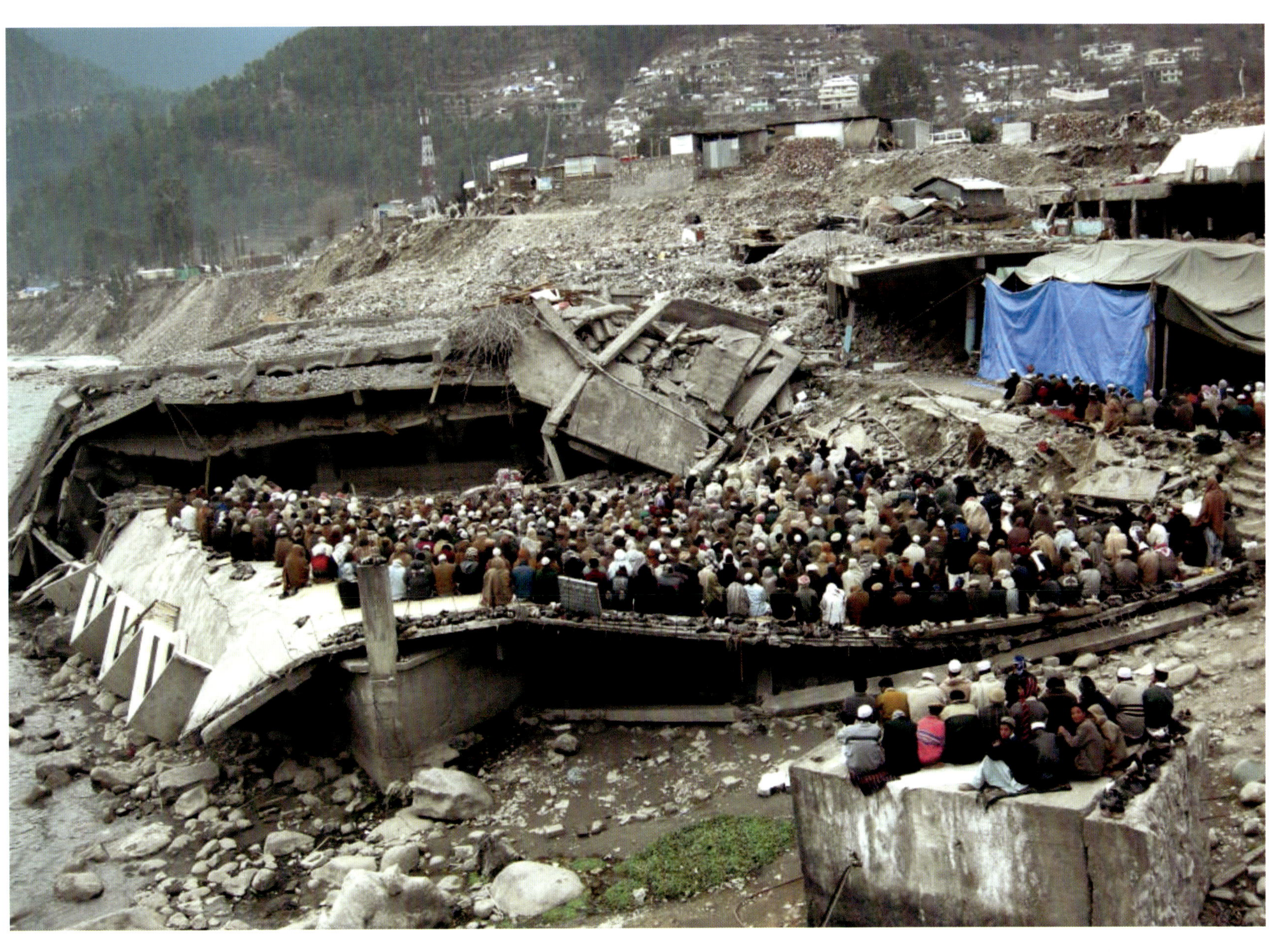

Pakistan 2005
IMC staff

Within 12 hours of the quake, International Medical Corps supplied emergency medical care, vaccinations, blankets, tents, and hygiene and cooking kits to earthquake victims. During the initial disaster-response phase, IMC airlifted more than 5 tons of medical supplies and provided improved sanitation and access to potable water to 10 large displacement camps and numerous communities.

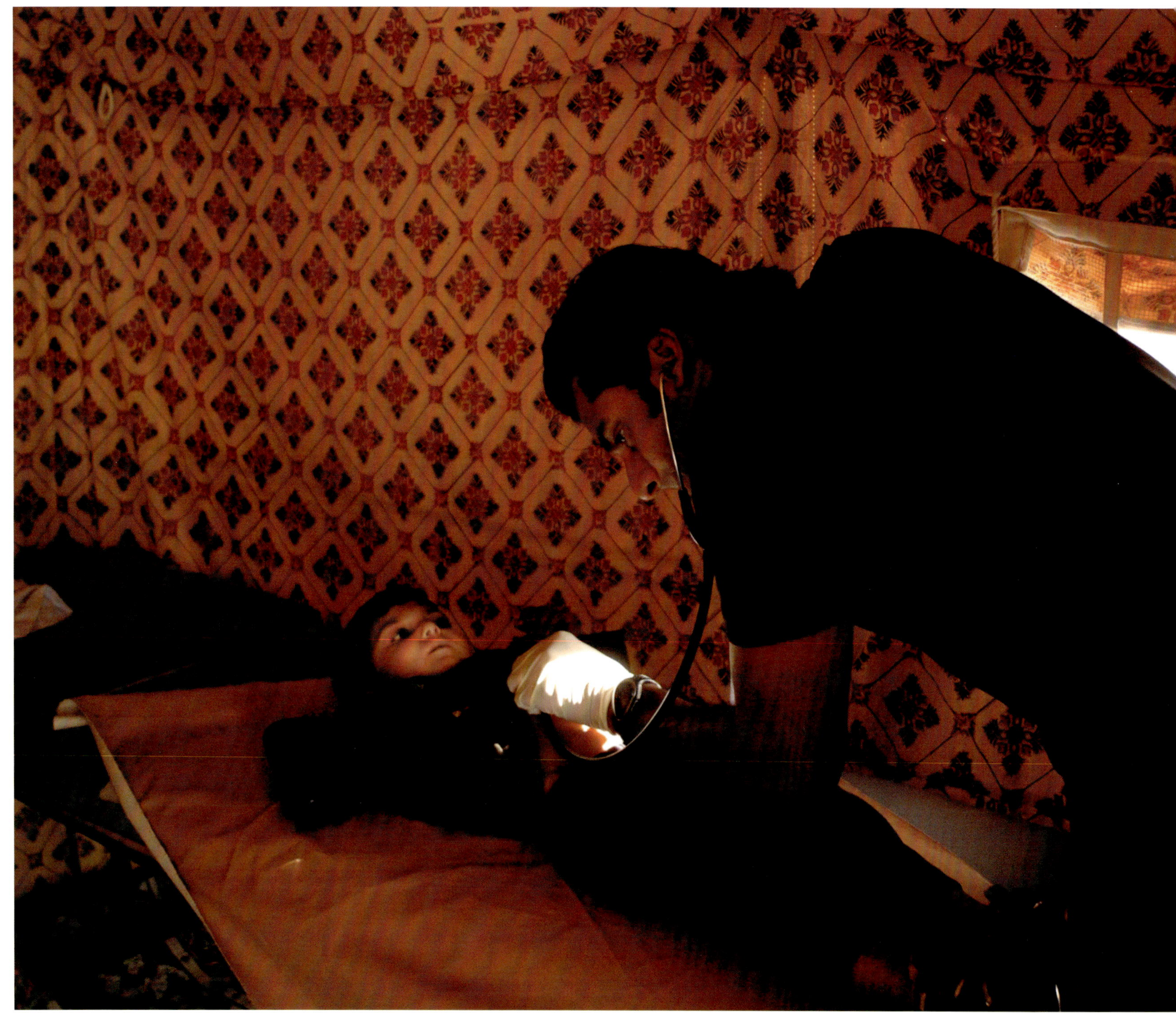

Pakistan 2002
Asim Rafiqui

With more than 20 years' experience in Pakistan, International Medical Corps was able to mobilize its health care teams already working there to reach the extremely poor and underserved areas where more than 80,000 people were killed and millions were left homeless. IMC mobilized numerous local teams of Pakistani and Afghan health care workers to respond to the earthquake crisis.

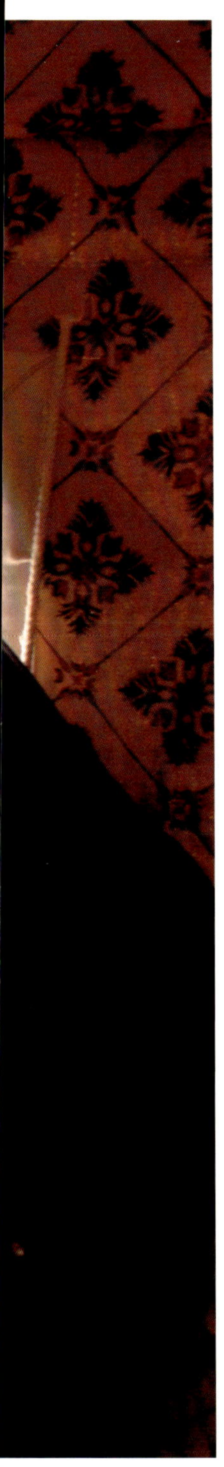

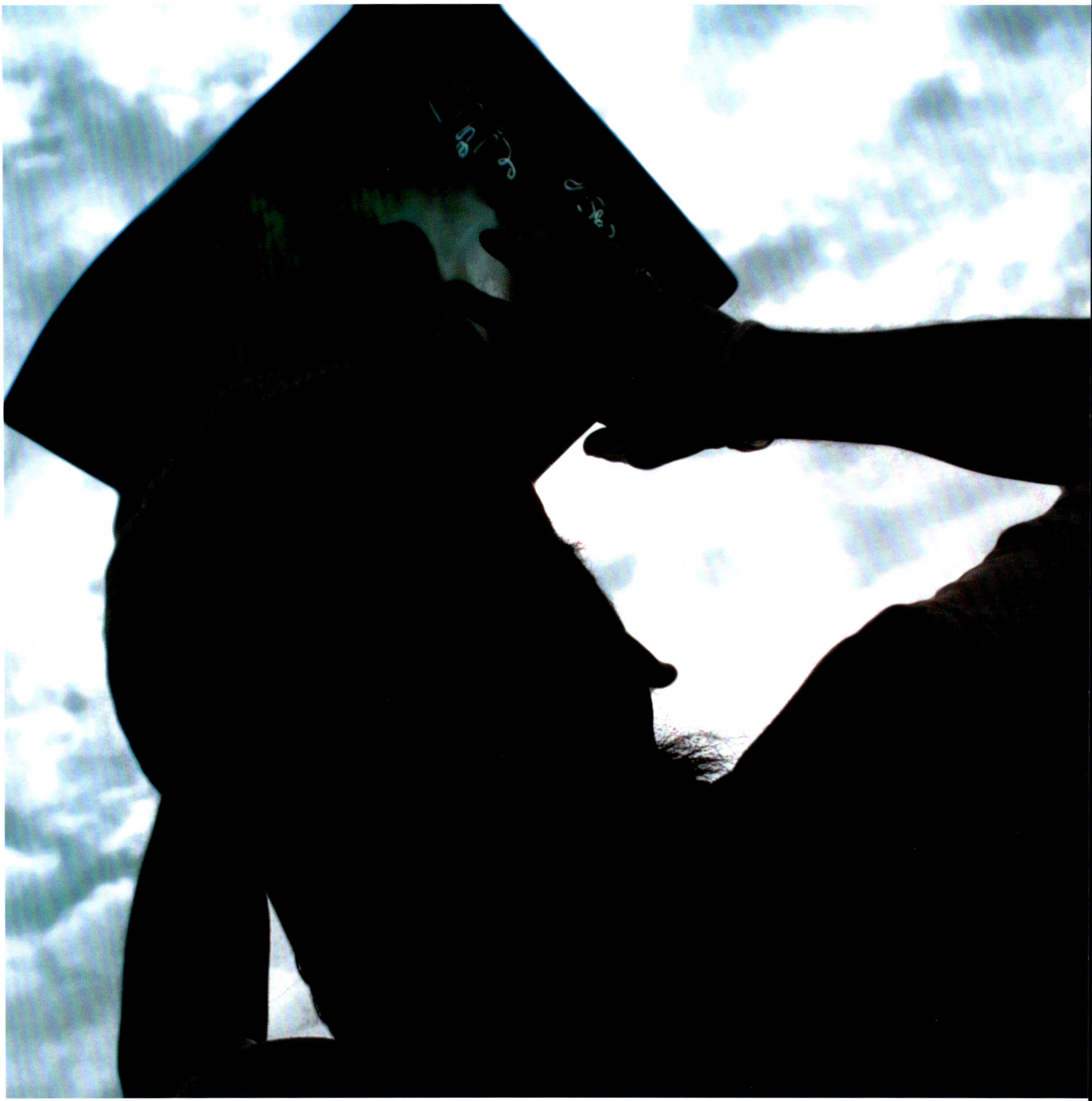

Pakistan 2005
Asim Rafiqui

A volunteer doctor examines a patient at one of International Medical Corps' Basic Health Units, set up in Ghari Habibullah after the Pakistan earthquake. IMC administered vital emergency health care services to thousands of victims of the devastating quake.

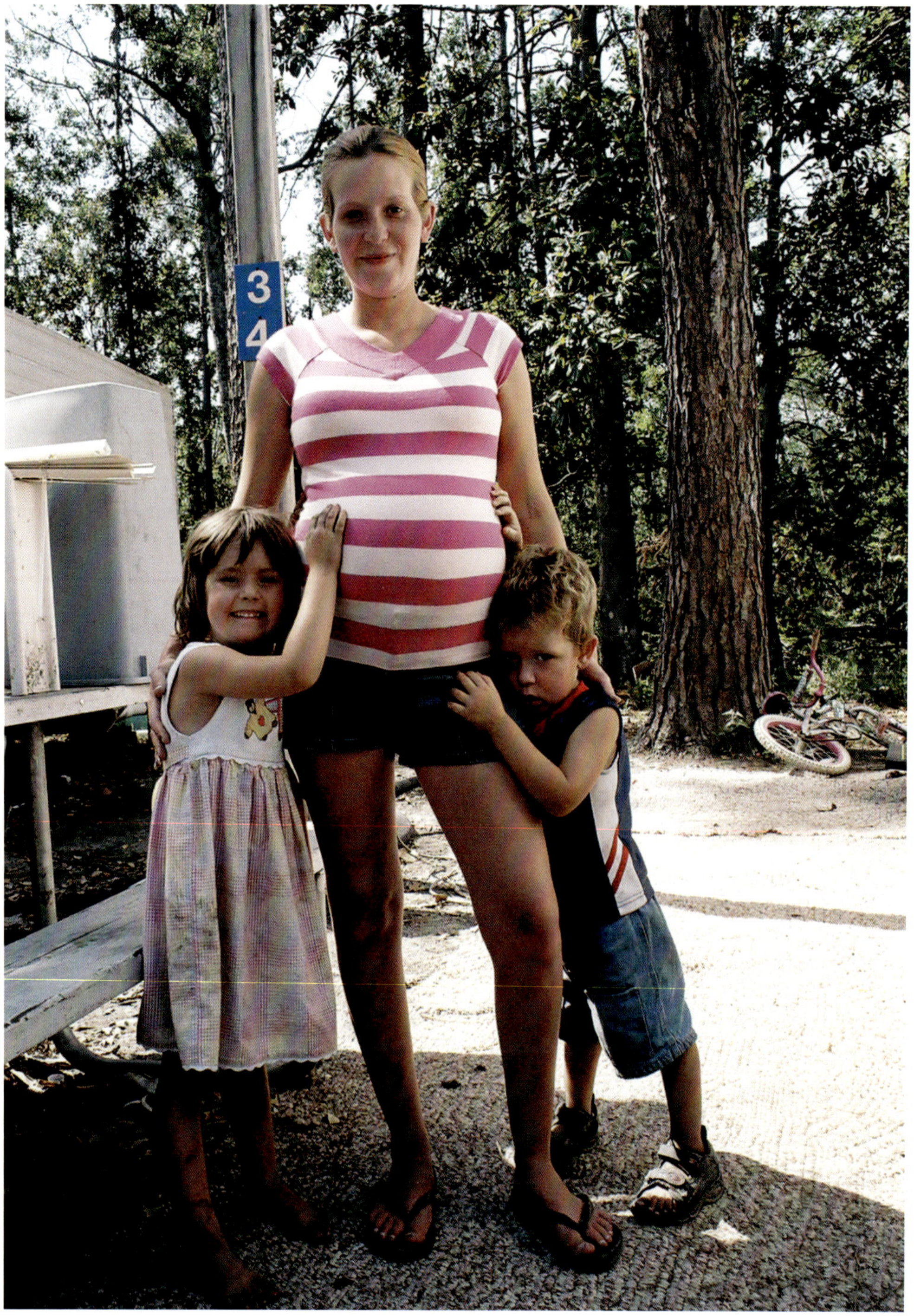

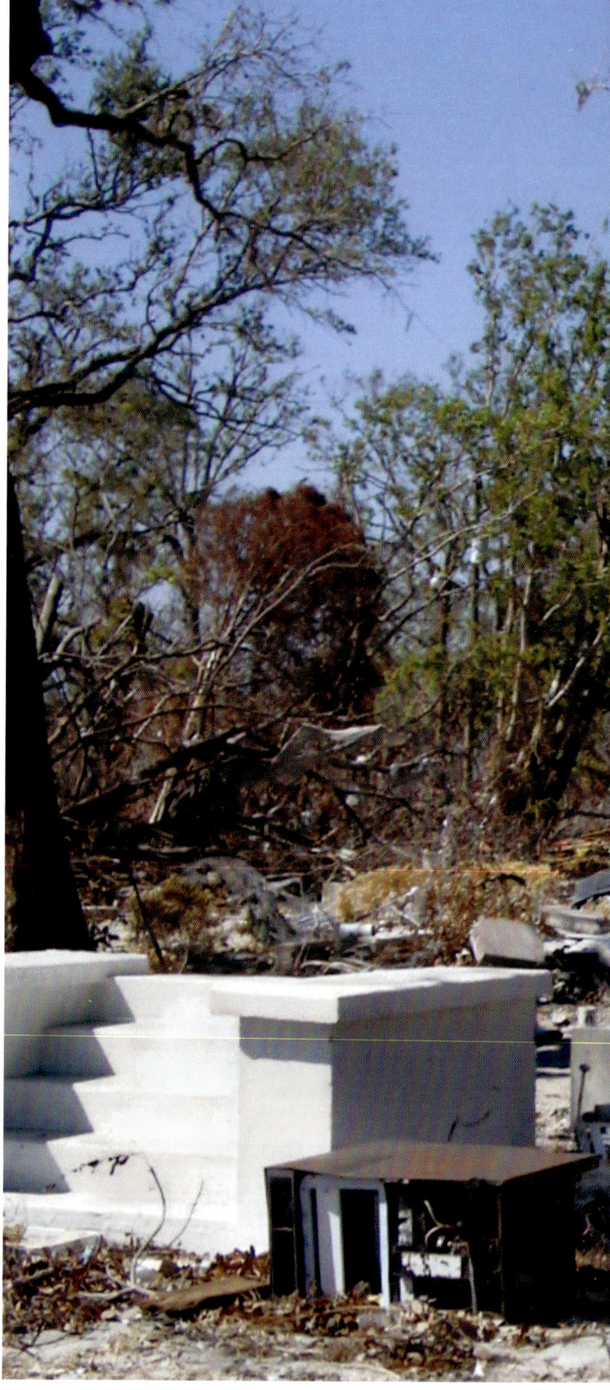

New Orleans USA 2005
IMC staff (above)
Julie Jiang (opposite)

Hurricane Katrina marked the first time in International Medical Corps' history that it responded to a domestic disaster. Within days of the storm's devastating strike, IMC used techniques proven effective in other disaster arenas around the world and was one of the first humanitarian groups on the ground in Baton Rouge, Louisiana.

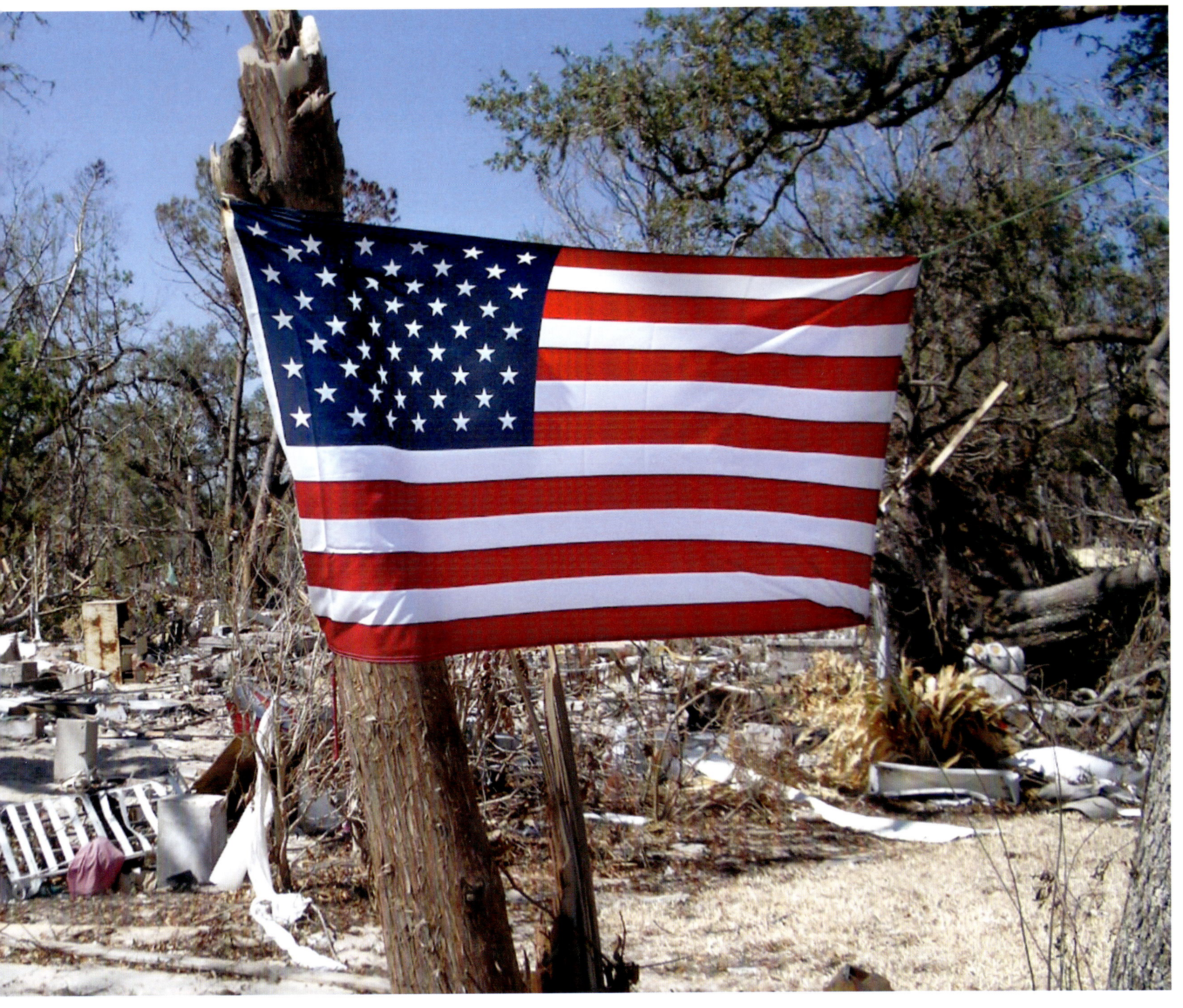

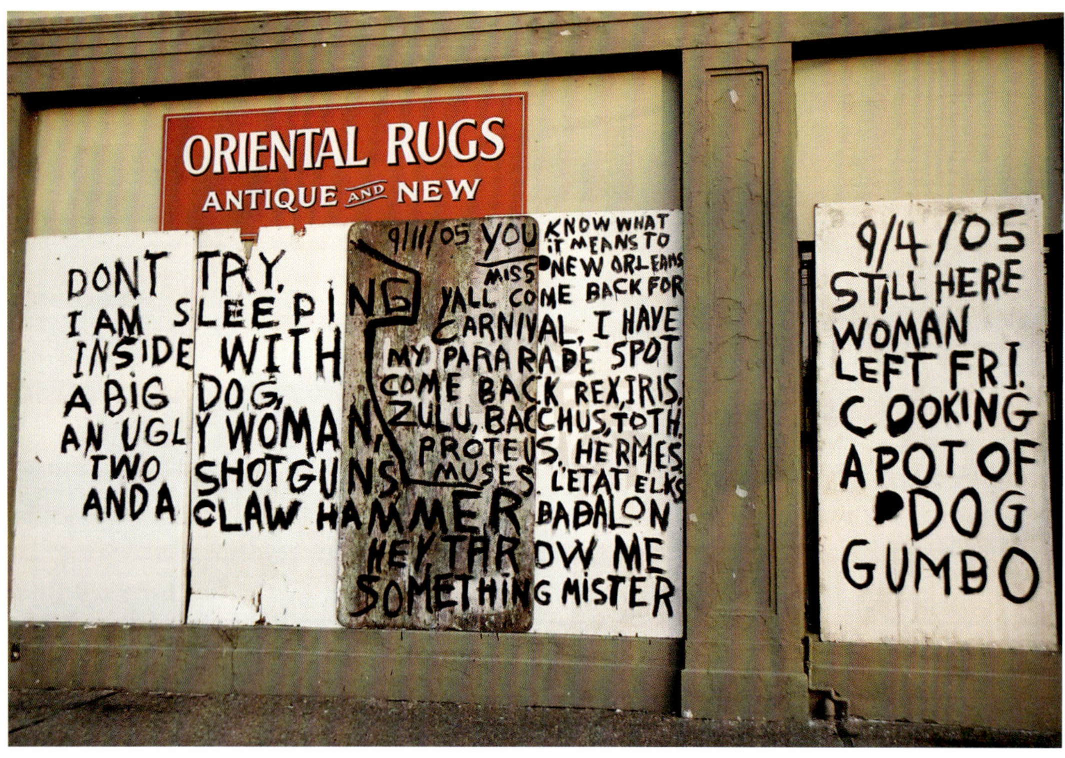

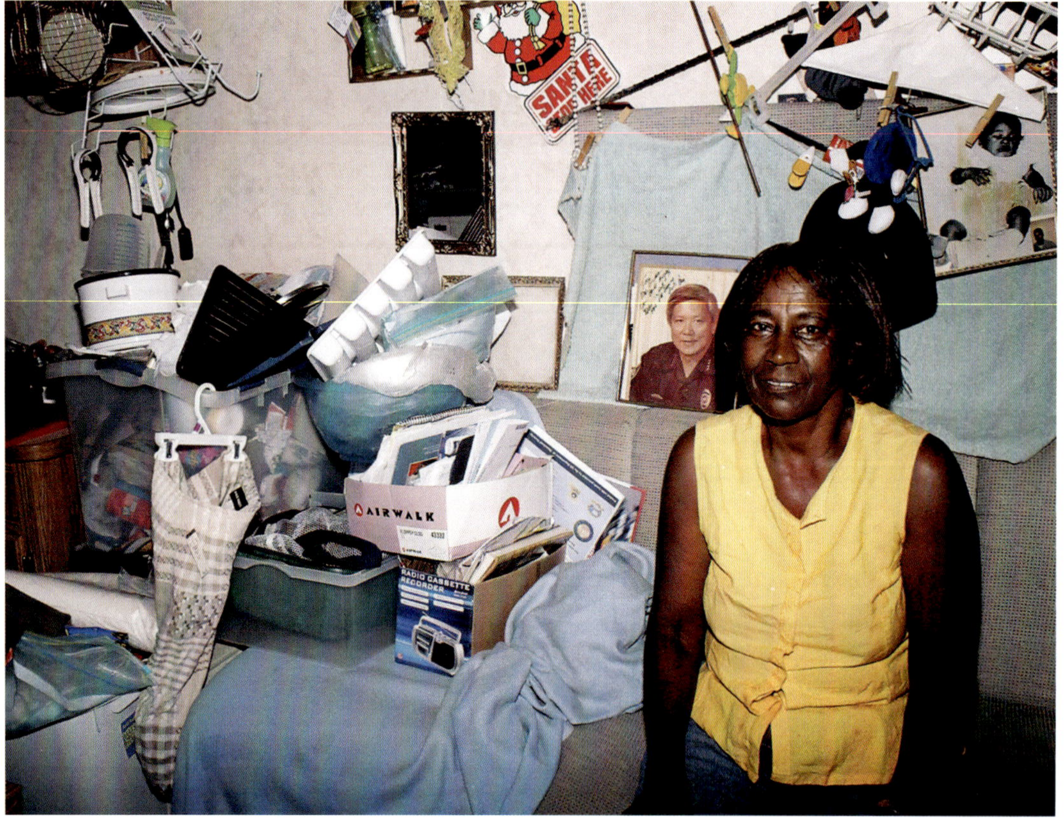

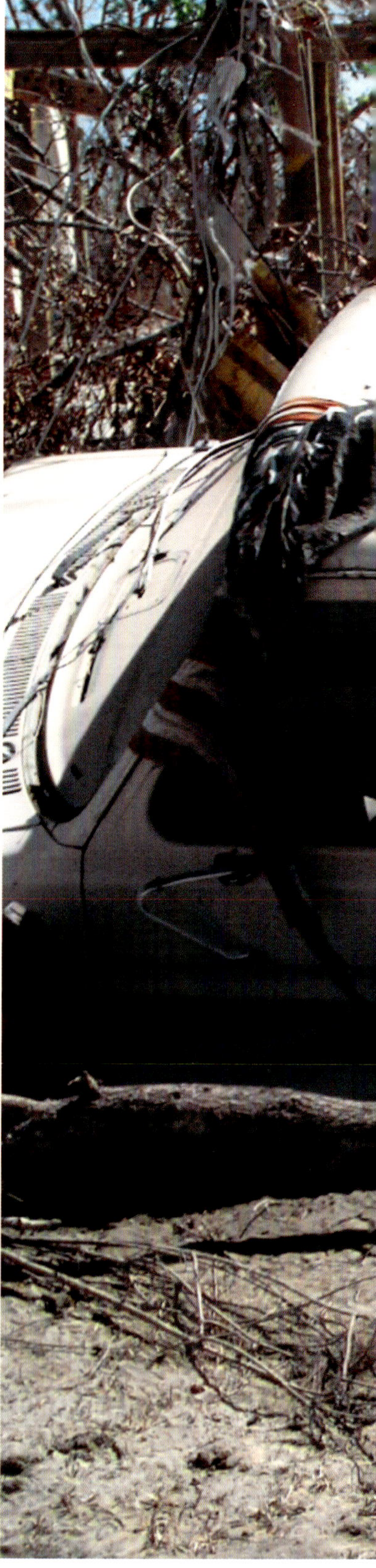

New Orleans USA 2005
IMC staff (both)

Gulf Coast survivors experienced a plight dramatically similar to those in some of the poorest countries in which International Medical Corps had worked previously. With more than two million people left homeless, there were deplorable living conditions in many towns and a fractured, sometimes nonexistent health care system—not unlike those IMC has witnessed in poorer nations around the globe.

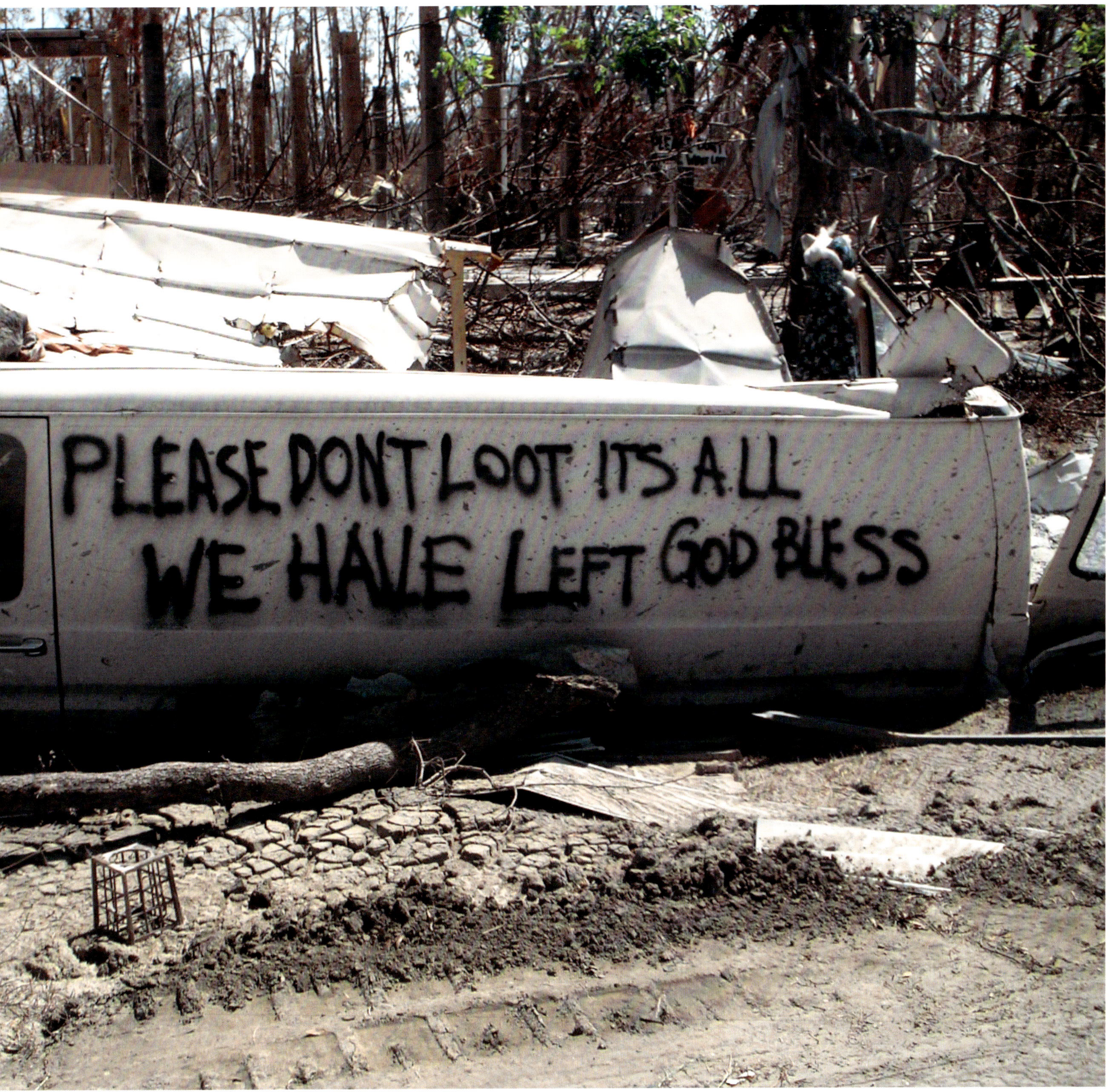

New Orleans USA 2005
Julie Jiang
International Medical Corps' Katrina response teams prioritized relief activities in three areas: primary health care support, psychosocial support, and direct assistance through targeted grants for community-based organizations responding to the disaster.

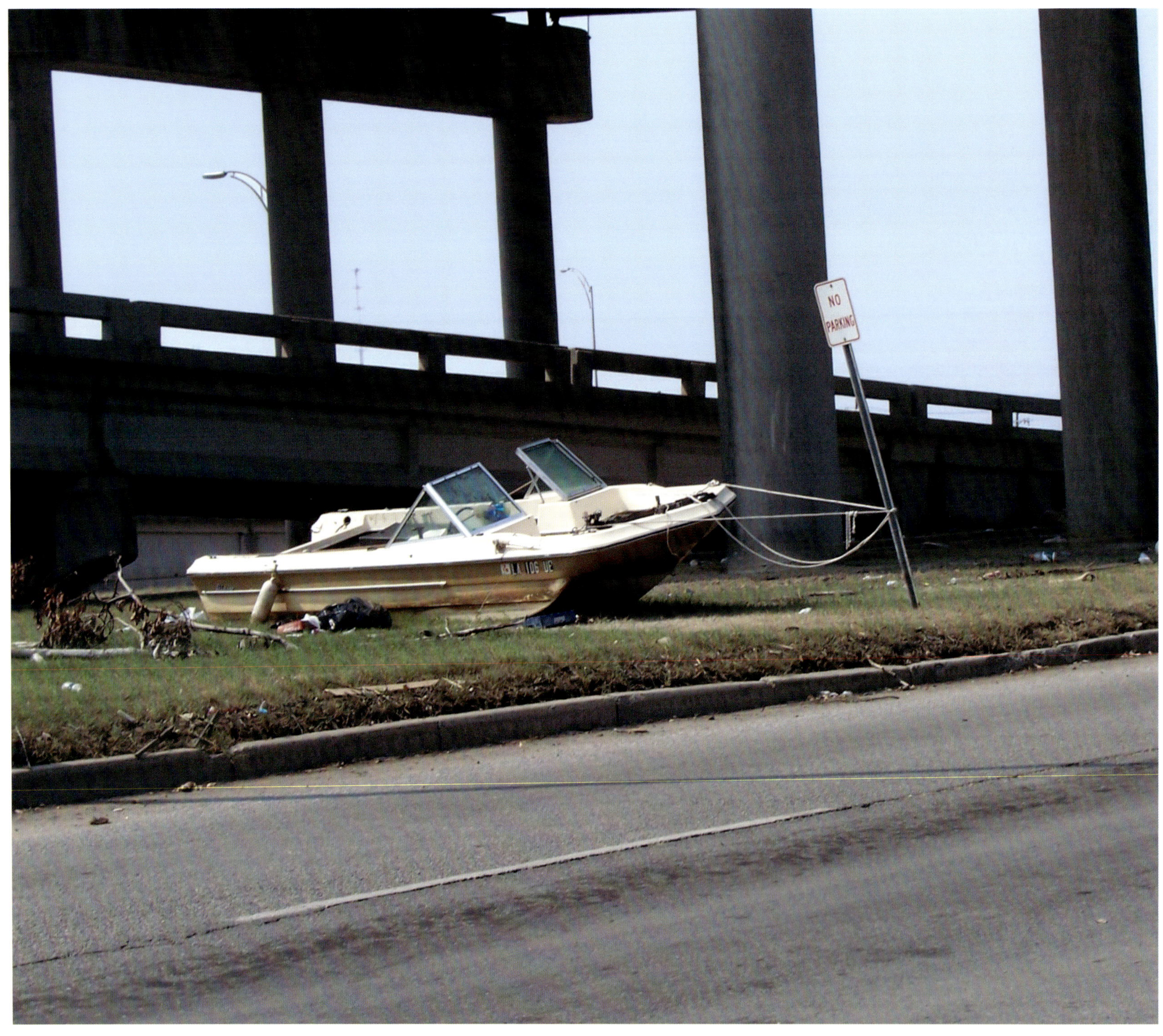

New Orleans USA 2005
IMC staff (both photos)

Working with the U.S. Public Health Service and other relief organizations, International Medical Corps conducted assessments and provided care to urban and rural areas outside of New Orleans, including St. Bernard Parish, where thousands of evacuees resided in shelters.

Opposite page: Collaborating with local health centers, International Medical Corps provided volunteer physicians and nurses to meet the health care needs of residents and evacuees. Both the IMC health center and its mobile clinics treated approximately 200 patients per day for several weeks after the hurricane hit.

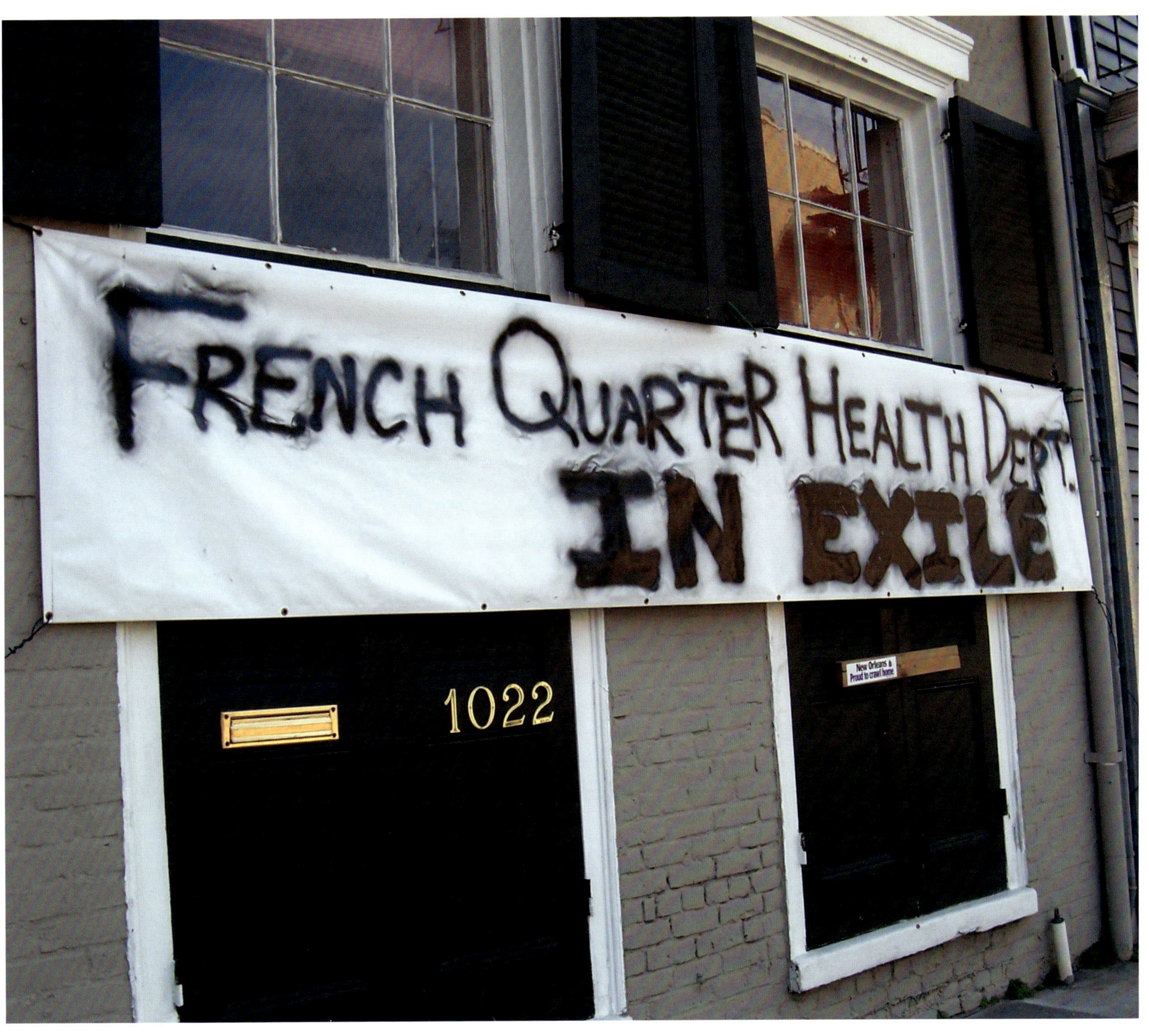
FRENCH QUARTER HEALTH DEPT.
IN EXILE
1022
New Orleans &
Proud to crawl home

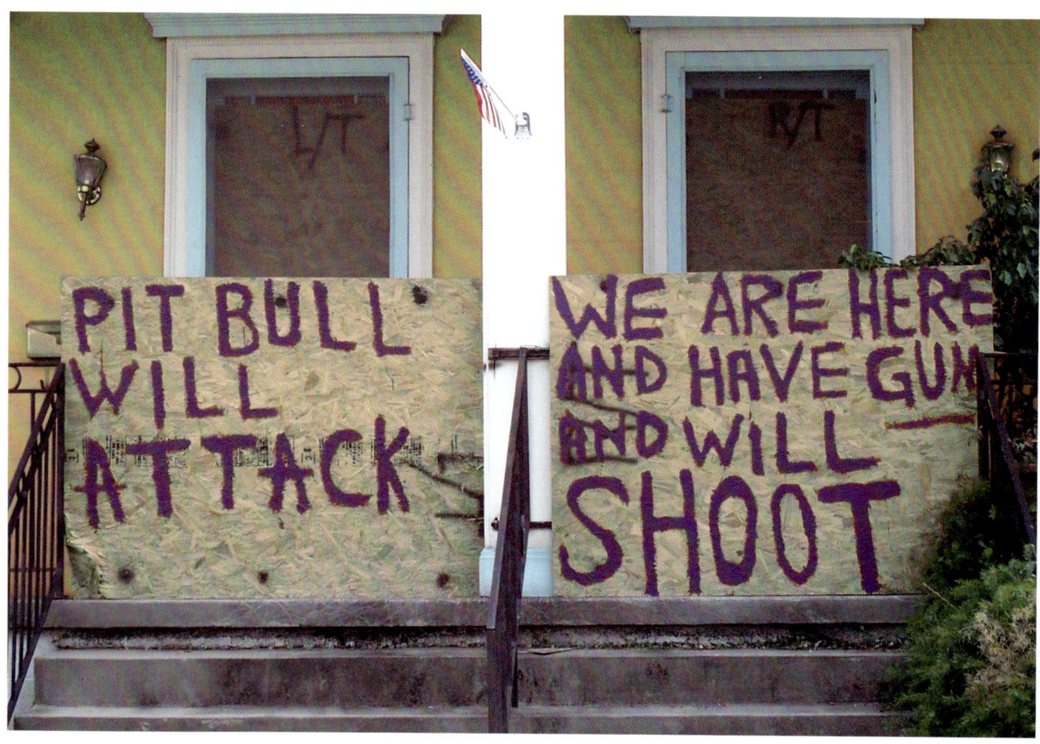

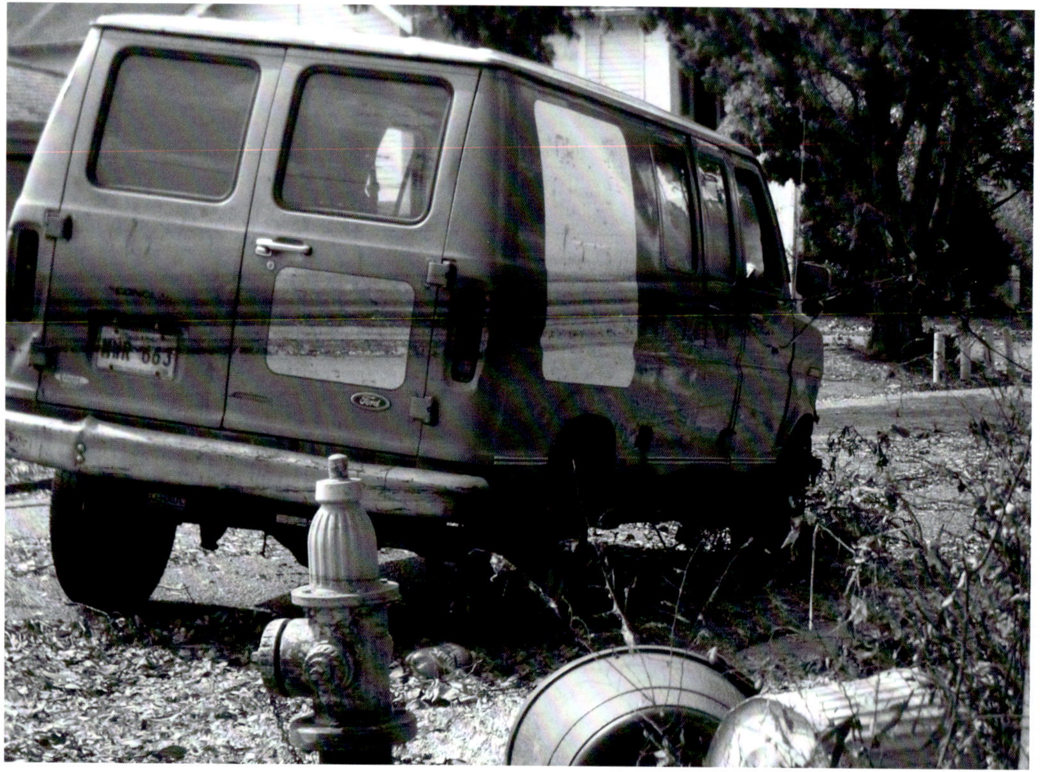

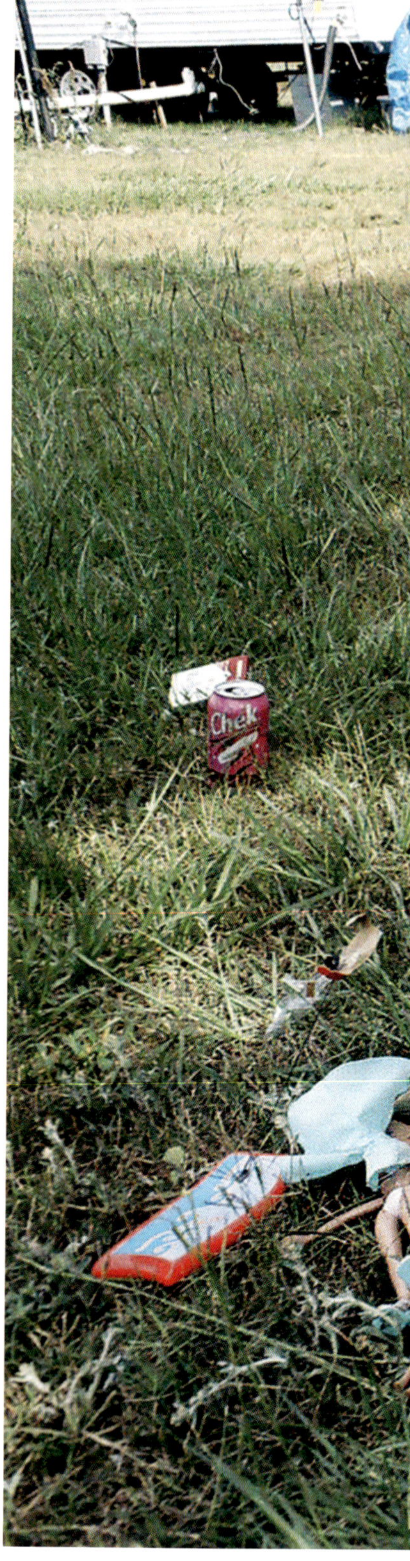

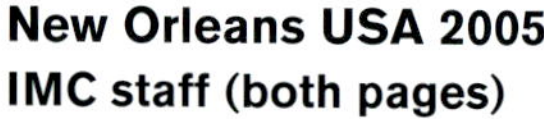

New Orleans USA 2005
IMC staff (both pages)

Through its small grants program, International Medical Corps distributed more than $100,000 in grants to existing community-based nonprofit organizations in disaster-affected areas to build internal capacity and to support relief efforts where communities needed help the most.

Opposite page: International Medical Corps provided structured psychosocial activities for families at a temporary trailer park housing approximately 1,000 individuals living in 193 mobile homes as a result of Hurricane Katrina.

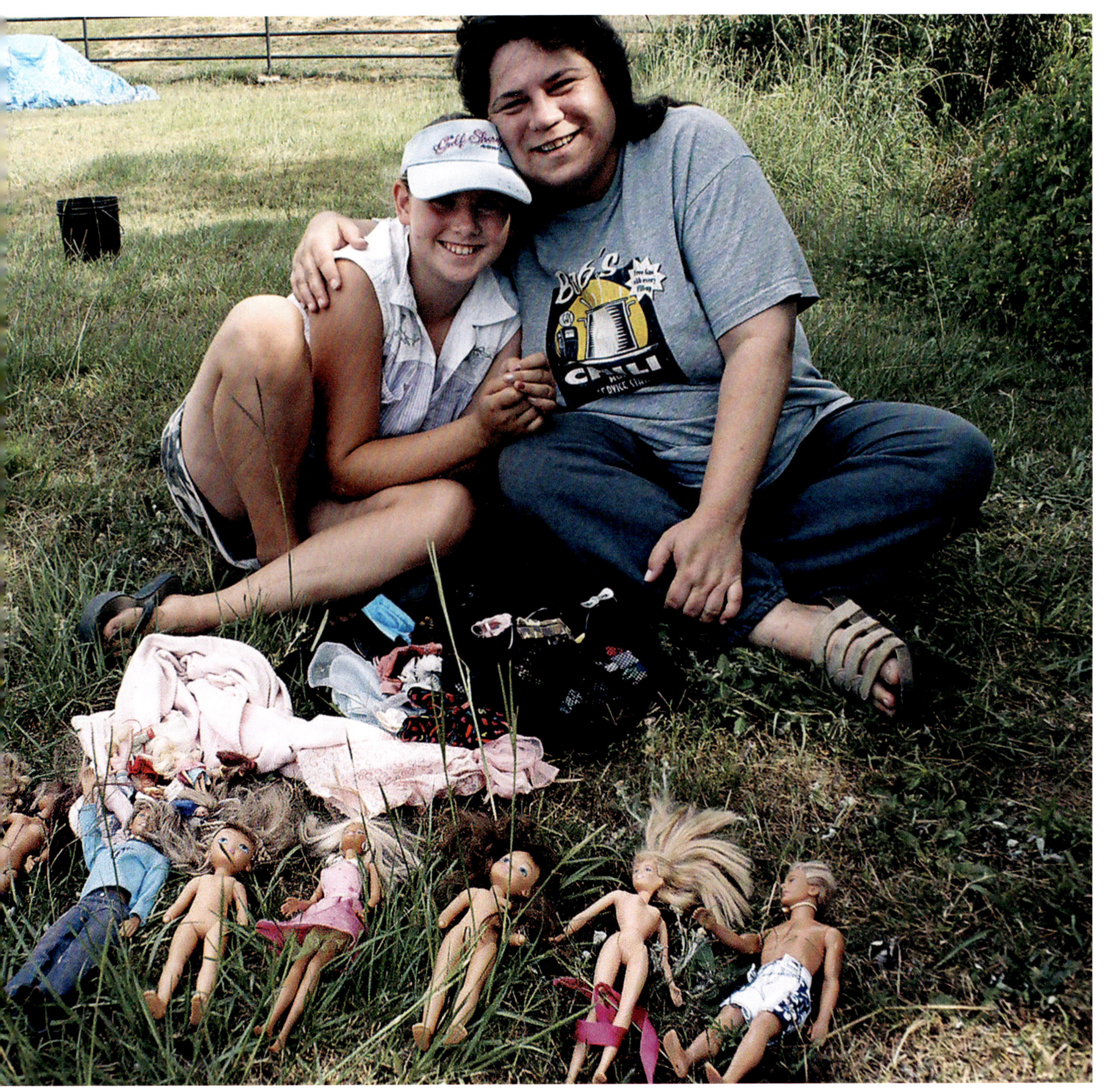

EPIDEMIC HIV/AIDS

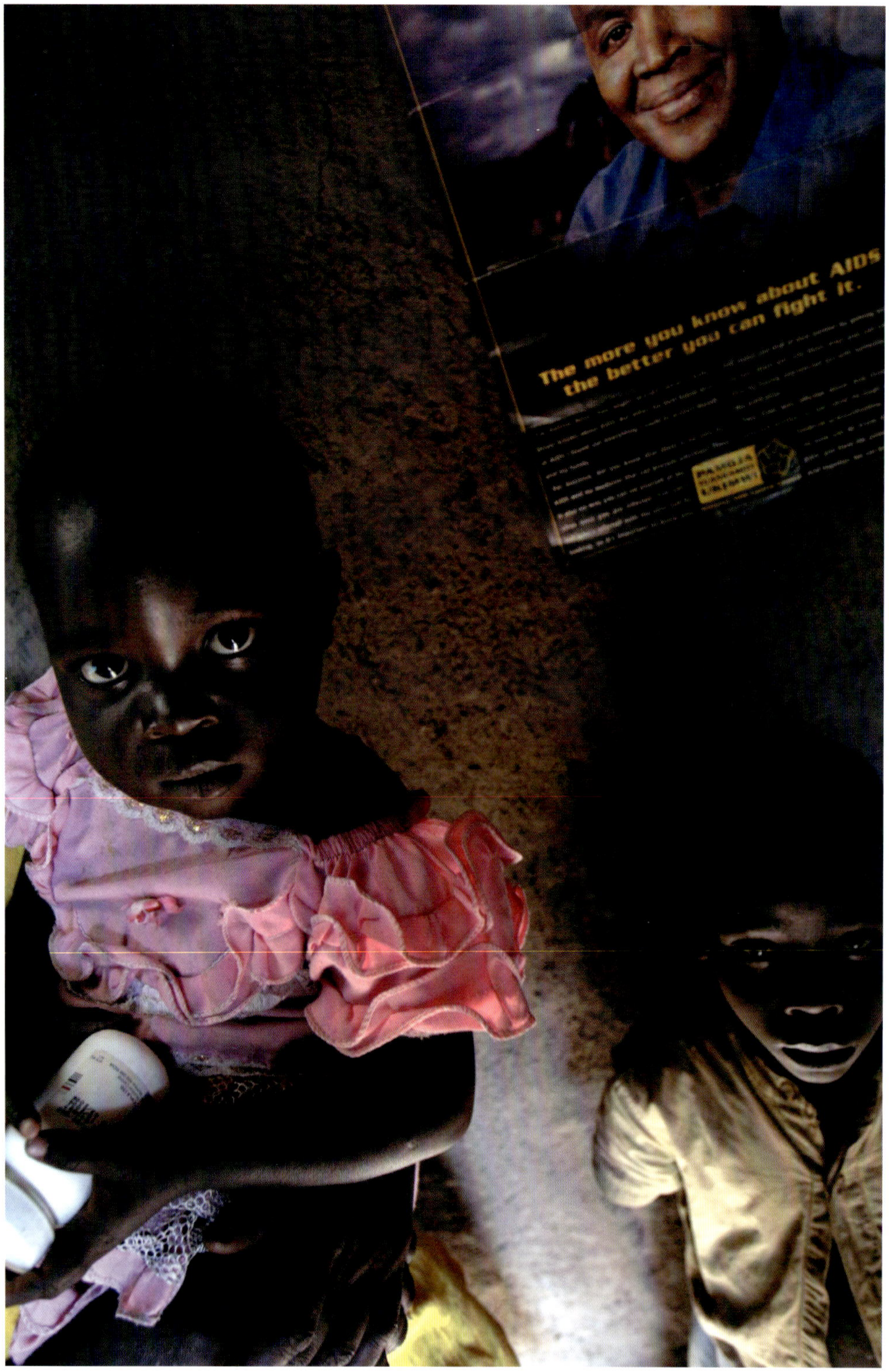

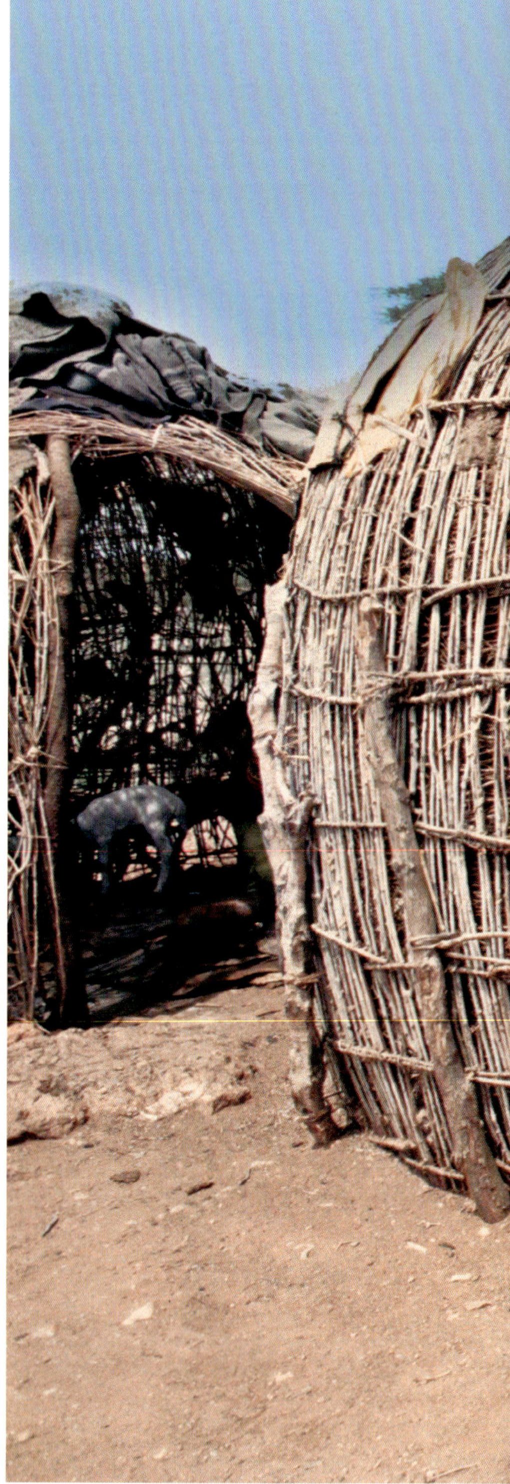

Kenya 2006
Jeffrey Austin

Like many sub-Saharan countries, Kenya has been hard-hit by the HIV/AIDS epidemic. International Medical Corps has dedicated its efforts in Kenya to treating the estimated 2.5 million Kenyans who are currently infected with HIV. Many of them are under the age of 15.

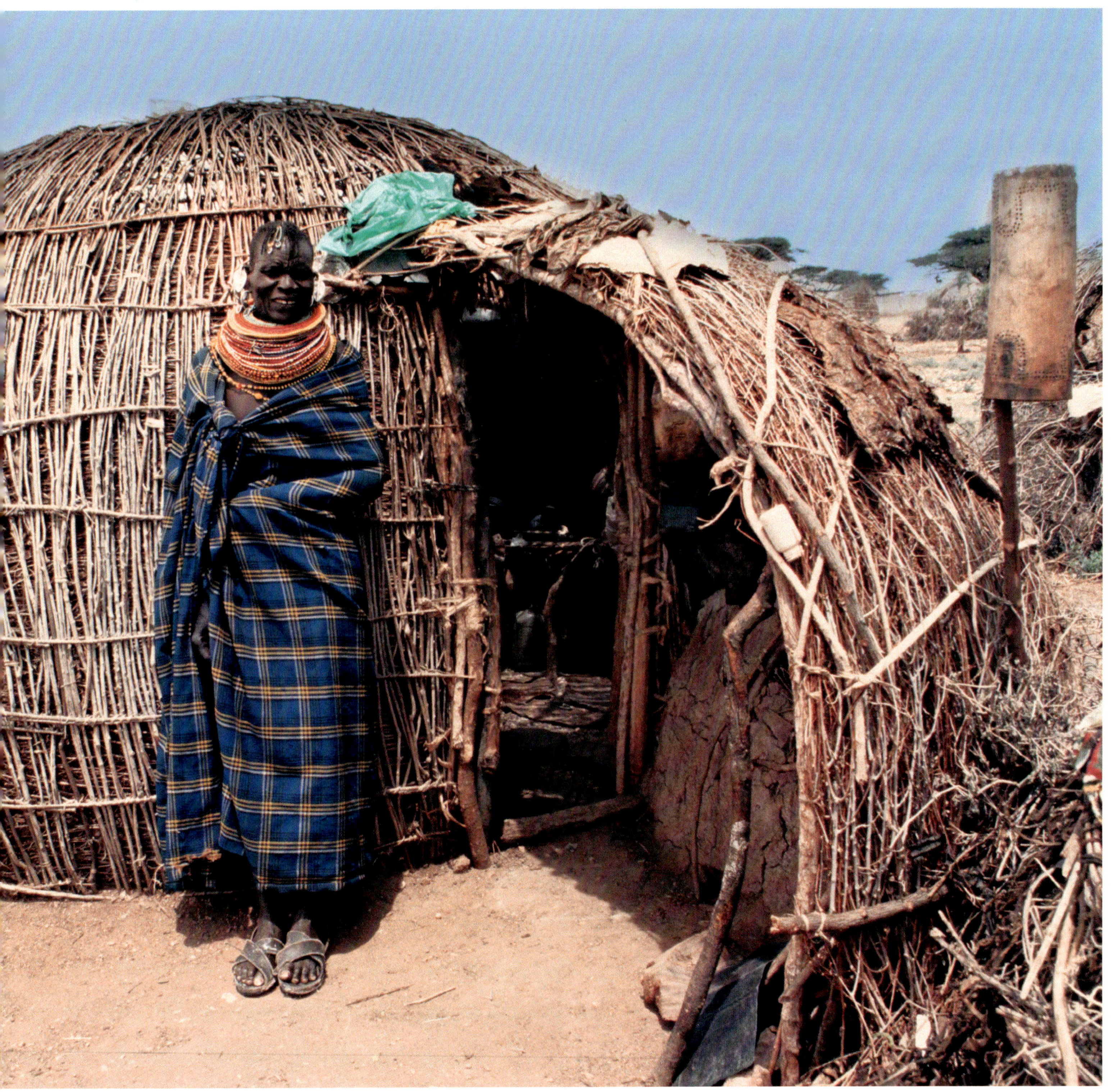

Kenya 2002
Jenny Chu

In 2002, International Medical Corps began a community-based campaign to improve the lives of those living with HIV/AIDS in Kenya by providing HIV/AIDS education to more than 30,000 people throughout the country, including some of its hardest-to-reach regions.

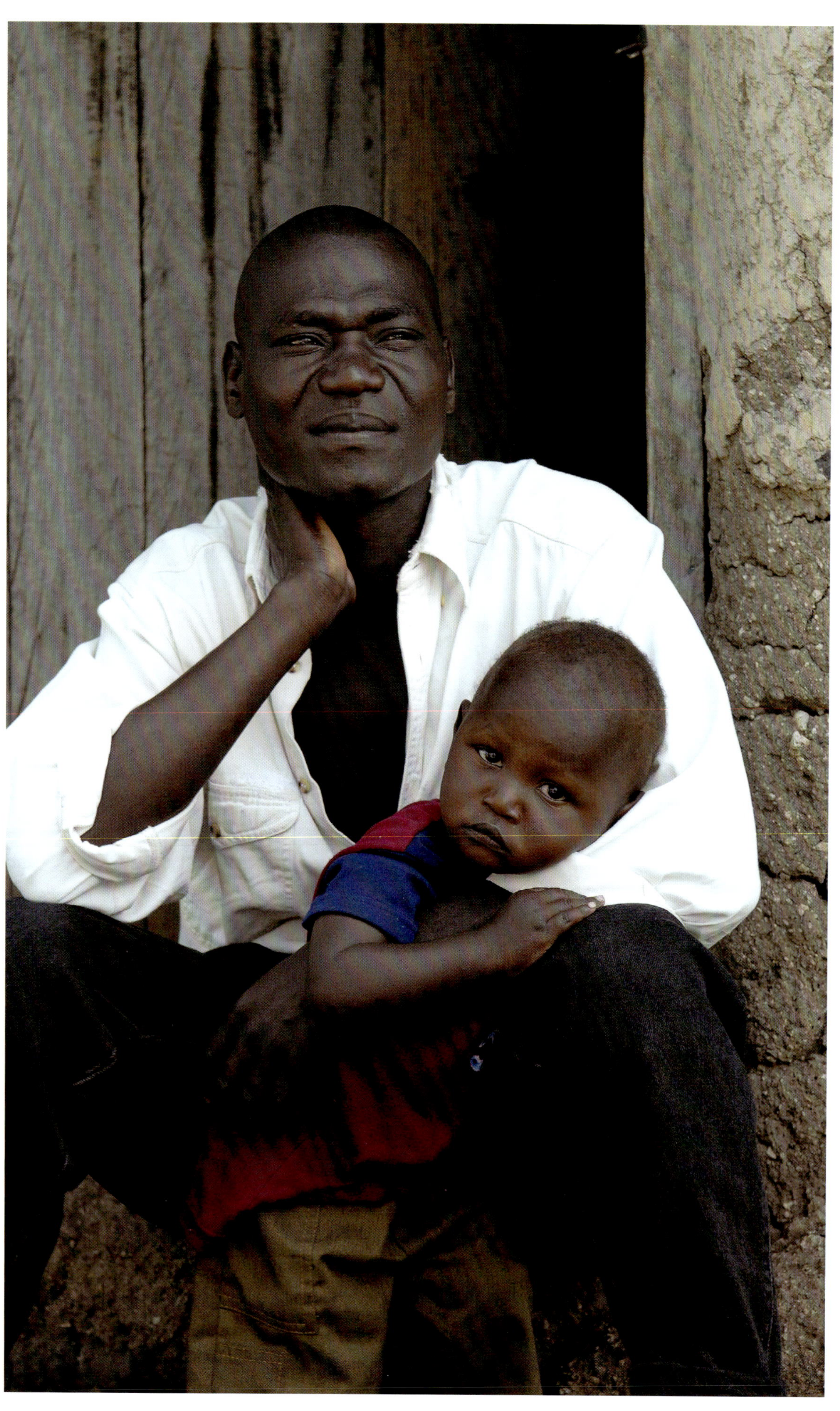

Kenya 2006
Jeffrey Austin (both pages)

The HIV/AIDS devastation is particularly evident in an area of Nairobi called Kibera, the largest urban slum in sub-Saharan Africa. International Medical Corps has focused much of its HIV/AIDS efforts in Kibera, which is home to an estimated 1.2 million people. Among adults here, one in four has HIV/AIDS.

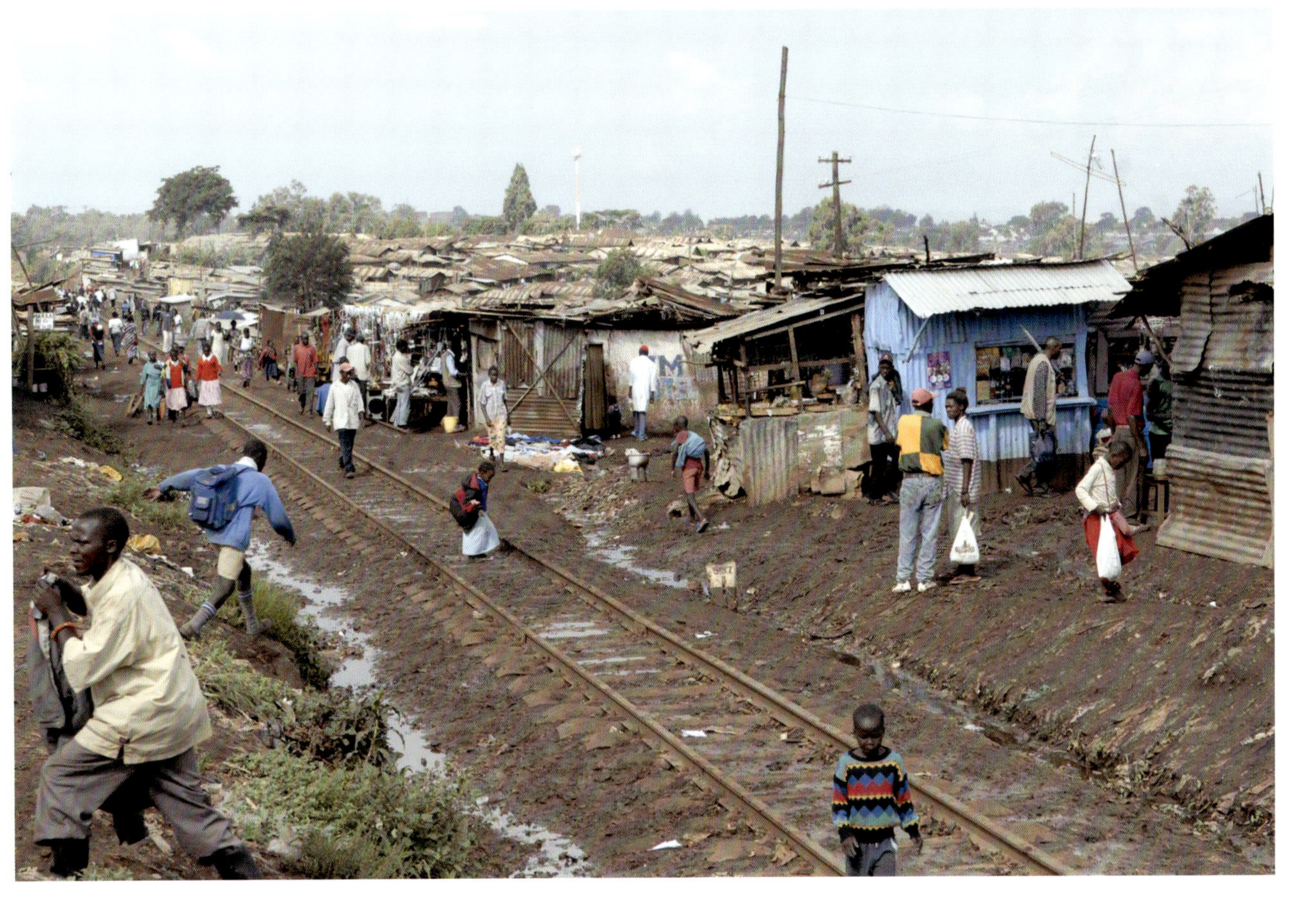

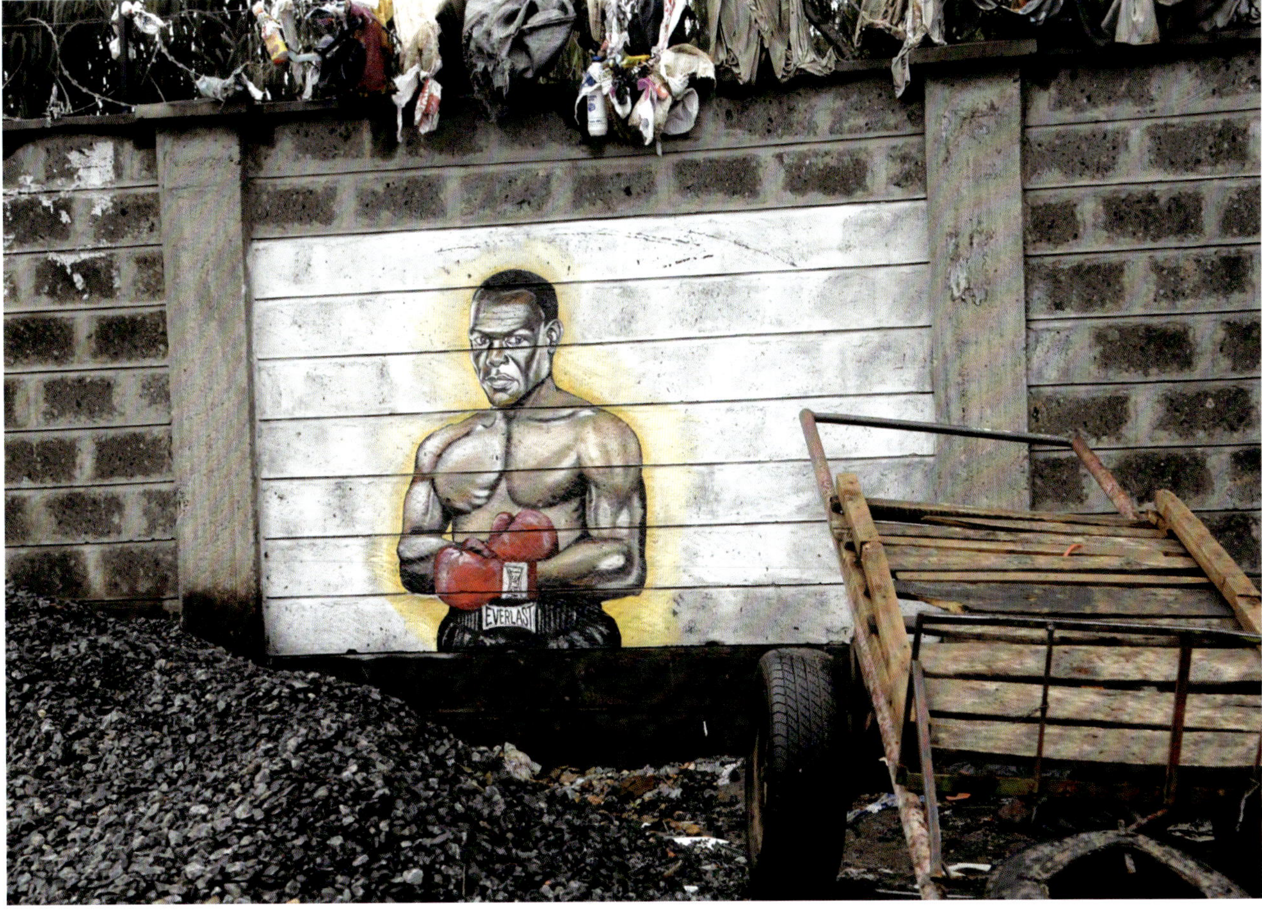
EVERLAST

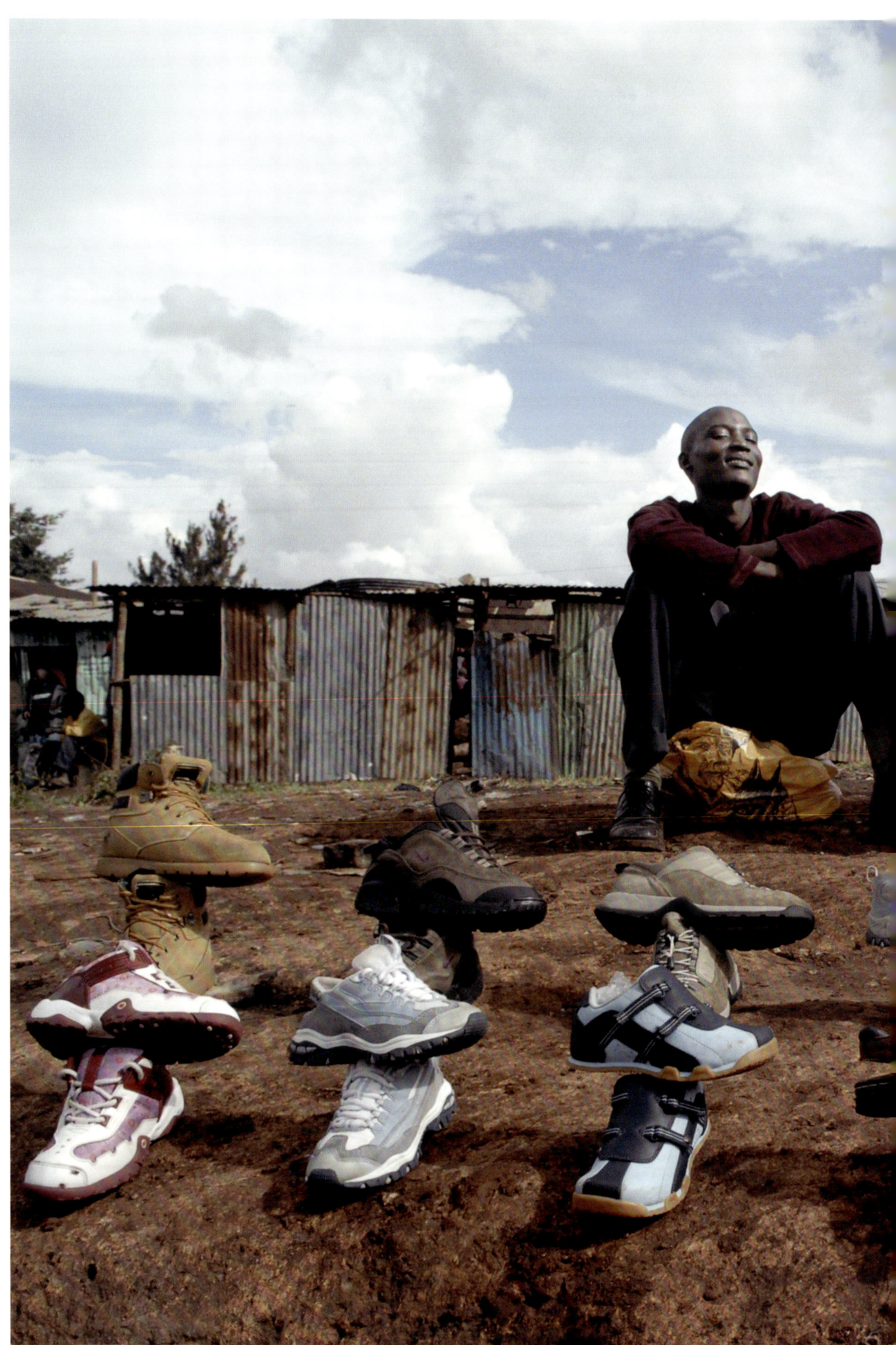

Kenya 2006
Jeffrey Austin

In the Kibera Slums, unemployment is widespread, and many of those who have jobs take home less than $1 per day. In such an economically deprived climate, most residents lack access to adequate health care, and International Medical Corps' HIV/AIDS program is often their primary source of health care.

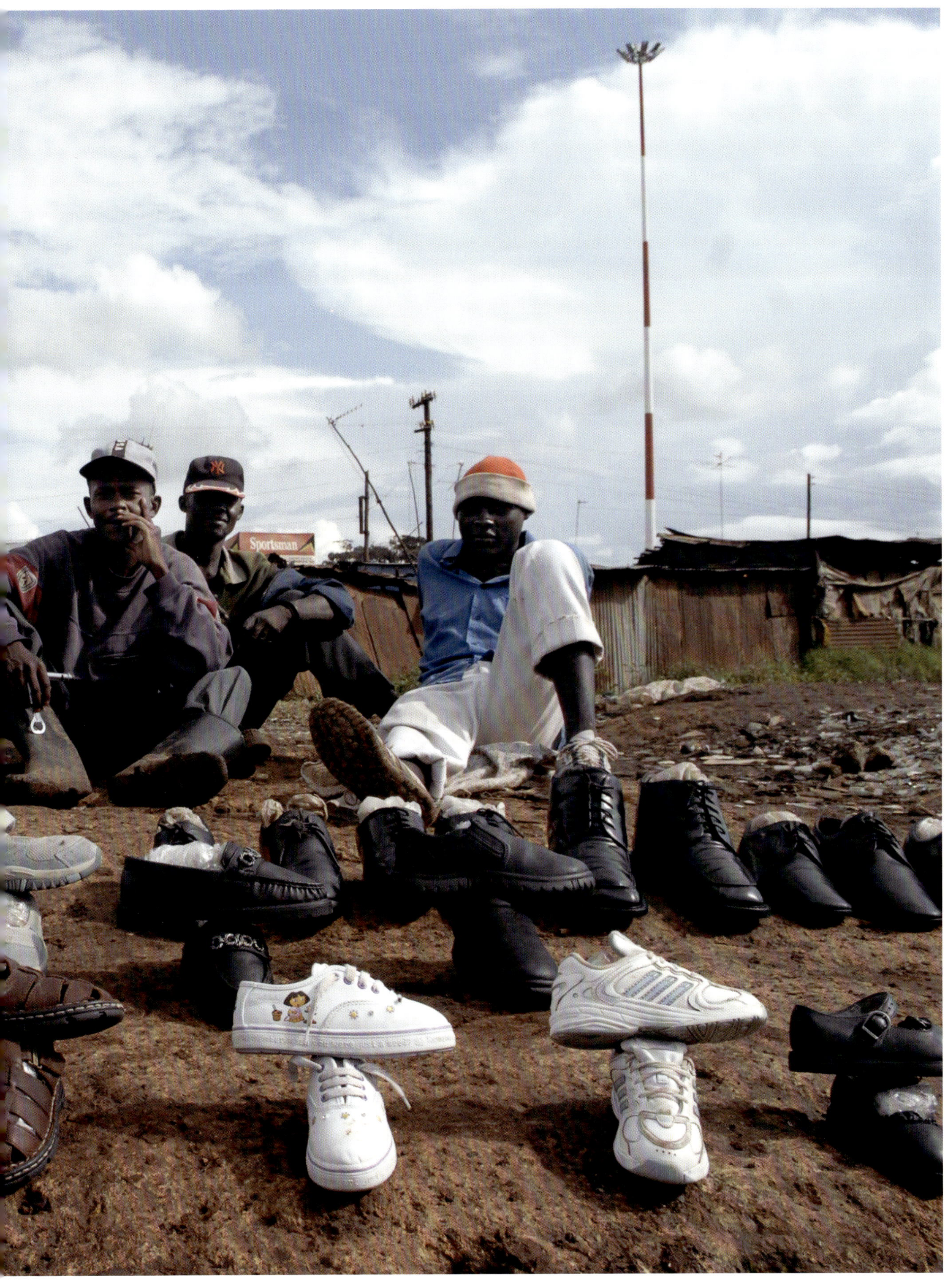
Sportsman

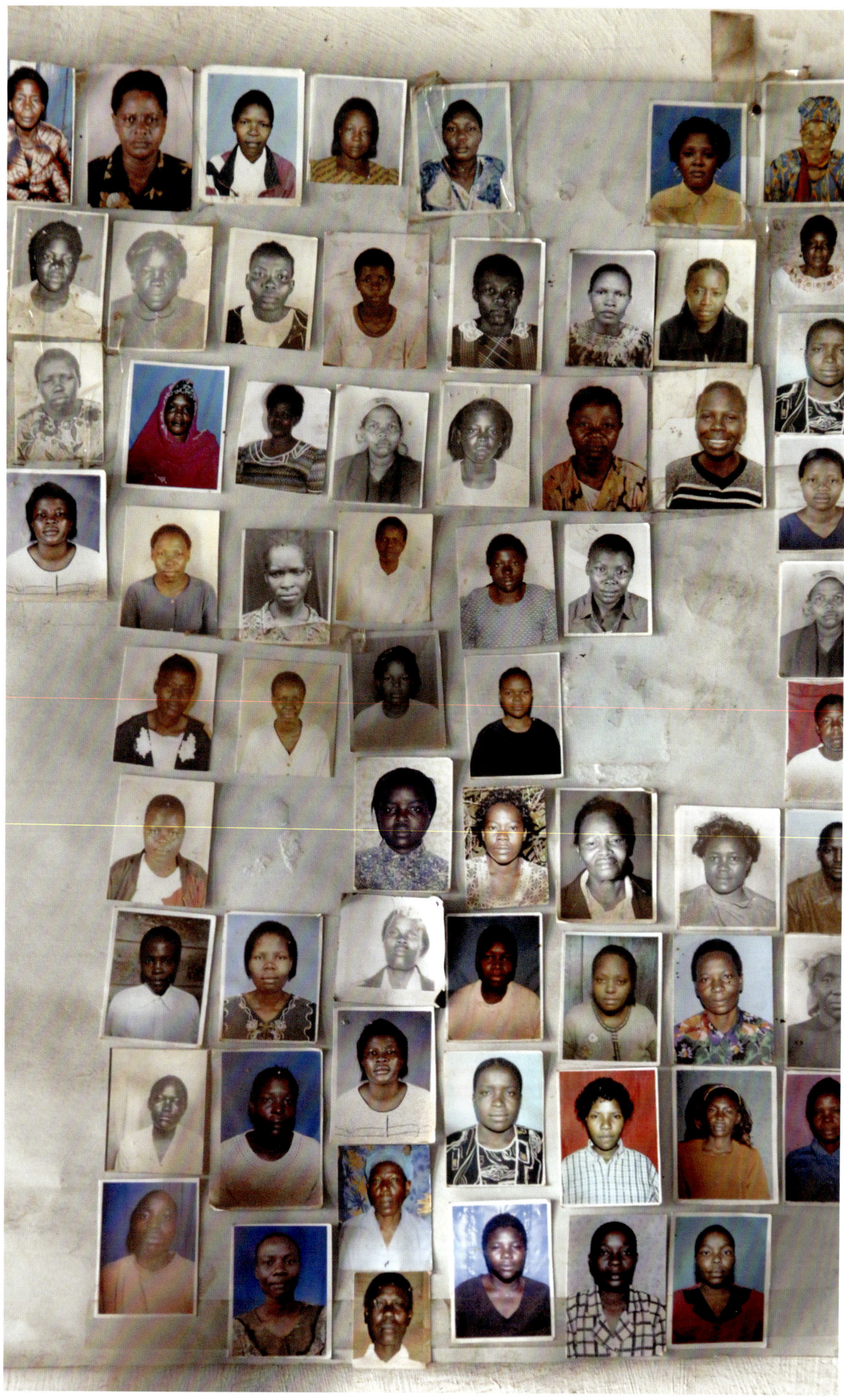

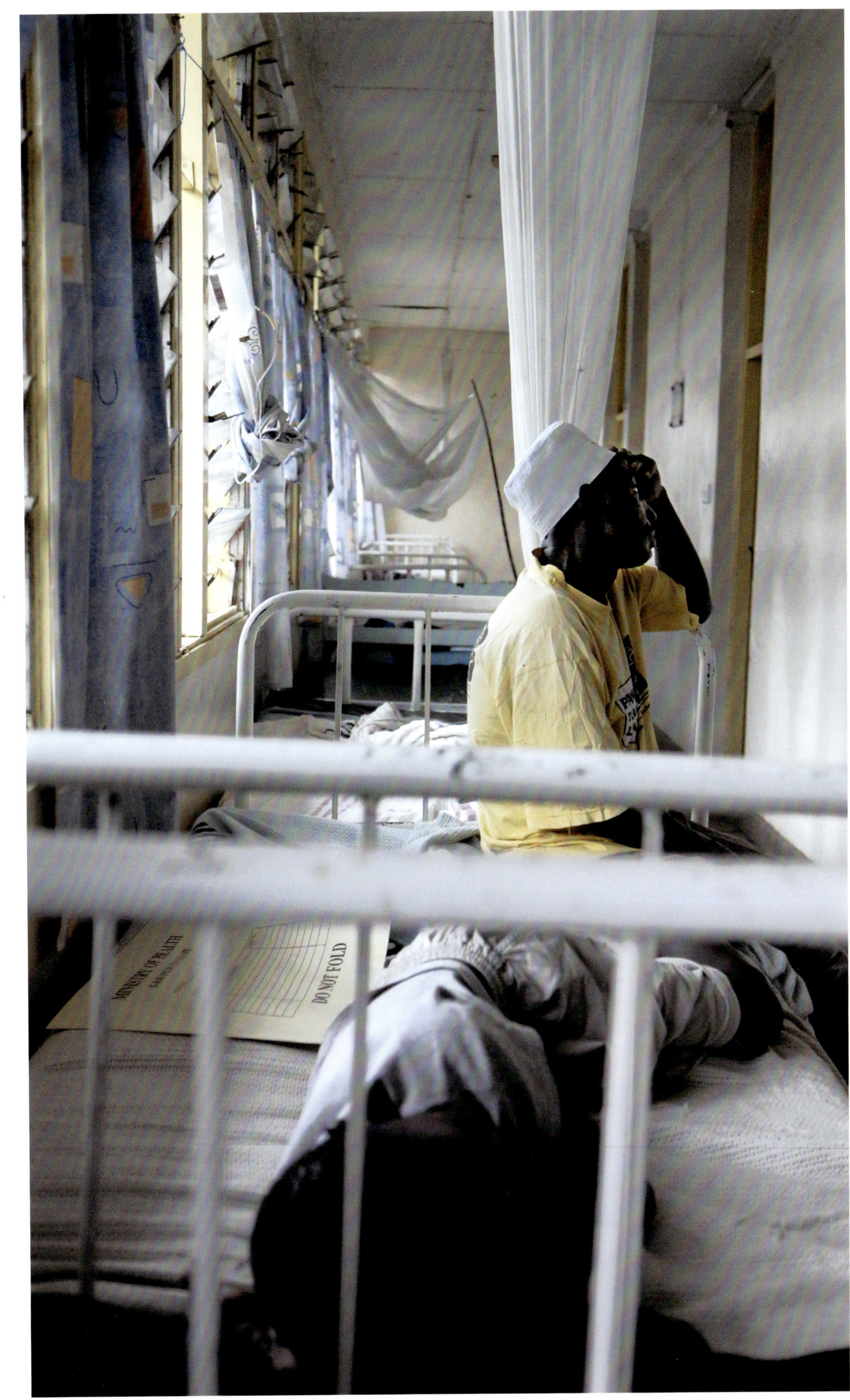

Kenya 2006
Jeffrey Austin (both pages)

In the International Medical Corps' Suba Hospital, a father sits at the bedside of his ailing child. In sub-Saharan Africa, more than three million children under the age of 15 carry the HIV virus. In 2004, IMC began to direct its efforts toward children infected with HIV/AIDS.

Opposite page: In Kibera, IMC and its local partner organization, KICOSHEP, identify and enroll the most vulnerable people affected by HIV/AIDS and provide them and their families with medical care, as well as social, emotional and moral support.

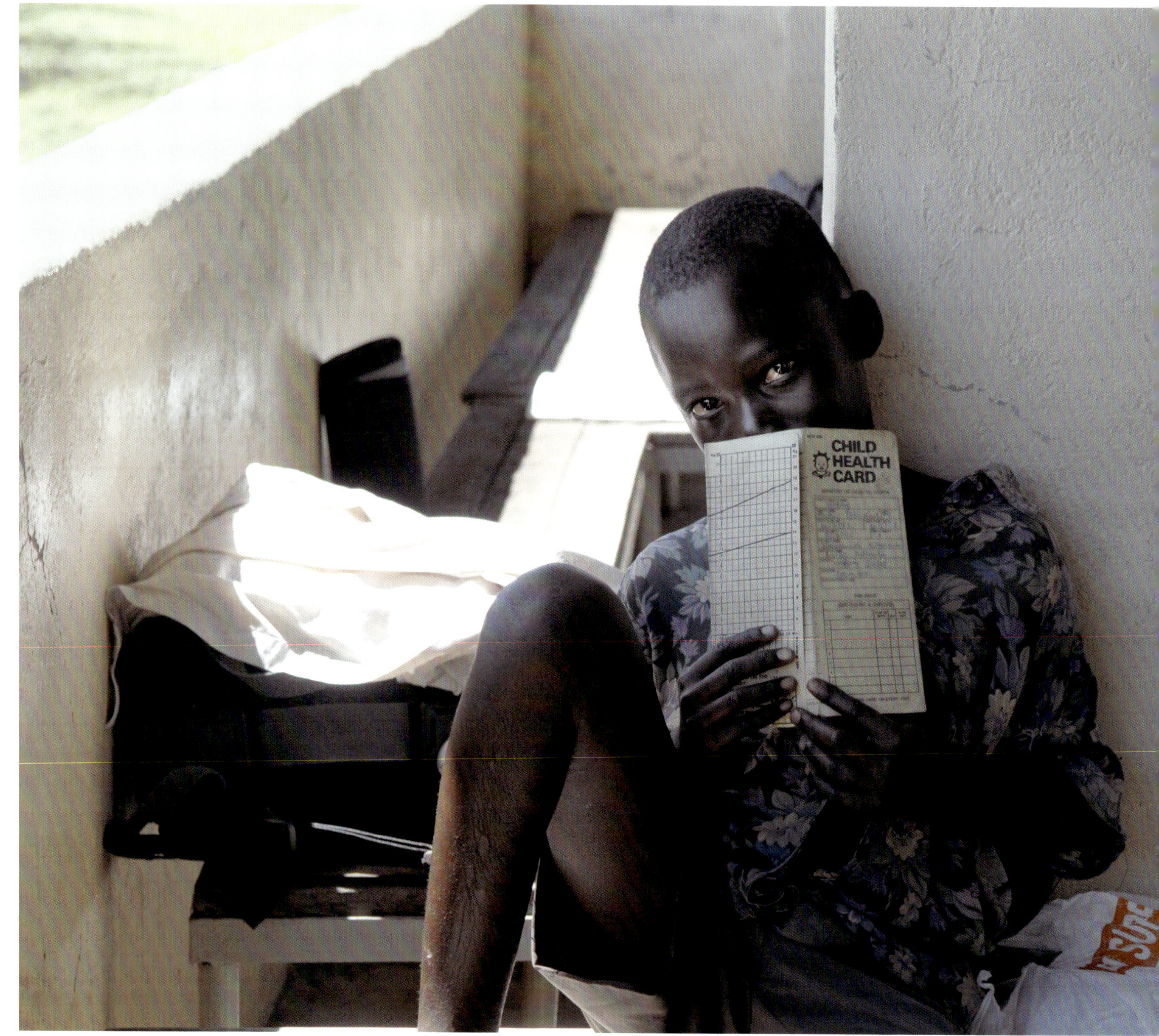

Kenya 2006
Jeffrey Austin (both pages)

A young boy holds his child health card while waiting outside an International Medical Corps clinic in Suba, Kenya. Through educational outreach activities, International Medical Corps works with the community and local youth to provide accurate information that challenges social stigmas and reduces the population's chances of contracting HIV.

Opposite page: A local poet visits the International Medical Corps clinic in Suba.

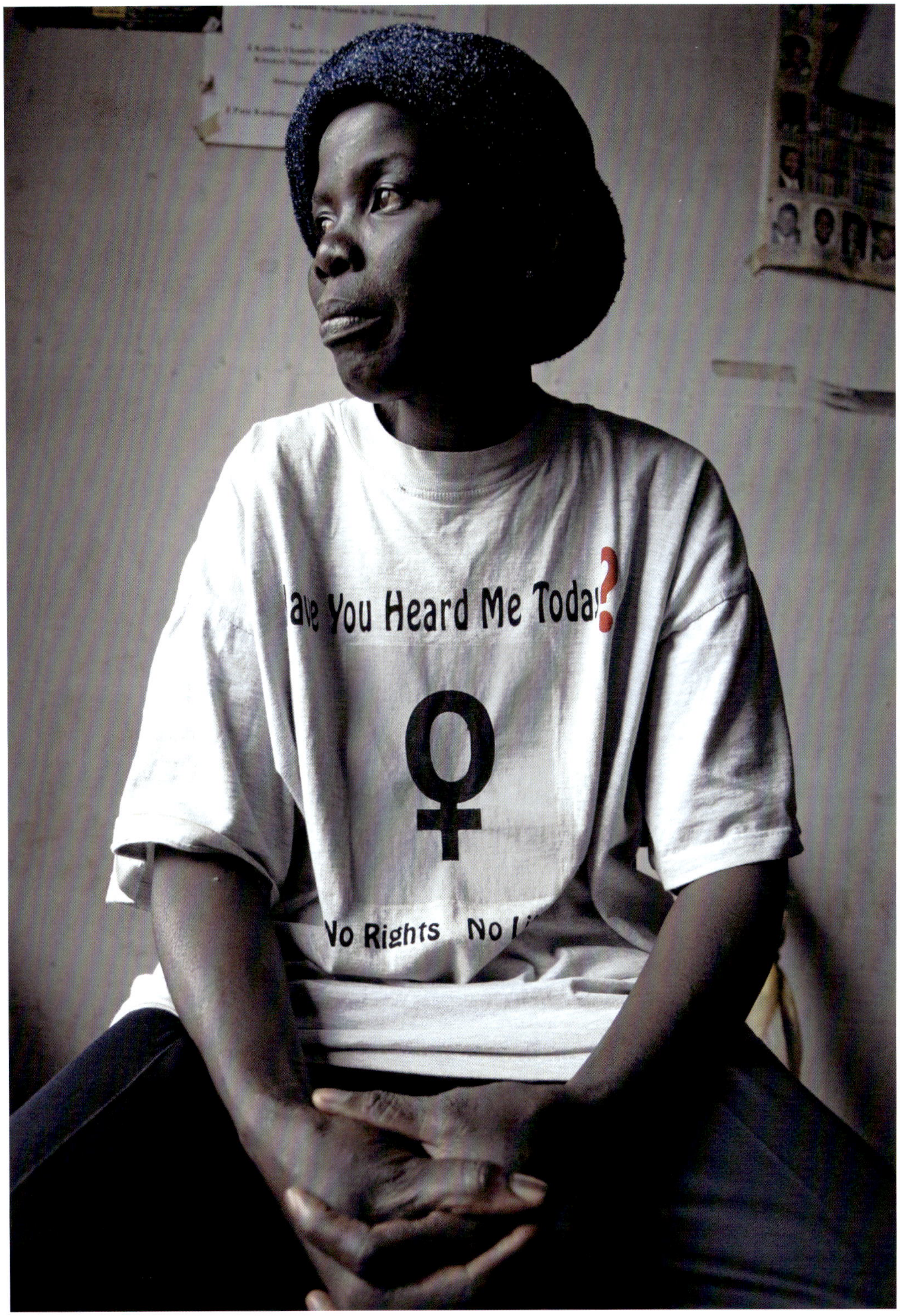

Kenya 2006
Jeffrey Austin

One of the main goals of International Medical Corps' HIV/AIDS programs is to change the attitude about HIV/AIDS in villages in Kenya. As a result, more Kenyans are being tested for HIV and are encouraging others in their community to know their status, like this man at IMC's HIV testing center.

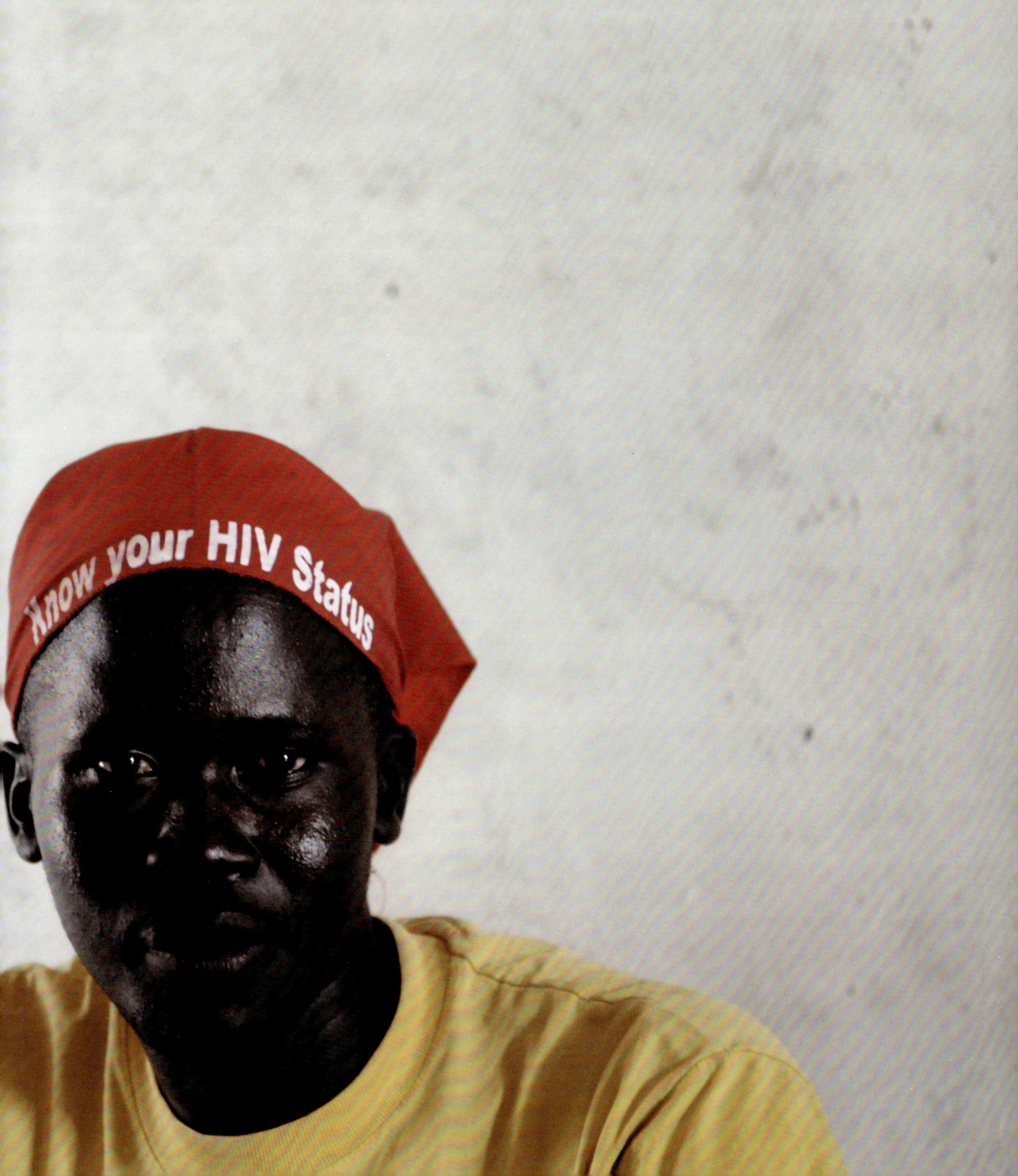
now your HIV Status

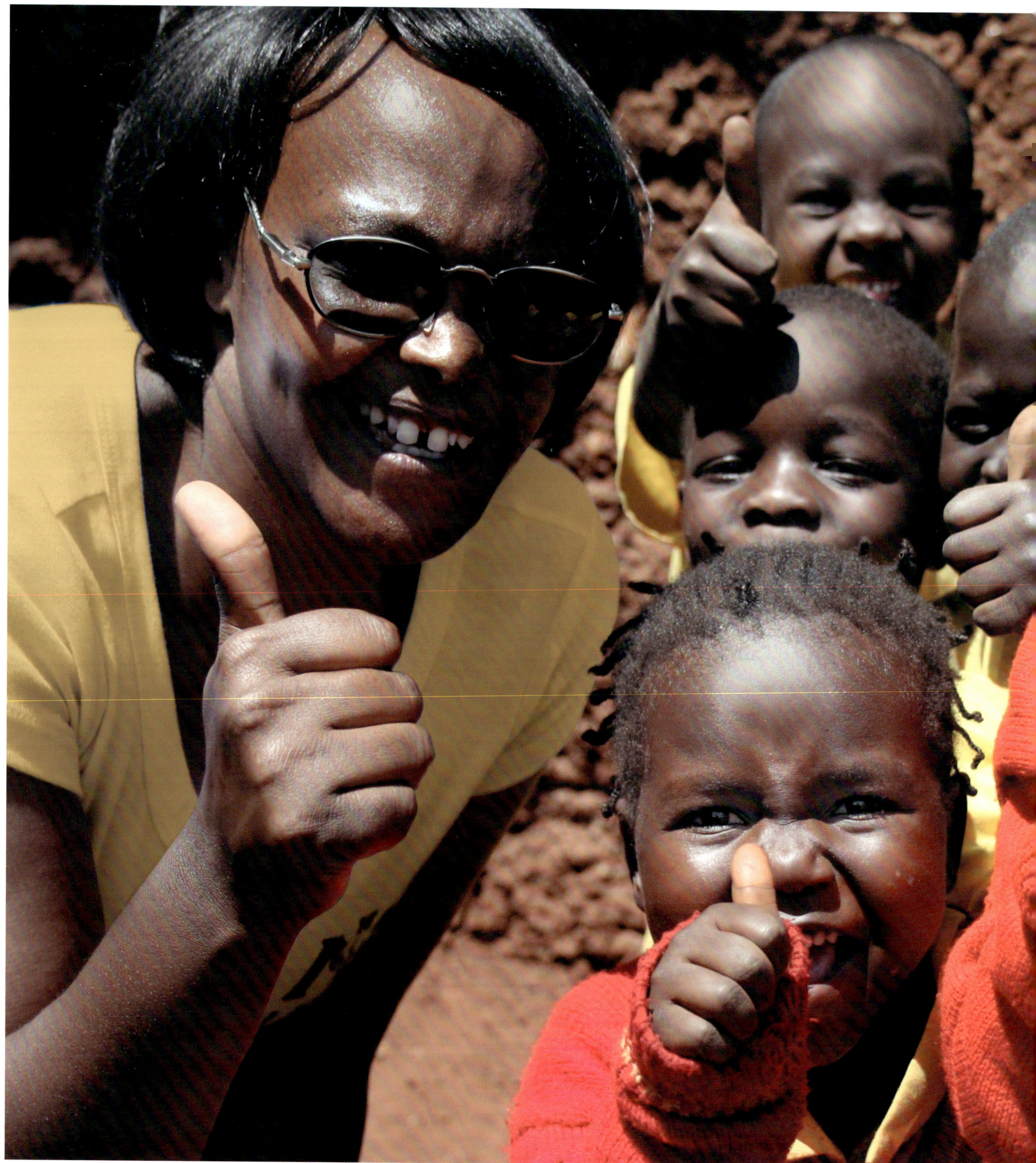

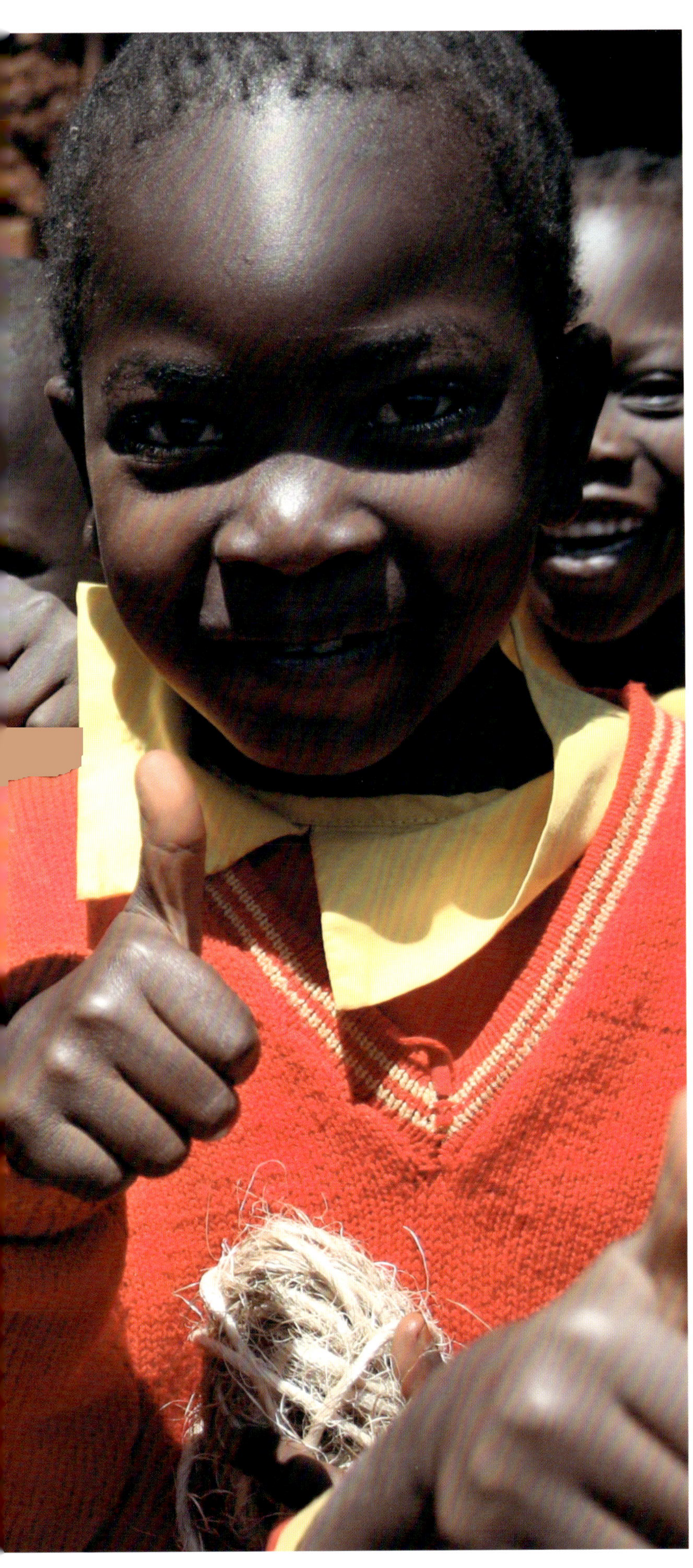

Kenya 2007
IMC staff

International Medical Corps' HIV/AIDS programs have been successful in treating and managing the HIV/AIDS epidemic in Kenya. Grace Muthumbi, a nurse and one of IMC's project coordinators in Kenya, is shown with many of the children she has treated.

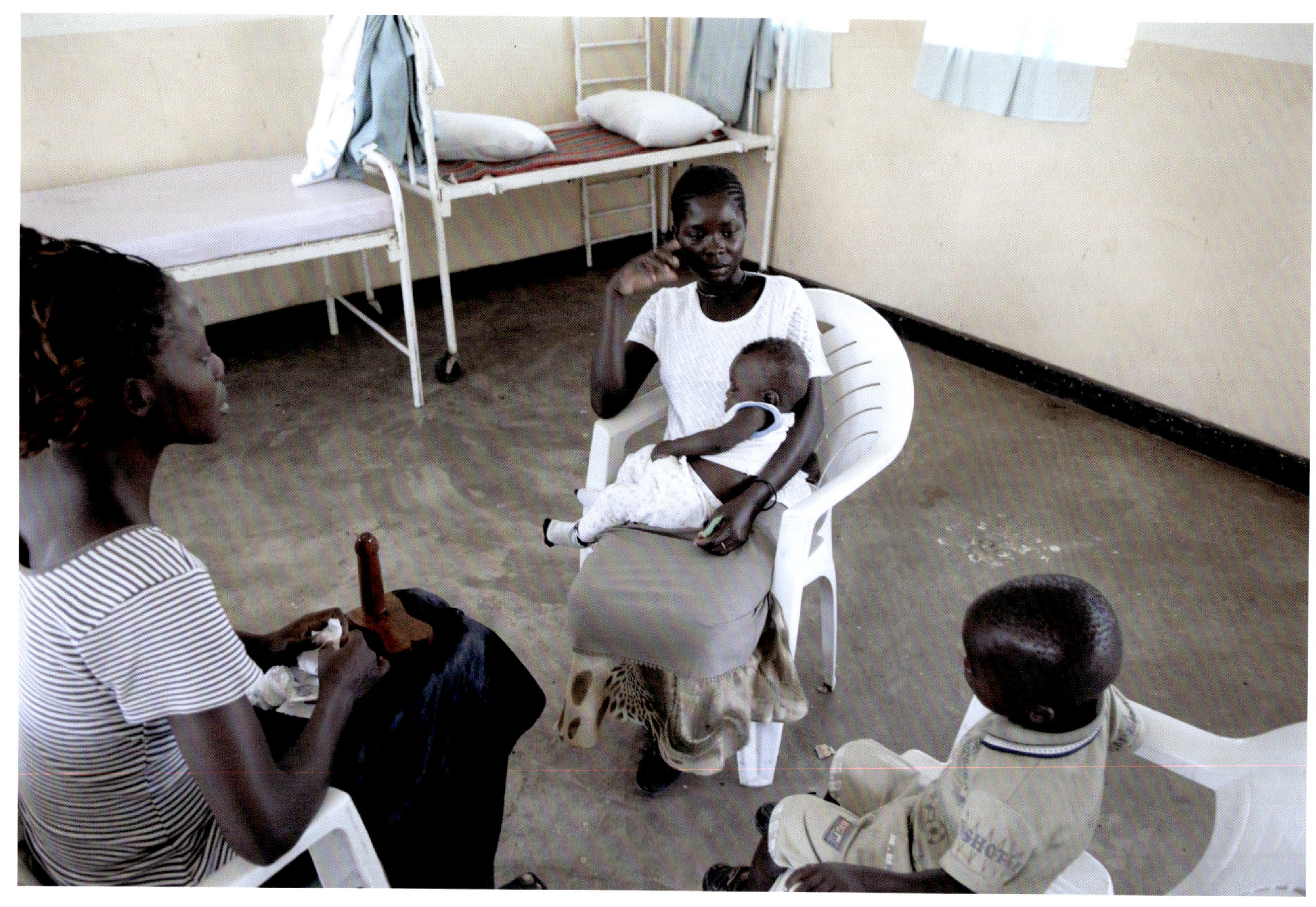

Kenya 2006/2002
Jeffrey Austin (above; opposite, top)
Jenny Chu (opposite, bottom)

In Suba, local International Medical Corps health care workers have counseled and tested more than 9,000 pregnant women and 4,000 others by providing advanced treatment to HIV-positive mothers and their infants. The IMC clinic has become a cornerstone to a community hard-hit by HIV/AIDS, providing hospital services and home-based care to those infected with and impacted by HIV/AIDS, particularly women and children.

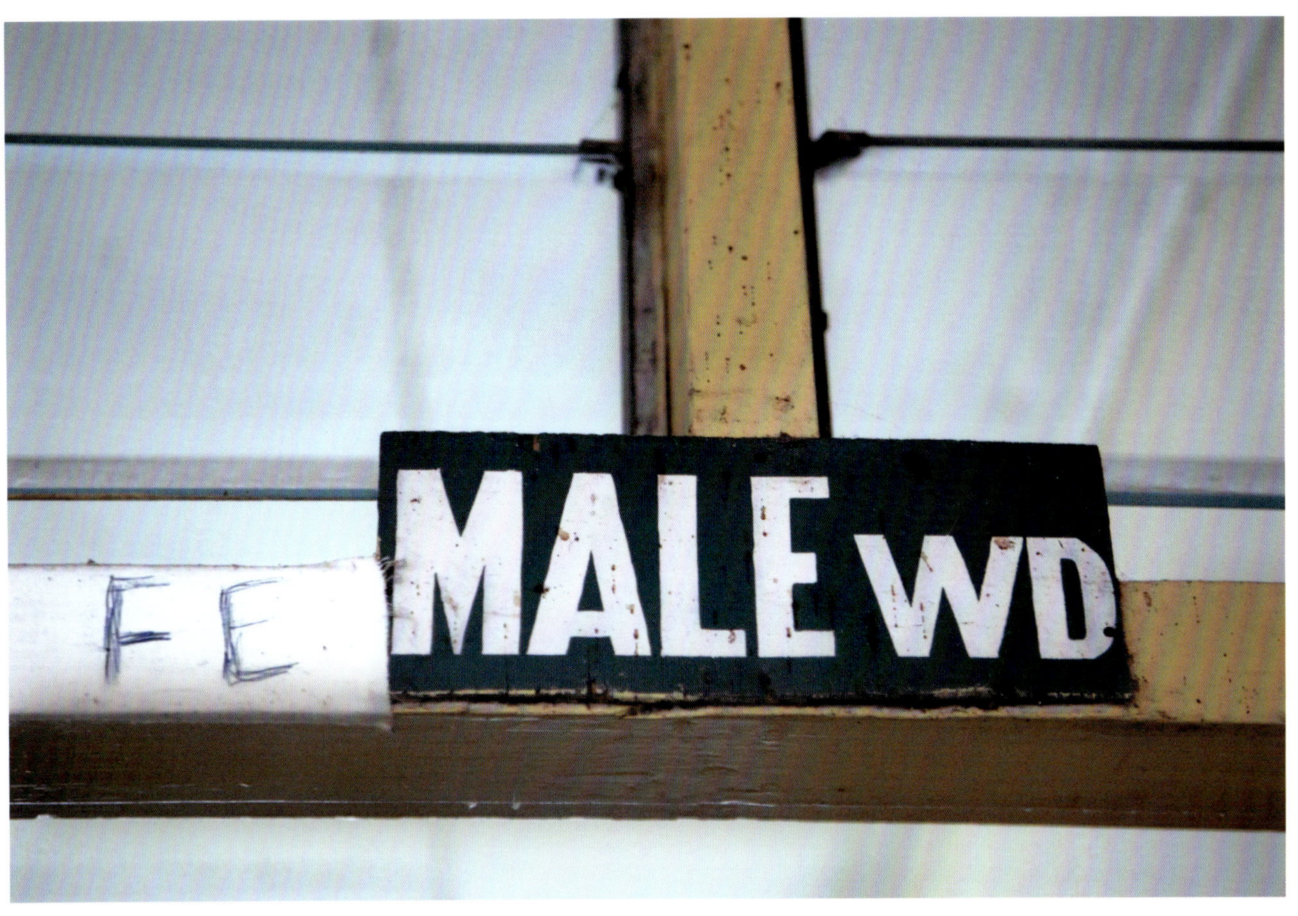
FE
MALE WD

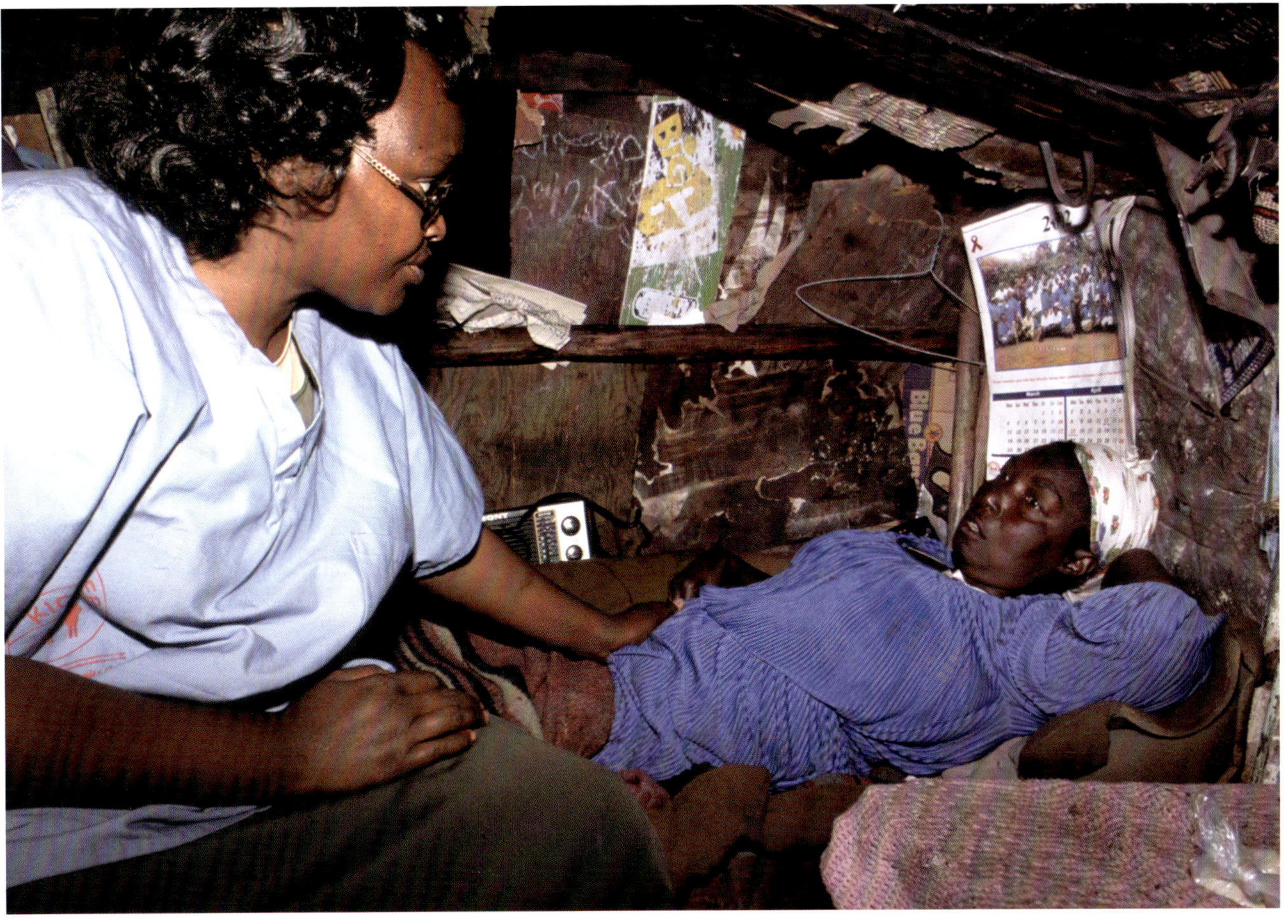

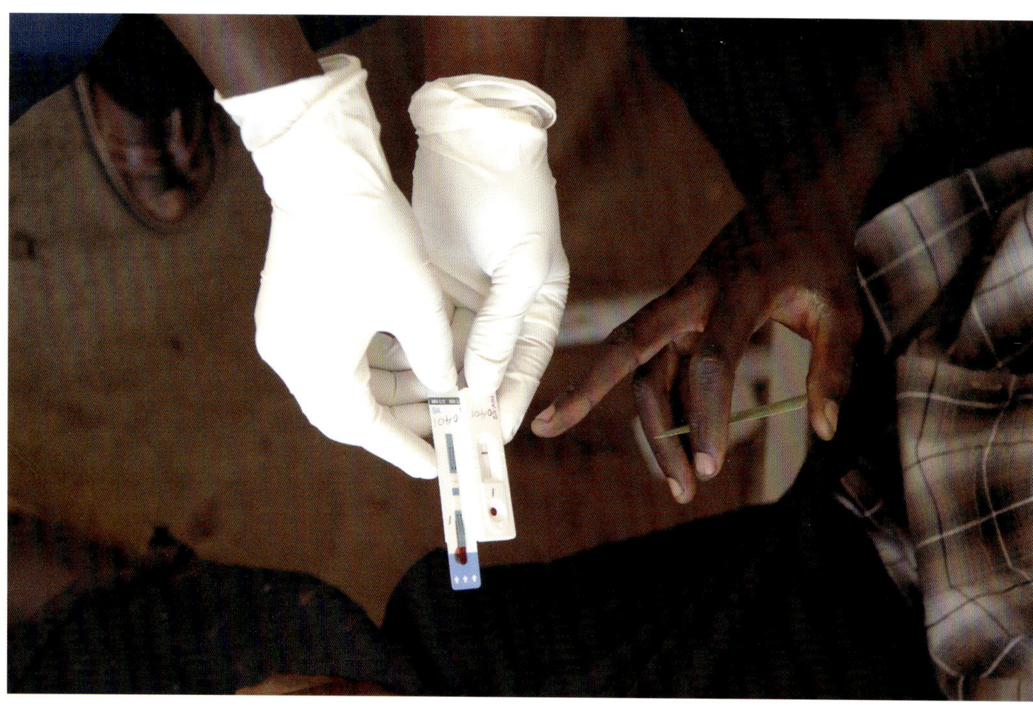

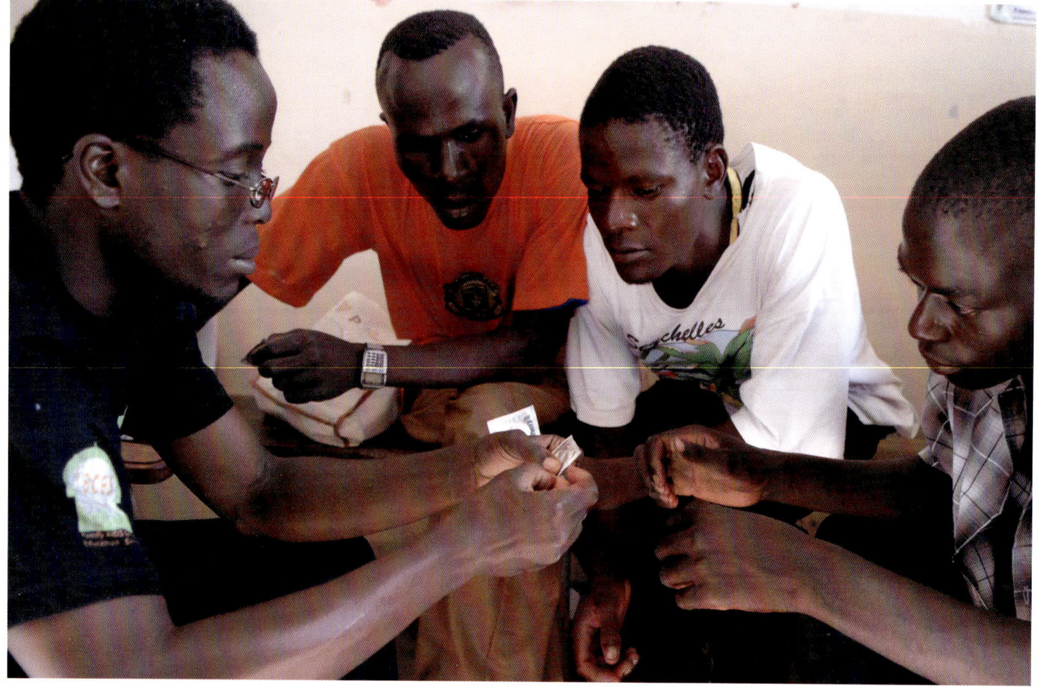

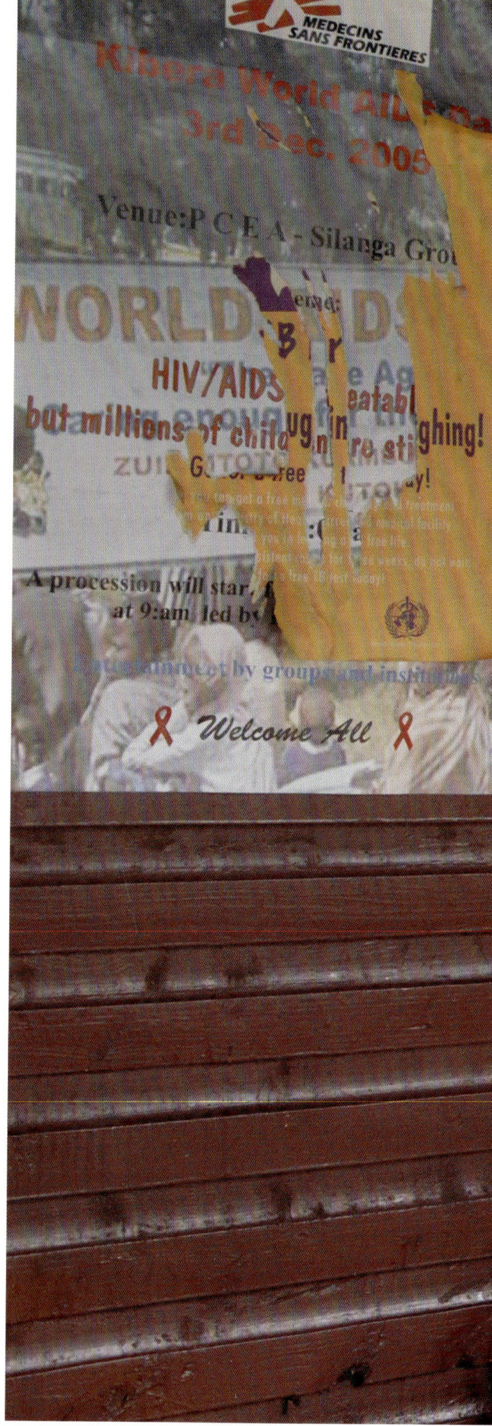
MEDECINS SANS FRONTIERES
3rd Dec. 2005
Venue:P C E A - Silanga
HIV/AIDS
A procession will
at 9:am
Welcome All

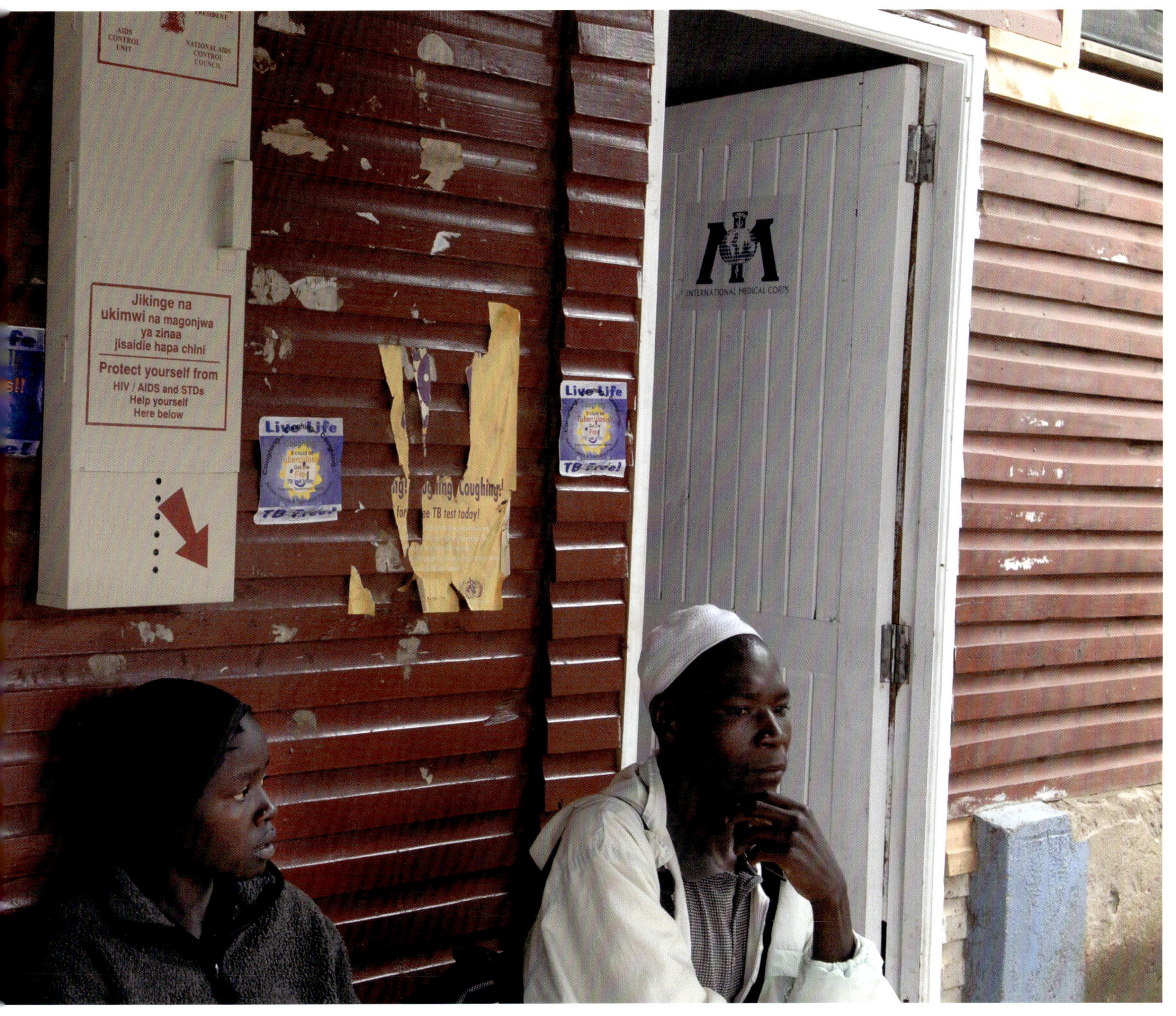

Kenya 2006
Jeffrey Austin (both pages)

At International Medical Corps' Suba Clinic, the improvement in the quality of life of those receiving care led others whose status was unknown to seek testing. IMC staff and local volunteers have been very successful in convincing community members to be tested for HIV, to know their HIV status, and to prevent the spread of HIV.

FOOD AND WATER

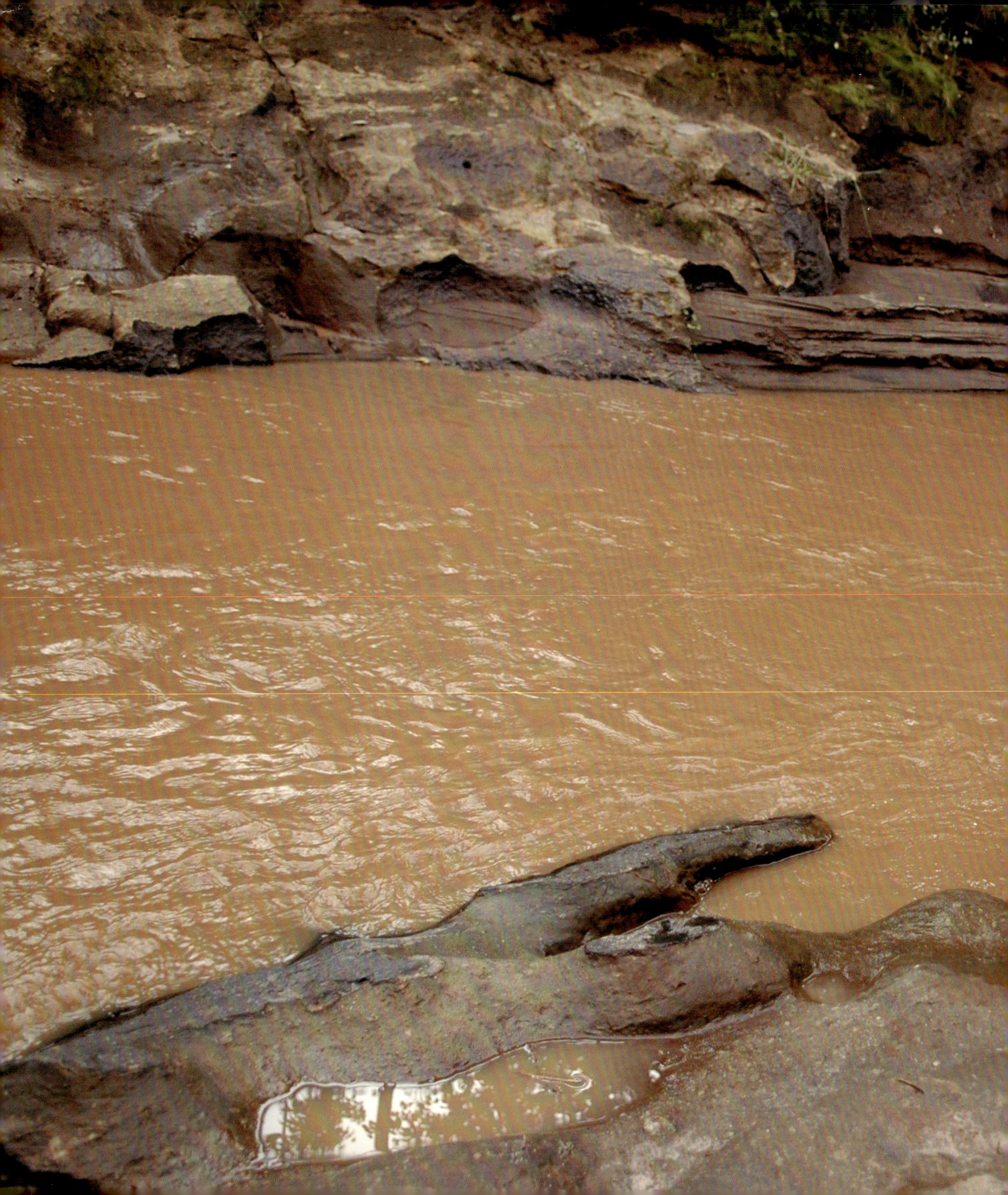

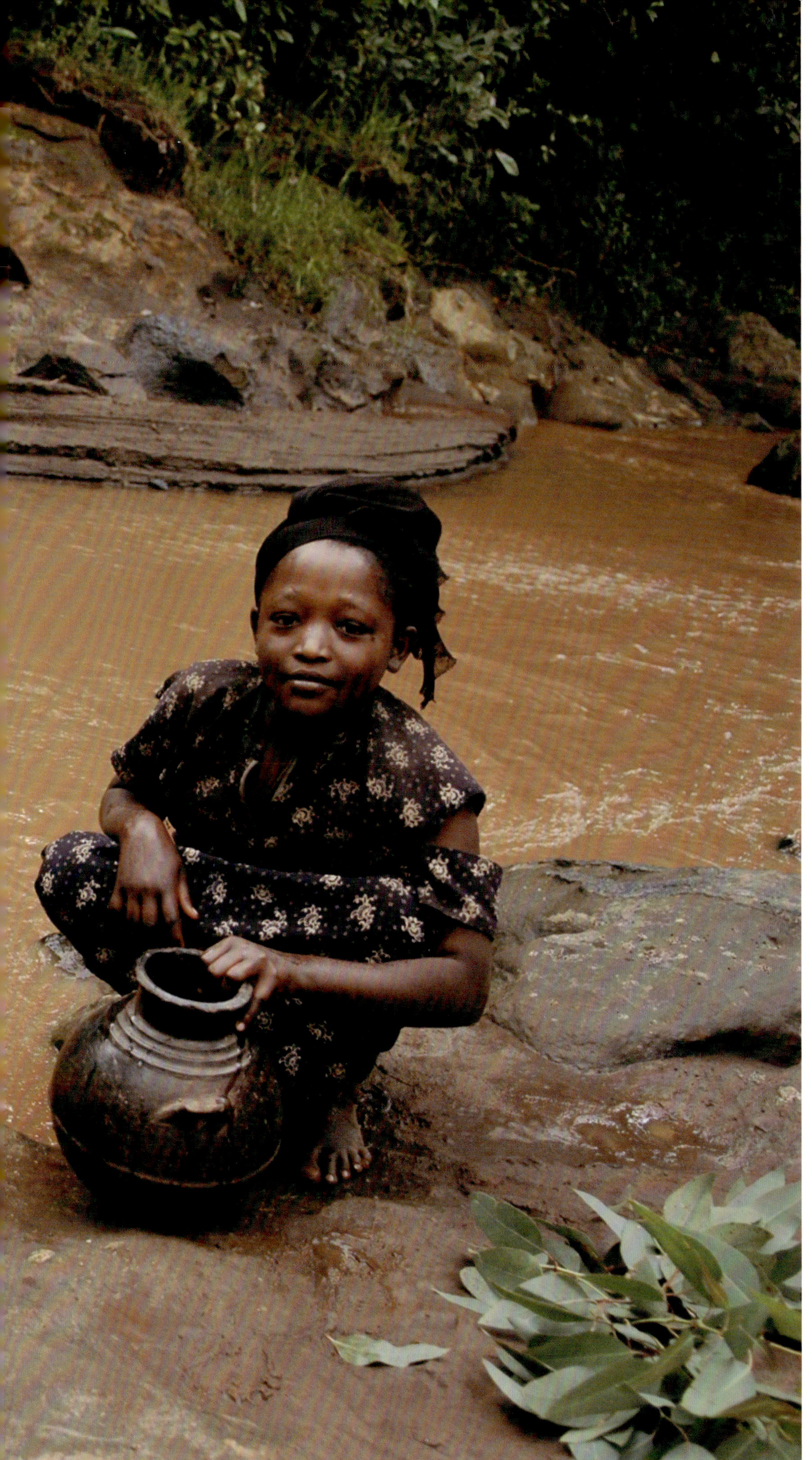

Ethiopia 2006
Julie Pudlowski

The combination of extreme poverty and cyclical droughts forced many Ethiopians to get their water supplies from contaminated sources, which caused a variety of health problems. In an effort to address this issue, International Medical Corps began several water/sanitation and irrigation projects throughout Ethiopia in 2002.

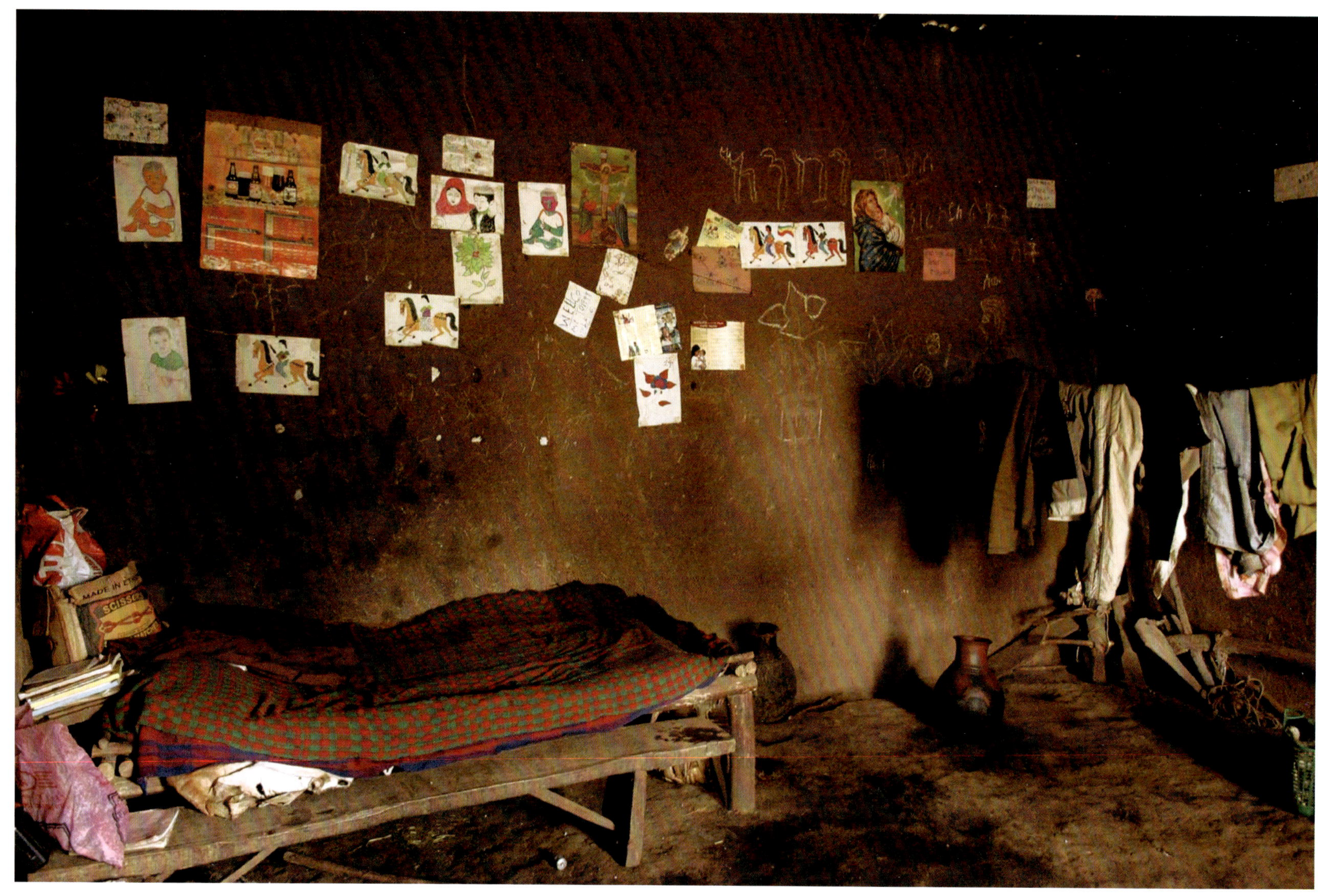

Ethiopia 2006
Julie Pudlowski (both pages)

With this view inside a home in the Sodo region of Ethiopia, it becomes clear that the families in this village do not have much. By purifying polluted water sources, International Medical Corps worked to stop the spread of illnesses, such as typhoid, cholera and diarrhea, to which children are especially susceptible. In 2006, one in six Ethiopian children died before turning 5.

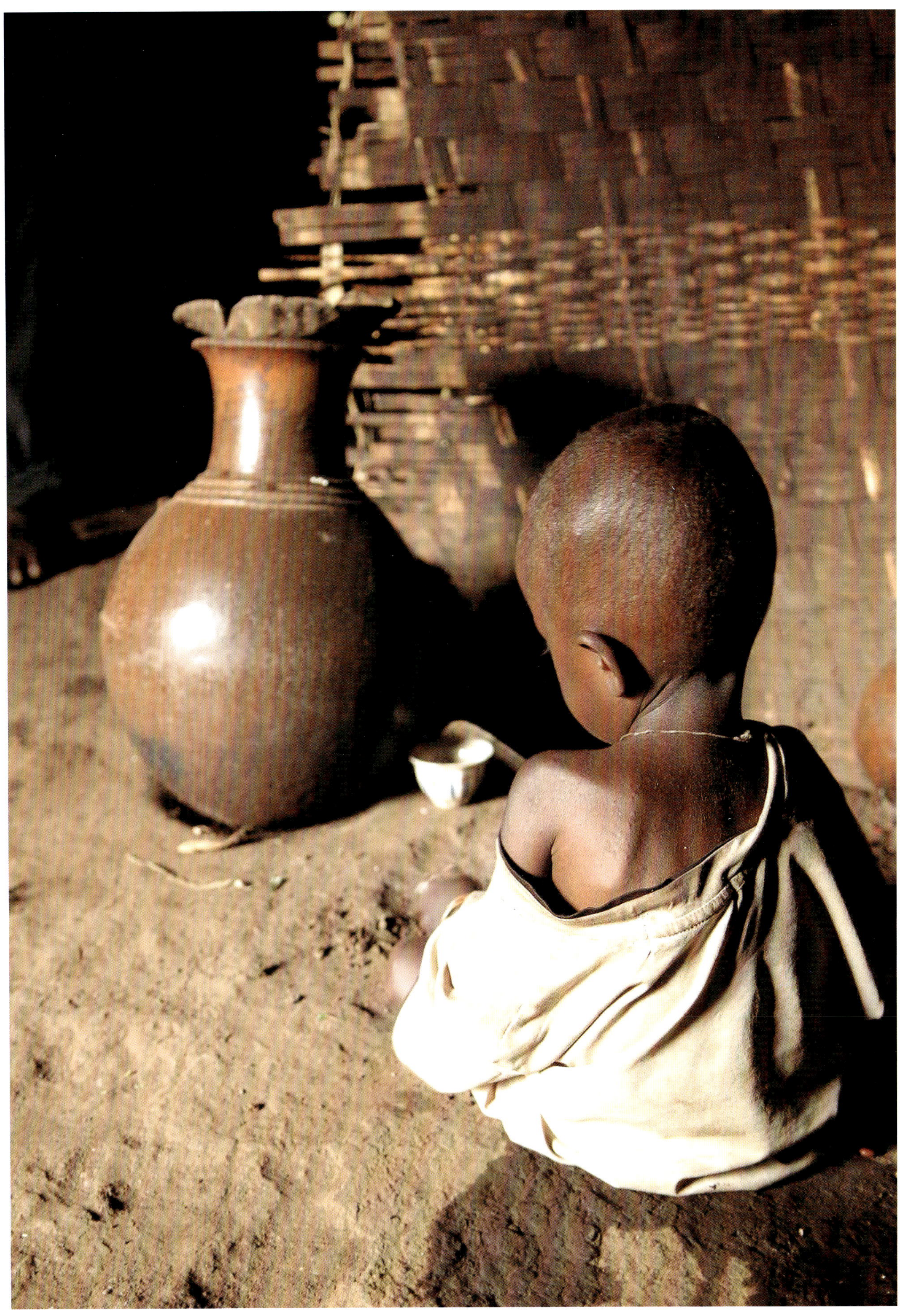

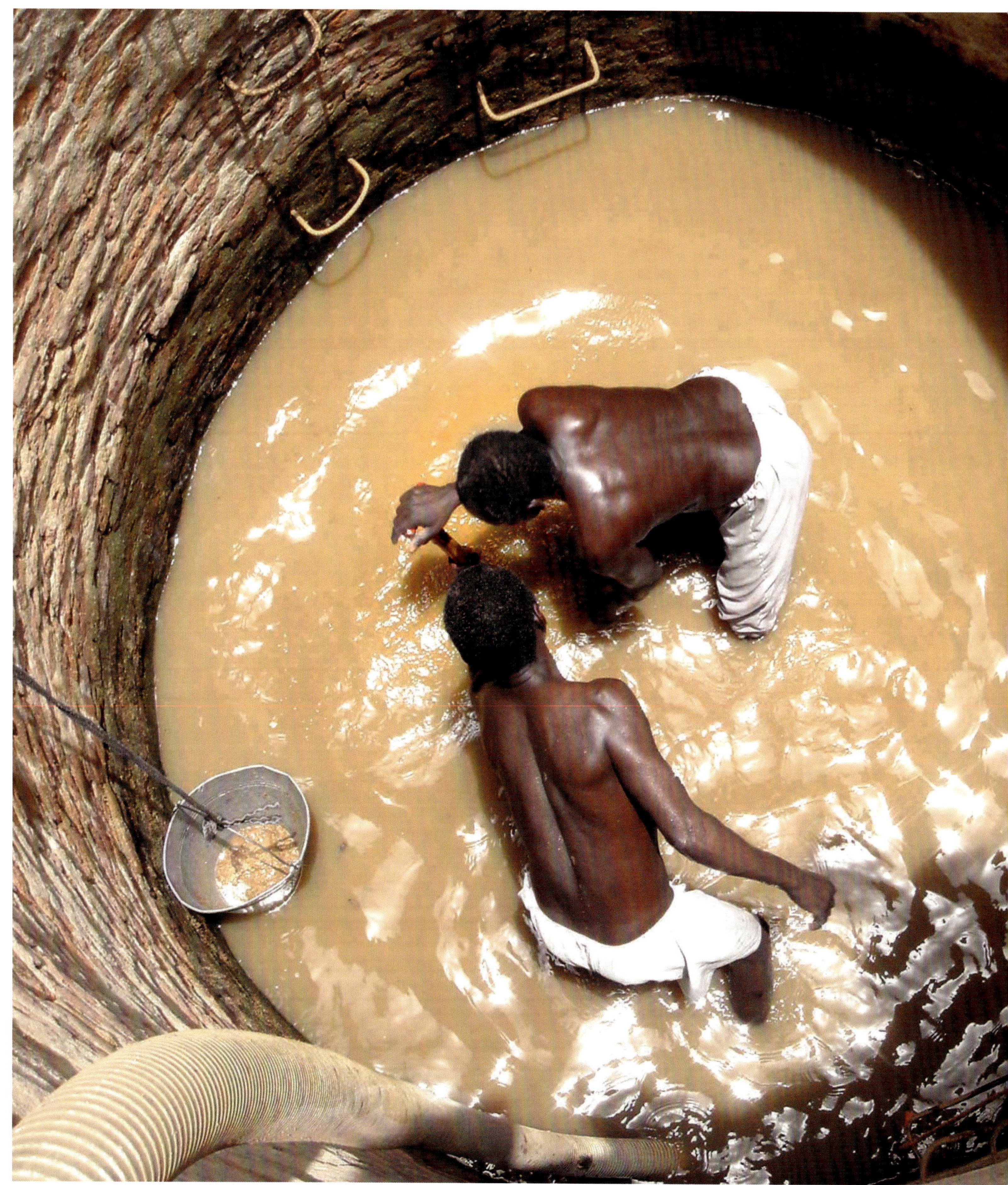

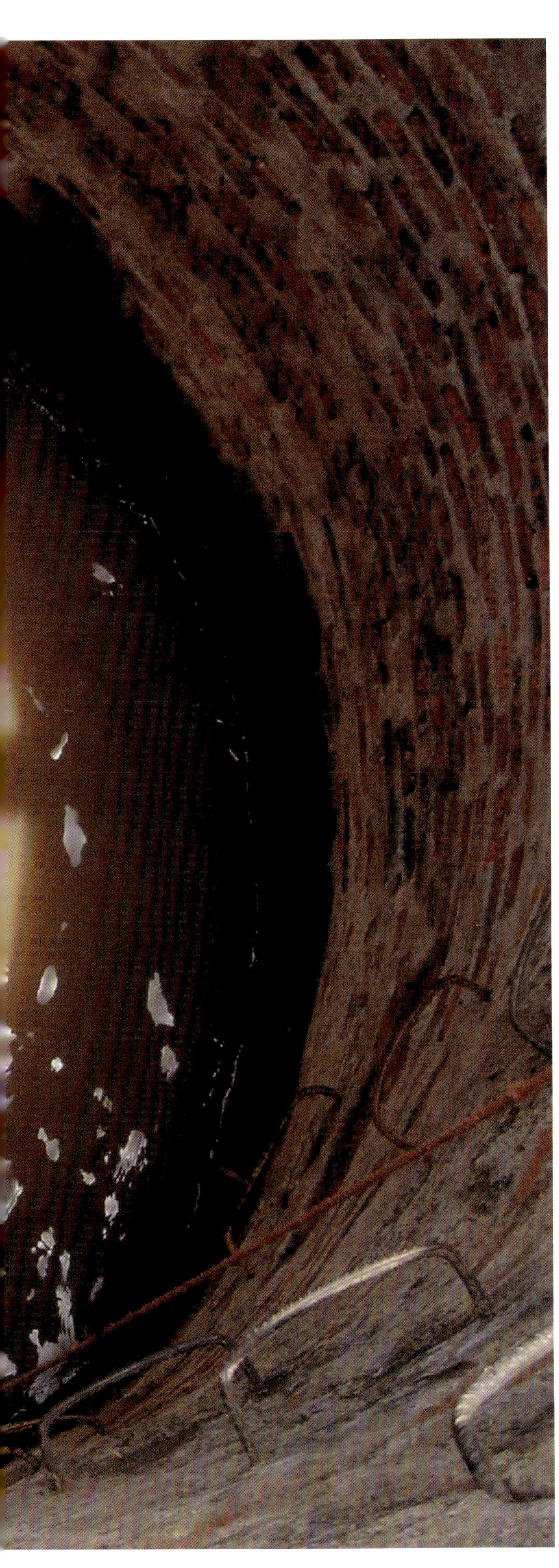

Darfur 2006
IMC staff

As part of a comprehensive approach to health care, International Medical Corps initiated a variety of water and sanitation projects that renovated aging systems and built new wells like this one at Garsila market in Darfur.

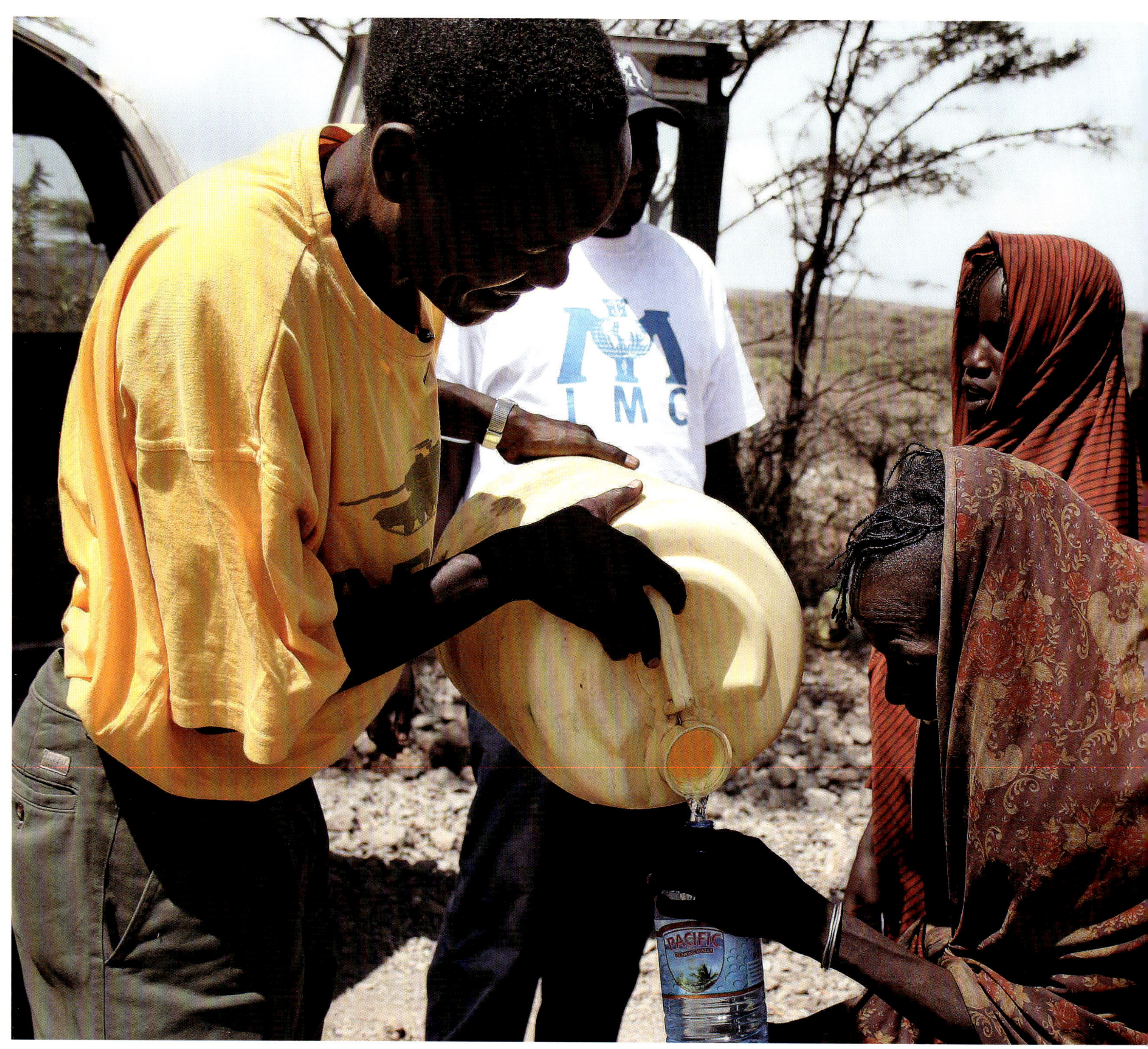
IMC
PACIFIC

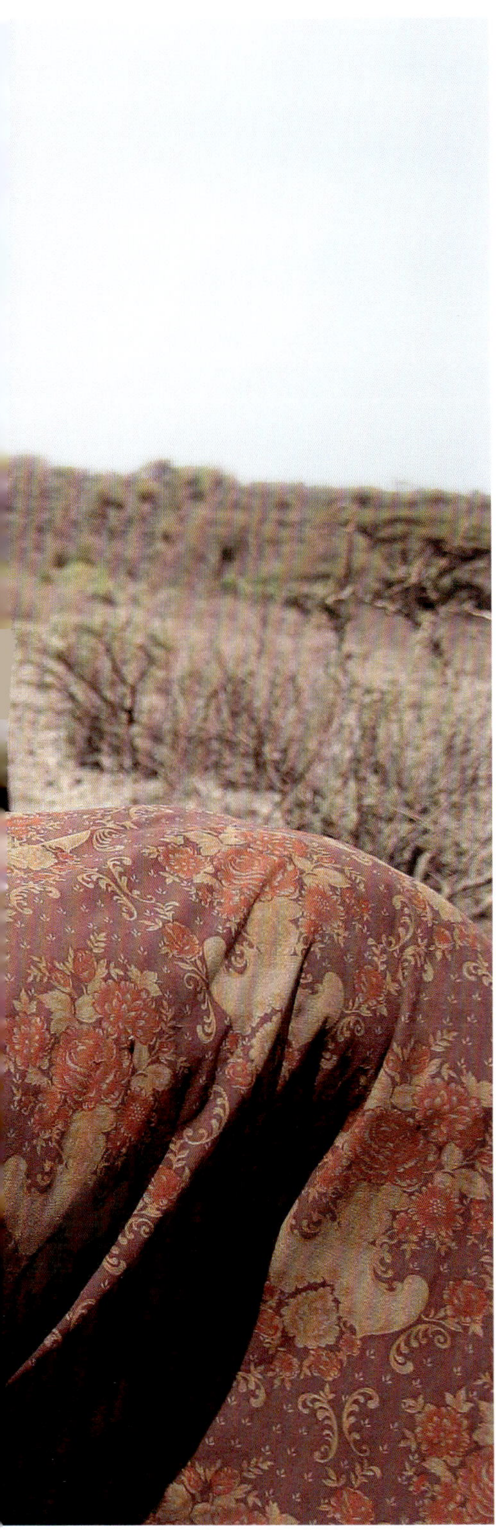

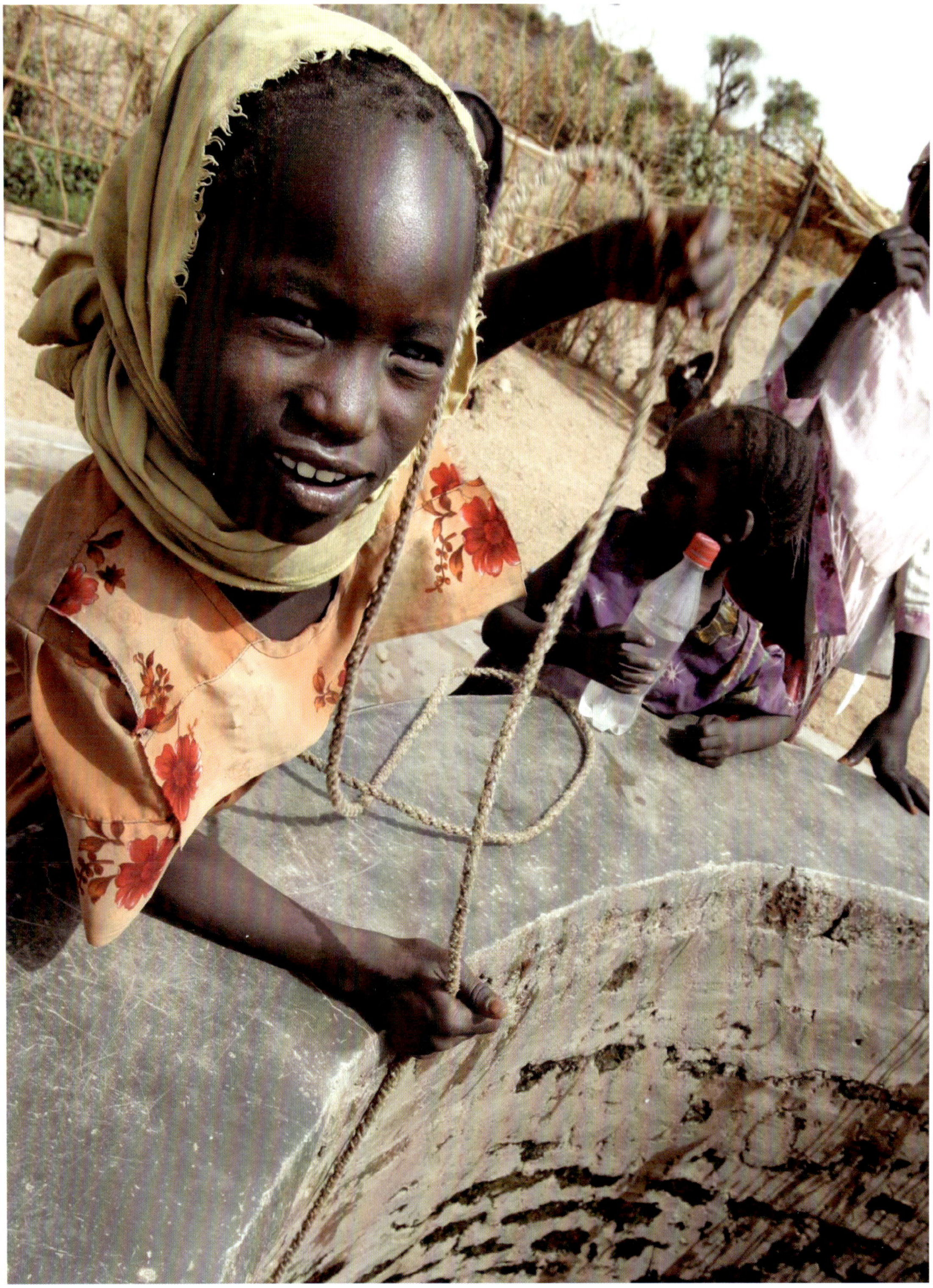

Kenya 2007 (opposite page)
Darfur 2006 (this page)
IMC staff

Throughout Africa, the lack of clean water is a growing problem and a priority for International Medical Corps. Africa is the only continent within which the people are expected to get poorer over the next century. To make matters more challenging, it is estimated that 25 African countries will not have enough water by 2025.

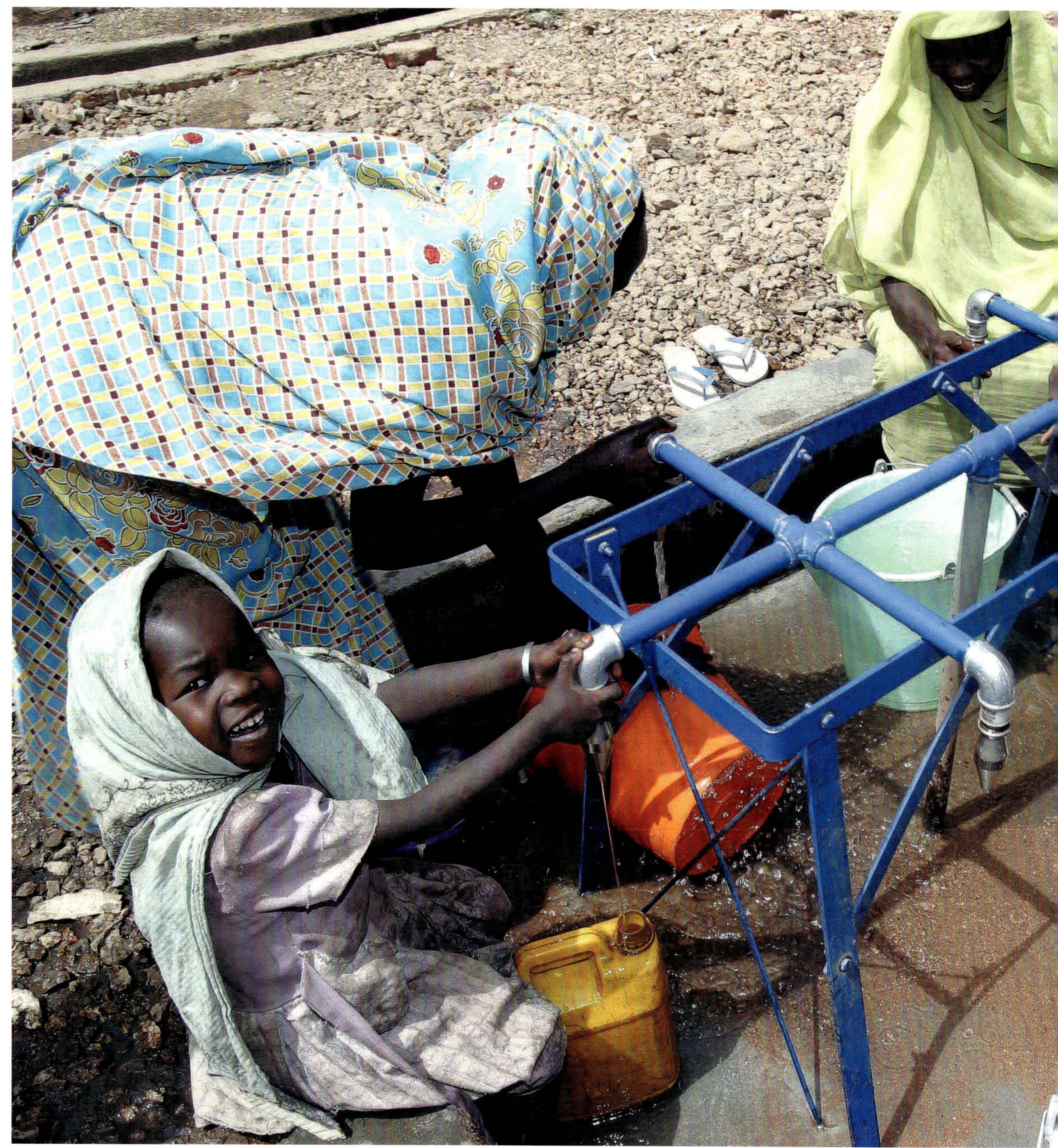

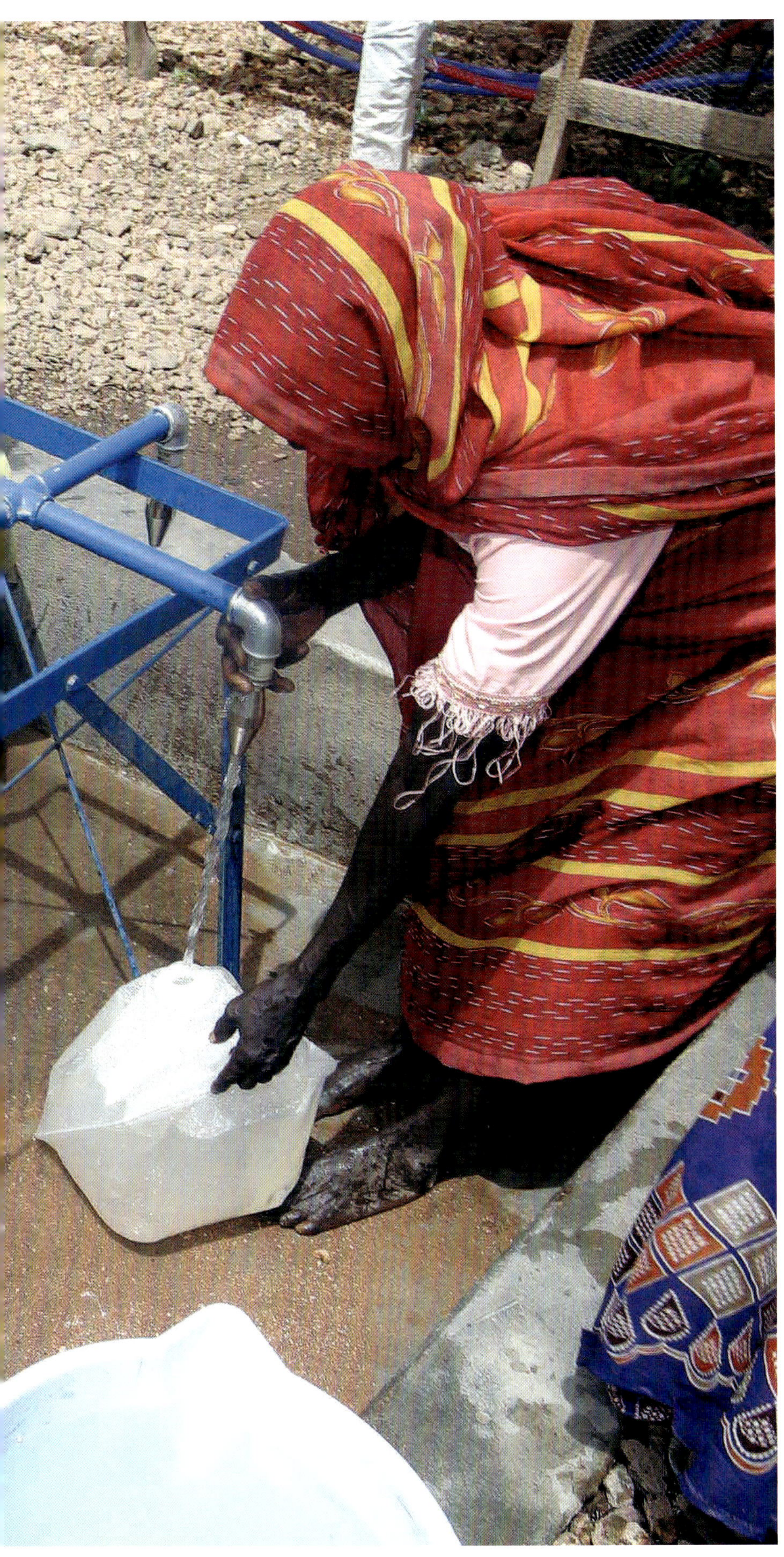

Darfur 2006
IMC staff

International Medical Corps believes clean water is vital to its health care initiatives and seeks to control the spread of waterborne diseases through a variety of water and sanitation projects. By renovating aging systems, constructing pipelines where none existed, and purifying polluted water sources, IMC is stopping the spread of illnesses such as typhoid, cholera and diarrhea.

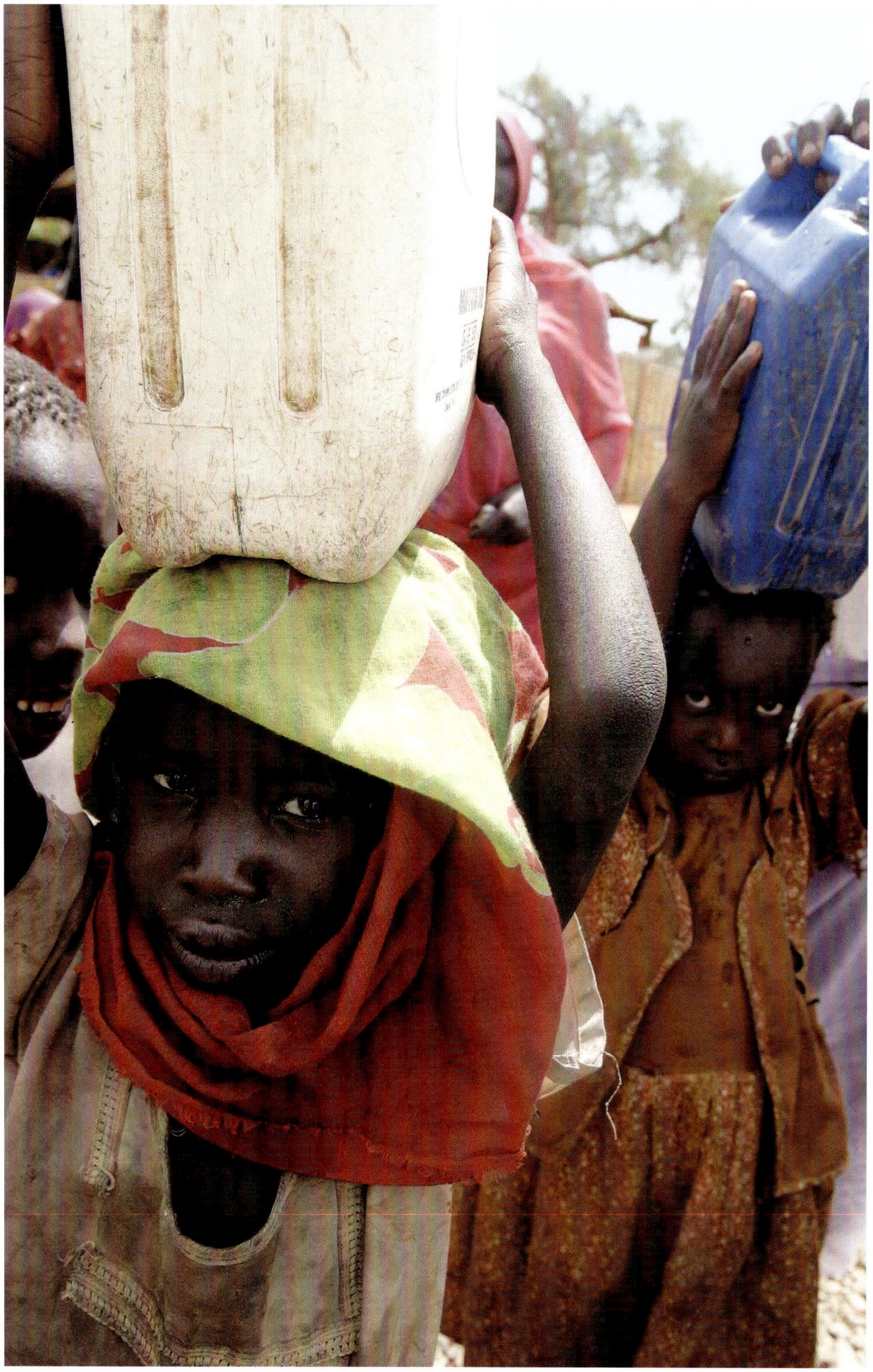

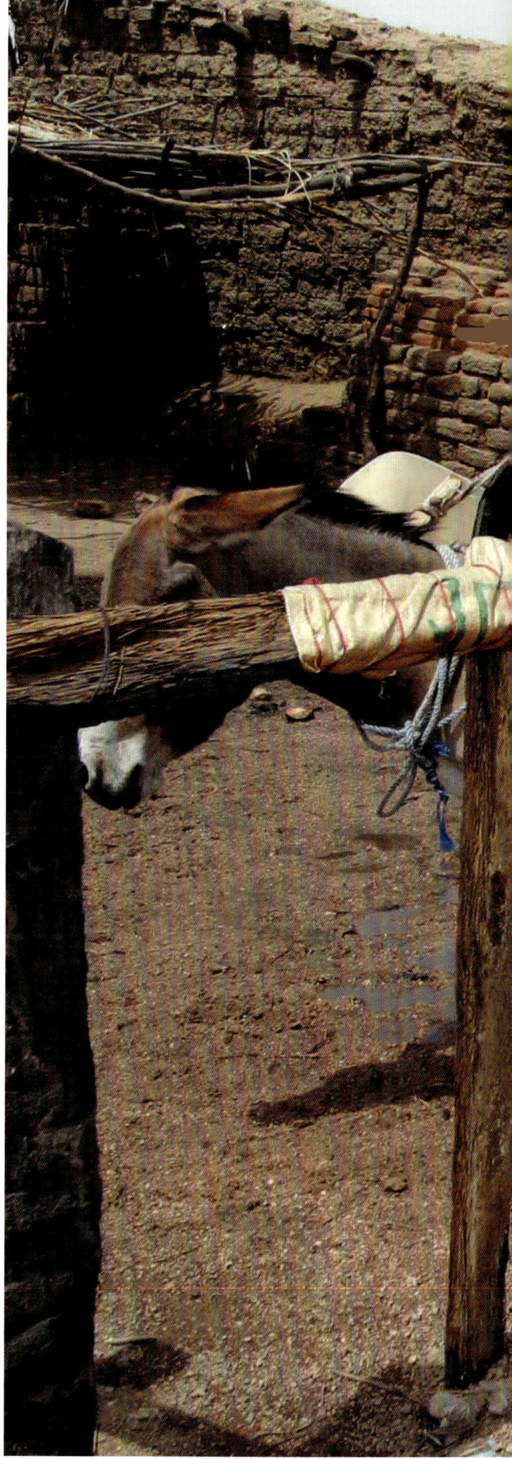

Darfur 2006
IMC staff (both photos)

In Darfur, International Medical Corps assisted with the water and sanitation crisis resulting from the ongoing conflict by distributing thousands of water tanks, which served as the only source of fresh water in settlements for internally displaced persons like the one in Garsila in Sudan.

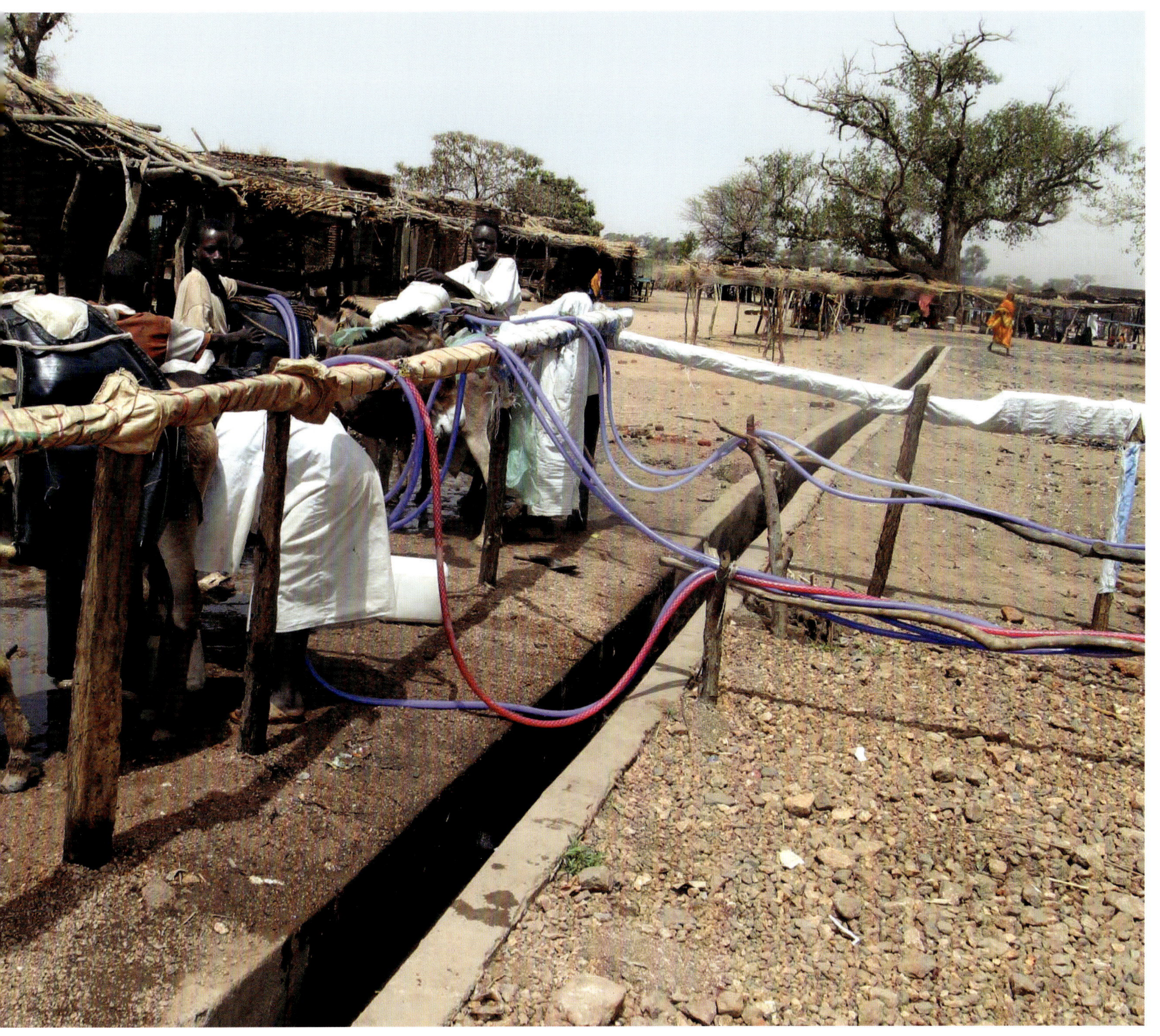

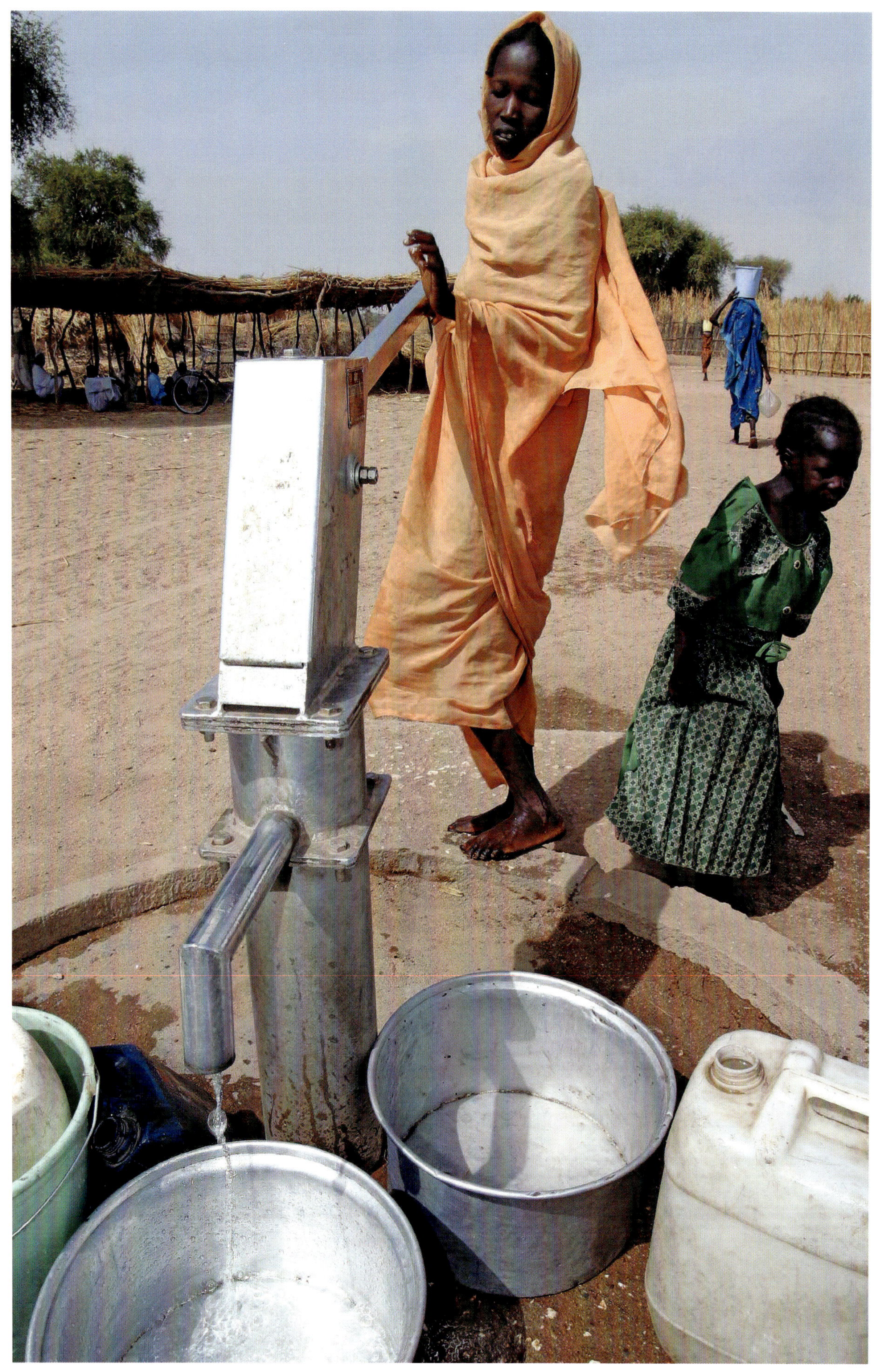

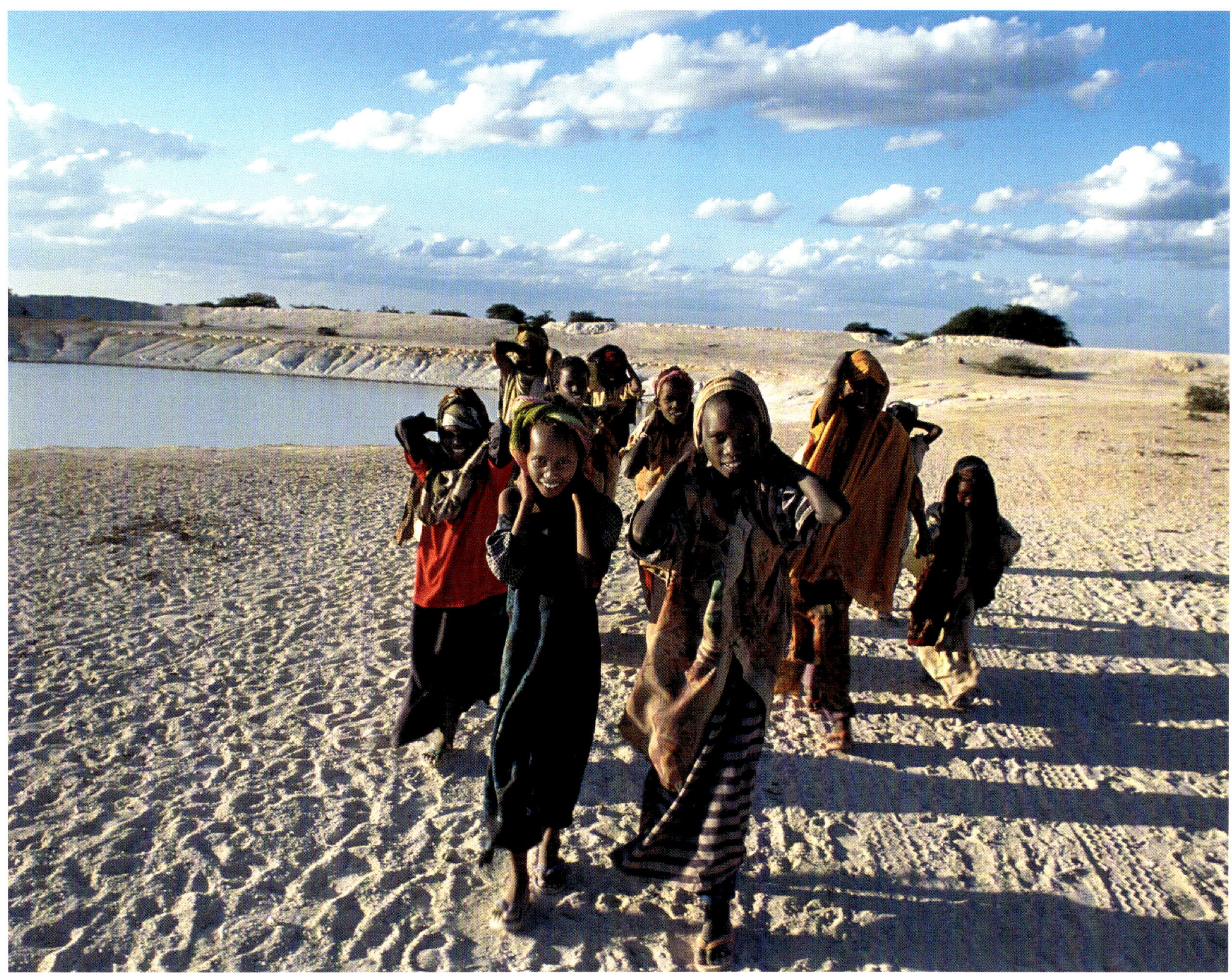

Darfur 2006
IMC staff

Opposite page: International Medical Corps water programs bring small and large-scale water and sanitation projects to many beneficiaries through new water sanitation centers and wells.

Somalia 2002
Jenny Chu

Above: International Medical Corps also renovated watering holes like the one from which children collect water in Sudder, Somalia.

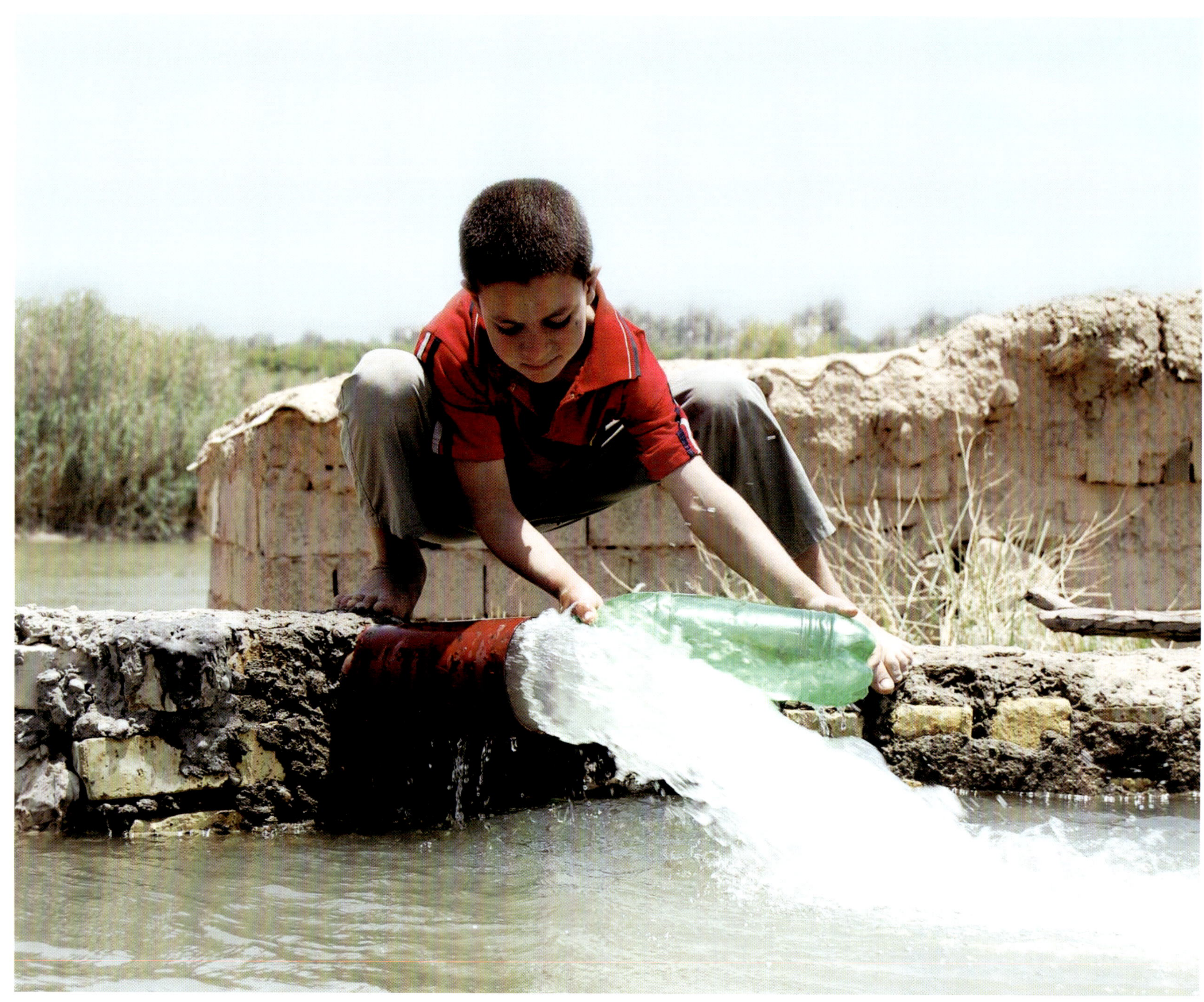

Iraq 2008
IMC staff (both pages)

Lack of clean water was the most prevalent health issue for Iraqi displaced people. Raw sewage flowed directly into water supplies and even ran across hospital floors. International Medical Corps rehabilitated and constructed water and sanitation facilities in dozens of locations throughout Iraq, including eight internally displaced persons camps, 30 villages and 29 hospitals. Because of IMC, half a million Iraqis in the region have clean water and sanitary sewage systems in their villages and hospitals.

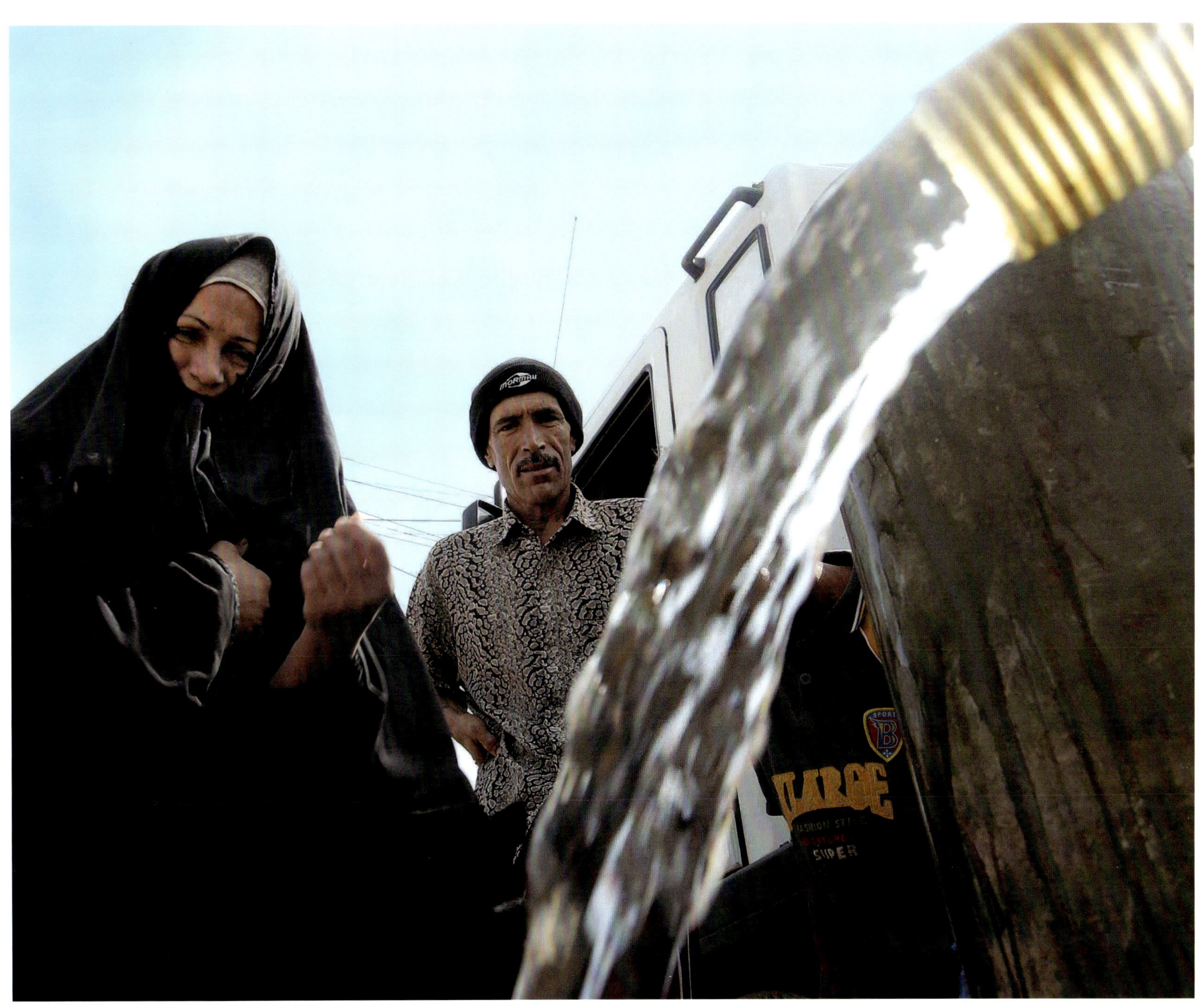
SPORT
B

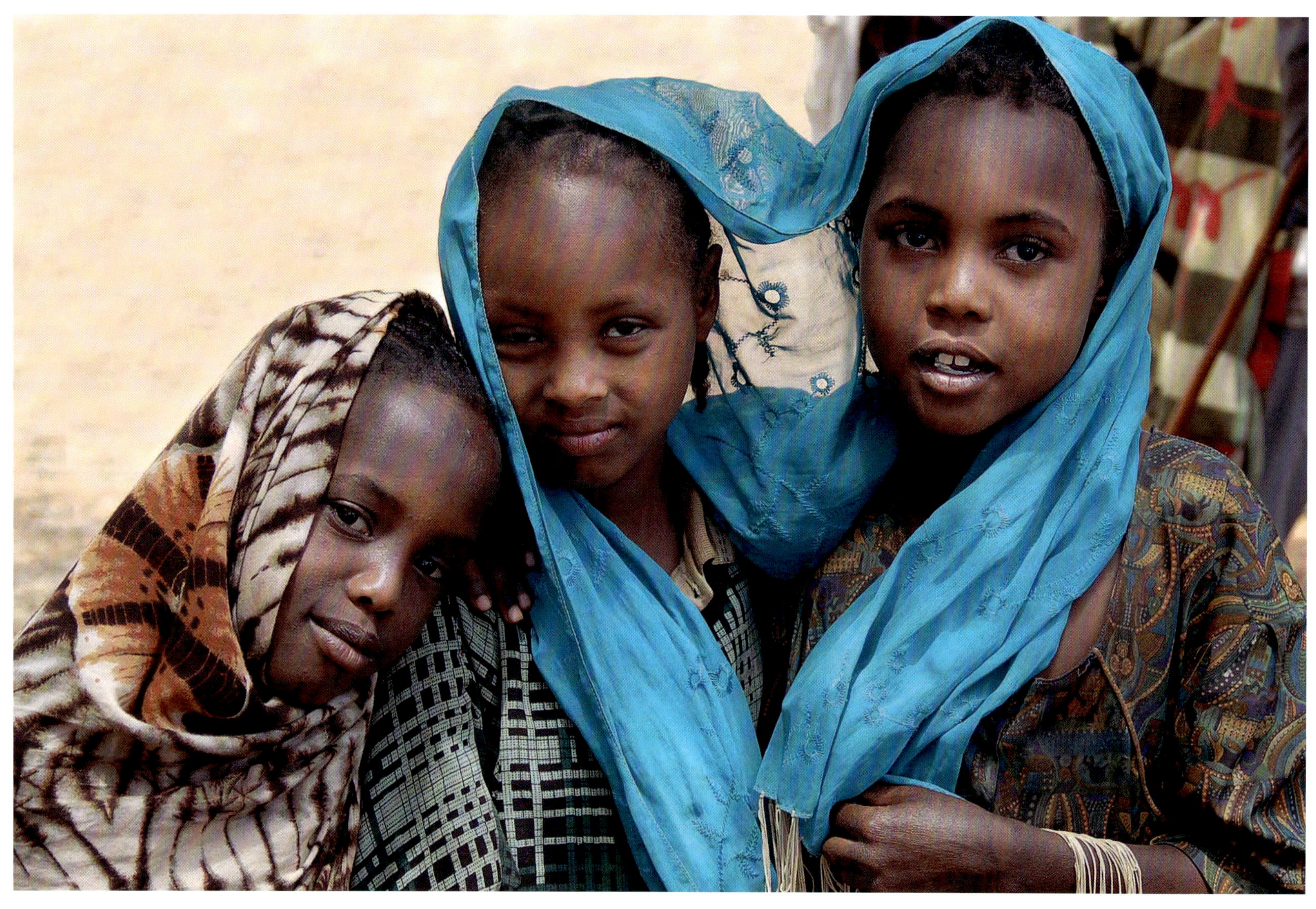

Ethiopia 2006/2002
IMC staff (above)
Jenny Chu (opposite)

In 2000, severe drought left a staggering 15.3 million Ethiopians vulnerable to famine. Faced with a food crisis far more threatening than the 1984 famine, which killed nearly one million people, International Medical Corps established food service programs in several regions of Ethiopia.

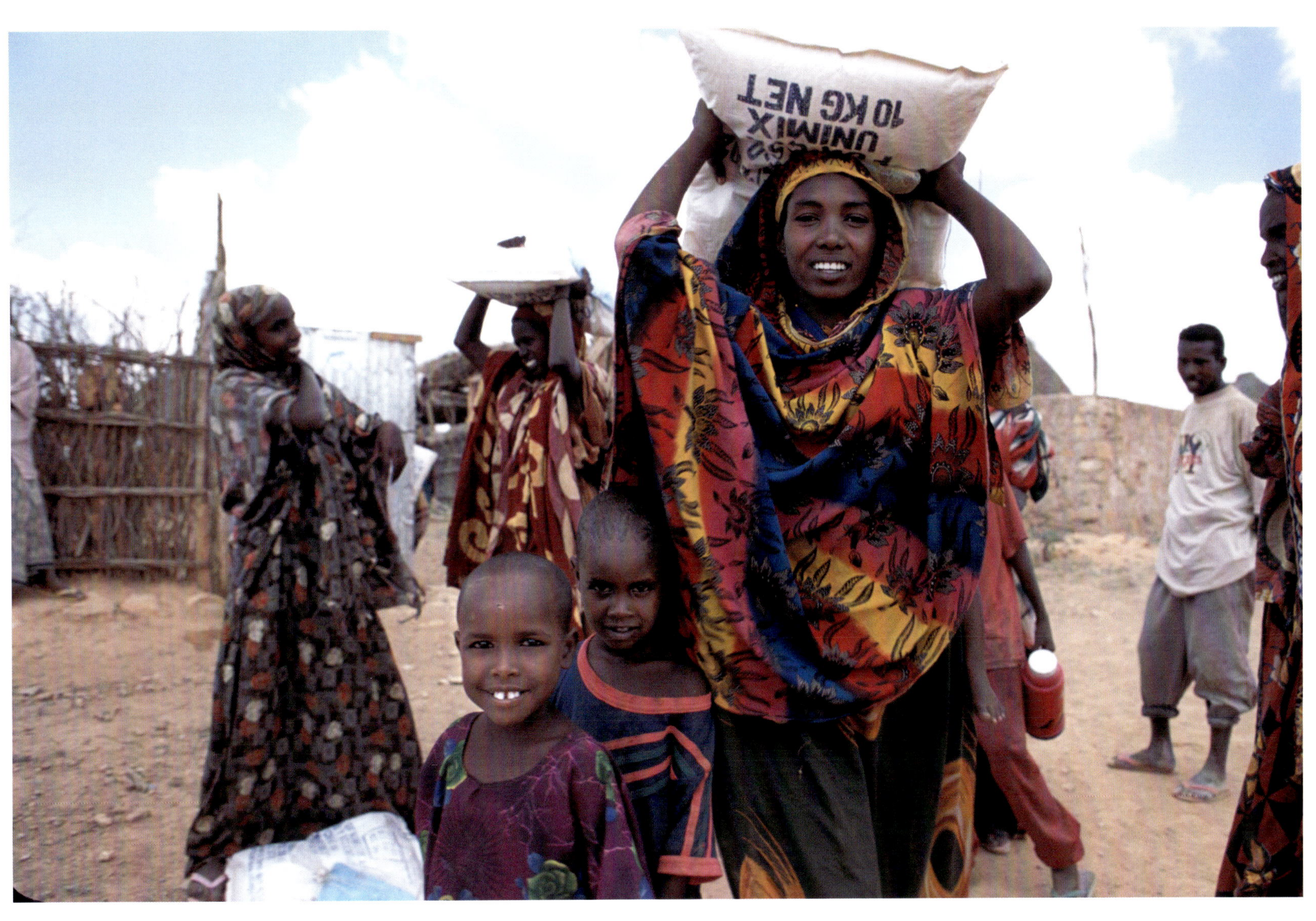
UNIMIX
10 KG NET

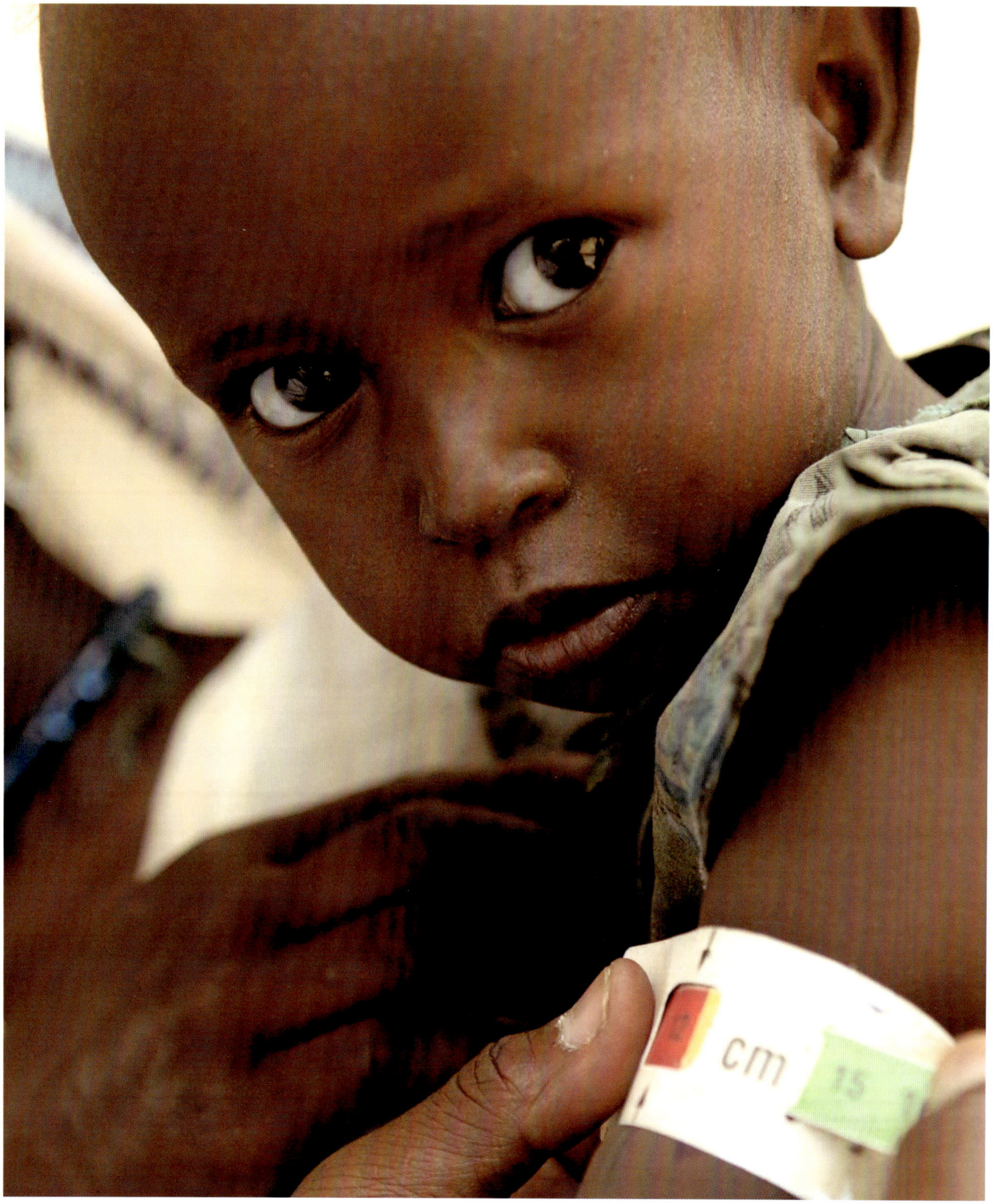

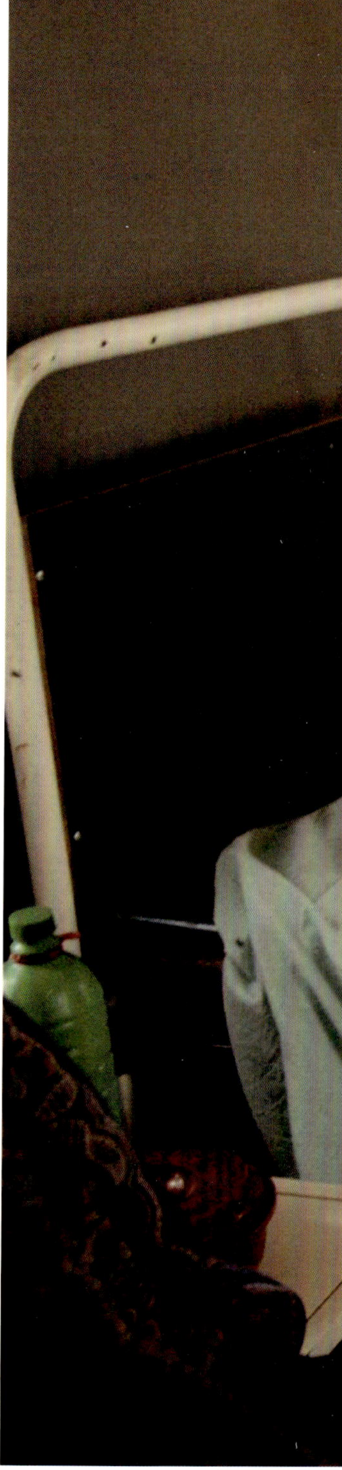

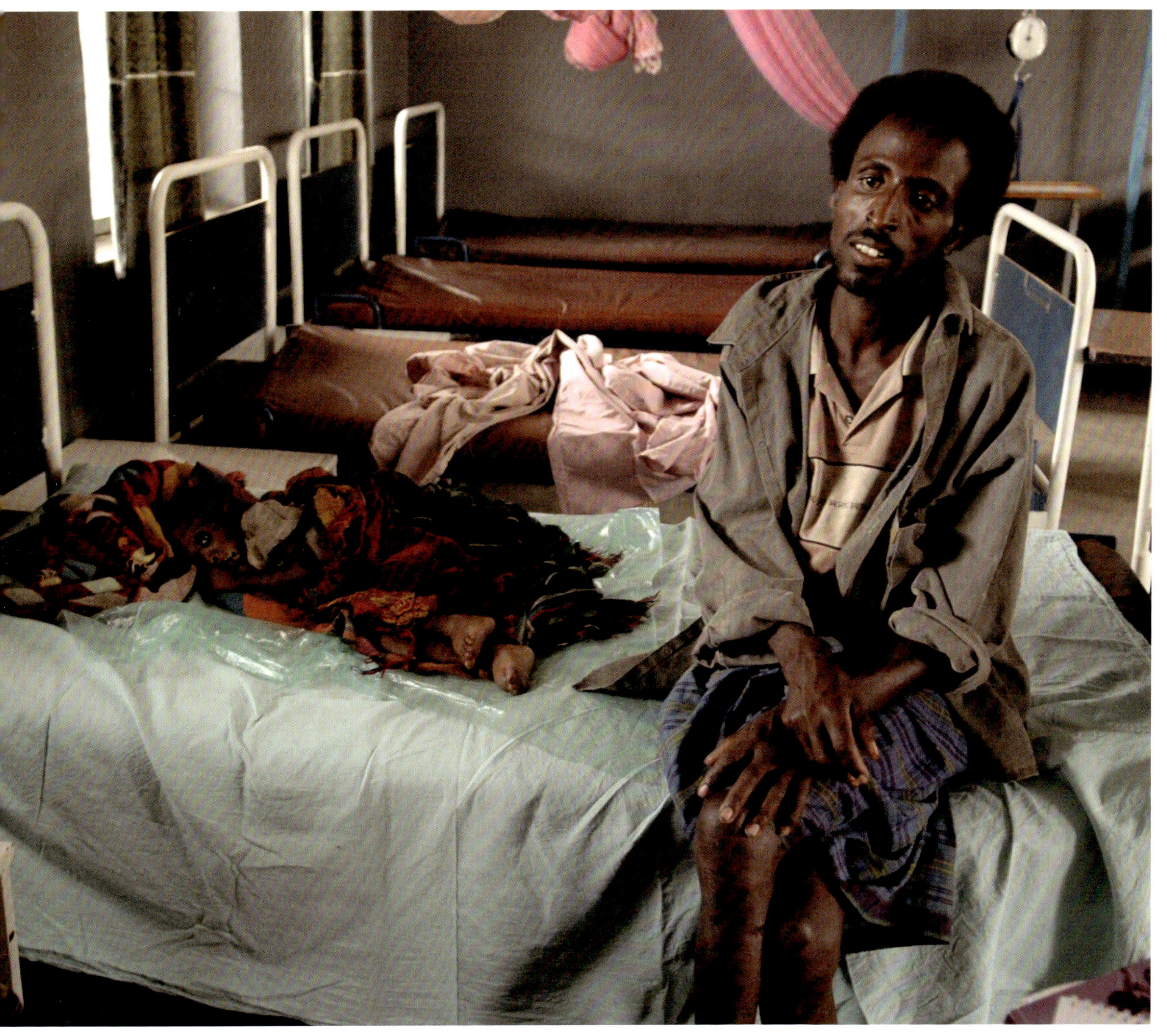

Julie Pudlowski (both photos)

Severely malnourished children are sent to local International Medical Corps hospitals, where they stay for anywhere from 5 to 10 days to receive intensive care. A 2-year-old Ethiopian boy was hospitalized for a week, and his father did not leave his bedside.

Opposite page: International Medical Corps also established nutritional centers, where children under 5 are screened for malnutrition. A young Ethiopian child has her upper arm circumference measured. It is a key factor in determining malnutrition.

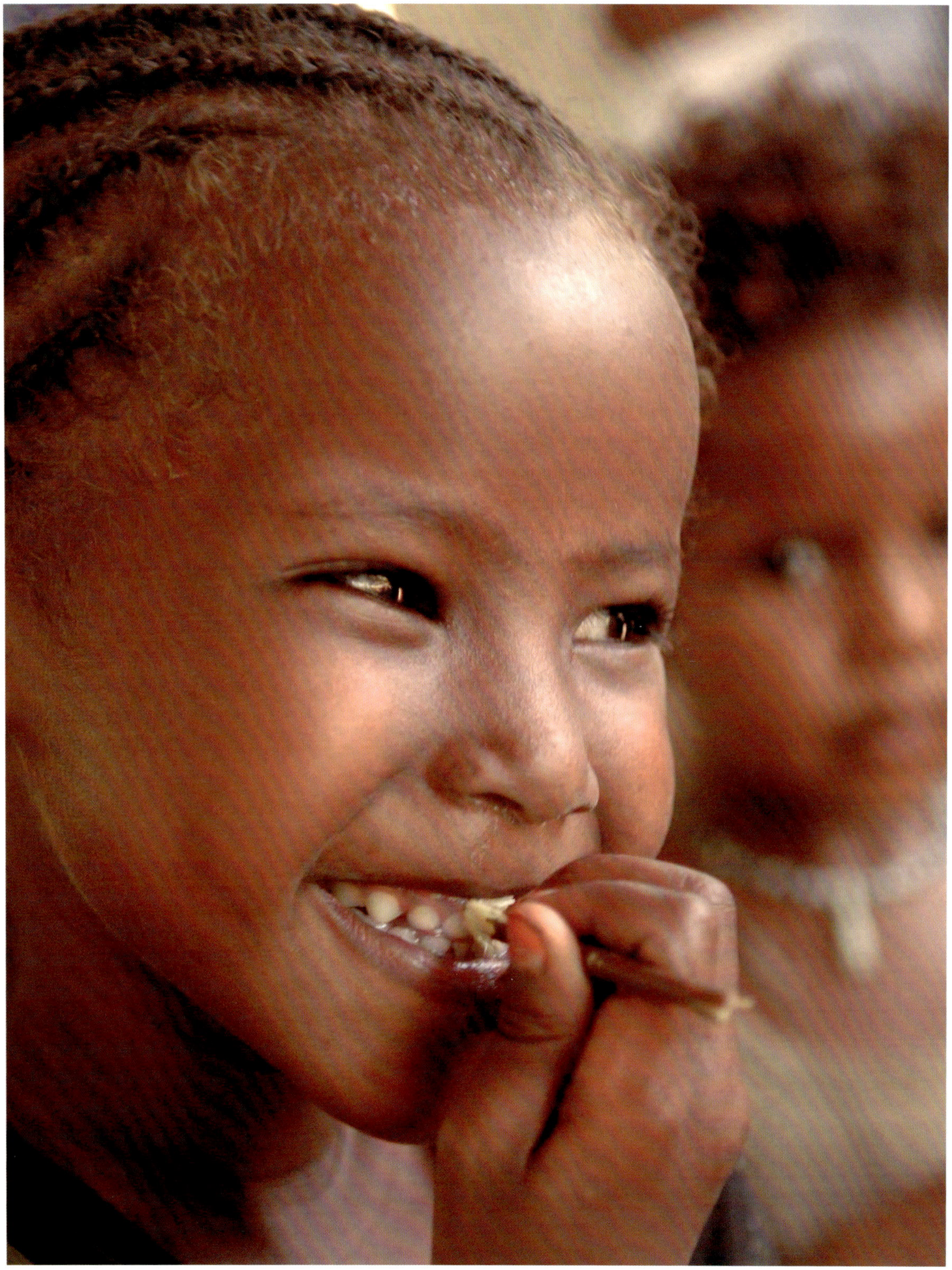

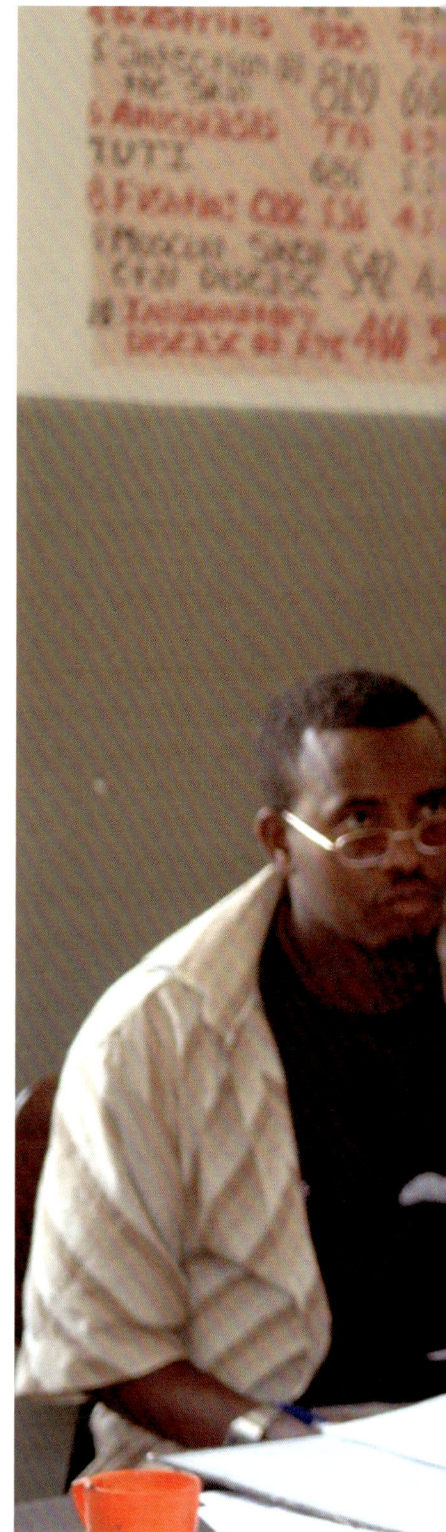

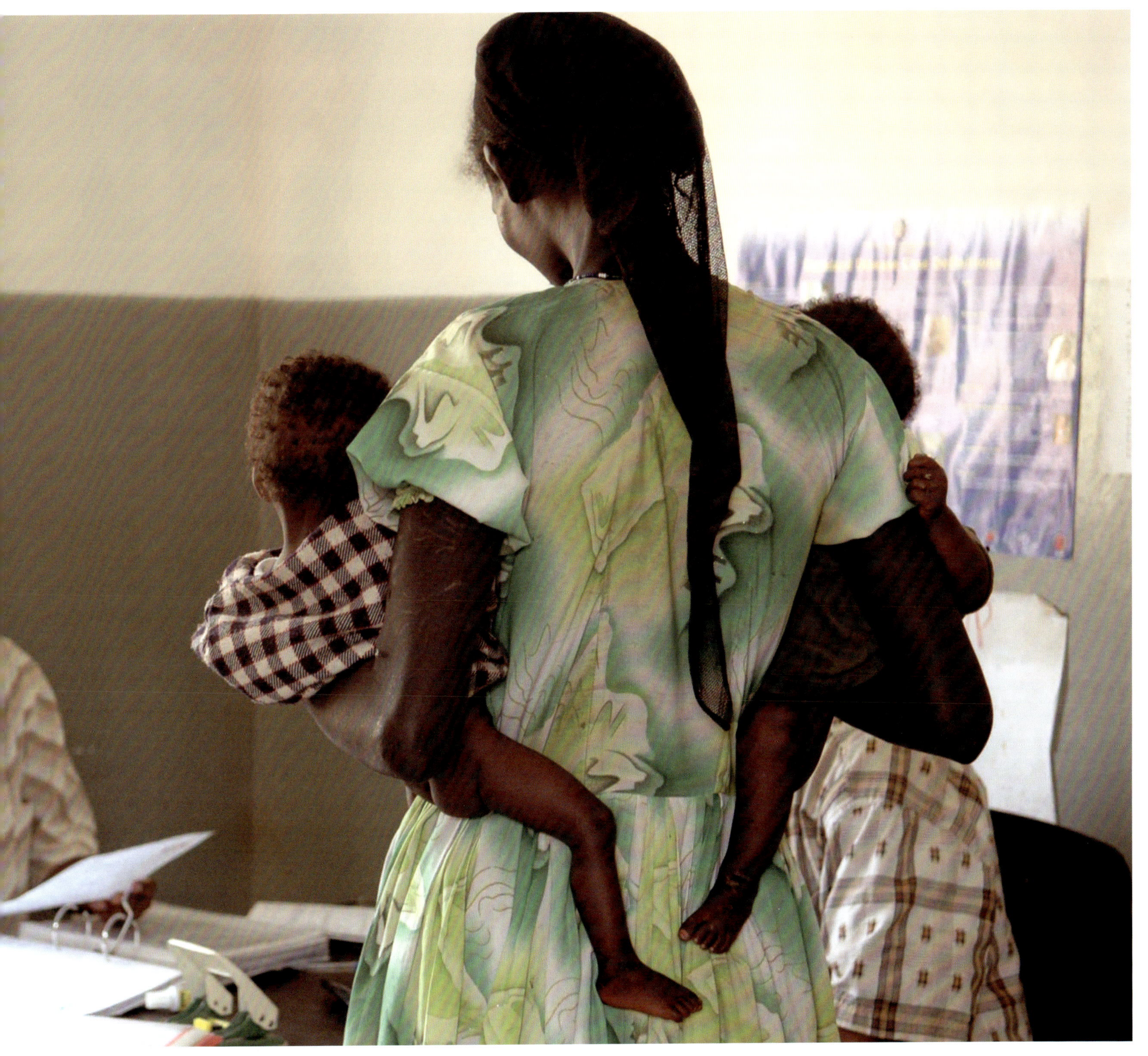

Ethiopia 2006
Julie Pudlowski (both pages)

A local Ethiopian mother came to the International Medical Corps clinic in Dire Dawa to receive food supplements for her twins, who were severely malnourished. Her breast milk completely dried up due to her poor diet.

Opposite page: A 4-year-old girl, whose mother received IMC nutritional training, learns to brush her teeth with IMC-supplied toothbrushes.

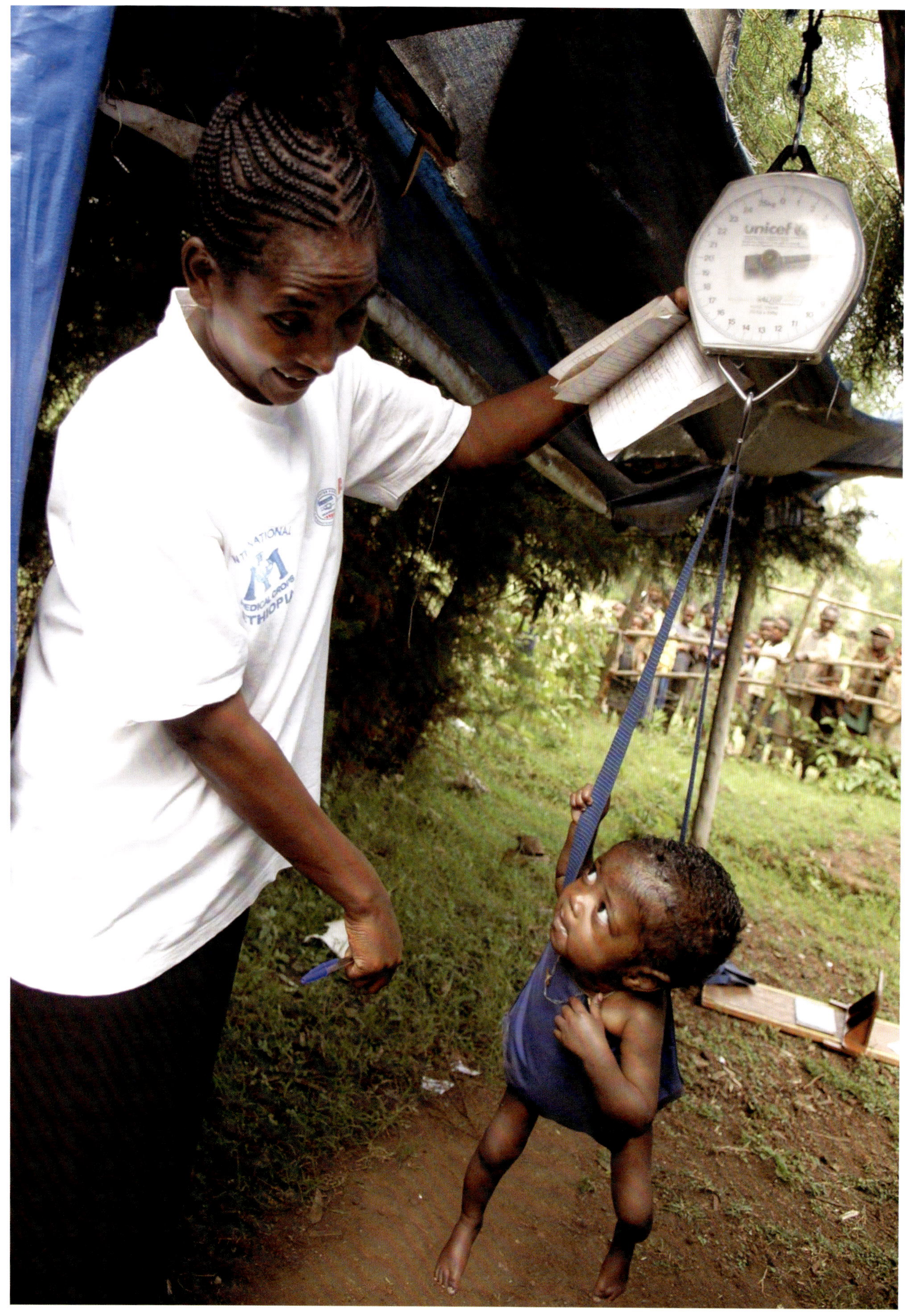
unicef

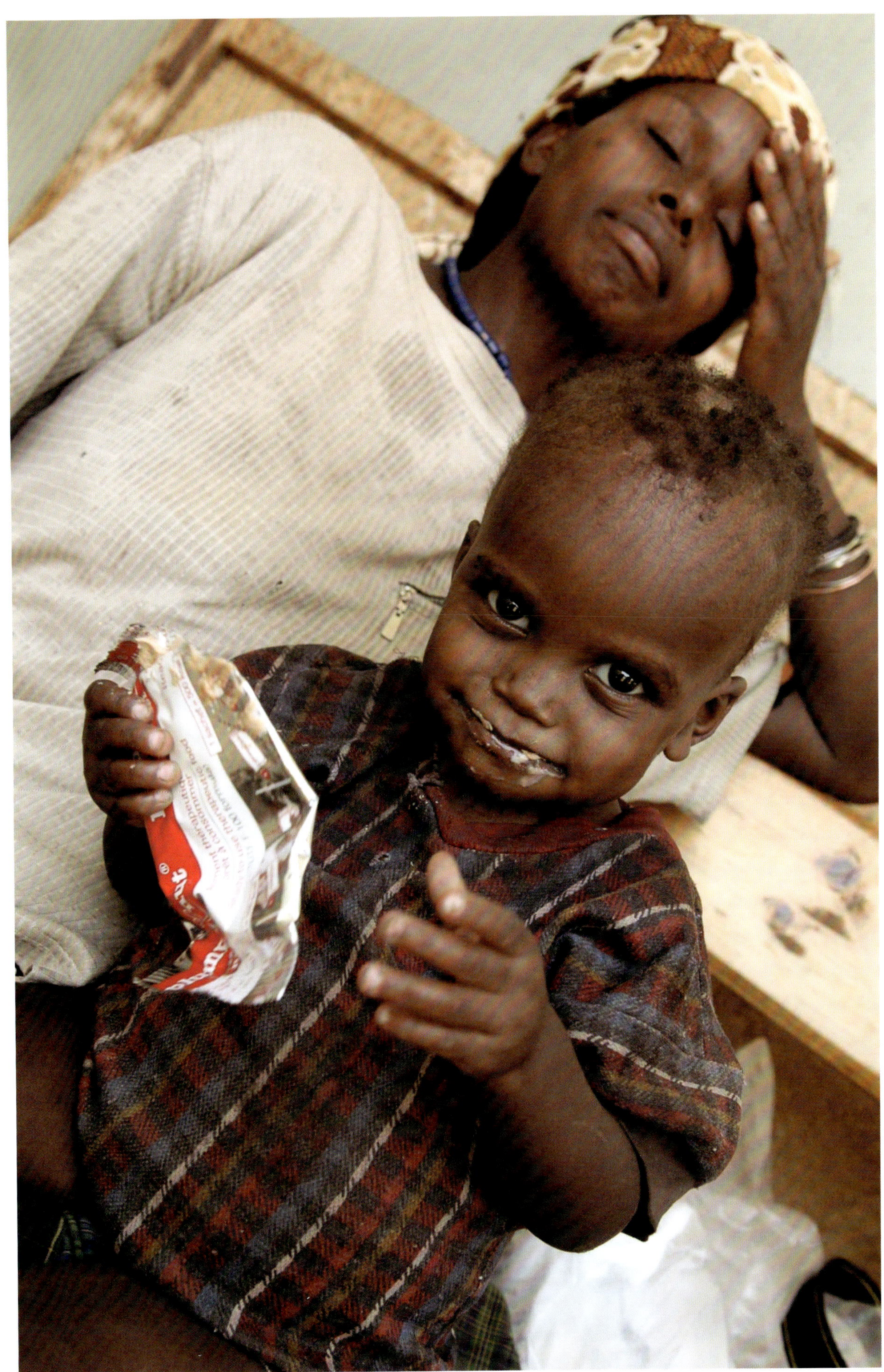

Ethiopia 2006
Julie Pudlowski (both pages)

An Ethiopian boy came regularly with his mother to the International Medical Corps outpatient site. The child's health improved after he started eating the Plumpy' Nut that IMC provided. Plumpy' Nut, often produced locally, is a nut paste similar to peanut butter that contains 500 kcal per packet and is given to moderately and severely malnourished children to help them regain weight quickly.

Opposite page: A 1-year-old child weighing just 3.5 kilograms was so small she almost fell out of the little leg hole of the weighing sack. She suffered from severe malnutrition and was enrolled in IMC's outpatient program, where she received Plumpy' Nut packets.

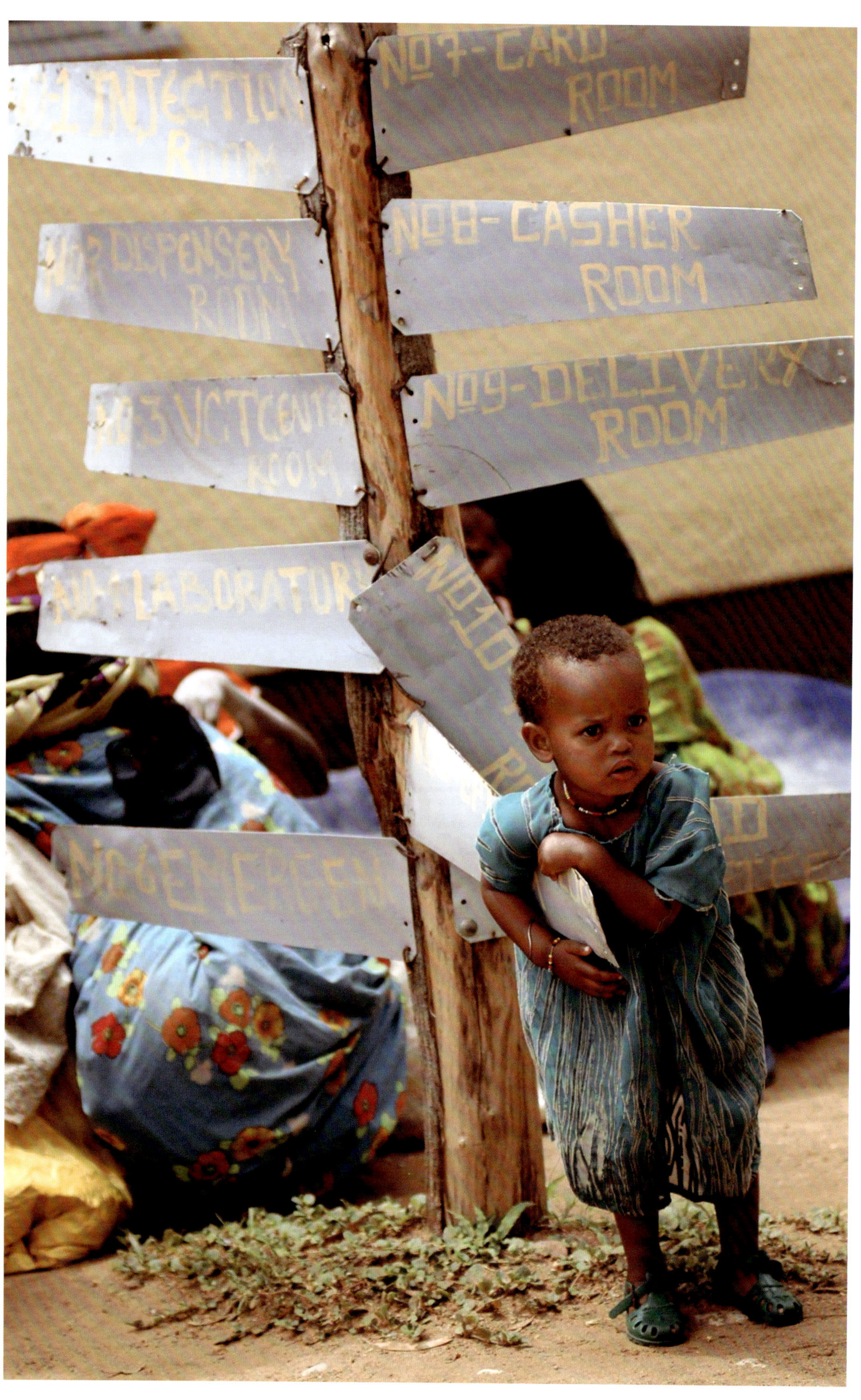

Ethiopia 2006
Julie Pudlowski (both pages)

The International Medical Corps outpatient center in East Hararghe opened in 2005 to treat cases of moderate malnutrition. There are 25 IMC centers in the East Hararghe program alone.

Opposite page: Local heath care workers teach parents who come to IMC's nutritional centers about nutrition, sanitation for their environment, and personal hygiene. Topics such as using latrines, washing hands, cleaning clothes, maintaining households and bathing children to prevent germs from causing disease are discussed.

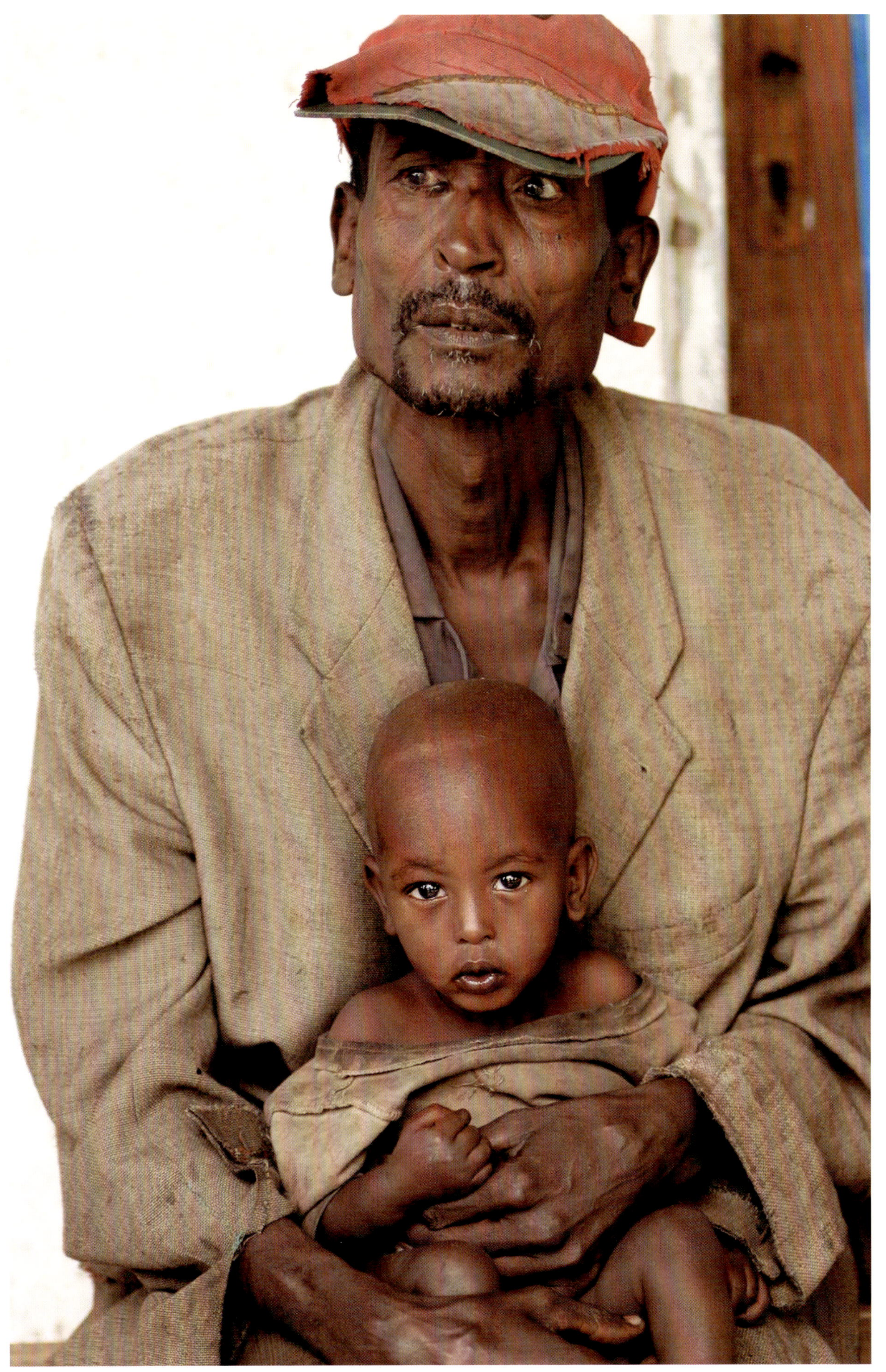

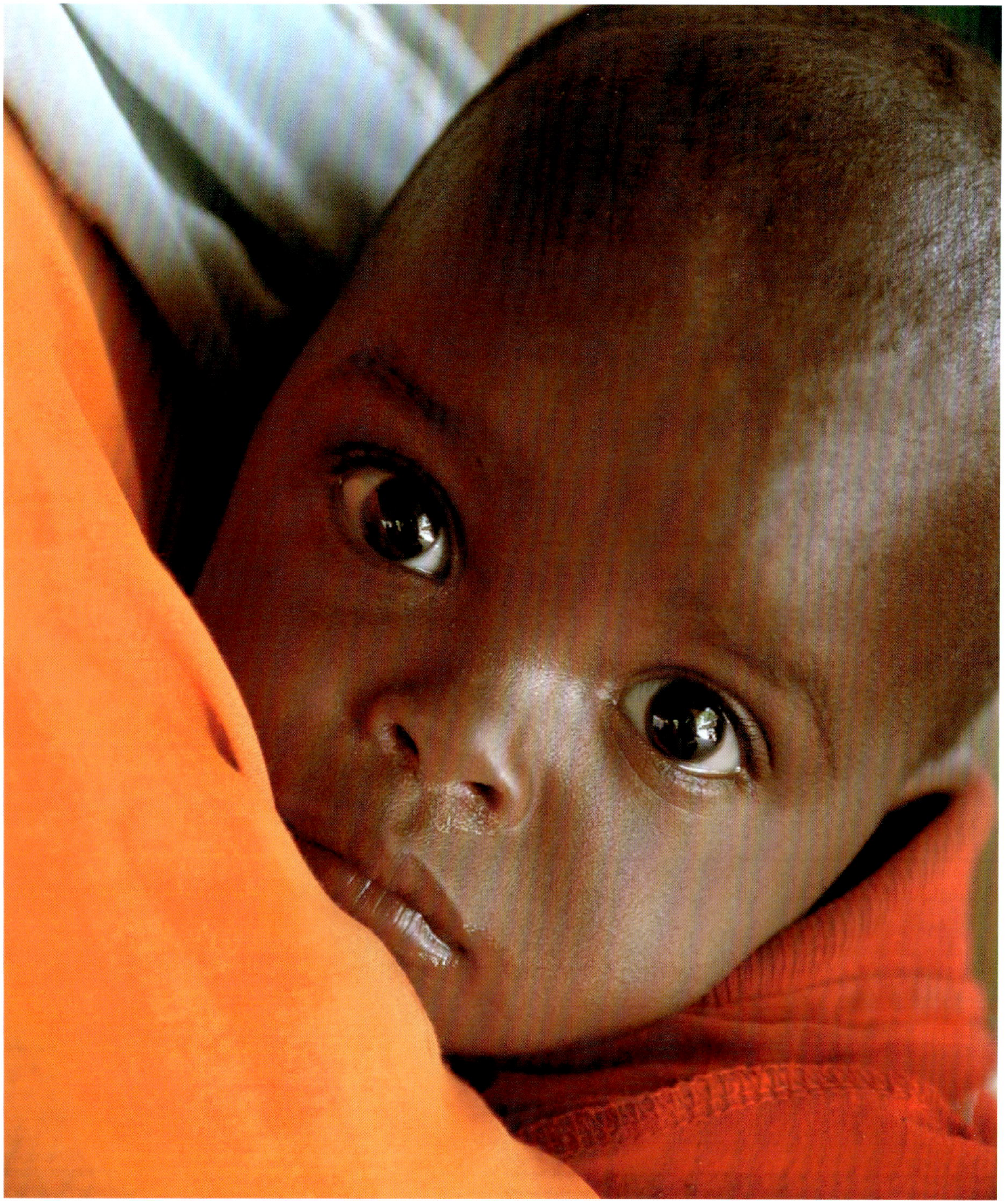

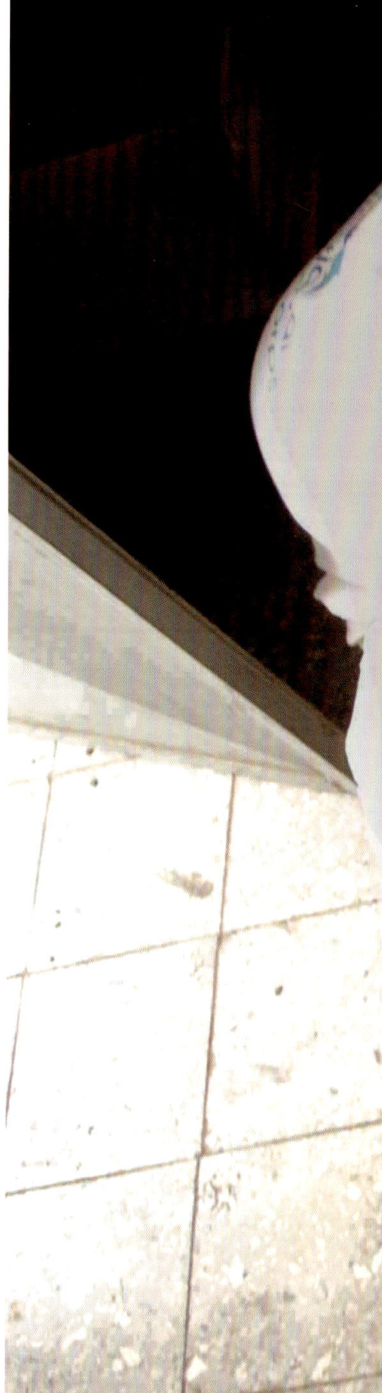

Ethiopia 2006
Julie Pudlowski (both photos)

Together with a team of local, regional and national health workers, in one year International Medical Corps successfully treated more than 5,000 malnourished children through 10 therapeutic feeding centers and 30 supplemental feeding centers in Ethiopia. In addition, IMC trained almost 250 Ethiopian health workers to continue the program.

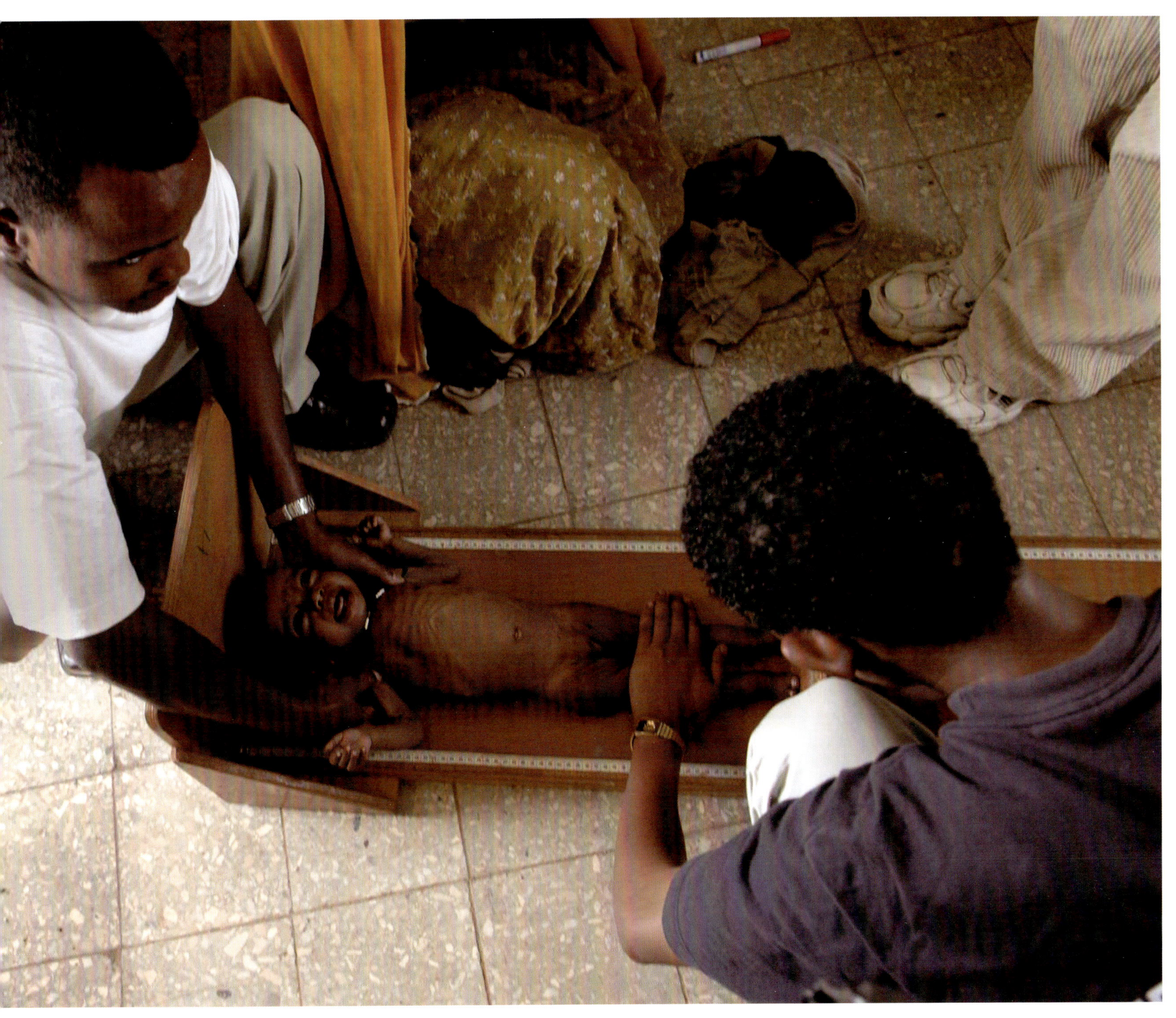

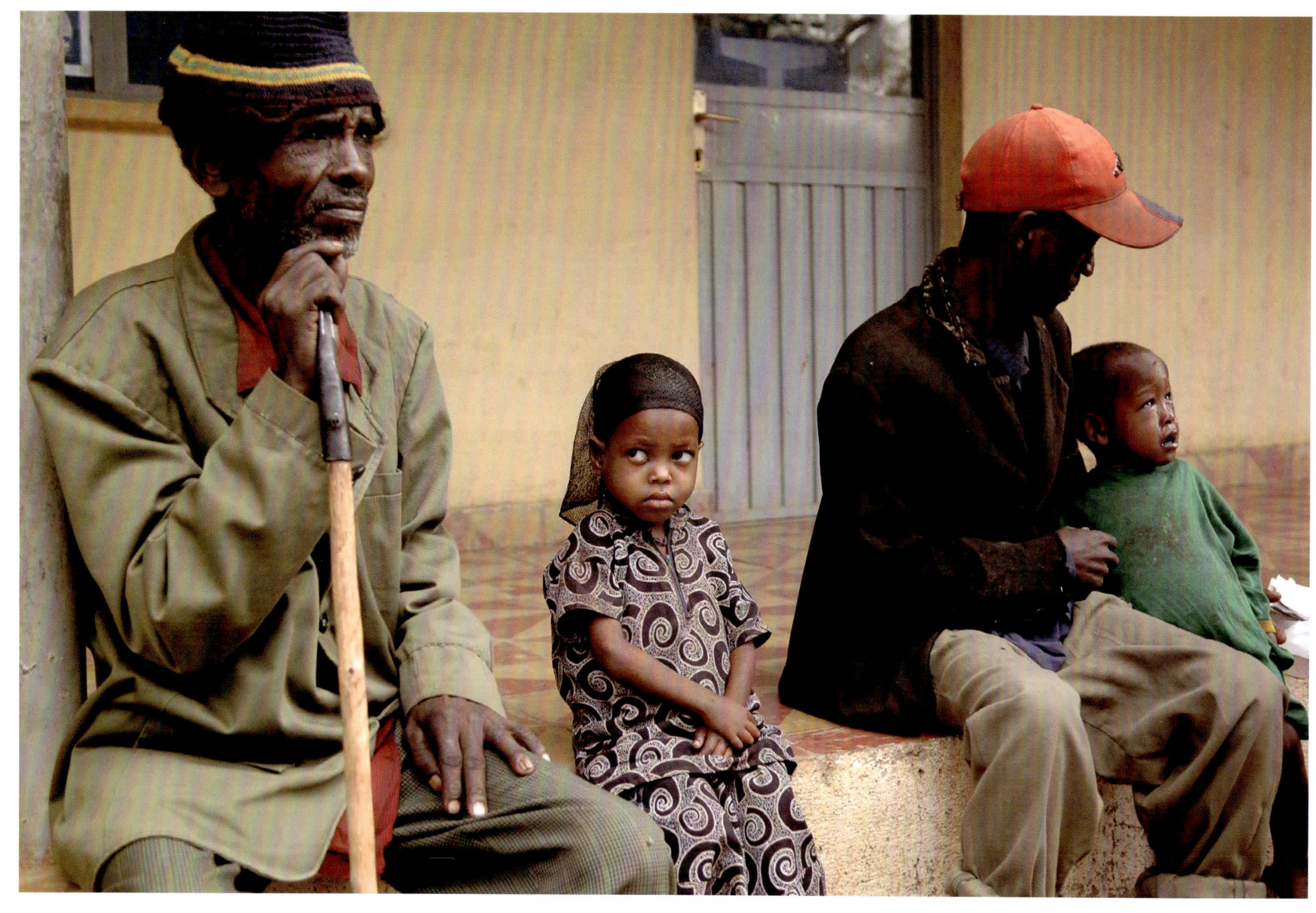

Ethiopia 2006
Julie Pudlowski (both photos)

International Medical Corps transitioned its clinic-based therapeutic feeding programs to community-based centers where malnourished children first receive treatment at an inpatient facility and, once their conditions are no longer critical, are then referred to an outpatient program to be administered at home. The community-based approach has improved outreach while empowering communities to help themselves.

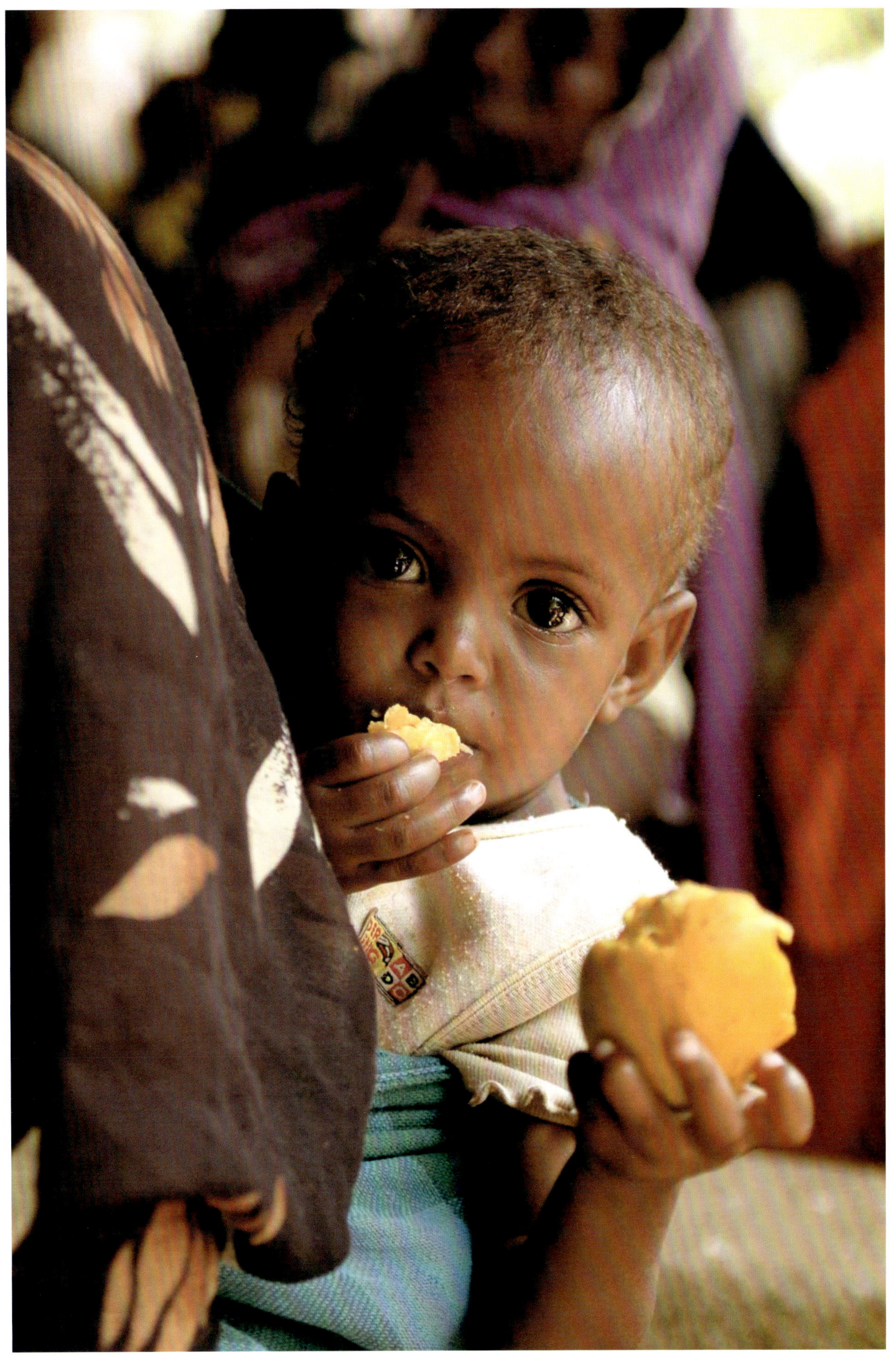

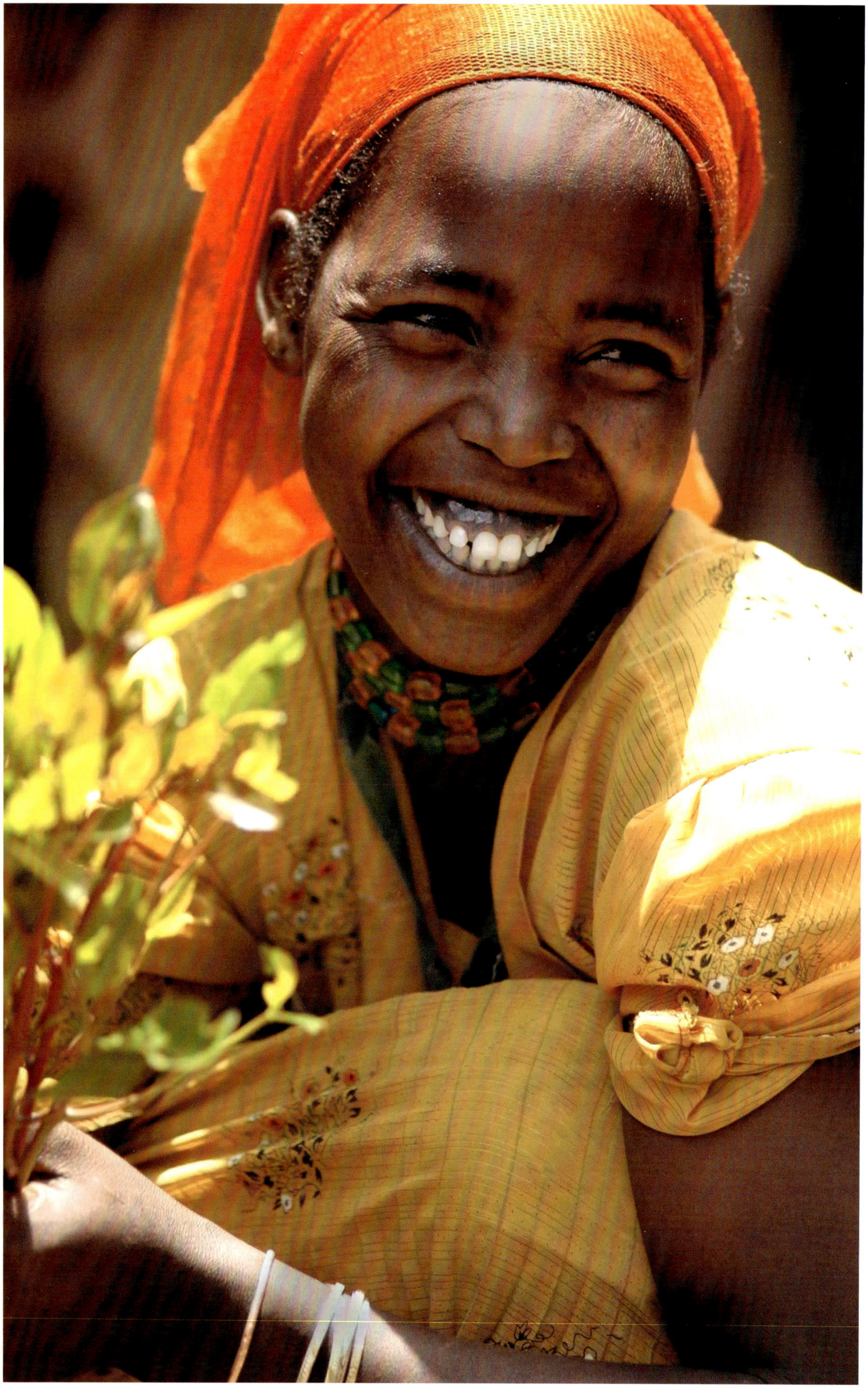

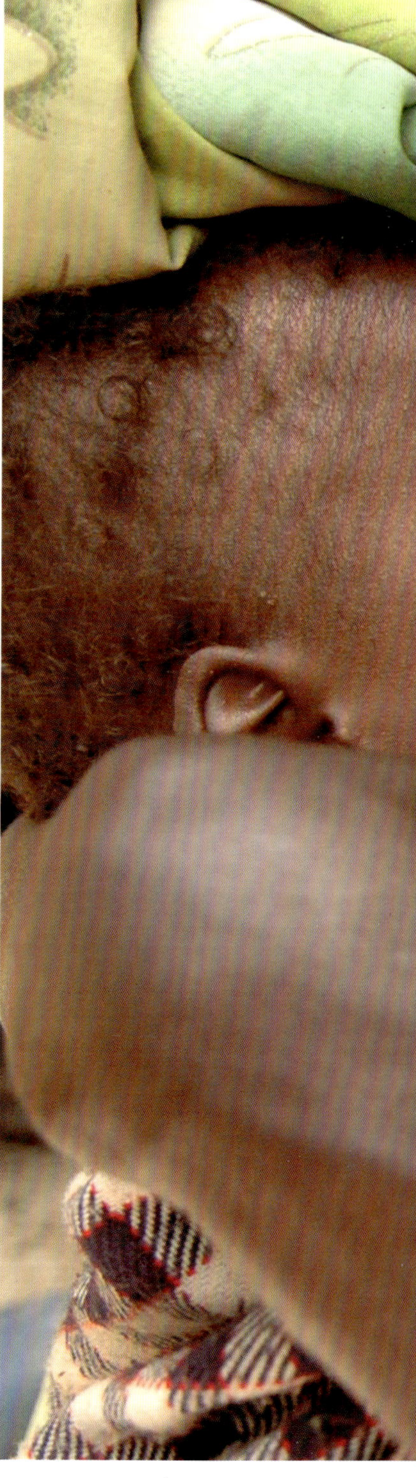

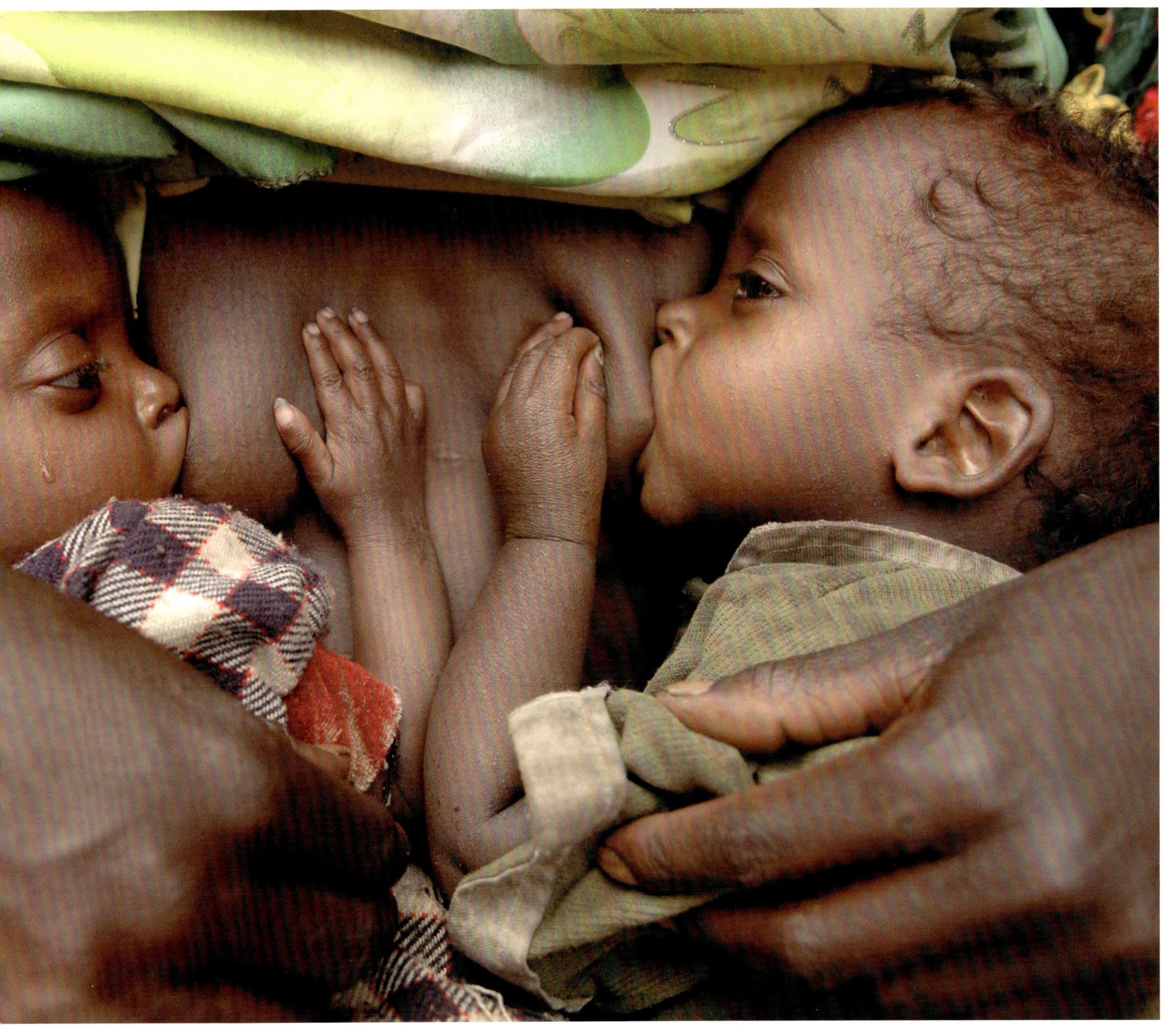

Ethiopia 2006
Julie Pudlowski (both photos)

International Medical Corps stresses the importance of maternal health and nutrition in Ethiopia. With proper maternal nutrition, mothers can continue to breast-feed their young children with an adequate and nutritional milk supply. Weaning children prematurely is a common cause of malnutrition in Ethiopia.

Opposite page: A 42-year-old widow has been raising her six young children alone since her husband died six years ago. She comes to the International Medical Corps demonstration plot to learn to sow seeds. Chat, potatoes and tomatoes are today her biggest sources of income, and she is now learning how to diversify her crops thanks to IMC livelihood projects.

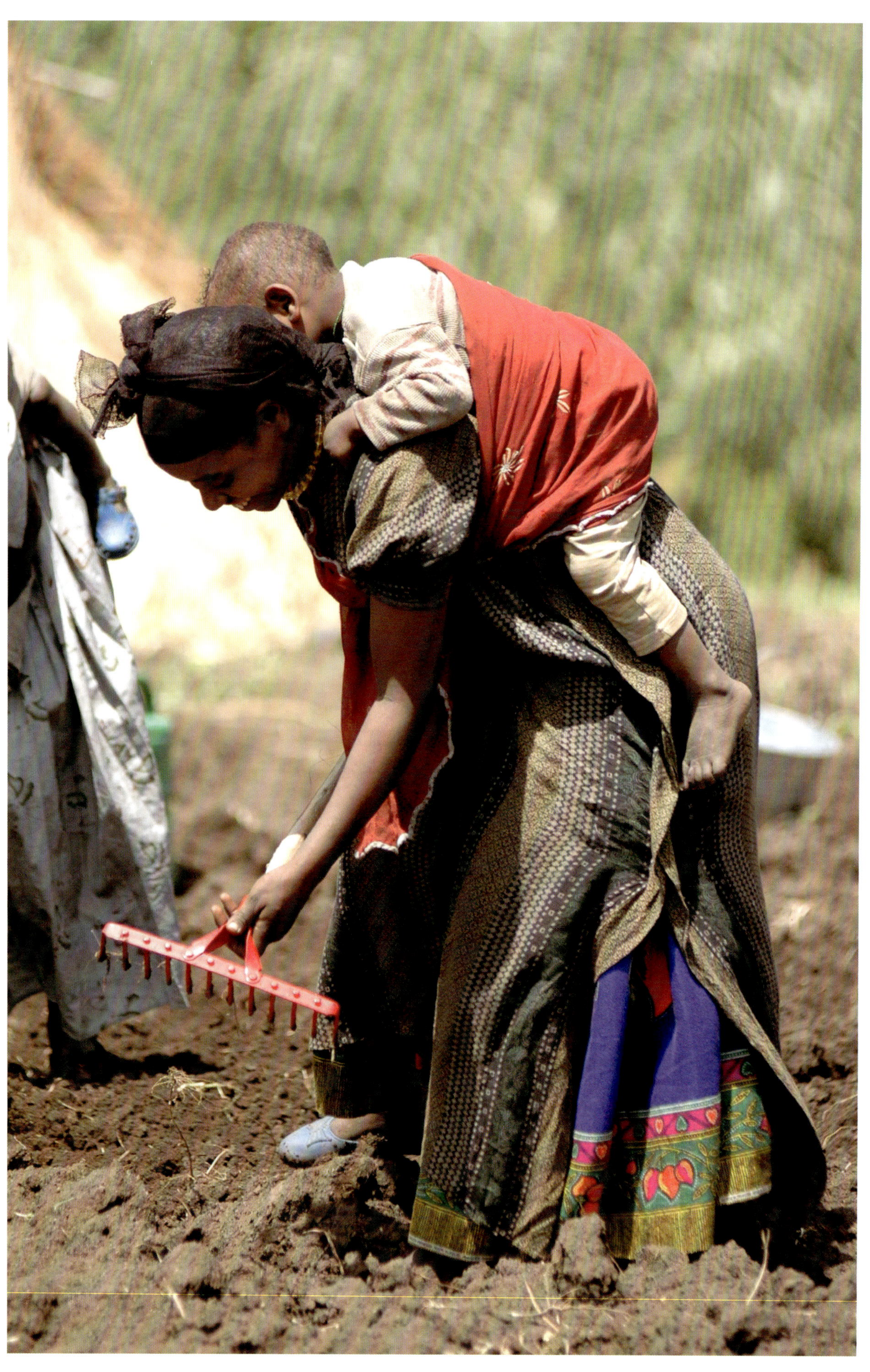

Ethiopia 2006
Julie Pudlowski

A pregnant woman in West Harargh, with a child on her back, is learning to sow seeds to provide nutritional variety for her children's diets as well as provide extra income for her family. International Medical Corps' micro-enterpise projects teach local women how to grow and sell their own food.

IMC staff

Opposite page: The entire community is involved in International Medical Corps' development programs. A local IMC meeting takes place in Dire Dawa and attracts a diverse crowd.

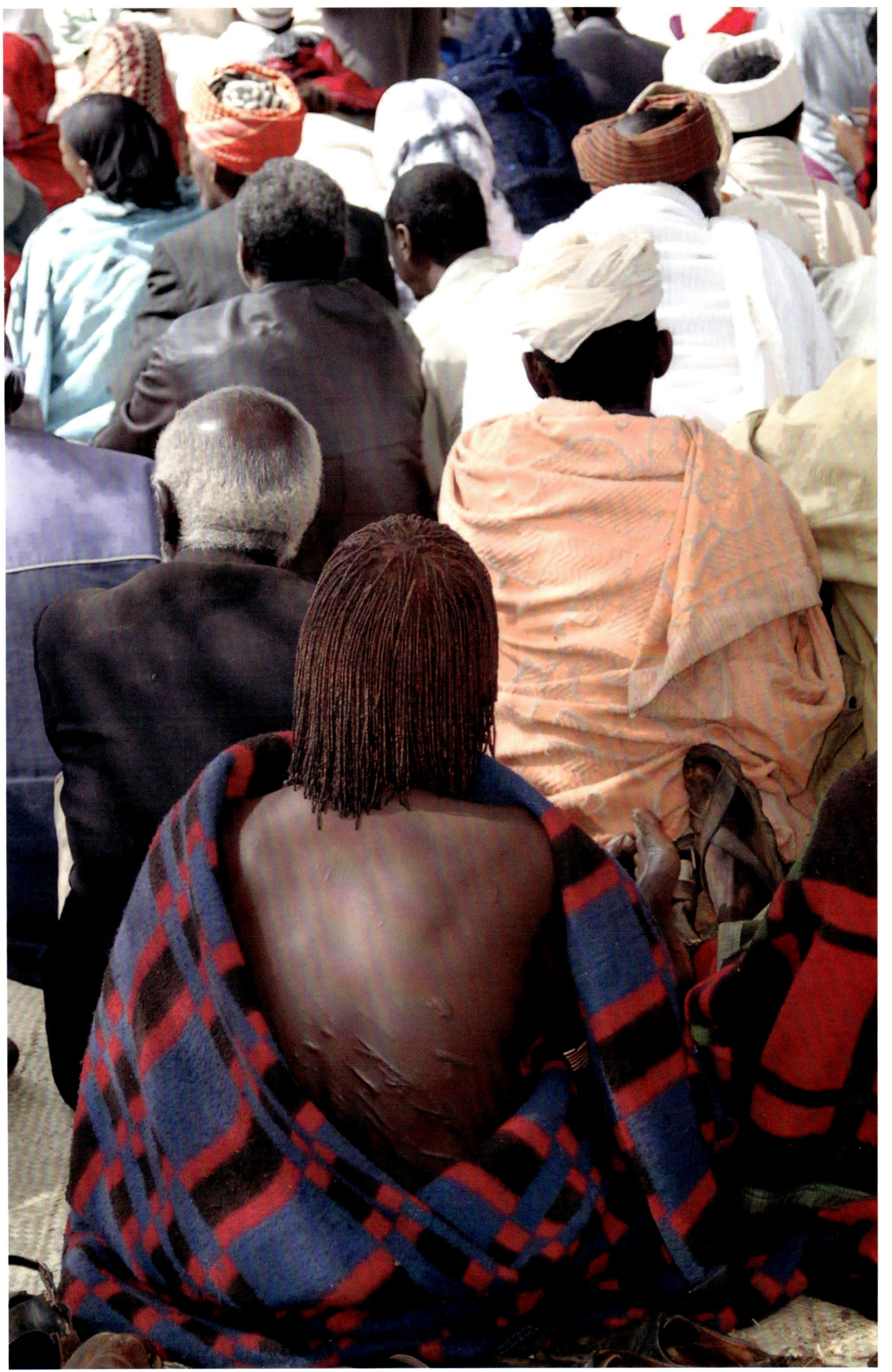

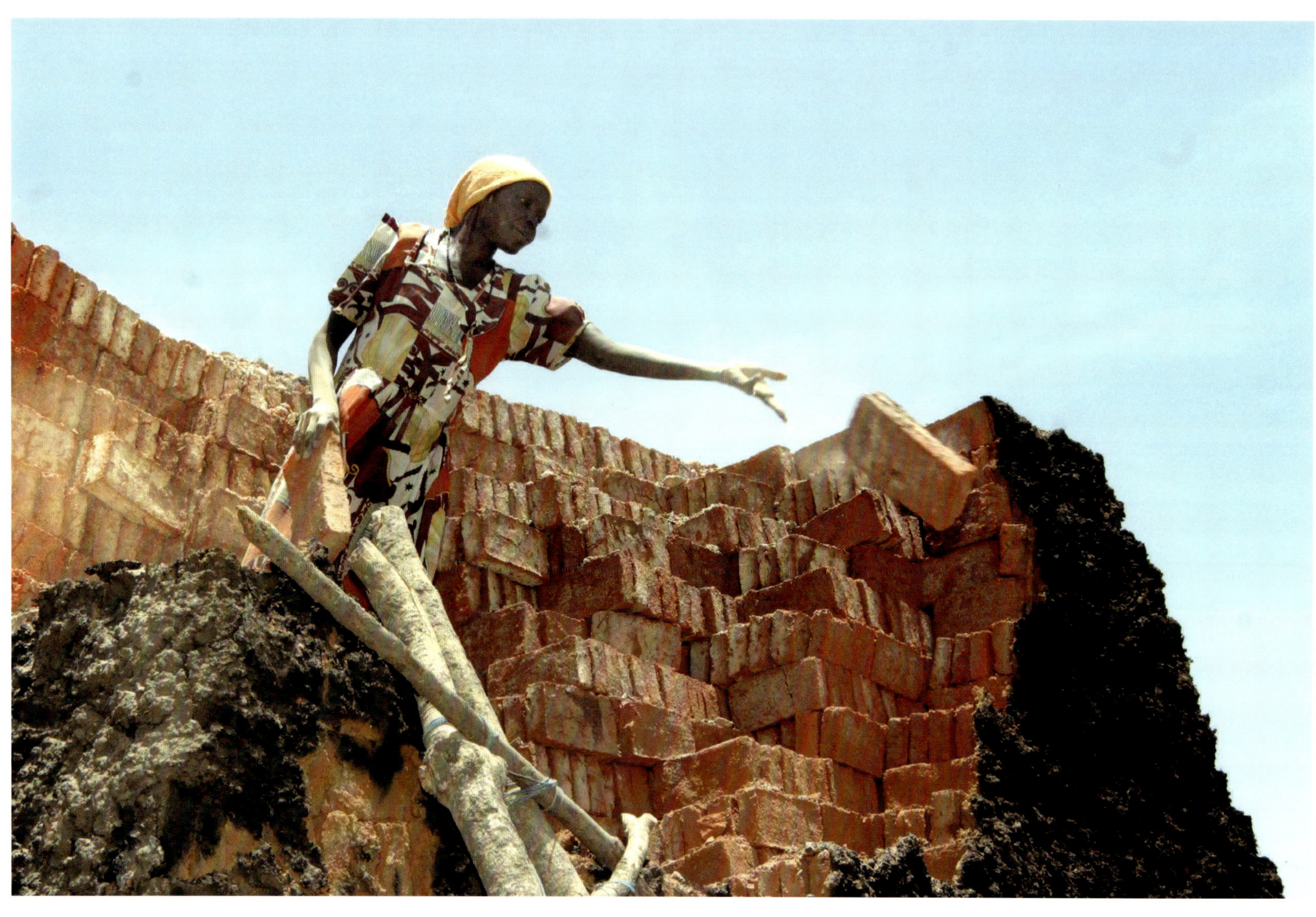

Darfur 2005
Tanya Hobjouqua

Locally made bricks are used to build new International Medical Corps health clinics and housing for thousands of people, and to provide work for local villagers. Brick-making is a part of International Medical Corps' development projects in Darfur. Bricks are made from mud at water runoff points. After being formed, they are stacked into 10-foot-tall pyramids and set ablaze. The fire makes them hard and turns them bright pink.

Ethiopia 2006
Julie Pudlowski

Opposite page: International Medical Corps' food programs in Ethiopia focus on training women in agricultural livelihoods. IMC specialists teach beneficiaries to sow tomato and cabbage seedlings by putting shallow dirt over the seedlings, covering them with straw, and then watering the seeds down to prevent erosion.

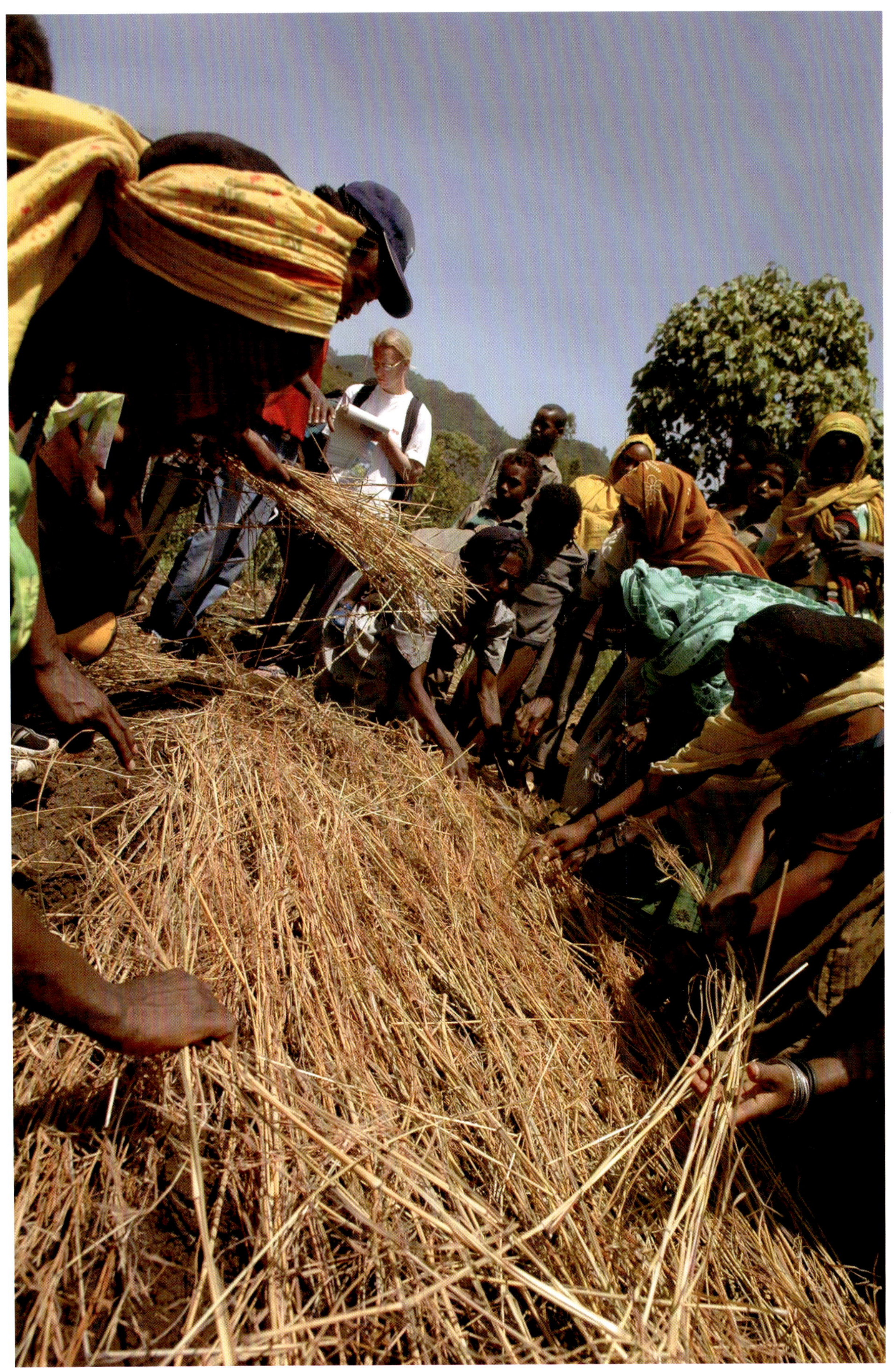

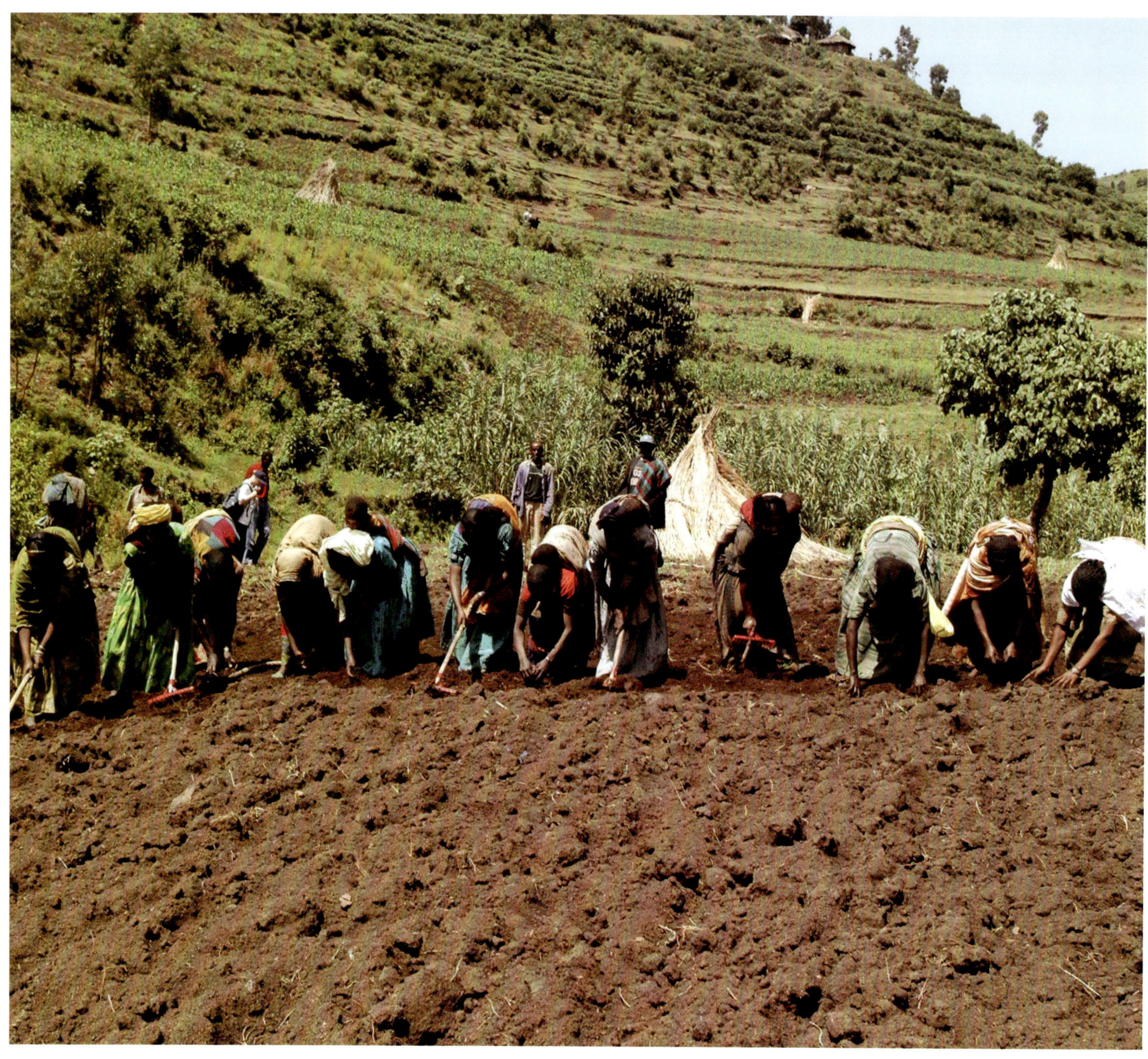

Ethiopia 2006
Julie Pudlowski (both photos)

In West Hararghe, International Medical Corps' livelihood project has targeted 2,500 beneficiaries in one year. IMC trainers give women seeds and tools and teach them how to better harvest their land. At the end of the training, each family is given five different seeds (carrots, beets, tomatoes, lettuce and cabbage) that they will plant in their fields.

Opposite page: For 25 years, International Medical Corps' food and water projects have helped millions of people to achieve economic self-reliance.

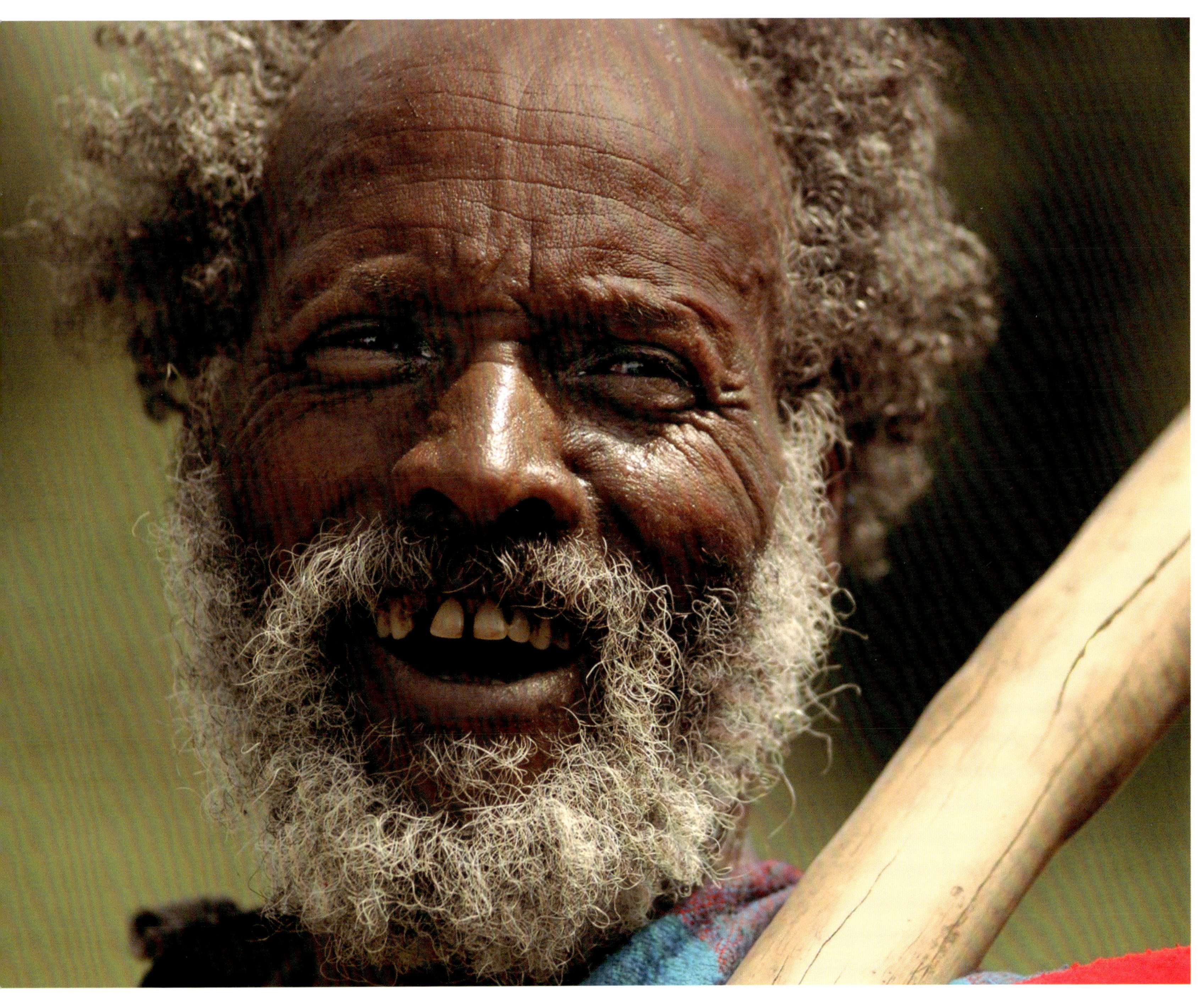

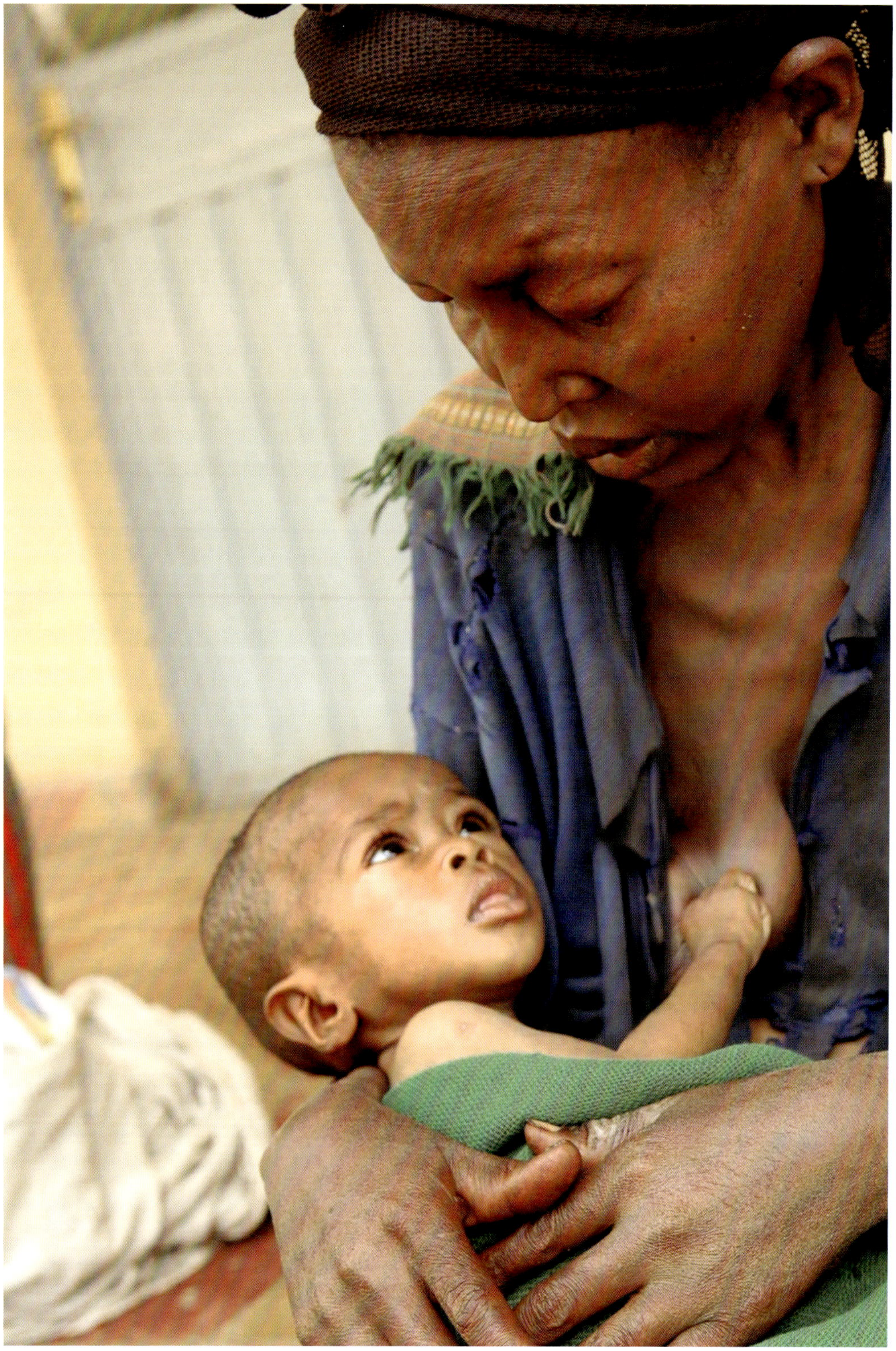

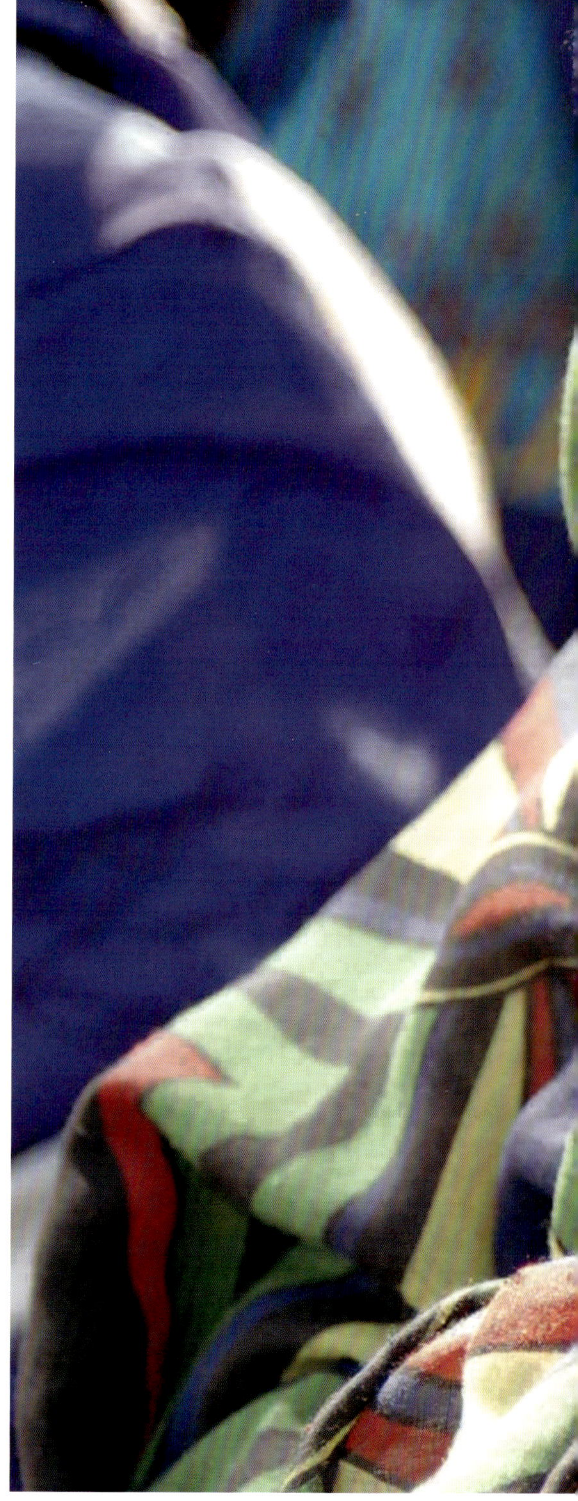

Ethiopia 2006
Julie Pudlowski (above)
IMC staff (opposite page)

For 25 years, International Medical Corps' training programs have provided lifesaving health care, medicine, clean water and nutrition to millions of people worldwide.

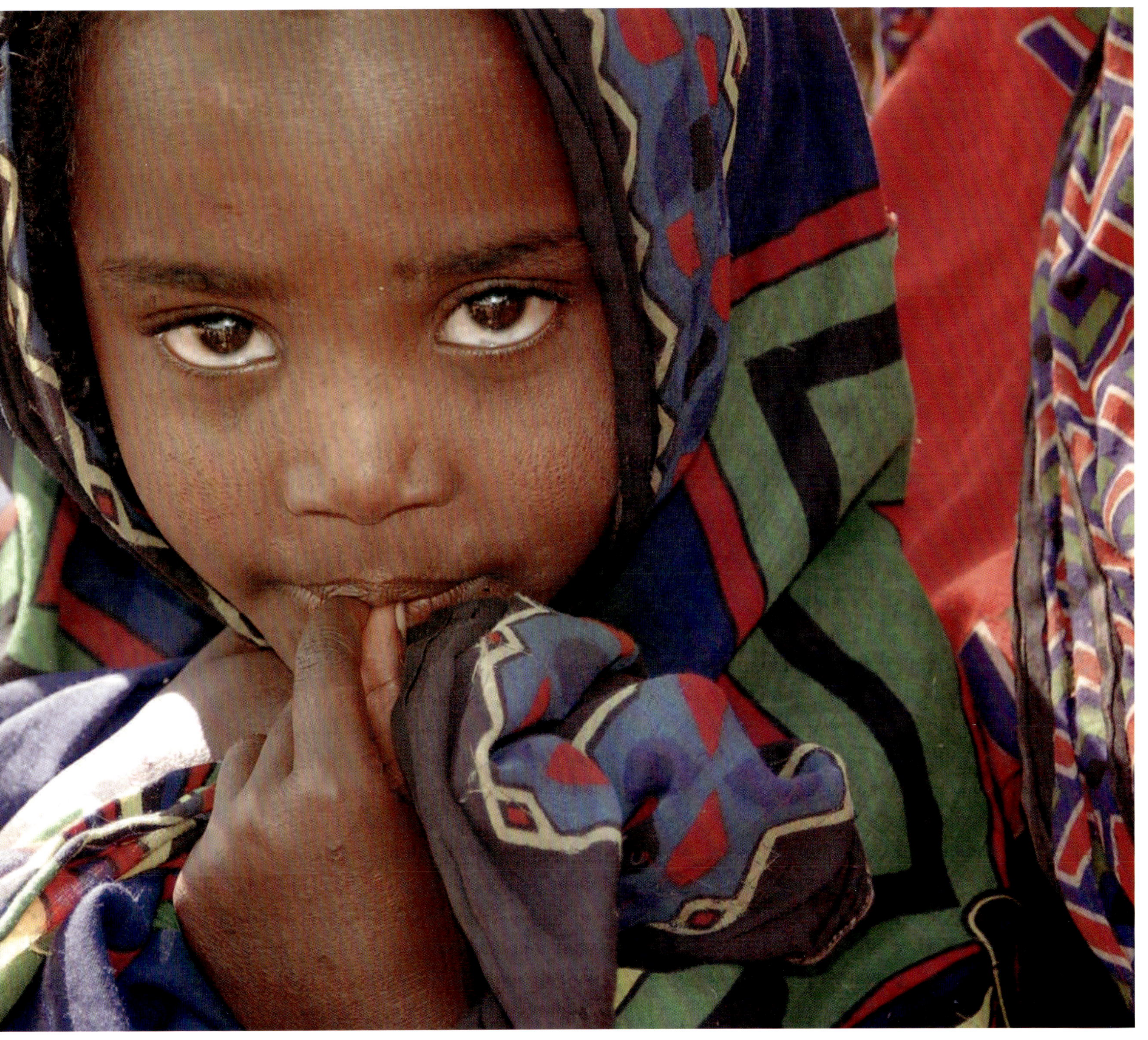

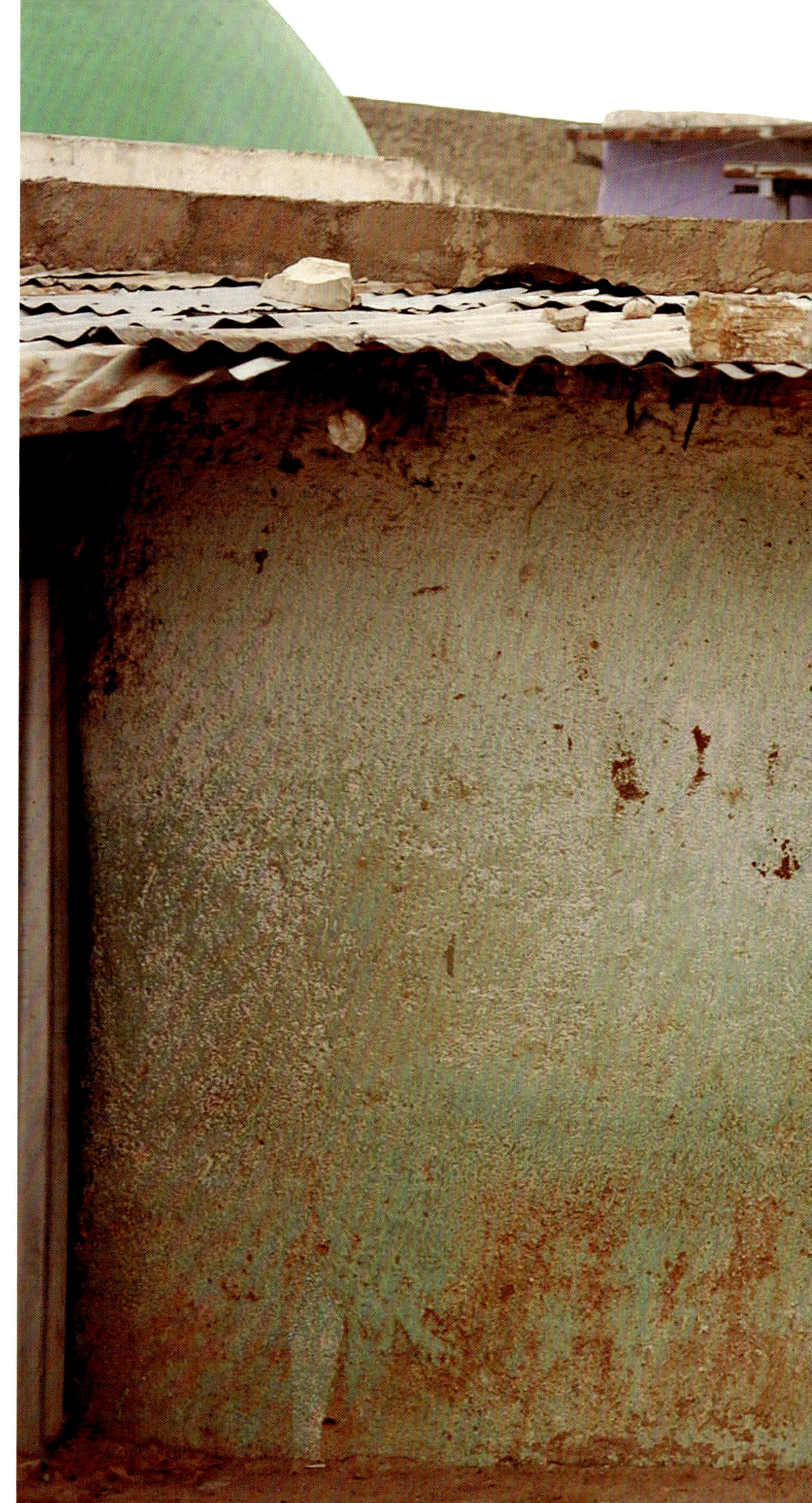

Ethiopia 2006
Julie Pudlowski
For 25 years, International Medical Corps has worked to improve the lives of millions of people by restoring hope and rebuilding self-reliance in communities around the globe.

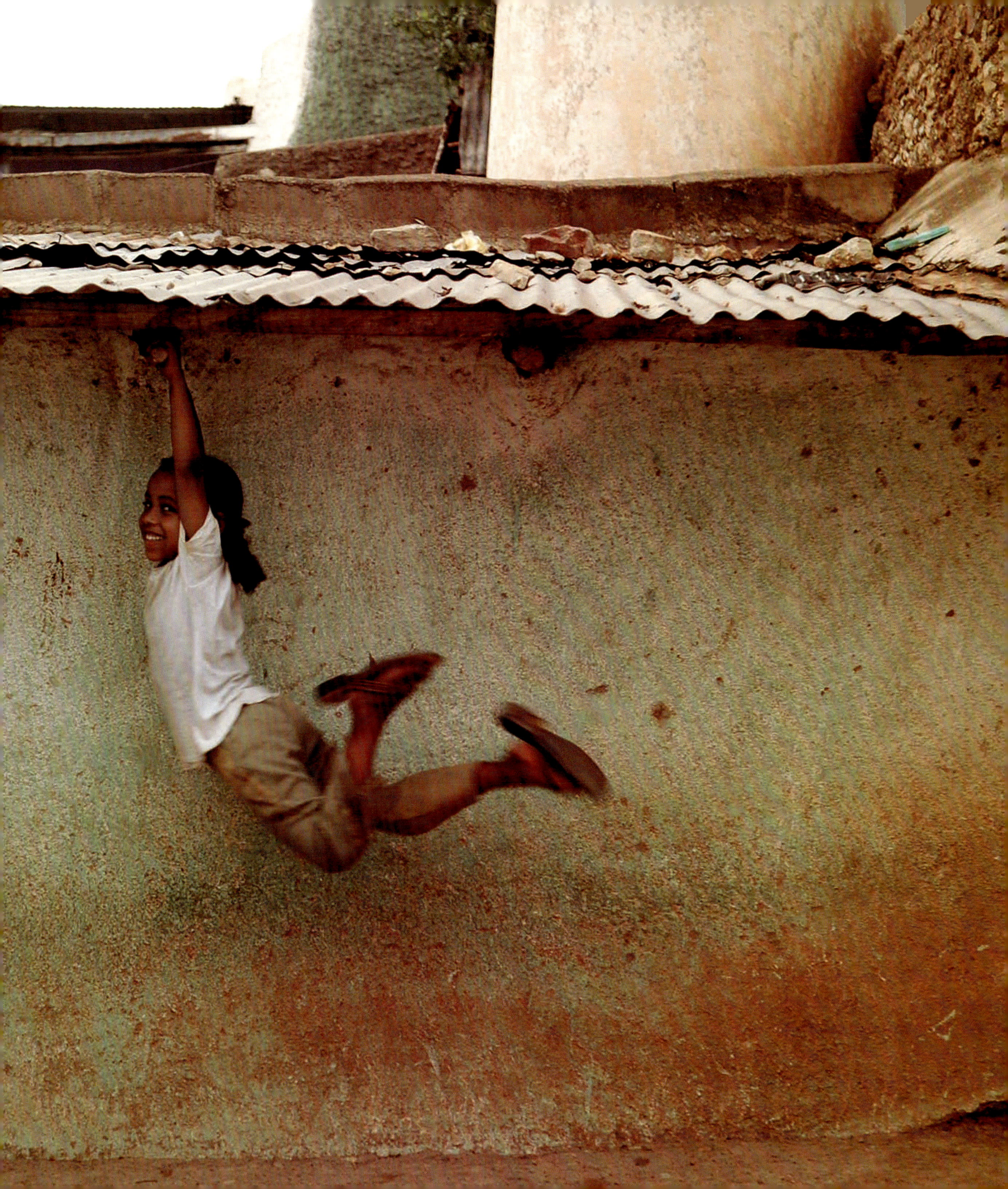

PHOTOGRAPHS IN THIS BOOK WERE CHOSEN FROM THE INTERNATIONAL MEDICAL CORPS ARCHIVE WITH HELP FROM:

Rebecca Morse, associate curator, photography
The Museum of Contemporary Art, Los Angeles

Judith Keller, curator of photography
J. Paul Getty Museum

Tim Wride, acting curator of photography (2007)
Los Angeles County Museum of Art

Artists and Collectors:
Bruce Berman, film producer, American photography collector
Ruth Bloom, art collector, MOCA Photography Committee chairperson
Richard Gere, actor, photographer, humanitarian, photography collector
Robert Graham, sculptor, artist, contemporary art collector
Anjelica Huston, actress, contemporary art collector
Shirley and Bernard Kinsey, African and contemporary art collectors
Eugenio Lopez, contemporary art collector
Judy Ovitz, contemporary art collector
Mario Testino, photographer, photography collector

PHOTOGRAPHERS

Thank you to all of the International Medical Corps doctors, nurses, volunteers and staff who continue to take photographs in the field, and to those whose photos were selected from the archives for this book, including:
Margaret Aguirre
Nancy Aossey
Miranda Bryant
Michael Gall
Kara Gaye
Dr. Jeff Goodman
Michael Holt
Dr. Henry Hood
Dr. Jill John-Kall
Dr. Lynne Jones
Dr. Neil Joyce
Jeanine Mahle
Dr. Bill Moore
Aosama Jaleel Nahey
Dr. Bob Simon
Bridget Steffen
Marin Tomas
Leo Tomlin

We have made every attempt to acknowledge every International Medical Corps staff member whose photographs were selected from the archives for this book. Our apologies if we have inadvertently left anyone out.

A special thanks to the professional photographers whose images were a part of the International Medical Corps archives over the years and whose photographs were chosen for this book, including:
Jeffrey Austin
Jenny Chu
Colin Finlay
Tanya Habjouqa
Tim Hetherington
Danny Hoffman
Julie Jiang
Robert Knoth
Peter Menzel
Julie Pudlowski
Asim Rafiqui
Chris Rainier
Tim Reese
Marissa Roth
Jennifer Rowland
Benny Sieu
Yael Swerdlow
Sara Terry
John Trotter
Judy Walgreen-Dehaas

ACKNOWLEDGEMENTS

I've been extremely lucky in my career to have worked on some very meaningful projects with several remarkable people. But this book project was an extraordinary experience. Everyone who took part in this project—without exception—generously donated their time, talent, expertise and resources to make it possible.

Thank you to **MODERN LUXURY MEDIA**, who generously donated its impressive magazine-publishing talents and production expertise to make this book come to life, beautifully.

Special thanks to **MODERN LUXURY CREATIVE DIRECTOR ANN SONG**, for designing the most stunning photography book, and to **MODERN LUXURY PRINT PROCUREMENT DIRECTOR SEAN BERTRAM** for painstakingly turning archival photos into printable, beautiful works of art. Thanks to **ANGELENO EDITOR-AT-LARGE JENN BALL** for your eagle-eye proofreading. And thank you to everyone in the Modern Luxury Media production department in Chicago for producing countless drafts of layouts, revisions and proofs.

A personal thank you to **MODERN LUXURY CEO MICHAEL KONG** for believing in this project and supporting it emotionally, intellectually and spiritually every step of the way. It was in so many ways a labor of love.

Thank you to the curators and collectors who helped select the photos for the book—**BRUCE BERMAN**, **RUTH BLOOM**, **RICHARD GERE**, **ANJELICA HUSTON**, **JUDITH KELLER**, **SHIRLEY AND BERNARD KINSEY**, **EUGENIO LOPEZ**, **REBECCA MORSE**, **JUDY OVITZ**, **MARIO TESTINO**, **TIM WRIDE** and **ROBERT GRAHAM**, who passed away before the printing of this book. When I asked each of you to select the final images from the International Medical Corps archives, I did so because of my great admiration for your critical eyes. But what became apparent through your selections and involvement in this book was also your generousity and humanitarian spirit. To all of you, I am truly grateful.

Thank you to **CHRISTIANE AMANPOUR** for writing the foreword for this book. Your lifetime of focusing on humanitarian issues and the plight of people around the globe is an inspiration, and we are grateful to you for continuing to share International Medical Corps stories with the world.

Thank you to **RICK GONZALEZ**, **SETH WEINBERGER** and **LEE SCHAUER** at **MAYER BROWN LLP** for making sure we did this right by publishing this book with the highest legal integrity.

Thank you to the International Medical Corps staff, who patiently and painstakingly answered question after question about every photograph in the book, particularly **MARGARET AGUIRRE**, **STEPHANIE BOWEN**, **MICHAEL HOLT**, **WENDY SMITH**, **STEPHEN TOMLIN** and **ROBIN TORBAY**. A special and personal thank you to **INTERNATIONAL MEDICAL CORPS CEO NANCY AOSSEY**. Your tireless dedication to this book and to International Medical Corps staff and beneficiaries it depicts continues to inspire me.

Thank you to the many friends and colleagues who helped and supported this project along the way, especially (in alphabetical order, because you all should come first!) **MARGARET AGUIRRE**, **RUTH BLOOM, JANE BUCKINGHAM**, **TRISHA CARDOSO**, **CHRIS CORTAZZO**, **CHARLOTTE COTTON**, **MANDY EISENHART**, **DEBBIE FISHER**, **KAREN KLOSE**, **NINA KOTICK**, **LISA MARK**, **ESTELLA PROVOS**, **SHANNON ROTENBERG**, **LEA RUSSO** and **DESIREE UNDERWOOD**.

Thank you to my daughters, **PHOEBE**, **ISABELLA AND TESSA**, who inspire me every day. May you be inspired by the hopeful stories and courageous people in this book.

Thank you to **THE ISABEL TRUST** and **THE FARO FOUNDATION** for generously donating the funds we needed to print the first run of this book.

But above all, thank you to all of the **PHOTOGRAPHERS** whose images appear in this book and who, under circumstances most could not imagine, took the time to take a picture and to share a bit of their world—our world—with us. It has been an honor to present your work here in this book. –ST

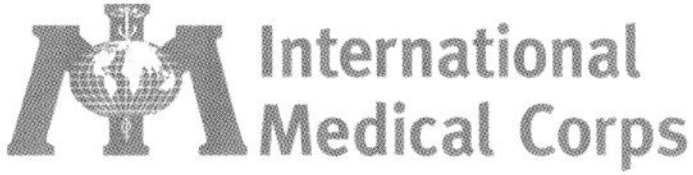

DONATE TO INTERNATIONAL MEDICAL CORPS

www.imcworldwide.org
imc@imcworldwide.org
24-Hour Donation Hotline: 800-481-4462

INTERNATIONAL MEDICAL CORPS HEADQUARTERS
1919 Santa Monica Blvd.
Suite 400
Santa Monica, CA 90404
Phone 310-826-7800
Fax 310-442-6622

INTERNATIONAL MEDICAL CORPS DC OFFICE
1313 L St. NW
Suite 220
Washington, DC 20005
Phone 202-828-5155
Fax 202-828-5156

INTERNATIONAL MEDICAL CORPS UK
3rd Floor
254-258 Goswell Rd.
London
EC1V 7EB
Phone +44 (0) 207 253 0001
Fax +44 (0) 207 250 3269

www.imcworldwide.org.uk
imc@imcworldwide.org.uk